# THE USE OF FORCE AND THE INTERNATIONAL LEGAL SYSTEM

This book provides in-depth coverage and analysis of the international law rules and principles that govern the use of force. Through a unique intra-disciplinary perspective, it examines how the law on the use of force functions within the international legal system and how it interacts with other relevant areas of the law. This includes arms control law, the law governing the use of the international commons, the law of armed conflict and human rights law, and the law of international responsibility. It offers an accessible guide to the law on the use of force to students and practitioners, alongside providing a unique perspective on the place and function of the law on the use of force within the wider legal landscape which will appeal to both academic professionals and others interested in how law regulates the use of force.

TERRY D. GILL is Emeritus Professor of Military Law at the University of Amsterdam and is a globally recognized authority on the law of armed conflict. He is founder and co-director of the Research Program on the Law of Armed Conflict and Military Operations (LACMO) at the Amsterdam Centre for International Law and is co-convenor of the Netherlands Research Forum on the Law of Armed Conflict and Peace Operations (LACPO).

KINGA TIBORI-SZABÓ is a post-doctoral guest researcher in the Role of Law in Armed Conflict and Military Operations (LACMO) research programme. She has been publishing and conducting research on the use of force in public international law for the past two decades and has sixteen years of experience working for international criminal tribunals. Since 2023, she has been working on criminal investigations for the United Nations in Iraq. Her views expressed in this book do not necessarily reflect those of her employer.

# THE USE OF FORCE AND THE INTERNATIONAL LEGAL SYSTEM

TERRY D. GILL
*University of Amsterdam*
KINGA TIBORI-SZABÓ
*University of Amsterdam*

CAMBRIDGE
UNIVERSITY PRESS

CAMBRIDGE
UNIVERSITY PRESS

Shaftesbury Road, Cambridge CB2 8EA, United Kingdom

One Liberty Plaza, 20th Floor, New York, NY 10006, USA

477 Williamstown Road, Port Melbourne, VIC 3207, Australia

314–321, 3rd Floor, Plot 3, Splendor Forum, Jasola District Centre,
New Delhi - 110025, India

103 Penang Road, #05–06/07, Visioncrest Commercial, Singapore 238467

Cambridge University Press is part of Cambridge University Press & Assessment,
a department of the University of Cambridge.

We share the University's mission to contribute to society through the pursuit of
education, learning and research at the highest international levels of excellence.

www.cambridge.org
Information on this title: www.cambridge.org/9781009407328

DOI: 10.1017/9781009407342



First published 2024

*A catalogue record for this publication is available from the British Library*

*A Cataloging-in-Publication data record for this book is available from the Library of Congress*

ISBN 978-1-009-40732-8 Hardback
ISBN 978-1-009-40735-9 Paperback

*To Annelies: 'always and forever'*
Terry

*To my family*
Kinga

CONTENTS

# BOXES

## Fact Boxes

## Summary Boxes

ACKNOWLEDGEMENTS

We are grateful to our support base at the Amsterdam Center for International Law (ACIL) of the University of Amsterdam and the Law of Armed Conflict and Military Operations Research Programme within ACIL for helping to facilitate this project.

We would like to thank Mitja Ličar of DEWESoft (Slovenia) for permission to use a hypertext link to the diagram of satellites in orbit (https://tinyurl.com/4ftkc2sk). Likewise, we are grateful to Dr Valentin Schatz for his kind permission to use the diagram of maritime zones in Chapter 13.

We would also like to thank Marianne Nield and her colleagues at Cambridge University Press for their support and assistance in making the book accessible. A vote of thanks also goes to our copy-editor, Virginia Hamilton, for her invaluable assistance. Any shortcomings or errors are wholly our own.

# TABLE OF CASES

## Reports of International Arbitral Awards (RIAA)



## Permanent Court of International Justice (PCIJ)



## International Court of Justice (ICJ)

## Nuremberg and Tokyo Tribunals

## Human Rights Bodies



## Other International and Domestic Courts

# TABLE OF TREATIES

## Pre-Charter Treaties



## UN Charter



## Post-Charter Treaties and Conventions

## Seminal UNGA Resolutions

# PART I

# Development of the Contemporary *jus ad bellum* in International Law

# 1

# Introduction

There is abundant literature on the use of force under international law; much of which is of a very good quality, so why add another book to the tall stacks of publications that already exist on the topic? This book will certainly not resolve all the controversies relating to the use of force. Nevertheless, we do hope to make a worthwhile contribution to the discussion on controversial issues, including on intervention for humanitarian purposes, the use of force in self-defence against attacks by non-State actors and how the law on the use of force applies to new and emerging technologies and in response to so-called hybrid threats. We also aim to set out the scope of the law governing the use of force, while not ignoring the areas of contention both in academic literature and in the practice of States and other actors. To some extent, this book will thus cover topics which have received attention elsewhere, from restating the main points of the law to discussing points of view on various controversial issues. Of course, we aim to do so from the perspective of our respective backgrounds and insights, incorporating our previous research and the work of others in this field and providing a considered viewpoint on issues where there is a significant difference of opinion. Consequently, we think the book will offer some new insights, even on those topics which have received considerable attention elsewhere.

The title of the book also reveals one aspect of our approach that differs from that adopted in most other literature on this topic. International law has become increasingly compartmentalized over the years, sometimes to such an extent that the individual components are no longer seen as part of a whole. This 'fragmentation' of the legal system is partly due to the increasing complexity of the law and the corresponding tendency to (over-)specialization in the legal profession. We are convinced that the law on the use of force has a central place in the contemporary international legal system and should be viewed not only through a microscope but also through a telescope, to see how it is connected to the wider legal system governing international relations. To this end, we have devoted one part of this book to exploring the relationship of the contemporary *jus ad bellum* with other areas of international law and its function within the broader legal landscape. We have done so, not to conflate the rules from one sub-system with those of another but to provide some insight into how they interrelate and to reconcile the apparent and real overlaps as well as occasional clashes of obligations which can arise between them. To put it simply, we see international law as a coherent and interlocking system, comparable to or imaginable as a metro map, with different coloured lines intersecting and serving different destinations. We also think that understanding contemporary law requires some attention to the historical evolution of the rules relating to the use of force; hence, another part of the book gives a historical overview of those rules, an aspect which is often overlooked nowadays in other works on the topic.

Who is the book addressed to? We have at least three audiences in mind. First, for our colleagues in the academic legal community as a contribution to the ongoing debate on issues relating to the use of force. Second, since we are both practitioner lawyers who have been and are engaged in providing legal advice to non-academic professionals (to the armed forces and to international tribunals respectively), we sincerely hope this book will be of use to a professional and practitioner public and assist in providing clear answers to difficult questions. This is not a 'manual' on how to apply the law in a practical setting, but if it assists those who write such manuals in providing usable answers to hard questions, it will have served one of its intended purposes. Last but not least, the book is intended as a research tool and further reading for the (post-)graduate level student and PhD candidate who is interested in the topic. We have therefore endeavoured to keep the work as accessible as possible, highlighting areas of agreement and contention to help inform the conduct of research.

The book is divided into five parts comprising a total of sixteen chapters. Part I consists of three chapters, including this one. It provides an introduction to the book and a historical background to the contemporary legal framework for the use of force. Part II, consisting of three chapters, sets out the legal framework relating to the use of force and devotes attention both to areas of agreement and to aspects of the law where there is a degree of controversy. It deals with the prohibition on the use of force and the two recognized exceptions to it. Part III, consisting of five chapters, delves further into older and newer controversies. These include the longstanding debate on the legality of the use of force for the protection of human rights in the absence of a mandate from the UN Security Council, the impact of new technologies and new methods of warfare on the law governing the use of force and the modalities of countering so-called hybrid threats. Part IV consists of four chapters and explores the place of the *jus ad bellum* within the wider international legal system. In this part, we aim to clarify the relationship between *jus ad bellum* and other international legal regimes, such as the law of armed conflict, the law of neutrality, the law relating to State sovereignty in the context of consensual intervention, the law governing the use of the global commons (law of the sea, air law and the law of outer space), international human rights law, international criminal law and the law of international responsibility. Part V, consisting of a single chapter, provides a summary of the main findings and discusses how to harmonize and reconcile the rights and obligations arising from different legal subsystems. It also contains some reflections on the relevance of the law in a world that does not always abide by its rules and precepts.

As regards our methodology in this book, we take a modernized legal-positivist approach to the law in relation to both sources and interpretation. Hence, we consider the law to be found primarily in the sources enumerated in Article 38 of the Statute of the International Court of Justice (ICJ), with the addition of decisions of international organizations which have legally binding effect. For the interpretation of treaties we use the well-known methods set out in the Vienna Convention on the Law of Treaties. We consider customary law to be identified through the application of the criteria developed in ICJ case law for determining the existence and content of a rule of customary international law. We also apply historical legal analysis and cite past and more recent examples from State practice as a means of illustrating the law. We use open sources on weapons technology and military operational questions (such as targeting doctrine) where relevant. We follow a legal-doctrinal approach in applying the law to concrete examples and cases. Hence, while we use numerous examples and cite State practice and case law where relevant, this is neither an empirical study of any particular case or situation nor a critique of any State's record on the use of force.

Where there are parallel legal obligations or potential conflicts of obligations arising from different legal regimes, we try to resolve them by using tools such as complementarity of obligations and systemic harmonization, with the aim of maintaining the coherence of the legal system. We do this on the basis of several premises: first, that States are bound by the totality of their legal obligations; second, that such obligations should be given due consideration when determining how to give them effect and harmonize them as far as possible; third, in the case of conflict between obligations arising from different legal regimes, it must be determined which obligation takes precedence over another. The complementarity of obligations would mean, for instance, that while the law of armed conflict is separate from the law on the use of force and provides rules relating to the conduct of hostilities irrespective of the right to use force, it does not preclude the relevance of the law governing the use of force once hostilities commence. Likewise, the law governing the use of particular geographical areas, such as the law of the sea or the law relating to the peaceful use of outer space, must be given due regard when applying the law on the use of force.

Finally, while we fully acknowledge that the law does not develop in a vacuum and that it is not alone in shaping the policy and behaviour of States and other actors, we see the law as distinct from pure policy, morality, ethics or other extra-legal considerations. We see a clear divide between the law as it is and the law that we or anyone else would like to have or which may be in the process of crystallizing. So we consistently distinguish 'black letter law' from opinions or possible directions in which the law may be moving.

2

# From Just War to the Great War

## 2.1 Introduction

This chapter follows through the history of the Western just war tradition, as the one forming the basis of the contemporary international law on the use of force. In the following paragraphs the main tenets of the different eras and approaches of the Western just war tradition will be briefly discussed. This brief review is useful in order to understand many aspects of today's *jus ad bellum*, such as how the prohibition on the use of force came to be; what, to this day, continue to be its core ideas and concerns; how self-defence, as one of the two exceptions to the prohibition on the use force, evolved in customary law over the centuries; how its current customary law content should be interpreted; and what precedents there are for collective action by States against unlawful uses of force.

## 2.2 The Just War Tradition

Justifying war has for long been at the centre of morality and law. Most of the world's philosophical, ethical or religious traditions have viewed war as a public and collective undertaking of a community against a foreign enemy. They have therefore formulated principles and/or rules on the causes and conduct of war (see Fact Box 2.1).

## 2.3 Ancient Greece and Rome

Both the ancient Greeks and Romans recognized several causes for legitimate war, and no war was commenced before allegations of legitimacy (*justum bellum*, for Romans) were made.[1]

[1] C. Phillipson, *The International Law and Custom of Ancient Greece and Rome* (Macmillan, 1911), vol. 2, pp. 167, 182; K. Tibori-Szabó, *Anticipatory Action in Self-Defence* (Springer, 2011), p. 32.

### FACT BOX 2.1 JUST WAR PERSPECTIVES AROUND THE WORLD

Justifications for war were embedded in the different philosophical, ethical or religious traditions governing a particular society and reflected these traditions' variations, schisms or changes over time. It is near impossible to speak about just war 'theory' or 'tradition' in the sense of a settled system of ideas; it is easier to speak of views and perspectives on war. With this in mind, the brief descriptions below identify some of the basic and relatively enduring ideas characterizing various just war perspectives around the world.

**Ancient Egyptian perspectives:** Seen as quasi-divine beings, pharaohs possessed incontestable legitimacy to wage wars on behalf of the kingdom, which was regarded as the terrestrial embodiment of the principle of order and justice (*Ma'at*). Defending the *Ma'at* against forces of chaos, embodied by foreign peoples (barbarians) or rebellious factions within the kingdom was regarded as just. Pharaohs frequently expanded this concept to include aggressive wars waged beyond their borders, as the conception of Egypt as the sole residence of order and justice meant that all Egyptian wars were defensive, fought against enemies who constantly threatened peace and security.

**Ancient Chinese thought:** A righteous war (*yi zhan*) could be both defensive and offensive as long as the use of arms and soldiers was for a righteous cause (*yi bing*), the war was ordered by a legitimate ruler and it was publicly announced. The main righteous causes were self-defence, punishment of wrongs and the preservation of peace. The latter also allowed for war against those viewed as barbarians, thereby spreading civility and harmony among them. Necessity and proportionality had to be observed in the conduct of war.

**Classic South Asian perspectives:** These include Hindu, Sikh and Buddhist thoughts about war. Under Hinduism, just war was fought to uphold the *dharma* – that is, to maintain peace and security through law and order within the larger cosmic order. The *dharma* could be endangered by aliens or nationals alike; force had to be used as a last resort and the conduct of war had to be as humane as possible. According to Sikh thought, the use of force was sanctioned in the defence of the *dharma*, which included resistance to the oppressor and fighting for liberty. War had to be waged as a last resort and a Sikh could never be the first to draw a sword. Buddhism condemned war unreservedly and attested to its futility in gaining a meaningful resolution to any conflict. A righteous war was one fought with ideas, not arms. Recognizing, however, the reality of war, Buddhism cautioned against indiscriminate and excessive use of force during hostilities.

**Islamic perspectives:** Just war in classical Muslim sources revolves around the concept of *jihad* (struggle, striving). Originally, this term was synonymous with self-defence. Under this early interpretation, wars were fought in defence of the caliphate or of the Muslim religion. Later on, *jihad* was expanded to accommodate wars for the conquest of new lands and the expansion of Islam. Such wars had to be ordered by a sovereign possessing uncontested political and religious legitimacy. Classical

FACT BOX 2.1 *(cont.)*

Muslim texts also contained detailed rules on the initiation, conduct and conclusion of wars.

**Western thought (discussed in this chapter):** Its roots can be traced back to the customs and laws of ancient Greece and Rome. Early Christian philosophy took over these prescriptions and gave them Christian foundations. During the Middle Ages, just war principles were codified and different sub-traditions emerged. Thinking about war was intrinsically connected to natural law concepts, according to which certain natural rights and intuitions accrued simply from the fact of being human or sovereign. Starting in 1600, secularism and positive law gradually replaced the Christian and natural law tenets of the just war tradition, although elements of it remain in the discourse on the ethics of war to the present day.

**Sources**: R. Cox, 'Expanding the History of the Just War: The Ethics of War in Ancient Egypt' (2017) 61 *International Studies Quarterly* 371–84; A. J. Bellamy, *Just Wars: From Cicero to Iraq* (Polity Press, 2006), 7–10, 120–1; P. Robinson (ed.), *Just War in Comparative Perspective* (Ashgate, 2003); L. Jayasuriya, 'Just War Tradition and Buddhism' (October 2009) 46 *International Studies* 371–480; H. M. Hensel (ed.), *The Prism of Just War: Asian and Western Perspectives on the Legitimate Use of Military Force* (Ashgate, 2010); M. C. Bassiouni and A. Guellali, *Jihad and Its Challenges to International and Domestic Law* (Hague Academic Press, 2010); R. J. Hoffmann, *The Just War and Jihad: Violence in Judaism, Christianity and Islam* (Prometheus Books, 2006); V. Morkevičius, *Realist Ethics: Just War Traditions as Power Politics* (Cambridge University Press 2018).

The most frequent grounds for resorting to war were violation of a treaty, withdrawal from an alliance, offence committed against an ally, breach of neutrality, offence against envoys, infringement of territorial rights, desecration of sacred places and unjust refusal of extradition.[2] Before the Peloponnesian War, Greek city-states followed customary practices for limiting war; later, however, written treaties were preferred.[3] Matters of war in Rome were regulated by the *ius fetiale*, a set of religious laws related to the conclusion of treaties and declarations of war.[4] Commencement of hostilities was 'just' only when it was carried out in conformity with these laws.[5] Adherence was ensured and overseen by the *fetiales*, a college of priests who had special responsibility for maintaining peaceful relations. The fetials, although required to discuss

[2] Phillipson, *International Law* (n. 1), p. 182.
[3] A. J. Bellamy, *Just Wars: From Cicero to Iraq* (Polity Press, 2006), pp. 15–16.
[4] G. M. Reichberg et al., *The Ethics of War: Classic and Contemporary Readings* (Blackwell, 2006), p. 47.
[5] Ibid., p. 47.

only the mere formalities of war, often analysed the legitimacy of the reasons invoked.[6]

The Roman jurist and philosopher Marcus Tullius Cicero (106–43 BC), developed a more comprehensive account of the legitimacy of war. According to him, '[w]ars ... ought to be undertaken for this purpose, that we may live in peace, without injustice'.[7] Cicero believed that no wars were just unless waged after a formal demand for restoration or unless formally declared by the appropriate authority.[8] He also advised restraint in the punishment of enemies once victory was secured.[9]

The concepts of just cause and appropriate authority developed by Roman law and ethics found their way into early and medieval Christian philosophy and greatly influenced the just war tradition for centuries to come.

## 2.4 Early and Medieval Christian Views

After three centuries of pacifist Christian philosophy prohibiting participation in military action, from the fourth century onwards Christian philosophy required justifying grounds to make the resort to war acceptable to both divine and earthly authority.[10]

Contemporaneous religious writings mirrored these changes.[11] One of the most important thinkers of early Christianity was Augustine of Hippo, who gave expression to an early Christian understanding of just war, based on precepts of 'natural law', which he regarded as knowledge that the divinely created natural order placed in every human being.[12] Relying on Roman concepts and early Christian thinking, Augustine identified several 'just causes', such as: obeying a divine command; defending the safety or the honour of the State; avenging injuries; punishing a nation for failure to take corrective action for wrongs committed

[6] I. Brownlie, *International Law and the Use of Force by States* (Clarendon Press, 1963), p. 4; Tibori-Szabó, *Anticipatory Action* (n. 1), pp. 33–4.

[7] Reichberg et al., *Ethics of War* (n. 4), p. 52, citing from Cicero, 'On Duties', bk I, s. 34, in M. T. Griffin and E. M. Atkins, *Cicero: On Duties* (Cambridge University Press, 1991).

[8] Ibid., citing from Cicero, 'On Duties' (n. 7), bk I, s. 36.

[9] Ibid., citing from Cicero, 'On Duties' (n. 7), bk I, s. 34; Bellamy, *Just Wars* (n. 3), pp. 19–20.

[10] Tibori-Szabó, *Anticipatory Action* (n. 1), pp. 35–6.

[11] Ibid., p. 36.

[12] Bellamy, *Just Wars* (n. 3), p. 25; R. Dougherty, 'St Augustine on Natural Law', in J. Crowe and C. Y. Lee (eds.), *Research Handbook on Natural Law Theory* (Edward Elgar, 2019), pp. 67–8.

by its citizens; and coming to the defence of one's allies.[13] According to Augustine, natural law did not allow wars to be fought for territorial expansion or without the approval of the appropriate public authority.[14]

After the fall of the Roman empire, several smaller kingdoms and principalities were established and the Catholic Church acquired ever greater responsibility in European affairs. After the establishment of the Holy Roman Empire, the Church shared power with the emperor and medieval popes often acted as political rulers to maintain a frail public order.[15] Between the fourth and eighth centuries, the barbarian invasions took place, forcing the Church to take a more realistic view on issues of military action.[16] From the tenth century onwards, the secular functions of the Catholic Church came to occupy a prominent place alongside its divine functions, and towards the end of the first millennium the Church started engaging in military affairs.[17] In 1095, Pope Urban II called the first crusade, against the Muslims and the Jews in ancient Palestine.[18] In the twelfth and thirteenth centuries, eight other crusades took place, most of them for the conquest of ancient Palestine.[19]

The justification for war as understood in the time of the crusades was aptly described by the *Decretum*, attributed to Gratian, a twelfth-century canon lawyer from Bologna.[20] The *Decretum* had three main parts, the second of which was a compilation of cases (*causae*), in which Gratian raised a number of legal questions. According to Case 23, war was just if waged in order to regain what had been stolen or to repel the attack of enemies.[21] Gratian further indicated that defending the

[13] J. M. Mattox, *Saint Augustine and the Theory of Just War* (Continuum, 2006), p. 74.

[14] Augustine, 'City of God', bk XIX, chap. 7, repr. in E. L. Fortin et al., *Augustine: Political Writings* (Hackett, 1994), p. 149.

[15] A. Nussbaum, *A Concise History of the Law of Nations* (Macmillan, 1947), pp. 23–7; Bellamy, *Just Wars* (n. 3), pp. 30–1.

[16] Nussbaum, *Concise History* (n. 15), pp. 23–7; Tibori-Szabó, *Anticipatory Action* (n. 1), p. 37.

[17] S. C. Neff, *War and the Law of Nations: General History* (Cambridge University Press, 2005), p. 48.

[18] 'Pope Urban II's Speech at Clermont, November 27, 1095', as reported by Robert the Monk, in R. G. D. Laffan, *Select Documents of European History: 800–1492* (Henry Holt, 1929), pp. 54–6.

[19] Tibori-Szabó, *Anticipatory Action* (n. 1), p. 38.

[20] The *Decretum* was a collection of canon law compiled and written in the form of a legal textbook. The collection was continuously annotated by canonists (Decretists, later coined Decretalists) in the second half of the twelfth century. Reichberg et al., *Ethics of War* (n. 4), p. 104; Bellamy, *Just War* (n. 3), pp. 34–6.

[21] Gratian, *Decretum*, pt II: 'Decreti Pars Secunda', Case 23, question II, canon 1, repr. in Reichberg et al., *Ethics of War* (n. 4), p. 113.

homeland from the barbarian invasions and engaging in holy wars were just causes.[22]

At the time when the *Decretum* was compiled, a new approach to combining ancient philosophy with Christian theology emerged under the name of scholasticism.[23] Thomas Aquinas was a prominent scholastic author and his best-known work, the *Summa Theologiae*, compiled all principal theological teachings of the time.[24] In the same work, building on pre-existing concepts, Aquinas put forward a detailed discussion of natural law, which he regarded as every human being's participation in the 'eternal law' that emanated from God. According to Aquinas, natural law was observed whenever humans engaged in correct practical reasoning about what was good for them overall in any given situation, as long as a number of precepts were respected. The first and fundamental precept was that anything good was to be pursued and the opposite of this good, evil, was to be avoided in all human acts.[25]

SUMMARY BOX 2.1 JUST WAR CONDITIONS ACCORDING TO AQUINAS

- Ordered by a public authority;
- for a just cause; and
- fought with the right intention.

These ideas also influenced Aquinas's discussion on the legitimacy of war. In Question 40 ('On War'), Aquinas named three conditions for a war to be just: the war had to be ordered by a public authority; it had to have a just cause; and it had to be fought with the right intention. As to the just causes of war, Aquinas cited Augustine and agreed that war ought to be fought to avenge wrongs; to punish a nation for failure to take

[22] Gratian, 'Decretum', pt II: 'Decreti Pars Secunda', Case 23, question III, canon 5, repr. in Reichberg et al. (n. 4), p. 114; Gratian, 'Decretum', pt II: 'Decreti Pars Secunda', Case 23, question V, canon 46, repr. in Reichberg et al. (n. 4), p. 119.

[23] Tibori-Szabó, *Anticipatory Action* (n. 1), p. 40. Earlier used by the Muslim scholars of Al-Andalus, this method of teaching was based on the critical analysis of the main work(s) of a renowned scholar, and in this way the students learned to understand and appreciate the theories of the author.

[24] Thomas Aquinas (ca. 1225-74) wrote the *Summa Theologiae* between 1265 and 1274.

[25] T. Aquinas, 'Summa Theologiae', pt I-II, qq. 90–4, in D. Bigongiari (ed.), *The Political Ideas of St. Thomas Aquinas: Representative Selections* (Hafner, 1969), pp. 3–54.

corrective action for wrongs committed by its citizens; or to restore what was seized unjustly.[26] In addition, Aquinas believed that religious wars ought to be fought only in defence of the faith or to overcome persecutions, but not for religious expansion.[27]

## 2.5 Christian Legalist Views

The tenets of early and medieval Christian thinking about war were partly retained by authors in the fifteenth to seventeenth centuries. Nonetheless, some aspects underwent important changes as a result of key events during that period. The middle of the fifteenth century saw the fall of Constantinople, marking the rise of the Ottoman Empire, and the end of the Hundred Years War between France's main contenders for the crown. The fifteenth century also saw the emergence of the Italian Renaissance and of French humanism. The discovery of new overseas territories fuelled new expansionist plans in sixteenth-century Spain, while the Catholic Church waged war against Protestant reformers. Meanwhile, Europe's boundaries were being endangered by the growing Ottoman threat.[28] Against this background, the fifteenth- and sixteenth-century Christian ideas about just war combined the more traditional theological teachings with evolving natural law perspectives and new humanist thought.[29]

### *2.5.1 Spanish Scholastics*

Spanish scholastics were the first proponents of the previously mentioned combined approach.[30] Francisco de Vitoria was the first philosopher to write an independent treatise on the problem of war between nations.[31] Following Aquinas, Vitoria linked the morality of war to natural law precepts, which he saw as reflected in the customs of all nations. In 1539 he delivered two lectures, *De Indis* and *De iure belli*, which were

26 Aquinas, 'Summa Theologiae', pt. II-II, q. 40, art. 1, in Reichberg et al., *Ethics of War* (n. 4), pp. 176–7.

27 Aquinas, 'Summa Theologiae', pt. II-II, q. 10, art. 8, in Reichberg et al. (n. 4), pp. 192–3.

28 Nussbaum, *Concise History* (n. 15), pp. 53, 58–9; Tibori-Szabó, *Anticipatory Action* (n. 1), p. 43.

29 Bellamy, *Just Wars* (n. 3), pp. 49–50; Nussbaum, *Concise History* (n. 15), p. 57.

30 Tibori-Szabó, *Anticipatory Action* (n. 1), p. 45.

31 Ibid.

first published in 1557.[32] Both lectures discussed recourse to war and were used as points of reference by subsequent authors.

In *De Indis*, Vitoria discussed illegitimate and legitimate titles of conquest in relation to Spain's claim to dominion in the New World.[33] He followed Aquinas's lead in rejecting war for religious differences and ruled out the idea that the Catholic Church or the Holy Roman Empire had a universal right to wage war.[34]

In *De jure belli*, Vitoria discussed the conditions for recourse to war. He rejected the enlargement of an empire and the personal glory of the sovereign as legitimate causes for war.[35] Vitoria differentiated between offensive and defensive wars.[36] Regarding the former, he asserted that offensive war was for the avenging of injuries and the admonishment of enemies. However, there could be no vengeance where there was no culpable offence in the first place.[37] Concerning defensive wars, Vitoria saw them as justified by natural law inasmuch as it was lawful to resist force with force.[38] According to Vitoria, only the most serious offences justified recourse to war, and he cautioned against inflicting cruel punishment for trivial offences.[39] Vitoria devoted a separate section in his *De jure belli* lecture on limits to be observed in a just war and discussed proportionality in both cautioning against excessive war and urging moderation in the conduct of hostilities.[40]

Francisco Suarez, another Spanish scholastic, echoed Vitoria's opinion about war in his treatise *Metaphysical Disputations*. Suarez similarly distinguished between defensive and offensive wars and believed that war was just if waged by a sovereign ruler to redress an injury or defend the homeland.[41] Like Vitoria, Suarez believed that only the most serious causes, as opposed to slight injuries, justified war.[42]

32 F. de Vitoria, 'De Indis', repr. in A. Pagden and J. Lawrance (eds.), Vitoria, *Political Writings* (Cambridge University Press, 1991), pp. 233, 293.
33 Ibid., pp. 250–2.
34 Ibid., pp. 250–2, 269–70; Bellamy, *Just Wars* (n. 3), pp. 50–1.
35 F. de Vitoria, 'De jure belli', repr. in Pagen and Lawrence (eds.), Vitoria, *Political Writings* (n. 32), pp. 302–3.
36 Ibid., p. 300.
37 Ibid., p. 303.
38 Ibid., p. 297.
39 Ibid., p. 304.
40 Ibid., pp. 314–26.
41 F. Suárez, 'The Three Theological Virtues: On Charity', disputation XIII, ss. 2 and 4, repr. in J. S. Scott (ed.), *Selections from Three Works of Francisco Suarez* (Clarendon Press, 1944), pp. 802–4, 815–16.
42 Ibid., pp. 802–4, 815–17.

### 2.5.2 *Protestant Jurists*

While Spanish scholastics were criticizing the Catholic Church's war against so-called non-believers, European sovereigns were dragged into their own holy war: the conflict between the Catholic Church and the Protestant Reformation movement. The roots of this movement went back to the fourteenth and the fifteenth centuries, but open and organized dissent manifested itself only from 1517 onwards, with the protests of Martin Luther, a Roman Catholic monk and academic. Despite the fact that contemporaneous jurists and theologians attempted to depart from the concept of religious wars, the firm opposition of the Catholic Church to the Reformation process added to the political arguments for holy war. Such ideas dominated the first half of the seventeenth century, when the Thirty Years War[43] engaged virtually all European powers in conflict.[44]

During this time, the tradition of the Spanish scholastics was taken further by Protestant jurists, who brought new insights into Christian thinking about war. Human reason, reflected in the customs of all nations, was gradually emerging as a source of natural law, alongside divine or eternal law. The effect of natural law concepts on the morality of war was no different, however: war had to be waged in moderation, for a just cause and by a just authority.

Alberico Gentili is most famous for his *De jure belli libri tres*, first published in 1588–9.[45] In his treatise, Gentili affirmed that war was a 'just and public contest of arms' between sovereign equals and that only 'supreme princes', who had no superior, could resort to war. According to Gentili, war had to be the last resort: 'whereas there are two modes of contention, one by argument and the other one by force, one should not resort to the latter if it is possible to use the former.'[46] Like his predecessors, Gentili also rejected religious motives as a justification for war, explicitly breaking away from the idea of holy war.[47]

Hugo Grotius's *De jure belli ac pacis libri tres* (The Law of War and Peace in Three Books), published in 1625, was an instant hit. Translations in Dutch, English, French, German, Swedish and Spanish quickly followed and the treatise became the textbook par excellence on the laws of

[43] The Thirty Years War (1618–48) began as a religious conflict between Catholics and reformer Protestants but ended up involving many other issues, such as territorial annexations and consolidation of power.

[44] Tibori-Szabó, *Anticipatory Action* (n. 1), p. 48.

[45] Nussbaum, *Concise History* (n. 15), p. 94.

[46] A. Gentili, *De Jure Belli Libri Tres* (Clarendon Press, 1933), bk I, chap. 3, p. 15.

[47] Ibid., bk I, chap. 9, pp. 38–9.

war.[48] Reflecting Grotius's ambition to cover all relevant topics in one treatise, *De jure belli ac pacis* addressed not only the definition, permissibility and causes of war but also the delineation of State boundaries; common use of land, rivers and seas; procedures for making treaties; rights of burial and diplomacy; division of booty; use of hostages; right of conquest; proper treatment of prisoners of war; prohibitions on rape, assassination and use of poison in battle; duties of allies; responsibilities of neutrals; the calling of truces; and the negotiation of peace treaties.[49] By the eighteenth century, the treatise had gone through fifty editions in Latin alone.[50] To this day, it is acknowledged as marking the advent of a more modern conception of the law of nations, 'valid apart from religious sanctions, supra-sectarian and human in spirit and still embodying the tradition of Christian piety and morality'.[51]

Grotius named four 'just causes' for war: defence; recovery of property; punishment; and pursuing an obligation not fulfilled by the other.[52] Grotius also subscribed to the view that religious motives did not justify war.[53] Like his predecessors, Grotius also distinguished between offensive and defensive wars. Punishment had to be exercised only in cases where the recovery of property or the undoing of wrong were no longer possible.[54] Defence, on the other hand, had to do with 'an injury not yet inflicted, which menaces either one's body or one's property'.[55]

Building on Vitoria's initiative of discussing the limits on warfare as a separate matter, Grotius devoted an entire book to this topic.

SUMMARY BOX 2.2 JUST CAUSES ACCORDING TO GROTIUS

- Defence
- Recovery of property
- Punishment
- Pursuit of an obligation not fulfilled

[48] Nussbaum, *Concise History* (n. 15), pp. 110–11; O. A. Hathaway and S. J. Shapiro, *The Internationalists and Their Plan to Outlaw War* (Penguin Books, 2018), p. 21.

[49] Hathaway and Shapiro, *Internationalists* (n. 48), p. 21; Nussbaum, *Concise History* (n. 15), pp. 102–10.

[50] Hathaway and Shapiro, *Internationalists* (n. 48), p. 21.

[51] Nussbaum, *Concise History* (n. 15), p. 2.

[52] H. Grotius, *De Jure Belli Ac Pacis Libri Tres* (Oceana 1964), bk II, chap. 1(ii), pp. 171–2.

[53] Ibid., bk II, chap. 20(xlviii), pp. 516–17.

[54] Ibid., bk II, chap. 20(i), p. 462.

[55] Ibid., bk II, chap. 1(ii), p. 172.

Accordingly, in Book III of his *De jure belli ac pacis*, Grotius extensively discusses righteous and moderate conduct in war as permitted by the law of nature and established by the law of nations.[56] As a consequence of his detailed emphasis on the conduct of warfare, subsequent authors began to treat this topic separately, as distinct from the causes of war.[57]

## 2.6 Early Positivist Views

Starting in the seventeenth century, the natural law doctrine of just war gradually became confined to the realm of ethics, while realist and positivist views gave secular (positive) law a dominant role in State affairs. This process was completed during the course of the late seventeenth century and first half of the eighteenth century, after which the law of nations was no longer based on theological precepts and Christian morality. Resort to war became increasingly a matter of sovereign prerogative and *raison d'État*, as the natural law tradition was increasingly replaced by the positivist secular, 'voluntary' law. As part of this process, the law of war became separated from the question of the legality of the resort to war, although the expressions *jus ad bellum* and *jus in bello* did not come into general use until much later.

Early signs of the changes to come could already be observed in writings from the fourteenth and fifteenth centuries, which advanced the idea that war was just if it was declared by a competent public authority, regardless of the ethical aspects of just causes.[58] Such arguments were put forward by Raphael Fulgosius (1367–1427),[59] Balthazar Ayala (1548–84)[60] and Niccolò Machiavelli (1469–1527). Machiavelli, the most prominent realist of the sixteenth century, believed that war was just when it was necessary and that morality played no role in restricting it.[61]

[56] Ibid., bk III, chap. 1(i), p. 599.

[57] A. Roberts, 'The Equal Application of the Laws of War: A Principle under Pressure' (2008) 90(872) *International Review of the Red Cross* 931–62, at 938.

[58] Tibori-Szabó, *Anticipatory Action* (n. 1), p. 43.

[59] Fulgosius, *In Primum Pandectarum Partem Comentaria*, repr. in Reichberg et al., *Ethics of War* (n. 4), pp. 228–9.

[60] B. Ayala, 'De Jure et Officiis Bellicis et Disciplina Military Libri', bk I, chap. 2, cited in Brownlie, *International Law* (n. 6), p. 10.

[61] N. Machiavelli, *The Prince* (Collector's Library, 2004), chaps. 15 and 26, pp. 79, 130; Reichberg et al., *Ethics of War* (n. 4), p. 257, citing from B. Crick (ed.), *Machiavelli: The Discourses* (Penguin Books, 1970), bk III, chap. 41, p. 515.

The Peace of Westphalia (1648) reinforced these early ideas.[62] With the birth of the principles of sovereign equality and balance of power, war became the absolute prerogative of the sovereign, who had no legal superior and could decide on efficient action when the State's vital interests were at stake.[63]

Jurists of the seventeenth and eighteenth centuries echoed this new understanding, while still retaining aspects of the natural law tradition of just war. For instance, Samuel von Pufendorf (1632–94), while still contending that humans had to obey natural duties commanded by God,[64] departed from this concept inasmuch as he saw war as exclusively regulated by positive law.[65] Still, Pufendorf maintained the distinction between offensive and defensive wars and identified as just causes: the preservation and protection of life and property against unjust attack; the collection of what is due from others; reparations for wrongs inflicted; and assurances for the future.[66] Notwithstanding his traditional approach to justifying war, Pufendorf saw the right to wage war as the prerogative of the sovereign, in line with the emerging views at the time.[67]

Another such jurist was Emerich de Vattel (1714–67), whose *Le Droit des gens*, published in 1758, is acknowledged as being at the crossroads of the just war tradition and the emergent international law of the eighteenth century.[68] Like many thinkers before him, Vattel differentiated between offensive and defensive wars. Offensive wars stemmed from the right to use force to obtain justice, if it could not otherwise be secured, or to follow up one's rights through the force of arms. Defensive war meant resisting by force any attack upon a State or its rights.[69] The preservation of the State was an obligation laid upon the sovereign by natural law, and therefore, in Vattel's view, any action that was necessary for the survival

[62] Tibori-Szabó, *Anticipatory Action* (n. 1), p. 60; J. Baylis and S. Smith, *The Globalization of World Politics* (Oxford University Press, 2001), p. 43.

[63] Tibori-Szabó, *Anticipatory Action* (n. 1), pp. 59–60.

[64] S. von Pufendorf, *On the Duty of Man and Citizen according to Natural Law* (Cambridge University Press, 1991), bk II, chap. 1(11), pp. 118–19.

[65] S. von Pufendorf, *De Jure Naturae et Gentium Libri Octo*, vol. 2 (Clarendon Press, 1934), bk VIII, chap. 6(7), p. 1325.

[66] Pufendorf, *Duty of Man and Citizen* (n. 64), bk II, chap. 16(2), p. 168.

[67] Ibid., bk II, chap. 1(11), p. 119.

[68] Reichberg et al., *Ethics of War* (n. 4), p. 504.

[69] E. de Vattel, *The Law of Nations or the Principles of Natural Law: Applied to the Conduct and to the Affairs of Nations and of Sovereigns* (Oceana, 1964), bk II, chap. 5, ss. 67–8, and bk III, chap. 1, s. 5, pp. 135, 236.

of the State was allowed, including the use of force, as long as the war was conducted in due form.[70]

If war was ordered by a public authority, initiated after a formal declaration and conducted in due form, a formal 'state of war' was instituted and the war was a 'perfect' one, affording the sovereign the full panoply of rights for conducting an offensive or defensive war.[71] When a declaration of war was lacking, the war was deemed irregular or imperfect. Although Vattel denounced wars launched without observing formal requirements, the seventeenth and eighteenth centuries saw an abundance of armed conflicts without an official state of war being instituted.[72] Imperfect wars were waged for a variety of reasons, such as self-defence and reprisals, all under the general umbrella of the self-preservation of the State, which was seen as a right and a duty of the sovereign.[73]

## 2.7 War as a Political Instrument and the Principle of Self-Preservation

Early and more developed positivist approaches were further developed in the eighteenth and nineteenth centuries, increasing the gap between the natural law tradition of just war and the realist, balance-of-power approach. The French Revolutionary Wars (1792–1802) and the Napoleonic Wars (1805–15) saw the enrolment into the army of huge masses of people, leading to a new method of warfare: the devastating defeat of the enemy army in a single blow. During the same period, the French and the British developed the system of 'total war' – that is, large-scale blockading and manipulation of neutral commerce while engaged in hostilities.[74]

Although State practice at this time did not result in any important changes as regards the legality and legitimacy of war, the view that the right to resort to war was a question of morality or policy outside the sphere of law was further strengthened.[75] In this regard, Carl von

70 Ibid., bk I, chap. 2, ss. 16 and 18, pp. 13–14.

71 Ibid., bk III, chap. 2, pp. 237–42.

72 Ibid., bk III, chap. 4, s. 67, p. 257; W. G. Grewe, *The Epochs of International Law* (De Gruyter, 2000), pp. 525–30.

73 Vattel, *Law of Nations* (n. 69), bk II, chap. 4, s. 49, pp. 130; Tibori-Szabó, *Anticipatory Action* (n. 1), pp. 66–8.

74 Neff, *War and the Law of Nations* (n. 17), pp. 92–3; Nussbaum, *Concise History* (n. 15), p. 246.

75 Tibori-Szabó, *Anticipatory Action* (n. 1), pp. 68–9.

Clausewitz (1780–1831) was greatly influenced by the ideas advanced by Machiavelli.[76] Clausewitz defined war as 'an act of violence intended to compel our opponent to fulfil our will'[77] and accordingly as 'a real political instrument, a continuation of political commerce, a carrying out of the same by other means'.[78] According to him, 'self-imposed restrictions, almost imperceptible and hardly worth mentioning, termed usages of international law, accompany [war] without essentially impairing its power'.[79] War was inherently brutal: 'to introduce into the philosophy of war itself a principle of moderation would be an absurdity'.[80]

SUMMARY BOX 2.3 PERFECT AND IMPERFECT WARS

**Perfect wars:** Ordered by the public authority, initiated after a formal declaration of war and carried out in accordance with the voluntary rules of war.

**Imperfect wars/measures short of war:** Uses of force without a declaration of war, typically justified under the principle of self-preservation of the State.

Seen as an exercise of will on the part of the State, war in nineteenth-century State practice was a subjective notion, coupled with a concept of 'measures short of war' equally open to interpretation. States could on their own judge whether they found themselves in a state of war, and if they did so find, a declaration of war was considered necessary to justify the taking of belligerent measures. Most governments, however, were eager to avoid a state of (perfect) war while still retaining the possibility to engage in armed action, if necessary.[81] In this context, the Concert of Europe, founded after the end of the Napoleonic Wars, aimed at maintaining the balance between the major powers and preventing another significant armed conflict in Europe (see Fact Box 2.2).[82] Therefore, resorting to measures short of war (imperfect

[76] P. Paret, 'Machiavelli, Fichte, and Clausewitz in the Labyrinth of German Idealism' (2015) 17(3) *Ethics & Politics* 78–95, at 80–2.

[77] C. von Clausewitz, *On War* (Wordsworth Editions, 1997), bk I, chap. 1, s. 2, p. 5.

[78] Ibid., bk I, chap. 1, s. 24, p. 22.

[79] Ibid., bk I, chap. 1, s. 2, p. 5.

[80] Ibid., bk I, chap. 1, s. 3, p. 6.

[81] Brownlie, *International Law* (n. 6), pp. 45–7.

[82] S. Jeannesson, 'The Concert of Europe', in *Digital Encyclopedia of European History*, https://tinyurl.com/4xwu2esm. See also Brownlie, *International Law* (n. 6), pp. 19–20.

## FACT BOX 2.2 THE CONCERT OF EUROPE (1815–1914)

The Concert of Europe, also known as the Congress System or the Vienna System, began its existence at the 1814 Vienna Congress held during the final stage of the Napoleonic Wars. It was founded by Austria, Britain, Prussia and Russia, with the immediate objective of defeating France and the more general purpose of maintaining peace in Europe and avoiding another major conflict.

The Concert of Europe involved a series of congresses and conferences between its members at the highest level, which was an innovative approach in international relations at the time. It was to become the main method of diplomacy governing relations between the great powers in Europe throughout the nineteenth century. It was based on the principle that those relations should be governed by the maintenance of a balance of power, and that any dispute among members that threatened the maintenance of that balance should be resolved through dialogue rather than resort to force, unless there was no option to resorting to force to prevent a breakdown of the balance of power.

Up until the early 1860s, the Concert of Europe recorded several successes in preventing or containing conflicts. Examples include the subduing of local rebellions in Italy and Spain (early 1820s) as well as interventions leading to the independence of Greece from the Ottoman Empire (Greek War of Independence, 1821–9) and of Belgium from the Netherlands (Belgian Rebellion, 1830–1). To some extent, even the Crimean War (1853–6) managed to be contained due to the functioning of the Congress System. In the second half of the nineteenth century, the effectiveness of the Concert of Europe gradually decreased. The existing balance of power was disrupted by, among others, the unification of Germany and Italy, as well as the pressure that the rise of nationalism exerted on multinational empires such as Austria-Hungary and the Ottoman Empire. After the Franco-Prussian War (1870–1), Germany emerged as the most powerful State on the European continent. During the chancellorship of Otto von Bismarck following the formation of the German Empire, a delicate balance was maintained through a complex set of treaty relations aimed at preventing the rise of a diplomatic rival to German power in the Concert system. After Bismarck's dismissal in 1890, the treaty system he had crafted was gradually replaced by a rival set of military alliances that faced each other in a situation of armed peace until the outbreak of the First World War brought about the definitive demise of the by then moribund Concert system.

Despite its demise, the principles and functioning of the Concert of Europe render it a precursor of the collective security systems of both the League of Nations and the United Nations in the twentieth century.

**Sources**: S. C. Neff, *War and the Law of Nations: General History* (Cambridge University Press, 2005), pp. 220–2; S. Jeannesson, 'The Concert of Europe', in *Digital Encyclopedia of European History*, https://tinyurl.com/4xwu2esm; O. Wright, 'Concert of Europe', in G. Martel (ed.), *The Encyclopedia of Diplomacy* (Wiley Online Library, 2018), https://doi.org/10.1002/9781118885154.dipl0058; C. J. Bartlett, *Peace, War and the European Powers 1814–1914* (Palgrave Macmillan, 1996); G. F. Kennan, *The Decline of Bismarck's European Order: Franco-Russian Relations, 1875–1890* (Princeton University Press, 1979), pp. 223–398; C. Clark, *The Sleepwalkers: How Europe Went to War in 1914* (Penguin Books, 2013), pp. 121–60.

wars) proved less costly and more efficient, in both political and financial terms. These measures came in a variety of forms – discussed below – and they were typically justified as expressions of the right or duty of self-preservation.[83]

Legal authors in the nineteenth century gave the principle of self-preservation a privileged place in the system of the law of nations, subordinating almost all State duties to this concept.[84] One important category of measures justified by self-preservation was reprisals. These measures were characterized as 'amicable' methods of dispute settlement not amounting to war, permitted when justice had been plainly denied or unreasonably delayed.[85] Another category comprised 'interferences' or 'interventions' in self-defence, to secure obligations of treaty stipulations, on humanitarian grounds, to preserve the balance of power or for the purpose of participating in civil wars.[86] Not all of these measures survived into the twentieth century. Interventions to secure obligations of treaty stipulations or for the purpose of participating in civil wars were gradually renounced as illegal.[87] Conversely, interventions in self-defence and on humanitarian grounds continued to be invoked in twentieth-century State practice.[88] A related category of necessity-driven measures comprised hot pursuit, punitive expeditions or the rescue of nationals.[89] The demarcation line between these measures was often blurred in nineteenth-century State practice, and the notions of self-defence and self-preservation were often used interchangeably.[90]

One famous incident analysed at the time as a case of self-preservation was a string of events involving a steam vessel named *Caroline*.

83 Tibori-Szabó, *Anticipatory Action* (n. 1), pp. 69–72.

84 R. Phillimore, *Commentaries upon International Law*, vol. 1 (W. Benning, 1854), p. 225; T. Twiss, *Law of Nations Considered as Independent Political Communities*, vol. 2 (Oxford University Press, 1863), p. 3; W. E. Hall, *International Law* (Clarendon Press, 1880), p. 226.

85 R. Phillimore, *Commentaries Upon International Law*, vol. 3 (W. Benning, 1857), pp. 10–13; H. W. Halleck, *International Law or Rules Regulating the Intercourse of States in Peace and War* (H. H. Bancroft, 1861), p. 297; Hall, *International Law* (n. 84), pp. 306, 308.

86 Phillimore, *Commentaries*, vol. 1 (n. 84), p. 434; Halleck, *International Law* (n. 85), p. 83; Hall, *International Law* (n. 84), pp. 242–50; L. F. L. Oppenheim, *International Law: A Treatise*, vol. 1 (Longmans, Green, and Co., 1905), pp. 181–3.

87 Halleck, *International Law* (n. 85), pp. 83–4; Hall, *International Law* (n. 84), pp. 242–50; Oppenheim, *International Law*, vol. 1 (n. 86), pp. 181–3.

88 Tibori-Szabó, *Anticipatory Action* (n. 1), pp. 70–1.

89 Phillimore, *Commentaries*, vol. 3 (n. 85), pp. 225–31; T. Twiss, *Law of Nations Considered as Independent Political Communities*, vol. 1 (Oxford University Press, 1860), pp. 143–5.

90 R. Y. Jennings, 'The Caroline and MacLeod Cases' (1938) 32 *American Journal of International Law* 82–99, at 82 .

### FACT BOX 2.3 THE CAROLINE INCIDENT (1837)

During the 1837 insurrection in Canada, small disturbances, undertaken by sympathizers of the insurrection, occurred at various places in the United States, especially along the Canadian border. The US government took measures to enforce neutrality laws, but upon being defeated insurgents repeatedly sought refuge on US territory, where they resumed the recruitment of their forces. The *Caroline* was a steam vessel owned by American sympathizers of the insurgents and was used for transporting aid and supplies to the rebel forces. To put an end to this practice, in December 1837 British forces crossed into US territory without the consent of the American government, took possession of the *Caroline,* and sent it over the Niagara Falls, with the loss of life in the process. The case was settled between the two countries in 1842 and friendly relations were never interrupted.

The *Caroline* incident bears importance because of the correspondence that ensued between the parties. In January 1838, the then US secretary of state, John Forsyth, officially complained to Henry Fox, the British minister in Washington, and asked for redress. In his response, Fox invoked, inter alia, the principles of self-defence and self-preservation as justifying the action of the British forces. After another two years the discussion was renewed as a result of the arrest of British citizen Alexander McLeod by the American authorities. McLeod claimed that he took part in the destruction of the *Caroline* and was consequently arrested and charged with murder. On 24 April 1841, the new American secretary of state Daniel Webster addressed a letter to Henry Fox, in which he took up both the issue of *Caroline* and McLeod's arrest.

With a formula which has become famous, Webster further defined absolute necessity as a 'necessity of self-defence, instant, overwhelming, leaving no choice of means, and no moment for deliberation'. On this basis, Webster looked in detail at the circumstances of the *Caroline* incident in order to demonstrate that there was no absolute necessity to justify the destruction of the vessel. Accordingly, Webster called upon the British government to show that the legal authorities of Canada 'did nothing unreasonable and excessive' and that seizure of the vessel during daylight was impossible; that simply detaining the vessel, as opposed to destroying it, was not enough; and that attacking the crew on board, killing some and injuring others 'was a necessity, present and inevitable'.

**Sources**: K. Tibori-Szabó, *Anticipatory Action in Self-Defence* (Springer, 2011), pp. 72–5; R. Y. Jennings, 'The Caroline and MacLeod Cases' (1938) 32 *American Journal of International Law* 82–99, at 82–84.

The *Caroline* incident is famous today because of the ensuing correspondence between Daniel Webster, the US secretary of state, and Henry Fox, the British minister in Washington, relating to the limits of self-defence.[91] The importance of that discussion will be elaborated in Chapter 6. For the purposes of the present chapter, the *Caroline* incident is instructive for three reasons. First, the British-American correspondence confirmed the contemporary requirement to provide legal justification for armed actions outside a state of war. Second, the analysis of the incident and the ensuing correspondence by nineteenth-century jurists confirms the dominant position of the principle of self-preservation as an overarching concept justifying measures short of war. Third, the incident shows that self-defence was viewed as a sub-category of the principle of self-preservation, and the only one to survive into twentieth-century State practice.[92]

## 2.8 Towards a Prohibition on Waging War

Starting in the late nineteenth century, the concept of war as a last resort began gaining momentum. At the same time, there was growing ambivalence towards general war and in relation to various types of measures short of war. In parallel, peaceful means of dispute settlement received increasing attention.[93] As a result of these new tendencies, the principle of self-preservation started losing its dominant position. German jurist Lassa Oppenheim (1858–1919) went as far as to say that violations in the interest of self-preservation were no longer excused unless based strictly on necessity.[94]

Concomitantly, the scientific and technological revolution of the second half of the nineteenth century created the need for a network of international agreements for a variety of measures, such as to oversee worldwide postal deliveries, lay cables and link telegraph systems or regulate major waterways.[95] Hundreds of conferences were held during this period to address issues such as sanitation, police regulations, patents and copyrights.[96] In 1863, thanks to the work of Henry Dunant, the International Committee for Relief to the Wounded (later to be known as the International Committee of the Red Cross) was established.[97]

[91] Tibori-Szabó, *Anticipatory Action* (n. 1), pp. 73–5.
[92] Ibid., p. 74.
[93] Ibid., pp. 81–2.
[94] Oppenheim, *International Law*, vol. 1 (n. 86), p. 178.
[95] R. Henig, *The Peace That Never Was: A History of the League of Nations* (Haus, 2019), p. 2.
[96] Ibid.
[97] Nussbaum, *Concise History* (n. 15), pp. 218–21.

The first signs of an 'international civil society' appeared with the regular organization of the Universal Peace Congresses, which had the cessation of the arms race as one of their objectives.[98] The first Universal Peace Congress took place in Paris in June 1889, and meetings followed almost every year until 1913. After the third Universal Peace Congress in November 1891, the International Peace Bureau was established. The Bureau's mission was to co-ordinate activities of various societies and promote peaceful solutions to international conflicts.[99] After the First World War, congresses resumed in 1921. The last Universal Peace Congress convened in Zurich in August 1939.[100]

### FACT BOX 2.4 THE ALABAMA CLAIMS

The *Alabama Claims* arbitration took place in Geneva in 1871 to resolve claims made by the United States against Great Britain arising from the latter's conduct as a neutral State during the American Civil War (1861–5).

Following the outbreak of the war in April 1861, US president Abraham Lincoln declared a blockade of all ports in the seceding Confederate states. The Confederate states needed ships to break this blockade, to import munitions and attack enemy shipping. Lacking any significant naval or shipbuilding capacity, these states commissioned vessels built in England for use as warships against the North. A number of ships were acquired in this way, including the *Alabama* (initially called *Enrica*). The *Alabama* was responsible for the burning or sinking of sixty-four US vessels before it was itself sunk in June 1864.

The arbitration was conducted by an international tribunal, which found that Britain had breached its neutrality duties by failing to use due diligence to prevent the arming or equipping within its jurisdiction of any vessel to be used against a State with which Britain was at peace, the departure of such a vessel and the use of its ports or waters as a base of naval operations for similar purposes. The tribunal awarded the United States damages of $15,500,000 in gold. The award was duly honoured.

**Sources**: 'Alabama Claims of the United States of America against Great Britain: Award rendered on 14 September 1872 by the tribunal of arbitration established by Article I of the Treaty of Washington of 8 May 1871', RIAA, vol. XXIX (1871), pp. 125–4; T. Bingham, 'Alabama Arbitration', in *Max Planck Encyclopedia of Public International Law* (Oxford Public International Law, 2006), https://tinyurl.com/mrxfs7tw.

[98] Tibori-Szabó, *Anticipatory Action* (n. 1), p. 82.

[99] World Summit of Nobel Peace Laurates, 'International Peace Bureau – IPB', www.nobelpeacesummit.com/international-peace-bureau-ipb/ (accessed 23 April 2023).

[100] P. Laity, *The British Peace Movement* (Oxford University Press, 2002), pp. 114–44.

The use of arbitration to settle disputes grew considerably towards the end of the nineteenth century and beginning of the twentieth century.[101] In this context, the peaceful resolution of a diplomatic dispute between the United States and Great Britain regarding the role of the Confederate warship *Alabama* during the American Civil War set an important precedent for solving serious international disputes through arbitration.

The first Hague Peace Conference, in 1899, reflected this trend and established the Permanent Court of Arbitration. The conference also reflected the growing trend towards the regulation of warfare and resulted in the adoption of several conventions codifying the laws and customs of war. A second Hague Peace Conference, held in 1907, expanded the provisions on arbitration, updated some of the conventions regulating warfare and adopted additional ones, further regulating the conduct of hostilities.

Although both conferences tacitly accepted the right of States to wage war, the adopted conventions set out procedures to be followed before resorting to armed force. In this regard, Article 1 of the Hague Convention III of 1907 provided that hostilities between contracting parties could not commence without a prior and unambiguous warning in the form of either a reasoned declaration of war or an ultimatum containing a conditional declaration of war.[102] Moreover, Article 1 of the Hague Convention II of 1907 prohibited, under certain conditions, recourse to force for the recovery of contractual debts, thereby vindicating the view held at the time that recovery of property and debts was no longer a legitimate reason for waging war.[103] Together, the Hague Peace Conferences marked the beginning of attempts to restrict the freedom to resort to war.[104]

[101] Henig, *Peace That Never Was* (n. 95), p. 3.

[102] Convention (III) relative to the Opening of Hostilities (signed at The Hague, 18 October 1907), art. 1: 'The contracting Powers recognize that hostilities between themselves must not commence without previous and explicit warning, in the form either of a declaration of war, giving reasons, or of an ultimatum with conditional declaration of war.'

[103] Convention (II) respecting the Limitation of the Employment of Force for the Recovery of Contract Debts (signed at The Hague, 18 October 1907), art. 1: 'The Contracting Powers agree not to have recourse to armed force for the recovery of contract debts claimed from the Government of one country by the Government of another country as being due to its nationals. This undertaking is, however, not applicable when the debtor State refuses or neglects to reply to an offer of arbitration, or, after accepting the offer, prevents any *compromis* from being agreed on, or, after the arbitration, fails to submit to the award.' See also Nussbaum, *Concise History* (n. 15), p. 244.

[104] A. Randelzhofer and O. Dörr, 'Article 2(4)', in B. Simma et al. (eds.), *The Charter of the United Nations: A Commentary*, vol. 1 (Oxford University Press, 2012), p. 204.

Another important initiative at the time was the series of bilateral agreements 'for the advancement of general peace' negotiated by US secretary of state William Jennings Bryan and concluded between the United States and a number of other States shortly before the outbreak of the First World War.[105] Known today as the Bryan Treaties, these agreements obligated the contracting parties to refer their future disputes to a permanent international commission of inquiry, and not to resort to war until the commission delivered its report, thereby creating a cooling-off period.[106] A number of these agreements were signed prior to the outbreak of the war and about twenty were ratified afterwards, primarily with Latin American States, but also with other countries, notably Britain, Italy and Russia.[107] The significance of the Bryan Treaties lies not merely in their purpose of advancing general peace, but also in their

SUMMARY BOX 2.4 IMPORTANT STEPS TOWARDS A PROHIBITION ON WAR

- International Committee for Relief to the Wounded (1863)
- Universal Peace Congresses (1889–1913)
- The Hague Conferences (1899 and 1907)
- The Bryan Treaties (1913–14)

initiative of using commissions of inquiry where other methods of settling disputes had failed.[108]

Despite the peace movement of the early twentieth century, foreign policy was still dominated by the balance-of-power system and the Clausewitzian approach to war. This resulted in the first global war, which profoundly changed society and morality and exposed the fragility of the existing legal instruments regulating war. At the same time, as will be shown in Chapter 3, the First World War led to the creation of the first international organization and collective security system aimed at preventing further wars.

[105] H.-J. Schlochauer, 'Bryan Treaties (1913–14)', in *Max Planck Encyclopedia of Public International Law* (Oxford Public International Law, 1984), para. 1, https://tinyurl.com/565kz4u5.

[106] Nussbaum, *Concise History* (n. 15), p. 245; Schlochauer, 'Bryan Treaties' (n. 105), para. 1.

[107] Nussbaum, *Concise History* (n. 15), p. 245.

[108] Schlochauer, 'Bryan Treaties' (n. 105), para. 7.

## 2.9 Conclusion

In this chapter, we traced the evolution of the Western just war tradition, from its ancient roots to its Christian, and later secular, natural law precepts. Although, starting in the seventeenth century, the just war tradition was gradually replaced by positive law and a balance-of-power system, many of its elements endured and remain at the basis of the contemporary discourse on the morality and/or legality of war. For instance, the limitation of just causes to defensive wars has informed centuries of moral and legal doctrine on the legitimacy and legality of self-defence, culminating in today's Charter- and custom-based exception to the prohibition on the use of force. Equally, contemporary arguments favouring armed interventions for humanitarian purposes have, at their core, an implicit natural law and just cause rationale – a responsibility to protect people from large-scale human rights violations. Alongside these just war elements, other concepts presented in this chapter have also survived into contemporary law on the use of force. For example, the balance-of-power system embodied in the Concert of Europe served as a precursor of the collective security systems of both the League of Nations and the United Nations in the twentieth century. Likewise, the nineteenth-century movement towards peaceful dispute settlement and the prevention of war laid the early foundations for the twentieth-century efforts to regulate and prohibit war, which are discussed in Chapter 3.

# 3

# From the Regulation of War to the Prohibition on the Use of Force

## 3.1 Introduction

This chapter looks at the evolution of the law governing the use of force from the end of the First World War until the UN Charter was adopted. The creation of the League of Nations, as well as its successes, failures and final demise, receive attention, as do the adoption and impact of the Kellogg-Briand Pact. This brief review is useful in order to understand many aspects of today's *jus ad bellum*, such as what the strengths and weaknesses of the League's collective security system were and how they influenced the movement towards the prohibition of war; what events and considerations led to the prohibition on the use of force in the UN Charter; and what sort of understanding and importance the drafters of the Charter attached to the novel prohibition.

## 3.2 The First World War

The so-called Great War was precipitated by escalating tensions between Austria-Hungary and Serbia over the former's annexation of Bosnia-Herzegovina, previously under Ottoman occupation.[1] The spark that ultimately ignited the war was the June 1914 assassination by Serbian nationalist Gavrilo Princip of Archduke Franz Ferdinand, the heir presumptive to the throne of Austria-Hungary.[2] Within a few months the crisis erupted into war between two rival coalitions: the Triple Alliance of Austria-Hungary, Germany and Italy, formed in

[1] R. Henig, *The Origins of the First World War* (Routledge, 2002), pp. 17–23; C. Clark, *The Sleepwalkers: How Europe Went to War in 1914* (Penguin Books, 2012), pp. 121–364; J. Keegan, *The First World War* (Bodley Head, 2014), pp. 55–7.

[2] Henig, *Origins* (n. 1), pp. 23–8; Keegan, *First World War* (n. 1), pp. 57–67; O. A. Hathaway and S. J. Shapiro, *The Internationalists and Their Plan to Outlaw War* (Penguin Books, 2018), pp. 101–2.

1882, on the one hand,[3] and the Triple Entente consisting of Britain, France and Russia, also relying on prior alliances, on the other. [4] Upon being subsequently joined by allies, the two coalitions came to be known as the Central Powers (Austria-Hungary, Bulgaria, Germany and the Ottoman Empire) and the Allied Powers (Britain, China, France, Greece, Japan, Portugal, Romania, Russia, Serbia, the United States and others). In April 1915, as a result of the continued deterioration of its historical rivalry with Austria-Hungary, Italy left the Triple Alliance and entered the war on the side of the Allied Powers.[5] The war lasted four years and ended in November 1918, with the Allied Powers claiming victory.

The First World War led to the collapse of four great empires (Austria-Hungary, Germany, the Ottoman Empire and Russia) and caused tremendous physical damage, especially across France and Belgium, and massive financial indebtedness, as well as the outbreak of revolutions and social unrest in Europe and elsewhere.[6] Due to novel military technologies used in the conflict and protracted trench warfare, especially on the Western Front, the First World War resulted in unprecedented levels of destruction and carnage.[7] By the time the war was over, more than 19 million people – soldiers and civilians alike – were dead.[8]

## 3.3 The Creation of the League of Nations

### *3.3.1 Preliminaries*

While the war was ongoing, pacifist groups in France, the United Kingdom and the United States amplified their call for the creation of an international organization to maintain peace.[9] In 1917, British foreign secretary Arthur Balfour set up a committee to examine the abundant literature that had by then appeared on the subject of a post-war

[3] C. J. Bartlett, *Peace, War and the European Powers 1814–1914* (Palgrave Macmillan, 1996), p. 110.

[4] Henig, *Origins* (n. 1), pp. 12–14.

[5] J. A. Vasquez, *Contagion and War: Lessons from the First World War* (Cambridge University Press, 2018), pp. 183–9; Keegan, *First World War* (n. 1), p. 244.

[6] R. Henig, *The Peace That Never Was: A History of the League of Nations* (Haus, 2019), p. 1.

[7] S. Bull, *Trench: A History of Trench Warfare on the Western Front* (Osprey, 2014), pp. 59–120; Keegan, *First World War* (n. 1), pp. 191–202; M. Howard, *The First World War: A Very Short Introduction* (Oxford University Press, 2002), pp. 100–1, 106, 122.

[8] N. Mougel, 'World War I Casualties', trans. J. Gratz, *REPERES* (2011), pp. 1–4.

[9] Henig, *Peace That Never Was* (n. 6), pp. 9–14.

international organization and to produce a report formulating a practical scheme for such an organization.[10] Echoing the Bryan Treaties, the final report of the committee proposed the creation of an international assembly of States, whose members would agree not to resort to war before submitting their disputes to some form of settlement, thus going through a cooling-off period.[11] In 1918, the French government also set up a commission to propose a model for a future world organization. Unlike the British model, the French proposal entailed a robust world organization with an international armed force and the capacity to impose sanctions on member States that disobeyed its decisions.[12] On the American side, in January 1918 US president Woodrow Wilson set out before the United States Congress fourteen points for 'the programme of the world's peace'.[13] The last of his 'Fourteen Points' called for the establishment of 'a general association of nations . . . for the purpose of affording mutual guarantees of political independence and territorial integrity to great and small States alike'.[14] Building on the British and French reports, Wilson's advisers prepared an American proposal for a new organization.[15] Also influential in the drafting process was a pamphlet entitled *The League of Nations: A Practical Suggestion*, written by South African General Jan Christian Smuts. In his pamphlet, Smuts advocated for a League 'not only as a possible means for preventing future wars, but much more as a great organ of the ordinary peaceful life of civilization, as the foundation of the new international system which will be erected on the ruins of this war'.[16] Relying on the British and American drafts and the South African proposal, Wilson personally oversaw the drafting of the League's Covenant at the Paris Peace Conference.[17]

[10] Ibid., pp. 15–16.

[11] Ibid., p. 16.

[12] Ibid., p. 17.

[13] President Woodrow Wilson's Fourteen Points, available in the Avalon Project digital document collection, Lillian Goldman Law Library, Yale Law School (Avalon Project), https://avalon.law.yale.edu/20th_century/wilson14.asp.

[14] Ibid.

[15] Henig, *Peace That Never Was* (n. 6), pp. 18–20; C. J. Tams, 'League of Nations', in *Max Planck Encyclopedia of Public International Law* (Oxford Public International Law, 2006), para. 1, https://tinyurl.com/m7cxd4s8.

[16] J. C. Smuts, *The League of Nations: A Practical Suggestion* (Hodder and Stoughton, 1918), p. 8.

[17] Henig, *Peace That Never Was* (n. 6), pp. 22–48.

### 3.3.2 The Paris Peace Conference

On 18 January 1919, the opening of the Paris Peace Conference marked the beginning of the formal peace process, which lasted until July 1923.[18] The centrepiece of the conference was the Treaty of Versailles, signed on 28 June 1919, which ended the state of war between the Allied Powers and Germany.[19] By the first week of May 1919, the full draft of the treaty was ready.[20] It consisted of fifteen parts, the first of which was the Covenant of the League of Nations (see Fact Box 3.1). The remaining parts set out the territorial, military, political and economic sanctions against Germany.[21]

Germany had hoped that the treaty would reflect Wilson's Fourteen Points and thus be couched in moderate terms.[22] However, when presented with the treaty on 7 May 1919, the German delegation was outraged and denounced its terms as hypocritical and unjust.[23] Their many objections to the sanctions that were to be imposed included fierce criticism of the so-called war-guilt clause in Article 231 of the treaty, which created a legal basis for imposing reparations.[24] Article 231, in Part VIII of the treaty, called upon Germany to accept its own and its allies' responsibility 'for causing all the loss and damage to which the Allied and Associated Governments and their nationals have been subjected as a consequence of the war imposed upon them by the aggression of Germany and her allies'. Furthermore, Articles 227–30, in Part VII of the treaty, called for the creation of special tribunals to try persons accused of having committed acts in violation of the laws and customs of war, including Emperor Wilhelm II of Hohenzollern 'for a supreme offence against international morality and the sanctity of treaties'. The German representatives also complained about not having been

[18] The formal peace process entailed the signing of several treaties, such as the Treaty of Versailles with Germany (1919), the Treaty of St Germain with Austria (1919), the Treaty of Neuilly with Bulgaria (1919), the Treaty of Trianon with Hungary (1920) and the Treaty of Sèvres with Turkey (1920), renegotiated as the Treaty of Lausanne (1923). M. S. Neiberg, *The Treaty of Versailles: A Concise History* (Oxford University Press, 2007), pp. ix–x.

[19] Ibid., p. x. The Treaty of Versailles entered into force on 10 January 1920.

[20] Ibid., p. 51.

[21] Treaty of Peace with Germany (Treaty of Versailles), 28 June 1919, Library of Congress, www.census.gov/history/pdf/treaty_of_versailles-112018.pdf.

[22] Neiberg, *Treaty of Versailles* (n. 18), pp. xi–xii.

[23] M. MacMillan, *Paris 1919: Six Months That Changed the World* (Random House, 2003), pp. 465–80; Neiberg, *Treaty of Versailles* (n. 18), p. xii; Henig, *Peace That Never Was* (n. 6), p. 49.

[24] Neiberg, *Treaty of Versailles* (n. 18), pp. 58–9.

permitted to contribute to the drafting of the Covenant and that Germany was excluded from original membership of the League.[25] The treaty was also criticized by many other commentators, including participants at the Paris Peace Conference. To this day, the Treaty of Versailles is considered by some commentators as one of the principal reasons that led to the Second World War.[26]

### FACT BOX 3.1 THE TREATY OF VERSAILLES AND THE LEAGUE COVENANT

The Covenant establishing the League of Nations formed an integral part of the Treaty of Versailles. It was signed by forty-two founding members at the Paris Peace Conference. The League officially started its existence on 10 January 1920, when the Covenant, together with the rest of the Treaty of Versailles, entered into force.

The Covenant consisted of a preamble and 26 articles. The preamble set out the League's principal objective – to promote international co-operation and to achieve international peace and security through: (a) the acceptance of obligations not to resort to war; (b) the prescription of open, just and honourable relations between nations; (c) the firm establishment of the understandings of international law as the actual rule of conduct among governments; and (d) the maintenance of justice and a scrupulous respect for all treaty obligations in dealings between organized peoples.

The Covenant set out the principal organs of the League: the Assembly and the Council, plus a permanent Secretariat. While the Assembly comprised representatives of all members of the League, the Council was to consist of the representatives of the 'Principal Allied and Associated Powers' – that is, Britain, France, Italy, Japan and the United States (permanent members), as well as the representatives of four other member States of the League, to be selected by the Assembly from time to time at its discretion (non-permanent members). In 1926, Germany joined the League and became a permanent member of the Council. The seat of the League was established in Geneva.

In order to fulfil the preamble's undertaking, the Covenant set out a collective security system (discussed at more length later in this chapter), which was a revived and more organized version of the functions fulfilled by the Concert of Europe in the nineteenth century (see Chapter 2). The League went on to have some major successes, but also many failures (see details later in this chapter).

In any event, the inclusion of the Covenant in the Treaty of Versailles was certainly one of the reasons for the subsequent failure of the League. Although all

[25] Henig, *Peace That Never Was* (n. 6), p. 49.

[26] Neiberg, *Treaty of Versailles* (n. 18), pp. x–xviii; N. A. Graebner and E. E. Bennett, *The Versailles Treaty and Its Legacy: The Failure of the Wilsonian Vision* (Cambridge University Press, 2014), pp. 57–60. See, however, MacMillan, *Paris 1919* (n. 23), pp. 492–4.

FACT BOX 3.1 (*cont.*)

the defeated powers would join the League, the new organization was bound to be viewed as an instrument in the hands of the victorious powers.

**Sources**: R. Henig, *The Peace That Never Was: A History of the League of Nations* (Haus, 2019), p. 211; C. J. Tams, 'League of Nations', in *Max Planck Encyclopedia of Public International Law* (Oxford Public International Law, 2006), para. 3.

## 3.4 The League's Collective Security System

Further to the undertaking expressed in the preamble, Articles 10–13 and 15 of the Covenant set up a collective security system among the members of the League. The most significant provision in this regard is Article 10, according to which League members undertook 'to respect and preserve as against external aggression the territorial integrity and existing political independence of all Members of the League'. Article 10 set up a collective security system against external aggression. Nonetheless, read in conjunction with Articles 12–13 and 15, Article 10 cannot be interpreted as unequivocally prohibiting war between League members. Certainly, the Covenant made it more difficult for League members to go to war against each other. In line with Articles 12, 13(1) and 15(1), members were required to submit their dispute to arbitration, judicial settlement or to the League Council and could not go to war against each other until three months after the rendering of the decision resolving the dispute. Most notably, recourse to war was forbidden against a League member complying, in accordance with Articles 13(4) and 15(6), with the arbitration award, the judicial decision or a report of the League Council unanimously agreed to by its members. Nonetheless, if the Council failed to reach a unanimous decision, League members could reserve the right to take such action as they considered necessary 'for the maintenance of right and justice' (Article 15(7)). Likewise, nothing stopped one member resorting to war against a non-complying member, provided applicable procedural requirements were observed. Moreover, the right of self-defence of any League member against an external aggression can be inferred from the wording of Articles 10, 12 and 15. This was explicitly acknowledged in one of the preliminary reports on the draft Geneva Protocol on the Pacific Settlement of International Disputes, which stated that the prohibition in the

Covenant affected only aggressive war and left intact the right to legitimate self-defence.[27] In any event, Article 16(1) provided that if a League member resorted to war in disregard of Articles 12, 13 or 15, it was deemed to have committed an act of war against all other members of the League, which in turn were required to subject the aggressor to various sanctions.[28]

**SUMMARY BOX 3.1 ARTICLE 10 OF THE LEAGUE COVENANT**

'The Members of the League undertake to respect and preserve as against external aggression the territorial integrity and existing political independence of all Members of the League. In case of any such aggression or in case of any threat or danger of such aggression the Council shall advise upon the means by which this obligation shall be fulfilled.'

The system thus set up by the Covenant was a peculiar combination of three of the aforementioned regulative frameworks: the just war doctrine, Clausewitzian realism and legal positivist thinking. Accordingly, while the Covenant did not resurrect the concept of just cause and did not set out *substantive* grounds for waging war, as did the just war doctrine, it nevertheless required *procedural* options for peaceful dispute settlement to be exhausted before war could occur.[29] Furthermore, echoing the dynamics of the Paris Peace Conference, the composition of the League Council ensured that great power politics continued to influence the functioning of the new organization. At the same time, the very existence of the Covenant and its collective security system clearly reflected the positivist approach of regulating war through legal instruments. As a multilateral treaty, the Covenant was also a historic milestone in the emerging international framework regulating war.

[27] E. Benes and N. Politis, 'Report on the Protocol, Submitted to the Fifth Assembly' (1924) 23 *League of Nations Official Journal*, Spec. Supp. 479–502, at 483.

[28] See also K. Tibori-Szabó, *Anticipatory Action in Self-Defence* (Springer, 2011), p. 86.

[29] S. C. Neff, *War and the Law of Nations: General History* (Cambridge University Press, 2005), pp. 292–3.

## 3.5 The Early Years of the League

Despite the historical importance of the Covenant, the League had its inherent and acquired vulnerabilities. As mentioned above, one of its weaknesses was the Covenant's incorporation in the Treaty of Versailles. Another blow suffered soon after the signing of the treaty was the refusal of the US Senate to ratify it. At the time, the US Senate had a small Republican majority, which largely opposed unconditional American membership of the League.[30] After returning from Europe, and in a bid to convince the American people to support the treaty, Wilson embarked on a speaking tour of the country to explain the treaty and promote his vision of the role of the League in preserving future peace. He was met with popular enthusiasm, but on 25 September 1919, while on tour, Wilson collapsed and was rushed back to Washington, where a few days later he suffered a near-fatal stroke.[31] His illness proved to be a decisive setback in the campaign to promote the League. In November 1919, the Republicans proposed fourteen reservations to the Treaty of Versailles, which, inter alia, had the effect of exempting the United States from any League obligations in relation to limitation of armaments or guarantees of territorial integrity and political independence of member States and allowing Congress to define unilaterally what constituted a 'domestic' issue over which the League had no jurisdiction and to demand American withdrawal from the League at any time.[32] Thanks to Wilson's insistence, a motion to pass the treaty with these reservations was rejected, but the treaty also failed to pass without reservations.[33] In March 1920, another set of reservations was put forward, but the motion again failed to pass, dashing any chance of US membership of the League.[34]

Another important absentee from the original membership of the League was Russia, embroiled in a civil war between the Bolshevik Red Army, led by Vladimir Lenin, and the counter-revolutionary, monarchist White Army. Throughout the Paris Peace Conference, the former Allies, mainly Britain and France, supported the counter-revolutionary side, and for that reason the Bolshevik government unequivocally condemned

[30] F. P. Walters, *A History of the League of Nations* (Oxford University Press, 1965), p. 69.

[31] Ibid., p. 70; Henig, *Peace That Never Was* (n. 6), pp. 51–2.

[32] Henig, *Peace That Never Was* (n. 6), p. 53; Walters, *History of the League of Nations* (n. 30), pp. 70–1.

[33] MacMillan, *Paris 1919* (n. 23), pp. 488–92; Henig, *Peace That Never Was* (n. 6), pp. 53–4.

[34] Henig, *Peace That Never Was* (n. 6), p. 56.

the work of the conference, including the drafting of the Covenant.[35] Another fourteen years elapsed before the Soviet Union finally joined the League in 1934.

Despite this difficult start, the first meeting of the League took place in Paris in January 1920, and its second meeting was held in London the following month. By the summer of that year, the League was already dealing with potential disputes.[36] One such conflict was the Åland islands crisis between Sweden and Finland. The islands had been part of the Grand Duchy of Finland when it was part of the Russian Empire. Though still nominally at war with Russia in the summer of 1920, the new Finnish government was in effective control of the whole country, including the Åland islands. The islanders, however, were mainly of Swedish origin and they wanted to become part of Sweden. The dispute was referred to the League Council in June 1920. A commission was set up and dispatched to the Baltic to draw up recommendations. The report drawn up by the commission recommended that the islands remain under Finnish sovereignty, but that the League should ensure that the rights and interests of the inhabitants were not threatened in any way and that the islands should not be used as military or naval bases. In June 1921, the League Council endorsed these recommendations in spite of strong Swedish opposition and Finnish concerns about the League's control over the islands. Nonetheless, both governments complied with the Council's decision, giving the League its first major success.[37]

Amidst the turbulent political landscape, the early years of the League looked reasonably promising. In December 1920, Austria and Bulgaria joined the League, followed by Hungary in September 1922. As a result of the improving relations between the former Allies and Germany following the signing of the Locarno Pact in October 1925,[38] the latter joined the League in September 1926 and also became a permanent member of

[35] Walters, *History of the League of Nations* (n. 30), p. 94.

[36] Henig, *Peace That Never Was* (n. 6), pp. 63–4.

[37] Walters, *History of the League of Nations* (n. 30), pp. 103–5; Henig, *Peace That Never Was* (n. 6), pp. 64–5.

[38] The Treaty of Mutual Guarantee between Germany, Belgium, France, Great Britain and Italy (Locarno Pact) was signed on 16 October 1925 and contained, inter alia, Germany's formal recognition of its western borders as set out in the Treaty of Versailles (Article 1). Furthermore, Germany, Belgium and France pledged that 'they will in no case attack or invade each other or resort to war against each other' except in cases of self-defence or League action (Article 2). Available in Avalon Project, https://avalon.law.yale.edu/20th_century/locarno_001.asp.

the Council. In total, fourteen countries joined the League before 1930 and another seven between 1930 and 1937.[39]

## 3.6 The Kellogg-Briand Pact

Notwithstanding the existence of the League and Germany's joining in 1926, France saw its own security and, implicitly, the security of Europe greatly endangered by its former enemy. Consequently, between 1920 and 1927 the French government managed to secure alliances with all important States bordering Germany (Belgium, Czechoslovakia and Poland) as well as States in the Balkans (Romania and Yugoslavia).[40]

Having secured these alliances, French foreign minister Aristide Briand commenced talks with the United States with a view to entering into an agreement that would preclude any future war between the two. Lengthy negotiations, spanning sixteen months, ensued (see Fact Box 3.2).

### FACT BOX 3.2 NEGOTIATING THE PACT OF PARIS (KELLOGG-BRIAND PACT)

On 6 April 1927, in a statement issued through the Associated Press, French foreign minister Aristide Briand proposed that the United States and France enter into an agreement never to use war as an instrument of national policy against each other. This suggestion was formalized in June that year as a draft treaty containing two articles. The first enunciated the parties' condemnation of recourse to war and their renunciation of war as an instrument of national policy towards one another. The second stated that the settlement of any disputes would be by pacific means.

Briand's American counterpart, US secretary of state Frank Kellogg, was initially sceptical about entering into any agreement with France and being drawn into the European system of security alliances. He deferred answering Briand's invitation for months. Finally, the American reply came in December 1927 with Kellogg's suggestion that they obtain 'the adherence of all the principal powers of the world to a declaration renouncing war as an instrument of national policy'. Kellogg was in fact hoping to quell the idea of a bilateral treaty without outrightly rejecting it. He suspected that France would be much less enthusiastic about a multilateral agreement on the same terms. While Briand was initially inclined to reject the American counter-proposal, he nevertheless engaged in negotiations with the Americans. The main questions discussed concerned the extent of the prohibition – that is, whether

[39] Walters, *History of the League of Nations* (n. 30), pp. 64–5.

[40] R. H. Ferrell, *Peace in Their Time: The Origins of the Kellogg-Briand Pact* (Yale University Press, 1952), pp. 63–4.

FACT BOX 3.2 (*cont.*)

aggressive war or war as such would be prohibited, the status of the right of self-defence and how the prohibition would be enforced. Despite his initial calculations behind the proposal of a multilateral treaty, Kellogg gradually warmed to his own idea. He took an active part in the debates and believed that the treaty should not differentiate between aggressive and defensive wars and considered the right of self-defence as a given. By the end of March 1928 Briand had reluctantly come to accept the idea of a multilateral treaty, but insisted on three fundamental points: the treaty had to be universal; a breach of its terms would release the signatories from their obligations; and the treaty must not prejudice the right of self-defence.

In April 1928, Kellogg submitted to Germany, Italy, Japan and the United Kingdom an official invitation to enter the anti-war discussion and sent a draft proposal of a multilateral treaty that was very similar to Briand's original proposal. One week later, Briand sent a counter-proposal, which explicitly reserved the right of self-defence and exempted from the prohibition any exercise of force undertaken pursuant to treaty obligations, such as the League Covenant. On 23 June 1928, Kellogg sent a revised draft together with an explanatory note addressing the comments, reservations and concerns expressed by the French and the other governments.

After sixteen months of negotiations, in August 1928, the Pact of Paris was finally signed. At the outbreak of the Second World War in 1939 it had sixty-three parties, which included almost all independent States at that time.

**Sources**: A. C. Watkins, *The Paris Pact: A Textbook for Schools and Colleges* (Harcourt Brace, 1932), pp. 6–20; O. A. Hathaway and S. J. Shapiro, *The Internationalists and Their Plan to Outlaw War* (Penguin Books, 2018), pp. 122–7; R. H. Ferrell, *Peace in Their Time: The Origins of the Kellogg-Briand Pact* (Yale University Press, 1952), pp. 164–5, 169–71, 187–8; D. H. Miller, *The Peace Pact of Paris: A Study of the Briand-Kellogg Treaty* (G. P. Putnam's Sons, 1928), pp. 213–14; K. Tibori-Szabó, *Anticipatory Action in Self-Defence* (Springer, 2011), pp. 88–9.

The Pact was signed by fifteen States on 27 August 1928.[41] It consisted of three articles: two substantive and one procedural. In Article I the contracting parties condemned recourse to war for the solution of international controversies and renounced it as an instrument of national policy in their relations with one another. Article II referred to the settlement of disputes and recorded the parties' agreement that the solution of 'all disputes or conflicts of whatever nature or of whatever

[41] The initial signatories were Australia, Belgium, Canada, Czechoslovakia, France, Germany, India, the Irish Free State, Italy, Japan, New Zealand, Poland, South Africa, the United Kingdom and the United States. R. Lessaffer, 'Kellogg-Briand Pact (1928)', in *Max Planck Encyclopedia of Public International Law* (Oxford Public International Law, 2015), para. 2, https://tinyurl.com/mwmx2jum.

SUMMARY BOX 3.2 KELLOGG ON THE RIGHT OF SELF-DEFENCE

'[The] right [of self-defence] is inherent in every sovereign State and is implicit in every treaty. Every nation is free at all times and regardless of treaty provisions to defend its territory from attack or invasion and it alone is competent to decide whether circumstances require recourse to war in self-defence.'

Frank B. Kellogg, Note, 23 June 1928

origin' that might arise among them would never be sought other than by pacific means. Article III concerned the procedure for further signatures and ratification.[42]

The terms of the Pact departed from the classic formulas of 'aggressive war' or 'external aggression' and instead outlawed war 'as an instrument of national policy', signalling a clear departure from Clausewitzian realism.[43] Admittedly, the new phraseology had its own weakness, as it did not clarify whether only declared wars or also measures short of war – with the exception of self-defence – were outlawed by the Pact.[44] It also did not stop several States from making reservations that further narrowed the prohibition, such as the British reservation for actions against interference in 'certain regions of the world the welfare and integrity of which constitute a special and vital interest for our peace and safety',[45] or the distinction Germany drew in 1930 between war as an instrument of national policy and war as 'a means of international action which may be considered necessary for the maintenance of order in international life'.[46] Furthermore, despite the extensive negotiations on the consequences of breaching the Pact and the American reassurance in the final note of

[42] Treaty Between the United States and Other Powers Providing for the Renunciation of War as an Instrument of National Policy, 27 August 1928, available in Avalon Project, https://avalon.law.yale.edu/20th_century/kbpact.asp; Tibori-Szabó, *Anticipatory Action* (n. 28), pp. 89–90.

[43] Tibori-Szabó, *Anticipatory Action* (n. 28), p. 90.

[44] Lessaffer, 'Kellogg-Briand Pact' (n. 41), para. 11.

[45] Telegram of 19 May 1928, 'The Ambassador in Great Britain (Houghton) to the Secretary of State' (1928) 1 *Papers Relating to the Foreign Relations of the United States* Doc. No. 56, para. 10, https://tinyurl.com/5f5kas4n; Lessaffer, 'Kellogg-Briand Pact' (n. 41), para. 12.

[46] 'Amendment of the Covenant of the League of Nations in Order to Bring It into Harmony with the Pact of Paris, Observations of the Governments, Germany' (May 1930) 11(5) *League of Nations Official Journal* 353–83, at 368; Lessaffer, 'Kellogg-Briand Pact' (n. 41), para. 13.

23 June 1928 that 'if a State resorts to war in violation of the treaty, the other contracting parties are released from their obligations under the treaty to that State',[47] the prohibition in Article I of the Pact was practically unenforceable. Despite these weaknesses, the Kellogg-Briand Pact was a further stepping stone in the emerging international framework regulating war and the evolution towards the prohibition on the use of force in the UN Charter.

## 3.7 The 1930s and the Collapse of the League

Although the Kellogg-Briand Pact was received with enthusiasm and was seen as an additional consolidation of the Covenant, State practice in the 1930s revealed the fatal weaknesses of the League system. The widely perceived unfairness of the post-war peace treaties and especially the Treaty of Versailles, the fact that the United States never became a member and the political and military vulnerability of France and Britain were some of the inherent weaknesses of the League, which were further exacerbated by the events of the 1930s. The financial crisis of 1929–33, the rise of fascism in Italy and Germany, the growing antagonism between Council members, and the withdrawal of Japan, Germany, Italy, Spain, the Soviet Union and others ultimately led to the League's demise.

The collapse of the League was facilitated by the Council's inability to tackle three major conflicts: the Japanese invasion of Manchuria (1931–2), the conflict between Bolivia and Paraguay (1932–3) and the Italian invasion of Abyssinia, or Ethiopia (1935). All three conflicts have been analysed (by parties and commentators) in terms of aggression and response to aggression.

By the time Italy had captured the Ethiopian capital in the spring of 1936, the world was irreversibly heading towards the Second World War. In March 1936, Hitler deployed German troops into the Rhineland, in breach of both the Treaty of Versailles and the Locarno Pact. In the summer of the same year, the Spanish Civil War broke out, bringing Mussolini and Hitler together in the assistance they afforded General Franco. One year later, the conflict between China and Japan turned into open war. Finally, in December 1939, the Council expelled the Soviet

[47] Telegram of 20 June 1928, 'The Secretary of State to the Ambassador in France (Herrick)' (1928) 1 *Papers Relating to the Foreign Relations of the United States* Doc. No. 71, https://tinyurl.com/2674anv6.

### FACT BOX 3.3 MID-1930S CONFLICTS AND THE RESPONSE OF THE LEAGUE OF NATIONS

#### The Japanese invasion of Manchuria (1931–2)

After winning the Russo-Japanese war of 1904–5, Japan was given control of a Russian-built railway running through Chinese Manchuria. Over the next two and a half decades, Japan turned the railway into a large and very lucrative corporate enterprise. However, the success and the expansion of the railway fuelled growing tensions between China and Japan, which reached a culmination in the autumn of 1931. On the night of 18 September 1931, an explosion occurred on the Japanese-run South Manchurian Railway in the south of Manchuria (now Shenyang). The incident was used to justify the deployment of Japanese army units across South Manchuria, which, by the end of 1931, resulted in the Japanese occupation of the entire region of Manchuria. In 1932, Chinese regulars and guerrillas strengthened their resistance, causing the conflict to spread beyond the region to other areas of China. During this time, neither China nor Japan declared the existence of a state of war. In May 1933 an armistice agreement was concluded.

Three days after the initial incident, China referred the matter to the League Council and asked for assistance from the United States under the Kellogg-Briand Pact. Addressing the Council, Japan initially reassured its members that it had no territorial desires and that most of its troops had already been withdrawn, while the rest would be evacuated as soon as Japanese citizens and property in Manchuria were no longer endangered. But as the situation in Manchuria worsened, the Council began to doubt the assurances given by Japan. Faced with criticism for its actions, the Japanese government advanced another justification, which was that China had breached the Kellogg-Briand Pact by boycotting Japanese goods throughout its territory and that Japan was thus entitled to take forcible counteraction. Negotiations overseen by the Council and the United States started in October 1931 but were inconclusive. The military situation grew increasingly worse, with the Japanese army further extending its territorial control and, in early 1932, establishing the new State of Manchukuo on Manchurian territory.

The League decided to dispatch a commission of inquiry to Manchuria. Led by Victor Bulwer-Lytton, the commission spent six weeks in Manchuria in the spring of 1932 piecing together the facts. Meanwhile, Japan continued to maintain that there were no warlike intentions and that its action was justified as a defence of rights and interests on which its very existence depended. The report of the Lytton Commission was published in the fall of 1932 and served as an authoritative record of facts. The report stated that the actions of the Japanese army after the initial incident could not be viewed as legitimate self-defence and intimated that the Japanese military campaign had been planned beforehand. The report recommended the re-establishment of Chinese sovereignty over Manchuria.

In response, Japan reiterated its argument of self-defence and rejected the recommendations of the report. On 27 March, following a statement adopted by the Assembly of the League in February 1933, which endorsed the findings and

FACT BOX 3.3 (*cont.*)

recommendations of the commission's report, Japan announced its withdrawal from the League. Despite the considerable efforts by Council members and the United States to secure a settlement of the conflict, and notwithstanding widespread praise of the commission's report for its accuracy and impartiality, the League's ability to deal with major international conflicts was dealt a serious blow.

**Sources**: O. A. Hathaway and S. J. Shapiro, *The Internationalists and Their Plan to Outlaw War* (Penguin Books, 2018), pp. 153–6; J. T. Shotwell and M. Salvin, *Lessons on Security and Disarmament: From the History of the League of Nations* (King's Crown Press, 1949), p. 81; R. Henig, *The Peace That Never Was: A History of the League of Nations* (Haus, 2019), pp. 127, 139; F. P. Walters, *A History of the League of Nations* (Oxford University Press, 1965), pp. 470, 473–5, 491–5; I. Brownlie, *International Law and the Use of Force by States* (Clarendon Press, 1963), pp. 294, 385–6; 'League Council Meeting, 25 January 1932' (1932) 13(3) *League of Nations Official Journal* 326–33, at 332; K. Tibori-Szabó, *Anticipatory Action in Self-Defence* (Springer, 2011), pp. 93–4.

### The Bolivia-Paraguay conflict (1932–3)

The conflict between Bolivia and Paraguay involved the Gran Chaco, a vast area separating the territory of the two countries. As a result of the 1879–84 war between Bolivia, Peru and Chile, Bolivia lost its narrow strip of coast and became landlocked. The Gran Chaco remained the only route which permitted Bolivia to reach the Atlantic coast through the Rio de La Plata estuary. Both the Bolivian and the Paraguayan governments claimed the whole area and each was in effective control of a small sector near its own territory. Although early clashes in the late 1920s were anesthetized by the League, in 1932 the two parties launched hostilities against each other.

In 1933, the League agreed to dispatch a commission of its own to solve the conflict. After several failures to secure agreement between the two parties, in 1934, the commission returned to Geneva. The League Council nevertheless succeeded in imposing an embargo on the selling of weapons and ammunition to the warring parties by European and American States. A last attempt of the Council to broker peace between the two countries failed in November 1934, when Paraguay did not accept the terms of the proposed treaty.

Reaching a state of mutual exhaustion, the two belligerents finally agreed on a truce in June 1935 and the war was declared over in November the same year. A peace treaty was finally signed in Buenos Aires in July 1938, but the League was no longer formally associated with the proceedings.

**Sources:** F. P. Walters, *A History of the League of Nations* (Oxford University Press, 1965), pp. 526–36; B. W. Farcau, *The Chaco War: Bolivia and Paraguay, 1932–1935* (Praeger, 1996), p. 8; A. Nussbaum, *A Concise History of the Law of Nations* (Macmillan, 1947), p. 249; K. Tibori-Szabó, *Anticipatory Action in Self-Defence* (Springer, 2011), pp. 91–2.

FACT BOX 3.3 (*cont.*)

### The Italian invasion of Ethiopia (1935–6)

Admitted to the League in 1923 and under the rule of Hailie Selassie from 1928, Ethiopia was bordered on the north and south by Italian colonies. The ancient kingdom had made considerable progress under the rule of Hailie Selassie but still lacked full control over its frontier regions. The ambition of Italian dictator Mussolini was to turn the Mediterranean Sea into 'an Italian lake' and one of his targets was the Abyssinian (Ethiopian) kingdom. He began planning an attack on the country as early as 1933, but a pretext was needed to launch hostilities. Such an excuse finally presented itself in December 1934, when armed bands of Somalis employed by the Italian Royal Corps clashed with Ethiopian militia in the disputed area between Italian Somaliland and the Ogaden province inhabited by Ethiopian tribes.

Selassie duly referred the matter to the League Council for arbitration. Italy rejected that option and demanded an apology and reparations. Action on behalf of the Council was delayed because France and Britain, for fear of upsetting Mussolini, on whose assistance they were counting to hold back Nazi aggression, wished to solve the matter on their own with Italy. Meanwhile, Italian preparations for the invasion of Ethiopia were manifestly intensifying. During the following months, Selassie reiterated his request to the League Council and an arbitral commission was eventually put in place, but its work was delayed. Selassie also appealed to the US government to avert a threatened violation of the Kellogg-Briand Pact, but the United States took no action other than expressing its hopes that a peaceful solution would be found.

The League Council met again in September 1935 and drafted a plan of international assistance for Ethiopia, which was rejected by Italy. The Italian government claimed that Ethiopia had failed to comply with its obligations under various treaties, that it had committed a long series of outrages against Italian diplomats and that, in fact, it could not qualify as a true member of the League because it was not an organized State and had not succeeded in abolishing slavery, as promised when joining the League. On this basis, Italy claimed that it was defending its own colonies and the prestige and good name of the League of Nations.

The Italian offensive began on 3 October 1935 and quickly turned into a full-scale invasion. Although the League proposed sanctions against Italy, the French prime minister Pierre Laval and the British chancellor Sir Samuel Hoare secretly decided not to enforce the sanctions as part of their plan to partition Ethiopia and give much of its territory to Mussolini. The plan was leaked to the French press and never came to fruition. The mild economic sanctions imposed thereafter did not hamper the Italian intervention. Addis Ababa was captured in May 1936 and Selassie was forced to flee. The Council's complete failure to manage the Ethiopian crisis and the exposure of its members' secret machinations permanently damaged the reputation and functioning of the League.

FACT BOX 3.3 (*cont.*)

**Sources**: R. Henig, *The Peace That Never Was: A History of the League of Nations* (Haus, 2019), pp. 146–8, 157–61, 164–5; J. T. Shotwell and M. Salvin, *Lessons on Security and Disarmament: From the History of the League of Nations* (King's Crown Press, 1949), pp. 92, 95, 100; E. de Bono, *Anno XIIII: The Conquest of an Empire* (Cresset Press, 1937), pp. 13–14; O. A. Hathaway and S. J. Shapiro, *The Internationalists and Their Plan to Outlaw War* (Penguin Books, 2018), p. 172; F. P. Walters, *A History of the League of Nations* (Oxford University Press, 1965), pp. 626–39, 642–4; K. Tibori-Szabó, *Anticipatory Action in Self-Defence* (Springer, 2011), pp. 94–5.

Union from the League for having invaded Finland and for having concluded a non-aggression pact with Hitler three months earlier.[48] With this, the fate of the League was sealed. Hailed as an innovative construct to prevent war and ensure peace, the League eventually succumbed to great power politics and the revanchist ambitions of the States that felt 'cheated' by the post-war peace settlement of 1919. The League was formally dissolved in 1946, but in reality it did not survive the Second World War.

## 3.8 The Second World War

For decades, the First World War was called 'The Great War', reflecting the unprecedented enormity of the casualties and destruction ensuing from that conflict. At its end, there was widespread hope that nothing comparable would ever happen again.[49] Nonetheless, in 1939, twenty years after the end of the Great War, the Second World War broke out and lasted six years. The war began on 1 September 1939 with the German invasion of Poland. Two days later, Britain and France delivered separate ultimatums demanding the immediate withdrawal of German troops from Poland. Upon their expiry, a state of war ensued between the two countries and Germany. Within less than a year, Europe was engulfed in the war between the Allied and the Axis powers. In June 1941, Germany began its invasion of the Soviet Union, which lasted until January 1944. On 7 December 1941, Japanese warplanes bombarded the American

48 Henig, *Peace That Never Was* (n. 6), pp. 163–6.

49 G. L. Weinberg, *Word War II: A Very Short Introduction* (Oxford University Press, 2014), p. 1.

naval base at Pearl Harbor, triggering the formal entry of the United States into the war and opening the Pacific war operations zone. US troops reached the French shores on 6 June 1944, also joining the European war theatre. Hostilities in Europe ended in May 1945, with the victory of the Allies, while in the Pacific theatre the war ended in August 1945, after Japanese capitulation following the US bombing of Hiroshima and Nagasaki.[50]

When the war finally ended, some 60 million people had been killed, the majority of them civilians. Massive destruction and economic hardship befell much of Europe, East and South East Asia and portions of North Africa. The war also resulted in massive population movement and displacement. Millions of prisoners of war, enslaved labourers and camp detainees were trying to return home or were struggling to find a safer place to live.[51]

It was against this background that States came together once again to create a new world organization to prevent war and ensure peace.

## 3.9 The Adoption of the UN Charter

The Charter of the United Nations was negotiated and drafted at the San Francisco Conference, formally known as the United Nations Conference on International Organization, which began on 25 April 1945 and lasted two months.[52] Delegates of fifty States came together to produce a ground-breaking founding document for the new world organization.[53] The idea of such an organization and the blueprint for its founding document came from previous, years-long preliminary declarations and negotiations, some of which started while the Second World War was still raging across the world. The most important of these was the 1944 Dumbarton Oaks Proposals (see Fact Box 3.4).

50 J. Keegan, *The Second World War* (Pimlico, 1997); Weinberg, *Word War II* (n. 49).

51 Weinberg, *Word War II* (n. 49), pp. 123–5.

52 'Chapter K: The United Nations Conference on International Organization', in *UN Yearbook* (1946–7), pt 1 ('The United Nations'), s. 1 ('Origin and Evolution'), pp. 12, 33.

53 Ibid., p. 14. The agenda of the conference was agreed to be 'the Dumbarton Oaks Proposals, as supplemented at the Crimea Conference, and by the Chinese Proposals agreed to by the sponsoring Governments, and the comments thereon submitted by the participating countries'.

### FACT BOX 3.4 THE ROAD TO THE SAN FRANCISCO CONFERENCE

During the Second World War, representatives of the Allied States met several times to discuss and adopt common positions regarding international peace and security.

In June 1941, at St James's Palace in London, the Allied States and several governments in exile signed a declaration in which they recorded their intention to work together for the furtherance of peace. The participants were Australia, Britain, Canada, New Zealand, the Union of South Africa and the exiled governments of Belgium, Czechoslovakia, Greece, Luxembourg, the Netherlands, Norway, Poland, Yugoslavia and the Free French government headed by General de Gaulle.

Two months later, in August 1941, the US president Franklin D. Roosevelt and the UK prime minister Winston Churchill signed the Atlantic Charter, which declared that 'all of the nations of the world, for realistic as well as spiritual reasons, must come to the abandonment of the use of force'. The bilateral agreement also stated that 'no future peace can be maintained if land, sea or air armaments continue to be employed by nations which threaten, or may threaten, aggression outside of their frontiers' and for that reason the disarmament of such States was essential 'pending the establishment of a wider and permanent system of general security'.

The Atlantic Charter was followed by the United Nations Declaration of 1 January 1942, signed initially by Churchill, Roosevelt, the Soviet ambassador to the United States Maxim Litvinov and the Chinese minister of foreign affairs Tse-Ven Soong. The following day the representatives of twenty-two other nations added their signatures.

Further agreements signed during the war were the Moscow Declaration of October 1943 and the Tehran Declaration of December 1943. The Moscow and Tehran Declarations were followed in October 1944 by the four-power (China, Soviet Union, the United Kingdom and the United States) conversations at Dumbarton Oaks, Washington, DC. The discussions were finalized on 7 October 1944, and the so-called Dumbarton Oaks Proposals relating to the principles and the structure of the new world organization were submitted to all the signatories of the United Nations Declaration. The Dumbarton Oaks Proposals later served as blueprints for the negotiation and drafting of the United Nations Charter in 1945 in San Francisco.

At the Yalta Conference of February 1945, Churchill, Roosevelt and Soviet chairman Joseph Stalin agreed to call a 'Conference of the United Nations' to meet in San Francisco to prepare the charter of 'a general international organization to maintain peace and security'.

**Sources:** 'Chapter E: The Dumbarton Oaks Conversations', in *UN Yearbook* (1946–7), pt 1 ('The United Nations'), s. 1 ('Origin and Evolution'), p. 4; 'Chapter F: The Yalta Agreement' in *UN Yearbook* (1946–7), pt 1 ('The United Nations'), s. 1 ('Origin and Evolution'), p. 9; 'Dumbarton Oaks and Yalta Conference (1944–45)' at 'History of the United Nations', www.un.org/es/node/44721; K. Tibori-Szabó, *Anticipatory Action in Self-Defence* (Springer, 2011), pp. 101–2.

The Charter of the United Nations was adopted on 25 June 1945 at the final plenary session of the San Francisco Conference.[54]

## 3.10 The Drafting and Content of Article 2(4) of the UN Charter

Reflecting the intention expressed in earlier declarations to abandon the use of force, Chapter II, paragraph 4, of the Dumbarton Oaks Proposals read as follows: 'All members of the Organization shall refrain in their international relations from the threat or use of force in any manner inconsistent with the purposes of the Organization.'[55] The language of paragraph 4 set out an unprecedented prohibition on the threat or use of force, going decisively beyond the undertakings formulated earlier in the League Covenant or the Kellogg-Briand Pact.

Having been submitted to the delegates of the Conference, the proposed text was addressed in the second plenary session by the Australian representative, who contended that a specific undertaking should be inserted for all members to refrain from force or the threat of force against the territorial integrity or political independence of another State.[56] Australia followed up its comment with a proposed amendment to Chapter II, paragraph 4, which read: 'All members or the United Nations shall refrain in their international relations from the threat or use of force against the territorial integrity or political independence of any member or State, or in any other manner inconsistent with the purposes of the United Nations.'[57]

The discussion of Chapter II and related amendment proposals fell within the mandate of Committee I/1.[58] Representatives of

[54] Ibid., p. 33; Verbatim Minutes of the Ninth Plenary Session, 24 June 1945 (Doc. 1210, P/20, 27 June 1945), in *Documents of the United Nations Conference on International Organization San Francisco, 1945* (1945) (*Documents of the UNCIO*), vol. 1, pp. 612–32, at 631.

[55] The United Nations Dumbarton Oaks Proposals for a General International Organization (For the Use of the Delegates) (Doc. 1, G/1), chap. II, para. 4, in *Documents of the UNCIO* (n. 54), vol. 3, pp. 1–23, at 3.

[56] Verbatim Minutes of the Second Plenary Session, 27 April 1945 (Doc. 20, P/6, 28 April 1945), in *Documents of the UNCIO* (n. 54), vol. 1, pp. 165–95, at 174.

[57] Amendments to the Dumbarton Oaks Proposals Submitted on Behalf of Australia (Doc. 2, G/14(l), 5 May 1945), in *Documents of the UNCIO* (n. 54), vol. 3, pp. 543–53, at 543.

[58] The conference was divided into four commissions and twelve technical committees. Commission I dealt with the general provisions and Committee I/1 the preamble, purpose and principles (chaps. I and II). 'Chapter K' (n. 52), p. 14.

other States, such as Bolivia,[59] Brazil,[60] Czechoslovakia,[61] Ecuador,[62] Egypt,[63] Ethiopia,[64] Honduras,[65] Iran,[66] Mexico,[67] New Zealand,[68] Paraguay,[69] Peru[70] and Uruguay,[71] also highlighted the importance of preserving territorial integrity and political independence and proposed

[59] Proposals of the Delegation of the Republic of Bolivia for the Organization of a System of Peace and Security (Doc. 2, G/14(r), 5 May 1945), in *Documents of the UNCIO* (n. 54), vol. 3, pp. 577–86, at 578.

[60] Brazilian Comment on Dumbarton Oaks Proposals: Memorandum of Brazilian Acting Minister for Foreign Affairs to American Chargé d'Affaires, 4 November 1944 (Doc. 2, G/7(e), 2 May 1945), in *Documents of the UNCIO* (n. 54), vol. 3, pp. 232–5, at 233; Brazilian Comment on Dumbarton Oaks Proposals Submitted to Inter-American Conference on Problems of War and Peace (Doc. 2, G/7/(e), 2 May 1945), in *Documents of the UNCIO* (n. 54), vol. 3, pp. 236–42, at 237.

[61] 'Observations of the Czechoslovak Government on the Dumbarton Oaks Proposals (Doc. 2, G/14(b), 1 May 1945), in *Documents of the UNCIO* (n. 54), vol. 3, pp. 466–71, at 467.

[62] Delegation of Ecuador to the United Nations Conference on International Organization: Comments and Amendments to the Proposals for the Establishment of a General International Organization as Submitted by the Dumbarton Oaks Conference, pt 1 (Doc. 2, G/7(p), 1 May 1945), in *Documents of the UNCIO* (n. 54), vol. 3, pp. 393–418, at 399.

[63] Amendments to the Dumbarton Oaks Proposals Presented by the Egyptian Delegation (Doc. 2, G/7(q)(1), 5 May 1945), in *Documents of the UNCIO* (n. 54), vol. 3, pp. 453–63, at 454.

[64] Amendments to the Proposals for the Maintenance of Peace and Security Agreed on at the Four Powers Conference at Dumbarton Oaks Supplemented as a Result of the Conference of Yalta, Submitted by the Ethiopian Delegation' (Doc. 2, G/14(n), 5 May 1945), in *Documents of the UNCIO* (n. 54), vol. 3, pp. 558–61, at 558.

[65] Comment of Honduran Government on Dumbarton Oaks Proposals (Doc. 2, G/7(m), n. d.), in *Documents of the UNCIO* (n. 54), vol. 3, pp. 349–52, at 349.

[66] Iran Proposal Submitted to Committee I/1 (Doc. 215, I/1/10, 11 May 1945), in *Documents of the UNCIO* (n. 54), vol. 6, p. 542.

[67] Opinion of the Department of Foreign Relations of Mexico Concerning the Dumbarton Oaks Proposals for the Creation of a General International Organization (Doc. 2, G(7)(c), 23 April 1945), in *Documents of the UNCIO* (n. 54), vol. 3, pp. 54–174, at 65.

[68] Amendments to the Dumbarton Oaks Proposals (Document 1 G/1) Submitted by the Delegation of New Zealand (Doc. 2, G/14(f), 2 May 1945), in *Documents of the UNCIO* (n. 54), vol. 3, pp. 486–9, at 486.

[69] Summary of Remarks Presented by the Government of Paraguay on the Dumbarton Oaks Proposals, 27 February 1945 (Doc. 2, G/7(l)), in *Documents of the UNCIO* (n. 54), vol. 3, pp. 345–8, at 347.

[70] Peru Proposal Submitted to Committee I/1 (Doc. 215, I/1/10, 11 May 1945), in *Documents of the UNCIO* (n. 54), vol. 6, p. 566.

[71] The Position of the Government of Uruguay Respecting the Plans of Postwar International Organization for the Maintenance of Peace and Security in the World, 28 September 1944 (Doc. 2, G/7(a)), in *Documents of the UNCIO* (n. 54), vol. 3, pp. 26–33, at 30.

comparable amendments, albeit not always in connection with Chapter II, paragraph 4.[72]

Other proposals concentrated on the nature of the prohibition. For instance, Brazil proposed to prohibit 'the threat or use of economic measures' alongside force.[73] Ecuador submitted an amendment proposal for the 'formal repudiation by the States of the exercise of moral or physical force in their mutual relations'.[74]

Several States sought to introduce the concept of 'aggression' in Chapter II, paragraph 4, or elsewhere in the Charter. For instance, Colombia recommended amending the preamble by declaring that any war of aggression constituted a crime in international law and involved not only the responsibility of the aggressor State but also the personal responsibility of the political and military leaders of that country.[75] Bolivia proposed to add the following sentence to Chapter II, paragraph 4: 'All threats or acts of violence committed by any State to the detriment of any other State shall be considered as acts of aggression committed against all the other members of the Organization.'[76] New Zealand proposed adding to Chapter I an undertaking 'to preserve as against external aggression the territorial integrity and political independence of every member of the Organisation'.[77] These proposals, especially the latter, were extensively discussed in relation to amendments to Chapter II, paragraph 4.[78] New Zealand later revised its proposal to fit Chapter II, rewording it as: 'All members of the Organization undertake collectively to resist every act of aggression against any member'.[79]

72 Summary Report of the Fourth Meeting of Committee I/1, 11 May 1945 (Doc. 272, I/1/11, 14 May 1945), in *Documents of the UNCIO* (n. 54), vol. 6, pp. 286–7, at 286; Summary Report of the Seventh Meeting of Committee I/1, 16 May 1945 (Doc. 382, I/1/19, 17 May 1945), in *Documents of the UNCIO* (n. 54), vol. 6, pp. 303–5, at 304.

73 Documentation for Meetings of Committee I/1 (Doc. 215, I/1/10, 11 May 1945), in *Documents of the UNCIO* (n. 54), vol. 6, pp. 525–69, at 559.

74 Ibid., p. 561.

75 Colombia Proposal Submitted to Committee I/1 (Doc. 215, I/1/10, 11 May 1945), in *Documents of the UNCIO* (n. 54), vol. 6, pp. 525–69 at 528.

76 Documentation for Meetings of Committee I/1 (Doc. 215, I/1/10, 11 May 1945), in *Documents of the UNCIO* (n. 54), vol. 6, pp. 525–69, at 558.

77 Amendments to the Dumbarton Oaks Proposals (Document 1 G/1) Submitted by the Delegation of New Zealand (Doc. 2, G/14(f), 2 May 1945), in *Documents of the UNCIO* (n. 54), vol. 3, pp. 486–9, at 486.

78 Summary Report of the Seventh Meeting of Committee I/1, 16 May 1945 (Doc. 382, I/1/19, 17 May 1945), in *Documents of the UNCIO* (n. 54), vol. 6, pp. 303–5, at 304.

79 Report of the Rapporteur of Subcommittee I/1/A to Committee I/1 on Chapter II (Doc. 739, I/1/A/19(a), 1 June 1945), in *Documents of the UNCIO* (n. 54), vol. 6, pp. 717–23, at 721.

Although supported by many delegates, these amendments ultimately failed, because they were perceived as narrowing the scope of the prohibition to cover only aggression and not other types of use of force.[80]

Other proposals addressed the limits of the prohibition. Costa Rica proposed to omit the last part of paragraph 4 – that is, the words 'in any manner inconsistent with the purposes of the Organization' – in order that 'the principle of abstention from the use of force may be absolutely established.'[81] Norway proposed that paragraph 4 be amended to clarify that no force should be used if not approved by the UN Security Council (UNSC, or Security Council).[82] Norway argued that its proposed amendment was necessary because the language of paragraph 4, as it stood, seemed to allow use of force consistent with the purposes of the Organization but without the prior approval of the Security Council.[83] The proposal received mixed reactions, as many delegates feared that the text thus amended might curtail the right of States to use force in self-defence.[84] Representatives agreed, however, that any use of force other than in self-defence would be in furtherance of a measure taken by the Organization.[85] The Netherlands raised a question concerning the standard of conduct to be applied in determining what acts would endanger international peace and security, and thus what use of force would be inconsistent with the purposes of

[80] Ibid.; Summary Report of Twelfth Meeting of Committee I/1, 5 June 1945 (Doc. 810, I/l/30, 6 June 1945), in *Documents of the UNCIO* (n. 54), vol. 6, pp. 342–8, at 344. See also N. Schrijver, 'The Ban on the Use of Force in the UN Charter', in M. Weller (ed.), *The Oxford Handbook of the Use of Force in International Law* (Oxford University Press, 2017), p. 470.

[81] Comments of the Government of Costa Rica on the Dumbarton Oaks Proposals (Doc. 2, G/7(h)(1), 4 May 1945), in *Documents of the UNCIO* (n. 54), vol. 3, pp. 278–81, at 278.

[82] Amendments and Observations on the Dumbarton Oaks Proposals, Submitted by the Norwegian Delegation, 3 May 1945 (Doc. 2, G/7(n)(1), 4 May 1945), in *Documents of the UNCIO* (n. 54), vol. 3, pp. 365–75, at 366.

[83] Summary Report of the Seventh Meeting of Committee I/1, 16 May 1945 (Doc. 382, I/1/19, 17 May 1945), in *Documents of the UNCIO* (n. 54), vol. 6, pp. 303–5, at 304.

[84] Report of the Rapporteur of Subcommittee I/1/A to Committee I/1 on Chapter II (Doc. 739, I/1/A/19(a), 1 June 1945), in *Documents of the UNCIO* (n. 54), vol. 6, pp. 717–23, at 721.

[85] Summary Report of Eleventh Meeting of Committee I/1, 4 June 1945 (Doc. 784, I/1/27, 5 June 1945), in *Documents of the UNCIO* (n. 54), vol. 6, pp. 331–5, at 334–5; Report of the Rapporteur of Committee 1 to Commission I (Doc. 885, I/1/34, 9 June 1945), in *Documents of the UNCIO* (n. 54), vol. 6, pp. 387–401, at 400 (text of the amended report of 13 June 1945 is identical, see Doc. 944, I/1/34(l), in *Documents of the UNCIO* (n. 54), vol. 6, pp. 446–60, at 459, and Appendix, Doc. 945, I/1/34(l)(a), ibid., pp. 461–3, at 463).

the organization.[86] While refraining from proposing an amendment to the text, the Netherlands nevertheless suggested that an independent body be created 'to pronounce upon decisions of the UNSC whenever an appeal to that effect were addressed to them'.[87]

Ultimately, the only amendment incorporated in Chapter II, paragraph 4, and submitted by Committee I/1 to the Coordination Committee, was the Australian proposal.[88] Further to the work of the Coordination Committee, chapters were turned into articles and the new amended prohibition became Article 2(4).[89] The meaning of the phrase 'any member or State' received some attention from the Coordination Committee.[90] Eventually, 'member or' was found to be redundant and discarded.[91]

At the final plenary session of the San Francisco Conference on 25 June 1945, the Charter of the United Nations was unanimously approved.[92]

For the first time in history, States agreed upon a broad prohibition on the threat or use of force and incorporated it in a multilateral treaty establishing a worldwide organization. The delegates at the San Francisco Conference understood the momentum, which was well reflected in the words of US president Harry Truman as he addressed the final session: 'The Charter of the United Nations which you are now signing is a solid structure upon which we can build for a better world. ... For it is a

86 Suggestions Presented by the Netherlands Government Concerning the Proposals for the Maintenance of Peace and Security Agreed on at the Four Powers Conference of Dumbarton Oaks as Published on October 9, 1944, January 1945 (Doc. 2, G/7(j)), in *Documents of the UNCIO* (n. 54), vol. 3, pp. 306–21, at 311–12.

87 Ibid., p. 313.

88 Text of Chapter II as Agreed upon by the Drafting Committee (Doc. 656, I/1/A/16, 28 May 1945), in *Documents of the UNCIO* (n. 54), vol. 6, pp. 687–8, at 687.

89 Revision of Technical Committee Text Suggested by the Secretariat as Submitted to the Coordination Committee, Alternative A (Doc. WD 303, CO/94(2), 14 June 1945), in *Documents of the UNCIO* (n. 54), vol. 18, pp. 115–16, at 115.

90 Summary Report of Twenty-Second Meeting of Coordination Committee, 15 June 1945 (Doc. WD 410, CO/170, 20 June 1945), in *Documents of the UNCIO* (n. 54), vol. 17, pp. 141–51, at 146; Summary Report of Twenty-Fourth Meeting of Coordination Committee, 16 June 1945 (Doc. WD 424, CO/188, 25 June 1945), in *Documents of the UNCIO* (n. 54), vol. 17, pp. 162–8, at 164.

91 Summary Report of Thirty-Ninth Meeting of Coordination Committee, 22 June 1945 (Doc. WD 439, CO/203, 14 September 1945), in *Documents of the UNCIO* (n. 54), vol. 17, pp. 336–59, at 346.

92 'Chapter K' (n. 52), p. 33; Verbatim Minutes of the Ninth Plenary Session, 25 June 1945 (Doc. 1210, P/20, 27 June 1945), in *Documents of the UNCIO* (n. 54), vol. 1, pp. 612–32, at 631.

> SUMMARY BOX 3.3 THE FINAL ADOPTED TEXT OF ARTICLE 2(4)
>
> 'All Members shall refrain in their international relations from the threat or use of force against the territorial integrity or political independence of any State, or in any other manner inconsistent with the Purposes of the United Nations.'

declaration of great faith by the nations of the earth – faith that war is not inevitable, faith that peace can be maintained.'[93]

## 3.11 Conclusion

In this chapter, we traced the evolution of the law governing the use of force from the end of the First World War to the adoption of the UN Charter. The chapter shed light on the differences between the prohibitions at the core of the League Covenant and the Kellogg-Briand Pact, on the one hand, and those at the heart of the Charter, on the other. It also delved into the debate among the drafters of the Charter over, and their understanding of, the prohibition on the use of force. This gives important insights into what lay at the root of that ground-breaking rule in the mid-twentieth century. This will in turn assist the analysis in the following chapters on how that prohibition has since been interpreted and adapted. It will also assist in discussing the prohibition's relationship with other aspects of the law on the use of force.

[93] Verbatim Minutes of the Closing Plenary Session, 26 June 1945 (Doc. 1209, P/19, 27 June 1945), in *Documents of the UNCIO* (n. 54), vol. 1, pp. 658–85, at 680.

# PART II

## Scope and Content of the Contemporary *jus ad bellum*

# 4

# The Prohibition on the Use or Threat of Force

## 4.1 Introduction

Article 2(4) of the UN Charter (see Summary Box 3.3) is generally recognized as a cornerstone of the contemporary international legal order and the starting point for any discussion on the law governing the use or threat of force. Despite this general consensus, there are still areas of disagreement on both fundamental and less important points relating to the scope of the prohibition and its relationship to other notions such as armed attack and aggression. In this chapter we identify the most important contested points and set out the leading interpretation of this key provision. We first analyse the meaning of the term 'force' and some of the other terms used in the provision. We then explore some of the other controversies relating to the scope of Article 2(4) and provide arguments in support of a broad interpretation of this provision. Finally, we examine its relationship to related, but distinct, concepts such as armed attack and aggression, and its overall role and function in the contemporary *jus ad bellum*.

## 4.2 Meaning of 'Force'

An examination of both the negotiating history of the Charter and subsequent practice makes clear that the term 'force' signifies 'armed force'.[1] The rejection of a proposal to include other forms of coercion, put forward by Brazil during negotiations on the drafting of Article 2(4), alongside consistent practice, including the authoritative

[1] Y. Dinstein, *War, Aggression and Self-Defence* (Cambridge University Press, 2017), p. 90; C. Henderson, *The Use of Force and International Law* (Cambridge University Press, 2018), pp. 52–3; B. Simma et al. (eds.), *The Charter of the United Nations: A Commentary*, vol. 1 (Oxford University Press, 2012), p. 208.

Friendly Relations Declaration adopted by the UN General Assembly in 1970, reflect a consensual interpretation of the Charter and are clear evidence supporting this interpretation.[2] This means that political or economic pressure, theft of intellectual property (even on a large scale), various forms of non-armed interference, subversion and disinformation, while in some cases (potentially) violating other rules of international law, do not fall within the scope of the prohibition of force. This interpretation is also mirrored in the case law of the International Court of Justice (ICJ) and in the opinions of most writers on the topic.[3]

Armed force can take various forms ranging from the application of direct military force to indirect use of force through a State organizing and equipping armed bands to undertake incursions into, or engage in violent acts directed against, another State. It also includes the fomenting of internal armed conflict in another State and the provision of material or logistical support for terrorist groups engaging in acts of violence directed against a State. There are further examples enumerated in the Friendly Relations Declaration.[4] Accordingly, in its Article 1 the Declaration reiterates the prohibition in Article 2(4) of the Charter and goes on to list both direct and indirect uses of force falling under the scope of the prohibition (see Fact Box 4.1).

Potential manifestations of armed force not envisaged in 1970 include non-kinetic actions in the cyber domain. The question of whether armed force can include such acts when they have similar consequences to conventional kinetic force in terms of physical damage to objects and injury to persons has not yet been conclusively determined in case law or through a UN Security Council decision. It seems

[2] Documentation for Meetings of Committee I/1, (Doc. 215, I/1/10, 11 May 1945), in *Documents of the United Nations Conference on International Organization San Francisco, 1945* (1945) (*Documents of the UNCIO*), vol. 6, pp. 525–69, at 559; Declaration on Principles of International Law Concerning Friendly Relations and Co-operation among States in accordance with the Charter of the United Nations, Annex to Resolution 2625 (XXV), adopted by the UN General Assembly on 24 October 1970, UN Doc. A/RES/25/2625. See also Chapter 3, Section 3.10, below.

[3] In the *Nicaragua* case, the International Court of Justice dealt with the question of the use of force separately from allegations of economic coercion of Nicaragua, and it is clear that the passages relating to the use of force in the decision related to armed force. *Military and Paramilitary Activities in and against Nicaragua* (*Nicaragua* v. *United States*) (Merits), Judgment, 27 June 1986, ICJ Reports 1986, paras. 187–91. See also n. 1, above.

[4] See also *Nicaragua* (n. 3), para. 191.

### FACT BOX 4.1 THE FRIENDLY RELATIONS DECLARATION (1970) – EXCERPTS

A war of aggression constitutes a crime against the peace, for which there is responsibility under international law.

In accordance with the purposes and principles of the United Nations, States have the duty to refrain from propaganda for wars of aggression.

Every State has the duty to refrain from the threat or use of force to violate the existing international boundaries of another State or as a means of solving international disputes, including territorial disputes and problems concerning frontiers of States.

Every State likewise has the duty to refrain from the threat or use of force to violate international lines of demarcation, such as armistice lines, established by or pursuant to an international agreement to which it is a party or which it is otherwise bound to respect. [. . .]

States have a duty to refrain from acts of reprisal involving the use of force.

Every State has the duty to refrain from any forcible action which deprives peoples referred to in the elaboration of the principle of equal rights and self-determination of their right to self-determination and freedom and independence.

Every State has the duty to refrain from organizing or encouraging the organization of irregular forces or armed bands including mercenaries, for incursion into the territory of another State.

Every State has the duty to refrain from organizing, instigating, assisting or participating in acts of civil strife or terrorist acts in another State or acquiescing in organized activities within its territory directed towards the commission of such acts, when the acts referred to in the present paragraph involve a threat or use of force.

The territory of a State shall not be the object of military occupation resulting from the use of force in contravention of the provisions of the Charter. The territory of a State shall not be the object of acquisition by another State resulting from the threat or use of force. [. . .]

**Source**: Declaration on Principles of International Law Concerning Friendly Relations and Co-operation among States in Accordance with the Charter of the United Nations, Annex to Resolution 2625 (XXV) adopted by the UN General Assembly on 24 October 1970, UN Doc. A/RES/25/2625.

clear, however, that an increasing number of States, as well as many authors, accept this possibility. Consequently, cyber acts conducted by, at the behest of or under the control of a State and which result in, or are intended to cause, physical harm to persons or damage to objects would fall within the scope of the prohibition, alongside the use of other potentially lethal non-kinetic weapons (such as radiological or biological weapons).[5]

## 4.3 'Threat of Force'

A threat of force is an explicitly or implicitly stated or expressed intention to engage in any of the previously mentioned acts which is credible in the prevailing circumstances and can reasonably be substantiated on the basis of conduct or statements.[6] A threat is credible when the State making it is capable of carrying it out and the threat appears objectively to be serious and not simply rhetorical.

Threats to use force can be expressed in various forms, such as explicit oral or written statements, a succession of communications mounting in pressure, a sequence of acts conveying a threatening situation and so forth.[7] It is worth noting, however, that the prevailing circumstances will determine whether the threat is credible and reasonably substantiated. For instance, in its *Nicaragua* judgment the ICJ refused to find that the military manoeuvres conducted by the United States near the Nicaraguan border constituted a threat of force within the meaning of Article 2(4).[8]

Only threats of unlawful use of force would in themselves violate Article 2(4). As said by the ICJ in its *Nuclear Weapons* advisory opinion:

> The notions of 'threat' and 'use' of force under Article 2, paragraph 4, of the Charter stand together in the sense that if the use of force itself in a given case is illegal – for whatever reason – the threat to use such force will likewise be illegal. In short, if it is to be lawful, the declared readiness of a State to use force must be a use of force that is in conformity with the Charter.[9]

Hence, a declaration that an armed attack against an allied State will be considered as an armed attack against all members of an alliance or (regional) organization does not constitute an unlawful threat of force,

[5] Dinstein, *War, Aggression and Self-Defence* (n. 1), p. 90; Henderson, *Use of Force* (n. 1), p. 56; M. N. Schmitt (ed.) *Tallinn Manual 2.0 on the International Law Applicable to Cyber Operations* (Cambridge University Press, 2017), pp. 330–7 (Rule 69). See also Chapter 11, below.

[6] R. Sadurska, 'Threats of Force' (1988) 82 *American Journal of International Law* 239–68, at 242.

[7] Ibid., pp. 242–3.

[8] *Nicaragua* (n. 3), para. 227.

[9] *Legality of the Threat or Use of Nuclear Weapons*, Advisory Opinion, 8 July 1996, ICJ Reports 1996, para. 47.

nor would an ultimatum given to a State engaging in an unlawful use of force to stand down or face consequences violate the prohibition.

## 4.4 'In Their International Relations'

The phrase 'in their international relations' in Article 2(4) is an important limitation in the scope of the provision. Only non-consensual armed force directed by a State against another State or across an international frontier, demarcation or ceasefire line falls within the scope of Article 2(4).[10] This includes territory whose status or title is disputed between parties and which is under the peaceful administration of one of them.[11] It is immaterial whether the use of force takes place on the territory of the State which uses force, on the territory of the targeted State, or in international waters or airspace, so long as it is conducted by a State against another State. It thus covers conduct anywhere within either States' territory, as well as force used against military units stationed abroad and against State vessels, aircraft and spacecraft located in international waters, airspace or outer space; in some cases, it may also include force directed against the merchant vessels and civil aircraft of the targeted State.[12] It can also cover force used by, or at the behest of, a State against the nationals of another State located abroad when they are deliberately targeted because of their nationality and connection to their parent State or as a means of forcibly coercing the parent State to do, or abstain from doing, something (see Chapter 8).[13]

On the other hand, force used within a State's borders which does not involve another State, whether in the context of an internal armed conflict between the State and one or more organized armed groups or in the context of routine law enforcement, does not fall within the scope

[10] Simma et al. (eds.), *Charter* (n. 1), p. 214; Dinstein, *War, Aggression and Self-Defence* (n. 1), pp. 89–90.

[11] Ethiopia/Eritrea Claims Commission, *Jus Ad Bellum* – Ethiopia's Claims 1-8, Partial Award, 19 December 2005, Reports of International Arbitral Awards, vol. XXVI, paras. 15–16, 467.

[12] See Definition of Aggression Annex to UNGA Res. 3314 (XXIX) (14 December 1974), art. 3(d); Simma et al. (eds.), *Charter* (n. 1), p. 215. See also Chapter 13, below.

[13] D. Bowett, 'The Use of Force for the Protection of Nationals Abroad', in A. Cassese (ed.) *The Current Legal Regulation of the Use of Force* (Nijhoff, 1986), p. 39; R. Higgins, *Problems and Process: International Law and How We Use It* (Oxford University Press, 1994), p. 244; O. Schachter, *International Law in Theory and Practice* (Nijhoff, 1991), p. 166; C. H. M. Waldock, 'The Regulation of the Use of Force by Individual States in International Law' (1952) 81 *Collected Courses of the Hague Academy of International Law* 455–517, at 467.

of Article 2(4), as this in no way affects the 'international relations' of any State.[14] Nor, for the same reason, does the exercise of routine law enforcement in maritime areas adjacent to a State over which it has functional jurisdiction fall within the ambit of Article 2(4).[15] It also follows that if a State consents to the presence of foreign military forces on its territory and the consent granted includes authorization to use armed force against a non-State actor for a specific purpose, no violation of Article 2(4) occurs if the foreign forces conduct their operation within the scope of the consent granted.[16] So if, for example, State Alpha were to grant permission to State Delta to conduct an operation aimed at neutralizing an armed group operating against Delta from Alpha's territory, no violation of Article 2(4) would occur. However, if Delta maintained a military base on Beta's territory pursuant to an agreement and used its forces in contravention of the terms of that agreement, this would constitute a breach of Article 2(4), as Beta's sovereignty would be violated by that use of force, thereby causing their international relations to be affected.

There is no persuasive evidence, in our view, that the prohibition in either its treaty-based or customary form was intended to have any direct application to entities other than States.[17] This is not to say that international organizations, armed groups or individuals are free to use force,

[14] Simma et al. (eds.), *Charter* (n. 1), p. 214; Dinstein, *War, Aggression and Self-Defence* (n. 1), p. 89. Law enforcement here refers to the exercise of routine enforcement jurisdiction (police powers) over private individuals, aircraft or vessels on the basis of a recognized legal ground for the exercise of such jurisdiction under national, or in some cases international, law. It does not include uses of force on the ground of self-defence or enforcement action mandated by the UN Security Council.

[15] This relates to functional jurisdiction over matters allocated to coastal States under the UN Law of the Sea Convention (Montego Bay, 10 December 1982). See Chapter 13, below.

[16] See International Law Commission, 'Draft Articles on Responsibility of States for Internationally Wrongful Acts, with Commentaries' (2001), in Report of the International Law Commission on the Work of Its Fifty-Third Session, UN Doc. A/56/10 pp. 72–4 (Commentary to Article 20). See also T. D. Gill, 'Military Intervention with the Consent or at the Invitation of a Government', in T. D. Gill and D. Fleck (eds.), *The Handbook of the International Law of Military Operations* (Oxford University Press, 2015), pp. 252–5. See also Chapter 12, below.

[17] Most authors agree that the customary and Charter norms prohibiting the threat or use of force are virtually identical. See, for example, Dinstein, *War, Aggression and Self-Defence* (n. 1), pp. 104-5; Henderson, *Use of Force* (n. 1), p. 18; V. Lanovoy, 'The Use of Force by Non-State Actors and the Limits of Attribution' (2017) 28(2) *European Journal of International Law* 563–585, at 568–70. For a comparatively rare contrary opinion, see R. Buchan and N. Tsagourias, *Regulating the Use of Force in International Law: Stability and Change* (Edward Elgar, 2021), pp. 18–19.

but such use is subject to rules of law other than the prohibition to use force in international relations. States acting through international organizations are equally bound by the prohibition as when they act unilaterally. Armed groups and individuals may violate other rules of international law, as well as the national law of any affected State, by engaging in acts involving force directed against a State or its nationals, but the prohibition in Article 2(4) of the Charter and in customary law is not directly relevant to such actions. Note that the question of whether the prohibition applies to non-State actors is distinct from that of whether a State which is the object of an attack by a non-State armed group has the right to exercise self-defence. That question will be dealt with separately in a subsequent chapter (see Chapter 6). Likewise, the attribution to a State of acts involving the use of force by individuals is governed by the law of international responsibility, but this is distinct from whether the prohibition on the use of force is applicable to individuals or other non-State actors.

## 4.5 Minimum Threshold?

Is there a *de minimis* threshold which must be crossed for a particular act to qualify as a use of armed force? In other words, does force have to be severe, prolonged or have particular consequences for it to amount to armed force? Note that this question is distinct from that of whether the use of force has to meet a certain threshold of severity in order to qualify as an armed attack under Article 51 of the Charter (see Chapter 6). In our view, an ordinary reading of the terms of Article 2(4) and subsequent practice and interpretation suggest that there is no requirement of a minimum threshold of intensity for an act to qualify as armed force.[18] So any use of armed force by a State against another State would constitute a use of force, even if did not result in (serious) harm

[18] Opinions are divided in the literature on this point. In support of a 'gravity threshold' are, inter alia, M. E. O'Connell, 'The Prohibition on the Use of Force', in N. D. White and C. Henderson (eds.), *Research Handbook on International Conflict and Security Law* (Edward Elgar, 2013), p. 102; Independent International Fact-Finding Mission on the Conflict in Georgia, *Report*, vol. II (September 2009), p. 242, referring to the opinion of R. Kolb, Ius contra bellum: *Le droit international relatif au maintien de la paix* (Helbing Lichtenhahn/Bruylant, 2009), p. 247. Those against a minimum threshold include Dinstein, *War, Aggression and Self-Defence* (n. 1), pp. 90–1; T. Ruys, 'The Meaning of "Force" and the Boundaries of the *Jus Ad Bellum*: Are "Minimal" Uses of Force Excluded from UN Charter Article 2(4)' (2014) 108(2) *American Journal of International Law* 159–210. We are in agreement with the second body of opinion.

to persons or (significant) damage to objects. Since armed force always has at least potentially harmful consequences, there is no need to require a further degree of intensity or for the force used to have actually resulted in the intended consequences. So, the act of a State agent (deliberately) firing a shot across a border is a use of force even if it misses its intended target. With non-kinetic force in the form of cyber acts, the situation may be somewhat different. A cyber act does not necessarily have potentially harmful consequences comparable with those resulting from the use of physical force. In order to distinguish between mere cyber interference and a cyber act constituting a use of force, the generally accepted position is that there have to be harmful consequences in the form of injury to persons or material damage of some type and degree.[19] Accordingly, while the use of kinetic, physical force does not require harmful consequences to fall within the scope of the prohibition, a cyber act does. This implies a minimal threshold of harm, but where exactly this threshold lies has not yet been agreed upon or settled in State practice.

A somewhat related question is whether the use of force has to be deliberate to constitute a breach of Article 2(4) of the Charter. An unintentional use of armed force that resulted in harmful consequences such as death, injury or material damage would not fall within the prohibition, as long as the State which had inadvertently caused the harm made clear that it was accidental, issued assurances of non-repetition and was prepared to offer compensation where this was necessary or as an indication of good faith. The same would apply to an ultra vires act by a State agent (such as a border guard or member of the armed forces) who voluntarily discharged one or more shots into another State's territory or against public vessels or aircraft of that State and who was acting beyond or outside official authority. So long as the State to which the State agent was affiliated made clear that the incident was not officially sanctioned and took the necessary measures to prevent repetition and provide compensation or satisfaction to the injured State, there is no violation of the prohibition on the use of force.[20]

[19] M. Schmitt, 'Computer Network Attacks and the Use of Force in International Law: Thoughts on a Normative Framework' (1998–9) 37 *Columbia Journal of Transnational Law* 885–937, at 890, 914–16. See also Schmitt, *Tallinn Manual 2.0* (n. 5), p. 330 (Rule 69). See also Chapter 11, below.

[20] Henderson, *Use of Force* (n. 1), pp. 75–8; T. Ruys, *'Armed Attack' and Article 51 of the UN Charter: Evolution in Customary Law and Practice* (Cambridge University Press, 2010), p. 192; O. Corten, *The Law against War: The Prohibition on the Use of Force in Contemporary International Law* (Hart, 2010), pp. 76–84. On the duty to make reparations for unlawful acts related to the use of force, see Chapter 15, below.

A use of armed force would also include the non-consensual intentional presence (not connected to distress, navigational error or equipment failure) of armed forces, warships or military aircraft of one State on another State's territory in violation of international agreements or coupled with a refusal to leave when ordered to do so. If the non-consensual presence became evident and the intruding military forces, aircraft or vessels had been ordered to leave but refused to do so, this would cross the line between being a mere violation of sovereignty and constituting a use of force even in the absence of actual shots being fired.[21] This is not to say that territorial intrusion in itself amounts to a use of force. Only if the intrusion is deliberate and is followed by a refusal to vacate the State's territory even when ordered to do so may it amount to a use of force.[22] These conditions will be detailed in Chapters 6 and 12.

## 4.6 Broad vs Narrow Interpretation

The second half of Article 2(4), referring to 'territorial integrity, political independence or in any other manner inconsistent with the Purposes of the United Nations', has given rise to a debate on whether this phrase narrows the scope of the prohibition by limiting it to situations related to violations of territorial integrity or independence or are otherwise in violation of the Charter's other main purposes and principles. In particular, proponents of force used in the context of self-determination and for humanitarian

[21] It should be stressed that forcible reaction against unauthorized aerial intrusion is in principle restricted to intruding State aircraft used solely for governmental purposes, in particular military aircraft, and does not extend to civil airliners or private aircraft, except in very exceptional circumstances (see also Chapters 12 and 13, below). The classical treatment of this topic is by O. Lissitzyn, 'The Treatment of Aerial Intruders in Recent Practice and in International Law' (1953) 47 *American Journal of International Law* 559–89. Various authors treat the legal basis for using force against aerial intrusion or unauthorized passage by warships in internal waters or non-innocent passage by warships in the territorial sea differently. Dinstein views any unauthorized crossing of a frontier by military units, aircraft or submerged passage of submarines in national waters as an (incipient) armed attack. Dinstein, *War, Aggression and Self-Defence* (n. 1), pp. 213–15. This view is supported by, inter alia, T. Gazzini, *The Changing Rules on the Use of Force in International Law* (Manchester University Press, 2005), pp. 133–4. On the other hand, Simma et al. (eds.), *Charter* (n. 1), p. 215 states that Article 2(4) 'does not apply to military acts of protection against intruding persons ships or aircraft on the State's own territory'.

[22] Lissitzyn, 'Treatment of Aerial Intruders' (n. 21); Schachter, *International Law* (n. 13), pp. 112–13. See also Chapter 12, below.

purposes have argued that force used in the context of self-determination or for humanitarian purposes does not impinge upon the prohibition.[23]

However, this narrow interpretation has no basis in law, as it is neither consistent with the intentions of the drafters of the Charter nor supported by State practice or authoritative interpretations of the Charter in General Assembly resolutions, such as the Friendly Relations Declaration.[24] Nor does it not find support in case law or in the writings of most publicists. Acceptance of such an interpretation would render the prohibition largely nugatory, as it would open the door to subjective claims that a particular use of force would be lawful as long it did not aim to deprive a State of part of its territory or subjugate a State's independence, or that the use of force was undertaken with benign intentions to further the Charter's purposes and principles. It is noteworthy that the phrase was added at the request of several smaller States to ensure that their independence and territorial integrity would not be sacrificed on the altar of preserving the peace. This happened to Czechoslovakia in 1938 as a consequence of the Munich Agreement, when it was forced to cede a portion of its territory to Nazi Germany as a means of avoiding war. Moreover, in the *Corfu Channel* judgment, the ICJ rejected the United Kingdom's argument that since its actions were not aimed at Albania's territorial integrity or independence, it had not violated the prohibition. The Court made it clear that such an interpretation was

[23] Proponents of this approach include R. Lillich, 'Humanitarian Intervention: A Reply to Ian Brownlie and a Plea for Constructive Alternatives', in J. N. Moore (ed.), *Law and Civil War in the Modern World* (John Hopkins Press, 1974), p. 229; W. M. Reisman, 'Humanitarian Intervention and Fledgling Democracies' (1994–5) 18 *Fordham International Law Journal* 794–805; J. Stone, *Aggression and World Order* (University of California Press, 1958), p. 43; A. D'Amato, *International Law: Process and Prospect* (Transnational Publishers, 1987), pp. 107–8. Opponents include Schachter, *International Law* (n. 13), pp. 112–26; Dinstein, *War, Aggression and Self-Defence* (n. 1), pp. 72–7; I. Brownlie, *International Law and the Use of Force by States* (Clarendon Press, 1963), pp. 338–42. An intermediate approach, whereby intervention in the absence of a UN Security Council mandate is acknowledged as unlawful but excusable in certain circumstances, is taken by, inter alia, T. M. Franck, *Recourse to Force: State Action against Threats and armed Attacks* (Cambridge University Press, 2002), pp. 138–9. See also Chapter 7, below.

[24] On the role of smaller States in support of adding this phrase to Article 2(4), see Summary Report of the Seventh Meeting of Commission I/1, 16 May 1945 (Doc. 382, I/1/19, 17 May 1945), in *Documents of the UNCIO* (n. 2), vol. 6, pp. 303–5, at 304; Summary Report of the Eleventh Meeting of Commission I/1, 4 June 1945 (Doc. 784, I/1/27, 5 June 1945), in *Documents of the UNCIO* (n. 2), vol. 6, pp. 331–5, at 334–5. See also UNGA Res. 2625 (n. 2) *Charter* (n. 1), pp. 216–17; Dinstein, *War, Aggression and Self-Defence* (n. 1), pp. 93–8; Schachter, *International Law* (n. 13), pp. 110–13.

fundamentally incompatible with the Charter's intent.[25] Consequently, the phrase should be seen as reinforcing the total ban on the use of armed force between States except in those situations in which force is allowed under the Charter, not as a clause limiting the prohibition.

## 4.7 Peremptory Character of the Prohibition

As well as being widely acknowledged as both a customary and a treaty-based rule, Article 2(4) is a clear example of a norm possessing a peremptory character. Assuming this is true, what does this signify and how can a peremptory norm include 'exceptions'?[26] If a norm is deemed peremptory, it is one from which no derogation is permitted, except as set out in the norm itself. It is also a rule which requires a very large majority of States to alter, and then only if it is clear that they intend to discard or alter the rule by another rule of equal weight. In short, the bar for creating a (new) exception to a peremptory rule (also referred to as *jus cogens)* is very high, considerably higher than is necessary for altering an 'ordinary' rule of customary or treaty law (*jus dispositivum*). Does Article 2(4) in fact qualify as peremptory considering that States have not always acted in conformity with the rule and have indeed violated it on numerous occasions and that there are at least two 'exceptions' to the prohibition which do not appear in the rule itself?

[25] See, for example, E. Gordon, 'Article 2(4) in Historical Context' (1985) 10 *Yale Journal of International* Law 271–8, at 275–6. See also Simma et al. (eds.), *Charter* (n. 1), p. 216.

[26] The ICJ acknowledged the customary status of the prohibition in *Nicaragua* (n. 3), paras. 98–102. On Article 2(4) as a peremptory norm, see, for example, Simma et al. (eds.), *Charter* (n. 1), p. 231; Dinstein, *War, Aggression and Self-Defence* (n. 1), pp. 109–12 (excepting 'threat of force' from peremptory status); Higgins, *Problems and Process* (n. 13), pp. 20–2; International Law Commission, Commentary to Article 50 of Draft articles on law of treaties, *Yearbook of the International Law Commission 1966*, vol. II (1966), p. 247. For a rare contrary opinion, see J. Green, 'Questioning the Peremptory Status of the Prohibition of the Use of Force' (2011) 32 *Michigan Journal of International Law*, 215–57, at 215, arguing that a peremptory norm cannot have 'exceptions'. Other arguments include the assertion that frequent violations of the norm show that States do not consider the norm as peremptory. The assertion that peremptory norms cannot have exceptions is not persuasive if such exceptions are in fact built into the norm itself, as is the case with the UN collective security system and Article 51 of the Charter guaranteeing the 'inherent' right of self-defence. See, for example, K. Hossain, 'The Concept of *Jus Cogens* and the Obligation under the UN Charter' (2005) 3 *Santa Clara Journal of International Law*' 72–98, at 86–95; P. M. Butchard, 'Back to San Francisco: Explaining the Inherent Contradictions of Art. 2(4) of the Charter' (2018) 23 *Journal of Conflict and Security Law* 229–67.

The binding character of a rule of customary law is not vitiated by it being violated, unless it is clear that by violating the rule the majority of States wished to alter or replace it or to dispense with the rule altogether. There has to be a clear legal intention behind a violation and the support of the bulk of the international community is needed to change a rule or make it no longer binding.[27] This is true of any rule of customary international law; in the case of a *jus cogens* rule, even dissenting or abstaining States are bound by it. The violation of a peremptory norm would bring about a change in the rule only if the entire international community concurred with the abandonment or alteration of the rule. With a multilateral treaty like the UN Charter, the situation is essentially the same. A (material) breach of a treaty does not release the parties from the obligation to comply with it unless all other parties agree to terminate the treaty or suspend its operation in whole or in part.[28] The prohibition on the use of force is a rule of both conventional and customary law. Hence, there is no basis for asserting that because the prohibition on the use of force has been violated on numerous occasions, the rule has lost its binding character.

It also seems clear that when the Charter was adopted, the prohibition on the use of force was intended to bind not just the signatory States but all States. The prohibition is based and builds on a pre-existing rule of international law relating to the renunciation of war as an instrument of national policy (see Chapter 3). The Charter also clearly gives the United Nations the power to ensure that non-member States do not endanger international peace and security (see Article 2(6) of the UN Charter). Hence, the prohibition is not dependent upon consent, whether it be that of its individual members or even of non-member States.[29] No State, member or otherwise, has ever taken the position that it is not bound by the prohibition or that a violation of the prohibition by any State on any occasion has diminished its binding effect in any way. Whenever States have used force, they have consistently argued that they have done so in conformity with the Charter, regardless of whether this was in fact the case, and, as the ICJ has pointed out, recourse to an exception to a rule reinforces the rule and does not necessarily undermine or vitiate it.[30] The various organs of the United Nations, with the endorsement of all States,

[27] *Nicaragua* (n. 3), para. 186.
[28] Article 60(2) of the Vienna Convention on the Law of Treaties (Vienna, 23 May 1969).
[29] I. Brownlie, *Principles of Public International Law* (Oxford University Press, 1990), p. 694; Hossain, 'Concept of *Jus Cogens*' (n. 26), pp. 92–4.
[30] *Nicaragua* (n. 3), paras. 183–6.

have repeatedly declared the prohibition to be binding on all States and as having a fundamental character, as, for example, in the Friendly Relations Declaration. In short, notwithstanding numerous violations of the rule since 1945, there is ample evidence of the binding, *erga omnes* and peremptory nature of the prohibition on the use of force in the practice of States inside and outside the United Nations.[31]

What, if anything, does the fact that there are recognized 'exceptions' to the use of force mean in relation to the peremptory character of the norm? Can there be exceptions to a peremptory rule when no derogation is allowed? First, it is abundantly clear that the framers of the Charter never intended to ban force used in the maintenance or restoration of international peace and security. On the contrary, the Charter is permeated with provisions relating to that central purpose underlying it. For example, the prohibition of UN intervention in the domestic affairs of its members does not apply to the Security Council's power to maintain international peace and security. Likewise, the rights and obligations States have under other treaties or rules of general international law (except for other rules of a peremptory character) do not impede the use of enforcement measures, including the use of force by, or with the authorization of, the Security Council for the maintenance of international peace and security. Consequently, if the use of force in the context of the UN collective security system is an 'exception' to the prohibition, it was built into the system from the outset and is a corollary to the prohibition. The other 'exception' is the right of self-defence. The right of self-defence is recognized as 'inherent' in Article 51. Consequently, while the Charter was clearly intended to lay down a comprehensive ban on the use of force, it was never intended to cover the use of force to maintain or restore international peace and security or the exercise of the right of self-defence.[32] So if these uses of force are exceptions to the prohibition, they are built into the UN collective security system. The prohibition and its exceptions together form a consistent whole and should be seen in conjunction with each other and with the Charter's fundamental purposes of restraining force, maintaining international peace and security and ensuring the territorial integrity and political independence of UN member States. Hence, there is no contradiction between the peremptory character of the prohibition on the use of force and the incorporation of these lawful uses of

[31] Ibid.

[32] Butchard, 'Back to San Francisco: (n. 26), pp. 266–7.

SUMMARY BOX 4.1 THE MAIN CHARACTERISTICS OF THE PROHIBITION ON THE USE OF FORCE

The prohibition on the threat or use of force in Article 2(4) of the Charter is a *jus cogens* norm that allows for only two exceptions: enforcement measures under Chapter VII and the exercise of the right of self-defence.

The prohibition and its exceptions form a consistent whole in the context of the fundamental purposes of the Charter.

force into the system. Nor, for that matter, is there any reason why a norm of a peremptory nature should not have built-in or recognized exceptions in a more general sense. There is a fundamental difference between a deviating/conflicting norm and an exception to a rule which is built into the rule or the overall norm itself.[33] For example, the right to life is generally considered to have a peremptory character, but this does not preclude the applicability of exceptions in which the use of lethal force is permitted by law.[34]

[33] Green, 'Questioning the Peremptory Status' (n. 26), p. 232 n. 82; U. Linderfalk, 'The Effect of *Jus Cogens* Norms: Whoever Opened Pandora's Box, Did You Think about the Consequences?' (2007) 18 *European Journal of International Law* 853–71.

[34] On the peremptory character of the right to life, see, for example, UN Human Rights Committee, General Comment 6, Article 6 (Sixteenth session, 1982), in Compilation of General Comments and General Recommendations Adopted by Human Rights Treaty Bodies, UN Doc. HRI/GEN/1/Rev.1 (29 July 1994), pp. 9–7, at 6. In both the International Covenant on Civil and Political Rights (New York, 16 December 1966) (ICCPR) and the European Convention for the Protection of Human Rights and Fundamental Freedoms (Rome, 4 November 1950) (ECHR), certain situations are recognized as providing a lawful basis for using lethal force under strict conditions. Article 6 ICCPR forbids arbitrary deprivation of life, which does not include lawful use of force in defence of oneself or others, lawful acts of war, etc. Article 2 ECHR provides for certain exceptions to protection of the right to life, and Article 15(2) ECHR expressly allows a derogation for lawful acts of war. Buchan and Tsagourias, *Regulating the Use of Force* (n. 17), pp. 36–8, contest the peremptory character of the norm on the grounds that since the threat of force is not deemed peremptory by some authors, it is not logical to 'cherry-pick' the use of force as having peremptory status. They also do not see how different primary rules (the 'exceptions' of collective security and self-defence) can be integrated into the primary rule prohibiting force and, finally, they point out that 'threat to the peace' (in Article 39 of the Charter) is given a 'progressive interpretation' by the UN Security Council covering situations not amounting to a 'threat or use of force'. The present authors disagree with this view. As pointed out by the ICJ in its *Nuclear Weapons* Advisory Opinion (n. 9), the threat and use of force are both covered by the peremptory character of the rule. They 'stand together', so there is no 'cherry-picking'. The concept of 'threat to the peace' in Article 39 of the Charter is completely separate and distinct from the 'threat of force' (see

## 4.8 Force and Its Relationship to Armed Attack, Aggression and Related Concepts in the *jus ad bellum*

As we have set out above, force has a specific meaning and function in the law governing its use. It signifies an act of armed coercion directed by one State against another State. It can take various forms and can be carried out in different ways, but all of them have in common the use (or threat) of armed force. The threshold for the use of force under the UN Charter is purposely set low so as to encompass any form or degree of armed coercion by one State against another. Its function is to demarcate acts which fall within the prohibition on the use of armed force from other forms of pressure or coercion and to set a standard that helps determine when a State has engaged in, or been the target of, a use of force. The term is related to, but distinct from, a number of other concepts which play a role within the law relating to the use of force. The two most important of these are 'armed attack', used in Article 51 of the Charter, and 'aggression', referred to in Article 39 of the Charter and a number of General Assembly resolutions, which forms the basis of the crime of aggression set out in the Rome Statute of the International Criminal Court (ICC Statute).

The first question to be answered is whether a use of force is synonymous with an armed attack. Does any use of force constitute an armed attack, or only when it exceeds a certain minimum threshold? We examine the right of self-defence below in Chapter 6; here, suffice it to say that opinions and the positions of States differ on this question. The ICJ seems to take the view that only acts involving a use of force of a particular degree of intensity qualify as 'armed attacks', although its position on this is not altogether consistent.[35] At the other end of the scale is the belief, held by certain States and authors, that any use of force can qualify as an armed attack. There is a middle position which accepts some gap or distance between the two concepts, but does not require an

Chapter 5, below) and the exceptions of collective security and self-defence are wholly integrated into, and compatible with, Article 2(4) for the reasons set out above.

35 In *Nicaragua* (n. 3), para. 195, the ICJ set a high threshold for a use of force to amount to an armed attack. This position was subsequently modified somewhat in ICJ, *Oil Platforms (Islamic Republic of Iran* v. *United States of America)*, Judgment, 6 November 2003, ICJ Reports 2003, para. 64. Wilmshurst takes the position that there is no gap between the use of force under Article 2(4) and an armed attack under Article 51 of the Charter. E. Wilmshurst, 'The Chatham House Principles of International Law on the Use of Force by States in Self-Defence' (2006) 55 *International & Comparative Law Quarterly* 963–72.

intensive or grave use of force to activate the right of a State to defend itself. That is the position we take, which will be explained in Chapter 6.

With regard to the distinction between force and aggression, the latter is used in two ways. First, it is referred to in Article 39 of the Charter as a ground for the taking of enforcement measures by the Security Council and is defined in a General Assembly resolution (see Fact Box 4.2).[36] Second, it refers to the element of State conduct that characterizes an act involving the use of force by a person in a position of authority, which, by its character, gravity and scale, is manifestly unlawful and constitutes an international crime under the ICC Statute (see Chapter 15, below).

### FACT BOX 4.2 DEFINITION OF AGGRESSION (1974) – EXCERPT

**Article 1**

Aggression is the use of armed force by a State against the sovereignty, territorial integrity or political independence of another State, or in any other manner inconsistent with the Charter of the United Nations, as set out in this Definition. [. . .]

**Article 2**

The First use of armed force by a State in contravention of the Charter shall constitute prima facie evidence of an act of aggression although the Security Council may, in conformity with the Charter, conclude that a determination that an act of aggression has been committed would not be justified in the light of other relevant circumstances, including the fact that the acts concerned or their consequences are not of sufficient gravity.

**Article 3**

Any of the following acts, regardless of a declaration of war, shall, subject to and in accordance with the provisions of article 2, qualify as an act of aggression:

(a) The invasion or attack by the armed forces of a State of the territory of another State, or any military occupation, however temporary, resulting from such invasion or attack, or any annexation by the use of force of the territory of another State or part thereof,
(b) Bombardment by the armed forces of a State against the territory of another State or the use of any weapons by a State against the territory of another State;
(c) The blockade of the ports or coasts of a State by the armed forces of another State;

[36] See Article 39 of the Charter; UNGA Res. 3314 (n. 12). See also Article 8 bis of the Rome Statute of the International Criminal Court.

FACT BOX 4.2 (*cont.*)

(d) An attack by the armed forces of a State on the land, sea or air forces, or marine and air fleets of another State;

(e) The use of armed forces of one State which are within the territory of another State with the agreement of the receiving State, in contravention of the conditions provided for in the agreement or any extension of their presence in such territory beyond the termination of the agreement;

(f) The action of a State in allowing its territory, which it has placed at the disposal of another State, to be used by that other State for perpetrating an act of aggression against a third State;

(g) The sending by or on behalf of a State of armed bands, groups, irregulars or mercenaries, which carry out acts of armed force against another State of such gravity as to amount to the acts listed above, or its substantial involvement therein.

**Article 4**

The acts enumerated above are not exhaustive and the Security Council may determine that other acts constitute aggression under the provisions of the Charter.

**Source**: Definition of Aggression, Annex to Resolution 3314 (XXIX), adopted by the UN General Assembly on 14 December 1974, UN Doc. A/RES/29/3314.

## 4.9 Conclusion

To sum up, 'force' is a generic term within the *jus ad bellum*, denoting any type of armed force, whether legal or illegal under international law. 'Armed attack' has a specific function as a precondition for exercising the right of self-defence, which, depending on the position one takes, is triggered either by any use of force or only by a particularly intense and grave thereof. Finally, 'aggression' denotes either a particularly grave threat to, or breach of, international peace and security constituting a situation for which the Security Council may take measures under Chapter VII, or a manifestly unlawful use of armed force constituting an international crime. Each of these three terms has its own particular meaning and function within the law on the use of force.

# 5

# The Use of Force in the UN Collective Security System: Maintenance and Restoration of International Peace and Security through Collective Measures

## 5.1 Introduction

This chapter looks at the scope and content of the UN collective security system. It examines the powers of the UN Security Council (UNSC, Security Council) in maintaining and restoring international peace and security. As a corollary, it also looks at the inherent limits to those powers, their source and scope. The chapter also discusses how the UN collective security system has evolved since the Charter was adopted and the role it plays in maintaining international peace and security through a variety of measures ranging from enforcement action to consensual peacekeeping.

## 5.2 Collective Security: Ideal and Reality

Article 1(1) of the Charter identifies the maintenance and restoration of international peace and security as the most important purpose of the United Nations and sets out a system to effectuate that purpose through the attribution to the Security Council of far-reaching powers to employ collective measures, including measures involving the use of force. This underlying purpose and the instruments and measures serving to realize it run as a leitmotiv throughout the Charter.[1] Nevertheless, the reality of how the Security Council has functioned over most of its existence makes clear that the collective security system has never been a world police force or even a guarantor of peace in many situations. For some commentators,

[1] B. Simma et al. (eds.), *The Charter of the United Nations: A Commentary* (Oxford University Press, 2012), vol. 1, pp. 101–6; L. Goodrich et al., *Charter of the United Nations* (Columbia University Press, 1969), pp. 25–9.

this means that the notion of a UN collective security system is a complete myth or a failed experiment that has not lived up to the expectations and intentions of the drafters of the Charter.[2]

The fact that the UN collective security system has clearly not lived up to the aspirations of the drafters of the Charter is undeniable. That being said, one has to accept that the notion of collective security was never meant to supplant State sovereignty, eliminate international rivalry or substitute the collective good for the interests of its members, especially the permanent members of the Security Council. The system is dependent upon the will of its members, and especially the permanent members of the Security Council, to use it as a means of managing international crises and is only as effective as its members are willing to make it. The UN collective security system is an instrument of international diplomacy, and in particular crisis management, not an international law enforcement mechanism or a centralized authority replacing the role of States in providing for their security against any threat that might arise. It has more in common with previous, non-institutional systems of balancing State interests and crisis management, such as the nineteenth-century Concert of Europe than it does with a centralized security system possessing a monopoly of force.[3] This is a consequence of any action undertaken by the Security Council being subject to the approval of its permanent members and dependent upon their support, or at least their non-opposition.[4]

## 5.3 The Charter and the Use of Force in the Maintenance and Restoration of International Peace and Security

Article 1(1) of the Charter provides for the maintenance or restoration of international peace and security through the use of effective collective measures. This objective is worked out in various provisions and parts of

[2] G. Egerton, 'Collective Security as Political Myth: Liberal Internationalism and the League of Nations in Politics and History' (1983) 5(4) *International History Review* 496–524, at 502–5; M. S. Helal, 'The Myth of U.N. Collective Security' (2018) 32 *Emory International Law Review Recent Developments* 1063–97; I. Scobbie, 'War', in J. d'Aspremont and S. Singh (eds.), *Concepts for International Law: Contributions to Disciplinary Thought* (Edward Elgar, 2019), pp. 900–12.

[3] Helal, 'Myth of U.N. Collective Security' (n. 1), p. 1066; S. Neff, 'A Short History of International Law', in M. D. Evans (ed.) *International Law* (Oxford University Press, 2003), pp. 48–9.

[4] This is the consequence of the so-called veto power of the permanent members as per Article 27(3) of the Charter.

the Charter. The prohibition of the use of force and the other main objectives of the Charter (e.g. the peaceful settlement of disputes, the promotion of friendly relations between the member States, the affirmation of the territorial integrity and political independence of the member States and the promotion of self-determination of peoples and human rights) were – despite their undoubted importance independently – also seen as factors contributing to the maintenance of international peace and stability.[5] But the ultimate guarantor of the peace was to be the major powers working through the Security Council, which was given primary responsibility in carrying out this task in Article 24 of the Charter. The same provision provides that the Security Council acts on behalf of the entire membership in discharging this responsibility. As a corollary, Article 25 declares that all members agree to accept and carry out UNSC decisions in accordance with the Charter. Article 2(6) extends the application of decisions relating to the maintenance and restoration of international peace and security to non-members. Article 2(7), while preserving the internal affairs or *domaine réservé* of the members from outside interference, makes clear that this is without prejudice to the exercise of enforcement powers by the Security Council in the maintenance of international peace and security.[6]

The enforcement powers of the Security Council are set out in detail in Chapter VII of the Charter, specifically in Articles 39–42. In Article 39, the Council is given wide discretion to determine that a given situation constitutes a threat to, or breach of, the peace or an act of aggression and to address such a situation through the use of collective enforcement measures, including measures involving the use of force. Article 39 is a key provision in the UN collective security system, since a finding that a particular situation constitutes a threat to, or breach of, the peace or an act of aggression is both a legal and a political requirement for taking any sort of enforcement action.[7] Enforcement measures are by their nature

[5] Simma et al. (eds.), *Charter* (n. 1), vol. 1, pp. 109–12.

[6] Ibid., pp. 254–5, 307–8, 763–4; T. D. Gill, 'Legal and Some Political Limitations on the Power of the UN Security Council to Exercise Its Enforcement Powers under Chapter VII of the Charter' (1995) 26 *Netherlands Yearbook of International Law* 33–138, at 38–41.

[7] Gill, 'Legal and Some Political Limitations' (n. 6); L. M. Goodrich, *The United Nations and the Maintenance of International Peace and Security* (Brookings Institution, 1955), pp. 346–7. Note that the term 'threat to the peace' has no relationship to the term 'threat of force' under Article 2(4) of the Charter and can include situations which have nothing to do with a threat or use of force in international relations (e.g. institutionalized racial discrimination in Southern Africa, a *coup d'état* in Haiti or piracy off the coast of Somalia). A 'breach of the peace' denotes a significant use of force across an international frontier

proactive, coercive and directed against a particular State or entity.[8] They have the objective of restoring the peace or dealing with any threat to it that the Council sees fit to address and is able to agree upon.

Article 40 provides for the imposition of interim measures, such as ceasefire orders, orders to parties to allow relief supplies to reach civilians, calls for parties to enter into negotiations with the aim of reaching a settlement to a dispute and so forth. Article 41 deals with coercive measures not involving the use of force, such as embargoes on categories of goods, economic and financial sanctions, the setting up of ad hoc international tribunals or other bodies to investigate and adjudicate specific types of violations of international law and so forth. Article 42 provides for enforcement measures involving the use of force.[9] These can range from authorizing peace operations to use force for particular purposes or authorizing naval and air forces of member States to conduct aerial and maritime interception and interdiction operations, such as non-consensual boarding of vessels to enforce an embargo or enforcement of no-fly zones, all the way to full-scale warfare, referred to rather euphemistically in Article 42 as 'other operations'. Article 42 is not dependent upon consent by the State or entity against which the force is directed, nor upon the prior exhaustion of other measures. The Security Council is given the discretion to determine when and under what conditions it considers that other measures have proven to be inadequate or would be inadequate in the prevailing circumstances.[10]

The UN General Assembly also plays a role in the context of the UN collective security system. The Charter provides the General Assembly with the power to discuss and recommend measures related to the maintenance of peace and security, but these are secondary to the primary role of the Security Council under the Charter. General Assembly Resolution 377 of 3 November 1950, usually referred to as the 'Uniting for Peace' resolution,

(e.g. the conflict between the United Kingdom and Argentina over the Falkland/Malvinas Islands in 1982, the Iran-Iraq War in 1980–8 and the invasion of Kuwait by Iraq in 1990). An 'act of aggression' denotes a particularly serious breach of the peace (see Chapter 4, Section 4.8, above).

8 D. W. Bowett, *United Nations Forces* (Praeger, 1964), p. 267.

9 Simma et al. (eds.), *Charter* (n. 1), vol. 2, p. 1330; O. Schachter, *International Law in Theory and Practice* (Nijhoff, 1991), pp. 391–3; Gill, 'Legal and Some Political Limitations' (n. 6), pp. 39–50.

10 Gill, 'Legal and Some Political Limitations' (n. 6), p. 50; Report of Mr Paul Boncour, Rapporteur, on Chapter VIII, Section B (Doc. 881, III/3/46, 10 June 1945), in *Documents of the United Nations Conference on International Organization San Francisco, 1945* (1945), vol. 12, pp. 502–14, at 507.

provided a relatively contentious basis in the early years of the United Nations for the General Assembly to make recommendations in the context of setting up peacekeeping and other military missions if the Security Council was unable to act due to the veto of (one of) its permanent members. This practice led to a crisis within the UN when two permanent members refused to pay contributions to finance peace (enforcement) operations based on a mandate of the General Assembly pursuant to this resolution. That crisis was resolved by the Security Council reasserting its prerogatives and primacy under the Charter, and no military operations have been undertaken on the basis of General Assembly recommendation since the early 1960s.[11] Nevertheless, the Assembly has convened on a limited number of occasions in the context of 'emergency sessions' based on Resolution 377 to discuss specific situations where the Council has failed to take action. Most recently, the General Assembly convened an emergency session to discuss and resoundingly condemn the military invasion of Ukraine by Russia in February 2022.[12]

[11] The crisis related to the refusal of two permanent members of the Security Council (France and the Soviet Union) to pay contributions for peace operations set up by the General Assembly (UNEF I and ONUC relating to the Suez crisis of 1956 and the Congo crisis of 1960–5, respectively). This led to a situation where these two members were faced with losing their right to vote as a result of being in arrears (Article 19 of the Charter), which in all probability would have led to them leaving the United Nations. To avoid that possibility, the General Assembly did not proceed to vote on any issue or adopt an agenda during its nineteenth session in 1965. Although the International Court of Justice (ICJ) had determined that the General Assembly had not acted ultra vires in recommending the establishment of the two peacekeeping missions, the solution was found in a political compromise, whereby the members agreed that the Security Council would be solely responsible for establishing peacekeeping missions and the General Assembly would refrain from using the 'Uniting for Peace' procedure to recommend military action while the Security Council was seized of an issue. ICJ, *Certain Expenses of the United Nations (Article 17, paragraph 2, of the Charter)*, Advisory Opinion, 20 July 1962. See Simma et al. (eds.), *Charter* (n. 1), vol. 2, pp. 1176–7; *UN Yearbook* (1964), pt 1 ('The United Nations'), s. 1 ('Political and Security Questions'), chap. 1, pp. 3–50.

[12] On the powers of the General Assembly in relation to the collective security system, see Articles 11, 12 and 24 of the Charter. On the background to and legal status of Resolution 377, see C. Tomuschat, 'Uniting for Peace' (2008), UN Audiovisual Library of International Law, https://legal.un.org/avl/ha/ufp/ufp.html. On the resolution condemning the invasion of Ukraine in 2022, see 'Aggression against Ukraine', UNGA Res. ES-11/1 (2 March 2022), https://news.un.org/en/story/2022/03/1113152. In the vote on that resolution, 141 States voted in favour of condemnation of the invasion, qualifying it as an act of aggression; 5 States, including Russia, opposed the resolution; and 35 abstained. This vote, while symbolic, also has practical consequences in filling a gap left by the inability of the Security Council to declare the invasion an act of aggression due to a veto by Russia of a draft resolution on 25 February 2022, which had 11 votes in favour and 3 abstentions.

## 5.4 Command Arrangements in the Implementation of Enforcement Measures: Authorizations for Military Enforcement Action and the Place of Regional Organizations in Collective Security

The original idea behind the employment of enforcement measures involving the use of force was that the Security Council would itself conduct enforcement operations using forces placed at its disposal by member States through agreements under Article 43. The Military Staff Committee was to exercise operational command over forces provided by member States. Nevertheless, this has never been the way the Security Council actually operates. No member has to date placed any unit of its armed forces at the disposal of the UNSC by means of a special agreement under Article 43 of the Charter. Any forces or other military assets provided by member States to carry out decisions of the Council are made available on a purely ad hoc and voluntary basis.[13] The Military Staff Committee has no command function whatsoever and is a largely dormant institution.[14] Likewise, no State is obliged to actively participate in enforcement action involving the use of force, although no State, member or otherwise, can lawfully actively interfere with the use of coercive measures, including the use of force, once the decision to implement such measures has been taken by the Security Council.[15] Consequently, the law of neutrality (albeit in a somewhat modified form) remains relevant, at least to some extent, to collective security measures involving the use of force.[16]

When enforcement action involving the use of force was utilized as a basis for the military operation known as Desert Shield/Desert Storm to

[13] Y. Dinstein, *War, Aggression and Self-Defence* (Cambridge University Press, 2017), p. 354; T. Franck, *Recourse to Force: State Action against Threats and Armed Attacks* (Cambridge University Press, 2002), pp. 24-27; Simma et al. (eds.), *Charter* (n. 1), vol. 2, pp. 1335–7.

[14] Simma et al. (eds.), *Charter* (n. 1), vol. 2, pp. 1362–3.

[15] Dinstein, *War, Aggression and Self-Defence*, (n. 13), p. 354; Schachter, *International Law* (n. 9), p. 394.

[16] Dinstein, *War, Aggression and Self-Defence* (n. 13), pp. 186–7. In relation to the exercise of collective enforcement measures, the law of neutrality is modified in the sense that while no State can be compelled to provide forces or otherwise actively participate in armed action, it is not open for a State not to comply with binding non-military enforcement measures or otherwise hinder UN forces in carrying out a mandate. See Institut de Droit international, Session of Wiesbaden (1975), 'Conditions of Application of Rules, other than Humanitarian Rules, of Armed Conflict to Hostilities in which United Nations Forces may be Engaged', www.idi-iil.org/app/uploads/2017/06/1975_wies_02_en.pdf. See Chapter 14, below, on neutrality law and its place in relation to the contemporary legal system regulating the use of force and the law of armed conflict.

force Iraq to end its occupation and annexation of Kuwait in 1990–1, some scholars and certain States questioned whether the use of collective military enforcement measures by means of an authorization by the Security Council could be reconciled with the Charter.[17] A literal reading of Articles 42–7 does not at first sight appear to open the way for collective military enforcement action by means of authorization. However, this has not proven to be the determining factor. While special agreements whereby member States would place contingents of their armed forces at the disposal of the Security Council may have been the original idea, there is no reason why other means of achieving the primary purpose of the Charter are not open to the Security Council and would not qualify as collective enforcement measures. This is how the Council has functioned for at least thirty years since this practice was (re-)introduced, and it is (now) accepted by most authors and States as a legitimate means to maintain or restore international peace and security.[18] The (command) arrangements envisaged in Articles 43–7 are a means to an end and not an end in themselves.[19] Hence, the legality of enforcement measures is not affected by the fact that they are not conducted directly by the Security Council, as was originally envisaged.

Although most authors now accept the legality of such authorizations, some still question whether enforcement measures based on such authorization fall under Article 42 or have a *sui generis* legal basis under Chapter VII, without being traceable to a specific provision in the Charter.[20] This discussion is rather academic, since it is clear that after at least thirty years of practice, conducting enforcement measures through authorization has become well established and is the only feasible way for the Council to employ such measures in the present political circumstances. Nevertheless, from a legal perspective it is preferable to

[17] N. Blokker, 'Is the Authorization Authorized? Powers and Practice of the UN Security Council to Authorize the Use of Force by Coalitions of "The Able And Willing"' (2000) 11 (3) *European Journal of International Law* 541–68. Blokker mentions objections to the practice of authorizations by, inter alia, Cuba and Malaysia in the period leading up to the adoption of UNSC Resolution 678 authorizing the use of force against Iraq (ibid., pp. 544–5).

[18] Schachter, *International Law* (n. 9), pp. 392–3; Simma et al. (eds.), *Charter* (n. 9), vol. 2, pp. 1337–8; R. Higgins, *Problems and Process: International Law and How We Use It* (Oxford University Press, 1994), pp. 257–9.

[19] Gill, 'Legal and Some Political Limitations' (n. 6), pp. 56–7, with accompanying notes citing, inter alia, Kelsen, White and Bowett.

[20] Dinstein is one notable scholar who opines that collective action authorized by the UNSC does not fall within the ambit of Article 42 of the Charter. Dinstein, *War, Aggression and Self-Defence* (n. 13), pp. 358–60.

conclude that Article 42 has evolved through subsequent practice (just as various other provisions of the Charter have), rather than attempt to introduce a new legal basis for the implementation of collective enforcement action. A *sui generis* basis is more difficult to reconcile with the Charter than reliance on a modified interpretation of an existing provision.

As regards the conducting of enforcement operations exceeding the threshold of peace operations of various kinds, the practice of the Security Council, for many years, has been to authorize the use of force by issuing a mandate to that effect, in which a particular State, group of States or regional organization is authorized to employ force for (a) specific purpose(s) against a specified State or non-State entity, usually, but not invariably, for a specified period of time. In such cases, the Security Council retains overall authority at the political-strategic level to extend, amend or withdraw the authorization and to exercise whatever level of oversight it deems appropriate, while the actual conduct of the enforcement operation involving the use of force is delegated to the State(s) or organization authorized to carry out the mandate.[21] Command of the forces participating in the operation is usually exercised by the State providing the bulk of the forces. In some cases, a (regional) organization or arrangement such as the African Union (AU), the European Union (EU), or the North Atlantic Treaty Organization (NATO) will exercise command over the forces provided by participating member States, relying on its own command arrangements to do so.[22]

The situation in relation to Peace Operations conducted directly by the Department of Peace Operations (DPO) of the UN Secretariat is somewhat different, with a civilian head of mission appointed by the Secretary General and a military commander (and sometimes a police commander) designated by the DPO to command the participating member State units conducting the mission. Most such missions are not primarily tasked with peace enforcement, although they are often provided with Chapter VII mandates by the Security Council, which retains overall

[21] Ibid., pp. 360–1; N. White, *Keeping the Peace* (Manchester University Press, 1997), pp. 225–84.

[22] Examples include UNSC Resolution 386 (2001) establishing the International Security Assistance Force (ISAF), which NATO commanded with the authorization of the UNSC in August 2003 and which continued until 2014; the AMISOM mission conducted by the AU, based on authorization given by the UNSC in Resolution 1744 (2007) and renewed periodically since; Operation ATALANTA authorizing the EU to combat piracy off the coast of Somalia under UNSC Resolution 1814 (2008), renewed periodically since.

political authority, just as with the above-mentioned (peace) enforcement operations delegated to coalitions of States and regional organizations.[23] The command arrangements can have an effect upon various matters, ranging from the status of the forces and rules of engagement to questions of attributing acts performed in the context of the mission to the United Nations, to another (regional) organization or arrangement designated to execute the mandate or to the member State(s) participating and exercising command over its or their forces.[24]

It is worth noting that the concept of regional organizations and arrangements and the way they operate in the context of the collective security system as set out in Chapters VII and VIII of the Charter has in some important respects worked differently from the original blueprint laid out in the Charter.[25] First, there is no 'one size fits all' definition of what a regional organization actually is. The term has come to mean any intergovernmental organization at a regional or sub-regional level which: (i) has a number of powers attributed to it by its members in the realm of international crisis management and/or in maintaining peace and security; (ii) is acceptable to the Security Council; and (iii) is willing and reasonably able to execute mandates involving the application of enforcement powers under Chapter VII. Hence, the term is not limited to traditional regional organizations such as the AU or Organization of American States (OAS), but has also come to include organizations such as the Economic Community of West African States (ECOWAS), the EU and NATO, none of which fit neatly into the definition of a 'regional organization'.[26] Second, the practice of the Security Council when relying on such organizations to apply enforcement powers has been to authorize them to conduct enforcement action under Chapter VII, rather than under Chapter VIII dealing with the role of regional organizations. Yet this, too, is of secondary importance, given the Security Council's wide discretion to carry out itself the Charter's primary purpose of maintaining and restoring international peace and security and to choose any

[23] For specifics on the command arrangements in UN peace operations, see T. D. Gill et al. (eds.), *Leuven Manual on the International Law Applicable to Peace Operations* (Cambridge University Press, 2017), pp. 41–51.

[24] Ibid., pp. 278–84. See also B. Cathcart, 'Command and Control in Military Operations', in T. D. Gill and D. Fleck (eds.), *The Handbook of the International Law of Military Operations* (Oxford University Press, 2015), pp. 259–68.

[25] Simma et al. (eds.), *Charter* (n. 1), vol. 2, p. 1192.

[26] Gill et al. (eds.), *Leuven Manual* (n. 23), p. 36. See also N. White and E. Myjer, 'Peace Operations Conducted by Regional Organizations and Arrangements', in Gill and Fleck (eds.), *Handbook* (n. 24), pp. 186–9.

arrangement it finds useful or expedient for performing that task in co-operation with member States and other organizations willing to assist it.

The Council has made frequent use of the services of various regional and sub-regional organizations.[27] There is significant complementarity between the legitimacy provided by an authorization from the Security Council and the consent of the State where the intervention occurs. On the other hand, the participation of a regional organization can itself enhance the effectiveness of a military intervention in some types of situations, whether because the degree of force contemplated in the intervention may go well beyond what the United Nations itself is prepared to undertake and is capable of undertaking, or because of the specialized nature of the operation, such as counter-piracy or enforcement of a no-fly zone. Moreover, the active engagement and support of a regional organization in executing a mandate can itself enhance the legitimacy of military enforcement measures, in terms of their political acceptability, as they might otherwise be seen as a form of outside interference.[28]

## 5.5 Political Restraints and Legal Regulation of the Use of Force by or under Authorization of the Security Council

The political restraints on the ability of the Council to order enforcement measures, especially measures involving the use of force, include some which are built into the system and others which are a consequence of the prevailing power distribution and state of international relations. The first category includes the requirement provided for in Article 27 of the Charter that a two-thirds majority of the members of the Security Council reach agreement on any decision of a substantive nature, including any decision to implement enforcement measures. The voting requirement also includes the veto power of the permanent members, whereby a negative vote on a substantive matter by one of them means no decision is reached. In essence, the drafters of the Charter built in the

[27] See n. 22, above. Additional examples include the authorization to NATO in relation to Libya (2011), to the AU in Darfur (2007–present). For more detailed treatment of regional peacekeeping, see, for example, P. D. Williams, 'Global and Regional Peacekeepers: Trends Opportunities, Risks and a Way Ahead' (2017) 8 *Global Policy* 124–9.

[28] Williams, 'Global and Regional Peacekeepers' (n. 27), p. 127.

impossibility of the Security Council conducting any kind of action in the face of opposition from a permanent member.[29]

Obviously, this has had, and continues to have, major consequences for how the collective security system works. Contrary to what is often said, this is not a 'failure' of the system, or even arguably a major departure from the original intention of the drafters of the Charter, since if they had expected to live in perfect harmony, they presumably would not have insisted upon the veto in the first place. The veto was the price that the most influential States insisted upon as a condition for their membership and support for the organization at the time the Charter was being drafted, and in all likelihood that remains as much the case today as it was then.[30] Consequently, the support of the permanent members is essential to the successful functioning of collective security. A system in which the most influential and powerful States were not represented would be severely crippled or even impotent. This was evidenced in the interbellum period, when the League of Nations was unable to respond to the crises in the international system, in no small measure because it did not have the support or even acceptance of several of the major powers of the day (see Chapter 3, above).

The second category of political restraints refers to the fact that the Security Council is a mirror of the prevailing power distribution and state of international relations at any given moment and is only as effective as the members are willing to make it. This was obviously the major reason for the Council's failure to reach agreement on most situations relating to international peace and security during the Cold War era, in which international relations were dominated by the rivalries between the United States and the Soviet Union. The end of the Cold War saw a comparatively brief period of relative unity within the Council resulting in a more frequent use of the collective security machinery. This coincided with a period of American predominance in military and political terms and the willingness of many States to co-operate, or at least not actively oppose, a more interventionist role on the part of the Council.

The most recent period saw the 2003 US invasion of Iraq, the disunity within the Council regarding the implementation of enforcement

29 Simma et al. (eds.), *Charter* (n. 1), vol. 1, pp. 913–15.

30 Ibid., pp. 931–3. On the role of the major powers in establishing the voting system and their predominance within it during the drafting history of the Charter, see, for example, A. Boyd, *Fifteen Men on a Powder Keg: A History of the United Nations Security Council* (Methuen, 1971), pp. 56–8; R. Hiscocks, *The Security Council: A Study in Adolescence* (Longman, 1973), pp. 82–4.

measures in Libya, the strains in the international system caused by the rapid rise of China and the invasion of Ukraine by Russia. Against this background, the relative unity within the Council has been gradually superseded by a much sharper rivalry between the permanent members, other influential States and other actors. The situation since at least 2011 has also been characterized by a more multipolar distribution of power and more fluid alignments and interaction between States than in either of the preceding periods. This makes co-operation possible in certain areas where interests coincide. In other cases, co-operation is difficult, or even impossible. It seems likely that this will remain the case for the foreseeable future, although caution is always advisable when predicting future events.[31]

The legal restraints on the Security Council are referred to in Article 24 of the Charter, according to which the Council, in discharging its responsibilities and powers under the Charter, must act in conformity with the UN purposes and principles. These are set out in Articles 1 and 2 of the Charter. In addition, it is clear that the Council must respect peremptory rules of international law in executing its functions. Nevertheless, the Council retains wide discretion to qualify any situation as a threat to, or breach of, the peace or as aggression and to apply any measures it feels necessary and can agree upon, including the use of force.

That translates into the Council's prerogative to set aside or suspend the application of rules of international law which do not form part of the UN purposes and principles or which do not have the status of peremptory rules. That is not to say that the Council can disregard international law, but that it has the power to set aside the rights of States under international treaties and customary rules of a non-peremptory nature if it feels that necessary for carrying out its tasks in the maintenance and restoration of international peace and security. This is in fact inherent in the implementation of enforcement measures of any kind. Hence, the Council can suspend the right of States to engage in trade and maritime and aerial commerce and can even use force against a State to maintain or restore international peace and security, but it must respect peremptory rules of the law of armed conflict and international human rights law in doing so. Also, the Council cannot take measures which would permanently deprive a State of its territorial integrity and political independence,

[31] T. D. Gill, 'The *Jus Ad Bellum Anno* 2040: An Essay on Possible Trends and Challenges', in M. Waxman and T. Oakley (eds.), *The Future Law of Armed Conflict* (Oxford University Press, 2022), pp. 36–9.

or its population of fundamental human rights and self-determination. Indeed, the Council has consistently stated the need to respect international humanitarian law and human rights law in conducting its duties under the Charter.[32]

## 5.6 Responsibility to Protect and the Security Council

The 'responsibility to protect' (R2P) principle grew out of the reaction of some segments of the international community to the failure to prevent or adequately address the humanitarian crises in Rwanda and the former Yugoslavia in the 1990s. It began as a Canadian-sponsored international proposal advocating for a responsibility to protect people from atrocities, incumbent on the entire international community. This responsibility was to include a right of humanitarian intervention even in the absence of a Security Council authorization (see Fact Box 5.1).[33] The R2P principle was subsequently adopted by the United Nations in 2005, but any military intervention was subject to the authorization of the Security Council on a case-by-case basis.

In short, no change was contemplated to the existing collective security mechanism or to the rules relating to the use of force.[34] R2P as a ground for military intervention in the absence of State consent has lost much traction in the aftermath of the 2011 NATO-led Libya intervention and the division within and outside the Council over the way that intervention was conducted.[35] Nevertheless, some role for the concept remains, as it forms an underpinning for another, related policy objective: the 'protection of civilians' (PoC) and the way this policy has been integrated into and implemented in UN(-mandated)

[32] On the legal restraints on the UNSC in exercising enforcement powers, see, for example, Simma et al. (eds.), *Charter* (n. 1), vol. 1, pp. 780–2; E. de Wet, *The Chapter VII Powers of the United Nations Security Council* (Hart, 2004), pp. 133–310; Gill, 'Legal and Some Political Limitations' (n. 6), p. 64.

[33] International Commission on Intervention and State Sovereignty (ICISS) Report (2001), pp. 54–5.

[34] World Summit Conference Outcome Document, UNGA Resolution 60/1 (24 October 2005), paras. 138–9. On the place of the R2P principle within the UN System, see G. Zyberi (ed.) *An Institutional Approach to the Responsibility to Protect* (Cambridge University Press, 2013). On the role of the Security Council in the implementation of the R2P principle, see T. D. Gill, 'The Security Council', in Zyberi (ed.), *Institutional Approach*, pp. 83–108.

[35] S. Brockmeier et al., 'The Impact of the Libya Intervention Debates on Norms of Protection' (2016) 30(1) *Journal of Global Society* 113–33; R. Thakur, 'R2P after Libya and Syria: Engaging Emerging Powers' (2013) 36(2) *Washington Quarterly* 61–76.

### FACT BOX 5.1 THE RESPONSIBILITY TO PROTECT

In the aftermath of the atrocities at Srebrenica (Bosnia-Herzegovina) and in Rwanda in the 1990s, the then UN secretary general, Kofi Annan, called on member States to submit proposals on how to react to gross and systematic violations of human rights. The Canadian government initiated the International Commission on Intervention and State Sovereignty (ICISS), consisting of a group of high-level diplomats, lawyers and politicians from a number of countries, to prepare a report in response to this call. The report issued by the Commission in 2001, entitled 'The Responsibility to Protect' (ICISS Report), argued that States had a primary responsibility to protect their peoples from atrocities and that when States proved either unwilling or unable to fulfil that duty, the responsibility was transferred to the international community. The ICISS Report also set out conditions for (pre-emptive) military intervention in cases where there was a grave risk of large-scale human rights violations and the State where this threat existed was either directly implicated or clearly unable to act. While the ICISS Report urged member States to secure the approval of the Security Council before any such intervention, it also left the door open for unilateral military action.

In 2003, Kofi Annan commissioned the High-Level Panel on Threats, Challenges and Change to, inter alia, examine the current challenges to peace and security and consider what collective action could address such challenges. In its final report, presented in December 2004, the Panel endorsed 'the emerging norm that there is a collective international responsibility to protect' and supported the conditions proposed in the ICISS Report in relation to military intervention, but within the existing Chapter VII procedures of the UN Charter.

In 2005, more than 170 UN member States debated the issues and recommendations raised in the ICISS Report and adopted the concept of R2P at the 2005 World Summit Conference (A/RES/60/1, 24 October 2005). The original framework of the ICISS Report was essentially retained, with the caveat that any military intervention was predicated upon a decision of the Security Council acting within the existing procedures of the UN Charter. In short, R2P was not an acknowledgement of a right of humanitarian intervention by individual States; instead, as a last resort and on a case-by-case basis, the Security Council could use its enforcement powers to address human rights violations (paras. 138–9).

In 2009, the then UN secretary general, Ban Ki-moon, presented a new report entitled 'Implementing the Responsibility to Protect'. Bringing together the proposals and parameters of the aforementioned documents, this new report set out a normative framework for the responsibility to protect consisting of three 'pillars'. The first pillar concerned the primary responsibility of States to protect their populations – whether nationals or not – from genocide, war crimes, ethnic cleansing and crimes against humanity, and from incitement to such crimes. The second pillar dealt with the responsibility of the international community to assist States in meeting those obligations, especially States faced with an internal breakdown in security or internal conflicts that threatened human rights. The third pillar set out the responsibility of member States to respond collectively and in a timely and

FACT BOX 5.1 (*cont.*)

decisive manner whenever a State was manifestly failing to protect its citizens. Such a response had to fully respect the provisions, purposes and principles of the Charter, including those related to Chapter VII measures.

**Sources**: United Nations Office on Genocide Prevention and the Responsibility to Protect, https://tinyurl.com/3wzmub4y; ICISS Report, pp. xi–xiii, 17–18, 31–7, https://tinyurl.com/45wxsufc; Report of the High-Level Panel on Threats, Challenges and Change, pp. 56–8, https://tinyurl.com/2s4easxm.

peace operations.[36] The policy objective of PoC forms part of the second pillar of R2P, which sets out the responsibility of the international community to assist a State in protecting human rights within its territory (see Fact Box 5.1). One tool in assisting States in such situations is UN peacekeeping, and PoC has become fully integrated into UN peace operation mandates in the last decade.

## 5.7 Peacekeeping and Its Place in the UN Collective Security System

Several references have been made in the preceding paragraphs to UN peacekeeping. It has its legal basis in the general powers of the Security Council (and the General Assembly) to maintain international peace and security. UN peace operations have traditionally been associated with Chapter VI of the Charter. Nevertheless, the Security Council need not refer to a specific chapter of the Charter when passing a resolution authorizing the deployment of a UN peacekeeping operation and has never invoked Chapter VI.

Peacekeeping grew out of the Cold War impasse within the Security Council as an alternative means of limiting conflicts and managing international crises and has since grown into a flagship activity of the United Nations, involving tens of thousands of uniformed peacekeepers and civilian personnel in dozens of countries spread all over the world (see Fact Box 5.2). The term 'peace operations' now encompasses both

[36] P. Williams, 'The R2P Protection of Civilians and UN Peacekeeping Operations', in A. J. Bellamy and T. Dunne, *The Oxford Handbook of the Responsibility to Protect* (Oxford University Press, 2016), p. 525.

### FACT BOX 5.2 UN PEACEKEEPING

Starting with small-scale UN observer missions that were set up in the early years of the United Nations to oversee ceasefire agreements in the Middle East and for India and Pakistan, the concept of UN peacekeeping has developed steadily and has gone through various stages. The first armed peacekeeping missions were those in the 1950s and early 1960s, which oversaw the withdrawal of foreign forces from Egypt following the Suez crisis of 1956 and addressed the breakdown in internal order and various insurgencies following the decolonization of the Congo in 1960. The Cold War made the use of enforcement powers unfeasible. As a result, UN peacekeeping involving troops from non-aligned and neutral States became an instrument for managing conflict on the basis of consent, impartiality and limited use of force. Such missions included those in Cyprus, the Dominican Republic, the Middle East, West New Guinea and Yemen.

Following the end of the Cold War, UN peacekeeping expanded both in numbers and in complexity; 'traditional' missions involving observational tasks performed by military personnel were increasingly replaced by complex 'multi-dimensional' enterprises, designed to ensure the implementation of comprehensive peace agreements, assist governments confronted with internal instability and conflicts in laying the foundations for sustainable peace and protecting civilians. Originally developed as a means of dealing with inter-State conflict, UN peacekeeping was increasingly applied to intra-State conflicts and civil wars. This trend saw peacekeeping evolve in new directions, with varying degrees of success and some notable failures, especially in the Balkans, Rwanda and Somalia. These operations came in for criticism, as peacekeepers faced situations where warring parties failed to adhere to peace agreements or where the peacekeepers were not provided with adequate resources. Despite these setbacks, the UN has made progress in developing the instrument of peacekeeping and allocating a more proactive role to such missions in the protection of civilians and promotion of internal stability.

As of late 2022, there have been a total of seventy-one peacekeeping and observer missions since 1948, with twelve currently in progress. These twelve missions involve a total of nearly 74,000 uniformed personnel (approximately 7,500 police and the rest military contingent personnel, staff officers and military observers) and some 12,000 civilian personnel divided between local civilians (nearly 8,200) and international civilian personnel (approximately 3,800). The total budget over the period 2021–2 was approximately USD 6.3 billion. It is no exaggeration to say that UN peacekeeping has become a flagship activity of the Organization.

**Sources:** United Nations Peacekeeping Data (February 2023) and UN website on peacekeeping, https://peacekeeping.un.org/en/data, https://peacekeeping.un.org/en/our-history.

traditional and multidimensional peacekeeping, peacebuilding and sometimes elements of peace enforcement. Peacemaking is a related activity taking the form of mediated diplomacy aimed at conflict resolution; it is either included as part of a peace operation or undertaken alongside or before a peace operation.[37]

There are inherent limitations to what peacekeeping can achieve, but if it did not exist, it would no doubt have to be invented, as it fulfils an essential function within the overall collective security system and one which cannot be easily duplicated.[38]

UN peacekeeping builds on several guiding principles, such as consent of the host State (on the territory of which the operation takes place), consent of the parties to a conflict to the maximum extent possible, impartiality and limited use of force.[39]

The requirement of consent is one of the main differences between consensual peace operations and 'pure' enforcement measures involving the use of force, such as the UN-authorized multinational operation to end the Iraqi occupation of Kuwait in 1991. UN-mandated peace enforcement missions, such as those in Afghanistan (ISAF) and Somalia (AMISOM), lie conceptually between 'pure' enforcement action and consensual peacekeeping. Nevertheless, this should not be seen as a neat division between Chapter VI operations and enforcement measures under Chapter VII, since in more recent practice most UN peace operations have a Chapter VII mandate enabling the mission to employ force for purposes other than strict self-defence, such as protection of civilians or assisting a government in re-establishing a stable environment throughout its territory.[40]

In UN parlance this is referred to as 'defence of the mandate', but since mandates have become steadily more ambitious, this has meant that force used to enforce or 'defend' the mandate often has as much to do with mission accomplishment as it does with self-defence and has its basis in the collective security powers of the Security Council.[41] If UN

[37] Simma et al. (eds.), *Charter* (n. 1), vol. 1, p. 1192; T. D. Gill, 'Peace Operations', in Gill and Fleck (eds.), *Handbook* (n. 24), pp. 156–8.

[38] This statement is a paraphrase of the famous remark by Ambassador Madeline Albright, made in a speech delivered in 2006 to the conference of the International Law Association in Toronto. See Policy Options, 'The UN: if it didn't exist, we would have to invent it' (1 October 2006), https://tinyurl.com/mwestt8x. For an overview of current and past UN peace operations, see the UN peacekeeping website at https://peacekeeping.un.org/en.

[39] United Nations Peacekeeping Operations: Principles and Guidelines (Capstone Doctrine, 2008), pp. 31–5.

[40] Gill, 'Peace Operations' (n. 37), pp. 154–5.

[41] J. F. R. Boddens Hosang, 'Personal Self-Defence and Rules of Engagement', in Gill and Fleck (eds.), *Handbook* (n. 24), pp. 478–81; M. Longobardo, 'Robust Peacekeeping Mandates: An Assessment in Light of *Jus Post Bellum*', in C. Stahn and J. Iverson (eds.), *Just Peace After Conflict: Jus Post Bellum and the Justice of Peace* (Oxford University Press, 2020), p. 165.

forces come under attack in the context of executing their mission, the right of 'self-defence' is not based on Article 51 of the UN Charter or the customary right of self-defence, since both of these pertain exclusively to States. Forces placed at the disposal and under the command of the United Nations, while still linked to their sending State, are operating as a subsidiary organ of the Security Council.[42] Hence, their right to use force as part of executing their mission, including in situations of self-defence, does not have its basis in the international law governing the self-defence of States but in the powers of the Security Council to take both proactive and reactive measures. These powers include not only the explicit reference to force in Article 42 of the Charter but also the general powers of the Security Council (and the General Assembly) in the context of maintaining and restoring international peace and security. Hence, peace operations, including those without a Chapter VII mandate, have the power to use force in the execution of this mission, both in the context of 'self-defence' and in the context of mission accomplishment.[43]

In operations carried out by States operating in the context of a regional organization or arrangement, the situation can be somewhat different. To the extent that the mandate provides for the use of force in the execution of the mission, it will form the legal basis for the use of force. If the forces come under attack, the right to use force will be based on the mandate, which will allow for both mission accomplishment and mission defence to the extent that the degree of control by the organization conducting the mission is comparable to operations carried out directly by the United Nations. If the sending States retain control over the forces conducting a mission mandated by the Security Council, the mandate will be the primary legal basis for the use of force, supplemented by the right of the State to use force in self-defence in the event their forces come under attack.[44]

42 See United Nations Security Council Subsidiary Organs: Overview, at https://tinyurl.com/yc4bhj2r.

43 See sources cited above, nn. 40, 41. Note that what is referred to here as 'self-defence' should not be confused with either the right of self-defence of States under international law or the right of individuals to defend themselves and (to varying degrees) defend others under national law, sometimes referred to as 'personal self-defence'. The right of self-defence of States is distinct from the powers of the UN Security Council to maintain or restore international peace and security. The right of individuals (including members of the armed forces) to defend themselves (and in some cases others) under national law falls outside the purview of this book, dealing as it does with the use of force under international law.

44 The application of the right of self-defence of States to localized attacks on their forces is dealt with in Chapter 6, Section 6.5.2, below.

The principles of impartiality and consent of the parties to a conflict often come under pressure when a mandate allows, and indeed expects, a peace operation to execute tasks with an element of enforcement. It is difficult, or often impossible, to maintain consent and be perceived as impartial when force is used against a specific group more than sporadically. On the other hand, traditional peacekeeping has proven inadequate in a number of cases where civilians were deliberately targeted by armed groups; this has demonstrated the inability of such operations to maintain or restore peace. Hence, contemporary peace operations often combine traditional elements of peacekeeping with more proactive peace enforcement in situations of internal armed conflict or systematic breakdown in the functioning of the host State. In other situations, the element of peace enforcement will be less relevant and the more traditional mode of peacekeeping will be more prominent. In either case, the reality in most contemporary operations is that the circumstances are inherently volatile and there is no easy way to maintain peace.[45] This is one of the reasons peace operations play such an essential role. They fill a gap between traditional war fighting in the form of military enforcement measures and non-forcible measures such as diplomacy and sanctions.[46] While this was not the original intent behind UN collective security as envisaged when the Charter was drafted, it has come to be recognized as playing a useful, and even invaluable, role within the collective security system.

## 5.8 Conclusion

Collective security as envisaged in the aspirations of the framers of the Charter is not reflected in the actual way the Security Council has operated and continues to operate. It is instead more of a traditional instrument of (great power) diplomacy and crisis management than a mechanism to resist aggression, much less a law enforcement agency for the international community. It has evolved considerably over the years as a consequence of the state of international relations, and some of its practices are difficult to trace back to specific provisions in the Charter.

Nevertheless, collective security is firmly grounded in the Charter and the practice of member States, as well as of the Organization itself. It is an

[45] See sources cited above, nn. 37–41.

[46] Gill et al. (eds.), *Leuven Manual* (n. 23), pp. 3–5.

instrument which is part of the law, but which, where necessary, can set aside particular rules of international law to achieve its objectives. It is a useful and reasonably effective instrument, notwithstanding a number of notable failures and shortcomings, some of which are built into the system and others a reflection of the state of international relations. Moreover, if it is to have any degree of success in preserving international stability and preventing at least some crises from spinning out of hand, collective security is dependent upon voluntary contributions from, and co-operation among, member States, especially the permanent members, and, increasingly, regional organizations. These are at once its strengths and its weaknesses, and they are unlikely to change essentially anytime soon.

# 6

# The Right of Self-Defence: Essence, Function, Legal Foundation, Requirements for Exercise, Scope and Modalities of Application

## 6.1 Introduction

This chapter sets out and examines the right of self-defence under international law. Self-defence is a recognized and well-established right, anchored in both the UN Charter and customary international law. The basic requirements and conditions relating to the exercise of self-defence are likewise well established. Nevertheless, despite this general understanding, there are various controversies surrounding its legal foundation, the scope of the right and certain modalities of its application. We examine the most important of those, without necessarily going into all the details of the various contending positions. This chapter is divided into four sections examining, respectively, (i) the essence and function of self-defence; (ii) its dual legal basis in the UN Charter and customary law, including some important points relating to its adoption in the Charter; (iii) the requirements for its exercise under both the Charter and customary law; and (iv) the general modalities of its application, including its temporal and geographical scope. Other aspects of self-defence, such as its relationship to other sub-disciplines within international law, and other possible justifications for the use of force outside its context receive attention in other chapters.

## 6.2 The Essence of Self-Defence and Its Function in the Contemporary International Legal Order

When one refers to self-defence, it is essential to have a clear understanding of what is being referred to. Self-defence is, of course, part of the national law of virtually all countries and, although it is defined and applied differently in each legal system, there are certain common characteristics. In national (criminal) law, it is a defence or justification invoked by an individual for using reasonable force to defend oneself or others against ongoing or imminent unlawful force, ranging from simple battery up to and including attempted murder. In most national legal systems, it serves as either a complete justification, when it meets certain criteria, or a(n) (partial) excuse, if some of the conditions are not met. It is sometimes applied differently to persons with an official function, such as police officers and members of the military acting on the basis of law and in the exercise of their official functions.[1]

Self-defence under international law is similar in some respects, but has some specific characteristics which distinguish it from self-defence in a national legal context. It refers to the right of a State to use force in response to ongoing or imminent unlawful force constituting an armed attack, which is directed against its territory, armed forces and, in some cases, its citizens and originates or is controlled from outside the State's territory. It can be exercised in two forms: individually (by one State in response to an armed attack directed against it), or collectively (by two or more States collectively resisting an armed attack directed at all of them, or by one or more States assisting (an)other State(s) in resisting an attack upon one or some of them, subject to either a standing commitment to provide mutual assistance in the event of an attack or an ad hoc request for such assistance from the State(s) under attack).[2]

### SUMMARY BOX 6.1 THE ESSENCE OF SELF-DEFENCE

Self-defence under international law is the *right* of a State to use force in response to *ongoing* or *imminent* unlawful force constituting an *armed attack*, which is directed against its territory, citizens or armed forces and originates or is controlled from *outside* the State's territory.

[1] On personal self-defence, see, for example, J. A. Hessbruegge, *Human Rights and Personal Self-Defense in International Law* (Oxford University Press, 2017), pp. 6–9; J. F. R. Boddens Hosang, *Rules of Engagement and the International Law of Military Operations* (Oxford University Press, 2020), pp. 80–93.

[2] On State self-defence under international law, see, for example, Y. Dinstein, *War, Aggression and Self-Defence* (Cambridge University Press, 2017), pp. 197–260; C. Gray, *International Law and the Use of Force* (Oxford University Press, 2018), pp. 120–99; I. Brownlie, *International Law and the Use of Force by States* (Clarendon Press, 1963), pp. 251–380; T. M. Franck, *Recourse to Force* (Cambridge University Press, 2002), pp. 45–108; R. Higgins, *Problems and Process: International Law and How We Use It* (Oxford University Press, 1994), pp. 238–53; K. Tibori-Szabó, *Anticipatory Action in Self-Defence* (Springer, 2011); O. Schachter, *International Law in Theory and Practice* (Nijhoff, 1991), pp. 135–83.

The defining characteristic of self-defence in international law is the lawful use of force by a State in response to unlawful transboundary force constituting an armed attack directed against that or another State. That is what sets it apart from other uses of force – both those that are lawful (the use of force under a mandate from the UN Security Council (UNSC, Security Council) to restore international peace and security, or at the request of another State to help it maintain law and order on its own territory) and those that do not have a recognized basis in international law (such as preventive war, armed intervention in support of an insurgency and armed reprisal).[3]

Self-defence is both a right of States to use force in defence against attack and a ground for precluding the wrongfulness of that use of force, both inside and outside the defending State's territory, including on the territory of the State from where the attack originated.[4] It is not subject to prior permission from the Security Council, any State or any other organization or entity. It is, however, subject to a number of conditions, all of which will be discussed below. Failure to meet those conditions renders the (further) exercise thereof unlawful. An invocation of self-defence is subject to subsequent approval or rejection by the Security Council and the exercise of self-defence must be terminated if the Security Council so orders, except when the Council has failed to take the measures necessary to halt an ongoing or imminent attack. Self-defence can also be subject to adjudication, provided there is a court or tribunal that has jurisdiction to hear a case relating to recourse to force on an invocation of self-defence. Hence, while a State makes the first call in invoking self-defence, it is always subject to subsequent acceptance or rejection by the international community.[5]

The essential function of the right of self-defence within the framework of the UN Charter is to recognize the right of States to defend themselves against armed attack until the Security Council takes the

[3] These instances of the use of force are addressed in subsequent chapters of this book.

[4] The recognition of self-defence in both the UN Charter and customary law are indications of its existence as a right under international law. Its function as a ground for precluding wrongfulness within the context of the law of international responsibility is set out in Article 21 of International Law Commission, Draft Articles on Responsibility of States for Internationally Wrongful Acts, 2001, Annex to UN General Assembly (UNGA) Resolution 56/83 (12 December 2001), UN Doc. A/RES/56/83.

[5] This was established conclusively in the writings of Sir Hersch Lauterpacht, *The Function of Law in the International Community* (Oxford University Press, orig. pub. 1933, repr. 2011), pp. 179–80, and followed by the International Military Tribunal in the Trial of Major War Criminals (1946–7), cited in Schachter, *International Law* (n. 2), p. 137.

necessary measures to restore international peace and security. Hence, it is embedded in the UN collective security framework and is subject to the Council's ultimate authority, but it is also an autonomous right that States have until such time as the Security Council takes necessary and effective measures.

## 6.3 The Dual Legal Foundation of Self-Defence

The right of self-defence in contemporary international law has two legal bases. First, it is incorporated in Article 51 of the UN Charter, which reads:

> Nothing in the present Charter shall impair the inherent right of individual or collective self-defence if an armed attack occurs against a Member of the United Nations, until the Security Council has taken measures necessary to maintain international peace and security. Measures taken by Members in the exercise of this right of self-defence shall be immediately reported to the Security Council and shall not in any way affect the authority and responsibility of the Security Council under the present Charter to take at any time such action as it deems necessary in order to maintain or restore international peace and security.

The Charter-based content of the right of self-defence thus contains some of the essential features mentioned in Section 6.2. Accordingly, Article 51 acknowledges the right of States to defend themselves individually or collectively in the event of an armed attack, provided their action(s) are reported to the Security Council and as long as such measure(s) do not affect the Council's authority to act.

Second, as suggested by the term 'inherent' in Article 51, the right of self-defence is also anchored in customary international law. As found by the International Court of Justice (ICJ, the Court):

> Article 51 of the UN Charter is only meaningful on the basis that there is a 'natural' or 'inherent' right of self-defence, and it is hard to see how this can be other than of a customary nature, even if its present content has been confirmed and influenced by the Charter.[6]

The customary content of the right of self-defence sets out conditions for the exercise of self-defence additional to those in the Charter. Accordingly, as will be discussed below, the requirements of necessity,

[6] International Court of Justice (ICJ), *Military and Paramilitary Activities in and against Nicaragua (Nicaragua* v. *United States)* (Merits), Judgment, 27 June 1986, ICJ Reports 1986, para. 176.

SUMMARY BOX 6.2 THE LEGAL BASIS OF SELF-DEFENCE

Self-defence has a **dual legal basis**:

- Article 51 of the UN Charter; and
- customary international law.

proportionality and an offshoot of necessity, which we refer to as immediacy,[7] stem from customary law.

The relationship between the two legal bases of self-defence is not wholly uncontroversial. Some authors contend that Article 51 supersedes the customary understanding of self-defence and limits it to the exact wording of the provision.[8] According to those authors, the term 'inherent' simply means that the right is vested in the sovereignty of every State and UN members may give assistance to a non-member falling victim to an armed attack.[9]

Other authors, including those of this book, maintain that through its use of the term 'inherent', Article 51 acknowledges the customary basis of self-defence.[10] This understanding is echoed by the ICJ in the extract

[7] The bulk of legal literature acknowledges the customary principles of necessity and proportionality. See, for instance, Brownlie, *International Law* (n. 2), pp. 257–61; B. Simma et al. (eds.), *The Charter of the United Nations. A Commentary*, vol. 2 (Oxford University Press, 2012), p. 1425; J. Gardam, *Necessity, Proportionality and the Use of Force by States* (Cambridge University Press, 2004), pp. 138–87. The ICJ has emphasized and applied these principles on several occasions: *Nicaragua* (n. 6), paras. 194, 237; *Oil Platforms (Islamic Republic of Iran* v. *United States of America)*, Judgment, 6 November 2003, ICJ Reports 2003, paras. 43, 51, 73–7; *Armed Activities on the Territory of the Congo (Democratic Republic of Congo* v. *Uganda)*, Judgment, 19 December 2005, ICJ Reports 2005, para. 147; *Legality of the Threat or Use of Nuclear Weapons*, Advisory Opinion, 8 July 1996, ICJ Reports 1996, para. 41. Some authors treat immediacy as a separate principle; see T. D. Gill, 'The Temporal Dimension of Self-Defence: Anticipation, Pre-emption, Prevention and Immediacy', in M. N. Schmitt and J. Pejić (eds.), *International Law and Armed Conflict: Exploring the Faultlines* (Nijhoff, 2007), pp. 113, 123–5; Dinstein, *War, Aggression and Self-Defence* (n. 2), pp. 249–52. Other authors incorporate immediacy in the principle of necessity; see Tibori-Szabó, *Anticipatory Action* (n. 2), pp. 192, 196, 256–258, 263, 291, 309; Simma et al. (eds.), *Charter* (n. 7), pp. 1425–7; Gray, *International Law* (n. 2), pp. 157–60; T. Ruys, *'Armed Attack' and Article 51 of the UN Charter: Evolution in Customary Law and Practice* (Cambridge University Press, 2010), pp. 99–108.

[8] Gray, *International Law* (n. 2), pp. 124–5; D. Tladi, 'An Assessment of Bethlehem's Principles on the Use of Force against Non-State Actors' (2013) 107 *American Journal of International Law* 572–5.

[9] Simma et al. (eds.), *Charter* (n. 7), p. 1403; Dinstein, *War, Aggression and Self-Defence* (n. 2), pp. 198–200, 249–52.

[10] D. W. Bowett, *Self-Defence in International Law* (Manchester University Press, 1958), p. 187; S. M. Schwebel, 'Aggression, Intervention and Self-Defence' (1972-II) 136 *Collected*

quoted above. Needless to say, this view does not imply, as contended by some, that a considerably wider, traditional form of self-defence, allowing measures of self-help outside the context of self-defence, has survived the Charter.[11] As a matter of fact, by the beginning of the twentieth century, the concept of self-defence was clearly distinguishable from other forms of self-help and was seen as the only legitimate remnant of the eighteenth- and nineteenth-century principle of self-preservation.[12] This narrower concept of self-defence was differentiated from armed reprisals, retaliations and preventive interventions, which were considered unlawful. To illustrate, German jurist Lassa Oppenheim wrote in 1905:

> Such acts of violence in the interest of self-preservation are exclusively excused as are necessary in self-defence, because otherwise the acting State would have to suffer or have to continue to suffer a violation against itself. If an imminent violation or the continuation of an already commenced violation can be prevented and redressed otherwise than by a violation of another State on the part of the endangered State, this latter violation is not necessary, and therefore not excused and justified.[13]

Similarly, the explanatory note of US secretary of state Frank B. Kellogg prior to the adoption of the Kellogg-Briand Pact[14] referred to self-defence as the inherent right of every sovereign State to defend its territory from attack or invasion.[15] Furthermore, the Locarno Pact defined self-defence as resistance to a violation of the States' undertaking

*Courses of the Hague Academy of International Law* pp. 479–83; C. Greenwood, 'Self-Defence', in *Max Planck Encyclopedia of Public International Law* (Oxford Public International Law, 2011), para. 3, https://tinyurl.com/2txyfx9j; D. Bethlehem, 'Self-Defence against an Imminent or Actual Armed Attack by Nonstate Actors' (2012) 106 *American Journal of International Law* 770–7; Gill, 'Temporal Dimension' (n. 7), pp. 116–17; Tibori-Szabó, *Anticipatory Action* (n. 2), pp. 109–14.

11 Simma et al. (eds.), *Charter* (n. 7), p. 1404.

12 L. Oppenheim, *International Law: A Treatise*, vol. 1 (Longmans Green, 1905), pp. 178, 181–3; E. Benes and N. Politis, 'Report on the Protocol, Submitted to the Fifth Assembly' (1924) 23 *League of Nations Official Journal*, Spec. Supp. 479–502, at 483; Tibori-Szabó, *Anticipatory Action* (n. 2), pp. 63–79, 81–99; T. D. Gill and K. Tibori-Szabó, 'Twelve Key Questions on Self-Defense against Non-State Actors' (2019) 95 *International Law Studies* 467–505, at 472.

13 Oppenheim, *International Law* (n. 12), p. 178.

14 See, in Chapter 3 above, Fact Box 3.2 and Summary Box 3.2.

15 D. H. Miller, *The Peace Pact of Paris: A Study of the Briand-Kellogg Treaty* (G. P. Putnam's Sons, 1928), pp. 213–14; Tibori-Szabó, *Anticipatory Action* (n. 2), p. 89; R. H. Ferrell, *Peace in Their Time: The Origins of the Kellogg-Briand Pact* (Yale University Press, 1952), pp. 187–88; A. C. Watkins, *The Paris Pact: A Textbook for Schools and Colleges* (Harcourt Brace, 1932), pp. 19-20.

not to attack, invade or resort to war against each other, or resistance to a 'flagrant breach' of the demilitarization provisions of the Treaty of Versailles (Articles 42 and 43) 'if such breach constitutes an unprovoked act of aggression and by reason of the assembly of armed forces in the demilitarized zone immediate action is necessary'.[16]

At the time the Charter was adopted, it was this narrower concept of self-defence that was widely viewed as the only legal exception to the future prohibition of the use of force (apart from the collective measures to restore international peace and security that were built into the Charter).[17]

As set out above in Chapter 3, the principal purpose of the 1945 San Francisco Conference, formally known as the United Nations Conference on International Organization, was to set up a general international organization to maintain peace and security.[18] It was in this context that the new prohibition on the threat or use of force was discussed and adopted.[19] Interestingly, the right of self-defence was not discussed in relation to the new prohibition, but rather in connection with the compatibility of pre-existing regional assistance treaties with that prohibition. The issue was first raised by delegates of the French and Turkish governments, who wanted to preserve their countries' right to initiate urgent security measures based on pre-existing regional arrangements without the prior approval of the future Security Council.[20] In addition, Turkey noted that such 'automatically functioning arrangements' should be allowed exclusively for purposes of self-defence.[21]

16 The Locarno Treaties were seven agreements negotiated in Locarno (Switzerland) in October 1925 and signed in London in December 1925 between Belgium, Britain, Czechoslovakia, France, Italy and Poland. The particular provision referred to in this section is Article 2 of the Treaty of Mutual Guarantee between Germany, Belgium, France, Great Britain and Italy, Locarno, 16 October 1925.

17 Tibori-Szabó, *Anticipatory Action* (n. 2), pp. 109–13.

18 'Chapter F: The Yalta Agreement', in *UN Yearbook* (1946–7), pt 1 ('The United Nations'), s. 1 ('Origin and Evolution'), p. 9; Tibori-Szabó, *Anticipatory Action* (n. 2), pp. 101–2.

19 See Chapter 3, Section 3.10.

20 Proposals from the French Government, 21 March 1945 (Doc. 2, G/7(o)), in *Documents of the United Nations Conference on International Organization San Francisco, 1945* (1945) (*Documents of the UNCIO*), vol. 3, pp. 376–82, at 379; Suggestions of the Turkish Government Concerning the Proposals for the Maintenance of Peace and Security Agreed at the Four-Power Conference at Dumbarton Oaks' (Doc. 2, G/14(e), 1 May 1945), in ibid., pp. 480–3, at 483.

21 Verbatim Minutes of the Sixth Plenary Session, 1 May 1945 (Doc. 55, P/13, 2 May 1945), in *Documents of the UNCIO* (n. 20), vol. 1, pp. 416–55, at 453.

The question of regional arrangements was placed on the agenda of Technical Committee 4 of Commission III, where the French and Turkish concerns were echoed by Czechoslovakia and taken up especially by the Latin-American States.[22] The concern of the Latin-American States related to the freshly adopted Act of Chapultepec,[23] according to which an attack against an American State was to be viewed as an attack against all signatory States. Moreover, the Act allowed action to be taken not only after such an attack occurred but also if there were 'reasons to believe that an aggression [was] being prepared'.[24] After ample debate on the subject in Technical Committee 4, as well as among the Five Powers (China, France, the Soviet Union, the United Kingdom and the United States), and following several rejected proposals concentrating on the autonomy of regional arrangements,[25] a new text was put forward couched in more general language, making no reference to regional arrangements and instead concentrating on the right of self-defence. According to this proposal, '[n]othing in this Charter shall invalidate the right of self-defence against armed attack, either individual or collective, in the event of the Security Council failing to take the necessary measures . . .'.[26] While the text referred explicitly to self-defence, the delegates of the Five Powers agreed that the Charter should refrain from specifying any conditions under which self-defence measures could be taken, as such attempts would raise many difficult issues.[27] A further amended proposal was then presented to the Latin American delegates, who, while not opposing the new text, reiterated their concern that such general phrasing might jeopardize the viability

[22] Terms of Reference of Committee III/4 (First Revision) (Chapter VIII, Section C, of the Dumbarton Oaks Proposals with Pertinent Excerpts from Comments and Draft Amendments Submitted by Delegations (Doc. 269, III/4/5, 14 May 1945), in *Documents of the UNCIO* (n. 20), vol. 12, pp. 764–84; Observations of the Czechoslovak Government on the Dumbarton Oaks Proposals, 25 April 1945 (Doc. 2, G/14(b), 1 May 1945), in *Documents of the UNCIO* (n. 20), vol. 3, pp. 466–71, at 470.

[23] The Act of Chapultepec was an agreement adopted at Chapultepec Castle (Mexico City) by the Inter-American Conference on the Problems of War and Peace held between 21 February and 8 March 1945. The Chapultepec Conference was attended by all States of North and South America, except Argentina.

[24] Section 4 of the Act of Chapultepec.

[25] Tibori-Szabó, *Anticipatory Action* (n. 2), pp. 106–7.

[26] 'Memorandum by Mr. Robert W. Hartley of the United States Delegation of a Conversation Held at San Francisco, Saturday, May 12, 1945, 3:30 p.m.', in *Foreign Relations of the United States*, Diplomatic Papers, 1945, General: The United Nations, vol. 1, pp. 698–704, at 704, https://tinyurl.com/5xk4zf2s.

[27] Ibid., p. 703.

of the Inter-American system.[28] To meet such concerns, the US delegate proposed the inclusion of a separate provision in the Charter clarifying the role of regional agreements in the peaceful settlement of disputes.[29] Having reached such an agreement, a consolidated proposal was put forward, having as sponsors the Five Powers and the Latin American States. The text of the proposal read:

> Nothing in the Charter impairs the inherent right of individual or collective self-defence if an armed attack occurs against a member State, until the Security Council has taken the measures necessary . . . .[30]

The text was unanimously adopted by Technical Committee 4.[31] On that occasion, one of the US delegates noted that the resulting text 'satisfies practically anybody'.[32] With minor wording adjustments, the text was adopted by the plenary session of the San Francisco Conference and became Article 51 of the Charter.[33]

The content and the limits of the 'inherent right of individual or collective self-defence' was consequently not discussed at the San Francisco Conference. Some viewed the right as implicit and subject to common sense; others considered it too difficult to define. For instance, during the discussions in Commission I, it was affirmed that 'the use of arms in legitimate defence remains admitted and unimpaired' and that no specific reservation was needed to safeguard such right.[34] On the other hand, UK delegate Anthony Eden repeatedly emphasized that self-defence (and aggression) was very difficult to define and that it was better to avoid interpretive formulations.[35]

28 'Notes on Second Informal Consultative Meeting with Chairmen of Delegations of Certain American Republics, Held at San Francisco, May 15, 1945, 2:45 p.m.', in ibid., vol. 1, pp. 730–6, https://tinyurl.com/3tw2pnss.

29 'Minutes of the Fourth Five-Power Informal Consultation Meeting on Proposed Amendments, Held at San Francisco, May 15, 1945, 5 p.m.', in ibid., pp. 737–9, at 737. The proposal for a separate provision on regional arrangements in the peaceful settlement of disputes became Article 33 of the UN Charter.

30 Proposal for the Amalgamation of Amendments Offered to Chapter VIII, Section C, Prepared by the Delegation of the United States in Consultation with the Other Sponsoring Governments and France, 21 May 1945 (Doc. 510, G/62, 23 May 1945), in *Documents of the UNCIO* (n. 20), vol. 3, pp. 634–6, at 635.

31 Tibori-Szabó, *Anticipatory Action* (n. 2), p. 109.

32 A. H. Vandenberg, Jr., *The Private Papers of Senator Vandenberg* (Houghton Mifflin, 1952), p. 198.

33 Tibori-Szabó, *Anticipatory Action* (n. 2), p. 109.

34 Report of the Rapporteur of Committee 1 to Commission I (Doc. 944, I/1/34 (1), 13 June 1945), in *Documents of the UNCIO* (n. 20), vol. 6, pp. 446–63, at 459.

35 'Memorandum by Mr Robert W. Hartley' (n. 26), p. 703.

In conclusion, Article 51 must be seen as 'codifying' the customary right of self-defence, with the content and limitations considered valid at that time, adding the requirement of the occurrence of an armed attack and the procedural conditions related to the Security Council. The incorporation of this customary right into the Charter was consequently not intended to either expand or limit the right beyond what its content was at the time the Charter was adopted.

## 6.4 The Requirements for the Exercise of Self-Defence

As stated above, there are a number of conditions for the lawful exercise of self-defence, some of which are based on the Charter while others are found in customary law. They are the requirement of an armed attack as set out in Article 51 of the Charter (Sections 6.4.1 and 6.4.2); the requirement under customary law that self-defence be carried out in conformity with the principles of necessity, proportionality and immediacy (Section 6.4.3); and the procedural requirements of reporting the defensive action immediately to the Security Council and of ceasing the exercise of self-defence if the Security Council takes measures which make the continued exercise of self-defence no longer necessary and orders that it cease (Section 6.4.4). Furthermore, there are some additional requirements relating to evidence pertaining to the extraterritorial source of the attack, which are derived from case law and international practice (Section 6.4.5) and a number of conditions for the exercise of collective self-defence (Section 6.4.6). We discuss these successively.

### *6.4.1 Armed Attack as a Prerequisite for the Exercise of Self-Defence*

According to Article 51, a State has recourse to self-defence 'when an armed attack occurs'. The article gives no further guidance as to what constitutes an armed attack or when an attack can be said to have occurred. While there is general agreement regarding the existence of this requirement, there is less consensus on what form or level of force qualifies as an armed attack. In the *Nicaragua* judgment of 1986, the ICJ set a relatively high threshold for the existence of an armed attack, which it distinguished from 'mere frontier incidents'.[36] The ICJ did, however, accept the possibility that an attack could be mounted by a State either directly, with its regular armed forces, or indirectly by 'sending' armed

[36] *Nicaragua* (n. 6), para. 195.

bands from its territory to carry out acts which were comparable, in terms of scale and effect, to an attack conducted by regular armed forces.[37] At the same time, the ICJ excluded not only strictly material support in the form of the provision of weapons to an armed band acting against another State but also 'logistical or other support' for such an armed group as qualifying as an armed attack.[38] The ICJ devoted no attention to the question of whether an armed group acting on its own volition would be capable of mounting an armed attack, as this possibility played no role in the factual or legal context of that case.[39]

This rather restrictive rendition of armed attack has come in for a substantial degree of criticism, both immediately following the decision and in the years since then. One of the most pointed critiques was set out in the dissenting opinion of Judge Sir Robert Jennings. He stated that the ICJ's rendition of armed attack was 'neither realistic nor just' and that the setting of such a high threshold made it impossible for a State to lawfully respond to lower-level uses of force, at least in so far as such a response could be based on a recognized right such as self-defence, and ignored the fact that lower-level uses of force and subversion can often be very destabilizing for a victim State.[40] In addition to these points raised by Jennings, the high threshold used by the Court has also potentially opened a fairly wide gap between prohibited armed force under Article 2(4) of the Charter and armed attack as a condition for self-defence under Article 51 of the Charter. As a result, various authors have struggled to find a plausible basis for using force to counter acts of a lower level than a substantial armed attack. This has sometimes resulted in rather convoluted solutions such as armed counter-measures, as put forward by the ICJ in the same decision, presumably to overcome its differentiation between force and armed attack, but which it considered subject to other criteria, including the non-collective exercise of such a right.[41]

[37] Ibid.

[38] Ibid.

[39] Gill and Tibori-Szabó, 'Twelve Key Questions' (n. 12), p. 478.

[40] *Nicaragua* (n. 6), Dissenting Opinion Judge Jennings, pp. 542–3.

[41] On the gap between 'use of force' in Article 2(4) and 'armed attack' in Article 51, see, for example, Dinstein, *War, Aggression and Self-Defence* (n. 2), pp. 205–8. On the attempt to bridge the gap with the construct of armed counter-measures, see, for example, *Oil Platforms* (n. 7), Separate Opinion of Judge Simma, pp. 331–2. On the ICJ's rendition of the conditions pertaining to such armed counter-measures short of self-defence, see *Nicaragua* (n. 6), para. 210.

SUMMARY BOX 6.3 LEVEL OF AN ARMED ATTACK

An armed attack can include any use of force above the *de minimis* level.

None of this is a logical rendition of either the text of Article 51 or its object and purpose, on the basis of which there is no reason to presume that an attack can consist only of armed acts 'on a significant scale'. It is true, however, that not any forcible act, no matter how attenuated and inconsequential, would necessarily open the way for the use of force in self-defence, particularly since it would be difficult in such a situation to make a case for the necessity of self-defence where there were no other feasible alternatives at hand. A few States and some experts argue the opposite – namely, that any use of force can qualify as an armed attack and that the scale of the unlawful force is immaterial to the question of whether self-defence is permissible in response, but that the scale of the response will be governed by the principles of necessity and proportionality.[42] This view seems more logical at first sight, but ignores the fact that most States and experts take the position that a certain minimum degree of force is required for it to qualify as an armed attack. This *de minimis* threshold is generally defined as one that causes neither loss of life nor significant damage or disruption in the target State.[43] Consequently, the most plausible answer to this problem seems to be that an armed attack can include any use of force above the level of an inconsequential (including an ordinary criminal) act involving armed force.

### 6.4.2 *Modalities of Armed Attack: Authorship and Forms of Execution*

The next questions to answer relate to the authors and forms of an armed attack.

Starting with the authorship of an armed attack, the most obvious and frequent author is another State, working either directly through its

[42] E. Wilmshurst, 'Chatham House Principles of International Law on the Use of Force by States in Self-Defence' (2006) 55 *International & Comparative Law Quarterly* 963–72, at 966: 'An armed attack means any use of armed force, and does not need to cross some threshold of intensity.'

[43] See, for example, Ruys, *'Armed Attack'* (n. 7), p. 155; M. Hakimi, 'Defensive Force against Non-State Actors: The State of Play' (2015) 91 *International Law Studies* 1–31, at 16–17; C. Henderson, *The Use of Force and International Law* (Cambridge University Press, 2018), p. 223.

armed forces or indirectly through an armed group under its direction, control or otherwise with its substantial involvement. Both of these alternatives were accepted as possible modes of attack by the ICJ in the previously mentioned *Nicaragua* judgment.[44] A classical armed attack is carried out by a State's armed forces through an invasion, bombardment or other 'act of war' directed against another State (or States). This is without doubt the type of armed attack that the framers of the Charter had in mind when Article 51 was drafted. However, this does not mean that other forms of transboundary armed force cannot qualify as an armed attack. Smaller-scale incursions and exchanges of fire can also qualify, whether conducted directly by a State or by a State acting through an armed group under its control. Likewise, 'hybrid' attacks using troops or armed bands without visible nationality indicators will also qualify as armed attacks if they are controlled or directed from abroad and the acts fit within the aforementioned definition of armed attack.[45] In some cases, a series of smaller-scale incidents which have the same source and are temporally and geographically connected (i.e. they are carried out in reasonable proximity to each other in both time and space) can be seen as a cumulative or phased armed attack. That would seem a reasonable conclusion to draw if the individual acts have a common author and their apparent purpose is to destabilize or coerce the target State or exact concessions from it. In such a case, the scale of the attack should be measured by viewing all the smaller incidents in combination rather than each of them separately.[46]

### SUMMARY BOX 6.4 AUTHORS OF AN ARMED ATTACK

An armed attack may be carried out by:

- a State (either directly through its armed forces, or indirectly through an armed group under the State's direction, control or with its substantial involvement); or
- an autonomous armed group (AAG) without any State control or support.

[44] *Nicaragua* (n. 6), para. 195.

[45] A textbook example of such a 'hybrid' armed attack was Russia's invasion of the Crimea in 2014. For a factual overview, see, for example, J. Simpson, 'Russia's Crimea Plan: Detailed, Secret and Successful', BBC News (19 March 2014), www.bbc.com/news/world-europe-26644082.

[46] On the accumulation of events and phased armed attack, see, inter alia, *Oil Platforms* (n. 7), para. 64; Dinstein, *War, Aggression and Self-Defence* (n. 2), pp. 211–12; Ruys, '*Armed Attack*' (n. 7), p. 177.

What about a State's support of an armed group where such support falls short of actual control? As said above, the question of material support (delivery of arms and other equipment) was also dealt with in the *Nicaragua* judgment and the Court's ruling on that issue seems to reflect State practice in that while outside material support for insurgent movements is widespread, it is rarely viewed on its own as an armed attack by either the injured State or others. While it may well in some cases violate international legal strictures on non-intervention, such support on its own is generally not seen as constituting an armed attack that would open the way for the exercise of self-defence. Even if this support were significant, it would not normally constitute an armed attack on its own. However, when material support is combined with direct support in the form of military advice, intelligence, logistical support and/or training, it becomes more than material support. Such a combination of material and direct support can be seen as a form of 'substantial involvement', which often also includes co-ordination of goals and activities between the State and an armed group without necessarily amounting to control. This too, by any reasonable standard, amounts to an armed attack conducted by a State, alongside the other forms of armed attacks discussed above.[47] All of these modes and authorships of attack are generally accepted as armed attacks by a substantial body of opinion.

However, in the case of attacks carried out by armed groups acting autonomously without any control or substantial involvement by a State,

[47] In *Nicaragua* (n. 6), the majority of the Court excluded material support (supply of arms) and 'logistical and other support'. This position was criticized by Judges Schwebel and Jennings (ibid., Dissenting Opinion of Judge Schwebel, paras. 162–71; Dissenting Opinion of Judge Jennings, pp. 542–3). It also attracted considerable opposition in the literature, not so much because of the exclusion of material support but because of the open-ended nature of the statement 'logistical and other support'. See Ruys, *'Armed Attack'* (n. 7), pp. 415–19; Dinstein, *War, Aggression and Self-Defence* (n. 2), pp. 237–8. The Court itself was relying on Article 3(g) of UNGA Resolution 3314, 'Definition of Aggression' (14 December 1974), which refers to 'substantial involvement' in acts amounting to aggression alongside 'sending armed bands', which it deemed expressive of customary international law. If the aforementioned forms of support (direct support in the form of military advice, intelligence, logistical support and the co-ordination of goals and activities) are added, it becomes synonymous with the 'overall control' standard used by the International Criminal Tribunal for the former Yugoslavia (ICTY). See ICTY, *Prosecutor* v. *Dusko Tadić*, Case No. IT-94-1-A, Appeals Chamber Judgment, 15 July 1999, paras. 118–20, 137, 145. This is also pointed out by Dinstein, *War, Aggression and Self-Defence* (n. 2), pp. 238–9. In any case, if substantial involvement means anything, it would seem reasonable that it would include a combination of these types of support.

opinions are more divided. Some States and authors, relying on a seeming exclusion of this possibility by the ICJ on two occasions and a restrictive interpretation of self-defence in a more general sense, take the position that only States are capable of mounting an armed attack activating the right to exercise self-defence.[48] Another group of States and authors accept the possibility of armed attacks being conducted by autonomous armed groups (AAGs) and the right of States to respond to such attacks through the exercise of self-defence.[49] In view of the form in which self-defence was incorporated into the Charter and, during the past two decades, the increasing practice by a number of States of using force in self-defence in response to attacks by AAGs, it seems fair to say that neither the Charter nor the customary dimension of the right of self-defence has ever excluded this possibility. The more challenging questions concern the modalities of using force against an AAG operating from another State's territory, rather than whether an armed group can mount an armed attack on its own in the first place. Certainly, in recent years there have been numerous examples of armed attacks of a substantial level conducted by autonomous armed groups across

48 See, for instance, O. Corten, 'Contre une invocation abusive de la légitime défense pour faire face au défi du terrorisme' RBTF (30 June 2016), https://tinyurl.com/47n3p9xb ('[i]n accordance with article 51 of the Charter, the use of force in self-defense on the territory of another State is only lawful if that State bears responsibility for a violation of international law tantamount to an "armed attack".'); O. Corten and F. Dubuisson, 'Opération "liberté immuable": Une extension abusive du concept de légitime défense' (2002) 106 *Revue générale de droit international public* 51–77, at 55; M. E. O'Connell, 'Dangerous Departures' (2013) 107 *American Journal of International Law* 380–6, at 382–3; D. Tladi, 'The Nonconsenting Innocent State: The Problem with Bethlehem's Principle 12' (2013) 107 *American Journal of International Law* 570–6, at 571–2.

49 Similarly, see Wilmshurst, 'Chatham House Principles' (n. 42), p. 969 (Principle 6 provides: 'Article 51 is not confined to self-defence in response to attacks by States. The right of self-defence applies also to attacks by non-state actors.'); Institut de Droit international, Session of Santiago – 2007, 10th Commission, Present Problems of the Use of Armed Force in International Law, Sub-group on self-defence, Resolution of 27 October 2007, www.idi-iil.org/app/uploads/2017/06/2007_san_02_en.pdf, Report of E. Roucounas, www.idi-iil.org/app/uploads/2017/06/Roucounas.pdf ('If [the territorial State] does not cooperate, individual and collective self-defence could be exercised in the territory of that State . . . under conditions obviously stricter than those of the traditional situation of State-to-State defence, since the requirement of cooperation requires a different *timing* and the aim will be the *neutralization* of the non-State entity.'); Bethlehem, 'Self-Defense' (n. 10), p. 775 ('[S]tates have a right of self-defense against an imminent or actual armed attack by non-State actors.'); N. Schrijver and L. van den Herik, 'Leiden Policy Recommendations on Counter-Terrorism and International Law' (2010) 57 *Netherlands International Law Review* 531–50 ('It is now well accepted that attacks by non-state actors, even when not acting on behalf of a state, can trigger a state's right of individual and collective (upon request of the victim state) self-defence.').

international borders. The modalities of exercising self-defence in this and other scenarios will be dealt with below in Section 6.5.3.

### *6.4.3 The Customary Law Requirements: Necessity, Proportionality and Immediacy*

Another indication of the dual legal basis for self-defence is the key role that customary law plays in determining when self-defence is a lawful response and regulating how it must be applied when it is lawful. These functions are inextricably bound up with the principles of necessity, proportionality and immediacy.[50] It is important to stress that we are referring to these principles in the context of self-defence and not in relation to other applications, such as in the context of international humanitarian law (also referred to as the law of armed conflict) or human rights law, where they have a different meaning and function (see Chapter 14, Summary Box 14.3).

Necessity *ad bellum* is *the* core principle in relation to self-defence. It serves as the driver of the right, as the existence of a necessity to act in response to an (imminent) armed attack, coupled with the lack of feasible alternatives to repel or overcome the attack, is the *conditio sine qua non* for the right of self-defence. At the same time, it serves as a limitation, since where there is no necessity, there can be no right to act in self-defence. The lack of necessity can lie in the feasibility of recourse to alternative courses of action sufficing to neutralize the threat, or in the absence of an ongoing or clear indication of an imminent armed attack requiring an armed response. Included in the availability of alternatives to self-defence is action undertaken by or under the authority of the Security Council which adequately removes the necessity to act in self-defence. In short, self-defence becomes a response available to a State if a necessity to act in self-defence exists and ceases to be a lawful response in the absence of a necessity to do so.[51]

Proportionality in the context of self-defence is a principle which regulates the scope of the response in terms of how much force may be used to ward off or overcome the attack and, in so doing, it can influence

[50] On these concepts or principles, see, for example, Gill and Tibori-Szabó, 'Twelve Key Questions' (n. 12), pp. 490–503; Dinstein, *War, Aggression and Self-Defence* (n. 2), pp. 249–53. The most comprehensive treatment is by Gardam, *Necessity* (n. 7).

[51] This can be traced back to the famous *Caroline* incident of 1837, where the components of necessity, proportionality and immediacy were first set out. See R. Y. Jennings, 'The Caroline and MacLeod Cases' (1938) 32 *American Journal of International Law* 82–99.

the manner and means of application of defensive force. For example, considerations of proportionality can influence the choice of targets, the locale of the response, or the choice of weapons to be employed, although those considerations will be predominately governed by the rules of the law of armed conflict (see Chapter 14). It has both a quantitative component, which requires the scale of the defensive response to be roughly in balance with the scale of the (imminent) attack, and a qualitative component, which is closely related to the principle of necessity in determining that force is proportionate in so far as it is required to ward off an attack or forestall an ongoing attack from the same source within the reasonably proximate future.[52] Force which exceeds what is required to serve this end is disproportionate and ceases to be lawful. The qualitative component is the more important of the two. Proportionality also serves both an enabling and a restrictive function. The enabling function lies in allowing for application of the force required to neutralize or overcome the attack. Obviously, the greater the scale of the attack, the greater the scale of defensive force required, and therefore lawful, in order to mount an effective defence and neutralize the threat, and vice versa. Proportionality also has a limiting function in that any force which is excessive in relation to the scale of the (imminent) attack and/or continued attack is not permitted and would be unlawful.

Immediacy is a term which has at least two applications in connection with self-defence. First, it relates to the temporal component of an armed attack as a consideration in determining when an attack is imminent. A threat of imminent attack is immediate and leaves no feasible window of opportunity open for alternative action. Second, as an independent criterion, it refers to the necessity for the victim of the attack to take defensive action within its capabilities as soon as this is possible subsequent to the attack, subject to a number of considerations of reasonableness. This is to differentiate self-defence from a purely punitive armed reprisal. Such considerations of reasonableness can include the ability of the defending State to adequately defend itself without delay or outside assistance, the need to mobilize or deploy forces to the locale of the attack, the need to obtain sufficient evidence of the author of the attack when this is not apparent, the need to consult allies or garner outside support when the victim is not capable of mounting an effective defence on its own and so forth.[53]

[52] Gardam, *Necessity* (n. 7), pp. 160–1; Gill, 'Temporal Dimension' (n. 7), p. 124.
[53] Gill, 'Temporal Dimension' (n. 7), pp. 151–4.

SUMMARY BOX 6.5 CUSTOMARY LAW REQUIREMENTS OF SELF-DEFENCE

**Necessity *ad bellum* means:**

- a need to act in response to an (imminent) armed attack; and
- the lack of feasible alternatives to repel or overcome the (imminent) armed attack.

**Proportionality *ad bellum* has:**

- a quantitative component (the defensive force must be proportionate to the scale of the imminent, ongoing or renewed attack); and
- a qualitative component (the defensive force must be proportionate to what is required to ward off or forestall an imminent or ongoing attack).

The qualitative element is the decisive one in determining proportionality.

**Immediacy *ad bellum* refers to:**

- the temporal component of an armed attack as a consideration in determining when an attack is imminent; and
- the necessity for the victim State to take defensive action within its capabilities as soon as this is possible subsequent to the attack.

Any exercise of self-defence will be governed by all three of these principles and must conform to all of them to qualify as a lawful exercise of self-defence. These criteria are on an equal footing with the requirements laid down in the Charter and are complementary to them.

### 6.4.4 *Self-Defence and the Security Council*

Article 51 lays down the procedural requirement that action taken in self-defence must be immediately reported to the Security Council. In addition, it provides that action taken in self-defence 'does not in any way affect the [power] of the Security Council to take any action it deems necessary to restore international peace and security'. This makes self-defence subject to the ultimate authority of the Security Council and partially embeds it within the collective security system of the Charter.[54]

[54] On the role of the Security Council in connection with the exercise of self-defence, see, for example, Dinstein, *War, Aggression and Self-Defence* (n. 2), pp. 253–60; Gray, *International Law* (n. 2), pp. 126–33, Henderson, *Use of Force* (n. 43), pp. 262–72;

Turning to the procedural requirement of reporting action taken in self-defence to the Security Council, the first point to make is that this is not in any way a requirement to request or receive permission or authorization for the exercise of self-defence. The decision to invoke self-defence rests with the State invoking it based on its perception of the necessity to do so and on the information available to it at the time the attack occurs or becomes manifestly imminent.[55] Nevertheless, the exercise of self-defence is subject to subsequent approval, noting or rejection by the Security Council. Once self-defence is invoked and has been reported to the Security Council, the latter can do one of three things: (i) it can endorse the invocation based on information at its disposal and possibly take further action; (ii) it can take note of the invocation, hear any justification for the resort to self-defence and decide to keep the matter under advisement and require the State invoking self-defence to keep the Council informed; or (iii) it can reject the invocation and enjoin the parties to stand down by issuing a binding ceasefire order. In the first two cases, the right of self-defence remains operative until the Council takes effective measures or until the conditions for continuing exercise of self-defence are no longer present. In any case, the action taken by the State invoking self-defence will usually be subsequently reviewed and discussed by the Council. The State invoking self-defence will have to (continue to) make a case for its action being in conformity with the substantive requirements for the exercise of self-defence. The Council can then accept the legality of the resort to self-defence, reject it or fail to endorse it. Dinstein refers to this as the 'two-phases rule', whereby a State makes the initial decision to resort to self-defence based on its own perception of the situation and subsequently the Council or, in the event the Council fails to reach consensus, the wider international community makes its own determination on the legality of the resort to self-defence.[56]

Failure to meet the reporting requirement does not in itself automatically have the effect of making the exercise of self-defence unlawful, provided such exercise meets the substantive requirements set out in the preceding Sections 6.4.1, 6.4.2 and 6.4.3. That being said, failure to report will most likely prejudice the subsequent assessment by the Security

T. D. Gill, 'Legal and Some Political Limitations on the Power of the UN Security Council to Exercise its Enforcement Powers under Chapter VII of the Charter' (1995) 26 *Netherlands Yearbook of International Law* 33–138, at 90–106.

[55] See, for example, Dinstein, *War, Aggression and Self-Defence* (n. 2), p. 253.

[56] Ibid., pp. 253–5.

Council of the action taken by the State resorting to self-defence and will increase the likelihood of it being deemed unlawful in the event any adjudication relating to the use of force were to take place.[57] Nevertheless, it is unlikely that a State acting under a clear necessity for self-defence in response to an unequivocal armed attack would be condemned simply because it failed to report its action immediately to the Security Council, provided it did so within a reasonable time.

As noted above, Article 51 makes clear that the Security Council's authority to take action to restore international peace and security is not affected by a recourse to self-defence. When this is viewed alongside the Council's primary responsibility for the maintenance of international peace and security and the enforcement powers allocated to the Council to implement this task, it is a clear indication of the Council's primacy and its authority to take measures which can endorse and complement, subsume or even terminate a State's recourse to self-defence. The Council has made use of all of these possibilities on occasion, but it is wholly up to the Council how it determines to act in relation to a State's recourse to self-defence. There is no requirement or guarantee that the Security Council will do anything other than take note of the situation. This is what the UNSC has done in many instances in which a State has had recourse to self-defence, particularly when that State was a permanent member or an ally of a permanent member, and when there was no consensus within the Council on whether measures should be taken to either complement or terminate the action taken in self-defence.[58]

It is important to stress that while the Security Council's primacy is clear and its discretion in the maintenance of international peace is virtually unlimited, the power of the Council to terminate a lawful recourse to self-defence is not. The measures ordered by the Security Council must be effective – that is, they must actually remove the necessity of acting in self-defence. Otherwise, the State's right to defend itself is not terminated. The primary responsibility given to the Council for

[57] This is also reflected in *Nicaragua* (n. 6, para. 235), where the Court viewed the failure to report the recourse to self-defence to the Security Council as prima facie evidence that the invocation of self-defence long after the alleged occurrence of an armed attack was not justified. For criticism of this position, *see* Dinstein, *War, Aggression and Self-Defence* (n. 2), pp. 258–60. While the present authors agree with the criticism, it is also realistic to expect that failure to report, whether justified or not, may have prejudicial effects.

[58] Dinstein, *War, Aggression and Self-Defence* (n. 2), pp. 255–6, on the options open to the Security Council once an act of self-defence is reported.

maintaining international peace does not translate into a discretionary power to order a State under attack to stand down, unless the orders given or the measures taken by the Council are in fact capable of restoring international peace and security and actually succeed in halting an ongoing or imminent attack (see Fact Box 6.1). This flows directly from Article 51, according to which a State has an inherent right to defend itself or assist in the defence of another State at the latter's request until the Council has taken the measures *necessary* to maintain or restore international peace and security. It also flows from the clear purpose underlying Article 51 and the fact that the Council may not act in violation of the purposes and principles of the Charter (see Chapter 5, above, and Chapter 15, below), which includes the right of States to

### FACT BOX 6.1 UNSC MEASURES UNDER ARTICLE 51 OF THE CHARTER

**Iran-Iraq War:** In July 1987, the Security Council adopted Resolution 598, in which it called upon Iran and Iraq to observe an immediate ceasefire, discontinue all military actions and withdraw all forces to the internationally recognized boundaries. In principle, this resolution would have suspended Iran's right of self-defence (as the war was initiated by Iraq in 1980), but only on condition that Iraq accepted and complied with the ceasefire and withdrawal of its forces from Iranian territory. However, it took the two States an entire year to accept the terms of the resolution and then it took another few weeks for their respective troops to withdraw to the international border. Resolution 598 became effective on 8 August 1988.

**The First Gulf War:** On 2 August 1990, Iraq invaded and occupied Kuwait. On the same day, the Security Council adopted its Resolution 660, condemning the invasion and demanding the immediate and unconditional withdrawal of Iraqi forces. After several further resolutions and Iraq's continuing refusal to withdraw, the Security Council adopted Resolution 678, according to which, if by 15 January 1991 Iraq had not fully implemented all of the Council's resolutions relating to the occupation of Kuwait, member States co-operating with Kuwait's legitimate government were authorized to use 'all necessary means' to compel Iraq to do so and restore international peace and security in the area. The deadline passed and on 16 January 1991 the armed forces of the States co-operating with the government of Kuwait began air attacks against Iraq, followed on 24 February by a ground offensive. In this case, the Security Council did not suspend or terminate Kuwait's right of self-defence, but it took measures that were complementary to that State's and its allies' defensive actions.

independence, territorial integrity and the safeguarding of the lives of its citizens from an attack.[59]

There is no inevitable incompatibility between the exercise of enforcement powers by the Council and the recourse to self-defence. In the event of a clash between the two, however, the former would prevail in so far as the measures taken by the Security Council effectively remove the necessity of recourse to self-defence.

### 6.4.5 *Additional Requirements: Providing Evidence of an Armed Attack*

States have typically not been required to substantiate their claims regarding the occurrence of an armed attack prior to the exercise of self-defence. Indeed, requiring a State to provide evidence of an imminent or ongoing armed attack before being allowed to defend itself would render the right of self-defence almost meaningless, as it would preclude or limit the possibility for the defending State to take the necessary measures in a timely manner. As said above, the decision to exercise the right of self-defence belongs to the State invoking it, based on its perception of the necessity of doing so in the light of the information available at the time.

Nonetheless, as previously discussed, States are required to report their defensive action to the Security Council. To date, three main types of reporting can be identified.[60] The first and most common is a letter from the permanent representative of the reporting State to the Security Council. The second is the submission of a document from a State official (head of State, head of government, foreign minister or other duly authorized government official) to the Council, typically appended to a letter of introduction by the permanent representative of the reporting State.[61] The third is an oral submission during a Security Council session, but this format is no longer in use.[62] Additionally, other forms of

[59] Gill, 'Legal and Some Political Limitations' (n. 54), pp. 94–5, 101–6.

[60] N. van der Steenhoven, 'Conduct and Subsequent Practice by States in the Application of the Requirement to Report under UN Charter Article 51' (2019) 6(2) *Journal on the Use of Force and International Law* 242–72.

[61] See, for instance, 'Letter dated 25 April 1980 from the Permanent Representative of the United States of America to the United Nations addressed to the President of the Security Council', UN Doc. S/13908 (25 April 1980); 'Letter dated 11 October 2014 from the Secretary-General addressed to the President of the Security Council', UN Doc. S/2014/730 (13 October 2014).

[62] Steenhoven, 'Conduct and Subsequent Practice (n. 60), p. 254.

reporting, such as memoranda or factsheets,[63] have also occurred.[64] In any case, there is no specific requirement as to the type or form of reporting, although the first two aforementioned types are the most commonly used.

As regards the content of the report, the question arises as to what form of substantiation or evidence the report must contain concerning the occurrence or imminence of the armed attack. Article 51 simply says that the measures taken by defending States must be immediately reported. It does not provide any parameters with regard to the substance of the reports. Nonetheless, given that the purpose of reporting is to allow the Security Council to decide on the measures to be taken, a mere notification of the defensive action would not suffice. To date, letters to the Security Council have typically provided a brief factual description of the events leading up to the invocation of self-defence.[65]

The present authors are of the view that the reporting State must provide clear, credible and persuasive information showing that the circumstances leading up to its exercise of self-defence led to the reasonable assumption: (i) that an armed attack had occurred (i.e. such an attack took place), was ongoing or there were clear indications that an attack from a specific source was imminent;[66] and (ii) that the attack was authored or controlled from abroad by an identified State or the non-State armed group against which the defensive action was (being) directed.

Beyond the reporting requirement under Article 51, defending States may have to prove the legality of their use of self-defence in subsequent judicial proceedings – namely, before the ICJ. In this regard, the question arises as to the applicable standard of proof for demonstrating the occurrence or imminence of an armed attack originating or controlled

[63] See, for instance, 'Letter dated 21 December 2001 from the Permanent Representative of Poland to the United Nations addressed to the Chairman of the Committee established pursuant to resolution 1373 (2001) concerning counter-terrorism, annexed to Letter dated 27 December 2001 from the Chairman of the Security Council Committee established pursuant to resolution 1373 (2001) concerning counter-terrorism addressed to the President of the Security Council', UN Doc. S/2001/1275 (27 December 2001), para. 3; 'Letter dated 4 March 2019 from the Permanent Representative of Armenia to the United Nations addressed to the Secretary-General', UN Doc. S/2019/211 (11 March 2019).

[64] Steenhoven, 'Conduct and Subsequent Practice' (n. 60), pp. 252–3.

[65] J. A. Green, 'The Article 51 Reporting Requirement for Self-Defense Actions' (2015) 55 *Virginia Journal of International Law* 563–624, at 602–6; Steenhoven, 'Conduct and Subsequent Practice' (n. 60), pp. 262–3.

[66] See Section 6.4.1, above.

from abroad and identifying its author. Such a standard would necessarily be more onerous than the aforementioned requirement to report to the Security Council, which is meant to assist the UNSC in decision-making. The standard of proof in ICJ proceedings has a different purpose: to set the evidentiary threshold for the parties to the dispute and for the Court to render its ruling. In this regard, the ICJ has not yet set out such a standard, although it has on a number of occasions rejected evidence as being 'insufficient' to determine the legality of a self-defence claim.[67] The failure of the Court to articulate an evidentiary standard has been criticized by some of its own judges. Notably, Judge Buergenthal, in his separate opinion to the *Oil Platforms* judgment, asked, 'What is meant by "insufficient" evidence? Does the evidence have to be "convincing", "preponderant", "overwhelming", or "beyond a reasonable doubt" to be sufficient?'[68] Despite refraining from the clear articulation of an evidentiary standard, the Court seems on many occasions to have implicitly relied upon a fairly elevated threshold of proof.[69] Accordingly, the Court has looked for 'some degree of certainty',[70] 'convincing evidence',[71] 'clear evidence'[72] or 'conclusive' evidence.[73] The Court has further rejected as insufficient to establish the alleged facts evidence that was 'suggestive, but no more',[74] merely 'indicative'[75] or 'highly suggestive, but not conclusive'.[76] It thus seems that the ICJ relies, implicitly and fairly consistently,[77] on a standard requiring clear and convincing or conclusive evidence in its findings.

67 *Nicaragua* (n. 6), paras. 54, 110, 159, 216; *Oil Platforms* (n. 7), para. 57. See also J. Green, 'Fluctuating Evidentiary Standards for Self-Defence in the International Court of Justice' (2009) 58 *International & Comparative Law Quarterly* 163–79, at 168.

68 *Oil Platforms* (n. 7), Separate Opinion of Judge Buergenthal, para. 41. See, similarly, ibid., Separate Opinion of Judge Higgins, paras. 30–6; Separate Opinion of Judge Owada, paras. 41–52.

69 Green, 'Fluctuating Evidentiary Standards' (n. 67), p. 172.

70 *Nicaragua* (n. 6), para. 29.

71 Ibid.

72 Ibid., para. 109.

73 *Oil Platforms* (n. 7), para. 71.

74 Ibid., para. 59.

75 Ibid., para. 61.

76 Ibid., para. 71.

77 Nonetheless, as Green shows, in the *Armed Activities* judgment, while apparently applying the same 'clear and convincing' threshold as in the *Nicaragua* and *Oil Platforms* cases, the ICJ appeared also to accept evidence (with regard to the establishment of an armed attack) based upon the notably lower standard of preponderance or prima facie evidence. Green, 'Fluctuating Evidentiary Standards' (n. 67), pp. 175–6.

### 6.4.6 *Requirements for Collective Self-Defence*

Collective self-defence denotes two possible situations. It can refer to an attack that is simultaneously directed at more than one State by the attacking State(s), in which case the attacked States can collectively resist the attack. It can also refer to one or more States coming to the assistance of a State under attack, either on the basis of a prior treaty commitment to provide such assistance or on the basis of an ad hoc request for such assistance.[78] Despite some opinions to the contrary, there can be no doubt that both of these situations are generally accepted in State practice and in fact reflect how States have consistently viewed collective self-defence from the time Article 51 was included in the Charter. The existence of military alliances such as the North Atlantic Treaty Organization (NATO), along with numerous bilateral arrangements which include mutual assistance clauses in the event of an attack on one of the members makes this abundantly clear. In the absence of such a predetermined trigger event to which the members of an alliance have previously agreed, an ad hoc request for assistance, or at least an agreement to accept assistance, will be required alongside all of the other requirements (Charter-based and customary) for the exercise of self-defence set out above. These are no different when collective self-defence is being exercised from when one State is exercising self-defence individually.

[78] On collective self-defence, see Dinstein, *War, Aggression and Self-Defence* (n. 2), pp. 301–27; Gray, *International Law* (n. 2), pp. 176–99; Schachter, *International Law* (n. 2), pp. 155–8. Article 51 was included at the behest of Latin American States to make allowance for mutual security arrangements between them in the form of the Treaty of Chapultepec (see Section 6.3, above). The supposed 'novelty' of collective self-defence, reportedly expressed by Anthony Eden at the time the Charter was drafted and echoed by some jurists since then, seems odd in the context of even State practice at the time the Second World War broke out. Great Britain and France declared war on Germany as a result of the latter's attack on Poland, and the declarations of war by the independent dominions in the British Commonwealth (Australia, Canada, New Zealand and South Africa) were likewise expressions of mutual solidarity and assistance. At the time, no attack had been perpetrated on either the United Kingdom or France, much less on the overseas dominions. That would seem to be proof positive that collective self-defence was already well accepted before the Charter, and it seems disingenuous to claim that it is a contradiction in terms. *Nicaragua* (n. 6, paras. 196–9) recognized both facets of collective self-defence and included a reference to a requirement of request for assistance.

## 6.5 The Modalities of the Exercise of Self-Defence

### *6.5.1 Introductory Note*

This section sets out and discusses the most important modalities for the exercise of self-defence. We first address different levels of self-defence, ranging from a tactical-level reaction by a military unit or a localized (imminent threat of a) one-off armed attack to full-scale warfare. We also devote some attention to particular forms of warfare which can play a role in the exercise of self-defence. Second, we devote attention to the modalities of exercising self-defence in response to an armed attack conducted by an AAG operating from another State's territory without the substantial involvement of, or control by, a State. In particular, the question of whether self-defence can be exercised on the territory of the State from where the armed group is conducting its attack without the consent of that State will be given attention. Third, the temporal dimension of self-defence is discussed and analysed. In that context, the elements of necessity and immediacy are discussed in relation to when defensive measures may be taken to forestall an imminent armed attack, as opposed to preventive measures against an attack which has not yet manifested itself. Likewise, the question of when self-defence must cease will be given attention. Finally, the last sub-section discusses the geography of self-defence – that is, where defensive measures may be taken and where not.

### *6.5.2 Levels of Self-Defence: From Local or Unit Self-Defence to Defensive War*

There is incontrovertibly only one right of self-defence under international law, but just as there are different modes and methods for conducting an attack, so there are different modes and 'levels' for the exercise of self-defence.[79] At the lower end of the scale is defensive action in response to localized, small-scale uses of force constituting an (imminent) armed attack. This level of response is referred to by different names by different authors, but they all denote the same manifestation of self-defence.[80]

[79] Two authors who explore these modalities in considerably more depth than is generally the case are Dinstein, in *War, Aggression and Self-Defence* (n. 2), pp. 261–300, and Ruys, in *'Armed Attack'* (n. 7), pp. 175–216.

[80] Dinstein refers to tactical-level exercise of self-defence in response to a small-scale local armed attack as 'on-the-spot reaction'; see Dinstein, *War, Aggression and Self-Defence* (n. 2), pp. 261–3. This is referred to by Boddens Hosang as 'unit self-defence'. See Boddens Hosang, *Rules of Engagement* (n. 1), p. 83.

This type of self-defence can be designated as 'local' or 'unit' self-defence for our purposes. It is a tactical-level exercise of self-defence by a discrete military unit such as a warship, flight of aircraft or platoon of soldiers upon coming under a (threat of imminent) localized attack and responding directly to neutralize that threat or attack. The response could be a one-off incident or could consist of a series of localized incidents, such as when a patrol comes under fire and returns fire, and within a relatively short time span is once again subjected to small-scale local attack a few kilometres down the line from the original attack. As long as the incidents do not accumulate to form a more substantial-level attack necessitating a larger-scale response, we are still dealing with a localized form of self-defence that will be carried out at the tactical level, and once the attack has ceased the incident(s) will be closed.[81] At the risk of stating the obvious, this mode of self-defence does not apply to the exchange of fire between hostile forces confronting each other in an ongoing armed conflict. We discuss the relationship between the law on the use of force and the law of armed conflict in Chapter 14, below.

One reason for designating this mode of self-defence as 'unit' self-defence is that it plays out at the level of discrete military units, which are subjected to localized attack, and it is the commander of the unit under attack, or in some cases an individual member of the unit, who has to tailor the response so as to react adequately within the law and the operational directives issued for the specific mission. In some organizations, such as NATO, there are specific authorizations for one unit to deliver tactical-level assistance to another unit which is part of the same operational command when the latter comes under a localized armed attack. The legal basis for this is collective self-defence, which in such a case is exercised at the tactical level.[82] This also applies to different contingents in a UN-led force conducting a peace operation when they come under localized attack. But in the UN context, the notion of self-defence extends beyond simply responding to an attack on one or more units to include forcible attempts to frustrate the lawful execution of the mandate and as such does not fall exclusively within the ambit of self-defence, but rather involves an element of mission accomplishment in the context of

[81] Dinstein, *War, Aggression and Self-Defence* (n. 2), p. 263.

[82] This is referred to in NATO parlance as 'extended self-defence'. See Boddens Hosang, *Rules of Engagement* (n. 1), pp. 77–80.

maintaining peace and security under the authority of the Security Council (see Chapter 5, above).[83]

A particular modality for the potential use of force in localized self-defence arises in the event of an unauthorized aerial or naval intrusion into a State's territory by a foreign military aircraft or warship. These situations have a number of specific characteristics and are subject to rules arising from air law and the law of the sea, in addition to considerations of when such intrusion can trigger measures in self-defence. These are dealt with in more detail below in Chapters 12 and 13. For the purpose of this chapter, suffice it to say that, in particular circumstances, an unauthorized and deliberate aerial intrusion into national airspace by military or other State aircraft, coupled with a refusal to heed warnings and instructions to leave or land, can trigger the right of self-defence if such intrusion poses a significant security threat to the State whose territory is violated. The same applies to unauthorized and deliberate entry into internal waters or non-innocent passage in the territorial sea by foreign warships when this is coupled with a refusal to desist from the unlawful conduct and forms a significant threat to the targeted State's security. In these scenarios, the modus of exercising self-defence, while localized in principle, is not best described as 'unit' self-defence, because the decision to move from interception and warning to actual use of force would typically not be made at unit level (individual pilot of a military aircraft or commander of a warship), but would be reserved for a higher authority. It seems therefore more appropriate to refer to this as localized self-defence in response to a hostile incursion into national territory.[84]

[83] Ibid., pp. 80–3. In view of the fact that self-defence applies at the inter-State level, and the significant element of mission accomplishment which is part of the UN doctrine of 'defence of the mandate', it is more plausible to see the use of force by UN-led peacekeeping missions as based on the powers of the Security Council to maintain international peace and security rather than on Article 51 of the Charter. See also Chapter 5, Section 5.7, above.

[84] On the use of force in response to aerial intrusions by military or State aircraft, see, for example, Ruys, *'Armed Attack'* (n. 7), pp. 184–98. Ruys accepts that certain types of aerial intrusion and unauthorized passage in territorial waters can trigger localized measures of self-defence and makes this largely dependent on a combination of factors, the most of important of which, alongside the factual context, he considers to be *animus agressionis* (hostile intent). See ibid., pp. 187–97. Other authors take similar views but sometimes for reasons other than self-defence or with less emphasis on subjective intentions and more on actual conduct. For example, Dinstein, *War, Aggression and Self-Defence* (n. 2), pp. 213–15, looks at the combination of unauthorized entry by military formations and deliberate conduct displaying the requisite degree of 'hostile intent' through, for example, refusal to comply with orders to leave the territory or other actions such as ignoring warnings. Indeed, the combination of unlawful entry into territory not due to accident or

That brings us to the next 'level' at which self-defence can potentially be exercised – namely, in response to a more than incidental use of force by attacking forces, but falling well short of a full-scale invasion or attack. Such a use of force could consist of a bombardment or aerial attack on specific locations in national territory; an attack upon or occupation of a (disputed) portion of territory under the sovereignty or control of the defending State; a cyber incident with deliberate violent effects resulting in human casualties, significant material damage or relatively severe and more than short-term or incidental disruption of (an) essential State function(s); or other possibilities similar in scale of intensity. This mode of self-defence would involve more than a localized defensive response by a discrete military unit, but would fall well short of a response to a full-scale armed attack triggering an all-out defensive war. It would consist of measures necessary to halt the attack and proportionate to the scale of the ongoing or recurrent attack, but with the definite objective of neutralizing the threat and ending the attack. This modality of self-defence would consequently not last longer or employ more force than was required for that purpose, unless the attacker persisted and/or intensified its efforts, in which case the defensive response would have to be upscaled in order to successfully ward off the attack. The national government and higher military command would be the responsible organs of the State in the exercise of this level of self-defence. We refer to this mode of self-defence as defensive action at the national level short of war (or defence short of war).

A further mode of self-defence consists of (a series of) extraterritorial targeted strikes or special operations directed against specific individuals, installations or other militarily relevant targets that were in the process of mounting or facilitating an (imminent) attack and which it was necessary to neutralize in order to halt the attack. This mode of self-defence might be carried out by remotely controlled platforms such as unmanned aerial vehicles (UAVs) or through digital means in the cyber domain, as well as by conventional aircraft or special operations forces. Operations aimed at extracting nationals in situations where their lives or physical safety are seriously threatened could fall within this mode of self-defence to the extent that self-defence is applicable to the rescue of nationals (see Chapter 8, below). Given some of the issues raised by the conducting of

distress and not based on consent in one form or another and the threat posed by the action are the determining factors in these authors' views. On the use of force below the threshold of localized armed attack in response to unauthorized territorial incursion, see Chapter 12, below.

targeted strikes and relating to the protection of nationals, this mode of self-defence is probably more controversial because of its susceptibility to abuse and the potential for escalation beyond what can be plausibly justified as self-defence. Nevertheless, there are some situations in which this mode of self-defence could conceivably be the only feasible way to successfully ward off an ongoing, or forestall an imminent, attack.[85] For lack of a better term, this modality of self-defence is referred to as a 'defensive contingency operation'.

Finally, in the event of an all-out armed attack in the form of an invasion or large-scale attack on national territory or the armed forces (of an ally), the defensive response can take the form of a defensive war with the object of defeating the attacking State and removing the threat of further aggression. This would be both a necessary and a proportionate response to an attack on that scale and could even result in the necessity to completely remove the government of the attacking State and temporarily occupy its territory until such time as a new government could take power. However, this – as in any case of self-defence – would wholly depend upon whether the total defeat of the attacking State were strictly necessary to restore the situation. In many cases, it is likely that at some point an attempt at some kind of negotiated settlement preceded by a ceasefire would be made by the Security Council or some other third party. It would depend upon whether such a settlement could be an adequate alternative to continuation of the defensive war by terminating and precluding further aggression and removing the necessity for continuation of the war. If it were, the defending State would have to make a good faith effort to end the war through a settlement which adequately removed the threat of further attack and provided acceptable redress for the harm inflicted. Conversely, the defending State would not be obliged to terminate the war if there were not a full and unconditional withdrawal of hostile forces, adequate guarantees of non-recurrence and some

[85] On self-defence in the cyber context, see, for example, M. N. Schmitt (ed.) *Tallinn Manual 2.0 on the International Law Applicable to Cyber Operations* (Cambridge University Press, 2017), pp. 339–56. On the use of unmanned vehicles for offensive strikes, see, for example, J. D. Ohlin (ed.) *Research Handbook on Remote Warfare* (Edward Elgar, 2019), pp. 213–334. On special operations forces, see, for example, B. Cathcart, 'Command and Control in Military Operations', in T.D. Gill and D. Fleck (eds.), *The Handbook of the International Law of Military Operations* (Oxford University Press, 2015), pp. 444–55. One specific possible application of this mode of self-defence is a rescue mission to neutralize a threat to the lives of the intervening State's nationals and extract them in situations where they have been targeted as a means of extracting concessions from their parent State. On the rescue of nationals, see Chapter 8.

provision for reparation. In a full-scale war, it is likely that all available resources would be mobilized; consequently, the full military, economic and human resources available to the defending State would in all likelihood be utilized.[86]

Any of these modalities can be exercised either individually or collectively, but self-defence in response to an unlawful territorial incursion or 'defensive action short of war' in response to a relatively localized and limited armed attack are less likely to be conducted collectively than the others. There is, however, no reason why, for example, units forming part of a multinational force cannot come to each other's assistance when one of them comes under attack and this is in fact quite commonly provided for in the context of multinational operations.[87] In any case, there is no legal impediment to exercising self-defence collectively at any of the levels dealt with here, provided the conditions pertaining to the exercise of collective self-defence are met (see Section 6.4.6, above).

### 6.5.3 *Exercising Self-Defence against Autonomous Armed Groups*

As stated in Section 6.4.2, during the past two decades the number of States using force in self-defence in response to attacks by AAG has been steadily increasing. That practice necessarily mirrors the growing number of substantial-level armed attacks across international borders conducted by such groups. The present authors subscribe to the view that States may use self-defence against attacks conducted by such AAGs, including on another State's territory from where the armed group is operating, without that State being necessarily responsible for the attack. The questions to be considered, therefore, are the modalities of the exercise of self-defence against such AAGs and the application of the customary principles of necessity, proportionality and immediacy in this context.

86 On defensive war as a mode of exercise of self-defence, see Dinstein, *War, Aggression and Self-Defence* (n. 2), pp. 279–88. Modern examples of such wars include the Korean conflict, the Iraq-Kuwait conflict (in both of which the collective security powers of the UNSC were also exercised), the Six-Day War, the Iran-Iraq War and the Ukraine-Russia War, among others.

87 J. F. R. Boddens Hosang, 'Force Protection, Unit Self-Defence and Personal Self-Defence: Their Relationship to Rules of Engagement', in Gill and Fleck (eds.), *Handbook* (n. 85), pp. 476–501.

#### 6.5.3.1 Necessity

As explained in Section 6.4.3, the principle of necessity refers to the existence of an ongoing or imminent armed attack and a lack of feasible alternatives, thereby making defensive action necessary. Necessity in the context of armed attacks mounted by AAGs entails these same considerations, but also presents additional challenges. When an AAG is preparing an armed attack in one State against a second State, feasible alternatives may obviate defensive action. These would include law enforcement measures taken by the territorial State; military action taken by the territorial State, unilaterally or in co-operation with the defending State; or Security Council action under Articles 41 or 42 of the UN Charter. Where the territorial State does not act, the defending State may still have the ability to take appropriate action on its own territory to stop the attack and preclude further attacks. Where this is feasible, extraterritorial defensive action by the defending State becomes unnecessary.

Only when none of these measures succeeds does the question of extraterritorial self-defence arise. In such a situation, the question is whether self-defence can be lawfully exercised by the defending State in another State that is unwilling or unable to prevent its territory from being used by an AAG carrying out attacks against the defending State. In particular, four follow-up questions arise: first, can self-defence be necessary merely because the territorial State failed in its duty to prevent its territory from being used? Second, what makes self-defence necessary on the territory of 'unable' States? Third, what makes self-defence necessary on the territory of 'unwilling' States? Finally, if resort to extraterritorial defensive action becomes necessary, does the defending State have a duty to request the consent of the territorial State? It is in this context that the controversial 'unwilling or unable' test has gained credence,[88] certain aspects of which will be touched upon below.

[88] The 'unable and unwilling' test is used by some States and commentators to determine when recourse to self-defence is justified. Under this test, the AAG's attack is not attributed to the territorial State. But, according to this test, its inability or unwillingness to prevent its territory from being used by the AAG to carry out armed attacks renders self-defence on its territory by the defending State lawful. The Chatham House Principles (n. 42), the Bethlehem Principles (n. 10) and, to a certain extent, the Leiden Policy Recommendations (n. 49) endorse this test. At the same time, critics characterize the unwilling or unable standard as incompatible with international law on the use of force. For those promoting the test, see A. Deeks, 'Unwilling or Unable: Toward a Normative Framework for Extraterritorial Self-Defense' (2012) 52 *Virginia Journal of International Law* 483–550, at 495; L. Moir, 'Action against Host States of Terrorist Groups', in

**Can self-defence be necessary merely because the territorial State failed in its duty to prevent its territory from being used?** It is important to note at the outset that exercising vigilance over one's territory and safeguarding the interests of other States is a core duty of the sovereign, confirmed in seminal decisions such as the 1928 *Island of Palmas* arbitral award[89] and the 1949 *Corfu Channel* judgment.[90] Furthermore, the duty of every State to prevent the use of its territory as a base for operations by an armed group against another State has been explicitly recognized in the Friendly Relations Declaration[91] and acknowledged as customary international law by the ICJ.[92] While failure to exercise these duties may give rise to responsibility and a duty of reparation towards the injured State, it does not automatically result in the necessity needed for the injured State to act in self-defence.[93] Where there are feasible alternatives, there is no necessity to act. Only the occurrence or imminence of an armed attack emanating from the AAG based in the territorial State coupled with the lack of feasible alternatives

M. Weller (ed.), *The Oxford Handbook of the Use of Force in International Law* (Oxford University Press, 2017), p. 730; Wilmshurst, 'Chatham House Principles' (n. 42), p. 969; Bethlehem, 'Self-Defence against an Imminent or Actual Armed Attack by Nonstate Actors' (n. 10), p. 776; Schrijver and van den Herik, 'Leiden Policy Recommendations' (n. 49), p. 42. For those criticizing the test, see, for example, O. Corten, 'The 'Unwilling or Unable' Test: Has it Been, and Could it Be, Accepted?' (2016) 29 *Leiden Journal of International Law* 777–99; M. E. O'Connell, 'Dangerous Departures' (n. 48), p. 384; M. Lehto, 'The Fight against ISIL in Syria. Comments on the Recent Discussion of the Right of Self-Defence against Non-State Actors' (2018) 87 *Nordic Journal of International Law* 1–25; J. Brunnée and S. J. Toope, 'Self-Defence against Non-State Actors: Are Powerful States Willing but Unable to Change International Law?', 67 *International & Comparative Law Quarterly* 263–86, at 267–9; T. Christakis, 'Challenging the "Unwilling and Unable" Test' (2017) 77 *Zeitschrift für ausländisches öffentliches Recht und Völkerrecht* 19–22, at 20; C. Martin, 'Challenging and Refining the "Unwilling and Unable" Doctrine' (2019) 52 *Vanderbilt Journal of Transnational Law* 387–461.

89 *Island of Palmas Case (Netherlands, USA)*, Award, 4 April 1928, Reports of International Arbitral Awards, vol. II, pp. 829–71.

90 ICJ, *The Corfu Channel Case (United Kingdom of Great Britain and Northern Ireland v. Albania)* (Merits), Judgment, 9 April 1949, ICJ Reports 1949, pp. 22–3.

91 Declaration on Principles of International Law Concerning Friendly Relations and Co-operation among States in accordance with the Charter of the United Nations, UNGA Res. 2625 (24 October 1970).

92 *Nicaragua* (n. 6), para. 191.

93 K. Tibori-Szabó, 'The "Unwilling and Unable" Test and the Law of Self-Defence', in C. Paulussen et al. (eds.), *Fundamental Rights in International and European Law* (Springer, 2016), pp. 73–97, at 90, 956.

gives rise to the necessity to act. Therefore, a lack of due diligence is not a stand-alone justification for the exercise of self-defence.[94]

**What makes self-defence necessary on the territory of 'unable' States?** The extent to which a State is unable to control its territory can vary considerably. Three main scenarios can be contemplated in this regard. First, the State may have imploded and ceased to be an effective sovereign with a functioning government.[95] Second, the State, while having a functioning government and a degree of control over its territory is too weak to take action against a more powerful armed group entrenched on its territory.[96] Third, the State may lose control over part of its territory due to internal fragmentation, civil conflict or other factors.[97] While there may be combinations of these scenarios, these three examples demonstrate situations in which an AAG is capable of operating freely from a State's territory. The term 'unable' thus indicates the inability of a State to prevent use of its territory by an armed group as a base for operations mounting attacks on other States. This inability is not a violation of an obligation the territorial State has towards the defending State. Consequently, the defending State may engage in self-defence actions in the territorial State *only* if there are no feasible alternatives to halt an armed attack by the AAG. Accordingly, once an attack has commenced, or is about to commence, and there are no alternatives to taking self-defence measures in the defending State to halt the attack, the defending State may resort to self-defence against the AAG in the territorial State.

[94] Gill and Tibori-Szabó, 'Twelve Key Questions' (n. 12), pp. 496, 498–9.

[95] For example, Somalia had no effective government for a prolonged period extending over years. This lack of governance was one of the reasons for various foreign military interventions on its territory, including Kenya's in 2011. See ibid., pp. 484-485, 497.

[96] An illustrative example is the inability of the Lebanese government to disarm Hezbollah or dislodge the group's control of the southern part of the country. Even Israel, a very credible military power, struggled in its confrontation with Hezbollah. See ibid., pp. 476, 483, 497.

[97] An illustrative example is the loss of territorial control in Syria between 2014 and 2019. During this time, the Syrian government continued to function and was engaged in clear efforts to regain control of its territory. Nevertheless, it was incapable of preventing ISIS from taking over a sizable part of its territory, and from there a large portion of Iraqi territory, and holding that territory for several years. In 2014, ISIS even threatened to take Baghdad after conquering Mosul, the second-largest city in the country. See ibid., pp. 486-487, 497–8. As of late 2022, there are substantial portions of Syrian territory over which the Syrian government does not exercise control, even though ISIS has been largely eliminated from the equation for the time being.

**What makes self-defence necessary on the territory of 'unwilling' States?** Where the territorial State has effective control over its territory and is capable of taking action to halt the use of its territory by an AAG as a base for operations but chooses not to do so, whether because of a certain degree of complicity with the armed group (falling short of control) or for any other reasons, the State is deemed 'unwilling'. Where the territorial State tolerates, encourages or supports an AAG operating against another State, it violates the customary principle of non-intervention.[98] In addition, certain forms of support will constitute violations of the prohibition on the use of force, even if they fall short of amounting to an indirect armed attack by the State itself.[99] That being said, as in the former scenarios, a territorial State cannot be held responsible for an armed attack by an AAG merely due to its unwillingness to prevent its territory from being used for that purpose. As in all cases, necessity arises from the combination of an ongoing or imminent armed attack and the lack of feasible alternatives. Certainly, the lack of feasible alternatives (such as law enforcement or co-operation with the defending State) may stem from the refusal of the territorial State to exercise its duty as a sovereign and, therefore, its unwillingness may well be a factor in assessing the need to act in self-defence. That being said, there is no self-reliant 'unable or unwilling' test replacing the principle of necessity, which remains the bedrock requirement for the exercise of self-defence.[100]

**Does the defending State have a duty to request the consent of the territorial State?** Several commentators maintain that the consent of the territorial State for the defensive action is an additional condition for using force or a necessary step to permitting the exercise of self-defence against AAGs on that State's territory.[101] The present authors do not share this view.[102] Self-defence is a lawful basis for using force, including extraterritorially. When necessity exists, self-defence actions do not

[98] See, for example, Declaration on the Inadmissibility of Intervention in the Domestic Affairs of States and the Protection of Their Independence and Sovereignty, UNGA Res. 2131 (XX) (21 December 1965). See also *Corfu Channel* (n. 90).

[99] UNGA Res. 2625 (n. 91), s. 1.

[100] Gill and Tibori-Szabó, 'Twelve Key Questions' (n. 12), p. 500.

[101] Deeks, 'Unwilling or Unable' (n. 88), p. 519; Christakis, 'Challenging' (n. 88), p. 21; P. Urs, 'Effective Territorial Control by Non-State Armed Groups and the Right of Self-Defence' (2017) 77 *Zeitschrift für ausländisches öffentliches Recht und Völkerrecht* 31–4, at 33.

[102] Gill and Tibori-Szabó, 'Twelve Key Questions' (n. 12), pp. 500–2.

require the permission of the territorial State or any other organization or entity. Certainly, the defending State must assess whether feasible alternatives to self-defence are available, and this may include military or law enforcement co-operation with the territorial State. However, there is no duty to seek consent when the necessity of self-defence is overriding or if doing so would significantly hamper the effectiveness of the defensive measures. Equally, the defending State is not obliged to subordinate its use of force to conditions imposed by the territorial State. This is especially true if such conditions would render the defensive action ineffective, infeasible or otherwise unacceptable. As set out below, the defending State has the corresponding duty to limit its intrusion into the territorial State to that required for its defence. In turn, the territorial State is obliged to co-operate with the targeted State[103] and has no right to interfere with proportionate defensive action directed against the AAG, as there is no self-defence against self-defence.[104] In any event, once the necessity of defence ceases, so too must any use of force on the territorial State's territory.

#### 6.5.3.2 Proportionality

Proportionality in the context of self-defence is generally understood as referring to two considerations. First, the scale of the defensive action must be roughly commensurate with the scale of the attack. Second, and more importantly, the measures taken must not exceed what is required to halt the attack and, where relevant, forestall continued attacks from the same source. For self-defence against AAGs conducted in the territory of a State that is not the author of the attack, proportionality has specific implications beyond those found in the inter-State context.[105]

Accordingly, in the case of 'unable' States, self-defence must be directed solely at neutralizing the ability of the AAG to conduct or continue its attack, and not at the territorial State. This requirement may limit the geographical area of operations and targets attacked, unless the territorial State forcibly interferes with the lawful exercise of self-defence. The defending State should inform and co-operate with the territorial State as far as possible. However, this would not be required if it were likely to significantly compromise the effectiveness of the defensive measures. The defending State must compensate for any damage to the territorial State

[103] Institut de Droit international, Resolution (n. 49), para. 10.

[104] *United States* v. *von Weizsaecker et al. (Ministries Case)*, in *Trials of War Criminals before the Nuremberg Military Tribunals under Control Law No. 10*, vol. 14 (1949), pp. 314, 329.

[105] Gill and Tibori-Szabó, 'Twelve Key Questions' (n. 12), pp. 502–3.

resulting from human error, equipment malfunction, faulty or reckless targeting or disproportionate force. Moreover, the defending State may also choose to compensate for damage caused by the use of lawful force.

As regards 'unwilling' States, defensive actions are again restricted to those necessary to neutralize the threat posed by the AAG without targeting assets of the territorial State, save in the event of forcible opposition. Given that, by definition, the 'unwilling' State has the means to act against the AAG operating in its territory, but chooses not to do so, there is no duty incumbent on the defending State to co-operate with the territorial State or compensate it for damages caused.

#### 6.5.3.3 Immediacy

As stated in Section 6.4.3, when it comes to the exercise of self-defence, immediacy requires the targeted State to take the defensive action as soon as the necessity of self-defence manifests itself through an actual or imminent armed attack, subject to exhausting any feasible alternatives. This is to differentiate self-defence from a purely punitive armed reprisal.

This requirement is no different in the case of AAGs. When the attack and/or the threat of an imminent attack is thwarted, the necessity required for self-defence is no longer present. At that point, defensive action must cease.[106] Self-defence is not a licence to target any armed group that poses a potential threat, irrespective of whether that threat is clear and present enough to justify armed measures on the territory of another State.[107] The timeliness of defensive action is elaborated below in Section 6.5.4.

### *6.5.4 The Temporal Scope of Self-Defence*

The specific meaning attributed to the phrase 'if an armed attack occurs' used in Article 51 of the UN Charter has sparked much debate over the temporal scope of self-defence. One school of thought adopts the view that Article 51, as an exception to the general prohibition to use force, must be interpreted restrictively as forbidding any action before an armed attack takes place.[108] Relying on the customary basis of self-defence, other

[106] T. D. Gill, 'When Does Self-Defence End?', in M. Weller (ed.), *The Oxford Handbook of the Use of Force in International Law* (Oxford University Press, 2017), pp. 750–1.

[107] Gill and Tibori-Szabó, 'Twelve Key Questions' (n. 12), pp. 503–4.

[108] G. Abi Saab, 'Cours général de droit international public' (1987) 207 *Collected Courses of the Hague Academy of International Law* 9–463, at 371; G. M. Badr, 'The Exculpatory Effect of Self-Defence in State Responsibility' (1980) 10 *Georgia Journal of International*

authors justify anticipatory action in self-defence against an imminent threat with reference to the 1841 *Caroline* criteria.[109] Yet other writers advocate for the legitimacy of 'preventive self-defence' against a threat that is more potential than imminent.[110] The wording of Article 51 has also had an impact on defensive action in the aftermath of an armed attack. Accordingly, a few authors maintain that self-defence is no longer a right when the armed attack has achieved its purpose and can be exercised only while the attack is still in progress.[111] Most authors, however, agree that

*and Comparative Law* 1–28, at 25; Brownlie, *International Law* (n. 2), pp. 275–8; A. Cassese, *International Law* (Oxford University Press, 2005), pp. 361–2 (Cassese proposes a possible future regulation of 'anticipatory self-defence', ibid., pp. 362–3); A. Constantinou, *The Right of Self-Defence under Customary International Law and Article 51 of the United Nations Charter* (Sakkoulas, 2000), pp. 120–1; O. Corten, *Le droit contre la guerre: L'interdiction du recours à la force en droit international contemporain* (Pedone, 2008), p. 619; Gray, *International Law* (n. 2), pp. 134–75; L. Henkin, 'The Use of Force: Law and US Policy', in *Right v. Might: International Law and the Use of Force* (Council on Foreign Relations Press, 1991), pp. 44–6; P. C. Jessup, *A Modern Law of Nations: An Introduction* (Macmillan, 1948), p. 166; D. N. Kolesnik, 'The Development of the Right of Self-Defence', in W. E. Butler (ed.), *The Non-Use of Force in International Law* (Nijhoff, 1989), p. 154; J. Kunz, 'Individual and Collective Self-Defence in Article 51 of the Charter of the UN' (1947) 41 *American Journal of International Law* 872–9, at 878; Ruys, *'Armed Attack'* (n. 7), pp. 259–62.

109 Bowett, *Self-Defence* (n. 10), pp. 188–9; D. Fleck, 'Rules of Engagement for Maritime Forces and the Limitation of the Use of Force and the UN Charter' (1988) 31 *German Yearbook of International Law* 165–86, at 176–7; R. Higgins, *The Development of International Law through the Political Organs of the United Nations* (Oxford University Press, 1963), p. 199; M. S. McDougal and F. P. Feliciano, *Law and Minimum World Public Order: The Legal Regulation of International Coercion* (Yale University Press, 1961), pp. 231–6; Schachter, *International Law* (n. 2), pp. 150–2; Schwebel, 'Aggression' (n. 10), p. 481; C. H. M. Waldock, 'The Regulation of the Use of Force by Individual States in International Law' (1952) 81 *Collected Courses of the Hague Academy of International Law* 455–517, at 497–9.

110 C. Hill, 'The Bush Administration Preemption Doctrine and the Future of World Order: Remark' (2004) 98 *American Society of International Law Proceedings* 329–31; C. Pierson, 'Preemptive Self-Defence in an Age of Weapons of Mass Destruction: Operation Iraqi Freedom' (2004) 33 *Denver Journal of International Law and Policy* 150–78, at 154–5; W. H. Taft and T. F. Buchwald, 'Preemption, Iraq, and International Law' (2003) 97 *American Journal of International Law* 557-563; R. Wedgwood, 'The Fall of Saddam Hussein: Security Council Mandates and Preemptive Self-Defence' (2003) 97 *American Journal of International Law* 576–85, at 584; J. Yoo, 'International Law and the War in Iraq' (2003) 97 *American Journal of International Law* 563–76, at 571–4.

111 Badr, 'Exculpatory Effect' (n. 108), p. 25; E. J. Myjer and N. D. White, 'The Twin Towers Attack: An Unlimited Right to Self-Defence?' (2002) 7 *Journal of Conflict and Security Law* 5–17, at 7. Abi Saab contends that if the armed attack is instantaneous (such as a bombardment or short incursion), self-defence cannot be exercised after the attack finishes. However, self-defence against occupation can be exercised, because that constitutes an attack extended in time. Abi Saab, 'Cours général' (n. 108), p. 373.

self-defence ceases when the necessity to act is no longer present.[112] Nonetheless, the exercise of self-defence against AAGs increasingly raises questions as regards the post-attack temporal scope of defensive action.

Before analysing the temporal scope of self-defence, it is useful to note that every armed attack has a preparation phase, an execution phase and an aftermath. The timing of defensive action will therefore depend on when the targeted State learns about the imminent attack and what measures are available at that time to thwart the attack. Typically, anticipatory action in self-defence is undertaken during the later stages of the preparation phase or just before the execution phase of an armed attack, while self-defence against ongoing armed attacks will take place during the execution phase of such attacks.

To set the question of temporal scope in context, a brief overview of pre-Charter and post-Charter developments is instructive. As said above in Section 6.3, at the time the Charter was adopted, customary law allowed only a relatively narrow right of self-defence. As the aforementioned texts by Oppenheim and Kellogg and in the Locarno Pact suggest, this narrower, pre-Charter concept had an intrinsic anticipatory aspect, entailing defence against imminent as well as ongoing attacks. This intrinsic anticipatory aspect echoed the famous words of US Secretary of State Daniel Webster, who, in 1841, defined the necessity of self-defence as 'instant, overwhelming, leaving no choice of means, and no moment for deliberation' (see Chapter 2, Fact Box 2.3).[113]

There is no reason to believe that this understanding of self-defence had further narrowed by the time of the San Francisco Conference in 1945. Admittedly, there is documentary evidence suggesting that some US delegates at the conference wanted to restrict self-defence to the time after an armed attack.[114] Their proposal, however, was met with scepticism by other US delegates who believed that the right would be unduly restricted.[115]

[112] See, for example, Gill, 'Temporal Dimension' (n. 7), pp. 152–4; Schachter, *International Law* (n. 2), p. 153.

[113] Letter from Daniel Webster, US Secretary of State, to Henry Fox, British minister in Washington (24 April 1841), in *British and Foreign State Papers 1840-1841*, vol. 29 (James Ridgway and Sons, 1857), pp. 1129–39, at 1138.

[114] 'Minutes of the Forty-Eighth Meeting (Executive Session) of the US Delegation, Held at San Francisco, Sunday, May 20, 1945, 12 Noon', in *Foreign Relations of the US* (n. 26), pp. 813–23, at 818. See also Franck, *Recourse to Force* (n. 2), p. 50; Ruys, *'Armed Attack'* (n. 7), p. 260.

[115] 'Minutes of the Forty-Eighth Meeting' (n. 114), p. 818; 'Minutes of the Thirty-Eighth Meeting of the United States Delegation, Held at San Francisco, Monday, May 14, 1945', in *Foreign Relations of the US* (n. 26), pp. 707–12, at 709.

Moreover, these proposals were not put forward before the relevant committee, so no intergovernmental discussion ensued on the topic.[116] Notably, as set out in Section 6.3, Article 51 was drafted with the clear purpose of accommodating regional security arrangements, including the Act of Chapultepec, which allowed anticipatory action against a threat of aggression. Therefore, the records alone do not allow any clear conclusion to be drawn about how the various negotiators understood the temporal dimension of self-defence. Likewise, there is no conclusive evidence of a common or at least generally shared intention of restricting the right of self-defence by excluding anticipatory action.[117] This is further confirmed by the Nuremberg and Tokyo judgments, both of which acknowledged the legality of self-defence against an imminent threat of invasion and did not reflect any other interpretation stemming from the freshly adopted Article 51 (Fact Box 6.2).[118]

That leaves us with post-Charter State practice and the impact it may have had on the temporal scope of self-defence.

As regards anticipatory action against *imminent* threats of armed attack, the 1967 Six-Day War was found by most commentators to be legitimate.[119] In June 1967, Israel used force against an imminent threat of invasion by its Arab neighbours.[120] The Israeli cabinet took into consideration the escalation of events beforehand and was able to predict both the manner and the purpose of the invasion. Furthermore, the American attitude during the 1962 Cuban missile crisis and the Israeli attitude before the outbreak of the 1973 Yom Kippur War were instances of State practice where anticipatory action was not resorted to, despite

116 Tibori-Szabó, *Anticipatory Action* (n. 2), pp. 110–11.

117 Ibid., pp. 111–13.

118 International Military Tribunal Nuremberg, Judgment of 1 October 1946, www.legal-tools.org/doc/45f18e/pdf/; International Military Tribunal for the Far East, Judgment of 4 November 1948, www.legal-tools.org/doc/8bef6f/pdf/; Tibori-Szabó, *Anticipatory Action* (n. 2), pp. 131–8.

119 L R. Beres, 'After the Gulf War: Israel, Preemption and Anticipatory Self-Defence Perspective' (1991) 13 *Houston Journal of International Law* 259–80, at 267; Dinstein, *War, Aggression and Self-Defence* (n. 2), p. 212 (Dinstein characterized the Six-Day War as an instance of 'interceptive self-defence'); Franck, *Recourse to Force* (n. 2), p. 105; Gill, 'Temporal Dimension' (n. 7), pp. 138–9; A. Shapira, 'The Six-Day War and the Right of Self-Defence' (1971) 6 *Israel Law Review* 65–80, at 75–6. Some authors rejected the legality of the Six-Day War; see S. Alexandrov, *Self-Defense against the Use of Force in International Law* (Kluwer Law International, 1996), pp. 153–4; J. Quigley, *The Six-Day War and Israeli Self-Defense* (Cambridge University Press, 2013).

120 Tibori-Szabó, *Anticipatory Action* (n. 2), pp. 144–6; J. Quigley, 'The Six Day War – 1967', in T. Ruys and O. Corten (eds.), *The Use of Force in International Law: A Case-Based Approach* (Oxford University Press, 2018), pp. 131–42.

### FACT BOX 6.2 IMMINENT THREAT OF INVASION IN THE NUREMBERG AND TOKYO JUDGMENTS

The issue of self-defence came up during the Major War Criminals' Trial in connection with the April 1940 invasion of Norway by Germany. Before the International Military Tribunal at Nuremberg (IMT), the prosecution argued that the German attack on Norway was a premeditated, thoroughly planned military action. The defence disputed this argument, contending that the attack against Norway was a measure of preventive self-defence in the face of numerous reports about the Allies' intention to occupy Norway. The IMT judges were not convinced by this argument. In their view, the invasion of Norway was a strategic move to secure a significant military advantage. There was no evidence of compelling circumstances that would have justified preventive use of force in self-defence. The judgment referred to the *Caroline* incident and affirmed that 'preventive action in foreign territory' was justified only in the case of 'an instant and overwhelming necessity for self-defence, leaving no choice of means and no moment for deliberation'. On the basis of the available evidence, the judges found that the plans for an attack on Norway were not made for the purpose of forestalling an imminent Allied landing but, 'at the most', were aimed at preventing an Allied occupation at some future date.

Self-defence also came up during the Trial of the Japanese War Criminals in relation to the so-called Pacific War, in particular the Japanese invasion of the then Dutch East Indies in January–March 1942. Before the International Military Tribunal for the Far East (Tokyo Tribunal), the prosecution argued that the Dutch East Indies were within Japan's area of interest and that Japan's preparations to invade this territory were part of a greater campaign to assert its military dominance in the Far East. The contention of the defence was that the Dutch East Indies, along with other East Asian territories, were invaded as a last resort response to economic aggression from Britain, France, the Netherlands and the United States and as a result of the Netherlands, the United Kingdom, the United States and other countries declaring war on Japan in December 1941. The judges of the Tokyo Tribunal were not convinced by this argument. In their view, the underlying reasons for Japan's acts were 'prompted by the desire to deprive China of any aid in the struggle she was waging against Japan's aggression and to secure for Japan the possession of her neighbours in the South'. The Tokyo Tribunal also found that in as much as the Netherlands took the initiative of declaring war on Japan, it did so in self-defence following the revelation that Japan was engaged in full preparations to invade the Dutch East Indies and after the Japanese bombing of Pearl Harbor on 7 December 1941. The Tokyo Tribunal held that '[t]he fact that the Netherlands, being fully apprised of the imminence of the attack, in self-defence declared war against Japan on 8th December and thus officially recognised the existence of a state of war which had been begun by Japan cannot change that war from a war of aggression on the part of Japan into something other than that'.

**Sources:** International Military Tribunal Nuremberg, Judgment of 1 October 1946, www.legal-tools.org/doc/45f18e/pdf/; International Military Tribunal for the Far East, Judgment of 4 November 1948, www.legal-tools.org/doc/8bef6f/pdf/; Tibori-Szabó, *Anticipatory Action in Self-Defence* (Springer, 2011), pp. 131–8.

being contemplated, because there was no perception of an imminent threat.[121] A reluctance to resort to self-defence in the absence of specific knowledge as to the imminence of the threat acknowledges the immediacy requirement of self-defence. Conversely, the 1956 Sinai Campaign was an example of State practice where resort to force was condemned because the purported threat, although serious, did not necessitate immediate action.[122]

To this day, the ICJ has avoided addressing the issue of anticipatory action against an imminent threat, as has the International Law Commission. Nonetheless, the High-Level Panel set up by former UN secretary general Kofi Annan in 2004 acknowledged the legality of self-defence before an attack as long as the threatened attack was imminent, there were no other means of deflecting it and the action was proportionate.[123] Additionally, the Bethlehem Principles, the Chatham House Rules and the Leiden Policy Recommendations all acknowledge the legality of self-defence against imminent threats of armed attack.[124]

The same cannot be said of instances of State practice where self-defence was exercised preventively against more removed, *potential* threats. For instance, in 1981 the Israeli government justified air strikes against the Osirak reactor as self-defence against the possibility of the Iraqi government developing a nuclear weapon in the foreseeable future.[125] The Israeli air strikes were criticized by States before the Security Council as exceeding the limits of anticipatory

121 Tibori-Szabó, *Anticipatory Action* (n. 2), pp. 149–50, 174–9; A. Orakhelashvili, 'The Cuban Missile Crisis - 1962', in Ruys and Corten (eds.), *Use of Force* (n. 120), pp. 97–107; F. Dubuisson and V. Koutroulis, 'The Yom Kippur War - 1973', in Ruys and Corten (eds.), *Use of Force* (n. 120), pp. 189–200.

122 Tibori-Szabó, *Anticipatory Action* (n. 2), pp. 142–4; A. Hofer, 'The Suez Crisis - 1956', in Ruys and Corten (eds.), *Use of Force* (n. 120), pp. 36–47.

123 'A More Secure World: Our Shared Responsibility', Report of the High-Level Panel on Threats, Challenges and Change, UN Doc. A/59/565 (2004), para. 188, p. 54.

124 Schrijver and van den Herik, 'Leiden Policy Recommendations' (n. 49), para. 41 ('The use of force in self-defence is justified only when force is necessary to bring an attack to an end, or to avert an imminent attack . . . .'); Wilmshurst, 'Chatham House Principles' (n. 42), p. 964 ('[T]he view that states have a right to act in self-defence in order to avert the threat of an imminent attack - often referred to as "anticipatory self-defence" - is widely, though not universally, accepted. It is unrealistic in practice to suppose that self-defence must in all cases await an actual attack.'); Bethlehem, 'Self-Defence' (n. 10), p. 775 (Principle 1: 'States have a right of self-defense against an imminent or actual armed attack by nonstate actors.').

125 Tibori-Szabó, *Anticipatory Action* (n. 2), pp. 179–81; T. Ruys, 'Israel's Airstrike Against Iraq's Osiraq Nuclear Reactor - 1981', in Ruys and Corten (eds.), *Use of Force* (n. 120), pp. 329–41.

action.[126] Similarly, the 2003 US invasion of Iraq was premised on the possession by Iraq of nuclear weapons. The 2002 US National Security Strategy (also known as the 'Bush Doctrine')[127] served as the basis for the invasion and occupation of Iraq and toppling of its regime without any evidence as to the existence, let alone imminent threat, of weapons of mass destruction. The preventive use of self-defence was criticized both by the Security Council and in legal doctrine.[128] Likewise, the aforementioned UN High-Level Panel asserted that unilateral preventive action against non-imminent threats carried great risks for the world order and the principle of non-intervention, and that such action should rather be taken after a collective endorsement under Chapter VII.[129] Comments advocating an alteration of the temporal dimension of self-defence to allow preventive action have been voiced in legal literature, but the opinion is still very much a minority view.[130]

Needless to say, there are numerous instances of State practice where self-defence was exercised against *ongoing* armed attacks. Before delving into some of the examples of ongoing attacks, it is useful to explore what such an attack entails. As already said, every armed attack has an execution phase. In some cases, especially those involving AAGs, the execution phase consists of a single, large-scale attack (which may include several

[126] Tibori-Szabó, *Anticipatory Action* (n. 2), pp. 180–1.

[127] R. N. Gardner, 'Neither Bush Nor the "Jurisprudes"' (2003) 97 *American Journal of International Law* 585–90, at 585–6; C. Henderson, 'The Bush Doctrine: From Theory to Practice' (2004) 9 *Journal of Conflict and Security Law* 3–24, at 6.

[128] UN Security Council Official Records (SCOR), 36th session, 2282nd meeting, UN Doc. S/PV.2282 (15 June 1981), paras. 14–19; 2283rd meeting, UN Doc. S/PV.2283 (15 June 1981), paras. 23–7, 46, 117, 146; 2284th meeting, UN Doc. S/PV.2284 (16 June 1981), para. 11; 2288th meeting, UN Doc. S/PV.2288 (19 June 1981), para. 115. In one instance, the concepts of 'anticipation' and 'preventive aggression' were equated and deemed unlawful; see 2283rd meeting, UN Doc. S/PV.2283 (15 June 1981), para. 146 (Sierra Leone). See also Alexandrov, *Self-Defense* (n. 119), p. 162; Franck, *Recourse to Force* (n. 2), pp. 105–7; Gardner, 'Neither Bush Nor the "Jurisprudes"' (n. 127), p. 587; Gill, 'Temporal Dimension' (n. 7), pp. 141–2; C. Greenwood, 'International Law and the Preemptive Use of Force: Afghanistan, Al-Qaida and Iraq' (2003) 4 *San Diego International Law Journal* 7–38, at 14; M. Sapiro, 'Preempting Prevention: Lessons Learned' (2005) 37 *NYU Journal of International Law and Politics* 357–71, at 367.

[129] 'More Secure World' (n. 123), para. 191, p. 55.

[130] Hill, 'Bush Administration Preemption Doctrine' (n. 110), pp. 329–31; Pierson, 'Preemptive Self-Defence' (n. 110), pp. 154–5; Taft and Buchwald, 'Preemption' (n. 110), pp. 557–63; Wedgwood, 'Fall of Saddam Hussein' (n. 110), p. 584; Yoo, 'International Law' (n. 110), pp. 571–4.

simultaneous incidents), such as 9/11. That being said, in most instances the execution phase entails protracted armed violence that can last days, weeks or even longer. In these cases, self-defence typically begins at an early execution phase of the armed attack, with the aim of thwarting the attack (i.e. responding to the use of force that has already occurred and preventing further uses of force within the same ongoing armed attack).

For example, the 1980–8 Iran-Iraq War was an instance in which Iran invoked and exercised the right of self-defence against a military invasion by Iraq. The armed conflict lasted for eight years.[131] The 1982 Falklands War involved the exercise of self-defence by the UK naval forces four weeks after the Junta regime invaded the Falklands Islands and South Georgia in the South Atlantic. While preparations for the use of force were made as soon as the armed attack had started, it took four weeks for the UK naval forces to reach the zone of operations and engage in self-defence.[132] Nonetheless, the legality of the UK action was widely accepted in the face of a persisting Argentinean invasion, which qualified as an ongoing, continuous armed attack.[133] More recently, the anti-ISIS coalition, consisting of twelve Western and six regional States under the military leadership of the United States, has used force in both Syria and Iraq against an ongoing attack by ISIS, which started with the mid-2014 invasion of Iraq.[134] All in all, what is important to remember regarding the exercise of self-defence against ongoing attacks is that as long as the necessity of self-defence persists, the use of force is legal. Indeed, the passage of time after the commencement of an armed attack would not preclude a State from exercising its right of self-defence as long as the attack is continuing, notwithstanding possible lulls between individual armed incidents. In any case, whether an attack is a large-scale incident or an ongoing invasion and occupation of territory, the necessity of self-defence will continue to apply as long as the author of the attack continues with action in support of the original attack and in clear preparation for renewed attacks.

Some instances of State practice have also involved defensive action against a series of separate, small-scale, sporadic attacks occurring over a period of weeks or months, which together were alleged to amount to

[131] Tibori-Szabó, *Anticipatory Action* (n. 2), pp. 150–2; A. de Guttry, 'The Iran-Iraq War – 1980–88', in Ruys and Corten (eds.), *Use of Force* (n. 120), pp. 315–28.

[132] Tibori-Szabó, *Anticipatory Action* (n. 2), pp. 153–5; E. Henry, 'The Falklands/Malvinas War – 1982', in Ruys and Corten (eds.), *Use of Force* (n. 120), pp. 361–72.

[133] Henry, 'Falklands/Malvinas War' (n. 132), p. 375 n. 107.

[134] Gill and Tibori-Szabó, 'Twelve Key Questions' (n. 12), pp. 486–7.

an armed attack. The difference between such sporadic attacks and an ongoing armed attack (as discussed above), is that the former are a sequence of smaller, one-off incidents with no use of force inbetween and not continuous enough to amount to an ongoing armed attack. They are rather 'needle-' or 'pinpricks',[135] meant to destabilize a country or a government. From the 1960s onwards, a small number of States began invoking self-defence against a sequence of such attacks, claiming that their accumulation amounted to an armed attack (accumulation of events theory). On these occasions, the defending States invoked self-defence at one and the same time *after* a series of attacks and *before* further attacks. For instance, in 1964 the United Kingdom justified the bombing of a Yemeni fort by claiming that a series of incidents indicated that 'a deliberate and increasing attack by Yemen against the [South Arabian] Federation was under way'.[136] In 1986 the United States justified the bombing of Libya by claiming that there was 'an ongoing pattern of attacks by Libya' as well as 'clear evidence that Libya was planning a multitude of future attacks'.[137] Likewise, in 1993 the United States defended its airstrike against the Iraqi Intelligence Headquarters by maintaining that there was no reasonable prospect that diplomatic initiatives or economic pressure could cause the Iraqi government to cease the planning of such attacks against US citizens.[138] Up until the early 1990s, these instances of self-defence received mixed reactions, because some commentators and States considered the accumulation of events theory as far-fetched: a string of sporadic, small-scale attacks could not in their view amount to an armed attack and justify the use of self-defence. Others took the position that if the incidents were sufficiently connected in time and locale to amount to a phased armed attack, the incidents should be treated cumulatively in gauging the permissible response.[139]

[135] Y. Z. Blum, 'State Response to Acts of Terrorism' (1976) 19 *German Yearbook of International Law* 223–37.

[136] *Repertoire of the Practice of the Security Council: Supplement 1964-1965* (United Nations, 1968), chap. 8, p. 128.

[137] SCOR, 41st session, 2674th meeting, UN Doc. S/PV.2674 (15 April 1986), p. 17.

[138] 'Letter dated 26 June 1993 from the Permanent Representative of the United States of America to the United Nations addressed to the President of the Security Council', UN Doc. S/26003 (1993); Franck, *Recourse to Force* (n. 2), p. 94.

[139] For authors endorsing the accumulation of events theory, see S. G. Baker, 'Terrorism and the Inherent Right of Self-Defence' (1987) 10 *Houston Journal of International Law* 25–49, at 42; Blum, 'State Response' (n. 135), p. 233; D. Bowett, 'Reprisals Involving Recourse to Armed Force' (1972) 66 *American Journal of International Law* 1–36, at 12; Brownlie, *International Law* (n. 2), p. 279; L. M. Gross, 'The Legal Implications of Israel's 1982 Invasion into Lebanon' (1983) 13 *California Western International Law Journal*

The past three decades have seen the increasing importance of non-State armed groups, especially AAGs. Such groups often resort to a string of separate, small-scale and sporadic attacks to achieve their purpose. Accordingly, defensive action against such groups has been on the increase. In this regard, the changing attitude of Security Council members to the 2006 Israeli invasion of Lebanon, the 2007–8 Turkish incursion into Northern Iraq and the 2008–9 Gaza crisis signalled an implicit acceptance of the accumulation of events theory, even though all these instances were criticized for their disproportionate use of force.[140] Additionally, growing concerns over the nature of twenty-first-century terrorism have also fuelled arguments for preventive self-defence, but these opinions form a minority part of the relevant legal doctrine.[141]

Lastly, defensive action against AAGs also raises the question of how long after the occurrence of (a series of) armed attacks should the exercise of self-defence remain legal. Can defensive action be lawful long after the armed attacks occurred and without any clear indication of further, imminent attacks?

The answer to the above question is the same as for any defensive action, whether against an imminent, ongoing or already executed armed attack. As long as the necessity of self-defence continues to exist, the defensive action remains lawful. In particular, where the defending State is faced with clear evidence of an imminent attack or where it is already subjected to an ongoing attack or an attack that has materialized, but it is still producing its effects, and there are no feasible alternatives to thwart or neutralize the effects of such an attack, self-defence remains necessary. This necessity cannot be measured in the abstract, it depends on the factual circumstances of the case. It may involve action during a few hours or days, but it may also necessitate a more ample strategy, extending over a longer period. The assessment of whether the necessity of self-defence persists is ultimately fact-based.[142]

458–92, at 478; Higgins, *Development of International Law* (n. 109), p. 201; M. R. Jacobson, 'War in the Information Age: International Law, Self-Defense, and the Problem of "Non-Armed" Attacks' (1998) 21(3) *Journal of Strategic Studies* 1–33, at 13, 16; O. Schachter, 'The Lawful Resort to Unilateral Use of Force' (1985) 10 *Yale Journal of International Law* 291–4, at 293. For authors criticizing the theory, see L. Henkin, *International Law: Politics and Values* (Nijhoff, 1995), pp. 126–7; N. Lubell, *Extraterritorial Use of Force Against Non-State Actors* (Oxford University Press, 2010), pp. 51–4.

[140] Tibori-Szabó, *Anticipatory Action* (n. 2), pp. 233–42.

[141] See above, n. 130.

[142] Gill, 'When Does Self-Defence End?' (n. 106), pp. 750–1.

### 6.5.5 The Geographical Scope of Self-Defence

As with its temporal scope, the question of where self-defence can be exercised is factually driven. A localized small-scale armed attack which can be effectively addressed by a one-off tactical-level, on-the-spot reaction will be geographically restricted to the immediate location of the attack. This would be the case both in situations of unit-level self-defence and in response to hostile localized territorial incursions or hostile significant armed violations of sovereignty. An attack on a somewhat larger scale conducted from a number of points against a variety of objects in different locations or against a particular segment of territory would allow for a defensive response with the object of neutralizing the ongoing (series of) attacks and forestalling continued attacks from the same sources. Nevertheless, unless the attacks continued or intensified, it would not, in principle, require defensive action being conducted far from the area where the attack occurred and where it was directed. An example of this was in the previously mentioned Falklands War, where the United Kingdom restricted its defensive measures to an area within the relative vicinity of the Falklands and did not extend them to the Argentinean mainland or further afield.[143] The facts (the scale and nature of the attack), together with the principles of necessity and proportionality *ad bellum*, determine the geographical scope of the defensive action (alongside considerations arising from the law of armed conflict). This would apply both to kinetic attacks and in cases where a digital attack had effects triggering self-defence (see Chapter 11, below).

In cases where defensive measures are directed against specific individuals or locations which must be neutralized in order to halt an attack, the scope of the defensive measures will be restricted to what is required in the prevailing circumstances to achieve that end and must not be extended to address other potential, as yet unmaterialized threats. As preventive self-defence has no basis in law, engaging potential targets located far from the original source of attack would be both unnecessary

[143] For a discussion of the effects of *ad bellum* necessity and proportionality on the geographical scope of self-defence measures, see C. Greenwood, 'Self-Defence and the Conduct of International Armed Conflict', in Y. Dinstein (ed.), *International Law in a Time of Perplexity: Essays in Honour of Shabtai Rosenne* (Nijhoff, 1989), p. 273; T. D. Gill, 'Some Considerations Concerning the Role of the *Ius ad Bellum* in Targeting', in P. A. L. Ducheine, M. N. Schmitt and F. P. B. Osinga (eds.), *Targeting: The Challenges of Modern Warfare* (Springer, 2016), pp. 101–19.

and disproportionate. This is one of the points that has understandably raised concern in relation to the seemingly limitless (and endless) reliance on self-defence in response to the 9/11 attacks on the World Trade Center and Pentagon in 2001. The use of remotely piloted aerial vehicles (drones) to attack individuals and targets far removed from the source of the original attack and long after its occurrence has generated considerable scepticism, even from States and authors supportive of the initial invocation of self-defence in response to those attacks.[144]

These considerations partly overlap with what has been previously said in relation to the modalities of responding to attacks conducted by AAGs. If an AAG is operating from the territory of a State which is not directly or indirectly involved in the attack, the defensive measures will be confined to the area of the State where the AAG is operating from. This is particularly true in the case of an 'unable' State, which may have no effective control over parts of its territory where an AAG is actively engaged in conducting cross-border attacks against other States.

Finally, in a situation of defensive war, the scope of the response is potentially much wider, depending on the scale of the attack, the military potential of the attacker and the nature of the operations. In some cases, the scope of the defensive measures could be global, as was the case in the two World Wars of the previous century; in this century, most conflicts are not fought at a global level, at least thus far. In any event, the facts determine what is necessary and proportionate in relation to the scope of the attack. Additionally, the territory of States not involved in the attack would be inviolable, as long as they did not permit a belligerent to conduct operations from or through their territory.

It should also be stressed that self-defence may be exercised within the territory of the State(s) under attack, on the territory of the State(s) from where the attack originated or was controlled and in international waters, airspace and possibly even in certain areas of outer space, all subject to the above-mentioned requirements of necessity and proportionality.

## 6.6 Conclusion

Despite the many controversies discussed above, and contrary to what is sometimes argued, the right of self-defence performs an essential function and retains a central place in the *jus ad bellum*. Its core (the right of a State

144 See contributions in Ohlin (ed.), *Research Handbook* (n. 85).

to defend itself in a necessary and proportionate manner against an armed attack) remains well-settled law, on which there is general agreement. Despite its 'old age', the right of self-defence provides States with sufficient scope to defend themselves, including against novel threats such as digital or cyber warfare. Nevertheless, it is not, and should not be(come), a licence to wage preventive war, a pretext for a modern-day version of imperial hegemony or an instrument of retribution for real or imagined past wrongs that may have been committed.

# PART III

# Controversies and Contested Justifications for the Use of Force

# 7

# Humanitarian Intervention and the Responsibility to Protect

## 7.1 Introduction

This chapter examines the question of whether there is a legally sanctioned right of unilateral humanitarian intervention by States to halt large-scale human rights violations. The chapter first looks at the concept of humanitarian intervention and whether the prohibition on the use of force applies to such interventions. It then examines existing legal and extra-legal justifications for humanitarian intervention.

## 7.2 The Ongoing Controversy Regarding Humanitarian Intervention

One of the most long-standing controversies in the law on the use of force has been the question of so-called humanitarian intervention. The controversy starts with what actually constitutes a 'humanitarian intervention' and extends to whether there is a stand-alone legal justification for using armed force to protect a population against gross and systematic human rights violations, and if not, whether it can otherwise be justified or excused. The debate involves proponents of both a wider and a narrower approach to the prohibition on the use of force. It also raises the question of the existence of a customary rule permitting unilateral military intervention to address large-scale violations of human rights. On occasion, the debate spills over into policy debates and into initiatives like the 'responsibility to protect' (R2P) doctrine (see Chapter 5, above), which is dealt with briefly in this chapter in a somewhat different light.[1]

[1] The majority of authors do not recognize a stand-alone right of humanitarian intervention without authorization of the UN Security Council (UNSC). They include I. Brownlie, 'Humanitarian Intervention', in J. N. Moore (ed.), *Law and Civil War in the Modern World* (John Hopkins University Press, 1974), pp. 217–28; Y. Dinstein, *War, Aggression and Self-Defence* (Cambridge University Press, 2017), pp. 75–7, 97–8; C. Henderson, *The Use of Force and International Law* (Cambridge University Press, 2018), pp. 379–407;

There have been a handful of cases of intervention with a purported humanitarian purpose or effect, to which reference will be made when examining the legal status of humanitarian intervention.

The starting point for this examination is to attempt a definition of what constitutes a humanitarian intervention from the point of view of the law on the use of force. If we exclude all non-forcible means of promoting and defending human rights (such as diplomatic action, non-military sanctions, humanitarian relief efforts not involving non-consensual armed intervention on another State's territory and legal efforts to bring suspects of human rights violations to justice), then we have narrowed the focus to include only armed intervention for the purpose of halting human rights violations. This would also exclude action undertaken in self-defence, as the purpose of self-defence is to ward off an armed attack and not to halt human rights violations on another State's territory, even if this were a side effect of action taken in self-defence. If we go on to further confine the issue to whether a stand-alone justification for such armed intervention exists under contemporary international law, we also have to exclude any intervention undertaken with the authorization of the UN Security Council (UNSC, Security Council), whether in the context of a UN peace (enforcement) operation with a mandate to protect civilians or by a State, ad hoc coalition of States or regional organization acting under a Chapter VII mandate of the Council to end human rights violations, with or without a reference to R2P, since the legal basis for such action lies within the UN collective security system.[2] Finally, we also have to exclude any armed action to protect human rights on another State's territory with that State's consent, since such action would neither violate the prohibition

O. Schachter, *International Law in Theory and Practice* (Nijhoff, 1991), pp. 117–26, There are some authors who do see a right arising either under a narrow interpretation of Article 2(4) of the Charter (allowing for interventions aimed at promoting the purposes and principles of the Charter) or under international customary law, or under both Charter and customary law. See, for example, R. Lillich, 'A Reply to Ian Brownlie and a Plea for Constructive Alternatives', in Moore (ed.), *Law and Civil War* (this note), pp. 229–51; F. Teson, *Humanitarian Intervention: An Inquiry into Law and Morality* (Transnational Publishers, 1997). A third group of authors argue that humanitarian intervention, though unlawful, can in certain cases be condoned. See n. 25, below.

2 The responsibility to protect (R2P) doctrine was recognized in '2005 World Summit Outcome', UN Doc. A/RES/60/1 (24 October 2005) and incorporated into the existing collective security framework of the Charter (see Chapter 5, Fact Box 5.1). It is related to 'protection of civilians', which is an aspect of UN peacekeeping doctrine and forms part of the mandates of most contemporary UN peace operations. See *The Protection of Civilians in United Nations Peacekeeping: Handbook* (United Nations, 2020), https://tinyurl.com/5v6f5j2w.

on the use of force in international relations nor constitute a forcible intervention (see Chapter 12, below).

We are thus left with two possible situations which could be designated as humanitarian intervention. One is an armed intervention to rescue and/or evacuate the intervening State's nationals and the other is an armed intervention to halt or prevent human rights violations inflicted on the citizens of the State where the intervention is conducted. We address the latter scenario in this chapter and discuss the rescue and/or evacuation of nationals in Chapter 8, as that contingency has a number of characteristics which distinguish it from the use of force to protect another State's nationals from violations on that State's territory.

## 7.3 Humanitarian Intervention and the Charter Prohibition on the Use of Force

Humanitarian intervention being thus defined as a non-consensual armed intervention on a State's territory to halt human rights violations, the first point to examine is how the Charter prohibition and a purported right of such intervention relate to each other. In other words, we need to ascertain whether there is any room to assume that the Charter prohibition does not apply to armed intervention for the purpose of halting large-scale violations of human rights. In Chapter 4, we explained that the scope of the prohibition to use force was to be interpreted broadly to encompass all forms of armed force not falling under the rubric of UNSC (-authorized) action to maintain or restore international peace and security or within the scope of the right to self-defence.

The reasons for this conclusion were to be found in the ordinary meaning of Article 2(4), the object and purpose of the prohibition, the drafting history of Article 2(4) and subsequent interpretations of the prohibition in authoritative UN General Assembly resolutions, such as the Friendly Relations Declaration, and case law, as well as in the views of the large majority of publicists.[3] In particular, we found that the phrase 'against the territorial integrity or political independence of any State, or in any other manner inconsistent with the Purposes of the United Nations' cannot be read as a limitation on the scope of the prohibition that would allow for uses of force which were (allegedly) intended to

[3] See nn. 1 above and 5 below. International Court of Justice (ICJ), *Military and Paramilitary Activities in and against Nicaragua (Nicaragua v. United States)* (Merits), Judgment, 27 June 1986, ICJ Reports, 1986, para. 268 ('the use of force could not be the appropriate method to monitor or ensure such respect [for human rights]').

promote purposes of the Organization such as human rights or self-determination.[4]

Accordingly, there is no reason to assume that the prohibition allows for any use of force not falling under the rubric of UNSC(-authorized) action to maintain or restore international peace and security or within the scope of self-defence. Consequently, the prohibition does not make an exception for armed intervention to halt or prevent ongoing or imminent large-scale human rights violations on another State's territory. There is no evidence that the drafters of the Charter or the overwhelming majority of the members of the United Nations have ever interpreted the Charter prohibition otherwise. On the contrary, there is ample evidence that the prohibition was meant to apply to any use of force that did not fall within one of the aforementioned exceptions to the prohibition or was undertaken at the invitation, or with the lawful consent, of the State where the intervention took place.[5] In short, humanitarian intervention outside the context of the UN collective security system is a violation of the Charter prohibition and hence unlawful, unless it can be persuasively demonstrated that there is some other legal justification for such action that precludes the wrongfulness of such an intervention or qualifies as an independent legal basis for the use of force.

## 7.4 Purported Justifications for Humanitarian Intervention

There are two possible legal justifications for humanitarian intervention put forward by its proponents. First, it is argued that humanitarian intervention is lawful on the basis of an alleged customary right, either having been carried over from pre-1945 international law or having emerged since the Charter came into force. Second, it is maintained that humanitarian intervention could be justified on the basis of the 'state of necessity' exclusion from wrongful activity under the law of international responsibility. We examine both in turn.

[4] See Chapter 4, Section 4.6, above.

[5] See Declaration on Principles of International Law Concerning Friendly Relations and Co-operation among States in accordance with the Charter of the United Nations, UN General Assembly (UNGA) Resolution 2625 (24 October 1970). See also Chapter 4, Section 4.2; Chapter 5, Section 5.6; Chapter 5, Fact Box 5.1; '2005 World Summit Outcome' (n. 2), paras. 77–9, 138–9.

### 7.4.1 *Customary Law as a Purported Basis*

There is evidence of the existence of significant support for a justification of armed intervention for humanitarian purposes in nineteenth-century international law.[6] The intervention of France in Lebanon in 1860 is often cited as an example of a 'purely' humanitarian intervention (one primarily motivated by humanitarian concerns).[7] Other candidates include the intervention of European powers in the Greek Independence War of 1821–32, the Russo-Turkish War of 1877–8 and the Spanish-American War of 1898, although the latter two are often seen as more doubtful examples of interventions for purely or primarily humanitarian considerations, since other considerations and interests played at least as significant a role as humanitarian ones in motivating resort to war by the intervening States. Nevertheless, even if we assume that there was such a right in the context of nineteenth-century international law, it does not mean that such a right still existed at the outbreak of the Second World War, nor that it was carried over into the

[6] Nineteenth-century advocates of humanitarian intervention believed that such interventions were lawful if (i) they were needed to counter gross mistreatment 'shocking the moral consciousness of mankind'; (ii) they were in some form collective, so as to acquire international legitimacy and limit abuse; and (iii) their main justification was humanitarian concern. See, for example, H. Wheaton, *Elements of International Law: With a Sketch of the History of the Science* (Carey, Lea and Blanchard, 1836), p. 91; A. W. Heffter, *Le droit international de l'Europe* (H. W. Muller/A. Cotillon, 1883), pp. 111–14; R. Phillimore, *Commentaries upon International Law*, vol. 1 (Butterworths, 1879), pp. 568–9, 622–3; T. D. Woolsey, *Introduction to the Study of International Law* (Sampson Low, Marston, Searle and Rivington, 1879), p. 44; P. Fiore, *Nouveau droit international public suivant les besoins de la civilization moderne*, 2nd ed., trad. C. Antoine, vol. 1 (A. Durant et Pedone-Lauriel, 1885), pp. 502–25; F. Martens, 'Étude historique sur la politique russe dans la question d'Orient' (1877) 9 *Revue de droit international et de législation comparée* 49–77, at 49; E. C. Stowell, *Intervention in International Law* (John Byrne, 1921), pp. 51–62, 472–525 (quoting several nineteenth-century authors). Those opposing humanitarian interventions relied on the principles of sovereignty and independence, with non-intervention as their corollary, as well as on practical grounds, especially abuse by powerful States. See, for example, Count Mamiani, *Rights of Nations, or the New Law of European States Applied to the Affairs of Italy* (W. Jeffs, 1860), pp. 140–1, 177–97; G. Carnazza Amari, 'Nouvel exposé du principe de non-intervention' (1873) 5 *Revue de droit international et de législation comparée* 352–89 (pt 1), at 370–377, and 531–65 (pt 2), at 552–9; T. Funck-Brentano and A. Sorel, *Précis du droit des gens* (Librairie Plon, 1887), pp. 215–16, 221, 223; P. L. Pradier-Fodéré, *Traité de droit international public européen et américain, suivant le progrès de la science et de la pratique contemporaines*, vol. 1 (A. Durand et Pedone-Lauriel, 1885), pp. 593–5. See also A. Heraclides and A. Dialla, *Humanitarian Intervention in the Long Nineteenth Century: Setting the Precedent* (Manchester University Press, 2015), pp. 57–80.

[7] I. Brownlie, *International Law and the Use of Force by States* (Clarendon Press, 1963), pp. 338–42; Heraclides and Dialla, *Humanitarian Intervention* (n. 6), pp. 134–47.

post-war period in the context of the emerging prohibition against the use of force. By the time the Second World War broke out, all of the justifications under the guise of 'self-help' in nineteenth-century international law had been narrowed down to self-defence under the influence of the League Covenant, the Kellogg-Briand Pact and other international treaties, as discussed above in Chapter 3.[8] During the negotiations leading to the adoption of the Charter, no party ever made any reference to a right of forcible unilateral intervention to safeguard human rights and no State made any attempt to incorporate such a right into the Charter.[9] Consequently, it is hardly tenable to assume that such a right, even if it did exist in the context of nineteenth-century international law, carried over into the Charter era without ever being mentioned during the negotiations leading to the Charter. To the extent that any such intervention was contemplated by the drafters of the Charter, it would have been within the context of the collective security provisions they were in the process of adopting and not as an independent right of States.

Turning to the possibility that since the adoption of the Charter a new rule of customary law providing legal justification for humanitarian intervention might have emerged, the question would be whether or not such a new rule meets the bar for acceptance of a new rule of customary law. As with any rule of customary law, such a rule would have to meet the criteria of evidencing a widespread, reasonably consistent and representative practice supported by clear indications that such practice was viewed as a legal right, creating a new exception to the prohibition on the use of force.[10] Even if one takes a less stringent approach to the formation of customary law, there would have to be clear evidence of support for the existence of such a right in the positions taken by States. There can be little doubt, however, that this test has not been met; there are only a handful of examples, most of which were based on other legal justifications or, in some cases, no legal justification at all.[11] Admittedly, after the end of the Cold War support for collectively

[8] See above Chapter 2, Sections 2.6 and 2.7.

[9] See above Chapter 3, Section 3.10.

[10] M. H. Mendelson, 'The Formation of Customary International Law' (1998) 272 *Collected Courses of the Hague Academy of International Law* 155–410; A. Roberts and S. Sivakumaran, 'The Theory and Reality of the Sources of International Law', in M. D. Evans (ed.), *International Law* (Oxford University Press, 2018), pp. 92–6.

[11] Examples most often cited include the Indian intervention in Eastern Pakistan (1971); the Vietnamese intervention in Cambodia (1978); the Tanzanian invasion of Uganda (1978–9); and the NATO bombing campaign of Serbia in response to the conflict in Kosovo (1999), all of which will be discussed below.

authorized military action aimed at safeguarding human rights did increase, at least until the consensus broke down in the aftermath of the 2011 UN-authorized intervention in Libya.[12] Nevertheless, the attitudes of the vast majority of States to such interventions do not point to anything close to a general acceptance of any new stand-alone right of humanitarian intervention.

The examples most often cited in the discussion related to the existence of a stand-alone justification for humanitarian intervention include (i) the Indian intervention in 1971 in response to massive human rights violations by the Pakistani Army against the Bengali population in what was then East Pakistan; (ii) the Vietnamese invasion and overthrow of the genocidal Khmer Rouge government in Cambodia in late 1978/early 1979; (iii) the Tanzanian invasion of Uganda in 1978–9 and overthrow of the government of Idi Amin, who had been responsible for large-scale human rights violations in Uganda; and (iv) the 1999 NATO aerial bombing campaign to end the humanitarian crisis in Kosovo.

None of these operations received authorization from the Security Council, but the first three were carried out on the basis of a claim of self-defence by the States conducting the interventions. It is not necessary to elaborate on whether the claims of self-defence were justified in the context of this discussion, but they make the incidents concerned less usable as evidence of a stand-alone justification for humanitarian intervention. In fact, the first three instances did not involve any claim of an independent right of humanitarian intervention, while the fourth instance relied only to a limited extent on such a claim.

#### 7.4.1.1 The 1971 Indian Intervention in East Pakistan

India claimed self-defence on the basis of the disruption caused by the mass exodus of over ten million Bengali refugees into India and air strikes

[12] The intervention in northern Iraq following the Iraq-Kuwait conflict (1991) and the interventions in Somalia (1992–3) are examples of collectively authorized interventions largely motivated by large-scale human rights violations and related humanitarian considerations such as securing relief efforts. Various collectively authorized interventions took place during the two decades between the end of the Cold War and the end of the first decade of the twenty-first century. These include the interventions in the former Yugoslavia (1991–5), Rwanda (1994) and Eastern Timor (1999). The intervention in Libya (2011) was the last collectively authorized humanitarian intervention in the post-Cold War period. These have, as indicated, a recognized legal basis in the guise of a Chapter VII authorization by the UNSC and are related to, or based on, the R2P doctrine (see Chapter 5, Section 5.6, above). By contrast, interventions lacking such collective authorization require another legal basis in order to be lawful.

by the Pakistani Air Force on forward positions of the Indian armed forces, along with artillery shelling of Indian territory. This argument formed the pretext for the large-scale invasion of East Pakistan by the Indian armed forces, which led to the defeat of Pakistan, independence of East Pakistan and its subsequent admission to the United Nations as Bangladesh in 1972.

While the human rights violations by the Pakistan Army in East Pakistan amounting to genocide were a significant factor behind the Indian intervention, India did not rely on a stand-alone justification of humanitarian intervention, despite some references to the humanitarian crisis in its public statements. Nor were the ensuing debates in the Security Council or the positions of outside powers directed towards the question of whether or not human rights violations, even on a massive scale, could serve as a justification for a military intervention.[13]

Consequently, although the intervention was related at least partly to a large-scale and systematic violation of human rights, it has little or no precedential value as support for the existence of a right of humanitarian intervention. India did not base its actions on such a right, nor did the question of whether such a right constituted a new exception to the prohibition on the use of force play any role (outside academic literature) in the assessment of the legality of the Indian intervention.

#### 7.4.1.2 The 1978–9 Vietnamese Invasion of Cambodia

The Vietnamese invasion of Cambodia (referred to at the time as Kampuchea) in December 1978 succeeded in ousting the genocidal regime of the Khmer Rouge. While the Cambodian genocide was responsible for the deaths of roughly a quarter of the country's population, this was not the primary, nor probably even a significant, reason for the Vietnamese

[13] For analysis of the Indian intervention in East Pakistan, see, inter alia, D. Kritsiotis, 'The Intervention of India into (East) Pakistan', in T. Ruys and O. Corten (eds.), *The Use of Force in International Law: A Case-Based Approach* (Oxford University Press, 2018), pp. 169–88; O. Marwah, 'India's Intervention in East Pakistan 1971–72' (1979) 13 *Journal of Modern Asian Studies* 549–80; T. Franck and N. Rodley, 'After Bangladesh: The Law of Humanitarian Intervention by Military Force' (1973) 67 *American Journal of International Law* 275–305. See also Question Considered by the Security Council at Its 1606th, 1607th and 1608th Meetings on 4, 5 and 6 December 1971, UNGA Res. 2793 (XXVI) (7 December 1971). This resolution called upon both parties to cease fire and was adopted by the UNGA after repeated Soviet vetoes of comparable draft resolutions in the UNSC. India rejected the resolution, even though it had been adopted by a vote of 104, with only 11 States (the USSR and its allies) backing India. See Marwah, 'India's Intervention' (this note), p. 578.

intervention, although the Vietnamese government referred to the atrocities in UN debates following the invasion. The Khmer Rouge had engaged in a series of attacks on Vietnamese territory starting in 1975 as a result of tension between the two States and a perception that Vietnam was engaged in a drive for hegemony in the region. Vietnam had carried out a punitive raid into Cambodia in late 1977 following large-scale Cambodian incursions into Vietnam in April of that year, but this had not compelled the Khmer Rouge to discontinue their hostile actions. Alongside the bilateral rivalry between the two States and strong anti-Vietnamese sentiment among the Khmer Rouge leadership was the larger geopolitical rivalry between the two major Communist powers, with the Soviet Union backing Vietnam and China backing the Khmer Rouge regime in Cambodia. The Vietnamese armed forces carried out a large-scale invasion of Cambodia in December 1978 and within two weeks had defeated the Khmer Rouge. The remnants of the ousted government escaped into eastern Thailand and conducted a guerrilla campaign against the Vietnamese-backed government. It also continued to be recognized as the lawful government of Cambodia by most States and the United Nations until the Vietnamese negotiated a settlement and withdrew in 1989.

The Vietnamese based their intervention on self-defence against the previously mentioned Khmer Rouge attacks and justified their continued presence in the country as being with the consent and at the invitation of the government installed and backed by Vietnam. At no time did Vietnam refer to a right of humanitarian intervention as the basis for their invasion. The attitude of the bulk of the international community in condemning the Vietnamese invasion and continuing to recognize the Khmer Rouge as the legitimate government after its expulsion from Cambodia likewise does not point to humanitarian considerations being accepted by the international community, despite the abundant evidence of massive human rights violations perpetrated by the Khmer Rouge during their rule of Cambodia.

In short, while the Vietnamese invasion had an undeniable humanitarian effect, this was a fortuitous by-product of the Vietnamese decision to oust the Khmer Rouge from power for reasons which had little or nothing to do with humanitarian considerations. Consequently, it too has virtually no precedential value as support for the existence or formation of a customary right of humanitarian intervention.[14]

[14] For analysis of the Vietnamese intervention in Cambodia, see, inter alia, G. Fox, 'The Vietnamese Intervention in Cambodia – 1978', in Ruys and Corten (eds.), *Use of Force* (n. 13), pp. 242–54; S. J. Morris, *Why Vietnam Invaded Cambodia: Political Culture and the Causes of War* (Stanford University Press, 1999); J. Wheeler, *Saving Strangers:*

#### 7.4.1.3 The 1978–9 Tanzanian Invasion of Uganda

The Tanzanian invasion and overthrow of the regime of Idi Amin in 1978–9 was based on a combination of arguments, one of which involved a plea of self-defence against the occupation and annexation in October 1978 of a portion of Tanzanian territory by Amin's forces known as the Kagera salient. The Tanzanian armed forces succeeded in driving out the Ugandan army by January 1979. The war continued, however, beyond a simple restoration of the status quo ante when the president of Tanzania assisted Ugandan exiles loyal to the former Ugandan president operating from Tanzania, who were engaged in an open rebellion against Amin and his supporters. These included, in addition to the Ugandan armed forces, several thousand Libyan troops sent by Amin's ally Colonel Gaddafi, who was then president of Libya, and a number of Palestinian fighters sent by the Palestine Liberation Organization. The Tanzanian intervention took on the role of open support for the Uganda National Liberation Front (UNLF). The Libyan intervention led to more open support by Tanzania for the UNLF, as it was clear that otherwise Amin would remain in control of the country. Tanzanian forces operating alongside UNLF fighters succeeded in defeating the Ugandan army and Libyan troops during March–April 1979, and by early April Amin had fled the country and the UNLF government had been recognized by most States.

While Amin's rule had seen massive human rights violations and was partly responsible for the influx of tens of thousands of refugees into Tanzania, the Tanzanian government did not claim to be acting on the basis of humanitarian intervention at any stage of the conflict. It based its intervention on self-defence and assistance to the UNLF as the representative government of Uganda.

In contrast to the condemnation that India and Vietnam had received for their interventions, Tanzania's action was neither condemned nor openly supported by the United Nations, nor by the bulk of the international community, including the Organization of African Unity (OAU) and most African States. The relative isolation of Amin and the indifference of most States to his fate was undoubtedly partly a result of his abysmal human rights record, but also a consequence of his

*Humanitarian Intervention in International Society* (Oxford University Press, 2002) pp. 78–110 (examining why Vietnam was condemned for its intervention and looking at the reasons the Khmer Rouge regime continued to receive the backing of the international community despite its genocidal policies during its period in power).

adventurous foreign policy and erratic behaviour as head of Uganda during most of his rule.[15] Nevertheless, failure to condemn cannot be construed as support for a customary right of humanitarian intervention. Equally, an intervention that is not based on a claim of humanitarian intervention cannot be viewed as State practice confirming or establishing such a right. It might be seen as an example of condoning a use of force that was not lawful but seen as necessary or legitimate from a policy or moral perspective, but that is not the same as a legal right under customary international law.

#### 7.4.1.4 The 1999 NATO Bombing Campaign Relating to the Humanitarian Crisis in Kosovo

The 1999 bombing campaign by NATO in response to human rights violations in Kosovo is an example of post-Cold War intervention often cited in support of the emergence of a right of humanitarian intervention.[16] In contrast to the earlier examples, it was undertaken not by a single State but by a collective military alliance. Moreover, this alliance had been directly involved in the ongoing conflict in the region and had played a significant role in support of UN peacemaking and enforcement efforts to end the security and humanitarian crisis resulting from the break-up of the former Yugoslavia over a period of several years immediately preceding the Kosovo crisis (see Fact Box 7.1). The aerial campaign was not authorized by the Security Council, but was partially justified by most of the participating NATO States as an enforcement of earlier UNSC resolutions and a response to a regional threat to peace and security.[17]

[15] For analysis of the Tanzanian intervention in Uganda, see, inter alia, K. Chan, 'The Ugandan-Tanzanian War – 1978–79', in Ruys and Corten (eds.), *Use of Force* (n. 13), pp. 255–68; G. Roberts, 'The Uganda-Tanzania War, the Fall of Idi Amin and the Failure of African Diplomacy' (2014) 8 *Journal of East African Studies* 692–709; O. Hathaway et al., 'Consent-Based Humanitarian Intervention: Giving Sovereignty Back to the Sovereign' (2013) 46 *Cornell International Law Journal* 499–568, at 514.

[16] For analysis of the NATO intervention in Kosovo, see, inter alia, D. Franchini and A. Tzanakopoulos, 'The Kosovo Crisis – 1999', in Ruys and Corten (eds.), *Use of Force* (n. 13), pp. 594–622; D. H. Joyner, 'The Kosovo Intervention: Legal Analysis and a More Persuasive Paradigm' (2002) 13 *European Journal of International Law* 597–619; L. Henkin, 'Kosovo and the Law of "Humanitarian Intervention"' (1999) 93 *American Journal of International Law* 824–8. For a factual perspective and for an examination of the main documents related to the crisis, see M. Weller, *The Crisis in Kosovo, 1989–1999: From the Dissolution of Yugoslavia to Rambouillet and the Outbreak of Hostilities* (Documents & Analysis Publishing, 1999).

[17] On the relationship between the UN and NATO positions and actions related to the Kosovo crisis, see B. Simma, 'NATO, the UN and the Use of Force: Legal Aspects' (1999) 10 *European Journal of International Law* 1–22.

### FACT BOX 7.1 THE SECURITY COUNCIL DEBATE ON THE NATO USE OF FORCE IN THE KOSOVO CRISIS

During the period leading up to the decision by NATO to use force in response to the humanitarian crisis in Kosovo, the situation steadily worsened from 1998 onwards. By mid-1998 the situation had escalated into a full-blown armed conflict between the Federal Republic of Yugoslavia (FRY) armed forces and police, on the one hand, and the ethnic Albanian Kosovo Liberation Army, on the other. The conflict resulted in several hundred deaths and large-scale displacement of ethnic Albanian Kosovar refugees over the border into Albania. In September 1998, the UNSC issued a ceasefire order and determined that the situation amounted to a threat to international peace under Article 39 of the Charter. An attempt at a negotiated settlement broke down in January 1999, with intensified fighting continuing into March against the background of ongoing hostilities, large-scale civilian displacement, a FRY declaration of state of emergency and the withdrawal of the monitoring mission of the Organization for Security and Co-operation in Europe (OSCE). NATO commenced a unilateral bombing offensive on 24 March 1999.

The Security Council met two days after the launch of the NATO offensive to consider a draft resolution put forward by Belarus, India and the Russian Federation, condemning the intervention as a violation of the UN Charter and calling for an immediate ceasefire. The draft resolution was rejected by twelve votes to three in the Security Council. While this did not amount to an endorsement of the NATO bombing campaign, it did provide support for the conclusion of the Independent International Commission on Kosovo, convened by the Swedish Government, that the NATO intervention was illegal but legitimate, in that all diplomatic avenues had been exhausted and the use of force was the only way to bring the atrocities in Kosovo to a halt. The refusal of such a large majority in the Council to condemn the intervention showed that a sizable segment of the international community was not prepared to view it as an act of aggression, notwithstanding the lack of a recognized legal basis for it.

**Sources:** UN Security Council Official Records (SCOR), 54th year, 3988th meeting, UN Doc. S/PV. 3988 (24 March 1999); SCOR, 54th year, 3989th meeting, UN Doc. S/PV. 3989 (26 March 1999); Independent International Commission on Kosovo, *The Kosovo Report* (Oxford University Press, 2000), https://reliefweb.int/report/albania/kosovo-report.

The intervention was controversial and opinion remains divided on the real or perceived motivation behind it, the way it was conducted and its long-term effect on international relations. The justifications put forward for the intervention by most NATO States were not based on the existence of a right of humanitarian intervention, notwithstanding references to violations of human rights committed by Serbia. The exceptions were Belgium and the United Kingdom, which did refer to a right or emergent right of humanitarian intervention as their principal justifications. The UNSC failed to adopt a draft resolution condemning the intervention and calling for an immediate ceasefire (see Fact Box 7.1).[18] This does not indicate support for the intervention as a new exception to the Charter prohibition on the use of force, but it does illustrate that a sizable portion of the international community was not prepared to condemn the action under the circumstances of an ongoing crisis on the territory of the former Yugoslavia which had destabilized the region for nearly a decade, reports of serious and ongoing human rights violations and a mass expulsion of ethnic Kosovar Albanians.[19] Together, these factors accounted for the degree of tolerance and even (conditional) support by many States. At the same time, an equally large segment of the international community was highly critical of, or openly opposed to, the intervention and the doctrine of humanitarian intervention, including two permanent members of the Security Council (China and Russia).

The division in the reaction of States, the reluctance of most NATO States to rely on a claim of humanitarian intervention and the clear lack of *opinio juris* across the different regional and political subdivisions in the United Nations show that the NATO intervention cannot be seen as evidence of an existing or emerging customary right of humanitarian intervention.

#### 7.4.1.5 Conclusions Relating to the Probative Value of State Practice in the Context of an Alleged Customary Right of Humanitarian Intervention

In sum, these examples of unilateral intervention do not provide sufficient evidence of an existing or emerging right of unilateral humanitarian intervention in the absence of a Security Council authorization. The examples lack the necessary acknowledgement of such a right by both the States actually conducting them and the wider international community. The reaction of most States was at best one of acceptance of the results and not one of recognition of a new exception to the Charter

[18] The text of the draft resolution sponsored by Russia condemning the intervention (UN Doc. S/1999/328) and the positions of the States supporting and opposing it can be found in 'Security Council Rejects Demand for Cessation of Use of Force against Federal Republic of Yugoslavia', UN Press Release SC/6659 (26 March 1999), www.un.org/press/en/1999/19990326.sc6659.html.

[19] The positions put forward by various NATO members are discussed in Franchini and Tzanakopoulos, 'Kosovo Crisis' (n. 16), pp. 598–603.

prohibition. The attitude of States during the negotiations relating to the incorporation of the R2P principle as UN policy in 2005 also points to a lack of willingness to accept a right of unilateral humanitarian intervention (see Chapter 5, Fact Box 5.1). Instead, States conditioned any use of force to protect populations against massive and systematic human rights violations upon Security Council authorization, regardless of whether the force was to be used by a regional organization or arrangement or by one or more States acting on their own.[20] Similarly, there have been no further examples of unilateral interventions based on humanitarian grounds since those referred to above. The most recent example of a reference to 'ending genocide' as a justification (alongside other alleged justifications) for the invasion of Ukraine by Russia in February 2022 lacks any credibility in fact or law and has gained no acceptance outside a narrow group of States which have openly supported the Russian invasion.[21]

### 7.4.2 *'State of Necessity' as a Justification or Excuse*

Article 25 of the Articles on the Responsibility of States for Internationally Wrongful Acts (ARSIWA) recognizes 'state of necessity' as a ground precluding the wrongfulness of an act in breach of an international obligation. It is subject to stringent conditions, which, taken together, prevent it from being invoked except as an emergency measure when a vital interest of a State is in question and no obligation of an equal or greater interest of

[20] See above, n. 5; Chapter 5, Fact Box 5.1; '2005 World Summit Outcome' (n. 2), paras. 77–9, 138–9.

[21] Russia's justifications for the full-scale invasion of Ukraine on 24 February 2022 were communicated by the Russian permanent representative to the United Nations directly following the invasion. They included, alongside a claim of self-defence, a reference to halting a 'genocide' against ethnic Russians in the Donbas region and elsewhere in Ukraine. The allegations were without factual basis. See, inter alia, ICJ, *Allegations of Genocide under the Convention on the Prevention and Punishment of the Crime of Genocide (Ukraine* v. *Russian Federation)*, Order of 16 March 2022. In this order on provisional measures, the ICJ noted that while a definite ruling on Ukraine's application would have to await the merits, it was able to conclude that 'the Court is not in possession of evidence substantiating the allegation of the Russian Federation that genocide has been committed on Ukrainian territory' (para. 59). For an analysis of the Russian claim, see J. Green, C. Henderson and T. Ruys, 'Russia's Attack on Ukraine and the *Jus ad Bellum*' (2022) 9 *Journal on the Use of Force and International Law* 4–30. For the UNGA reaction, see Aggression against Ukraine, UNGA Res. ES-11/1 (2 March 2022); UN News, 'General Assembly Resolution Demands End to Russian Offensive in Ukraine' (2 March 2022), https://news.un.org/en/story/2022/03/1113152. See also Chapter 16, Section 16.4, below.

another State is violated.[22] It is generally considered not to apply to the inter-State use of armed force, as the prohibition on the use of force is of a peremptory nature and does not allow for exceptions other than those which are recognized under the Charter.[23] Sometimes, necessity has been related to the use of force against non-State actors, for example in relation to the rescue of nationals in situations where a danger arises from a non-State armed group outside the control of the State where the nationals are located (see Chapter 8, below).[24]

Acceptance of a defence of necessity as precluding the wrongfulness of a military intervention on humanitarian grounds amounts to essentially the same as saying that the Charter prohibition should not apply to such interventions, which we have already discussed and concluded is not tenable. If the prohibition on the use of force is meant to apply broadly and the only exceptions to it are those that are built into the law and generally recognized as such, then an extra escape clause which would excuse the use of force on humanitarian grounds would end up making the prohibition subject to yet another exception and one which was not meant to serve as a circumvention of a peremptory rule of law. Likewise, if we conclude that State practice and *opinio juris* are insufficient to establish a rule of customary law allowing for humanitarian intervention, it is hardly likely that an exceptional plea of necessity which has been invoked by only one or two States with little sign of general acceptance is a plausible legal basis for such interventions.

One possible narrow exception might be in a situation where a State had completely lost control over a portion of its territory and one or more armed groups were committing acts amounting to international crimes against (a portion of) the population of that area. In a situation where the government had ceased to function or have any control over that portion of its territory, it could be argued that force used to halt the violations would not constitute an act of force directed against the State, if it met certain conditions and there were no other options available. But this type of situation would most likely be either consented to by the

22 Responsibility of States for Internationally Wrongful Acts, Annex to UNGA Resolution 56/83 (12 December 2001), UN Doc. A/RES/56/83.

23 International Law Commission, 'Draft Articles on Responsibility of States for Internationally Wrongful Acts, with Commentaries' (2001), in Report of the International Law Commission on the Work of Its Fifty-Third Session, UN Doc. A/56/10, p. 85 (Commentary to Article 26), para. (4): 'The plea of necessity likewise cannot excuse the breach of a peremptory norm'.

24 Schachter, *International Law* (n. 1), pp. 169–71.

government, if it was still functioning, or capable of being addressed by a Security Council authorization. In any case, it could not apply to situations where humanitarian intervention involved large-scale invasion resulting in the overthrow of the incumbent government or dismemberment of its territory. It would also not apply to any other form of force, such as 'surgical air strikes' or firing cruise missiles at specific targets on humanitarian grounds, since any use of force against a State requires a clear and unequivocal legal basis (see Chapter 9, below).

## 7.5 Extra-Legal Justification for or Mitigation of Humanitarian Intervention

Alongside legal considerations, moral and policy ones will almost inevitably play a role in the decision to resort to force. This is particularly the case with humanitarian intervention, which is undertaken on moral grounds to halt ongoing, large-scale human rights violations. Judging from the record of such interventions so far, States have put forward imperative policy concerns and/or overriding humanitarian considerations as a justification for military intervention in response to human rights violations more often than they have claimed a right of humanitarian intervention under international law. Usually, it is a combination of both sets of factors which triggers the decision to undertake a risky endeavour like a (generally large-scale) military intervention to, inter alia, end egregious human rights violations. Experience has shown that such massive human rights violations – in addition to their reprehensibility from a moral standpoint – will very often be the cause of a major threat to stability and security in the region where they occur. Hence, more often than not the intervening State(s) will have significant policy interests in addition to humanitarian motives for taking such action. This was true in all the cases we discussed earlier, as it was in the context of European diplomacy in the nineteenth century. Accordingly, the oft-heard consideration that the intervening State must have 'pure' humanitarian motives in order to be 'absolved' for taking unlawful military action does not reflect reality. More often than not, the intervening State will likely have more than purely humanitarian motives for putting an end to human rights violations in another country; such motives may include preventing the spillover of a conflict or massive refugee flows, maintaining influence or preventing outside intervention in the region, alongside (sometimes) genuine humanitarian concerns.

What weight should these considerations be given in assessing, if not the legality, then at least in some cases the acceptability or toleration of intervention? Such interventions could be mitigated or tolerated if (i) there was a clear case of large-scale human rights violations with potentially wider destabilizing effects; (ii) there was no likelihood of UNSC-mandated or -authorized enforcement measures; and (iii) the intervention was proportionate, in both how it was conducted and its likely effects on internal and international security and stability.[25]

Not all of the aforementioned examples were tolerated or mitigated, for a variety of reasons, mostly to do with the prevailing political climate and larger geopolitical considerations at the relevant time. India and Vietnam received less 'understanding' for their interventions than did Tanzania and NATO. The reasons for this are related to the political and security contexts at the time and in the relevant regions; they are less connected to moral or legal considerations. All were unlawful from a legal perspective, but the latter two were looked upon with a reasonable degree of acceptance or at least tolerance, and even the interventions of India and Vietnam are viewed less critically in retrospect than at the time they occurred. Undoubtedly, all such interventions ultimately undermine the prohibition on the use of force and may open the door to (even) less noble interventions, with the use of similar arguments to mask aggression or render the Security Council less effective.

Be that as it may, the possibility of a degree of mitigation of responsibility cannot be excluded if certain conditions are met. That should not be confused with a recognized legal basis, but neither is it without legal significance. Most legal systems recognize some possibility of mitigation of responsibility, without that making unlawful conduct legal. It might even be seen as a general principle of law that extra-legal considerations can have a bearing on the degree of culpability of a wrongful act. In the *Corfu Channel* judgment, the Court found that a declaration relating to the unlawfulness of the United Kingdom's minesweeping operation in Albanian waters was sufficient recompense in view of the circumstances,

[25] Various authors have put forward the proposition that humanitarian intervention, while illegal, might under certain conditions qualify for mitigation of responsibility or at least be condoned on extra-legal grounds. They include I. Brownlie, 'Thoughts on the Kind-Hearted Gunman', in R. Lillich (ed.) *Humanitarian Intervention and the United Nations* (University of Virginia Press, 1973), 139–48; Schachter, *International Law* (n. 1), p. 126; T. Franck, *Recourse to Force: State Action against Threats and Armed Attacks* (Cambridge University Press, 2002); T. D. Gill, 'Humanitaire Interventie: Rechtmatigheid, Rechtvaardigheid en Legitimiteit' (2001) 94 *Militair Rechtelijk Tijdschrift* 221–41; T. D. Gill, 'Humanitarian Intervention: Legality, Justice and Legitimacy' (2005) 1 *Global Yearbook of International Law* 51–76. See also below Chapter 9, Section 9.6 and Chapter 10, Section 10.6.

which included Albania's failure to prevent its territory from being used to harm other States. This may be seen as recognition that the wrongfulness of an act can be mitigated by factual and other considerations.[26] It is not outside the realm of plausibility to accept that interventions which meet the conditions set out above (or one similar to them) should qualify for at least some degree of mitigation and acceptance of the humanitarian outcome, if not necessarily of the means used to obtain it. Another way of phrasing this is that provided certain conditions are met, the international community may opt to tolerate or, to a certain extent, even excuse a 'genuine' humanitarian intervention – in other words, withhold from attaching significant condemnation or legal consequences to it, without necessarily seeing it as a precedent for the establishment of a new rule of law which would allow for such interventions.

## 7.6 Conclusion

To sum up, in the absence of a mandate by the Security Council, no recognized right allowing for humanitarian intervention exists, whether on the basis of an existing or emerging customary rule or on any other purported basis. That being said, such interventions could be mitigated or tolerated if there was a clear case of large-scale human rights violations, no likelihood of UNSC-mandated or -authorized enforcement measures, and the intervention was proportionate, in both how it was conducted and its likely effects on internal and international security and stability. In other words, in such cases the international community may opt to tolerate, mitigate or, to a certain extent, even excuse a humanitarian intervention and, consequently, to not attach significant condemnation or legal consequences to it. Such an approach should not, however, be seen as a precedent for the establishment of a new rule of customary law legalizing such interventions.

[26] ICJ, *The Corfu Channel Case (United Kingdom of Great Britain and Northern Ireland v. Albania)* (Merits), Judgment, 9 April 1949, ICJ Reports 1949, pp. 35–6.

# 8

# The Use of Force and the Rescue and Evacuation of Nationals

## 8.1 Introduction

This chapter examines the legality of intervention for the purpose of rescuing and evacuating nationals of the intervening State in response to acute danger to their lives or safety. It first looks at the concept of rescue and evacuation of nationals and its distinction from a broader concept of 'protection of nationals'. It then examines necessity and self-defence as possible justifications for the rescue and evacuation of nationals.

## 8.2 The Legality of Rescue and Evacuation of Nationals and Its Distinction from a Broader Concept of Protection of Nationals

The question of whether there is a right of non-consensual intervention on the territory of another State in order to safeguard the lives of citizens of the intervening State and assure their safe evacuation when there is a direct threat to their lives or physical safety is often conflated with a discussion on the legality of military intervention under the much broader heading of 'protection of nationals'. While the international law of the nineteenth century undoubtedly recognized a rather broad concept of intervention to protect the lives and property of the citizens of an intervening State within the context of armed self-help, such a broadly framed right to protect nationals no longer exists under contemporary international law.[1] The position of most States and writers is that a broadly based notion of protection of nationals allowing and serving as a pretext for large-scale

[1] Under the international law in force prior to the First World War, the right of States to intervene on behalf of their nationals was widely recognized. See, for example, S. Neff, *War and the Law of Nations: A General History* (Cambridge University Press, 2005), pp. 243–5; I. Brownlie, *International Law and the Use of Force by States* (Clarendon Press, 1963), pp. 289–91.

military interventions is neither compatible with Article 2(4) of the Charter nor has sufficient support in contemporary State practice and *opinio juris* to qualify as a rule of customary law.[2]

On the other hand, the question of whether a State may undertake a more limited intervention to rescue and/or evacuate nationals in situations where there is an acute threat to their lives or safety and no protection is forthcoming from the territorial State is distinct from the aforementioned broad concept of protection of nationals. A non-consensual intervention for the evacuation of nationals may be necessary when the normal protection of the territorial State is not feasible because of internal conflict, breakdown of State authority, temporary loss of control over a portion of territory or similar conditions, as a result of which the safety of foreign nationals is directly threatened and no other means of alleviating the danger is available. The legal basis for intervention in such situations is most credibly to be found in the doctrine of 'state of necessity' in our view (see Section 8.4, below).

By contrast, in situations where an organ of the territorial State or an armed group is directly responsible for armed violence, imminent and unequivocal threat of such violence or unlawful deprivation of liberty directed against a particular State's nationals as a way of exerting pressure on or coercing the parent State into a particular course of action, there are persuasive reasons for regarding such action as an indirect attack on the parent State itself. This would justify necessary and proportionate measures of self-defence to neutralize the (threat of) violence aimed at its citizens and conduct them to safety (see Section 8.5, below).

Intervention of a limited nature based on the two aforementioned grounds (state of necessity and self-defence) for the purpose of rescuing nationals in the circumstances described above may be lawful and should be distinguished from a broader notion of protection of nationals under both legal and policy considerations.[3] This more circumscribed right is

2 Most authors take the position that current international law does not recognize a broadly framed right of protection of nationals, but a more limited right of rescue and evacuation of nationals (on the basis of self-defence and/or necessity) may be allowed under certain conditions. See, for example, Brownlie, *International Law* (n. 1), pp. 298–301; T. M. Franck, *Recourse to Force: State Action against Threats and Armed Attacks* (Cambridge University Press, 2002), pp. 76–96; C. Henderson, *The Use of Force and International Law* (Cambridge University Press, 2018), pp. 247–56; T. Ruys, *'Armed Attack' and Article 51 of the UN Charter: Evolution in Customary Law and Practice* (Cambridge University Press, 2010), pp. 213–49; C. Gray, *International Law and the Use of Force* (Oxford University Press, 2018), pp. 165–70.

3 See, for example, O. Schachter, *International Law in Theory and Practice* (Nijhoff, 1991), pp. 165–7, 169–73. See also authors cited in n. 2, above: Franck and Henderson cautiously

referred to here by the wording used in the title of this chapter (i.e. 'rescue and evacuation of nationals'), in order to differentiate it from the broader notion of 'protection of nationals'. In military doctrine, this is often referred to as 'non-combatant evacuation', or by the acronym NEO for 'non-combatant evacuation operation'.[4] To set the scope of the discussion, we deal here exclusively with non-consensual and unilateral military interventions by a State in situations of acute threat to the lives or safety of citizens of the intervening State. In the case of lawful consent to conduct an evacuation of nationals, no intervention or violation of the prohibition on the threat or use of force occurs (see Chapter 12, below). In the case of a UN Security Council mandate clearly providing authority for an evacuation, either singly or in combination with other authorizations, an alternative legal basis exists which obviates the need to invoke any other justification. In any case, there can be no doubt that a military intervention on another State's territory without that State's lawful consent will always require a legal basis. Arguments that such interventions, whether broad or narrow, somehow fall outside the scope of the prohibition on the threat or use of force and the prohibition of intervention have no basis in law. Nonetheless, an emergency non-consensual evacuation of nationals which does not involve armed force does not in our view constitute a use of force in international relations, although it does constitute an unauthorized trespass on another State's territory which requires a justification.[5]

Likewise, it is clear that a narrowly formulated right to neutralize direct threats and/or to extract nationals of the intervening State from situations of acute danger to their lives or safety is completely separate from the question of the legality of humanitarian intervention in cases of widespread violence affecting the population of the State where the violations

recognize the possibility that self-defence could apply; Ruys, while concluding that there is insufficient evidence that a right of protection of nationals exists, is inclined to accept the legality of a more limited right of rescue and evacuation of nationals as either existing law or emerging law; Gray seems also to take this position, although it is not stated explicitly. Most authors who rule out the existence of such a right do so by pointing to the potential abuse of that right by States. For a reply to that position, see, for example, R. Higgins, *Problems and Process: International Law and How We Use it* (Oxford University Press, 1994), pp. 245–51 (although Higgins calls the protection of nationals 'humanitarian intervention', it is clear that she is talking about what is usually referred to as the protection/rescue of nationals).

4 'Non-combatant evacuation' is a term used widely in military doctrine. See, for example, A. W. Thompson, 'Doctrine of the Protection of Nationals Abroad: Rise of the Non-Combatant Evacuation Operation' (2012) 11 *Washington University Global Studies Law Review* 627–68, at 654–9.

5 On the minimum threshold for the use of force, see Chapter 4, Section 4.5, above.

are occurring. The essential difference, aside from the scale of the intervention, lies in the relationship of nationality between a State and its nationals. It should be obvious that a genuine link of nationality must exist for the State engaging in a rescue and evacuation of its nationals to be able to raise a valid claim of protection. This would preclude interventions on the basis of mere linguistic or ethnic kinship, either real or imagined, or on the basis of 'manufactured nationality' through mass conferral of passports on the inhabitants of a foreign country who have no appreciable link to the State doing so. It would not exclude the rescue and/or evacuation of any third-State nationals who might be co-located with the rescuing State's nationals and in a similar situation requiring removal from danger, should they wish to be removed.[6]

## 8.3 Necessity and Its Significance in Relation to the Rescue and Evacuation of Nationals

The conditions for a non-consensual and unilateral military intervention to rescue and evacuate nationals are based on necessity, both as a component of the right to self-defence and as an independent circumstance precluding the wrongfulness of an act.[7] Both forms of necessity have in common that action undertaken to safeguard nationals must not only be required to ward off a grave and ongoing or imminent peril to their lives, but must

[6] On the distinction between humanitarian intervention and the protection or rescue of nationals, see Chapter 7, Section 7.2, above. On nationality, see, for example, J. Crawford, *Brownlie's Principles of Public International Law* (Oxford University Press, 2019), pp. 495–511. On the practice of 'passportization' (i.e. wholesale conferral of nationality to inhabitants of another State on the basis of real or feigned ethnic or linguistic kinship as a pretext for (armed) interference in the State where the persons are resident), see A. Peters, 'Passportisation: Risks for International Law and Stability', *EJIL:Talk!* (9–10 May 2019), https://tinyurl.com/nm37cvh7 (Part I), https://tinyurl.com/2munkm84 (Part II).

[7] Necessity as a component of the right of self-defence is discussed above in Chapter 6, Section 6.4.3. The conditions for invoking necessity as a circumstance precluding wrongfulness are discussed in Section 8.4 of this chapter. The former is linked to the conditions for the lawful exercise of self-defence. As an excuse for otherwise unlawful conduct, no prior unlawful conduct is required or assumed. Rather, necessity in that context refers to emergency action intended to ward off a grave and imminent peril to a vital interest of a State or the international community and which does not violate an interest of equal or greater importance and can be excused if a number of conditions are met. See Responsibility of States for Internationally Wrongful Acts, Annex to UNGA Resolution 56/83 (12 December 2001), UN Doc. A/RES/56/83, Article 25; International Law Commission, 'Draft Articles on Responsibility of States for Internationally Wrongful Acts, with Commentaries' (2001), in Report of the International Law Commission on the Work of Its Fifty-Third Session, UN Doc. A/56/10, pp. 80–4 (Commentary to Article 25).

additionally be the only feasible means to end the threat under the prevailing circumstances. This would mean that as long as the authorities of the territorial State were engaged in a good faith effort to end the threat to the safety of the threatened foreign nationals and were capable of offering the necessary protection, there would be no grounds for use of force in self-defence by the parent State of the threatened nationals. Likewise, as long as there were alternative means for the nationals of any foreign State to safely leave an area, there would be no grounds for a state-of-necessity-driven, non-consensual intervention to speed the process along.

If, however, these considerations are not met, then any action undertaken by the parent State must conform to the formulation of the *Caroline* criteria set out in relation to the protection of nationals. These are: (i) an imminent or ongoing threat to the lives or safety of the nationals of the intervening State; (ii) a failure or inability on the part of the territorial State to protect the nationals of the intervening State from serious injury; and (iii) measures of protection strictly required and aimed at neutralizing the threat and removing the nationals of the intervening State to safety with as little as possible collateral effect on the territorial State or its inhabitants.[8]

Hence, large-scale interventions such as the US invasions of Grenada in 1983 or of Panama in 1989, or the Russian invasion of Georgia in 2008 and most recently of Ukraine in February 2022, all of which were ostensibly (partly) based on a doctrine of protection of nationals, would automatically be disqualified as either disproportionate or simply as pretexts for intervening to achieve other purposes. These examples receive no further consideration in the context of this chapter, as they *ipso facto* lack any legal basis.[9] The discussion of State practice will be limited to a few instances where these conditions were arguably met. Nevertheless, since such cases are limited in number, most of the

[8] C. H. M. Waldock, 'The Regulation of the Use of Force by Individual States in International Law' (1952) 81 *Collected Courses of the Hague Academy of International Law* 455–517, pp. 462–4, 503.

[9] Franck, *Recourse to Force* (n. 2), pp. 86–8 (Grenada), 91–4 (Panama); N. Hajjami, 'The Intervention of the United States and Other Eastern Caribbean States in Grenada: 1983', in T. Ruys and O. Corten (eds.), *The Use of Force in International Law: A Case-Based Approach* (Oxford University Press, 2018), pp. 385–94; N. Tsagourias, 'The US Intervention in Panama: 1989', in Ruys and Corten (eds.), *Use of Force*, pp. 426–38; C. Gray, 'The Conflict in Georgia: 2008', in Ruys and Corten (eds.), *Use of Force*, pp. 712–28; M. E. O'Connell, 'The Crisis in Ukraine: 2014', in Ruys and Corten (eds.), *Use of Force*, pp. 855–72. In the last example, Russia based its claim to use force on multiple grounds, only one of which was the protection of persons with Russian nationality or ethnicity. The US invasion of Panama is also discussed in Fact Box 8.1 as an example of an unlawful intervention.

discussion will be more doctrinal in nature, weighing the arguments for and against the recognition of such a right, whether on the basis of necessity as a narrow exclusion of wrongfulness for acts which would otherwise be unlawful or on the basis of the right of self-defence, depending on the nature of the threat and other relevant circumstances.

### FACT BOX 8.1 THE US INVASION OF PANAMA

During the mid and late 1980s, relations between the United States and Panama became increasingly strained. The then de facto leader of Panama, General Manuel Noriega, had co-operated with the United States against the left-wing government of Nicaragua and had been a long-serving paid informant of the US Central Intelligence Agency. He was, however, also suspected of being involved in the narcotics trade and money laundering activities. He was therefore indicted for these alleged crimes by a US federal court in 1988. Efforts to persuade Noriega to voluntarily relinquish power and leave Panama in return for dropping the aforementioned charges were unsuccessful.

After elections in Panama appeared to have been won by a civilian opposition leader, Noriega had the results annulled. Street violence erupted between his supporters and those of the opposition candidate. In mid-December 1989, a car carrying four off-duty US servicemen was fired upon by Panamanian military personnel, resulting in the fatal wounding of one of the serviceman in the vehicle and the non-fatal wounding of a second. Another off-duty US serviceman and his wife who had witnessed the shooting incident were also held in custody and allegedly seriously mistreated by Panamanian military personnel. On 20 December 1989, US president G. H. W. Bush launched the invasion by nearly 28,000 troops and around 300 aircraft. Over the course of approximately five weeks, the United States took complete control of the country, arrested General Noriega, who had taken refuge in the diplomatic mission of the Vatican, and installed the president-elect, Guillermo Endara, as president.

The invasion was condemned by the UN General Assembly as a 'flagrant violation' of the UN Charter after a draft resolution in the Security Council was vetoed by France, the United Kingdom and the United States. It was also overwhelmingly condemned as a violation of the Rio Treaty by the Organization of American States. The invasion resulted in the death of some 200–300 Panamanian combatants, at least 300 civilians and 23 US service personnel, as well as hundreds of wounded on both sides.

**Sources:** 'Operation Just Cause', *Britannica*, https://tinyurl.com/2hh8wsym; D. A. M. Rodolfo, 'Legality of the 1989 Panama Invasion and the Responsibility to Protect Doctrine' (2016) 3(1) *United Nations University Peace and Progress Graduate Student Journal* 50–63, https://postgraduate.ias.unu.edu/upp/journal-issues/.

## 8.4 Justification of Rescue and Evacuation on the Basis of 'State of Necessity'

State of necessity as a legal basis for the rescue and evacuation of nationals applies when, due to circumstances beyond its control, the territorial State is temporarily unable to provide a sufficient degree of protection to safeguard foreign nationals from grave and impending danger. This can be due to circumstances such as breakdown of authority or loss of control over (a portion of) territory due to serious internal unrest, natural disaster or internal conflict. It must additionally be clear that consent from the territorial State is either unfeasible, due to lack of an effective functioning government capable of providing lawful consent, or would not be likely to be forthcoming in time or in such a way as to enable a safe and orderly evacuation of the intervening State's nationals. In such cases, the most plausible justification for effecting a non-consensual evacuation on the territory of another State is on the basis of a 'state of necessity' as a circumstance precluding the wrongfulness of what otherwise would be an unlawful intervention in another State.

The conditions for the successful invocation of necessity as an independent justification or as a circumstance precluding wrongfulness are set out in Article 25 of the Articles on the Responsibility of States for Internationally Wrongful Acts (ARSIWA). These conditions are stringent, and while the ARSIWA are non-binding in themselves, many of their provisions are considered to be an accurate reflection of customary law (see Chapter 15, below). The commentary of the International Law Commission (ILC) to Article 25 provides persuasive evidence of the customary nature of the plea of necessity as a circumstance precluding wrongfulness and the conditions pertaining to its invocation. The question of an emergency evacuation in the absence of consent of the territorial State is not addressed in the commentary. Nevertheless, the conditions the ILC commentary lists for invoking necessity to preclude the wrongfulness of an otherwise unlawful action do not exclude such an emergency measure.[10]

The genuine link between a State and its nationals translates into an essential interest of any State to prevent serious harm to its nationals. A temporary and limited non-consensual intervention to conduct the safe and orderly evacuation of such nationals, while falling within the ambit of

[10] See n. 7, above.

prima facie unlawful intervention, would not constitute an act of aggression in the sense of attempting to usurp the territorial State's authority over its territory. Nor does such an evacuation constitute a use of armed force directed against the territorial State, unless that State forcibly opposed it. As long as any force used was not a pretext for using force against the State where the evacuation was conducted, but was aimed at ensuring the safety of the evacuees and the personnel involved in the mission and was strictly confined to what was required to effectuate the evacuation, it could be justified as an emergency measure. Hence, while there is an indisputable violation of the territorial State's sovereignty, the limited and temporary nature of an evacuation of nationals does not affect an interest of the territorial State that would clearly outweigh the interest of the intervening State to safeguard its nationals from grave and impending danger to their lives or safety. The intervening State must evacuate its nationals with as little use of force as the situation strictly requires (in many, indeed most, cases no force is necessarily used at all) and without undue delay in leaving the territory of the State where the evacuation is conducted. Likewise, such a limited and temporary military presence does not plausibly constitute violation of a peremptory norm that would preclude the invocation of necessity. This is true only as long as the intervention does not involve use of force against the State.[11]

Examples of such non-consensual emergency interventions include various evacuations by France of its nationals in Chad and the Central African Republic in the 1990s and in 2003, the evacuation by the United States of its nationals from Liberia in 1990, the evacuation of EU nationals from Albania in 1997 and the multinational evacuation of foreign nationals from Beirut during the 2006 Israeli war with Hezbollah in Lebanon.[12]

None of these operations encountered any significant criticism as being unlawful, whether from States or in the legal literature on the topic. On balance, there are good reasons for accepting such emergency evacuations of nationals as falling within the purview of 'necessity' as a ground precluding the wrongfulness of a violation of the territorial State's sovereignty, as no other justification plausibly applies to such evacuations in the absence of

[11] Schachter, *International Law* (n. 3), pp. 165–7, 169–73; N. Tsagourias, 'Necessity and the Use of Force: A Special Regime' (2010) *Netherlands Yearbook of International Law* 11–44, at 38–42; J. Vidmar, 'The Use of Force as a Plea of Necessity' (2017) 111 *American Journal of International Law Unbound* 302–6; A. Laursen, 'The Use of Force and (the State of) Necessity' (2004) 37 *Vanderbilt Journal of Transnational Law* 485–526.

[12] Ruys, *'Armed Attack'* (n. 2), pp. 230–1; Gray, *International Law*(n. 2), p. 169 n. 243. See also Fact Box 8.2.

## FACT BOX 8.2 EVACUATION OF FOREIGN NATIONALS (LIBERIA, ALBANIA AND LEBANON)

### Liberia 1990

In August 1990, amid fighting between Liberian government troops and rebel forces, US Marines evacuated fifty-nine foreign nationals from Monrovia, Liberia, after reports were made of a rebel threat to capture foreign nationals in order to provoke outside intervention in the Liberian civil conflict. The Marines met with no resistance, and US officials stressed that the United States had no desire to become involved in the civil conflict or confront either side unless US nationals were directly threatened. The evacuation was reported to the Liberian president and to two of the rebel factions.

**Source**: M. A. Hiltzik, 'Marines Fly Americans from War-Torn Liberia', *Los Angeles Times*, 6 August 1990, https://tinyurl.com/mr272vfw

### Albania 1997

In January 1997, a meltdown of the Albanian economy, caused by the failure of various pyramid schemes that had emerged with the transition to a market economy, led to massive protests that deteriorated into widespread civil unrest, with criminal gangs and various groups arming themselves with weapons from the government arms depots. Widespread looting and mob violence followed, and various governments, including a number from the European Union (France, Germany, Greece, Italy, Romania and others), Turkey and the United States began evacuating their nationals from the country to ships offshore and to nearby Montenegro by helicopter. There were some incidents of the troops conducting the evacuation and the evacuees being fired on by gunmen, and defensive fire was returned. No evacuees or evacuating forces were injured and there was no organized armed attempt to prevent the evacuation. Subsequently, the Security Council authorized a multinational peace force led by Italy to assist the Albanian government in restoring order.

**Sources**: T. Wilkinson, 'Foreigners by the Hundreds Flee Anarchy in Albania', *Los Angeles Times*, 15 March 1997, https://tinyurl.com/3j2aamss; Riccardo Marchiò, '"Operation Alba": A European Approach to Peace Support Operations in the Balkans' (2000) US Army War College Research Paper, https://apps.dtic.mil/sti/pdfs/ADA378201.pdf.

### Lebanon 2006

As the Israel-Lebanon War of 2006 intensified and fighting spread, many foreign governments conducted large-scale evacuation of their nationals from Beirut and other parts of the country. Thousands of foreign nationals were evacuated by sea and air from the country in July 2006, reportedly under strict conditions imposed by Israel. There were no armed incidents nor any opposition from the Lebanese authorities.

**Source**: B. Whitaker, 'Mass Evacuation from Beirut Under Way', *The Guardian*, 18 July 2006, https://tinyurl.com/bdez3ebe

consent by the territorial State. This basis fits such situations better than the justification of self-defence would under such circumstances, since in the absence of a clear intention to use or threaten the use of force against a given State's nationals, it is not credible to view a mere emergency situation as an armed attack on the State. The alternative of basing such acts on a vague stand-alone right of protection of nationals is even less persuasive as a matter of law, and less acceptable from a policy viewpoint as potentially opening the door to other supposed justifications for using force.

## 8.5 Self-Defence as a Justification for Rescue and Evacuation of Nationals

In the second type of scenario, where the lives or safety of nationals are directly threatened, either by the authorities of the State where they are located or by an armed group as a means of coercion against the parent State of the nationals, there are plausible grounds for viewing such a threat as an (incipient) armed attack on the parent State of the threatened nationals justifying measures of self-defence in the form of a rescue and forcible evacuation. The reason for this is that violence directed against a State by threatening the lives of its nationals who happen to be on the territory of the State which is the source of the threat is plausibly seen as a form of indirect armed attack on the State whose nationals are threatened, despite the extraterritorial location of the threatened nationals. The purpose of the threat is to coerce the parent State and force it to do, or abstain from doing, something.[13]

Clearly, an attack on troops, State vessels and aircraft lawfully present on another State's territory would be regarded as an attack on the State. The same would apply to an attack on high-level State officials or State representatives on an official mission. The same probably applies to an attack on a diplomatic mission. Likewise, an attack on a passenger vessel or civil passenger aircraft having the nationality of a particular State, assuming it was done to coerce the flag State, would also qualify as an attack on the State (see Chapter 13, below). There is no reason to exclude an attack on a parent State's nationals located in another State from qualifying as an armed attack on the parent State when there is a serious risk to the lives and/or safety of those nationals and the attack is clearly intended to coerce the parent State

[13] This line of argument has been put forward by various authors, including D. W. Bowett, *Self-Defence in International Law* (Manchester University Press, 1958), pp. 91–105; Y. Dinstein, *War, Aggression and Self-Defence* (Cambridge University Press, 2017), pp. 219–20; Schachter, *International Law* (n. 3), p. 166.

into taking or refraining from certain action. In other words, when violence is directed against a group of persons who not only have a clear relationship of nationality with their parent State but have been targeted specifically because of that relationship with their parent State, there is a strong case that the use or threat of violence directed against them constitutes an attack on their parent State. This, in our view, applies regardless of whether the number of nationals subjected to (the threat of) violence is substantial or more limited. We have already explained why there are good reasons for not excluding smaller-scale uses of force against a State from the notion of 'armed attack'. Self-defence does not, in our view, depend on the number of persons who are the object of the attack, although the scale of the attack will obviously influence the level of the permissible response.[14]

If the attack is carried out by or with the substantial involvement of the State where the threatened nationals are located, the author of the attack would obviously be the State which is responsible for the (threatened) violence. If, on the other hand, the threat to the lives of the nationals originates from an autonomous armed group (AAG) operating on another State's territory, the author of the attack would be the AAG and not the State where the armed group was operating. In either case, the principles of necessity, proportionality and immediacy would require that the measures of self-defence be aimed at ending the threat by safely evacuating the threatened nationals with the use of no more force than is strictly required to neutralize the ongoing or threatened violence and ensure the safe evacuation of the threatened nationals, the personnel conducting the operation and any nationals of a third State who might find themselves under the same threat and wish to be evacuated along with the intervening State's nationals. The other conditions related to the exercise of self-defence in response to attack by AAGs have been discussed in Chapter 6 and need not be repeated here.[15]

Some examples of operations to protect nationals based on self-defence have been criticized (sometimes quite justifiably) as being excessive or simply as pretexts for armed intervention on another State's territory for reasons unrelated to the protection of nationals. These include the previously mentioned examples. Nevertheless, neither the International Court of Justice (ICJ) nor the Security Council has made a blanket assertion that

[14] See Chapter 6, Section 6.4.1, above, where we argue that an armed attack is any use of force above the level of an inconsequential act involving armed force which causes neither loss of life nor significant damage or disruption in the target State.

[15] On the modalities of exercising self-defence against attacks mounted by autonomous non-state armed groups, see Chapter 6, Section 6.5.3, above.

self-defence is *ipso facto* inapplicable to rescue of nationals as a matter of law.[16] Likewise, while many States and some authors have been critical of the assertion of self-defence as a justification for armed intervention under the banner of the protection of nationals, most of this criticism has targeted real or alleged excessive use of force on particular occasions or viewed such use of force as prone to misuse. Be that as it may, there is no reason why the right of self-defence in the context of the rescue of nationals should be considered inapplicable. The argument that the right of self-defence in connection with the protection of nationals has been misused in the past, or that it is capable of being misused, can apply to virtually any right without implying that the particular right should in such instances be considered void or as having lapsed. Misuse or abuse of any right will have the consequence of rendering the individual reliance on that right *in that instance* inoperative or void. That does not, however, vitiate the right itself as a matter of law.[17]

While self-defence has been frequently asserted in relation to the protection of nationals, only a very limited number of cases would qualify as rescue and evacuation operations based on self-defence. Probably the most plausible and accepted example of such an operation was the Israeli rescue operation in Kampala in 1976, in which Israel successfully evacuated a group of nationals taken hostage by terrorists (see Fact Box 8.3). Despite the release of the non-Israeli passengers (apart from a number of non-Israeli nationals who were Jewish and the crew of the hijacked aircraft, who refused to leave without their passengers), there was strong evidence of complicity with the hijackers on the part of the Ugandan authorities and a clear threat to the lives of those still in the hands of the hijackers. The hostages were used as a means of pressure on the Israeli government to release persons in custody – which was an act aimed at the Israeli State. Moreover, negotiations were almost certainly not conducted in good faith by the Ugandan government given its open collusion with the hijackers, and there was little prospect of the hostages' release unless Israel accepted the hijacker's conditions. The rescue operation was conducted in a manner designed to bring about the safe extraction of the hostages with as little

[16] Various instances of force declared as self-defence to protect nationals but widely criticized as disproportionate or as a pretext to use force for other purposes include the US invasions of Grenada and Panama and the Russian invasions of Georgia and Ukraine. See references in n. 9, above. No blanket assertion that rescue operations are *ipso facto* unlawful has hitherto been made by either the UN Security Council or the International Court of Justice, despite the matter having come before these organs on various occasions.

[17] Higgins, *Problems and Process* (n. 3), pp. 245–51.

### FACT BOX 8.3 THE ENTEBBE RESCUE

On 27 June 1976, while en route from Tel Aviv to Paris, an Air France airliner was hijacked by a group of Palestinian and German extremists belonging respectively to a breakaway faction of the Popular Front for the Liberation of Palestine (PFLP) and the Revolutionary Cells terrorist group. The hijackers, purporting to be passengers, boarded the aircraft during a short landing at Athens airport. The aircraft was flown to Entebbe in Uganda, where it was met by Ugandan troops who apparently knew in advance of the hijacking and appeared to know the hijackers. The plane had 248 passengers and 12 crew members on board at the time of the hijacking. The four hijackers were later joined in Entebbe by six additional armed men. Ugandan president Idi Amin greeted the hijackers and assured the hostages that they were 'innocent' but that the cause of the Palestinians was 'just' and that they would be released as soon as Israel met their demands for the release of fifty-eight persons held for various offences in France, Germany, Israel, Kenya and Switzerland. Negotiations with the hijackers by the French government led to the release of forty-seven elderly and infirm hostages, who were flown to Paris and who provided some information on the situation, including the apparent co-operation between the hijackers and the Ugandan authorities. The remaining hostages were then separated into a group of 148 non-Israelis, who were subsequently released, and a group of 94 Israeli and other Jewish passengers, along with the aircrew, who insisted on staying with them. The hijackers threatened to execute the latter group if their demands were not met by 1 July, a deadline subsequently extended to 4 July at 11:00 a.m. after it appeared that Israel was ready to meet their demands.

During the early morning hours of 4 July an Israeli commando group of some 100 men in three transport aircraft landed at Entebbe airport, having flown some 4,000 km. Within an hour that saw a firefight with Ugandan troops in the control tower and the destruction of eleven Ugandan fighter planes on the ground to prevent pursuit, the hostages were freed and evacuated to the waiting aircraft. One Israeli commando died during the firefight and five others were wounded. Three hostages were also killed during the rescue along with all of the hijackers. In addition, between twenty and forty-five Ugandan soldiers involved in guarding the hostages and in the firefight also lost their lives. On its way back to Israel, the aircraft made a refuelling and medical stop in Nairobi, where one of the five wounded Israeli soldiers succumbed to his injuries. The aircraft landed in Israel later the same day. Kenya was accused by President Amin of complicity in the raid, and some 245 Kenyans resident in Uganda were massacred and several thousand forced to flee. An elderly female hostage, Dora Bloch, who was at a hospital in Kampala when the rescue took place was murdered by Ugandan agents, along with several medical personnel who were attending her and attempted to intercede on her behalf.

Debates in the Security Council were inconclusive. Three African States sponsored a resolution condemning the mission as an act of aggression, and three Western States sponsored another one condemning terrorism and aircraft hijacking. Neither resolution was adopted. No attempt was made by the opponents of the

FACT BOX 8.3 (*cont.*)

rescue mission to bring the matter before the General Assembly after the Security Council failed to reach a decision.

**Sources:** *Keesing's Record of World Events*, vol. 22, August 1976, pp. 27888, 27891; 'Israelis Rescue Entebbe Hostages' (*BBC On This Day*, 4 July 1976), https://tinyurl.com/2ycn7643; UNSCOR, 31st yr, 1943rd meeting, UN Doc. S/PV. 1943 (14 July 1976).

collateral effect as possible. Although the operation was criticized as being unnecessary or excessive by some States (probably at least as much for political as for legal reasons), there was widespread acceptance of its necessity and the manner in which it was conducted at the time.[18]

## 8.6 Conclusion

There is no good reason to try to establish a new customary right of rescue of nationals, since the Charter prohibition only permits force used within the established 'exceptions' to the prohibition on the use of force. Equally, there is no need to prove the existence of the right of self-defence or the recognition of a 'state of necessity' as a justification for an otherwise unlawful act. No State has claimed a new right of rescue of nationals; in the absence of any such claim, there is no need to consider whether such a right meets the criteria for the emergence of a new rule of

[18] For analysis of the Entebbe rescue mission, see, inter alia, Franck, *Recourse to Force* (n. 2), pp. 82–6; C. Kreß and B. Nußberger, 'The Entebbe Raid: 1976', in Ruys and Corten (eds.), *Use of Force* (n. 9), p. 220; U. Beyerlin, '*Die israelische Befreiungsaktion von Entebbe in völkerrechtlicher Sicht*' (1977) 37 *Zeitschrift für ausländisches öffentliches Recht und Völkerrecht* 213–43. For a factual and operational perspective, see S. Dunstan, *Entebbe: The Most Daring Raid of Israel's Special Forces* (Rosen, 2011). The Security Council debates were heated and reached no conclusion, with neither a condemnation of Israel nor a resolution condemning terrorism being adopted. The positions of most States had arguably as much to do with political considerations as with a considered appraisal of the legal dimension of the parties' positions as presented in the Security Council. The oft-repeated statement that only Western States were prepared to support or condone the Israeli operation is inaccurate. The rescue operation flew over the territory of Ethiopia and Kenya and was allowed to land and refuel at Nairobi airport. Other non-Western States (Panama, Romania) were not prepared to support a condemnation of Israel in the Security Council. Uganda and other States that supported a condemnation did not refer the matter to the UN General Assembly under the 'Uniting for Peace' procedure, because they were not convinced of sufficient support to obtain such a condemnation for this action. See Franck, *Recourse to Force* (n. 2), p. 85.

customary international law. There can be no doubt that self-defence is a well-established right and that there is no need to prove its existence. On the other hand, it must be established that it can apply in the type of scenario set out here. We think we have provided persuasive arguments to that effect – as have others before us. While there is certainly room for discussion on whether these arguments are conclusive, there are in any event cogent reasons for believing that self-defence can be applicable and successfully invoked if the relevant conditions are met. Likewise, while the justification of 'state of necessity' is subject to stringent conditions and has been openly invoked only on a limited basis, there is persuasive evidence of it constituting a recognized ground under customary law for precluding the wrongfulness of an otherwise unlawful act, where the conditions pertaining to its successful invocation are met. We provided arguments for why it could well serve as a justification for a non-consensual evacuation of nationals along the lines set out above.

# 9

# Armed Reprisals and the Law on the Use of Force

## 9.1 Introduction

The present chapter discusses armed reprisals that take place outside a situation of armed conflict. It does not address 'belligerent reprisals', which occur during armed conflict. In particular, when referring to 'reprisals' throughout this chapter, unless otherwise noted, we are referring to cross-border incidental uses of armed force by a State against another State in response to a prior wrongful act, or one perceived as such.

While the bulk of the chapter addresses reprisals by one State against another, the history of reprisals by individuals or communities against foreigners or their communities is also given brief attention. The chapter then looks at the evolution and legality of inter-State reprisals both before and after the adoption of the UN Charter.

## 9.2 Pre-Charter History of Reprisals

### *9.2.1 Private Reprisals*

So-called private reprisals, by individuals or communities, were practised among the City-States of the ancient Mediterranean world and were regulated both by treaty and by local law.[1] A community could be held responsible for the wrong committed by one of its members against a foreigner if it failed to give the latter justice. In such a case, property or members of that community could be seized by the victim's own community.[2] The expansion of the Roman Empire seems, however, to have put an end to such practices on the territories under Roman rule.[3]

[1] E. Colbert, *Retaliation in International Law* (King's Crown Press, 1948), p. 10.
[2] C. Wampach, *Armed Reprisals from Medieval Times to 1945* (Nomos, 2020), p. 50.
[3] Colbert, *Retaliation* (n. 1), p. 11.

They reappeared with the decay of the Roman Empire and the ensuing disappearance of a superior authority that could dispense justice.[4]

During the centuries immediately following the fall of the Roman Empire, private reprisals developed unconstrainedly and constituted an obstacle to trade and peaceful relations.[5] From the tenth century onwards, attempts were made to restrict such reprisals,[6] and by the thirteenth century they had become regulated by both local and treaty law,[7] albeit not in a homogenous way.[8]

Generally speaking, for a private reprisal to be lawful, treaty and local law required (i) an initial wrong suffered by the victim; (ii) the exhaustion of local remedies by the victim in the wrongdoer's community; (iii) followed by a 'denial of justice' by the wrongdoer or his or her community.[9] Only then could the victim (iv) apply for a licence (letter of reprisal or letter of marque), from his or her own sovereign, to engage in a (v) proportionate reprisal against the wrongdoer and/or his community.[10] These conditions were generally echoed in Bartolus Saxoferrato's *Tractatus Represaliarum*, completed in 1354, which was the first academic work to examine thoroughly the matter of reprisals and explain contemporaneous practice.[11] These requirements were reiterated by subsequent jurists, including Giovanni da Legnano, Francisco de Vitoria, Alberico Gentili and Hugo Grotius.[12]

While the analogies between private reprisals and (just) wars were many at the time, private reprisals were in fact an exercise of delegated law enforcement and were not regarded as war between sovereigns.[13] Reprisals also differed from self-defence: the latter was designed to prevent an injury from occurring; the former was remedial and designed to obtain redress for an injury after it had occurred.[14] Reprisals were also differentiated from retorsion, which entailed a sovereign enacting

[4] Wampach, *Armed Reprisals* (n. 2), p. 51, citing Bartolus de Saxoferrato and Giovanni da Legnano.

[5] Ibid.

[6] Ibid.

[7] Ibid., p. 52; Colbert, *Retaliation* (n. 1), p. 12; H. W. Spiegel, 'Origin and Development of Denial of Justice' (1938) 32 *American Journal of International Law* 63–81, at 69.

[8] Wampach, *Armed Reprisals* (n. 2), p. 59.

[9] Colbert, *Retaliation* (n. 1), pp. 15–27; Wampach, *Armed Reprisals* (n. 2), p. 53.

[10] Wampach, *Armed Reprisals* (n. 2), pp. 53, 68.

[11] Ibid., p. 59; Spiegel, 'Origin and Development' (n. 7), p. 70.

[12] Spiegel, 'Origin and Development' (n. 7), pp. 71–8.

[13] S. Neff, *War and the Law of Nations: A General History* (Cambridge University Press, 2005), p. 80.

[14] Ibid., p. 123.

discriminatory measures against foreigners in response to similar measures being enacted by the country of said foreigners.[15] Finally, reprisals were different from retaliation, which involved inflicting on one's enemy the very same wrong that the latter had originally committed.[16]

### 9.2.2 *Public Reprisals Prior to the UN Charter*

With the emergence of modern States, private reprisals began to be replaced by so-called public reprisals, which entailed action by a State against another State. By the beginning of the eighteenth century, the practice of private reprisals had declined,[17] although States still issued letters of marque (licences) for privateering, following the practice of private reprisals. Privateering was abolished in 1856.[18] Gradually, States became the only actors in the practice of reprisals.[19] The new types of reprisal were not confined to the sequestering of property; they could entail any act, including the use of armed force to occupy part of the targeted State's territory or impose a naval blockade.[20] Moreover, their purpose was not only to obtain compensation for a past injury but also to coerce a State to alter its conduct and comply with a (purportedly) violated obligation.[21]

The practice of public reprisals flourished throughout the nineteenth century,[22] especially in the form of so-called pacific blockades,[23] and continued into the first two decades of the twentieth century. As the nineteenth century was seen as the 'classic epoch of reprisals',[24] the legality of reprisals was accepted, although the lawfulness of pacific blockades was the subject of abundant doctrinal debate.[25] As regards

15 Ibid., p. 124.
16 Ibid., pp. 123–4.
17 Colbert, *Retaliation* (n. 1), pp. 57–8; Wampach, *Armed Reprisals* (n. 2), pp. 77–83.
18 Privateering declined after the end of the Napoleonic Wars and was formally abolished in the Declaration of Paris in 1856. For a discussion of one of the reasons behind this decline, see, for example, H. Hillmann and C. Gathmann, 'Overseas Trade and the Decline of Privateering' (2011) 71 *Journal of Economic History* 730–61.
19 Wampach, *Armed Reprisals* (n. 2), p. 97.
20 Neff, *War and the Law of Nations* (n. 13), pp. 226, 228–9; Wampach, *Armed Reprisals* (n. 2), pp. 135–40, 190–2.
21 Neff, *War and the Law of Nations* (n. 13), p. 226.
22 Wampach, *Armed Reprisals* (n. 2), pp. 121–2.
23 Ibid., pp. 158–3, 190; Neff, *War and the Law of Nations* (n. 13), pp. 234–5.
24 C. de Visscher, *Theory and Reality in Public International Law* (Princeton University Press, 1968), p. 296.
25 Wampach, *Armed Reprisals* (n. 2), pp. 182–8.

conditions of legality, reprisals still required an initial wrong, which was largely understood as an infringement of a State's rights. A denial of justice, in the sense used for private reprisals, was also required in theory; in practice, this meant that the defending State had to attempt to obtain redress by diplomatic means.[26] The fulfilment of this condition was, however, left to be determined by the defending State.[27] There was also a general requirement of proportionality between the amount of force being used and the initial wrong,[28] but this was not always reflected in State practice,[29] especially where the purpose was to coerce a State into fulfilling its obligations rather than to obtain compensation for a past offence.[30] Despite being practised by States against each other, such reprisals were seen as 'amicable', albeit 'compulsive', methods of dispute settlement that did not amount to war.[31]

The legality of reprisals was also confirmed in the Treaty of Versailles.[32] Accordingly, § 18 of Annex II to Part VIII of the Treaty of Versailles explicitly allowed Allied and Associated Powers to resort to, inter alia, reprisals in case of voluntary default by Germany on its obligations.[33]

As described above in Chapter 3, the Covenant of the League of Nations did not unequivocally prohibit war between League members. Moreover, the Covenant remained silent as regards the legality of reprisals. It did, however, require its members to submit their disputes to arbitration, judicial settlement or to the League Council and prohibited resort to war before a lapse of three months after the resolution was rendered.[34] This was not necessarily apparent in the League's tackling of the 1923 Corfu incident, which involved the bombing and occupation of Corfu by Italy in response to the assassination of Italian officials in Greece.[35] While the dispute was not settled by the Council,[36] a Special

26 Colbert, *Retaliation* (n. 1), pp. 51–4.
27 Wampach, *Armed Reprisals* (n. 2), pp. 76–7, 87.
28 Neff, *War and the Law of Nations* (n. 13), p. 226.
29 Colbert, *Retaliation* (n. 1), pp. 76–80.
30 Wampach, *Armed Reprisals* (n. 2), pp. 133–4.
31 K. Tibori-Szabó, *Anticipatory Action in Self-Defence* (Springer, 2011), p. 70 n. 62.
32 Wampach, *Armed Reprisals* (n. 2), p. 237.
33 Treaty of Peace with Germany (Versailles, 28 June 1919) (Treaty of Versailles), pt VIII, annex II, § 18, www.census.gov/history/pdf/treaty_of_versailles-112018.pdf,.
34 See Chapter 3, Sections 3.3 and 3.4.
35 Tibori-Szabó, *Anticipatory Action* (n. 31), p. 86; Wampach, *Armed Reprisals* (n. 2), pp. 247–8.
36 Wampach, *Armed Reprisals* (n. 2), pp. 251–2.

Commission of Jurists was set up by the League to answer a series of legal questions arising from the incident.[37] One of these questions was whether 'measures of coercion which are not meant to constitute acts of war' were consistent with the terms of the Covenant.[38] The jurists answered as follows: 'Coercive measures which are not intended to constitute acts of war may, or may not, be consistent with the provisions of Articles 12 to 15 of the Covenant, and it is for the Council, when the dispute has been submitted to it, to decide immediately, having due regard to all the circumstances of the case and to the nature of the measures adopted, whether it should recommend the maintenance or the withdrawal of such measures.'[39] The inscrutable answer of the jurists, giving the Council a wide margin of appreciation in the matter, showed that, notwithstanding the restrictive purpose of the Covenant, the outlawry of 'coercive measures' was still not generally acknowledged in the first decades of the twentieth century.[40]

That reprisals were not unlawful was further confirmed by the 1928 findings of a Special Arbitral Tribunal set up under the terms of the Treaty of Versailles in the *Naulilaa* case. The Tribunal was mandated to adjudicate a 1914 incident in which the German colony of South West Africa ordered reprisals on Portuguese targets after German officials were killed by Portuguese soldiers in the Angolan fortress of Naulilaa.[41] In its findings of 31 July 1928, the Tribunal described reprisals as measures of self-help responding to an internationally wrongful act. Reprisals had to be preceded by a request to remedy the wrong and had to be proportionate to the initial injury. Moreover, according to the Tribunal, reprisals were aimed at imposing on the offending State the reparation of the offence or the return to equality, in order to avoid new offences.[42] The *Naulilaa* arbitral award is generally seen as a key decision on the subject of reprisals: it not only set out the applicable legal conditions but also

37 Colbert, *Retaliation* (n. 1), pp. 83-84.

38 'Questions Resulting from the Corfu Incident Submitted September 28, 1923, by the Council of the League of Nations to the Special Commission of Jurists and the Replies of That Commission' *International Conciliation* No. 199 (June 1924) 158–63, at 159–60. See also Colbert, *Retaliation* (n. 1), p. 84.

39 'Questions Resulting from the Corfu Incident' (n. 38), pp. 159–60.

40 Tibori-Szabó, *Anticipatory Action* (n. 31), p. 86.

41 *Responsabilité de l'Allemagne à raison des dommages causés dans les colonies portugaises du Sud de l'Afrique*, Award, 31 July 1928, Reports of International Arbitral Awards, vol. II, pp. 1011–33.

42 Ibid., pp. 1026–7.

indicated that, at least during the interbellum period, reprisals were still considered to be lawful under the listed conditions.

The Kellogg-Briand Pact of 1928 outlawed war 'as an instrument of national policy' (see Chapter 3), but it remained silent on the issue of reprisals.

The legality of reprisals was finally addressed by the Institut de Droit international in its 1934 Resolution on the regime applicable to peacetime reprisals.[43] In Article 1 of the resolution, the Institut defined reprisals as coercive measures in breach of the ordinary rules of the Law of Nations that are taken by a State following unlawful acts committed against it by another State and which, through infliction of damage, are intended to compel the latter to comply with the law. Article 3 of the Resolution differentiated between armed and unarmed reprisals. The former category was defined as involving the use of force in any form, including military, naval or air force. Article 4 went on to prohibit armed reprisals 'under the same conditions as recourse to war'. The Resolution did not detail these conditions, but Article 6 put forward a list of six requirements that reprisals had to meet in order to be considered legal: (i) a request for redress had to be made to the offending State prior to any reprisal; (ii) reprisals had to be proportionate to the wrong; (iii) the effects of reprisals had to be limited to the offending State and the rights of third States and individuals had to be respected as much as possible; (iv) the laws of humanity and the dictates of public conscience had to be respected; (v) the object of reprisals must not change during their employment; and (vi) reprisals had to end as soon as the goal was achieved.[44]

Both the Resolution and the aforementioned findings of the *Naulilaa* Tribunal set out requirements that could be traced back to those applicable to private reprisals and which also reflected subsequent customary law regulating public reprisals. While the Resolution did not consider armed reprisals illegal, the tendency to restrict their use is apparent from the wording and conditions set out therein.

## 9.3 The Prohibition of Reprisals under the UN Charter

As detailed above in Chapter 3, the horrors of the Second World War gave a new urgency to moves to prohibit war. The UN Charter, adopted in 1945, contained in Article 2(4) a broad prohibition on the threat or use

43 Institut de Droit international, Session of Paris – 1934, 'Régime des représailles en temps de paix' (Resolution, 19 October 1934), www.idi-iil.org/app/uploads/2017/06/1934_paris_03_fr.pdf.

44 Ibid., art. 6; Wampach, *Armed Reprisals* (n. 2), p. 276.

of force, which was not limited to war but encompassed any use or threat of force, except those permitted by other provisions of the Charter (see Chapter 4, above). Given that the only permitted uses of force were those in self-defence (enshrined in Article 51) and collective enforcement measures mandated by the UN Security Council (set out in Articles 39–42), it was clear that any other uses of force, including reprisals, would be banned.

The ban on reprisals, as measures of self-help, was confirmed by the International Court of Justice (ICJ) in its *Corfu Channel* judgment. The case concerned, inter alia, the legality of a UK minesweeping operation in Albanian territorial waters following the damage caused to British destroyers by exploding mines. The Court found that the minesweeping had violated Albanian sovereignty because the 'alleged right of intervention' was 'the manifestation of a policy of force, such as has, in the past, given rise to most serious abuses and such as cannot, whatever be the present defects in international organization, find a place in international law'.[45] The Court further held that the notions of 'self-help' or 'self-protection' asserted by the United Kingdom were unacceptable, as '[b]etween independent States, respect for territorial sovereignty is an essential foundation of international relations'.[46]

The illegality of reprisals was explicitly set out two decades later, in the UN General Assembly's Friendly Relations Declaration, which stated, inter alia, that 'States have a duty to refrain from acts of reprisal involving the use of force'.[47]

## 9.4 Post-Charter State Practice and *opinio juris*

Despite the new prohibition on the use of force, States continued to resort to reprisals in the second half of the twentieth century. Nonetheless, given that the only unilateral use of force permitted by the Charter was in self-defence, many States sought to justify their cross-border armed incursions, including reprisals, as defensive action. This led to arguments that, at least to all appearance, conflated the purpose and scope of self-defence with those of reprisals.

[45] ICJ, *Corfu Channel (United Kingdom of Great Britain and Northern Ireland* v. *Albania)* (Merits), Judgment, 9 April 1949, ICJ Reports 1949, p. 35.

[46] Ibid., p. 35.

[47] Declaration on Principles of International Law Concerning Friendly Relations and Co-operation among States in accordance with the Charter of the United Nations, UNGA Res. 2625 (24 October 1970).

Most controversies arose in relation to those instances of State practice where a State was responding with armed force to an attack that had already ended, resulting in loss of life and/or property damage but no occupation of territory. Such instances often involved uses of force against attacks carried out by non-State actors and relied on the 'accumulation of events' theory purportedly justifying such uses of force as self-defence. As set out above in Chapter 6, the 'accumulation of events' or 'needle-prick' test is increasingly recognized today as a form of self-defence against armed attacks by non-State actors.[48] Nevertheless, for much of the second half of the twentieth century, this argument was rejected by the UN Security Council (UNSC, Security Council) and many States.[49] Armed actions relying on this theory were condemned as disproportionate and/or unprovoked acts of reprisal, retaliation or invasion.[50]

For instance, in December 1968 Israeli forces launched an attack on Beirut airport in response to an attack two days earlier in Athens on an Israeli passenger plane (see Fact Box 9.1). Before the Security Council, Israel claimed that it was duty-bound to take action in self-defence 'designed to prevent any repetition of this nefarious attack',[51] which it also described as 'the culmination of a long sustained and officially encouraged campaign'.[52] At least four members of the Security Council explicitly described the raid as an unlawful reprisal or retaliation;[53] a UNSC resolution condemned it as a 'premeditated' and 'grave' attack against Beirut airport.[54]

Israel used the above argument throughout the period 1950s–1980s to justify its armed incursions into the territory of its Arab neighbours. Similar arguments were put forward by other States, such as Portugal,

[48] See Chapter 6, Section 6.5.4.

[49] F. McKinnon, 'Reprisals as a Method of Enforcing International Law' (1991) 4 *Leiden Journal of International Law* 221–48, at 226.

[50] See, for instance, UNSC Resolutions S/RES/101 (1953) (expressing 'the strongest censure' of Israel's 'retaliatory actions'); S/RES/188 (1964) (condemning reprisals as 'incompatible with the purposes and principles of the United Nations' and deploring the British military action in Yemen); S/RES/228 (1966) (censoring Israel for 'actions of military reprisal'); S/RES/290 (1970) (strongly condemning Portugal for the 'invasion of the Republic of Guinea'). See also S/RES/106 (1955); S/RES/111 (1956); S/RES/248 (1968); S/RES/256 (1968); S/RES/262 (1968); S/RES/265 (1969); S/RES/270 (1969); S/RES/ 280 (1970).

[51] UN Security Council Official Records (SCOR), 23rd session, 1460th meeting, 29 December 1968, UN Doc. S/PV.1460, para. 59.

[52] Ibid., para. 52.

[53] Ibid., paras. 74, 89, 137–8, 144.

[54] S/RES/262 (1968).

**FACT BOX 9.1 THE BEIRUT AIRPORT RAID (1968)**

On 26 December 1968, two members of the Popular Front for the Liberation of Palestine (Popular Front) attacked an Israeli El Al aircraft on a lay-over at Athens airport en route to New York. The attackers used automatic weapons and grenades. One passenger was killed and a crew member was injured in the attack. Both were Israeli citizens. The plane caught fire and was severely damaged. Both attackers were captured by the Greek authorities. The Popular Front issued a statement from its office in Beirut, claiming responsibility for the attack.

In response, Israel launched Operation Gift two days later. On the evening of 28 December 1968, six helicopters carrying Israeli special forces landed at Beirut airport. After landing, the special forces split into three groups and attacked planes and facilities at the airport with explosives and machine guns. The attack lasted around twenty to thirty minutes before the Israeli forces withdrew using the same helicopters. Fourteen aircraft were destroyed, all belonging to Lebanese airlines: Middle East Airlines (MEA), Air Libea (Lebanese International Airways) and Trans-Mediterranean Airlines. Additional damage to hangars and other airport installations was reported.

**Sources**: 'Editorial Note', in *Foreign Relations of the United States*, 1964–8, vol. XX, Arab-Israeli Dispute 1967–8, Doc. No. 367 https://tinyurl.com/3kks5keb; R. A. Falk, 'The Beirut Raid and the International Law of Retaliation' (1969) 63 *American Journal of International Law* 415–43, at 415–20; F. McKinnon, 'Reprisals as a Method of Enforcing International Law' (1991) 4 *Leiden Journal of International Law* 221–48, at 225; SCOR, 23rd session, 1460th meeting, 29 December 1968, UN Doc. S/PV.1460, paras. 15, 27–8; 'Israel's Wars & Operations: Operation Gift', AICE Jewish Virtual Library, www.jewishvirtuallibrary.org/operation-gift.

South Africa, the United Kingdom and the United States, most of which were likewise condemned.[55]

The reasons for this condemnation and apparent conflation with reprisals stemmed from the very nature of the 'accumulation of events' theory, as well as from the manner in which it was implemented. By its nature, this theory justified defensive action against both past and future small-scale attacks; these attacks, accumulated over time, were said to amount to an actual armed attack within the meaning of Article 51 of the UN Charter.[56] As a consequence, the defending State was permitted to resort to self-defence against the totality of the attacks as opposed to

[55] *Repertoire of the Practice of the Security Council: Supplement 1964–1965* (United Nations, 1965), chap. 8, p. 128; SCOR, 41st session, 2674th meeting, 15 April 1986, UN Doc. S/PV.2674, p. 17; Tibori-Szabó, *Anticipatory Action* (n. 31), pp. 157–9, 208.

[56] See Chapter 6, Section 6.5.4, above.

individual acts; for this reason, the defensive action envisaged under the 'accumulation of events' test could be larger in scale than the individual small-scale attacks, as its purpose was to respond to all such attacks and deter future ones. Accordingly, proponents of this theory argued that in order to assess the necessity and proportionality of such action one had to take into consideration the entire conflictual context and not just the last incident preceding the defensive action.[57]

Most States and the Security Council refused to interpret self-defence in this manner. Needless to say, reasons were often political.[58] Reluctance to accept the 'accumulation of events' theory also stemmed, however, from genuine concern about the interpretation of the law. Relying on the wording of Article 51 of the Charter, self-defence was seen as necessitating a singular, large-scale armed attack that could be thwarted only by the use of force in self-defence. Small-scale attacks, albeit frequent, were not considered to fall under Article 51 of the Charter. Accordingly, armed action by States against repeated small-scale attacks was seen as a reprisal against the last such attack and, by definition, a disproportionate one, as the purpose of deterring future attacks was not accepted either.

These concerns were understandable to a certain extent. First, the very nature of reprisals dictated a response post-dating an attack – which was always the case with the aforementioned State practice. Since small-scale attacks were not seen as armed attacks within the meaning of Article 51, the response of the defending State was seen as an illegal incursion or reprisal. Second, because of the wording of Article 51, many States and commentators did not accept that self-defence could be used to anticipate future attacks, so the response of the defending State was seen as aimed at punishing another State or coercing it into altering its conduct to comply with an obligation – which happened to be the main purpose of reprisals. Third, whatever purpose the defending State's actions might have, this was very difficult to elucidate, especially when an entire context of repeated attacks and ongoing conflict had to be considered. Fourth, many instances of State practice relying on the 'accumulation of events'

[57] D. Bowett, 'Reprisals Involving Recourse to Armed Force' (1972) 66 *American Journal of International Law* 1–36, at 2–4. See also 'Addendum to the Eighth Report on State Responsibility, by Mr. Roberto Ago: The internationally wrongful act of the State, source of international responsibility (part 1) (concluded)', UN Doc. A/CN.4/318/Add.5–7, *Yearbook of the International Law Commission 1980*, vol. II(1) (1980), pp. 69–70.

[58] Tibori-Szabó, *Anticipatory Action* (n. 31), pp. 209, 215–17.

argument used a disproportionate amount of force by any measure, exacerbating concerns over the illegality of the action.

To address these difficulties, various solutions were put forward, mainly by legal scholars. Characterizing the 1968 Beirut raid by Israel as illegal, even as an instance of reprisal, Falk proposed a legal framework for 'retaliatory' use of force against prior terrorist acts. The framework set out a number of conditions, most of which reflected prior customary practice regarding reprisals, but it also required an overall defensive purpose.[59] Inspired by and relying on Falk's framework, Bowett suggested slightly simplified 'reasonableness criteria' that would prevent reprisals from being condemned by the Security Council,[60] and which did not necessarily require a defensive aim. Dinstein proposed the concept of 'defensive armed reprisals' as a permissible form of self-defence exercised after an armed attack and meeting the requirements of necessity, proportionality and immediacy.[61]

The ICJ stayed clear of these matters, even when it had a chance to address them. In the *Nicaragua* judgment, the Court ruled that States did not have a right of 'collective' armed response to acts which did not constitute an armed attack.[62] While the Court held that certain acts of Nicaragua 'could only have justified proportionate counter-measures on the part of the State which had been the victim of these acts' and that '[t]hey could not justify counter-measures taken by a third State, the United States, and particularly could not justify intervention involving the use of force', it did not clarify whether counter-measures *by the defending States* could involve the use of force.[63] The matter of forcible counter-measures resurfaced in the separate opinion of a member of the Court. In the 2003 *Oil Platforms* judgment, the Court found that, in view of all the circumstances, including the inconclusiveness of the evidence, it was unable to hold that the attacks on the Iranian platforms had been shown to have been in self-defence.[64] The Court did not, however, expand on whether the US action was therefore an unlawful

59 R. A. Falk, 'The Beirut Raid and the International Law of Retaliation' (1969) 63 *American Journal of International Law* 415–43, at 440–2.

60 Bowett, 'Reprisals' (n. 57), pp. 26–8.

61 Y. Dinstein, *War, Aggression and Self-Defence* (Cambridge University Press, 2017), pp. 264–75.

62 ICJ, *Military and Paramilitary Activities in and against Nicaragua (Nicaragua* v. *United States)* (Merits), Judgment, 27 June 1986, ICJ Reports 1986, para. 211.

63 Ibid., para. 249.

64 ICJ, *Oil Platforms (Islamic Republic of Iran* v. *United States of America)*, Judgment, 6 November 2003, ICJ Reports 2003, paras. 195–6.

use of force or whether it could be justified in any other way. By contrast, in his Separate Opinion accompanying the judgment, Judge Simma asserted that 'proportionate defensive measures' below the threshold of Article 51 were lawful.[65] Judge Simma relied on the Court's *Nicaragua* ruling and stated that the reference to counter-measures in relation to defending States could have only meant 'defensive military action "short of" full-scale self-defence"'.[66] Some authors saw Judge Simma's opinion as an implicit justification for reprisals.[67] A careful look at Judge Simma's opinion shows, however, that he was referring to a category of 'proportionate defensive measures' below the threshold of Article 51, and not to armed measures aimed at inducing compliance. As a result, his opinion cannot be interpreted as a justification of reprisals. In any event, in its 1996 Advisory Opinion on the *Legality of the Threat or Use of Nuclear Weapons* the Court stated as a dictum that it did not have to examine the question of 'armed reprisals in time of peace', as these were considered unlawful. The Court did not expand on its assertion, and it is not clear whether the Court differentiated at any time between the concepts of forcible counter-measures and reprisals.[68]

The issue of counter-measures was of course addressed by the International Law Commission in its Articles on the Responsibility of States for Internationally Wrongful Acts. Counter-measures were clearly differentiated from self-defence (compare Articles 21 and 22) and the commentary to the Articles clarified that, traditionally, the term 'reprisals' was used to cover otherwise unlawful action, including forcible action, taken by way of self-help in response to a breach.[69] The commentary went on to explain that '[t]he term "countermeasures" covers that part of the subject of reprisals not associated with armed conflict'[70] – that is, reprisals in time of peace. Importantly, Article 50(1)

65 *Oil Platforms* (n. 64), Separate Opinion of Judge Simma, para. 12.

66 Ibid.

67 E. A. Heinze and R. Neilsen, 'Limited Force and the Return of Reprisals in the Law of Armed Conflict' (2020) 34(2) *Ethics and International Affairs* 175–88, at 179; S. Darcy, 'Revival of Classical Concepts? Retaliation and Reprisal', in M. Weller (ed.), *The Oxford Handbook of the Use of Force in International Law* (Oxford University Press, 2017), pp. 890–1.

68 ICJ, *Legality of the Threat or Use of Nuclear Weapons*, Advisory Opinion, 8 July 1996, ICJ Reports 1996, para. 46.

69 International Law Commission, 'Draft Articles on Responsibility of States for Internationally Wrongful Acts, with Commentaries' (2001), in Report of the International Law Commission on the Work of Its Fifty-Third Session, UN Doc. A/56/10, p. 128, para. (3).

70 Ibid.

clearly stated that counter-measures could not affect the obligation to refrain from the threat or use of force as embodied in the UN Charter. This provision unequivocally limited counter-measures to non-forcible actions and refuted any argument that reprisals could still be legal.

The view that reprisals are unlawful and counter-measures should be limited to non-forcible actions has undoubtedly endured the test of time. That does not necessarily mean that specific instances of reprisals cannot be mitigated if adequate extra-legal justifications apply. This possibility will be discussed below. That being said, the authors of this book consider that, in any event, the concepts of self-defence and reprisal should be kept apart. While the above summary of State practice undoubtedly shows the difficulties in distinguishing between the two concepts, there are three fundamental considerations that set self-defence apart from reprisals.

First, self-defence requires an armed attack. This can be a one-off, small-scale attack or a single, large-scale attack that is imminent, is unfolding or has already occurred (see Chapter 6, above). A series of repeated, small-scale attacks by the same actor that commenced in the past can also be considered to amount to a phased armed attack.

Second, the purpose of self-defence is to stop an ongoing armed attack, pre-empt an imminent armed attack, halt the effects of an armed attack that has already materialized or prevent future attacks following upon a string of past attacks. This purpose is narrower than that of reprisals, which is to coerce States into altering their conduct and induce compliance with a (purportedly) violated obligation. For example, bombing training camps of a non-State actor on the territory of a State may be considered a legitimate exercise of self-defence if it is aimed at destroying the armed group's capability of carrying out future attacks. At the same time, bombing a civilian airport to coerce a State's government to stop supporting a non-State actor on its territory goes well beyond a defensive purpose as outlined above, although it fits into the purpose of a reprisal. Simply put, it is imperative to keep the purpose of the armed action in focus. Is it – based on the available evidence – likely and plausible that the armed measures are taken in order to halt or forestall (the effects of) an attack (or repetition of attacks), or does it seem likely that the action was punitive in nature and/or aimed at altering the conduct of a State and inducing compliance with a (purportedly) violated obligation?

Third, while both self-defence and reprisals require necessity and proportionality, the former also presupposes an element of immediacy. This requirement refers to the need for the defending State to take defensive action within its capabilities as soon as this is possible, subject to a number of considerations of reasonableness, such as the ability of the defending State to adequately defend itself without delay or outside assistance, the need to mobilize or deploy forces to the locale of the attack, the need to obtain sufficient evidence of the author of the attack when this is not apparent, the need to consult allies or garner outside support when the victim is not capable of mounting an effective defence on its own and so forth.[71]

Ultimately, the assessment whether an armed action is a lawful exercise of self-defence or an unlawful reprisal is to be done on a case-by-case basis, taking into consideration the factual background and arguments raised in each case.

## 9.5 The Return to Reprisals?

The controversy regarding the 'accumulation of events' theory as a substitute for reprisals gradually disappeared with the advent of global terrorist networks capable of carrying out repeated, often large-scale attacks. Use of force against such attacks carried out by non-State actors is increasingly seen today as a legitimate exercise of self-defence if certain conditions apply (see Chapter 6, above). The question of whether reprisals could be legal re-surfaced, however, in the second decade of the twenty-first century, this time in relation to the use of weapons of mass destruction (see Chapter 10, below).

On 7 April 2017, US planes struck and severely damaged an airbase in Syria believed to be the source of an earlier chemical attack by the Syrian government on its own civilians (see Fact Box 9.2).[72] The United States justified the strike as 'a proportional response to Assad's heinous act', aimed at deterring the Syrian regime 'from using chemical weapons again'.[73] Neither the United States nor the countries expressing support for the air strike made any explicit reference to its legality under international law.[74]

[71] T. D. Gill, 'The Temporal Dimension of Self-Defence: Anticipation, Pre-emption, Prevention and Immediacy', in M. N. Schmitt and J. Pejić (eds.), *International Law and Armed Conflict: Exploring the Faultlines* (Nijhoff, 2007), pp. 151–4.

[72] SCOR, 72nd year, 7919th meeting, 7 April 2017, UN Doc. S/PV.7919, p. 2; US Department of Defense, 'Statement by Secretary of Defense Jim Mattis on the U.S. Military Response to the Syrian Government's Use of Chemical Weapons', news release (10 April 2017), https://tinyurl.com/yuk3urua.

[73] US Department of Defense, 'Statement from Pentagon Spokesman Capt. Jeff Davis on U.S. Strike in Syria', news release (6 April 2017), https://tinyurl.com/ktcs3nb9.

[74] UN Doc. S/PV.7919 (n. 72), pp. 5 (United Kingdom), 9 (France), 8 (Italy), 16 (Ukraine). Other countries supporting the US airstrikes were Australia, Canada, Japan, Saudi Arabia and Turkey. See A. Lagerwall, 'Threats and Actual Military Strikes Against Syria – 2013

### FACT BOX 9.2 AIR STRIKES ON SYRIA AS REPRISALS FOR THE USE OF CHEMICAL WEAPONS

Starting in 2012, there have been increasing reports of chemical weapons being used by the Syrian government against its own civilians during the Syrian civil war. Several steps were taken by the international community to stop Syria's action by non-forcible means. In particular, thanks to Russian diplomatic involvement, Syria ratified the Chemical Weapons Convention in 2013 and submitted to the monitoring and destruction or removal of its chemical arsenal. It also accepted several inspections by the Organisation for the Prohibition of Chemical Weapons (OPCW). Moreover, in 2015, the Security Council adopted Resolution 2235 and established a joint investigative mechanism to identify perpetrators using chemical weapons in Syria. Nonetheless, incidents involving the use of chemical weapons continued well into 2017.

On 4 April 2017, reports emerged of a Syrian government warplane attacking the rebel-held town of Khan Sheikhoun in the Idlib Governorate with a nerve agent, killing at least ninety people, including thirty children.

In response, in the early hours of 7 April 2017 fifty-nine Tomahawk cruise missiles were launched from the US warships USS Ross and USS Porter in the eastern Mediterranean. They hit the Al Shayrat airbase near Homs, which was said to be the location from which Syrian forces launched the chemical attack on Khan Sheikhoun. The missiles were aimed at Syrian fighter jets, hardened aircraft shelters, radar equipment, ammunition bunkers, sites for storing fuel and air-defence systems.

One year later, on 8 April 2018, reports emerged of another chemical attack attributed to the Syrian government, this time on the besieged town of Douma in the enclave of Eastern Ghouta, near Damascus. The attack, carried out in close proximity to bomb shelters, killed dozens of people and injured several hundreds.

In response, on 13 April 2018, the United States, United Kingdom and France fired missiles at three targets in Syria: a scientific research facility in Damascus, allegedly connected to the production of chemical and biological weapons; a chemical weapons storage facility west of Homs; and a chemical weapons equipment storage site and an important command post, also near Homs.

The use of chemical by the Syrian government in both of the above-mentioned attacks was confirmed by the OPCW and the Independent International Commission of Inquiry on the Syrian Arab Republic (IICI).

**Sources**: Syria ratified the Chemical Weapons Convention on 14 September 2013, www.opcw.org/about-us/member-states/syria; Joint Framework on Destruction of Syrian CW, Annex B of Framework for Elimination of Syrian Chemical Weapons (14 September 2013), EC-M–33/NAT.1, https://tinyurl.com/2p8jy9xh; UNSC Res. 2209 (2015); UNSC Res. 2235 (2015); OPCW reports: UN Doc. S/1212/2014 (10 September 2014), UN Doc. S/1230/2014 (18 December 2014), UN Doc. S/1319/2015 (29 October 2015), UN Doc. S/1320/2015 (29 October 2015), UN Doc. S/1318/2015/Rev.1 (17 December 2015), UN Doc. S/1444/2016 (21 December 2016), UN Doc. S/2017/904 (26 October 2017); UN Doc. S/1731/2019 (1 March 2019); IICI Reports: UN Doc. A/HRC/36/55 (8 August 2017), UN Doc. A/HRC/39/65 (9 August 2018); Human Rights Watch, 'Death by Chemicals: The Syrian Government's Widespread and Systematic Use of Chemical Weapons' (1 May 2017), https://tinyurl.com/5ce6p7xs; M. R. Gordon, H. Cooper and M. D. Shear, 'Dozens of U.S. Missiles Hit Airbase in Syria', *New York Times* (6 April 2017), https://tinyurl.com/5b86ea98; K. Shaheen, 'Dozens Killed in Suspected Chemical Attack on Syrian Rebel Enclave', *The Guardian* (8 April 2018), https://tinyurl.com/3wn3d7ak; BBC News, 'Syria Air Strikes: US and Allies Attack "Chemical Weapons Sites"' (14 April 2018), www.bbc.com/news/world-middle-east-43762251.

Iran, Russia and Syria condemned the air strike, while a number of other countries expressed their concern as to the compatibility of the strike with international law.[75]

One year later, on 13 April 2018, following reports of another chemical attack by the Syrian regime,[76] the United States, the United Kingdom and France bombed a research facility and two storage facilities in Syria allegedly connected to the production or storage of chemical and biological weapons (see Fact Box 9.2).[77] As with the 2017 air strikes, the United States, the United Kingdom and France did not explicitly refer to international law in their justifications, but indicated that the bombings were meant to deter from future use of chemical weapons.[78] Russia and Syria condemned the bombings as acts of aggression, while other countries expressed their concern as to the strikes' compatibility with international law.[79] That being said, a draft resolution proposed by Russia condemning the air strikes as acts of aggression was opposed by eight members of the Council.[80]

Some commentators attempted to justify the air strikes as anticipatory and/or collective self-defence. These arguments are discussed and rejected below in Chapter 10. For present purposes, suffice it to say that the three fundamental differences between self-defence and reprisals outlined above also apply to the 2017 and 2018 air strikes. First, none followed an armed attack by the Syrian regime or a threat thereof against the States carrying out the air strikes. While the Syrian regime's use of chemical weapons against its own people was clearly unlawful, it did not constitute an (imminent threat of an) armed attack against the United

and 2017', in T. Ruys and O. Corten (eds.), *The Use of Force in International Law: A Case-Based Approach* (Oxford University Press, 2018), pp. 848–9; G. Aisch, Y. Joseph and A. Singhvi, 'Which Countries Support and Which Oppose the U.S. Missile Strikes in Syria', *New York Times* (9 April 2017), https://tinyurl.com/yhf9kw5c.

75 UN Doc. S/PV.7919 (n. 72), pp. 3 (Bolivia), 7 (Uruguay), 10 (Russia), 13 (Senegal, Kazakhstan), 14 (Sweden), 18 (Syria). See also Lagerwall, 'Threat ' (n. 74), pp. 849–50.

76 BBC News, 'Syria War: At Least 70 Killed in Suspected Chemical Attack in Douma' (8 April 2018), www.bbc.com/news/world-middle-east-43686157.

77 US Department of Defense, 'Department of Defense Press Briefing by Pentagon Chief Spokesperson Dana W. White and Joint Staff Director Lt. Gen. Kenneth F. McKenzie Jr. in the Pentagon Briefing Room', transcript (14 April 2018), https://tinyurl.com/3mjt5936; BBC News, 'Syria Air Strikes: US and Allies Attack "Chemical Weapons Sites"' (14 April 2018), www.bbc.com/news/world-middle-east-43762251.

78 SCOR, 73rd year, 8233th meeting, 14 April 2018, UN Doc. S/PV.8233, pp. 5 (United States), 6 (United Kingdom), 9 (France).

79 Ibid., pp. 3 (Russia), 10 (China, Kazakhstan), 14 (Bolivia), 18 (Equatorial Guinea), 19–20 (Syria).

80 Ibid., pp. 22–3.

States or its allies. Second, the purpose of the air strikes was to stop the Syrian regime from using chemical weapons against its own people and not to defend the United States and its allies. Third, while the strikes were carried out soon after the alleged use of chemical weapons, there was no consideration of immediacy within the meaning of self-defence. The strikes were carried out promptly to teach Syria a lesson; they were neither informed by nor subject to the ability of the United States and its allies to defend themselves adequately.

According to some commentators, the Syria air strikes were paving the way for a more limited type of humanitarian interventions – one responding to the extreme nature of the harm, not necessarily its scale.[81] Others have opined that any such future, narrowly tailored intervention should be justified on a number of more general, legal, policy and/or legitimacy grounds.[82] Several authors criticized these arguments as incompatible with international law or not reflecting the rationale of humanitarian interventions.[83] Viewing the Syria air strikes as humanitarian interventions is problematic for at least two reasons. First, the concept of humanitarian intervention does not have a recognized legal basis in contemporary international law.[84] Second, past humanitarian interventions tended to be tolerated and excused on moral or policy grounds when they were undertaken (i) in the face of a clear case of human rights violations on a large scale with (potential) wider destabilizing effects; (ii) with no feasible possibility of gaining

[81] M. N. Schmitt and C. M. Ford, 'The Use of Force in Response to Syrian Chemical Attacks: Emergence of a New Norm?', *Just Security* (8 April 2017), https://tinyurl.com/54tr67f4; M. N. Schmitt and C. M. Ford, 'Assessing U.S. Justifications for Using Force in Response to Syria's Chemical Attacks: An International Law Perspective' (2017) 9 *Journal of National Security Law and Policy* 283–303, at 302–3.

[82] A. Deeks, 'How Does the Syria Situation Stack up to the "Factors" that Justified Intervention in Kosovo?', *Lawfare* (7 April 2017), https://tinyurl.com/5pb9jbet; H. Hongju Koh, 'Not Illegal: But Now the Hard Part Begins', *Just Security* (7 April 2017), www.justsecurity.org/39695/illegal-hard-part-begins/; C. Dunlap, 'Yes, the Attack on Syria Was Justifiable, and International Law Will Benefit from It', *Lawfire* (7 April 2017), https://tinyurl.com/254cm7mbo.

[83] S. Krishnan, 'The Alleged Use Of Chemical Weapons against the Syrian People' (2017) 21 (2) *World Affairs: The Journal of International Issues* 22–33, at 31–2; A. Henriksen, 'Trump's Missile Strike on Syria and the Legality of Using Force to Deter Chemical Warfare' (2018) 23 *Journal of Conflict & Security Law* 33–48; A. C. de Beer and D. Tladi, 'The Use of Force against Syria in Response to Alleged Use of Chemical Weapons by Syria: A Return to Humanitarian Intervention?' (2019) 79 *Heidelberg Journal of International Law* 205–39; M. Milanovic, 'The Syria Strikes: Still Clearly Illegal', *EJIL: Talk!* (15 April 2018), www.ejiltalk.org/the-syria-strikes-still-clearly-illegal/.

[84] See Chapter 7, Sections 7.3 and 7.4, above.

a mandate from the Security Council and (iii) in a proportionate manner as regards the conduct of the intervention and its likely effects on international security and stability.[85] The 2017 and 2018 air strikes were undertaken in response to specific uses of chemical weapons by the Syrian regime. The strikes occurred against the background of abundant evidence of large-scale, systematic and egregious violations of humanitarian and human rights law amounting to war crimes and crimes against humanity attributable to the Syrian regime. The strikes, however, did not respond to such large-scale violations, but to the specific use of chemical weapons against civilian targets. For this reason, the case for the strikes being a form of humanitarian intervention is not convincing. Why respond to just one form of human rights violation and leave the others out of the equation? In fact, the 2017 and 2018 air strikes were not intended to alleviate the suffering of the entire Syrian population and definitely did not have that effect. They therefore should not be viewed as (new forms of) humanitarian interventions.

Despite the considerable efforts on the part of various commentators to justify the air strikes as self-defence or humanitarian intervention, it is quite obvious that they amounted to reprisals. This was also pointed out by a number of authors.[86] Notably, the language used by the United States, the United Kingdom, France and other States in justifying or supporting the air strikes evoked the rationale of reprisals, implying the punitive and coercive nature of the strikes for the purpose of deterring future use of chemical weapons. The statement of the French president went as far as to say that any 'use of chemical weapons would result in reprisals and an immediate riposte, at least where France is concerned'.[87] Other countries expressed their support by coining the strikes as a 'proportionate', 'measured' and/or 'necessary' 'response', echoing the language of reprisals.[88]

85 See Chapter 7, Section 7.5, above.

86 M. Milanovic, 'The Clearly Illegal US Missile Strike in Syria', *EJIL:Talk!* (7 April 2017), https://tinyurl.com/ckh6k94u; Milanovic, 'Syria Strikes' (n. 83); M. Hakimi, 'The Attack on Syria and the Contemporary *Jus ad Bellum*', *EJIL:Talk!* (15 April 2018), https://tinyurl.com/y5n3sk3t; de Beer and Tladi, 'Use of Force' (n. 83), pp. 224–6; M. E. O'Connell, 'The Popular but Unlawful Reprisal' (2018) 44 *Ohio Northern University Law Review* 325–50, at 325–7.

87 Reuters, 'Chemical Weapons a Red Line in Syria, France's Macron Says' (29 May 2017), https://tinyurl.com/2p93ttv9.

88 A. G. Dunkelberg et al., 'Mapping States' Reactions to the U.S. Strikes against Syria of April 2018: A Comprehensive Guide', *Just Security* (7 May 2018), https://tinyurl.com/bdupuujj. Turkey called the strikes 'an appropriate response to the chemical attack which caused

In this respect, it is important to note that the purpose of the air strikes was novel even in relation to reprisals, as there was no prior breach by Syria vis-à-vis the striking States. The violation was in relation to Syria's international obligations as a State towards its own people and, due to the international prohibition on the use of chemical weapons, towards the international community as a whole. The question then arises as to whether such a purpose – that is, coercing a State to abide by its *erga omnes* obligations – can create a new customary rule legitimizing reprisals under limited conditions.

## 9.6 Mitigation of Certain Reprisals

These air strikes, on their own, clearly do not constitute sufficient State practice to suggest a trend towards the legitimization of reprisals. Equally, the language used by the United States and its allies cannot be interpreted as clear *opinio juris* signalling a departure from the prohibition of reprisals. Of course, it cannot be excluded that future instances of State practice, if sufficiently frequent and consistent enough in their justifications to elicit a condoning reaction from the majority of States, could lead to the emergence of a new customary rule allowing limited use of reprisals. For the time being, however, they remain unlawful.

This does not mean, however, that the wrongfulness of certain instances of reprisals cannot be mitigated if adequate, extra-legal justifications apply. The 2017 and 2018 air strikes almost certainly qualify as reprisals. They were, however, driven by imperative humanitarian considerations in relation to the Syrian population suffering repeated attacks by chemical agents. The strikes came after years of concerns expressed by various States as regards Syria's use of chemical weapons and its egregious violations of human rights standards.[89] Furthermore, the strikes were carried out in a surgical manner, targeting only facilities connected to the production or

the deaths of many civilians'. Estonia stated that the strikes were 'a proper and proportionate response to the repeated use of chemical weapons by the Syrian regime against the Syrian people'. Spain stated that the strikes were 'a measured and proportionate response to the brutal attacks committed by the Syrian regime against the civilian population'. Romania characterized the strikes as 'a firm response to the atrocities that have resulted in numerous casualties among the civilian population in Douma'. Georgia stated that the strikes were 'an appropriate and needed response to chemical attacks against the civilian population'. The G7 viewed the strikes as 'limited, proportionate and necessary – and taken only after exhausting every possible diplomatic option to uphold the international norm against the use of chemical weapons'.

[89] See Chapter 10, below.

storage of such weapons and avoiding any unnecessary loss of life or damage to property. Moreover, they were carried out in want of any better solution; there was no prospect of the Syrian regime unilaterally stopping the use of such weapons and there was also no likelihood of a Security Council-mandated intervention.

As proposed above in Chapter 7 in relation to humanitarian interventions, such considerations should be taken into account when assessing whether these unlawful uses of force can nevertheless be accepted or tolerated, leading to a mitigation of responsibility in their respect. In other words, in cases where comparable conditions are met, the international community may opt to tolerate, mitigate or, to a certain extent, even excuse a reprisal and, consequently, to not attach significant condemnation or legal consequences to it. Such an approach should not, however, be seen as a precedent for the establishment of a new rule of customary law legalizing such interventions.

## 9.7 Conclusion

Since the adoption of the UN Charter, armed reprisals in times of peace remain prohibited under international law, despite various instances of State practice and scholarly opinion according them limited legality under certain circumstances. The authors of this book do not consider that the evolution of post-Charter State practice, including the abovementioned recent instances of reprisals, signal the emergence of a new customary rule legalizing reprisals in certain situations. That being said, the authors consider that in situations where there are overriding humanitarian considerations and a lack of other feasible alternatives, and where reprisals are resorted to in a proportionate manner to coerce a State to respect its obligations and stop egregious human rights violations, reprisals can, to a certain extent, be excused and not condemned in any significant way.

# 10

# The Use of Force and Weapons of Mass Destruction

## 10.1 Introduction

This chapter discusses the implications that weapons of mass destruction (WMDs) are purported to have for the international law governing the use of force. It first looks at the definition of the term WMD and briefly describes the use of such weapons in the past. It then analyses a number of instances of State practice involving the use or threat of use of nuclear and chemical weapons and draws conclusions on their implications as far as the law on the use of force is concerned.

## 10.2 Weapons of Mass Destruction: Background and Definitions

The expression 'weapons of mass destruction' is widely understood to refer to nuclear, chemical and biological weapons.[1] In 1948, the UN Commission for Conventional Armaments[2] defined WMDs as including 'atomic explosive weapons, radioactive material weapons, lethal chemical and biological weapons, and any weapons developed in the future which might have characteristics comparable in destructive effect to those of the atomic bomb or other weapons mentioned above'.[3] This definition was

1 H. A. Strydom, 'Weapons of Mass Destruction', in *Max Planck Encyclopedia of Public International Law* (Oxford Public International Law, 2017), https://tinyurl.com/2dzp59xb.

2 The Commission for Conventional Armaments was established by the UN Security Council (UNSC) in February 1947 with the aim of making proposals for the general regulation and reduction of armaments and armed forces. The Commission stopped functioning in 1950 owing to deadlock between its members. It was dissolved in 1952. See United Nations Office for Disarmament Affairs, 'The Commission for Conventional Armaments', in *United Nations and Disarmament 1945–1970* (United Nations, 1970), pp. 25–34, www.un-ilibrary.org/content/books/9789210579780s002-c002.

3 UN Doc. S/C.3/32/Rev.1 and Rev.1/Corr.1 (18 August 1948).

formally accepted by the UN General Assembly in 1977 and is still referenced today.[4]

As can be inferred from the above definition, the common element of these weapons is their large-scale and indiscriminately destructive effect on combatants and civilians alike.

Nuclear weapons are devices designed to release explosive energy as a result of the splitting (fission) or joining (fusion) of atoms, or a combination of the two processes.[5] The 'atomic' bomb that destroyed Hiroshima in 1945 was a fission weapon and had the explosive force of 14,000 tons of TNT.[6] The 'thermonuclear' or 'hydrogen' bomb tested by the United States in the Pacific in October 1952 was a fusion weapon and had the explosive force of 7 million tons of TNT and produced lethal radioactive fallout from gamma rays.[7] Although nuclear weapons have not been used in armed conflict since the Second World War bombings of Hiroshima and Nagasaki, the number of States with nuclear weapons has steadily increased since the 1940s. By the 1960s, not only the United States and the Soviet Union were known to possess nuclear weapons, but also the United Kingdom, France and China.[8] Since the 1970s, several other States have developed nuclear weapons (e.g. India, Israel, Pakistan, North Korea).[9] Other States possessed such weapons for a period of time before dismantling them (South Africa) or returning them to the Russian Federation (Belarus, Kazakhstan,

[4] UN General Assembly (UNGA) Resolution 32/84-B (12 December 1977), UN Doc. A/RES/32/84-B. For subsequent references to the definition, see, for example, UNGA Resolution 51/37 (10 December 1996), UN Doc. A/RES/51/37; UNGA Resolution 54/44 (23 December 1999), UN Doc. A/RES/54/44; UNGA Resolution 57/50 (30 December 2002), UN Doc. A/RES/57/50; UNGA Resolution 60/46 (6 January 2006), UN Doc. A/RES/60/46; UNGA Resolution 63/36 (13 January 2009), UN Doc. A/RES/63/36; UNGA Resolution 75/31(7 December 2020), UN Doc. A/RES/75/31. See also W. S. Carus, 'Defining "Weapons of Mass Destruction"' (revised and updated), Center for the Study of Weapons of Mass Destruction Occasional Paper No. 8 (National Defense University Press, January 2012), pp. 5–6.

[5] M. Chan, 'What Is the Difference between a Hydrogen Bomb and an Atomic Bomb?', *Time* (22 September 2017), https://time.com/4954082/hydrogen-bomb-atomic-bomb/; J. M. Siracusa, *Nuclear Weapons: A Very Short Introduction* (Oxford University Press, 2020), p. 2.

[6] Siracusa, *Nuclear Weapons* (n. 5), pp. 6, 20–3.

[7] Ibid., pp. 2–6.

[8] J. Baylis and S. Smith, *The Globalization of World Politics* (Oxford University Press, 2001), pp. 85–6.

[9] BBC News, 'Nuclear Weapons: Which Countries Have Them and How Many Are There?' (14 January 2020), www.bbc.com/news/newsbeat-51091897.

Ukraine).[10] Some States had invested (Iraq) or are purportedly still investing considerable effort in developing such weapons (Iran, Syria).[11] About 13,400 such weapons are known to exist today and there have been over 2,000 nuclear tests conducted to date.[12]

Chemical weapons are defined as any chemical used to cause intentional death or harm through its toxic properties, including any munitions, devices and other equipment specifically designed to weaponize toxic chemicals.[13] Chemical weapons have been used since the First World War, in the form of phosgene, mustard gas and other chemical agents put into standard munitions such as grenades and artillery shells. Poisonous (nerve) gasses and other chemical weapons were used during the Second World War in Nazi concentration camps and by Japan against Chinese targets.[14] Since the Second World War chemical weapons have been used several times, most notably in the Vietnam War,[15] the Iran-Iraq War,[16] by the Iraqi government against the Kurds[17] and in the Syrian civil war.[18] Since the First World War chemical weapons have caused more than a million casualties globally.[19]

[10] US Arms Control Association, 'Nuclear Weapons: Who Has What at a Glance' (August 2020), www.armscontrol.org/factsheets/Nuclearweaponswhohaswhat.

[11] Ibid.

[12] UN Office for Disarmament Affairs, 'Nuclear Weapons', www.un.org/disarmament/wmd/nuclear/.

[13] Article II of the Convention on the Prohibition of the Development, Production, Stockpiling and Use of Chemical Weapons and on Their Destruction (Paris, 13 January 1993). See also Organisation for the Prohibition of Chemical Weapons (OPCW), 'What Is a Chemical Weapon', www.opcw.org/our-work/what-chemical-weapon.

[14] United States Holocaust Memorial Museum, 'Gassing Operations', https://tinyurl.com/ymksf639; F. Schmaltz, 'Chemical Weapons Research on Soldiers and Concentration Camp Inmates in Nazi Germany', in: B. Friedrich et al. (eds.), *One Hundred Years of Chemical Warfare: Research, Deployment, Consequences* (Springer, 2017), pp. 229–58; W. E. Grunden, 'No Retaliation in Kind: Japanese Chemical Warfare Policy in World War II', in Friedrich et al. (eds.), *One Hundred Years*(this note), pp. 259–71.

[15] M. Meselson, 'From Charles and Francis Darwin to Richard Nixon: The Origin and Termination of Anti-Plant Chemical Warfare in Vietnam', in Friedrich et al. (eds.), *One Hundred Years* (n. 14), pp. 335–48.

[16] R. L. Russell, 'Iraq's Chemical Weapons Legacy: What Others Might Learn from Saddam' (2005) 59(2) *Middle East Journal* 187–208.

[17] K. Mlodoch, 'The Indelible Smell of Apples: Poison Gas Survivors in Halabja, Kurdistan-Iraq, and Their Struggle for Recognition', in Friedrich et al. (eds.), *One Hundred Years* (n. 14), pp. 349–62.

[18] R. Trapp, 'The Use of Chemical Weapons in Syria: Implications and Consequences', in Friedrich et al. (eds.), *One Hundred Years* (n. 14), pp. 363–75.

[19] UN Office for Disarmament Affairs, 'Chemical Weapons', www.un.org/disarmament/wmd/chemical/.

Biological weapons are micro-organisms (such as viruses, bacteria or fungi) or toxins (such as poisons derived from animals, plants or micro-organisms, or similar substances produced synthetically), which are produced and/or enhanced and deliberately released through a delivery mechanism to cause disease and death in humans, animals or plants.[20] Accounts of modern biological warfare date back to the late eighteenth century and include (purported and not always successful) efforts to spread smallpox and yellow fever.[21] The first decades of the twentieth century saw the multiplication of efforts to create biological programmes by several countries, including Germany and Japan.[22] Biological agents purportedly developed and/or used during this period included those causing anthrax, the plague, typhoid, typhus fever, brucellosis, tularaemia and botulism.[23] Since 1945, methods for the effective delivery of biological agents have developed significantly. Such delivery systems can take a variety of forms, such as missiles, bombs, rockets, hand grenades, or spray-tanks to be fitted to aircraft, cars, trucks and boats.[24] The secretive nature of these programmes makes it very difficult to assess the number of countries that have developed such weapons, although instances of their alleged use seem so far to be limited.[25]

In order to control, curb or prohibit the use of WMDs, several multilateral treaties have been adopted over the past sixty years. The best-known instruments in this regard are the Treaty on the Non-Proliferation of Nuclear Weapons (NPT),[26] the Biological Weapons

20 UN Office for Disarmament Affairs, 'What Are Biological Weapons?', https://tinyurl.com/2d39teu4; World Health Organization, 'Biological Weapons', www.who.int/health-topics/biological-weapons#tab=tab_1.

21 W. S. Carus, 'A Short History of Biological Warfare: From Pre-History to the 21st Century', Center for the Study of Weapons of Mass Destruction, Occasional Paper No. 12 (National Defense University Press, 2017), pp. 7–11; V. Barras and G. Greub, 'History of Biological Warfare and Bioterrorism' (2014) 20 *Clinical Microbiology and Infection* 497–502, at 499.

22 Barras and Greub, 'History of Biological Warfare' (n. 21), pp. 499–501; Carus, 'Short History' (n. 21), pp. 12–25.

23 Carus, 'Short History' (n. 21), pp. 12–25.

24 UN Office for Disarmament Affairs, 'Biological Weapons' (n. 20); Carus, 'Short History' (n. 21), pp. 28–39. See also The Hague Centre for Strategic Studies, 'The Increasing Threat of Biological Weapons' (2016), https://tinyurl.com/6majzdzp.

25 Carus, 'Short History' (n. 21), p. 28.

26 The Treaty on the Non-Proliferation of Nuclear Weapons (NPT) was adopted on 1 July 1968 and entered into force in 1970. One of its main objectives is to prevent the spread of nuclear weapons and weapons technology. As of late 2022, the NPT had 191 State parties, including five States recognized as possessing nuclear weapons (China, France, Russia, the United Kingdom and the United States).

Convention[27] and the Chemical Weapons Convention.[28] Other treaties aimed at banning nuclear weapons, such as the Treaty on the Prohibition of Nuclear Weapons, have also been adopted, but State adhesion to them is still limited.[29]

Despite the adoption of, and widespread adhesion to, these treaties, the development, possession, proliferation and (potential) use of WMDs continues to present a significant threat to international peace and security today. First, there is a continuing threat of States using such weapons against other States or their own citizens. Second, the emergence of (quasi-)independent non-State armed groups in recent decades has created a new and increasing threat of WMDs being acquired and used by such groups.

These threats also impact on the law governing the use of force by States. In particular, several instances of State practice involve the use of force in response to potential threats posed by nuclear weapons or (alleged) threats or uses of chemical weapons. These instances will be discussed below. While, to date, there have been no instances of States using force in relation to purported threats or uses of biological weapons, this topic will also receive brief attention.

[27] The Biological Weapons Convention was adopted on 10 April 1972 and entered into force in 1975. The Convention prohibits the development, production, acquisition, transfer, stockpiling and retention of biological and toxin weapons. As of late 2022, it had 184 State parties. The precursor of the Convention and the first international instrument banning the use of biological agents as weapons of war was the Protocol for the Prohibition of the Use in War of Asphyxiating, Poisonous or Other Gases, and of Bacteriological Methods of Warfare (Geneva, 17 June 1925), also known as the 1925 Geneva Protocol. The Protocol was adopted under the auspices of the League of Nations and entered into force in 1928. As of late 2022, it had 146 State parties.

[28] The Convention on the Prohibition of the Development, Production, Stockpiling and Use of Chemical Weapons and on Their Destruction was adopted on 13 January 1993 and entered into force in 1997. The Convention prohibits the development, production, acquisition, stockpiling, retention, transfer or use of chemical weapons by State parties. As of late 2022, it had 193 State parties.

[29] Other treaties on nuclear weapons are the Treaty Banning Nuclear Weapon Tests in the Atmosphere, in Outer Space and under Water, also known as the Partial Test Ban Treaty, which was adopted in Moscow on 5 August 1963 and entered into force the same year; the Comprehensive Nuclear-Test-Ban Treaty, which was adopted in New York on 24 September 1996 and has not yet entered into force; and the Treaty on the Prohibition of Nuclear Weapons (TPNW), which was adopted in New York on 7 July 2017 and entered into force in 2021. The TPNW prohibits, inter alia, the development, testing, production, acquisition, possession, stockpiling, use or threatened use of nuclear weapons. It also prohibits the deployment of nuclear weapons on national territory and the provision of assistance to any State in the conduct of prohibited activities. As of late 2022, the TPNW had 68 State parties, none of which are States recognized or known as possessing nuclear weapons.

SUMMARY BOX 10.1 MAIN TREATIES ON WMDS

The **Treaty on the Non-Proliferation of Nuclear Weapons** bans the possession of nuclear weapons for all States except nuclear-weapon States.

**Other nuclear weapons treaties**, such as the **Treaty on the Prohibition of Nuclear Weapons**, aim to ban, partially or totally, the possession or use of nuclear weapons, but adhesion to them remains limited.

The **Biological Weapons Convention** and the **Chemical Weapons Convention** respectively ban chemical and biological weapons per se.

FACT BOX 10.1 WMD TREATIES – EXCERPTS

**Treaty on the Non-Proliferation of Nuclear Weapons**

*Article I*

Each nuclear-weapon State Party to the Treaty undertakes not to transfer to any recipient whatsoever nuclear weapons or other nuclear explosive devices or control over such weapons or explosive devices directly, or indirectly; and not in any way to assist, encourage, or induce any non-nuclear-weapon State to manufacture or otherwise acquire nuclear weapons or other nuclear explosive devices, or control over such weapons or explosive devices.

*Article II*

Each non-nuclear-weapon State Party to the Treaty undertakes not to receive the transfer from any transferor whatsoever of nuclear weapons or other nuclear explosive devices or of control over such weapons or explosive devices directly, or indirectly; not to manufacture or otherwise acquire nuclear weapons or other nuclear explosive devices; and not to seek or receive any assistance in the manufacture of nuclear weapons or other nuclear explosive devices.

**Convention on the Prohibition of the Development, Production and Stockpiling of Bacteriological (Biological) and Toxin Weapons and on Their Destruction (Biological Weapons Convention)**

*Article I*

Each State Party to this Convention undertakes never in any circumstances to develop, produce, stockpile or otherwise acquire or retain:

1. microbial or other biological agents, or toxins whatever their origin or method of production, of types and in quantities that have no justification for prophylactic, protective or other peaceful purposes;

FACT BOX 10.1 *(cont.)*

2. weapons, equipment or means of delivery designed to use such agents or toxins for hostile purposes or in armed conflict.

*Article II*

Each State Party to this Convention undertakes to destroy, or to divert to peaceful purposes, as soon as possible but not later than nine months after the entry into force of the Convention, all agents, toxins, weapons, equipment and means of delivery specified in Article I of the Convention, which are in its possession or under its jurisdiction or control. In implementing the provisions of this Article all necessary safety precautions shall be observed to protect populations and the environment.

*Article III*

Each State Party to this Convention undertakes not to transfer to any recipient whatsoever, directly or indirectly, and not in any way to assist, encourage, or induce any State, group of States or international organisations to manufacture or otherwise acquire any of the agents, toxins, weapons, equipment or means of delivery specified in Article I of the Convention.

*Article IV*

Each State Party to this Convention shall, in accordance with its constitutional processes, take any necessary measures to prohibit and prevent the development, production, stockpiling, acquisition or retention of the agents, toxins, weapons, equipment and means of delivery specified in Article I of the Convention, within the territory of such State, under its jurisdiction or under its control anywhere.

**Convention on the Prohibition of the Development, Production, Stockpiling and Use of Chemical Weapons and on Their Destruction (Chemical Weapons Convention)**

*Article I: General Obligations*

1. Each State Party to this Convention undertakes never under any circumstances:
   (a) To develop, produce, otherwise acquire, stockpile or retain chemical weapons, or transfer, directly or indirectly, chemical weapons to anyone;
   (b) To use chemical weapons;
   (c) To engage in any military preparations to use chemical weapons;
   (d) To assist, encourage or induce, in any way, anyone to engage in any activity prohibited to a State Party under this Convention.
2. Each State Party undertakes to destroy chemical weapons it owns or possesses, or that are located in any place under its jurisdiction or control, in accordance with the provisions of this Convention.

FACT BOX 10.1 (*cont.*)

3. Each State Party undertakes to destroy all chemical weapons it abandoned on the territory of another State Party, in accordance with the provisions of this Convention.
4. Each State Party undertakes to destroy any chemical weapons production facilities it owns or possesses, or that are located in any place under its jurisdiction or control, in accordance with the provisions of this Convention.
5. Each State Party undertakes not to use riot control agents as a method of warfare.

**Treaty on the Prohibition of Nuclear Weapons**

*Article 1: Prohibitions*

1. Each State Party undertakes never under any circumstances to:
   (a) Develop, test, produce, manufacture, otherwise acquire, possess or stockpile nuclear weapons or other nuclear explosive devices;
   (b) Transfer to any recipient whatsoever nuclear weapons or other nuclear explosive devices or control over such weapons or explosive devices directly or indirectly;
   (c) Receive the transfer of or control over nuclear weapons or other nuclear explosive devices directly or indirectly;
   (d) Use or threaten to use nuclear weapons or other nuclear explosive devices;
   (e) Assist, encourage or induce, in any way, anyone to engage in any activity prohibited to a State Party under this Treaty;
   (f) Seek or receive any assistance, in any way, from anyone to engage in any activity prohibited to a State Party under this Treaty;
   (g) Allow any stationing, installation or deployment of any nuclear weapons or other nuclear explosive devices in its territory or at any place under its jurisdiction or control.

## 10.3 Nuclear Weapons and the Use of Force: State Practice

As said above nuclear weapons have to date not been used in armed conflict since the Second World War. There are, however, a few instances of State practice in which force was used in relation to the alleged possession, stationing or development of nuclear weapons. These cases are instructive for this chapter, as they show the legal justifications that States put forward for their use of force. The role of nuclear deterrence policies and nuclear weapons strategy in relation to the law relating to the use of force will also be given some attention.

### *10.3.1 The Cuban Missile Crisis (1962)*

The first such case dates back to 1962, when the United States was faced with Soviet nuclear missile deployment in Cuba. While Soviet arms shipments to Cuba were not a novelty in the early 1960s, the US government believed that such a build-up was confined to defensive systems.[30] By October 1962 it became clear, however, that the build-up included medium-range and intermediate range nuclear missiles, bomber and fighter planes capable of carrying nuclear weapons, as well as 22,000 Soviet military personnel for the construction, operation and defence of these weapons.[31]

The US government saw the build-up as a major security threat for the United States itself and the region as a whole and considered several options in response. Three of such options involved the use of armed force, be it in the form of surgical air strikes against the relevant sites, a large air campaign against a multitude of targets or a general ground invasion of Cuba.[32] All these options were, however, excluded because they were seen by the US government as not conforming to international law on the use of force.[33] First, it was clear that collective enforcement action by the UN Security Council (UNSC, Security Council) was out of the question, given that the Soviet Union was one of its permanent members.[34] Second, the conditions for the exercise of self-defence under Article 51 of the UN Charter were not seen to be met. In particular, while the US position was that an armed attack had to be construed broadly enough to permit some anticipatory action, the circumstances of the Cuban crisis would have required an exaggeratedly expansive view on the issue. The then legal adviser to the US State Department, Abram Chayes, considered that anticipatory action could not be expanded 'to include threatening deployments or demonstrations that do not have imminent attack as their purpose or probable outcome'.[35]

30 A. Chayes, *The Cuban Missile Crisis* (Oxford University Press, 1974), p. 8.

31 L. Chang and P. Kornbluh (eds.), *The Cuban Missile Crisis 1962: A National Security Archive Documents Reader* (The New Press, 1992), pp. 353–61.

32 G. T. Allison, *Essence of Decision: Explaining the Cuban Missile Crisis* (Little Brown, 1971), pp. 59–60; K. P. Mueller et al., *Striking First. Preemptive and Preventive Attack in U.S. National Security Policy* (RAND Project Air Force, 2006), pp. 176–7.

33 Chayes, *Cuban Missile Crisis* (n. 30), p. 65.

34 *Repertoire of the Practice of the Security Council: Supplement 1959–1963* (United Nations, 1965), pp. 201–2.

35 Chayes, *Cuban Missile Crisis* (n. 30), p. 65.

The option finally adopted was to impose a naval quarantine, interdicting the delivery of nuclear weapons and associated material to Cuba.[36] The United States justified the quarantine as a regional measure under the Inter-American Treaty of Reciprocal Assistance (Rio Treaty).[37] The US position was endorsed by a resolution adopted by the Organization of American States, which, invoking Articles 6 and 8 of the Rio Treaty, recommended that member States 'take all measures, individually or collectively, including the use of armed force, which they may deem necessary to ensure that the Government of Cuba cannot continue to receive from the Sino-Soviet Powers military material and related supplies which may threaten peace and security of the Continent and to prevent the missiles in Cuba with offensive capability from ever becoming an active threat to the peace and security of the Continent'.[38] Notwithstanding this resolution, the naval quarantine proved to be a controversial measure, as some States and commentators saw it as a veritable naval blockade involving the use of armed force without the authorization of the Security Council.[39] Despite this critique, the US

[36] *Public Papers of the Presidents of the United States*: John F. Kennedy, 1962 (US Government Printing Office, 1963), pp. 809–11.

[37] UNSC, 'Letter dated 22 October 1962 from the Representative of the United States of America addressed to the President of the Security Council', UN Doc. S/5181 (1962). The Rio Treaty was signed in 1947 between several American States, including the United States. The declared purpose of the treaty was 'to provide for effective reciprocal assistance to meet armed attacks against any American State, and in order to deal with threats of aggression against any of them' (preamble).

[38] UNSC, 'Letter dated 23 October 1962 from the Secretary-General of the Organization of American States addressed to the Acting Secretary-General of the United Nations', UN Doc. S/5193 (1962). Article 6 of the Rio Treaty provides that, in the event of an aggression, extra- or intracontinental conflict or other situation not amounting to an armed attack that affected the inviolability, territorial integrity, sovereignty or political independence of any American State, the OAS Organ of Consultation had to meet and discuss necessary measures. Article 8 of the Rio Treaty offered a list of measures that could be taken by the Organ of Consultation in such a situation: recalling chiefs of diplomatic missions; breaking off diplomatic relations; breaking off consular relations; partial or complete interruption of economic relations or of rail, sea, air, postal, telegraphic, telephonic and radiotelephonic or radiotelegraphic communications; and use of armed force.

[39] 'Questions Relating to the Americas', UN Yearbook 1962, pt 1, Political and Security Questions, chap. 8, pp. 105–8; UN Security Council Official Records (SCOR), 17th year, 1024th meeting, UN Doc. S/PV.1024 (24 October 1962), paras. 74, 106–10. See also Q. Wright, 'The Cuban Quarantine' (1963) 57 *American Journal of International Law* 546–65; A. Orakhelashvili, 'The Cuban Missile Crisis – 1962', in T. Ruys and O. Corten (eds.), *The Use of Force in International Law: A Case-Based Approach* (Oxford University Press, 2018), pp. 99–106.

action received widespread support from both its traditional allies and Latin American States.[40]

### *10.3.2 The Israeli Bombing of the Osirak Reactor (1981)*

A second instance of State practice in which force was used in relation to nuclear weapons was the Israeli bombing of the Osirak reactor in 1981. By the beginning of the 1980s, it was widely believed that Israel had succeeded in developing nuclear weapons,[41] while Iraq was suspected of being in the process of doing so.[42] According to Israel, Osirak, the nuclear reactor near Baghdad, was used by the Iraqi government to produce atomic bombs and it was to be fully operational by July or September 1981.[43] Israeli intelligence estimated that a crude nuclear device was to be finalized by 1985.[44]

The Israelis feared that, once in possession of a nuclear weapon, Saddam Hussein, the Iraqi president, would undoubtedly decide to use it against Israel and 'thus a mortal danger to the people of Israel progressively arose'.[45] That said, Israeli intelligence did not acquire any sort of information that might suggest Saddam Hussein had a plan to attack Israel.[46] Israel relied instead on the declared hostile intentions of Iraq,

[40] 'Questions Relating to the Americas' (n. 39), pp. 106–9. See also J. S. Campbell, 'The Cuban Missile Crisis and the U.N. Charter: An Analysis of the United States Position' (1963) 16 *Stanford Law Review* 160–76; M. S. McDougal, 'The Soviet-Cuban Quarantine and Self-Defense' (1963) 57 *American Journal of International Law* 597–604; L. C. Meeker, 'Defensive Quarantine and the Law' (1963) 57 *American Journal of International Law* 515–24; K. Tibori-Szabó, *Anticipatory Action in Self-Defence* (Springer, 2011), pp. 178–9.

[41] Stockholm International Peace Research Institute (SIPRI), 'World Nuclear Forces', in *SIPRI Yearbook 2020: Armaments, Disarmament and International Security*, pp. 375–7, www.sipri.org/sites/default/files/2020-06/yb20_10_wnf.pdf. Israel has neither officially confirmed nor denied that it possesses nuclear weapons.

[42] Baylis and Smith (eds.), *Globalization* (n. 8), p. 86; Mueller et al., *Striking First* (n. 32), p. 212.

[43] UNSC, 'Letter dated 8 June 1981 from the Permanent Representative of Israel to the United Nations addressed to the President of the Security Council', UN Doc. S/14510 (1981).

[44] Mueller et al., *Striking First* (n. 32), p. 212.

[45] UN Doc. S/14510 (n. 43); SCOR, 36thsession, 2288th meeting, 19 June 1981, UN Doc. S/PV.2288, paras. 78–9.

[46] T. M. Franck, *Recourse to Force: State Action against Threats and Armed Attacks* (Cambridge University Press, 2002), p. 106; T. D. Gill, 'The Temporal Dimension of Self-Defence: Anticipation, Pre-emption, Prevention and Immediacy', in M. N. Schmitt and J. Pejić, *International Law and Armed Conflict: Exploring the Faultlines* (Nijhoff, 2007), p. 141.

including a statement made by Saddam Hussein that the reactor was being constructed against Israel.[47]

Against this background, on 6 June 1981 Israeli bomber and fighter planes flew into Iraq, destroyed the reactor and killed or injured around ten persons in the process.[48] Before the Security Council, Israel justified its action as self-defence 'as understood in general international law and as preserved in Article 51 of the Charter of the United Nations'.[49] Referring to the *Caroline* incident and quoting several scholars, Israel claimed that the right of self-defence did not demand that its government 'stand idly by while an irresponsible, ruthless and bellicose regime, such as that of Iraq, acquired nuclear weapons'.[50] Israel further maintained that 'the concepts of "armed attack" and the threat of such an attack must be read in conjunction with, and are related to, the present-day criteria of speed and power, and placed within the context of the circumstances surrounding nuclear attack, including the preparations for it and the consequences resulting therefrom'.[51] Israel also averred that the bombing could not have waited, because once the reactor became operational, an attack thereon would have caused extensive civilian damage due to the release of large amounts of nuclear fallout.[52]

International reaction was negative. Iraq condemned the Israeli raid as an act of aggression, as could be expected.[53] Before the Security Council, several States expressed their criticism of the Israeli action.[54] Some representatives asserted that the Israeli action went well beyond the limits of pre-emptive or anticipatory defensive action against an imminent attack.[55] The Israeli air strike was also characterized as 'preventive war', the legality of which was seen as having been abolished by the Charter.[56] The Security Council

47 UN Doc. S/14510 (n. 43).
48 Mueller et al., *Striking First* (n. 32), p. 215.
49 SCOR, 36th session, 2280th meeting, 12 June 1981, UN Doc. S/PV.2280, para. 58.
50 UN Doc. S/PV.2280 (n. 49), paras. 96–101; UN Doc. S/PV.2288 (n. 45), paras. 79–85.
51 GAOR, 36th session, 52nd plenary meeting, 11 November 1981, UN Doc. A/36/PV.52, para. 63.
52 UN Doc. S/14510 (n. 43); UN Doc. S/PV.2280 (n. 49), para. 95.
53 UN Doc. S/PV.2280 (n. 49), paras. 48–51.
54 SCOR, 36th session, 2280th–2288th meetings, 12–19 June 1981, UN Docs S/PV.2280–S/PV.2288.
55 SCOR, 36th session, 2282nd meeting, 15 June 1981, UN Doc. S/PV.2282, paras. 14–19; 2283rd meeting, 15 June 1981, S/PV.2283, paras. 23–7; 2284th meeting, 16 June 1981, UN Doc. S/PV.2284, para. 11.
56 UN Doc. S/PV.2283 (n. 55), paras. 46, 117, 146; UN Doc. S/PV.2288 (n. 45), para. 115; UN Doc. S/PV.2283 (n. 55), para. 146.

unanimously adopted a resolution that condemned the Israeli action and found it to be in clear violation of the Charter and the norms of international conduct.[57] The Israeli raid was also criticized by legal scholars.[58]

### *10.3.3 The War against Iraq (2003)*

The 2003 Iraqi War (Second Gulf War) involved several complex legal arguments advanced by mainly the United States and the United Kingdom.[59] The principal argument, however, was the alleged existence of Iraqi nuclear, chemical and biological weapons programmes in violation of relevant Security Council resolutions. This argument was coupled with a novel policy put forward by the United States in its 2002 National Security Strategy, according to which the concept of imminent threat in the context of self-defence had to be adapted 'to the capabilities and objectives of today's adversaries', including 'the use of weapons of mass destruction – weapons that can be easily concealed, delivered covertly, and used without warning'.[60] According to the new policy, '[t]he greater the threat, the greater is the risk of inaction' and the United States could not afford to 'remain idle' in the face of the 'world's most destructive technologies'; hence, anticipatory action was necessary, 'even if

[57] UNSC Resolution 487 (1981), para. 1.

[58] A. D'Amato, 'Israel's Air Strike against the Osiraq Reactor: A Retrospective' (1996) 10 *Temple International and Comparative Law Journal* 259–60; G. Fischer, 'Le bombardement par Israël d'un réacteur nucléaire irakien' (1981) 27 *Annuaire français de droit international* 147–67; M. S. Nydell, 'Tensions between International Law and Strategic Security: Implications of Israel's Preemptive Raid on Iraq's Nuclear Reactor' (1984) 24 *Virginia Journal of International Law* 459–92, at 471, 483; S. Alexandrov, *Self-Defense against the Use of Force in International Law* (Kluwer Law International, 1996), p. 162; Franck, *Recourse to Force* (n. 46), pp. 105–6; Gill, 'Temporal Dimension' (n. 46), pp. 141–2; C. Greenwood, 'International Law and the Preemptive Use of Force: Afghanistan, Al-Qaida and Iraq' (2003) 4 *San Diego International Law Journal* 7–38, at 14. For a defence of the Israeli position, see N. J. Kaplan, 'The Attack on Osirak: Delimitation of Self-Defence under International Law' (1982) 4 *New York Law School Journal of International and Comparative Law* 131–56, at 155–6.

[59] C. Greenwood, 'Legality of the Use of Force: Iraq in 2003', in M. Bothe, M. E. O'Connell and N. Ronzitti (eds.), *Redefining Sovereignty: The Use of Force after the Cold War* (Transnational, 2005), pp. 399–404.

[60] *The National Security Strategy of the United States of America* (September 2002), pt V ('Prevent Our Enemies from Threatening Us, Our Allies, and Our Friends with Weapons of Mass Destruction'), p. 15. See also President G. W. Bush, State of the Union Address, 29 January 2002, https://tinyurl.com/2vcv253t; President G. W. Bush, Graduation Speech at West Point', 1 June 2002, https://tinyurl.com/53tkszvyl.

uncertainty remains as to the time and place of the enemy's attack'.[61] The policy was further characterized by the then legal adviser of the US State Department, William H. Taft IV, as relying upon 'the same legal framework applied to the British in *Caroline* and to Israel in 1981'.[62]

On 12 September 2002, in a speech before the General Assembly, US president George W. Bush warned that Iraq continued to withhold important information about its nuclear program, that it retained the physical infrastructure needed to build a nuclear weapon and that if it acquired fissile material, it would be able to build such a weapon within a year.[63] The US president characterized the actions of the Iraqi regime as a threat to peace. Therefore, Iraq was obliged, inter alia, to disclose and remove or destroy all of its weapons of mass destruction.[64]

During the following months, the Security Council adopted several resolutions dealing with Iraq.[65] Resolution 1441 of November 2002 found Iraq to be in 'material breach' of its obligations under previous resolutions, including Resolution 687 (1991), in particular through its failure to co-operate with United Nations and the International Atomic Energy Agency (IAEA) inspectors.[66] The resolution put forward several demands, with which Iraq was called upon to comply, and warned that Iraq would face serious consequences if it continued to disregard its obligations.[67] Although the resolution was adopted under Chapter VII of the Charter, there was no reference to collective enforcement actions.[68] Iraq agreed to comply with Resolution 1441 and to the re-entry of UN and IAEA inspectors,[69] who carried out several inspections and reported

61 *National Security Strategy* (n. 60).

62 W. H. Taft, 'The Legal Basis for Preemption', Council on Foreign Relations (18 November 2002).

63 'President's Remarks at the United Nations General Assembly' (12 September 2002), https://tinyurl.com/3u957v8ul.

64 Ibid.

65 UNSC Resolutions 1441, 1443, 1447 and 1454 (2002).

66 UNSC Resolution 1441 (2002), para. 1.

67 Ibid., para. 13.

68 An earlier draft of what became paragraph 4 of UNSC Resolution 1441 (2002) stated that 'such breach authorizes Member States to use all necessary means to restore international peace and security in the area'. The text was opposed by France and Russia and thus was erased from the final version of the resolution. D. McGoldrick, *From '9-11' to the Iraq War 2003: International Law in an Age of Complexity* (Hart, 2004), p. 62; Tibori-Szabó, *Anticipatory Action* (n. 40), p. 190.

69 E. MacAskill and O. Burkeman, 'Defiant Saddam Accepts UN Team', *The Guardian* (14 November 2002), www.theguardian.com/world/2002/nov/14/iraq.ewenmacaskill; 'UN Weapons Inspectors Arrive in Iraq', *The Guardian* (18 November 2002), www.theguardian.com/world/2002/nov/18/iraq.

a number of contraventions[70] but found no evidence of 'proscribed activities'.[71] Additionally, several States expressed strong support for a peaceful disarmament process.[72]

In these circumstances, the United States, the United Kingdom and Australia, supported by a number of other States (the 'Coalition of the Willing'), decided to take military action without a further resolution of the Security Council expressly endorsing it.[73] Their argument was a complex legal construction, according to which the 'material breach' of Resolution 687 (1991), as ascertained by Resolution 1441 (2002), in fact revived the mandate of Resolution 678 (1990) that authorized the use of force against Iraq.[74] Accordingly, by not complying with Resolution 1441, Iraq had, according to this view, squandered the last opportunity for a peaceful solution, thus reviving the mandate of Resolution 678 (1990) and removing options other than the use of force.[75] Next to this argument, the United

70 'Iraq Timeline: July 16 1979 to January 31 2004', Special Report Iraq, *The Guardian*, www.guardian.co.uk/Iraq/page/0,12438,793802,00.html; 'Iraq Weapons Inspectors Find Empty Chemical Warheads', *The Guardian* (17 January 2003), www.guardian.co.uk/world/2003/jan/17/iraq.ewenmacaskill; 'UN Team Finds Iraq Has Illegal Missiles', *The Guardian* (13 February 2003), www.guardian.co.uk/world/2003/feb/13/iraq.garyyounge.

71 M. ElBaradei, Director General IAEA, 'Statement to the United Nations Security Council: The Status of Nuclear Inspections in Iraq', 27 January 2003; H. Blix, Executive Chairman of the UN Monitoring, Verification and Inspection Commission (UNMOVIC), 'Briefing of the Security Council: An Update on Inspections', 27 January 2003; M. ElBaradei, Director General IAEA, 'Statement to the United Nations Security Council: The Status of Nuclear Inspections in Iraq – An Update', 14 February 2003; 'Hans Blix's Briefing to the Security Council', *The Guardian* (14 February 2003), www.theguardian.com/world/2003/feb/14/iraq.unitednations1; M. ElBaradei, Director General IAEA, 'Statement to the United Nations Security Council: The Status of Nuclear Inspections in Iraq – An Update', 7 March 2003, http://www.un.org/News/dh/iraq/elbaradei-7mar03.pdf; H. Blix, 'Briefing of the Security Council: Oral Introduction of the 12th Quarterly Report of UNMOVIC' (7 March 2003); SCOR, 58th session, 4714th meeting, 7 March 2003, UN Doc. S/PV.4714, p. 3.

72 UN Doc. S/PV.4714 (n. 71), pp. 9 (Germany), 11 (Syria), 17 (Russia), 18–19 (France), 21 (China), 32–3 (Pakistan).

73 Greenwood, 'Legality' (n. 59), p. 395; Tibori-Szabó, *Anticipatory Action* (n. 40), pp. 190–1.

74 UNSC, 'Letter dated 20 March 2003 from the Permanent Representative of the United States of America to the United Nations addressed to the President of the Security Council', UN Doc. S/2003/351 (2003); UNSC, 'Letter dated 20 March 2003 from the Permanent Representative of the United Kingdom of Great Britain and Northern Ireland to the United Nations addressed to the President of the Security Council', UN Doc. S/2003/350 (2003); McGoldrick, *From '9-11' to the Iraq War 2003* (n. 68), pp. 53–5, p. 286 (Appendix VII: 'The Advice of the United Kingdom Attorney-General, Lord Goldsmith, on "The Legal Basis for the Use of Force against Iraq", 17 March 2003').

75 UN Doc. S/2003/351 (n. 74); McGoldrick, *From '9-11' to the Iraq War 2003* (n. 68), pp. 53–5, pp. 264–80 (Appendix V: 'Presentation of Colin Powell, US Secretary of State, to the United Nations Security Council on "Iraq – Failing to Disarm", 5 February 2003').

States also maintained that the actions of the coalition forces were necessary steps 'to defend the United States and the international community from the threat posed by Iraq and to restore international peace and security in the area'[76] and that 'the President may also ... always use force under international law in self-defence'.[77] These statements were interpreted by many commentators as the first application of the novel policy advanced in the 2002 National Security Strategy.[78]

Operation Iraqi Freedom commenced on 19 March 2003. On 1 May 2003 President Bush announced the end of 'major combat operations'. In June 2004 the United States transferred sovereignty to Iraq, while the US combat mission ended in August 2010.[79] No WMDs were ever found in Iraq.[80] Today, the 2003 war is widely regarded as having been unlawful,

Greenwood asserted that the governments that resorted to force against Iraq were right to conclude that they could rely on the authorization of military action in UNSC Resolution 678, read together with Resolutions 687 and 1441. Greenwood, 'International Law' (n. 58), p. 36. For similar opinions, see C. Hill, 'The Bush Administration Preemption Doctrine and the Future of World Order: Remark' (2004) 98 *American Society of International Law Proceedings* 329–31; C. Pierson, 'Preemptive Self-Defence in an Age of Weapons of Mass Destruction: Operation Iraqi Freedom' (2004), 33 *Denver Journal of International Law and Policy* 150–78, at 154–5; W. H. Taft and T. F. Buchwald, 'Preemption, Iraq, and International Law' (2003) 97 *American Journal of International Law* 557–63; R. Wedgwood, 'The Fall of Saddam Hussein: Security Council Mandates and Preemptive Self-Defence' (2003) 97 *American Journal of International Law* 576–85, at 584; J. Yoo, 'International Law and the War in Iraq' (2003) 97 *American Journal of International Law* 563–76, at 571–4. Rejecting the US argument, see Conclusions to Davids Commission, 'Rapport Commissie van Onderzoek Besluitvorming Irak' (January 2010), https://tinyurl.com/2p89dh2u, paras. 18–20.

76 UN Doc. S/2003/351 (n. 74).

77 W. H. Taft, Remarks to the National Association of Attorneys General, 20 March 2003, http://usinfo.org/wf-archive/2003/030321/epf516.htm.

78 R. N. Gardner, 'Neither Bush Nor the "Jurisprudes"' (2003) 97 *American Journal of International Law* 585–90, at 588; C. Henderson, 'The Bush Doctrine: From Theory to Practice' (2004) 9 *Journal of Conflict and Security Law* 3–24, at 12; McGoldrick, *From '9-11' to the Iraq War 2003* (n. 68), p. 68; M. Sapiro, 'Iraq: The Shifting Sands of Preemptive Self-Defense' (2003) 97 *American Journal of International Law* 599–607, at 602. See also 'A Decade of Deception and Defiance: Saddam Hussein's Defiance of the United Nations' (12 September 2002), www.gwu.edu/~nsarchiv/NSAEBB/NSAEBB80/wmd13.pdf.

79 A. Silverleib, 'US Combat Mission in Iraq Ends', CNN News (1 September 2010), https://tinyurl.com/yr9f8wh4.

80 *Comprehensive Report of the Special Advisor to the DCI on Iraq's WMD, with Addendums, Revised* (April 2005), https://www.govinfo.gov/app/details/GPO-DUELFERREPORT. The report concluded that Saddam Hussein did not possess stockpiles of illicit weapons at the time of the US invasion in March 2003 and had not begun any programme to produce them.

including by the present authors.[81] In the absence of clear evidence that Iraq was in the process of preparing an attack on the United States or its allies, the only legal path to use force was through the Security Council, which retained overall authority over the implementation of its earlier resolutions.

### *10.3.4 The Israeli Air Strike in Syria (2007)*

On 6 September 2007 Israeli aircraft entered Syrian airspace and struck a nuclear research establishment in the north of the country. The facility, code-named al-Kibar, was said to be operating with the involvement of North Korea.[82] The incident and its aftermath was shrouded in mystery, with neither Israel nor Syria providing details about the air strikes or their target. Subsequent reports and accounts seemed to confirm the assumption that the facility destroyed was a nuclear reactor in the early stages of construction.[83]

Syria characterized the air strikes as an act of aggression against its territory,[84] while Israel issued no official comment and provided no legal justification.[85] In stark contrast to reaction to the 1981 Israeli raid, the 2007 air strike prompted virtually no response from other States, except

[81] Tibori-Szabó, *Anticipatory Action* (n. 40), pp. 197–8; Gardner, 'Neither Bush Nor the "Jurisprudes"' (n. 78), pp. 587–8; Henderson, 'Bush Doctrine' (n. 78), p. 14; V. Lowe, 'The Iraqi Crisis: What Now?' (2003) 52 *International & Comparative Law Quarterly* 859–71, at 865; M. Sapiro, 'Preempting Prevention: Lessons Learned' (2005) 37 *NYU Journal of International Law and Politics* 357–371, at 367; A. M. Slaughter, 'The Use of Force in Iraq: Illegal and Illegitimate' (2004) 98 *American Society of International Law Proceedings* 262–3.

[82] 'Israeli Nuclear Suspicions Linked to Raid in Syria', *New York Times* (18 September 2007), www.nytimes.com/2007/09/18/world/asia/18korea.html; 'Israeli Airstrike Was Aimed at Syrian Reactor, Report Says', *The Guardian* (15 October 2007), www.theguardian.com/world/2007/oct/15/syria.israel; R. Weitz, 'Israel Airstrike in Syria: International Reactions' (James Martin Center for Non-Proliferation Studies, 1 November 2007), https://tinyurl.com/k48buy63; L. Moir, 'Israeli Airstrikes in Syria – 2003 and 2007', in Ruys and Corten (eds.), Use of Force (n. 39), pp. 662–3.

[83] United States Office of the Director of National Intelligence (ODNI), 'Background Briefing with Senior U.S. Officials on Syria's Covert Nuclear Reactor and North Korea's Involvement' (24 April 2008), https://tinyurl.com/43xuzcxa; IAEA, 'Implementation of the NPT Safeguards Agreement in the Syrian Arab Republic: Report by the Director General', GOV/2011/30 (24 May 2011), p. 1, www.iaea.org/sites/default/files/gov2011-30.pdf.

[84] UNGA/UNSC, 'Identical letters dated 9 September 2007 from the Permanent Representative of the Syrian Arab Republic to the United Nations addressed to the Secretary-General and the President of the Security Council', UN Doc A/61/1041–S/2007/537.

[85] Moir, 'Israeli Airstrikes' (n. 82), p. 666.

for a North Korean statement condemning the Israeli air strike.[86] The United States, China, Russia and Arab States refrained from issuing statements.[87] The European Union limited its reaction to a request for 'cooler heads' to prevail.[88] Two years later, however, the Non-Aligned Movement unequivocally condemned the Israeli raid as a flagrant violation of the UN Charter.[89]

### 10.3.5 *Nuclear Deterrence and Strategy and the* jus ad bellum

One of the linchpins of alliances such as NATO during and since the Cold War has been the policy of nuclear deterrence, which was linked to the right of collective self-defence. The policy is based on the idea that a potential aggressor would not risk a nuclear response, whether to a nuclear first strike or a large-scale conventional attack, and that thereby the possibility of a war between nuclear powers and their allies would be reduced. Such a policy is effective only if the threat of a nuclear response is credible. In the early stages of the Cold War, the United States relied on a threat of massive retaliation in response to any large-scale attack that would result in 'mutually assured destruction' of all protagonists in the event of a war between the Soviet Union and the United States and their respective allies. This policy was gradually supplanted by a more flexible and graduated response to a potential attack, as a result of the increasing parity in nuclear capability between the two main nuclear rivals of the period, together with a changing political and strategic climate in the later stages of the Cold War that supported this shift in strategy.[90]

Nevertheless, the policy of nuclear deterrence was not abandoned and still has a place in the strategic posture of not only nuclear-weapon States but also many other States linked to them by political and military

[86] Korean Central News Agency of the DPRK, 'Israel Condemned for Intrusion into Syria's Territorial Air' (11 September 2007), in Federation of American Scientists, *A Sourcebook on the Israeli Strike in Syria, 6 September 2007* (8 September 2018), p. 14, https://fas.org/man/eprint/syria.pdf.

[87] Moir, 'Israeli Airstrikes' (n. 82), p. 666.

[88] CNN News, 'Syria Complains to U.N. about Israeli Airstrike'(11 September 2007), https://edition.cnn.com/2007/WORLD/meast/09/11/israel.syria/.

[89] 'Final Document', Fifteenth Summit of the Heads of State and Government of the Non-Aligned Movement, Sharm-el-Sheikh, Egypt, 11–16 July 2009 (NAM2009/FD/Doc.1, 16 July 2009), para. 125.

[90] L. Freedman, 'The First Two Generations of Nuclear Strategists', in P. Paret (ed.) *Makers of Modern Strategy: From Machiavelli to the Nuclear Age* (Princeton University Press, 1986), p. 735.

commitments. Although there is no explicit commitment to resort to nuclear weapons in any treaty of alliance, the threat of a potential nuclear response in the event of large-scale attack is probably still implicit.

The importance and potential downside of nuclear deterrence is also highlighted by the 2022 Russian war against Ukraine. Russia's possession of nuclear weapons has not deterred NATO countries from arming Ukraine and from imposing sanctions on Russia. Nonetheless, the United States and other NATO members are refraining from action that could be perceived as posing an existential threat to Russia, which could in turn push it to use nuclear weapons.[91] On the other hand, if Russia were to use nuclear weapons against Ukraine, this would have major repercussions on the position of Russia within the international community and could potentially lead to a further escalation of the conflict, aside from being indefensible legally or otherwise. This is also reflected in the US president's warning against the use of tactical nuclear weapons by Russia, an act that would 'change the face of war unlike anything since World War Two'.[92]

### *10.3.6 Implications for the* jus ad bellum

What the aforementioned instances of State practice have in common is the use of armed force by a State in response to alleged possession or development of nuclear weapons by another State. The justifications put forward seem to impact mainly on the right of self-defence, as one of the exceptions to the prohibition to use force enshrined in Article 2(4) of the Charter. In the Cuban crisis, the United States shied away from the direct use of armed force in the form of air strikes or ground invasion, as it did not view the Soviet build-up in Cuba as an imminent threat of an armed attack justifying resort to self-defence. It chose instead to rely on a regional arrangement and impose a naval quarantine that was a lesser form of force. Almost twenty years later, Israel took a much bolder view on the matter: it opted for surgical air strikes to destroy a reactor that was allegedly developing nuclear weapons. Israel justified its actions as self-defence, notwithstanding the fact that the reactor was at least five years away from producing such a weapon. Despite near-universal criticism of

[91] M. Harries, 'Putin's Brutal War Shows the Dilemmas of Nuclear Deterrence: Powerful Threats Could Too Easily Become Real Disasters', *Foreign Policy*, (22 March 2022), https://tinyurl.com/3tn2ferk.

[92] CBS News, 'President Biden Warns Vladimir Putin Not to Use Nuclear Weapons: "Don't. Don't. Don't."' (16 September 2022), https://tinyurl.com/yevbjft6.

the Israeli action at that time, the United States twenty years later followed the Israeli approach in its 2002 National Security Strategy. In invading Iraq, the United States nonetheless chose to rely primarily on a legal argument involving the other exception to the prohibition to use force – namely, collective enforcement actions under Chapter VII of the Charter. In 2007, Israel chose to remain silent and advanced no legal justification for its air strike against a purported Syrian nuclear facility.

It is thus clear that since 1962 there has been a gradual shift towards proactive and unilateral uses of force to prevent the development or possession of nuclear weapons. This shift transcends the contemporary limits of *jus ad bellum*, as it corresponds to neither of the two exceptions to the prohibition on the use force.

In particular, while the adoption of Chapter VII enforcement measures involving the use of force against the development or possession of nuclear weapons is possible, they must be ordered by the Security Council and States cannot unilaterally appoint themselves to carry out such measures. Moreover, the political divides in the Security Council could often pose difficulties for the adoption of such measures.[93] This is particularly apparent today, given the deepening divide between Russia and some other members of the Security Council as a result of the Ukrainian war.

Equally, self-defence cannot accommodate uses of force where no imminent threat of an armed attack exists. First, the possession or development of nuclear weapons is not, in itself, unlawful under the *jus ad bellum*.[94] As the International Court of Justice (ICJ) found in its 1996 *Nuclear Weapons* advisory opinion, the use or possession of nuclear weapons was not in itself contrary to Article 2(4) of the Charter.[95] In particular, the Court opined that the possession of nuclear weapons could be rendered an unlawful threat under Article 2(4) of the Charter only if the particular use of force envisaged were to be directed against the territorial integrity or political independence of a State or the purposes of the United Nations, or, where such possession was

[93] D. H. Joyner, 'The Implications of the Proliferation of Weapons of Mass Destruction for the Prohibition of the Use of Force', in M. Weller (ed.), *The Oxford Handbook of the Use of Force in International Law* (Oxford University Press, 2017), pp. 1048–52.

[94] Non-nuclear State parties to the NPT and State parties to the TPNW are prohibited from, inter alia, producing or possessing nuclear weapons, but this prohibition is based on their treaty obligations and not on the *jus ad bellum*.

[95] ICJ, *Legality of the Threat or Use of Nuclear Weapons*, Advisory Opinion, 8 July 1996, ICJ Reports 1996, paras. 39, 48.

> **SUMMARY BOX 10.2 POSSESSION OF NUCLEAR WEAPONS AS AN IMMINENT THREAT**
>
> Possession of nuclear weapons can translate into an imminent threat of an armed attack under Article 51 of the Charter only if there is credible information that steps are being undertaken to launch an attack involving such weapons in the near future.

intended as a means of defence, if it were to violate the principles of necessity and proportionality.[96] According to the ICJ, even if possession of such weapons showed preparedness to use them by the possessing State, a credible intention of using nuclear weapons was necessary for an effective policy of deterrence.[97] The Court thus took the view that a policy of nuclear deterrence would not violate the prohibition on the threat of force if the threat to use force was for a lawful purpose such as (collective) self-defence.[98]

Second, even if possession of nuclear weapons amounted to an inchoate threat of force under Article 2(4) of the Charter or a threat to international peace and security under its Article 39, such a threat does not automatically translate into an imminent threat of an armed attack. The Court did not suggest that possession of nuclear weapons in such cases would trigger the exercise of self-defence under Article 51 of the Charter. Accordingly, possession of nuclear weapons can translate into an imminent threat of an armed attack only if there is credible information that steps are being undertaken to launch an attack involving such weapons in the near future (see Chapter 6, above). Moreover, since the production of nuclear weapons typically takes years, an imminent threat of an armed attack cannot possibly materialize while the development process for such weapons is ongoing. In the event that nuclear weapons are used in self-defence, the principles of necessity and proportionality would apply. This would presuppose an armed attack on such a large scale that a nuclear response would become potentially necessary and proportionate in *ad bellum* terms. In addition, any such use would also have to comply with the law of armed conflict and other applicable law.[99]

[96] Ibid., para. 48.
[97] Ibid., para. 48.
[98] Ibid., paras. 47–8.
[99] *Nuclear Weapons* Advisory Opinion (n. 95), paras. 77–87.

The shift towards proactive and unilateral uses of force has become part and parcel of a relatively novel policy of 'counter-proliferation', developed in the post-9/11 international security climate. While 'non-proliferation' efforts traditionally relied upon diplomacy and the implementation of treaty obligations, counter-proliferation efforts are generally designed either to forcefully prevent specific States and non-State actors from developing or possessing WMDs or related materials and technologies or to compel the destruction of existing WMD capabilities.[100] Such counter-proliferation efforts include intelligence activities, early detection technologies, interdiction of suspected transfers of sensitive items, cyber operations, law enforcement and preventive uses of force.[101] The latter category is incompatible with the contemporary law on the use of force. That being said, it may be that such future instances, if sufficiently frequent and consistent enough in their justifications to elicit a condoning reaction from the majority of States, could lead to the emergence of a new customary rule condoning preventive uses of force under certain circumstances in the context of nuclear counter-proliferation. At this point, however, it is decidedly premature to speculate whether, or under what conditions, this might happen.

## 10.4 Chemical Weapons and the Use of Force

As said above, chemical weapons have been used several times in recent decades, most recently in the Syrian civil war. These instances have occurred in the context of international and/or non-international armed conflicts and have been widely condemned as illegal under international law. Recent efforts to prevent possession or use of such weapons have also, in a few instances, led to the use of force. This section will concentrate on these instances and their significance for the *jus ad bellum*.

### *10.4.1 US Air Strikes in Sudan and Afghanistan (1998)*

On 7 August 1998 twin bombings in Nairobi (Kenya) and Dar-Es-Salaam (Tanzania) killed or injured several hundred people and caused damage to the US embassies there, which were the targets of the

[100] Joyner, 'Implications' (n. 93), pp. 1036–7.

[101] D. H. Joyner, 'The Proliferation Security Initiative: Nonproliferation, Counterproliferation and International Law' (2005) 30 *Yale Journal of International Law* 507–48; M. Roscini, 'Cyber Operations as Nuclear Counterproliferation Measures' (2014) 19 *Journal of Conflict and Security Law* 133–57.

attack.[102] Two weeks later, on 20 August 1998, the United States fired Tomahawk missiles at targets in Afghanistan and Sudan. The United States contended that the Afghan targets were training camps associated with the so-called bin Laden network, in relation to which there was convincing information that it was responsible for the Kenya and Tanzania bombings. As regards the Sudanese target, the United States contended that it was a chemical plant involved in the production of chemical weapon agents and associated with the same bin Laden network.[103]

The United States promptly informed the Security Council about the air strikes and invoked the right of self-defence in the face of 'a series of armed attacks' against US embassies and nationals.[104] It also referred to the purported production of chemical weapons at the Sudanese target, without, however, maintaining that chemical weapons were used or about to be used by the bin Laden network.[105]

The reaction to the US air strikes was mixed and concentrated on the justification of self-defence against terrorist attacks.[106] It is nonetheless important to note that this was one of the first instances in which the unilateral use of force was justified also as a response to the production or possession of chemical weapons.

### *10.4.2 Air Strikes in Syria (2017, 2018)*

The civilian uprising in Syria began in 2011 and by 2012 had reached the threshold of a non-international armed conflict characterized by widespread human rights abuses and intentional uses of armed force against civilians by Syrian forces and authorities.[107]

[102] US Department of State, 'Discussion and Findings: Report of the Accountability Review Boards on the Embassy Bombings in Nairobi, Kenya and Dar es Salaam, Tanzania on August 7, 1998' (January 1999), https://tinyurl.com/34jfrsct.

[103] US Department of State, 'Address to the Nation by the President' (20 August 1998), https://tinyurl.com/fyfamds9; US Department of State, 'Fact Sheet: U.S. Strike on Facilities in Afghanistan and Sudan' (21 August 1998), https://tinyurl.com/yusn4smr.

[104] UNSC, 'Letter dated 20 August 1998 from the Permanent Representative of the United States of America to the United Nations addressed to the President of the Security Council', UN Doc. S/1998/780 (20 August 1998).

[105] Ibid.

[106] Tibori-Szabó, *Anticipatory Action* (n. 40), pp. 219–20.

[107] UNSC, 'Statement by the President of the Security Council', UN Doc. S/PRST/2011/16 (3 July 2011); International Committee of the Red Cross (ICRC), 'Syria: ICRC and Syrian Arab Red Crescent Maintain Effort Amid Increased Fighting' (17 July 2012), https://

In August 2012, in response to reports of possible uses of chemical weapons, US president Barack Obama warned all parties to the conflict that deploying such weapons would be to cross a 'red line' and lead to 'enormous consequences'.[108] The United Kingdom and France made similar statements.[109]

One year later, in August 2013, several attacks occurred, the effects of which pointed to use of the nerve agent Sarin.[110] The United States, the United Kingdom and France contemplated a military intervention in Syria but abandoned the plan once it became clear that neither the American nor the British legislatures would approve such action.[111] Instead, further to Russian diplomatic involvement, Syria agreed to ratify the Chemical Weapons Convention and to submit to the monitoring and destruction or removal of its chemical arsenal.[112] Despite these steps and several inspections by the Organisation for the Prohibition of Chemical Weapons (OPCW), incidents involving the use of chemical weapons

tinyurl.com/y46p759a; Human Rights Council, 'Report of the independent international commission of inquiry on the Syrian Arab Republic', UN Doc. A/HRC/21/50 (16 August 2012); K. Huszti-Orbán and N. Kalandarishvili-Mueller, 'Is it a Bird? Is it a Plane? Is it an Armed Conflict? The Classification of the Situation in Syria' (2012) 1 *Journal of International Law*; C. Phillips, 'Syria', in L. Arimatsu and M. Choudhury (eds.), *The Legal Classification of the Armed Conflicts in Syria, Yemen and Libya* (Chatham House, 2014), p. 15; A. Lagerwall, 'Threats and Actual Military Strikes against Syria – 2013 and 2017', in Ruys and Corten (eds.), *Use of Force*, pp. 828–9.

108 The White House, 'Remarks by the President to the White House Press Corps' (20 August 2012), https://tinyurl.com/yh4ar7hu.

109 'Prime Minister's phone calls with Presidents Hollande and Obama' (23 August 2012), https://tinyurl.com/4m7fxmx9; 'Discours Hollande aux ambassadeurs, XXème Conférence, 27 août 2017', https://tinyurl.com/2bt4pa7w.

110 'Syria: Reported Chemical Weapons Use', Letter from chairman of UK Joint Intelligence Committee, 29 August 2013, https://tinyurl.com/yjmpe8mr; The White House, 'Government Assessment of the Syrian Government's Use of Chemical Weapons on August 21, 2013' (30 August 2013), https://tinyurl.com/mr393yu2; French Defence Ministry, 'Syria/Syrian Chemical Programme: National Executive Summary of Declassified Intelligence' (3 September 2013), https://tinyurl.com/mrxp84x5 . See also UNGA/UNSC, 'Report of the United Nations Mission to Investigate Allegations of the Use of Chemical Weapons in the Syrian Arab Republic on the alleged use of chemical weapons in the Ghouta area of Damascus on 21 August 2013', UN Doc. A/67/997–S/2013/553 (16 September 2013).

111 Lagerwall, 'Threats and Actual Military Strikes' (n. 107), p. 830.

112 Syria ratified the Chemical Weapons Convention on 14 September 2013; see www.opcw.org/about-us/member-states/syria; OPCW, Joint Framework on Destruction of Syrian CW, Annex B of Framework for Elimination of Syrian Chemical Weapons (14 September 2013), EC-M-33/NAT.1, https://tinyurl.com/2p8jy9xh.

continued to be reported in 2014 and 2015.[113] As a result, in 2015 the Security Council condemned the use of chemical weapons and established a joint investigative mechanism to identify users of such weapons in Syria.[114] Notwithstanding, incidents involving the use of chemical weapons continued to be reported in 2016 as well.[115]

On 5 April 2017, following new reports of the Syrian regime having used chemical weapons the day before,[116] US ambassador Nikki Haley warned Security Council members that 'when the United Nations consistently fails in its duty to act collectively, there are times in the life of States in which we are compelled to take our own action'.[117] On 7 April US planes struck and severely damaged an airbase in the Homs Governorate, believed to be the source of the 4 April chemical attack (see Chapter 9, Fact Box 9.2).[118] The United States justified the strike as a 'proportional response to Assad's heinous act', aimed at deterring the Syrian regime 'from using chemical weapons again'.[119] Neither the United States nor the countries expressing support for the air strike made any explicit reference to its legality under international law.[120]

[113] OPCW, 'Second Report of the Fact-Finding Mission in Syria', UN Doc. S/1212/2014 (10 September 2014); 'Third Report of the OPCW Fact-Finding Mission in Syria', UN Doc. S/1230/2014 (18 December 2014); 'Report of the OPCW Fact-Finding Mission in Syria regarding alleged incidents in the Idlib Governorate of the Syrian Arab Republic between 16 March and 20 May 2015', UN Doc. S/1319/2015 (29 October 2015); 'Report of the OPCW Fact-Finding Mission in Syria regarding alleged incidents in Marea – August 2015', UN Doc. S/1320/2015 (29 October 2015); 'Report of the OPCW Fact-Finding Mission in Syria regarding the incidents described in communications from the Deputy Minister for Foreign Affairs and Expatriates and Head of the National Authority of the Syrian Arab Republic', UN Doc. S/1318/2015/Rev.1 (17 December 2015).

[114] UNSC Resolution 2209 (2015); UNSC Resolution 2235 (2015).

[115] OPCW, 'Report of the Fact-Finding Mission in Syria regarding the incident of 2 August 2016 as reported in the *Note Verbale* of the Syrian Arab Republic number 69 dated 16 August 2016', UN Doc. S/1444/2016 (21 December 2016).

[116] 'Worst Chemical Attack in Years in Syria; US Blames Assad', *New York Times*, (4 April 2017), https://tinyurl.com/5erwtaak; Human Rights Watch, 'Death by Chemicals: The Syrian Government's Widespread and Systematic Use of Chemical Weapons' (1 May 2017), https://tinyurl.com/5ce6p7xs.

[117] SCOR, 72nd year, 7915th meeting, UN Doc. S/PV.7915 (5 April 2017), p. 18.

[118] SCOR, 72nd year, 7919th meeting, UN Doc. S/PV.7919 (7 April 2017), p. 2; US Department of Defense, 'Statement by Secretary of Defense Jim Mattis on the U.S. Military Response to the Syrian Government's Use of Chemical Weapons', news release (10 April 2017), https://tinyurl.com/yuk3urua.

[119] US Department of Defense, 'Statement from Pentagon Spokesman Capt. Jeff Davis on U.S. Strike in Syria' (6 April 2017), https://tinyurl.com/yc6rwdxv.

[120] UN Doc. S/PV.7919 (n. 118), pp. 5 (United Kingdom), 9 (France), 8 (Italy), 16 (Ukraine). Other countries supporting the US airstrikes were Australia, Canada, Japan, Saudi Arabia and Turkey. See Lagerwall, 'Threats and Actual Military Strikes' (n. 107),

Syria, Russia and Iran condemned the airstrike, while a number of other countries expressed concerns over the compatibility of the strike with international law.[121]

One year later, on 13 April 2018, following reports of another chemical attack by the Syrian regime,[122] the United States, the United Kingdom and France bombed a research facility in Damascus alleged to be connected to the production of chemical and biological weapons and two chemical weapon storage facilities near Homs, one of which also operated as a command post (see Chapter 9, Fact Box 9.2).[123] As with the 2017 air strikes, the United States, the United Kingdom and France did not explicitly refer to international law in their justifications, but indicated that the bombings were meant to deter the future use of chemical weapons.[124] Russia and Syria condemned the bombings as acts of aggression, while other countries expressed concerns over the strikes' compatibility with international law.[125] That said, a draft resolution proposed by Russia condemning the air strikes as acts of aggression was opposed by eight members of the Council.[126]

### *10.4.3 Implications for the* jus ad bellum

The 1998 US air strikes' legality under *jus ad bellum* was debated at the time in relation to the use of self-defence against terrorist groups, but little emphasis was placed on the Sudanese chemical plant as a target. Conversely, the legality of the 2017 and 2018 strikes as uses of force in

pp. 848–9; G. Aisch, Y. Joseph and A. Singhvi, 'Which Countries Support and Which Oppose the U.S. Missile Strikes in Syria', *New York Times* (9 April 2017), https://tinyurl.com/yhf9kw5c.

121 UN Doc S/PV.7919 (n. 121), pp. 3 (Bolivia), 7 (Uruguay), 10 (Russia), 13 (Senegal, Kazakhstan), 14 (Sweden), 18 (Syria). See also Lagerwall, 'Threats and Actual Military Strikes' (n. 107), pp. 849–50. See also Chapter 9, above.

122 BBC News, 'Syria War: At Least 70 Killed in Suspected Chemical Attack in Douma' (8 April 2018), www.bbc.com/news/world-middle-east-43686157.

123 US Department of Defense, 'Press Briefing by Pentagon Chief Spokesperson Dana W. White and Joint Staff Director Lt. Gen. Kenneth F. McKenzie Jr. in the Pentagon Briefing Room', transcript (14 April 2018), https://tinyurl.com/3mjt5936; BBC News, 'Syria Air Strikes: US and Allies Attack "Chemical Weapons Sites"' (14 April 2018), www.bbc.com/news/world-middle-east-43762251.

124 SCOR, 73rd year, 8233rd meeting, 14 April 2018, UN Doc. S/PV.8233, pp. 5 (United States), 6 (United Kingdom), 9 (France).

125 Ibid., pp. 3 (Russia), 10 (China, Kazakhstan), 14 (Bolivia), 18 (Equatorial Guinea), 19–20 (Syria).

126 Ibid., pp. 22–23.

response to and for the prevention of the use of chemical weapons received significant attention from legal scholars, despite (or perhaps due to) the fact that the United States and its allies did not advance any specific legal justification. The arguments advanced revolved around three concepts: self-defence, humanitarian intervention and reprisals.

Some authors contended that the statements made by the United States and its allies on the occasion of the strikes echoed justifications of self-defence against the threat of chemical weapons.[127] There has been little doubting, however, that the 2017 and 2018 air strikes did not fit within the limits of Article 51 of the Charter, even when interpreted broadly to encompass anticipatory action against an imminent threat.[128] The Syrian regime's use of chemical weapons against its own people could not amount to an imminent threat of an armed attack against the United States or its allies (see Chapter 6, above). Others have suggested that such strikes could be justified as 'anticipatory collective self-defence', if the use of chemical weapons in Syria was likely to affect neighbouring countries and would therefore be seen as an armed attack on them.[129] This scenario has not, however, materialized and, in any event, the use of chemical weapons by the Syrian regime on its own people would not qualify as an armed attack on its neighbours simply because the poisonous particles might waft into their territory; there needs to be credible information about an intentional attack on the neighbouring States.[130] The 2017 and 2018 air strikes are accordingly not instances of anticipatory or collective self-defence.

Another argument that was advanced, and which sparked considerable debate, was that the 2017 and 2018 air strikes were a (new) form of

[127] R. Goodman, 'What Do Top Legal Experts Say about the Syria Strikes?', *Just Security* (7 April 2017), www.justsecurity.org/39712/top-legal-experts-syria-strikes/; M. N. Schmitt and C. M. Ford, 'Assessing U.S. Justifications for Using Force in Response to Syria's Chemical Attacks: An International Law Perspective' (2017) 9 *Journal of National Security Law and Policy* 283–303, at 285, 288; Lagerwall, 'Threats' (n. 107), p. 851.

[128] Schmitt and Ford, 'Assessing U.S. Justifications' (n. 127), pp. 288–90; Lagerwall, 'Threats' (n. 107), p. 851; S. Krishnan, 'The Alleged Use of Chemical Weapons against the Syrian People' (2017) 21(2) *World Affairs: The Journal of International Issues* 22–33, at 28–9.

[129] A. Deeks, 'Syria, Chemical Weapons, and Possible U.S. Military Action', *Lawfare* (10 December 2012), https://tinyurl.com/2d4jyzxw; A. Deeks, 'Chemical Weapons in Syria: Enough to Justify the Use of Force?', *Lawfare* (26 April 2013), https://tinyurl.com/yc38nztb; Krishnan, 'Alleged Use' (n. 128), pp. 28, 32.

[130] D. Akande, 'Does Use of Chemical Weapons Justify Intervention in Syria?', *EJIL:Talk!* (27 April 2013), https://tinyurl.com/ex4sj4ze.

humanitarian intervention.[131] These arguments were discussed and discarded in Chapter 9. For the purposes of this chapter, suffice it to say that the 2017 and 2018 air strikes were selective uses of force against one form of human rights violation against a background of widespread violations of human rights and humanitarian norms in the context of the Syrian conflict. They therefore were not conducted with the intention of, and definitely did not have the effect of, potentially alleviating the suffering of the entire Syrian population. They should therefore not be viewed as humanitarian interventions.

Several authors pointed out that the air strikes resembled armed reprisals.[132] These arguments were elaborated in Chapter 9. For the purposes of this chapter, suffice it to say that armed reprisals remain illegal under international law. That said, as observed above in relation to the use of force against the possession or development of nuclear weapons, it may be that such future instances, if sufficiently frequent and consistent enough in their justifications to elicit a condoning reaction from the majority of States, could lead to the emergence of a new customary rule allowing use of force against WMDs in certain circumstances. For the time being, however, such a new customary rule has not materialized. In any event, as proposed in Chapter 9, in cases of overriding humanitarian considerations and lack of other feasible alternatives, where reprisals are resorted to in a proportionate manner to coerce a State to respect its obligations and stop egregious human rights violations, reprisals can arguably be excused to a greater or lesser extent depending on the circumstances and the manner of their implementation. Such an approach should not, however, be seen as a precedent for the establishment of a new rule of customary law allowing for such interventions.

[131] Schmitt and Ford, 'Assessing U.S. Justifications' (n. 127), pp. 293–302; Goodman, 'What Do Top Legal Experts Say?' (n. 127).

[132] M. Milanovic, 'The Clearly Illegal US Missile Strike in Syria', *EJIL:Talk!* (7 April 2017), https://tinyurl.com/ckh6k94u; M. Milanovic, 'The Syria Strikes: Still Clearly Illegal', *EJIL:Talk!* (15 April 2018), https://tinyurl.com/y4fshkcf; M. Hakimi, 'The Attack on Syria and the Contemporary *Jus ad Bellum*', *EJIL:Talk!* (15 April 2018), https://tinyurl.com/y5n3sk3t; A. C. de Beer and D. Tladi, 'The Use of Force against Syria in Response to Alleged Use of Chemical Weapons by Syria: A Return to Humanitarian Intervention?' (2019) 79 *Heidelberg Journal of International Law* 205–39, at 224–6; M. E. O'Connell, 'The Popular but Unlawful Reprisal' (2018) 44 *Ohio Northern University Law Review* 325–50, at 325–7.

## 10.5 Biological Weapons and the Use of Force

While the development, possession or use of biological weapons has not so far led to use of armed force, the observations made above in relation to nuclear and chemical weapons also apply here. Accordingly, the use of force against the development, possession or use of biological weapons is legal only if it fits into one of the exceptions to the prohibition on the use of force – that is, if it is a collective enforcement action under Chapter VII ordered by the Security Council or an exercise of self-defence under Article 51 of the Charter and customary international law. Any other uses of force are currently illegal. It remains to be seen whether future instances of State practice will be capable of shaping customary international law to allow for an additional exception to the prohibition on the use of force, in relation to WMDs.

## 10.6 Conclusions

Chemical and biological weapons are banned outright under both conventional and customary international law, while possession of nuclear weapons is, in theory, banned for all States except nuclear-weapon States under the NPT. WMDs are not directly addressed by the UN Charter, but, as confirmed by the ICJ, the possession and potential use thereof does not in itself violate Article 2(4). Consequently, any use of force against the possession or use of WMDs must also accord with Article 2(4) of the Charter and, in particular, with the exceptions thereto (i.e. collective enforcement measures or self-defence). The instances of State practice discussed in this chapter have all pushed against, or in some cases clearly exceeded, the limits of the aforementioned provisions. They are precedents only in the sense that they happened. The critical question is whether other States will rely on such justifications in the future.[133] The indisputably abhorrent effect of WMDs is not in itself a justification for ignoring the law on the use of force, stringent as it may be. The relatively narrow scope of the exceptions to the prohibition on the use of force serve the very important purpose of preserving international peace and security. Instances of State practice violating such exceptions ultimately weaken the force of the law. It is also true, however, that the *jus ad bellum*

[133] Hakimi, 'Attack on Syria' (n. 132).

is not a static construct; it is shaped by the will of States, which, if sufficiently consistent and coherent, can lead to new treaty obligations or new customary rules. In the case of WMDs, it remains to be seen whether their feared nature and effects will engender an alteration of the existing limits of the *jus ad bellum*.

# 11

## New Technologies of Warfare and the Law on the Use of Force

### 11.1 Introduction

In this chapter we discuss how a number of new or emerging technologies and techniques of warfare affect the application of the law on the use of force. Most of these new or emerging means and methods of warfare have already received a substantial amount of attention in the literature and we do not intend to reproduce detailed discussions on cyber warfare, autonomous weapons, unmanned and remotely piloted aircraft (drones) or other new weaponry technologies. While some consideration has been given to the way such technologies might affect the *jus ad bellum*, most attention has been devoted to whether such weapons are compatible with international humanitarian law (commonly referred to as IHL and/or the law of armed conflict/LOAC).[1]

[1] For analysis of the application of international law to cyber warfare, see, inter alia, M. N. Schmitt (ed.) *Tallinn Manual 2.0 on the International Law Applicable to Cyber Operations* (Cambridge University Press, 2017). This publication devotes 30 pages to the application of the law on the use of force to cyber warfare in comparison to 181 pages devoted to the law of armed conflict in the cyber context. The compatibility of autonomous weapons with the law of armed conflict is the subject of ongoing discussions in the context of the Convention on Certain Conventional Weapons, which since 2016 have involved a group of governmental experts. See Convention on Prohibitions or Restrictions on the Use of Certain Conventional Weapons Which May Be Deemed to Be Excessively Injurious or to Have Indiscriminate Effects (Geneva, 10 October 1980, as amended 21 December 2001); UN Office for Disarmament Affairs, 'Overview: Group of Governmental Experts on Lethal Autonomous Weapons Systems', https://meetings.unoda.org/meeting/ccw-gge-2017/; UN Office for Disarmament Affairs, 'Background on LAWS in the CCW', https://tinyurl.com/yeyjk3pv. Numerous publications have discussed the compatibility of the use of armed drones with international law, especially the law of armed conflict, while the possible impact of drones on lowering the threshold for the use of force has also received attention. See, inter alia, M. N. Schmitt, 'Drone Attacks under the *Jus ad Bellum* and *Jus in Bello*: Clearing the "Fog of Law"' (2011) 13 *Yearbook of International Humanitarian Law* 311–26. On some key legal issues relating to both autonomous weapons systems and remotely piloted vehicles, see, for example, J. D. Ohlin (ed.), *Research Handbook on Remote Warfare* (Edward Elgar, 2019).

**FACT BOX 11.1 WEAPON SYSTEMS**

**CIWS (Close-In Weapon System):** Point-defence fully automated weapon system consisting of rapid fire guns and a radar system used on board warships to defend against incoming projectiles. Examples include the US Phalanx, Dutch Goalkeeper, Russian Kashtan and Chinese Type 730 systems.

**C-RAM (Counter Rocket, Artillery and Mortar):** Automated area-defence system similar to CIWS but used on land to defend a specific installation or position against incoming projectiles. A more sophisticated version of this is the Israeli Iron Dome area-defence system, which is designed for surface-to-air missile defence against incoming missiles, rockets and artillery shells and has proven to be highly effective in intercepting rockets targeting Israeli territory launched from Gaza and elsewhere.

**HAROP/HARPY:** A loitering munition developed by Israel consisting of a kamikaze drone which is designed to fly above a battlespace and engage selected targets by crashing into them and exploding. It can be used as a remotely piloted aerial vehicle with a human-in-the-loop controlling it or in autonomous mode, in which case it engages preselected targets such as enemy air-defence radar systems.

**LAWS (Lethal Autonomous Weapons System):** Used to denote an autonomous weapons system employing artificial intelligence (AI) to independently identify and engage prospective targets. There are various definitions of 'autonomy' in circulation. The US Department of Defense Policy on Autonomy in Weapons Systems defines autonomy as 'a weapon system that, once activated, can select and engage targets without further intervention by a human operator'. At present, there exists no fully autonomous weapon capable of independently selecting targets in an open environment, but the legal, ethical and policy dimensions of such weapons are being debated in various fora, including the UN Group of Governmental Experts (GGE) in the context of the UN Conventional Weapons Convention of 1980.

**Sources:** L. A. Letendre, 'Lethal Autonomous Weapons Systems: Translating Geek Speech for Lawyers' (2020) 96 International Law Studies 274–94; Airforce Technology, 'Harop Loitering Munitions UCAV System' (2 July 2015), www.airforce-technology.com/projects/haroploiteringmuniti/; Army Technology, 'Iron Dome Air Defence Missile System' (14 May 2021), www.army-technology.com/projects/iron-dome/; Raytheon, 'Phalanx Weapon System', https://tinyurl.com/y2hj5y96.

This is understandable, since the legal status of a weapon is related more to a weapon's capacity to conform to the targeting rules in IHL/LOAC than to whether a weapon affects the right to use force as such.[2]

[2] The obligation to ensure that new weapons and methods of warfare can be used in conformity with the law of armed conflict is based on Article 36 of the Protocol

Nevertheless, in view of the significant amount of controversy most of these weapons have engendered, we feel that some attention to their possible impact on the law governing the use of force is warranted. In that context, we briefly discuss whether and how cyber weapons and digital warfare techniques, drones and lethal autonomous weapons might impact and affect the application of the law governing the use of force. Another emerging technology is related to so-called hypersonic weapons, which have so far received less attention in the legal literature than the other previously mentioned technologies and warrant some discussion on how they may affect the application of the law governing the use of force.[3]

Alongside technologies, so-called hybrid warfare is also given attention. We use this term in a descriptive sense to denote a combination of various forms of coercion, both overt and covert, military and non-military, including intimidation, interference, subterfuge and sabotage, as well as full-blown inter-State warfare. Hybrid warfare has gained increasing attention in recent years. In this chapter, we attempt to answer a number of questions regarding the ability of the law to address the threat hybrid warfare can pose and how this technique of confrontation and intimidation might affect the way the law is applied.[4] As this book is about the law on the use of force, the technologies and techniques mentioned here are only cursorily described. Likewise, particular conflicts and instances in which they (may have) played a role are mentioned only to illustrate how they may affect the application of the law and do not receive detailed attention. Furthermore, since some of the types of weapons do not yet exist or have not been used in an operational context and some technologies have scarcely played a role in conflicts, the discussion is to some extent hypothetical.

Additional to the Geneva Conventions of 12 August 1949, and Relating to the Protection of Victims of International Armed Conflicts (Additional Protocol I) (Geneva, 8 June 1977).

[3] For a general discussion of what hypersonic weapons are, see, for example, R. Tiron, 'Hypersonic Weapons: Who Has Them and Why It Matters', Bloomberg News, (27 October 2021, updated 6 April 2022), https://tinyurl.com/3exbk924.

[4] 'Hybrid warfare' is a generic term referring to a variety of techniques of overt and covert coercion above and below the threshold for the use of force. For a general discussion and description, see, for example, A. Bilal, 'Hybrid Warfare: New Threats, Complexity, and "Trust" as the Antidote', *NATO Review* (30 November 2021), https://tinyurl.com/3c9eua3e.

## 11.2 The (Potential) Impact of New Technologies on the Law on the Use of Force

### *11.2.1 Lethal Autonomous Weapons Systems*

The term 'lethal autonomous weapons' (or 'LAWS') is used here to refer to weapons employing artificial intelligence which are designed to independently select and determine the status of the prospective targets and to engage the selected targets without human intervention. They differ from automated weapons by not being preprogrammed to perform a specific function in a closed setting, as is the case with, for example, the automated close-in weapon systems (CIWS) that have been mounted on board warships for decades. As of late 2022, there exists no autonomous weapons system not incorporating target preselection capable of operating in an open setting without human intervention. There are, however, weapon systems with a significant degree of autonomy, which, once activated, are capable of performing a particular function within a predetermined geographical and/or temporal radius.[5]

So-called loitering munitions, such as the Israeli Harpy and Harop kamikaze drones, are capable of operating in autonomous mode as well as under remote control with a human-in-the-loop capable of intervening in and controlling the functioning of the weapons system. But the weapon is designed to perform a specific function (engage adversarial air-defence radar systems) in a preselected operational area when it is operating in autonomous mode, which makes it less than fully autonomous. Other reasonably similar weapons include the Israeli Iron Dome anti-missile area-defence system; the Samsung sentry robot, used to detect persons in the demilitarized zone separating North and South Korea; and the US C-RAM system, which is a modified version of the naval Phalanx CIWS.[6] These and similar weapon systems are more

[5] There exist different definitions of what constitutes 'autonomy' in a weapons system. The approach followed here is that autonomy means the ability of the weapon to function completely free of any human involvement or preprogramming that predetermines the type of target and the environment. See, for example, L. A. Letendre, 'Lethal Autonomous Weapons Systems: Translating Geek Speech for Lawyers' (2020) 96 *International Law Studies* 274–94.

[6] For information concerning the Harop/Harpy loitering munitions systems, see Airforce Technology, 'Harop Loitering Munitions UCAV System' (2 July 2015), www.airforce-technology.com/projects/haroploiteringmuniti/. For the Phalanx and similar CIWS systems, see Raytheon, 'Phalanx Weapon System', https://tinyurl.com/y2hj5y96. For the Iron Dome area-defence weapons, see Airforce Technology, 'Iron Dome Air Defence Missile System' (14 May 2021), www.army-technology.com/projects/iron-dome/.

automated than autonomous and are designed to perform a specific function (usually to intercept incoming projectiles) and have no real independent capability to seek out, identify and engage targets without being preprogrammed to perform a specific function in a predetermined setting.

Undoubtedly, newer versions of these and other weapons will follow in due course, but even if at some point a weapon is designed and deployed to perform in a truly autonomous mode with the ability to independently select and engage targets in a dynamic setting, this will likely not have any appreciable effect on the *jus ad bellum*. Such weapons may well raise questions related to their ability to accurately classify and distinguish targets and conform to IHL/LOAC targeting rules. Their use may also raise ethical questions around allowing machines to independently 'decide' to kill human beings – if such a capability were ever to become feasible and operationally advantageous.[7]

But none of this relates to, or impacts upon, the *jus ad bellum*, as it is clear that any decision to engage in the use of force beyond immediate reaction to an instant and localized threat (e.g. from incoming projectiles, unmanned or remotely controlled drones, etc.) will always be taken at the political/strategic level and not left for a weapons system, however sophisticated, to decide independently of any human supervision and control. Therefore, we conclude that this weapon technology does not appear likely to raise significant questions relating to the law governing the use of force.

### *11.2.2 Cyber Weapons and Digital Warfare*

Cyber or digital 'warfare' has received a lot of attention – at least since the Russian cyber campaign against Estonia in 2007, which alerted both policy-makers and the academic community to the potential of cyber interference to have harmful and destructive consequences. From an international legal perspective, much of the attention has focused on the question of whether

[7] See above n. 1 referring to negotiations on autonomous weapons in the context of the Convention on Certain Conventional Weapons. Numerous articles have addressed the compatibility of lethal autonomous weapons systems with the law of armed conflict and ethical considerations. See, for example, M. Sassoli, 'Autonomous Weapons and International Humanitarian Law: Advantages, Open Questions and Legal Issues to be Clarified' (2014) 90 *International Law Studies* 308–40; K. Anderson, D. Reisner and M. Waxman, 'Adapting the Law of Armed Conflict to Autonomous Weapons Systems' (2014) 90 *International Law Studies* 386–411; International Committee of the Red Cross, 'ICRC's Position on Autonomous Weapons Systems' (12 May 2021), https://tinyurl.com/y3y9n272.

international legal norms and principles apply to cross-border cyber activity and the digital domain per se, and if they do, how they should be meaningfully interpreted in a domain quite different from the physical domain, for which the rules were originally designed.[8] At the UN level, States have gradually come to accept that the basic rules and principles of international law do apply to and in the digital domain, and hence to harmful cyber activity and interference.[9] Various States have produced policy statements on how they view the applicability of international law to cyber activity, including the question of under what conditions cyber interference could constitute an infringement of the duty of non-intervention and the prohibition on the use of force.[10] For the States that have done so, this has entailed setting a standard or a set of indicators to assess at what point harmful cyber activity goes beyond mere interference and amounts to an armed attack triggering the right of self-defence. Academic studies such as the *Tallinn Manual* on the application of international law to cyber warfare and operations have likewise attempted to provide guidance on how international law applies to cyber actions, including those which could constitute a use of force and in some cases amount to an armed attack.

These initiatives point to a general consensus that international law applies to cross-border cyber activity. There is also a substantial amount of agreement on the general guidelines as to when a cyber act could violate the prohibition on the use of force and potentially be deemed an armed

[8] Schmitt, *Tallinn Manual 2.0* (n. 1); N. Tsagourias and R. Buchan (eds.), *Research Handbook on International Law and Cyberspace* (Edward Elgar, 2021).

[9] In December 2018 the UN General Assembly adopted two resolutions on the application of international law to cyberspace and established two bodies: a new group of governmental experts backed by Western States and an open-ended working group sponsored by Russia and China. See, respectively, UNGA Res. 73/266 (22 December 2018), 'Advancing responsible State behaviour in cyberspace in the context of international security', UN Doc. A/RES/73/266; UNGA Res. 73/27 (5 December 2018), 'Developments in the field of information and telecommunications in the context of international security', UN Doc. A/Res/73/27. While they took different approaches, and the questions of the application of the right of self-defence, counter-measures in response to unlawful acts and the humanitarian law of armed conflict remained controversial, there was consensus that the UN Charter and international law apply in cyberspace. For further background, see A. Ponta, 'Responsible State Behavior in Cyberspace: Two New Reports from Parallel UN Processes' (2021) 25(14) *ASIL Insights*, www.asil.org/insights/volume/25/issue/14.

[10] Examples include the official statements and position papers of Australia, Estonia, France, Germany, Netherlands, the United Kingdom and the United States. See P. Roguski, *Application of International Law to Cyber Operations: A Comparative Analysis of States' Views*, The Hague Program for Cyber Norms Policy Brief (March 2020), https://tinyurl.com/3zxfs2wk (Policy Brief); and Annex thereto, 'Excerpts from Statements of States on How International Law Applies to Cyber Operations', https://tinyurl.com/yranh3st.

attack. An act of kinetic force in the physical domain need not necessarily cause physical injury or damage to be considered a use of force in the sense of Article 2(4) of the Charter.[11] This is because an act of kinetic force is always potentially physically harmful, even if no harm ensues. In the cyber context, however, this is not the case. Most cyber activity, including malicious or hostile cyber activity, has no measurable physical effects and cannot be deemed 'armed force', even if it is intrusive, disruptive or results in non-physical harm such as economic loss or the compromising of sensitive information. For this reason, a significant number of States and experts agree that a cyber act must have a measurable negative physical effect, comparable to an act of kinetic force, in order to constitute a violation of the prohibition on the use of force.[12] Likewise, while opinions differ on where the threshold of an armed attack lies, it is safe to say that if a cyber act were to cause significant casualties and/or physical damage it would be deemed an armed attack.[13] Such significant effects could include interference with aircraft in flight or the railway traffic system, causing aircraft to crash or passenger trains to collide. To date, no State has openly qualified a hostile stand-alone cyber act as either a violation of the prohibition on the use of force or an armed attack.

With regard to non-physical harmful consequences, there is much less clarity and agreement. Nevertheless, some States and experts take the position that, under certain conditions, a cyber act causing long-term and severe crippling effects on the ability of a State to perform essential functions, while not causing loss of life or physical damage, could trigger the right of self-defence. Examples of such harmful cyber action without (immediate) lethal consequences include disabling the military communications system of the target State in such a way as to seriously impair the command and control of the armed forces or disabling the critical

[11] See Chapter 4, Section 4.5, above.

[12] Roguski, Policy Brief (n. 10), p. 9, referring to the position that all the States accepted the application of the prohibition on the use of force and all employed the 'scale and effects' test based on the *Nicaragua* judgment. See International Court of Justice, *Military and Paramilitary Activities in and against Nicaragua* (*Nicaragua* v. *United States*) (Merits), Judgment, 27 June 1986, ICJ Reports 1986, para. 195. The same test was put forward by the group of experts who drafted the *Tallinn Manual*. See Schmitt, *Tallinn Manual 2.0* (n. 1), Rule 69.

[13] See Chapter 6, Section 6.4.1, above. On how states view the application of the right of self-defence in the cyber context, see, for example, Roguski, Policy Brief (n. 10), pp. 21–3, showing that all of the States accepted the applicability of the right of self-defence, with the Netherlands taking the position that self-defence could also apply to cyber-attacks without human casualties or physical damage but having substantial long-term effects harmful to core State functions.

infrastructure of the target State, for example the water supply or electricity grid. These acts differ from so-called economic warfare in the form of sanctions or trade embargoes through their impact on essential functions, their intrusiveness and their lack of reversibility. In our view, if a cyber act that causes no immediate physical harm nevertheless (i) has the effect of or is clearly aimed at preventing the State from performing essential functions for a prolonged period, (ii) cannot be (easily) reversed, and (iii) is attributable to a State or organized armed group, it could indeed amount to an armed attack.

As a result, the threshold for qualifying a cyber act as either a use of force or an armed attack is in our view likely to be appreciably higher than in the physical domain. This is partly due to the fact that malicious cyber activity is much more pervasive and generally more difficult to attribute to a specific actor than is hostile activity in the physical context.[14] There is a great deal of intrusive and disruptive cyber interference occurring on a daily basis in the form of cyber espionage, cyber interference and influence operations, cyber criminality (sometimes tolerated or encouraged by States) and even in some cases cyber sabotage, without these being deemed acts of armed force or armed attacks.

Much of this malicious or harmful cyber activity is of a criminal nature, such as extortion through the use of ransomware. While this can undoubtedly have significant negative consequences, it is not of such a nature as to be relevant to the application of the law on the use of force and therefore need not be discussed further. Likewise, cyber espionage, cyber election interference and clandestine cyber manipulation of facts and public opinion as a means of influencing political outcomes in the target State and/or causing confusion and dissension among the target audience, while potentially violating international law relating to non-interference, respect for sovereignty or certain human rights, does not impact on the *jus ad bellum*. Even cyber sabotage would have no bearing on the *jus ad bellum* unless it resulted in loss of life or physical damage or led to the long-term crippling of a State's essential functions.[15]

[14] Attribution of acts to particular actors is reasonably well settled in the law of international responsibility. But the technical attribution of specific acts to a specific actor poses particular challenges in the digital environment. Roguski, Policy Brief (n. 10), pp. 13–17; P. Ducheine, 'Military Cyber Operations', in T. D. Gill and D. Fleck (eds.), *The Handbook of the International Law of Military Operations* (Oxford University Press, 2015), pp. 456–75, at 463–5.

[15] On cyber influence operations and election manipulation, see, for example, B. M. J. Pijpers, *Influence Operations in Cyberspace and the Applicability of International Law*, Elgar (2023).

Until now, there have been very few known cyber actions which have resulted in such consequences (see Fact Box 11.2).[16] Even in the rare cases that might qualify, States have been extremely reluctant to qualify these cyber actions as acts of armed force, and much less to resort to armed force on the basis of self-defence. One reason for this reluctance is the problem of attribution (i.e. identifying the author of the attack). While attribution of authorship for malicious or hostile cyber activity is not impossible, it is nonetheless very difficult to provide convincing evidence of the author of hostile cyber activity and the location from which the action was directed. This makes it difficult to engage in a defensive measure involving the use of force.

In any event, most defensive measures against cyber-attacks involve action in the cyber domain and do not involve an act of force. Cyber security measures aimed at enhancing the ability of an information system to withstand hostile cyber intrusion are largely passive in nature. Active cyber defence in the form of hacking back to take down a server which is involved in a hostile cyber intrusion is also usually below the threshold of force, since it does not normally cause any measurable physical effects and has more in common with electronic warfare (e.g. jamming of a radio frequency) than with use of armed force. Most such measures will also not be given any notoriety, much less publicly

[16] For an overview of cyber warfare and cyber security incidents, see Center for Strategic and International Studies (CSIS), 'Significant Cyber Incidents', https://tinyurl.com/ycxkvzan. Of these, the Stuxnet/Olympic Games operation is the best-known example to date of a stand-alone cyber-attack at inter-State level that resulted in physical damage. See M. A. Kamiński, 'Operation "Olympic Games": Cyber-Sabotage as a Tool of American Intelligence Aimed at Counteracting the Development of Iran's Nuclear Programme' (2020) 29 *Security & Defence Quarterly* 63–71. See also Fact Box 11.2. Other examples of cyber-attacks include the 2008 Russian cyber-attacks on Georgian government websites and the 2007 Israeli air strike on a Syrian nuclear facility (Operation Orchard), which employed offensive cyber capabilities to neutralize the Syrian air-defence system. These attacks were part of a combined kinetic/digital operation which involved traditional warfare and cyber. For further information on Operation Orchard from NATO Cooperative Cyber Defence Center of Excellence (CCDOE), https://tinyurl.com/ycj4rmvp. More recently, Iran and Israel have reportedly engaged in a number of cyber-attacks, which have on occasion resulted in relatively limited but not inconsequential damage. In June 2022 a hack by the group known as Predatory Sparrow resulted in physical damage at an Iranian steel factory. See J. Tidy, 'Predatory Sparrow: Who Are the Hackers Who Say They Started a Fire in Iran?', BBC News (11 July 2022), www.bbc.com/news/technology-62072480. The Predatory Sparrow hackers are apparently acting on behalf of Israel, although the precise status of the group has not been positively identified.

### FACT BOX 11.2 STUXNET

Stuxnet was a malicious computer worm designed to degrade the Iranian nuclear programme. It was reportedly developed by US and Israeli intelligence (Operation Olympic Games) and was inserted into the air-gapped (not directly connected to the Internet) Iranian nuclear facility on a USB stick, where it damaged the centrifuges used to enrich uranium to potential weapons grade. It was reportedly first used in 2010, although its development apparently took several years and was successful in delaying the programme for as long as two years. To date, Stuxnet is one of the few known examples of an alleged cyber-attack by a State actor which resulted in physical damage.

**Computer worm:** A computer worm is a type of malware whose primary function is to self-replicate and infect other computers while remaining active on infected systems. A computer worm duplicates itself to spread to uninfected computers. It often does this by exploiting parts of an operating system that are automatic and invisible to the user.

**Air-gap:** A security measure that isolates a digital device component or private local area network (LAN) from other devices and networks, including the public internet. An air gap is also known as an air wall and the strategy of using air gaps to protect critical data is also known as security by isolation.

**Sources**: J. Fruhlinger, 'Stuxnet Explained: The First Known Cyber Weapon' CSO (31 August 2022), https://tinyurl.com/mr364u84; TechTarget, 'Definition: Computer Worm', www.techtarget.com/searchsecurity/definition/worm; Techopedia, 'What Does Air Gap Mean?', www.techopedia.com/definition/17037/air-gap.

proclaimed as measures of self-defence under international law. The alternative possibility of resorting to physical force in self-defence in response to a cyber armed attack is only a potentially plausible option in cases of loss of life, physical damage or long-term crippling effects on essential State functions, and where convincing evidence relating to the author of the attack is available. Neither of these scenarios is usually present or forthcoming, at least not on the basis of the record so far.

Accordingly, hostile cyber activity when used on its own will continue to serve primarily as a means of obtaining intelligence, stealing or corrupting data, disseminating (dis)information and as a means of sowing doubt and discord among the target audience through manipulation of information and public opinion. Such activities have little relevance to the *jus ad bellum*. For example, cyber espionage has resulted in a revolutionary change in how intelligence is gathered and has exponentially increased the vulnerability of sensitive information for most States.[17] That said, it has little or no connection to the law on the use of force. In the event the cyber domain were used as a weapon, it would be most likely in conjunction with other means of warfare. In such a case, cyber acts would be primarily governed by the targeting rules under IHL/LOAC, with the law on the use of force influencing the overall assessment of the legality of the recourse to force as a whole.

In conclusion, it seems rarely likely that cyber acts will have the necessary physical effects to qualify as falling within the purview of the *jus ad bellum*. To the extent they do, the rules relating to the prohibition on the use of force and the exercise of self-defence would be applicable in a manner comparable to the physical domain, albeit with the differences outlined above.

### *11.2.3 Remotely Piloted Aerial Vehicles (Drones)*

Remotely piloted aerial vehicles (or unmanned aerial vehicles/UAVs, or more popularly drones) differ from so-called autonomous weapons in that until now they have a human operator who is capable of intervening in automated functions and who controls the critical function of targeting persons or objects (if the vehicle is capable of carrying weapons and is used for the purpose of engaging targets), alongside its usual functions of observation and reconnaissance. UAVs are hardly 'new' technology, as they have been in use since the Vietnam War and have been employed as weapons platforms for over twenty years, since the commencement of the US response to the 9/11 attacks. Today, an increasing number of States and some non-State actors employ UAVs as weapons platforms.[18] Since their use has occasioned a lot of comment and criticism and has become steadily more widespread, it seems necessary to say something about their impact on the *jus ad bellum*.

Remotely piloted aerial vehicles have certain characteristics that make them a useful option in specific types of operations and which can also have a potential impact, if not on the law itself, probably on the degree to which the law can act as an effective restraint on their use. They are relatively inexpensive, reasonably easy to operate and certain versions

[17] Cyber espionage by States targets foreign governmental digital systems as well as corporate and other non-State entities and is extremely widespread and pervasive. The reason is that it is much easier to clandestinely obtain digital(ized) information than it is information stored through traditional means. See CSIS, 'Significant Cyber Incidents' (n. 16).

[18] For a succinct description and history of modern military drones, see 'Unmanned Aerial Vehicle', *Britannica*, www.britannica.com/technology/unmanned-aerial-vehicle.

(medium altitude long endurance platforms, or 'MALE') are capable of being deployed over a long distance for extended periods of time to perform a variety of tasks. Because they are not manned, the negative repercussions of losing one due to malfunction or it being shot down are significantly lower than would be the case if a manned aircraft were lost over hostile territory. They are not as visible or intrusive as manned combat aircraft, and therefore there are fewer obstacles involved in operating them in a potentially hostile environment. On the other hand, they are (until now) relatively slow and vulnerable to any party with a reasonably sophisticated and capable air-defence system. This makes them more useful in environments where a potential adversary lacks such a defensive capability than against an opponent with the capability to detect, intercept and shoot them down.[19]

Newer or planned versions are reportedly faster and capable of operating in a more autonomous mode, sometimes employing 'swarming' techniques to overwhelm defences and engage a prospective target, even when the opponent has a reasonably sophisticated air-defence capability. These new features may increase the propensity of States to use UAVs in environments which until now have been less amenable to the employment of such platforms. Various questions relating to whether they have consistently been used in compliance with IHL/LOAC targeting rules or human rights law are relevant to whether they have been lawfully employed in the context of those legal regimes, but do not directly affect their ability to conform to the law as such. Nor does the fact that an aircraft is remotely piloted, as opposed to having the pilot on board, in any way change the law regulating the use of force. However, their ease of use, low profile and relatively low 'cost' to deploy, together with their capability to operate over long distances and for extended periods of time against specific persons or armed groups, have undeniably made the use of force through such UAVs more likely than if manned aircraft or ground troops had been the only alternative to engage such targets.[20]

[19] T. D. Gill, J. V. Haaster and M. Roorda, 'Some Legal and Operational Considerations Regarding Remote Warfare: Drones and Cyber Warfare Revisited', in Ohlin (ed.), *Research Handbook* (n. 1), pp. 298–334.

[20] For discussion on how the characteristics of unmanned aerial vehicles have increased the propensity to use them for conducting strikes against individuals or groups of individuals in situations which do not necessarily fall within the context of the conduct of hostilities in armed conflict, see, for example, G. Corn, 'Drone Warfare and the Erosion of Traditional Limits on War Power', in Ohlin (ed.), *Research Handbook* (n. 1), pp. 246–72; C. Heyns et al., 'The International Law Framework Regulating the Use of Armed Drones' (2016) 65 *International & Comparative Law Quarterly* 791–827.

This has been the case both within and outside the context of the conduct of hostilities in an armed conflict. For example, there were a reported 430 US drone strikes in Pakistan between 2008 and December 2014. It is hard to imagine such a large number of strikes by manned aircraft being carried out in a country which was not actively engaged in an armed conflict with the country conducting the strikes.[21] Hence, while the use of remotely piloted vehicles as a weapons platform to conduct strikes in situations which do not readily fit within the 'hostilities paradigm' under IHL/LOAC do not change the law itself, they do make it more likely that a prospective actor which has them at its disposal will resort to them and, in doing so, sometimes test the limits of the law relating to the use of force. Those limits have not only been tested – and, at times, arguably pushed beyond what was formerly acceptable – but, more likely than not, clearly transgressed or, in some cases, simply ignored on the basis of the facts generally available.

Examples of pushing the limits of the law on the use of force beyond breaking-point include the use of drones in the context of the 'global war on terror' against targets and in locations far removed from the original attack on the United States in 2001, as well as probably in the January 2020 strike against a general of the Iranian Revolutionary Guards.[22]

[21] See Bureau of Investigative Journalism, 'Drone Warfare', www.thebureauinvestigates.com/projects/drone-war (providing statistics on the number of drone strikes in selected countries and estimated casualties).

[22] On the indeterminacy of the way in which the law has been applied in the context of the US drone campaign, see, for example, R. Brooks, 'Duck-Rabbits and Drones: Legal Indeterminacy in the War on Terror' (2014) 25 *Stanford Law and Policy Review* 301–16. On the US drone strike on General Soleimani from the perspective of the UN Special Rapporteur on Extrajudicial, Summary or Arbitrary Executions, see A. Callamard, 'The Targeted Killing of General Soleimani: Its Lawfulness and Why It Matters', *Just Security* (8 January 2020), https://tinyurl.com/3rw4wuj4. For the US reaction, see US Embassy in Georgia, 'Michael R. Pompeo, Secretary of State: UN Special Rapporteur Gives More Cause to Distrust UN Human Rights Mechanisms (July 9)' (9 July 2020), https://tinyurl.com/596rkcjt. This was the first instance of a drone strike against a State agent outside the clear context of an armed conflict. Because Iran and the United States were not openly engaged in an armed conflict, although Iranian-backed militias in Iraq had been involved in strikes against US military personnel there, the targeted killing of a high-level State agent (allegedly involved in co-ordinating pro-Iranian militia actions in Iraq and elsewhere) clearly pushed the 'grey zone' confrontation between Iran and the United States into a new phase of more open warfare. Whether or not it was lawful depends very much on the evidence of Iranian direct involvement (control over militia actions) in strikes on US personnel. The lawfulness would thus depend on whether the conditions for an exercise of self-defence by the United States on Iraqi territory against Iranian targets were met, which is questionable, to say the least. See 'U.S. Drone Strike in Iraq Kills Iranian Military Leader Qasem Soleimani' (2020) 114 *American Journal of International Law* 313–23.

It is likely that although the law is quite capable of being applied to their use, this tendency to use UAVs in situations where their use is of questionable legality will not disappear or significantly abate in the coming years. On the contrary, as UAVs become an increasingly capable means of conducting strikes and more widely available, their use is likely to increase, including in situations where such use would be unlawful under the *jus ad bellum.*

### *11.2.4 Hypersonic Weapons*

Another new or emerging technology relates to the development and actual or potential deployment of 'hypersonic weapons'. This term refers to missiles or other projectiles which are designed to travel at speeds of between five and ten times the speed of sound (Mach 5 – Mach 10).[23] This translates into speeds starting at around 3,800 mph and rising to in excess of 6,000 mph, which is far faster than any conventional aircraft or cruise missile. Several countries either claim to have already tested and deployed such weapons or are reportedly in the process of developing them.[24]

One might ask what the legal significance of such a development is. After all, the speed at which an aircraft, rocket or missile travels is not in itself a legal issue. Moreover, ballistic missiles and rockets already travel at speeds considerably higher than those which hypersonic weapons are supposed to be able to reach. But hypersonic weapons differ from ballistic rockets in the way they are designed to fly and their purported ability to manoeuvre towards the intended target, instead of following a fixed flight path, as is the case with missiles following a ballistic trajectory.[25]

The types of hypersonic weapons currently being developed are intended to be able to elude detection or missile defence systems to a significant degree. This would make such weapons potentially highly destabilizing as regards their effect on deterrence and decision-making. A highly manoeuvrable weapon which is capable of travelling at very high speeds and is capable of avoiding detection or interception would greatly increase the

[23] Tiron, 'Hypersonic Weapons' (n. 3).
[24] Ibid.
[25] Australian Broadcasting Corporation, 'What's the Big Deal about Hypersonic Weapons and Why Are Major Powers Vying for This Capability?' (28 October 2021), https://tinyurl.com/3xs6ubfe.

vulnerability of potential high-value targets such as warships, command centres and missile sites. This could in turn considerably increase the likelihood of pre-emptive or even preventive strikes (see Chapter 6, above) by either the party possessing such weapons or the potential recipient State. This would be a significant challenge to the current legal constraints on the use of force in the context of anticipatory self-defence and perhaps to the policy of nuclear deterrence.

While it is uncertain whether all claims regarding the capabilities of such weapons are accurate and realistic,[26] an arms race is already under way in the realm of hypersonic missile technology between such States as China, Russia and the United States.[27] Hypersonic weapons have also reportedly been used by Russia in the conflict in Ukraine, although their effects seem so far to be limited.[28] In the absence of an arms control agreement within the near future in relation to such weapons, there is a strong likelihood that, sooner or later, a number of States will possess weapons capable of hypersonic manoeuvrable flight and accurate engaging of a target with significantly less chance of detection or interception. That is a clear reason for concern on a number of fronts, including the possible impact of such weapons on the *jus ad bellum*. There are, however, ways in which the use of such weapons might be deterred or neutralized if no arms control agreement were possible. These include allowing for a more flexible interpretation of 'imminence' for pre-emptive defensive action if an attack appeared highly probable. Another possible option would be to provide for a second strike capability, akin to that used in the context of nuclear deterrence, and thereby make a first strike with hypersonic weapons less probable, since there would still be the possibility of effective retaliation. Finally, it might well be possible to develop an effective means of neutralizing the capabilities of hypersonic missiles through an automated defensive weapon system capable of intercepting the missiles or jamming the system.

[26] D. Wright and C. Tracy, 'The Physics and Hype of Hypersonic Weapons', *Scientific American* (1 August 2021), https://tinyurl.com/2yb85s67.

[27] M. Stone, 'U.S. in Hypersonic Weapon "Arms Race" with China – Air Force Secretary', Reuters (1 December 2021), https://tinyurl.com/yt39tsr2.

[28] 'Russia Says It Used Hypersonic Missiles in Ukraine Again', *Al Jazeera*, (20 March 2022), https://tinyurl.com/n7puk5hw.

## 11.3 Hybrid Warfare Techniques and the Law Governing the Use of Force

### *11.3.1 What is Hybrid Warfare?*

The term 'hybrid warfare' is a relatively recent designation (or buzzword) for a wide variety of long-standing and newer techniques of coercive behaviour, ranging from illegal cyber interference with elections to irregular or clandestine warfare. These forms of interference have received increasing attention since the Russian invasion and annexation of the Crimea in 2014 and are now the subject of attention in both policy and academic circles.[29] There is no generally agreed definition, but the definition used by the European Centre of Excellence for Countering Hybrid Threats is instructive: 'The term hybrid threat refers to an action conducted by State or non-State actors, whose goal is to undermine or harm a target by combining overt and covert military and non-military means.'[30]

Much of what is referred to as hybrid warfare takes place in a legal and factual 'grey zone'. This term is, however, misleading, since an act either does or does not constitute a use of force under international law, and to the extent an act is overt there is usually no doubt as to who the author is. Covert action is likewise nothing new, and the main obstacle as far as it is concerned is ascertaining with reasonable certainty who is responsible for it. Most covert action, unless it is so covert as to escape notice altogether, will have at least some characteristics and effects that make it possible to determine who is most likely responsible and whether it is of such a nature as to constitute an act of force. In any case, since we are dealing here with the law on the use of force, we do not consider forms of hybrid interference which clearly fall below the threshold of the use of force, such as election interference, information manipulation, espionage and, more recently, even the 'weaponization' of migrants as a means of destabilizing the target State.[31] For such action, however prejudicial it might be to security and stability, there is no question of armed force being employed and no place for an armed response outside the context of domestic law enforcement and maintenance of public order measures. Therefore, such threats will receive no further consideration here.

[29] Bilal, 'Hybrid Warfare' (n. 4); D. Stoker and C. Whiteside, 'Blurred Lines: Gray-Zone Conflict and Hybrid War – Two Failures of American Strategic Thinking' (2020) 73(1) *Naval War College Review* 13–48.

[30] See European Centre for Countering Hybrid Threats, www.hybridcoe.fi/hybrid-threats/.

[31] An example of this was the transfer of Iraqi and Afghan nationals by Belarus to the border with Poland and Lithuania in November–December 2021. See M. Galeotti, 'How Migrants Got Weaponized' *Foreign Affairs* (2 December 2021), https://tinyurl.com/3krnns2d.

### *11.3.2 The Role of the Law in Countering Hybrid Threats in the Use of Force Paradigm*

For hybrid threats which clearly or at least potentially reach or cross the threshold of the use of force, the situation is different. The first challenge will be to identify the author and nature of the threat, which is essentially a forensic and factual exercise and in some cases a question of probabilities. For example, the 'little green men' referred to in the context of the Russian annexation of the Crimea were simply Russian special forces troops not wearing the usual nationality indicators on their uniforms.[32] Since we can safely assume that the likelihood of an alien spaceship being involved was negligible, despite the reference to 'little green men', the nationality of these troops would not have been a difficult puzzle to solve, since the only likely candidate was self-evident. Moreover, for purposes of the applicable law it would not have made any difference where they came from, once it was clear that their presence was uninvited, intentional and hostile.

Another example of overt 'hybrid' action is the support given by Russia to militias operating in the eastern part of Ukraine in the period between 2014, when Russia annexed the Crimean Peninsula, and the full-scale invasion of Ukraine in February 2022.[33] This type of proxy irregular warfare was commonly engaged in by various States during the Cold War era and is therefore likewise nothing new. In the *Nicaragua* judgment, the International Court of Justice ruled that such support for an armed group constituted a breach of the principle of non-intervention and the prohibition on the use of force.[34]

Probably the most successful use of hybrid techniques to date is China's resort to a combination of physical intimidation, the creation of new facts or alteration of facts on the ground, lawfare (the use of (quasi-)legal arguments as a means to advance interests), coercive diplomacy and information operations to advance its interests in the South China and East China Sea regions. Despite some examples of armed intimidation which border on the threat or use of force, the threshold of actual use of

[32] BBC News, '"Little Green Men" or "Russian Invaders"?' (11 March 2014), www.bbc.com/news/world-europe-26532154.

[33] For an analysis of Russian hybrid strategy in the Crimea and eastern Ukraine, see T. Kuzio and P. D'Anieri, 'Annexation and Hybrid Warfare in Crimea and Eastern Ukraine' *E-International Relations* (25 June 2018), https://tinyurl.com/mvvdsn4a.

[34] *Nicaragua* (n. 12), paras. 191–5.

force has not been met.[35] One aspect of the Chinese hybrid strategy is the use of so-called maritime militias consisting of fishery craft ostensibly civilian in nature.[36] This complicates the question of whether their actions can be attributed to the Chinese government. China also uses its paramilitary Coast Guard to obscure the dividing line between military and law enforcement activity as a way of making it more difficult to identify the most appropriate response to its actions.[37] The fact that China's strategy and use of hybrid tactics have to date (largely) remained below the threshold of the use of force and avoided open confrontation is probably one reason why this strategy has been so successful as a means of advancing China's interests in recent years. By staying below the threshold of the use of force, China has hitherto avoided any outside direct challenge to its conduct, which might have occurred if it had crossed the line into open or irregular warfare against one or more of the neighbouring States.

In any case, if the support a State gives to a proxy armed group engaged in irregular warfare were of a level to be deemed substantial, most States and experts would agree that the threshold of armed attack had been reached. Identifying the applicable law and making this clear to the adversary and the wider international community is consequently the next step in reducing the 'greyness' of the grey zone. However, the law may possibly be open to more than one interpretation and, to the extent it gives rise to ambiguity, this can make it more difficult to counter misuse of the law as a cloak for coercion. This is one reason why it is imperative to reduce the degree of ambiguity in identifying the applicable law and the available legal responses to the maximum extent possible. In short, it is about removing, or at least reducing, the deniability and the 'greyness' of the threat so as to make the hybrid threat less hybrid, increase the 'cost' and, where possible, make the course of action less useful as a means of coercion. So, while ambiguity in the law can

[35] M. Clarke, 'China's Application of the "Three Warfares" in the South China Sea and Xinjiang' (2019) 63(2) *Orbis* 187–208; S. Miracola, 'Chinese Hybrid Warfare: Commentary', Italian Institute for International Political Studies (ISPI) (21 December 2018), https://tinyurl.com/bdcprffu; G. Grieger, European Parliamentary Research Service (EPRS), 'China Tightens Its Grip over the South China Sea' (24 February 2021), https://tinyurl.com/2p8p6664. Creating new facts or altering facts on the ground is an expression used in international relations and diplomacy. It denotes the capability to achieve clear results (realities, facts) in a particular location or region.

[36] B. Jebb and L. Jones, 'Little Blue Men in the South China Sea: Unmasking China's Maritime Militia' (podcast), Modern War Institute (5 June 2022), https://tinyurl.com/53h2sba6.

[37] J. Shida, 'China is Set to Wage Hybrid Warfare', *World Insight* (21 December 2021, updated 6 December 2022), https://tinyurl.com/347f2zh7.

sometimes be used as a cloak for hybrid action, the law can also serve to make such action more costly to the party engaging in it.[38]

## 11.4 Conclusion

To sum up, the law continues to apply to new technologies and methods of warfare, as it does to more conventional uses of armed force, albeit with certain modifications to take account of the different effects produced by such technologies and methods of coercion. Cyber warfare is now generally recognized as subject to the law on the use of force and the modalities of its application. Likewise, so-called autonomous weapons incorporating artificial intelligence pose few challenges to the *jus ad bellum*, regardless of the controversies they may provoke when it comes to the application of the law of armed conflict or from an ethical perspective. This is because determinations relating to the use of force are matters of State policy reserved in most cases to the State leadership and not to any weapons system. By contrast, remotely controlled vehicles, especially aerial drones, have increased the likelihood of the application of inter-State force because of their specific characteristics, including in situations where their use is of questionable legality. Furthermore, hypersonic weapons are also potentially destabilizing due to the difficulties involved in countering them and the pressure they can exert on the temporal scope of self-defence. It remains unclear, however, how well they are likely to be able to perform in reality. The present conflict between Russia and Ukraine has reportedly seen their use, but hitherto with little added effect as far as can be determined.

Finally, hybrid warfare is most effective (as is cyber warfare) in situations below the threshold of force, where the grey areas of the law allow some States to engage in forms of coercion that can disrupt their opponents and advance their interests, especially if there is a clear gap in relative power between the State applying the pressure and its target(s). By contrast, once the threshold of open force is crossed, hybrid warfare becomes essentially another name for irregular warfare, which is nothing new or particularly challenging from a legal perspective.

[38] Bilal, 'Hybrid Warfare' (n. 4).

# PART IV

## The Use of Force in the Wider Legal Landscape

In Part IV we relate the use of force to the most relevant sub-disciplines and regimes within international law which interact with it. We do so on the basis of our view that international law forms a more or less integrated system and is not simply a collection of rules and principles or a random selection of separate sub-disciplines which exist in isolation from each other.[1] The law relating to the use of force plays a very important role within the system but is, like the rest of international law, part of a whole and subject to interaction with other disciplines making up the system. All sub-divisions of international law are subject to a common set of principles relating to the nature of and purpose underlying the system, the sources of international obligations, the entities to which those obligations apply and the general consequences of breach of an international obligation. These sub-divisions, moreover, share a common methodology that determines how obligations relate to each other and how any conflicts of obligation arising from one or more sub-regimes within the system are resolved. Furthermore, while law is the subject of our focus, we do not ignore the fact that it is but one factor of importance within the context of international relations and the conduct of States' foreign policies.

Trying to relate the law on the use of force to the entirety of international law would be a well-nigh impossible endeavour. Therefore, we have chosen what we think are the most important principles, regimes and sub-disciplines which directly relate to the use of force. This part of the book is divided into five chapters. In Chapter 12, we discuss the relationship of State sovereignty to the use of force. In that context we examine so-called consensual interventions as an attribute of State sovereignty and give some attention to the rights of States to police their territory against non-consensual intrusions and other violations of sovereignty below the

[1] R. Higgins, *Problems and Process: International Law and How We Use It* (Oxford University Press, 1994), p. 1.

threshold of armed attack. In Chapter 13, we discuss how the rules and regimes of international law governing the use of the international commons and certain other areas subject to special regimes (international waters and airspace, Antarctica and outer space) relate to the law on the use of force. In Chapter 14, we discuss the relationship between the law relating to the use of force and the law of armed conflict. In our view this relationship goes further than simply acknowledging that the equal application of the law of armed conflict to all parties is not dependent upon the question of the legality of the resort to force under the *jus ad bellum*. We also discuss to what extent the regime of international human rights law is applicable to the use of force in international relations. Finally, in Chapter 15, we examine the law of international and criminal responsibility and how they relate to the use of force. We do not attempt to restate the different rules within these various sub-disciplines and regimes beyond what is strictly necessary. Likewise, we do not delve into specific controversial uses of force by one or another State, save for purposes of illustration. Instead, we focus on how the specific character and the specific rules of a given regime relate to the *jus ad bellum*.

# 12

## The Use of Force as an Attribute of State Sovereignty

### 12.1 Introduction

This chapter examines how and to what extent the principle and rule of State sovereignty provides the basis for a State's use of force in situations that fall outside the Charter prohibition. First, the chapter looks at the use of force founded on the consent or invitation of a State; it examines the basis, limitations and conditions for such consent or invitation. Second, the chapter analyses how the principle of sovereignty empowers a State to take action to halt unauthorized incursion on its territory below the threshold of an armed attack by foreign military aircraft, warships and military personnel and examines the legal basis for taking action in such situations.

### 12.2 The Use of Force on the Basis of Consent or Invitation

#### *12.2.1 Sovereignty as the Basis for Consent to the Use of Force by a Foreign State*

The power of a State to consent to the use of force by another State or to invite another State to assist it in the maintenance of order or in military action directed against an armed group or insurgency on its territory is based upon and directly related to the notion of the sovereignty of the State (see Fact Box 12.1).[2] Sovereignty is a multifaceted and elastic

[2] G. Hafner, 'Report on Intervention by Invitation' (2009) 73 *Institute of International Law Yearbook* 302–39, at 305–6, citing, inter alia, UN General Assembly (UNGA) Resolutions 2625 (Declaration on Principles of International Law Concerning Friendly Relations and Co-operation among States in accordance with the Charter of the United Nations, 24 October 1970); UNGA Resolution 3314 (Definition of Aggression, 14 December 1974); UN Security Council (UNSC) Resolution 387 (on South Africa's military activities against Angola, 31 March 1976); International Court of Justice (ICJ), *Military and Paramilitary Activities in and against Nicaragua* (*Nicaragua* v. *United States*) (Merits), Judgment, 27 June 1986, ICJ Reports 1986, para. 246.

SUMMARY BOX 12.1 POWER TO CONSENT OR INVITE

The power of a State to consent to or invite foreign military action on its territory stems from its sovereignty and is not an 'exception' to the prohibition on the use of force, as it does not involve a use of force in international relations as envisaged in Article 2(4) of the UN Charter.

concept in international law, which can lead to questions as to its content and scope. In our opinion, sovereignty is neither an immutable and invariably overriding consideration nor an obsolete notion pertaining to a bygone era, as is sometimes argued by either those in favour of an absolutist approach to sovereignty or those more inclined to dismiss it as outdated or irrelevant.[3]

Rather than embarking on a fruitless discussion of the opposing views on the nature of sovereignty, we refer to the definition set out in the *Island of Palmas* arbitral award: 'Sovereignty in the relations between States signifies independence. Independence in regard to a portion of the globe is the right to exercise therein, to the exclusion of any other State, the functions of a State.'[4] The plenary authority of the State over its territory and the exclusive right to exercise State functions without forcible outside interference within that territory entitles it to accede to a request by a foreign State to conduct a military operation on its territory against a hostile armed group situated therein; to ask for, or with its consent receive, assistance in maintaining internal order; and to resist a forcible overthrow of its government or forcible usurpation of its authority over (part of) its territory by an armed group or insurrectionary movement. Although the characterization of sovereignty in the *Island of Palmas* arbitral award predates the UN Charter, it mirrors how sovereignty is anchored in the Charter. It also corresponds to the

[3] On the different concepts of sovereignty in international law and international relations, see, for example, T. L. Ilgen (ed.), *Reconfigured Sovereignty: Multi-Layered Governance in the Global Age* (Ashgate, 2003); N. Walker (ed.), *Sovereignty in Transition* (Hart, 2003); S. Beaulac, *The Power of Language in the Making of International Law: The Word Sovereignty in Bodin and Vattel and the Myth of Westphalia* (Brill, 2004); D. Grimm, *Sovereignty: The Origin and Future of a Political and Legal Concept* (Columbia University Press, 2015).

[4] *Island of Palmas Case (Netherlands, USA)*, Award, 4 April 1928, Reports of International Arbitral Awards, vol. II, pp. 829–71, at 838.

contemporary interpretation of the prohibition of intervention and the related but distinct prohibition on the use of force in international relations.[5]

Nevertheless, it is important to emphasize that the power of a State to consent to or invite foreign military action on its territory is not a part of the contemporary *jus ad bellum* in the sense of being an 'exception' to the prohibition on the use of force set out in Article 2(4) of the Charter and in customary international law. Allowing or inviting another State to act within the consenting State's territory, whether against an armed group or in the context of a breakdown in public order, does not involve a use of force in international relations.[6] Nor is a consensual use of force a manifestation of armed intervention by a foreign State. Intervention characterized by Lauterpacht as 'dictatorial interference' always involves an element of coercion, and armed intervention by another State is by its nature coercive.[7] In contrast to this, when a State accedes to a request by another State to conduct a military operation directed against a non-State entity on its territory, or itself requests assistance in conducting such an operation, this constitutes neither a prohibited intervention nor a use of force between States. Hence, the term 'consensual intervention' is something of an oxymoron, despite its widespread use. The request of assistance by a State to mount a defence against an armed attack by another State or by an armed group operating from another State's territory falls within the specific scope of the right of collective self-defence and is governed by the law of self-defence discussed above in Chapter 6. It is distinct from a consensual use of force by one State on the consenting State's territory against a non-State actor which is the subject of this chapter.

5 In addition to the instruments cited above in n. 2, in which non-intervention and its relationship to sovereignty are referred to, see *Nicaragua* (n. 2), paras. 202–4, on non-intervention and its relationship to the prohibition on the use of force and respect for sovereignty. These observations are virtually identical to the portrayal of the rights relating to sovereignty in *Island of Palmas* (n. 4).

6 See Chapter 4, Section 4.4, above. See also O. Schachter, *International Law in Theory and Practice* (Nijhoff, 1991), p. 114; Y. Dinstein, *War, Aggression and Self-Defence* (Cambridge University Press, 2017), p. 127; C. Henderson, *The Use of Force and International Law* (Cambridge University Press, 2018), pp. 349–50.

7 For a contemporary discussion relating to the scope and status of the non-intervention principle, see, inter alia, R. Jennings and A. Watts, *Oppenheim's International Law* (Oxford University Press, 2008), pp. 428–51. On the reference to 'dictatorial interference', see ibid., p. 432. See also T. D. Gill, 'Non-Intervention in the Cyber Context', in K. Ziolkowski (ed.) *Peacetime Regime for State Activities in Cyberspace* (NATO CCD COE Publications, 2013), pp. 217–38.

Although reference is often made to consent as a circumstance precluding wrongfulness in the literature, the legality of the consensual use of force by another State does not have its basis in the law of international responsibility; it derives instead from the State's power to issue a valid consent in the first place – in short, from its sovereignty and independence. It is true that the Articles on the Responsibility of States for Internationally Wrongful Acts (ARSIWA) recognize consent as a circumstance precluding wrongfulness. However, this function within the law of international responsibility is not the source of the legality but simply a recognition of the fact that if a State validly consents to an act which would otherwise be unlawful, no responsibility is incurred. In the case of a consensual or invited use of force against a non-State entity, no rule of international law is violated in principle. So while the conditions for valid consent are to be (partially) found in Article 20 of ARSIWA, it is not the basis on which the State's power to consent or invite resides; this lies rather in the sovereignty of the State and the resultant power this gives it to grant consent or issue a request for a foreign State or international organization to deploy military forces on its territory and conduct actions that the State is competent to consent to or request, within the bounds of its consent or request and in conformity with general international law.[8] We now turn to the inherent limitations posed by international law governing consent.

### 12.2.2 *The Inherent Limits to Conducting Military Operations on the Basis of Consent under International Law*

Since the power to give consent or issue an invitation for a foreign military operation has its basis in the sovereignty of the consenting State over its territory, the limits to this power can be found in the selfsame concept. Sovereignty has never been absolute in the sense of not being subject to any legal restrictions. It is part of international law and subject to the limits such law places on States. All States are bound by international law, and although their legal obligations may differ

[8] In addition to the sources cited above in n. 6, see G. H. Fox, 'Intervention by Invitation', in M. Weller (ed.), *The Oxford Handbook of the Use of Force in International Law* (Oxford University Press, 2017), pp. 816–40. See also International Law Commission, 'Draft Articles on Responsibility of States for Internationally Wrongful Acts, with Commentaries' (2001), in Report of the International Law Commission on the Work of Its Fifty-Third Session, UN Doc. A/56/10 (ARSIWA Commentaries), pp. 72–4 (Commentary to Article 20).

### FACT BOX 12.1 IDI RESOLUTION ON INTERVENTION ON REQUEST – EXCERPTS

#### Article 1: Definitions

For the purposes of this Resolution:

a) 'Military assistance on request' means direct military assistance by the sending of armed forces by one State to another State upon the latter's request.
b) 'Request' means a request reflecting the free expression of will of the requesting State and its consent to the terms and modalities of the military assistance.

#### Article 2: Scope

1. This Resolution applies to situations of internal disturbances and tensions, such as riots, isolated and sporadic acts of violence and other acts of a similar nature, including acts of terrorism, below the threshold of non-international armed conflict . . ..
2. The objective of military assistance is to assist the requesting State in its struggle against non-State actors or individual persons within its territory, with full respect for human rights and fundamental freedoms.

#### Article 3: Prohibition of military assistance

1. Military assistance is prohibited when it is exercised in violation of the Charter of the United Nations, of the principles of non-intervention, of equal rights and self-determination of peoples and generally accepted standards of human rights and in particular when its object is to support an established government against its own population.
2. Military assistance shall not be provided where such provision would be inconsistent with a Security Council resolution relating to the specific situation, adopted under Chapter VII of the Charter of the United Nations.

#### Article 4: Request

1. Military assistance may only be provided upon the request of the requesting State.
2. The request shall be valid, specific and in conformity with the international obligations of the requesting State.

. . .

**Sources:** Institut de Droit international, Session of Rhodes – 2011, 10th Commission, Present Problems of the Use of Force in International Law, Sub-group on military assistance on request (Rapporteur M. Gerhard Hafner), Resolution of 8 September 2011, www.idi-iil.org/app/uploads/2017/06/2011_rhodes_10_C_en.pdf.

depending on the treaty relations they have entered into, they are all bound by the UN Charter and rules of customary law. Hence, consent to conduct any type of military operation will always be subject to any applicable legal obligations, including peremptory norms.

Moreover, inherent in the very notion of sovereignty are limitations on what a State can validly consent to. For example, a State cannot consent to the termination of its plenary authority over its territory and attendant power to exercise State functions over its territory and population. This would be incompatible with its independence and its citizens' right to self-determination,[9] unless the State's population and government freely elect to join or integrate into another State. Accordingly, the State giving consent is not ceding any part of its sovereignty by allowing (an)other State(s) or an international organization to conduct a military operation on its territory. Consequently, it can make consent subject to any conditions or restrictions it wishes to impose on the nature, purpose, location or duration of the foreign military presence on its territory, provided they do not violate the obligations of either party under international law. Likewise, consent can be modified or terminated at any time, subject to considerations of reasonableness and good faith, such as giving due regard to the other party's ability to accede to the modification or terminating the terms of consent within the communicated time frame.[10] So, if State A agrees to allow State B to conduct a military operation against a non-State entity under certain conditions on its territory without stipulating a particular time limit, it should allow the State that is operating in accordance with the conditions set out to make an orderly withdrawal if it decides to terminate its consent.

Hence, consent is subject to any limitations inherent in the exercise of sovereignty, such as respect for the independence of the consenting State and its authority over its territory, as well as to the international legal obligations of both the consenting State and the State(s) conducting the military operation. It goes without saying that any consent given must be freely obtained and not the result of a threat of force or any other form of

[9] Such a limitation flows from Article 2(1) of the Charter and the principles of international law contained in UNGA Res. 2625 (n. 2), which refers to sovereign equality and self-determination.

[10] Dinstein, *War, Aggression and Self-Defence* (n. 6), p. 128. This also follows from the text of Article 20 of ARSIWA, where reference is made to a given act undertaken on the basis of consent within the limits of that consent.

coercion. Likewise, consent cannot be obtained unlawfully, for example through corruption of a State official or deliberate misrepresentation of facts essential to the granting of consent.

As said above, any consent sought or given is always subject to restrictions based on a peremptory norm.[11] For example, no consent can be given to carry out acts amounting to an international crime, such as genocide, crimes against humanity, war crimes, apartheid, torture and inhumane treatment. Moreover, consent by the government of a State or entity that is under the control of the intervening State has no legal basis as it is not freely given. Consent by a State on the basis of its sovereignty also does not empower the threat or use of force against another State or against a non-State entity not located on the consenting State's territory. Such a use of force must have its basis in either a binding decision of the UN Security Council (UNSC, Security Council) or the right of (collective) self-defence.[12]

Apart from these requirements, the State(s) conducting the military operation must also abide by all applicable obligations arising from the law of armed conflict and/or international human rights law. The conduct of the operation may additionally be subject to other rules of international law, such as the law relating to the status of foreign military personnel on a State's territory, the law of international responsibility and other applicable law.[13]

In summary, the power of a State to give consent to another State to conduct a military operation on its territory, including one involving the use of force against a non-State entity, is an inherent part of the consenting State's sovereignty and plenary authority over its territory. The limits to the scope of such consent likewise have their basis in the very nature of sovereignty and its place within international law. Hence, no State can avoid its legal obligations by asking another State to perform an act contrary to its own legal obligations. Equally, no State receiving consent can perform any act which would violate its legal obligations or the obligations binding any State under general international law. These inherent limitations should not be conflated with the conditions relating to the valid granting of consent, to which we now turn.

[11] This is self-evident given the nature of peremptory rules and is reflected in Article 26 of ARSIWA on the limitation peremptory rules place on the invocation of any circumstance precluding wrongfulness, including consent.

[12] See Chapters 4, 5 and 6, above.

[13] For a detailed treatment of these and other legal regimes relevant to the conduct of any military operation, see T. D. Gill and D. Fleck (eds.), *The Handbook of the International Law of Military Operations* (Oxford University Press, 2015).

### *12.2.3 Conditions of Valid Consent to Conduct a Military Operation on Another State's Territory*

Alongside the above limits to the scope of permissible consent, there are a number of further conditions relating to the validity of granting consent. Some of these are substantive and others are of a more procedural nature, but they are all relevant to determining whether consent in a particular instance is valid and therefore lawful. As stated previously, some of these conditions are also set out in Article 20 of ARSIWA.

Consent by a State is given by its government exercising State functions over its territory and representing the State at the international level. The exercise of State functions by the government can be seen as a prima facie indication that it is capable and authorized to grant valid consent or issue a valid request for military assistance to another State. The capacity to exercise State functions depends on a reasonable degree of effective control over the territory of the State. This control need not be complete or even uncontested, but to the extent that the government has at least preponderant control over a significant part of its territory, it will also be capable of acting on behalf of the State. Effective control over a State's territory and exercise of core State functions by the government remain the most widely acknowledged criteria for accepting the authority of the government to act on behalf of the State, including through the issuing of a valid consent to or request for military assistance. Temporary or even prolonged loss of control over part of the State's territory through a breakdown in security, internal unrest or even internal armed conflict does not vitiate the government's ability to act on behalf of the State.[14]

Another indicator of the ability of the government of a State to act on behalf of that State is its ability to conduct international relations at the inter-State level through diplomatic representation and by representing

[14] On effective control, see, inter alia, Hafner, 'Report' (n. 2), pp. 321–2; Henderson, *Use of Force* (n. 6), pp. 355–6. An example of the continued validity of this test as prima facie evidence of the authority of a government to request assistance is the general recognition of the capacity of the Syrian government to request and receive assistance from Russia and Iran as the effective government of Syria. See C. Gray, *International Law and the Use of Force* (Oxford University Press, 2018), p. 107. See also ICJ, *Armed Activities on the Territory of Congo (DRC* v. *Uganda)* (Merits), Judgment, 19 December 2005, ICJ Reports 2005, paras. 49–54, 198–9. The Court did not question the authority of the government of the Democratic Republic of the Congo (DRC) to issue or withdraw consent, despite not having control over substantial parts of its territory for prolonged periods and having been torn by internal conflict for many years. The same could be said of Afghanistan, Iraq, Mali and many other States where foreign forces are or have operated on the basis of consent.

the State at a multilateral level through membership of and participation in international organizations, particularly the United Nations. While recognition may not normally be a qualification for statehood, it is a *conditio sine qua non* for the conduct of international relations in a practical sense, including the ability to enter into international agreements and issue a valid consent to or request for military assistance from a foreign State or an international organization. Irrespective of whether a particular government chooses to enter into diplomatic relations or recognize another State's government, the capacity of the government of a State to act in the international arena is not dependent on its being recognized as the legitimate government, except in the event of collective non-recognition by (virtually) the entire international community where the State or its government owes its existence to a violation of a peremptory norm or the UN Security Council acting under Chapter VII has passed a resolution designating a particular government as the legitimate authority to act on behalf of the State.[15]

Some authors take the position that only democratically elected governments are entitled to issue a valid consent to or request for military assistance.[16] This proposition begs the question of who decides whether a particular form of government qualifies as democratic. Acceptance of such a condition would subordinate the exercise of a legal right to issue valid consent to a political assessment of whether a particular form of government was sufficiently democratic.

A number of peremptory norms do impose a duty upon States not to recognize certain governments, such as those imposed by foreign military intervention or based on a violation of the right to external self-determination (apartheid or racist ideology, colonial domination or foreign occupation).[17] Such a duty does not, however, imply that only democratic States should be seen as having the power to validly consent.

[15] On recognition, see, for example, M. N. Shaw, *International Law* (Cambridge University Press, 2021), pp. 377–415. On collective non-recognition, see n. 16, below. On the role of the UNSC in relation to acceptance or rejection of the legitimacy of a government, see nn. 20 and 21, below.

[16] Two authors taking this position are R. Buchan and N. Tsagourias, *Regulating the Use of Force in International Law: Stability and Change* (Edward Elgar, 2021), pp. 107–8, citing E. de Wet, 'The Modern Practice of Intervention by Invitation in Africa and its Implications for the Prohibition of the Use of Force' (2016) 26 *European Journal of International Law* 979–98, at 983–90.

[17] ICJ, *Legal Consequences of the Construction of a Wall in the Occupied Palestinian Territory*, Advisory Opinion, 9 July 2004, ICJ Reports 2004, paras. 155–9. See also J. Dugard, *Recognition and the United Nations* (Cambridge University Press, 1987).

International law also recognizes the right of the citizens of a State to internal self-determination. Internal self-determination requires the State to permit its citizens some form of participation and representation in the governance of the State on the basis of equal rights and non-discrimination, but does not prescribe any form of government or the form or manner in which such participation and representation must be effectuated.[18] There is thus no rule of international law requiring a State to have a particular form of government, democratic or otherwise, in order to qualify as a fully sovereign State empowered to exercise the functions pertaining to statehood, including the issuing of valid requests for military assistance or consent to the conduct of a military operation on its territory.[19]

On occasion, the Security Council or a regional organization has designated a particular representative of a State as the legitimate government. It has done so on the basis of that representative having been elected to the function of head of State or head of government, despite having been forcibly deposed. In such cases, the fact of having been democratically elected in internationally recognized elections has indeed been an essential factor in determining any authority to request military

[18] On the internal right of self-determination, see Supreme Court of Canada, *Re Secession of Quebec*, Judgment, 20 August 1998, paras. 118–20, referring, inter alia, to UNGA Res. 50/6 (9 November 1995), which reaffirmed the right of self-determination as set out in UNGA Res. 2625 (n. 1) in the following terms: the UNGA will '[c]ontinue to reaffirm the right of self-determination of all peoples, taking into account the particular situation of peoples under colonial or other forms of alien domination or foreign occupation, and recognize the right of peoples to take legitimate action in accordance with the Charter of the United Nations to realize their inalienable right of self-determination. This shall not be construed as authorizing or encouraging any action that would dismember or impair, totally or in part, the territorial integrity or political unity of sovereign and independent States conducting themselves in compliance with the principle of equal rights and self-determination of peoples *and thus possessed of a Government representing the whole people belonging to the territory without distinction of any kind*' (emphasis added).

[19] That there is no requirement for a State to possess a 'liberal democratic' government in order to be able to exercise the prerogatives of a State is abundantly clear from State practice. Of the 193 UN member States, no more than half qualify as democracies according to the standards of free elections, rule of law, safeguarding of basic rights, etc. See, for example, Freedom House, 'Countries and Territories', https://freedomhouse.org/countries/freedom-world/scores. According to the Democracy Index of *The Economist*'s intelligence unit, only 6.4 per cent of the world population live in countries that are 'fully democratic'. See 'A New Low for Global Democracy', *The Economist* (9 February 2022), https://tinyurl.com/ysppzc4e. Other definitions of what constitutes a democratic government would obviously yield different results, which is one reason why such a condition is not part of international law.

assistance.[20] Nevertheless, consideration of whether the representative in question actually exercised office prior to being deposed and whether the forcible overthrow could be seen as a usurpation of the legitimate authority was equally essential. For example, the Security Council rejected the 1991 forcible overthrow of the Haitian government of Jean-Bertrand Aristide and designated him as the lawful government. The Security Council did so again with respect to the deposed president of Yemen, Abdrabbuh Mansour Hadi, in 2015. These examples should, however, be seen in context. While they indicate that the forcible overthrow of an elected government may be one factor in determining who the legitimate representative of the State is, it is not an indication that only democratically elected governments are competent to issue valid requests for military assistance.[21] Of course, it is open to any State to refuse a request to provide military assistance for any reason it sees fit on policy grounds, but this has no bearing on whether a State is entitled to seek and receive assistance within the limits of the law as a matter of principle.

Assuming that a State has a government effectively exercising State functions over its territory and representing the State at the international level, the next question concerns the official(s) authorized to act on behalf of that government in the context of issuing a valid consent to or request for military assistance. There is no exhaustive list of officials who possess that authority, but the person in question must have the capacity to represent the State at the international level and be authorized under that State's domestic law to make such decisions and representations. Under the law of treaties, heads of State, heads of government and foreign ministers are presumed to have such power, unless it is clear that they do not – as, for example, when a head of State exercises a purely ceremonial function. In some cases, other officials (e.g. deputy heads of State or government, (deputy) ministers of defence or justice) may have such authorization for specific purposes. If the requesting State has no reason to doubt the validity of a freely given consent by a State official of sufficient

[20] Fox, 'Intervention by Invitation' (n. 8), pp. 834–7.

[21] Ibid. See also UNSC Resolution 940 (1994) in relation to Haiti and UNSC Resolution 2216 (2015) on Yemen. It is clear from these resolutions that the specific factual context was a crucial factor behind the Security Council's decisions to back incumbent presidents who had been forcibly deposed in both of those cases. In Haiti, the breakdown in internal stability, the humanitarian situation inside the country and large refugee flows played a significant role. In Yemen, the ongoing internal armed conflict and its implications for regional security were key factors. That makes it implausible to view these examples as generally applicable to the question of whether a government that is less than democratic has the necessary legitimacy to represent the State.

rank, it may presume that the official is acting within his or her competence and it may rely on such consent, unless clear signs subsequently emerged that the official acted ultra vires and the consent was invalid. In such a case, the State would have to terminate its presence on the apparently consenting State's territory, save where it has since received valid consent from a duly authorized official to carry on with the operation. If the State seeking consent was acting in good faith and it is not readily apparent that the consent was invalid, the State would not be in violation of the prohibition on the use of force or the principle of non-intervention, provided it complied with any subsequent instructions from a duly authorized official of the consenting State.[22] The form a consent may take is another point which has engendered a certain amount of controversy. In any event, there is no requirement under international law that a consent to or request for assistance be expressed in any particular form, as long as it is freely given by an authorized official. It can be done through a written agreement between the requesting and consenting States; it can be communicated in a formal setting through a public statement made by an authorized official; or it can be accomplished without any form of publicity or public notification.[23] Hence, validity of consent is not subject to any requirements regarding the form in which it is given, as long as it meets the requirements set out above. Furthermore, it must be clear that consent has been duly given; military operations on another State's territory cannot be based on an assumption that consent will be given.[24] If the action for which consent is sought is undertaken prior to the granting of consent, it is prima facie unlawful in the absence of any other valid legal basis, unless the requesting State subsequently consents and waives any responsibility for the infringement of its territory.[25] This implies that consent should be sought before any incursion into another State's territory, so as to rule out the possibility of a violation of the other State's sovereignty or the perception that the action is hostile.

[22] See Article 7(2)(a) (authority of heads of State/government and foreign ministers to represent the State) and Article 8 (subsequent confirmation of an invalid act) of the Vienna Convention on the Law of Treaties (Vienna, 23 May 1969). While consent is not necessarily a treaty, the principles set out in these provisions can be applied by analogy.

[23] See, for example, E. Lieblich, 'Intervention and Consent: Consensual Forcible Interventions in Armed Conflicts as International Agreements' (2011) 29 *Boston University International Law Journal* 337–82, at 359, referring to the informal nature of the Lebanese consent to the presence of US Marines in 1958; Henderson, *Use of Force* (n. 6), pp. 371–2.

[24] See ARSIWA Commentaries (n. 8), p. 73 (Commentary to Article 20).

[25] Ibid.

Advance consent in the form of a treaty provision providing for the possibility of a military intervention in a State in particular circumstances does not constitute a legal basis for valid consent, unless at the time the treaty was invoked as a basis for intervention, the preconsenting State unequivocally reiterated its consent to the military operation in conformity with the treaty and any additional conditions it saw fit to stipulate. The reason for this is that a State always retains ultimate authority over its territory and will therefore have the last word on whether it agrees to a specific foreign military intervention. This means that the State can at any time withdraw its consent. Any treaty provision allowing for intervention despite the opposition of the government of the State would in fact contravene the prohibition on the use of force and would lack legal effect. Such treaty clauses making reference to advance consent to a military intervention by another State or international organization are therefore to be seen as a provisional undertaking.[26]

### *12.2.4 Consent in the Context of Civil Conflict*

In the preceding paragraphs we have alluded to the possibility of a State requesting assistance to help restore internal order or resist forcible overthrow of the government, including in situations of internal conflict. How does this possibility relate to the prohibition of intervention or to the duty not to participate in the armed suppression of the right to self-determination? We address the question of whether either of these rules of international law stand in the way of assisting a State that has requested military assistance in the context of an insurgency or internal armed conflict.

In the international law predating the UN Charter, a duty of neutrality for third States (i.e. States other than the one where a civil conflict was in progress) was presumed to exist in situations where an internal conflict had reached the stage of a full-scale civil war whereby the hostilities were subject to the law of war as a result of an implicit or explicit recognition of belligerency, unless the third State intervened on the side of one of the parties. If a third State recognized a rebellious

[26] Lieblich, 'Intervention and Consent' (n. 23), pp. 371–2; Henderson, *Use of Force* (n. 6), p. 374; B. Roth, 'The Illegality of Pro-Democratic Invasion Pacts', in G. Fox and B. Roth (eds.), *Democratic Governance and International Law* (Cambridge University Press, 2010), p. 328; Dinstein, *War, Aggression and Self-Defence* (n. 6), pp. 129–30.

movement as a belligerent, this signified that the law of neutrality would govern its relationship with both the incumbent government and the rebellious party.[27]

This did not mean that a State could not intervene, but that if it did so, it would find itself in a state of war with the opposing party. In that period, from roughly the latter half of the eighteenth century until the end of the First World War, there was no rule of international law which precluded resorting to war. As a result, if a State chose to intervene on the side of a rebellious party in the context of a civil conflict, as that concept was understood at the time, it would be tantamount to a declaration of war on the incumbent government and the intervening State would be a co-belligerent with the rebellious party. Examples include the intervention of France in the American War of Independence on the side of the American colonies in 1778–82, the intervention of Britain, France and Russia in the Greek War of Independence in 1827–9 and the intervention of the United States in the Cuban uprising against Spain in 1895–8.[28]

Likewise, there was no rule preventing a State from intervening on the side of an incumbent government to assist it in putting down a rebellion. Examples include the French intervention in support of the Spanish royalist government in 1823, the Russian intervention to assist Austria in suppressing a rebellion in Hungary against Austrian rule in 1849, and the Prussian intervention to suppress popular uprisings in Baden and the Palatinate in 1849.[29]

[27] On recognition of belligerency and its legal effects, see, for example, S. Sivakumaran, *The Law of Non-International Armed Conflict* (Oxford University Press, 2012), pp. 9–14; Y. Dinstein, *Non-International Armed Conflicts in International Law* (Cambridge University Press, 2014), pp. 108–13; L. Moir, *The Law of Internal Armed Conflict* (Cambridge University Press, 2002), pp. 3–11.

[28] On the intervention of France in the American War of Independence, see, for example, M. A. Jones, *The Limits of Liberty: American History 1607–1980* (Oxford University Press, 1983), pp. 51–4. On the intervention of Britain, France and Russia in the Greek War of Independence, see A. Heraclides and A. Dialla, *Humanitarian Intervention in the Long Nineteenth Century: Setting the Precedent* (Manchester University Press, 2015), pp. 105–33. On the US intervention in Cuba, see Heraclides and Dialla, *Humanitarian Intervention*, pp. 197–222.

[29] On the French intervention in Spain, see R. Weaver, *The Hundred Thousand Sons of St. Louis: The French Campaign in Spain April–October 1823* (Helion, 2018). On the Russian intervention in support of the Austrian suppression of the Hungarian Revolution in 1849, see A. J. P. Taylor, *The Struggle for Mastery in Europe 1848–1918* (Oxford University Press, 1954), pp. 30–2. On the Prussian intervention in the German states in 1849, see C. Clark, *Iron Kingdom: Rise and Downfall of Prussia 1600–1947* (Penguin Books, 2006), pp. 485–6.

### FACT BOX 12.2 THE GREEK WAR OF INDEPENDENCE (1821 – 1832)

The French Revolution and the principles of the Enlightenment triggered and influenced independence movements within European territories under the rule of the Ottoman Empire. One such movement was the 1821–32 Greek Independence War.

The way was paved for the rebellion in 1814 with the creation of a clandestine society in Odessa, the aim of which was to achieve Greek independence with Russian support. The revolt began in February 1821 when a small Greek armed group crossed from Russian territory into Moldavia, which was under Turkish rule at the time. While this initial rebellion was quashed by the Turks by June 1821, in March of the same year revolts against Turkish rule broke out in the Peloponnese, resulting in the deaths of thousands of Muslims. By January 1822 the rebels had gained control of the Peloponnese and declared Greek independence.

The Turks did not accept this state of affairs and during the following three years (1822–4) they attempted to take back the area, but without success. This changed in 1825, when Egyptian forces, sent to aid the Turks, successfully invaded the Peloponnese and went so far as to capture Athens and its acropolis in 1826–7. The European powers offered to mediate between the Turks and the Greeks in order to stop the conflict and establish an autonomous Greek State. While the Greek rebels nominally accepted the offer, the sultan refused. As a result, Britain, France and Russia decided to intervene on the Greek side and sent their naval fleets to Navarino Bay. After an unsuccessful blockade against the Turkish and Egyptian fleet, the three European powers engaged in battle and on 20 October 1827 destroyed the Turkish and Egyptian naval forces. Despite this loss, the Egyptian forces continued their campaign in the Peloponnese until September 1828, when they were expelled with the aid of a French expeditionary force.

While the conflict continued into 1830, insistent diplomatic efforts on the part of the European powers led to the sultan finally recognizing the independent Greek State in July 1832.

**Sources**: A. Heraclides and A. Dialla, Humanitarian Intervention in the Long 19th Century: Setting the Precedent (Manchester University Press, 2015), pp. 105–33; 'War of Greek Independence', Britannica, www.britannica.com/event/War-of-Greek-Independence; 'Battle of Navarino', Britannica, www.britannica.com/event/Battle-of-Navarino; National Geographic Visual History of the World (National Geographic, 2005) p. 408.

During the interbellum period, the freedom to resort to war was gradually curtailed in the League of Nations Covenant and subsequently further limited with the Kellogg-Briand Pact (see Chapter 3, above). However, this development did not have much impact on the propensity of States to intervene in civil conflicts in support of the rebellious party. For example, both the Russian (1918–20) and Spanish (1936–9) civil wars

### FACT BOX 12.3 THE HUNGARIAN REVOLUTION (1848–1849)

The 1848 February Revolution in France ignited several liberal uprisings in Europe. One such rebellion was the 1848–9 Hungarian Revolution against the Austrian Empire.

Between 1526 and 1867 the Kingdom of Hungary formed part of the Habsburg monarchy that became the Austrian Empire in 1804. On 15 March 1848, inspired by the February Revolution, a group of Hungarian intellectuals drew up a proclamation of twelve points demanding, inter alia, an autonomous Hungarian government, reunion with Transylvania, civil and religious equality and a free press. The twelve points were incorporated into laws adopted by the Hungarian legislature (Diet) and a new government was formed. In May 1848 the Transylvanian Diet ratified its reunion with Hungary. While the Habsburgs initially agreed to the new Hungarian government, tensions continued to grow during the following months, fuelled also by internal discord between revolutionaries and conservatives. The new Hungarian government was also faced with resistance from the Serbs of Vojvodina, Romanians of the newly unified Transylvania and the Kingdom of Croatia, which was in a personal union with Hungary under the Austrian Empire. In September 1848, on Austrian orders, the Croat provincial governor led imperial troops into Hungary, but these were defeated by an improvised Hungarian revolutionary army. In December 1848, under the new emperor, Franz Joseph, hostilities were renewed. In March 1849 the Habsburg government abolished the Hungarian laws adopted in March 1848. In response, Hungary declared independence; the revolution gained momentum and the Austrian forces were expelled from Hungary in April 1849.

Fuelled by its own strategic concerns, Russia offered to intervene on the side of the Habsburgs against the Hungarian revolutionaries. After an initial defeat in March 1849 in Transylvania, the Russian forces re-entered Hungary in May 1849 and successfully defeated the revolutionary army in the east of the country. At the same time, Austrian forces engaged the Hungarian army in the north, west and south. Hungary finally surrendered to Russia in August 1849.

**Sources:** A. J. P. Taylor, *The Struggle for Mastery in Europe 1848–1918* (Oxford University Press, 1954), pp. 30–2; 'The Nationalities of Hungary', *Britannica*, www.britannica.com/place/Hungary/The-nationalities#ref411290; *National Geographic Visual History of the World* (National Geographic, 2005) p. 372.

saw large-scale interventions by foreign powers on the side of the party in rebellion against the incumbent government.[30] Ideological, military and geopolitical factors seemingly overrode any considerations relating to a nascent prohibition of armed intervention on the side of a rebellion

[30] On the Allied intervention in the Russian Civil War, see 'Russian Civil War: Foreign Intervention', *Britannica*, https://tinyurl.com/d7b769z3. On the foreign intervention in the Spanish Civil War, see H. Thomas, *The Spanish Civil War* (Penguin Books, 1965), chap. 25, pp. 281–92.

against the incumbent government in both those conflicts. Consequently, it is not plausible to maintain that a prohibition of armed intervention in civil conflict existed prior to the Second World War, and there is in any case no evidence that any rule of international law at the time would have prohibited intervention on the side of an incumbent government. The emerging *jus ad bellum* was relevant only in relation to inter-State war, and a rebellious party in a civil conflict would not qualify as a State.

With the adoption of the UN Charter, the prohibition of war became the contemporary prohibition on the use of force in international relations. Hence, any armed intervention on the side of an insurgent movement in a civil conflict would be a use of force in the context of international relations and fall within the scope of the prohibition, irrespective of whether it constituted an act of war. However, this does not apply to interventions in support of the incumbent government. There is abundant State practice showing that, with the exception of interventions where a peremptory rule is at issue, there is no rule prohibiting a State to consent to or invite foreign military assistance in combatting an insurgency or ending a civil conflict. This is regardless of whether the insurgent party benefits from outside support. For instance, the Cold War saw many interventions on the side of governments fighting armed insurgencies, with the United States and the Soviet Union often supporting opposite sides in the same conflict. Such support was often couched in terms of 'counter-intervention'. Examples include the US intervention in the Dominican Republic in 1965, the US intervention in South East Asia between 1963 and 1975, the Cuban intervention in the Angolan Civil War between 1975 and 1991 and the Soviet intervention in Afghanistan between 1979 and 1987.

The tendency in more recent internal conflicts has been to politically justify the need for intervention in terms of counter-terrorism and protection of civilians rather than in terms of ideology or geopolitical rivalry. Examples are myriad and include the UN peace and peace-enforcement operations conducted over the past thirty years, from those in the Balkans and Somalia in the 1990s to the contemporary operations in the Democratic Republic of the Congo, Mali and elsewhere, most of which have been premised on support to an incumbent government in the throes of an internal conflict with one or more armed groups. Likewise, various UN-mandated operations conducted by regional organizations and ad hoc interventions by individual States and coalitions of States have been based on the consent of a host State which the operation was mandated to support in the face of an armed insurgency.

### FACT BOX 12.4 THE SOVIET INTERVENTION IN AFGHANISTAN (1979–1989)

Between 1933 and 1973 Afghanistan was a monarchy. Efforts to centralize power failed due to the traditional and autonomous tribal structures that dominated the country. In 1973 the king was deposed in a coup and Afghanistan proclaimed a republic. In 1978 the government was overthrown by the Communist-oriented People's Democratic Party. The new government had little popular support but forged close ties with the Soviet Union. In 1979, following purges of all domestic opposition and extensive land and social reforms that pursued leftist and secularist principles, Afghan tribes and parts of the army rebelled against the government. The insurgents – collectively known as the *mujahideen* – were of Islamic orientation. The uprising led to the collapse of public order in many regions of the country. The government asked the Soviet Union to assist in quelling the rebellion.

Soviet troops entered Afghanistan in December 1979 and toppled the incumbent government, installing an exiled, Soviet-friendly Afghan politician as head of State and government, but he was unable to attain significant popular support. The *mujahideen* rebellion, aided financially and militarily by the United States and other Arab countries, grew to new proportions and spread to all corners of the country. The Afghan army was ineffective in suppressing the rebellion, so Soviet troops (totalling around 100,000) engaged in controlling the larger localities and garrisons, while trying to crush the guerrilla war. The Soviets suffered around 15,000 dead and many more injured.

Eight years later, in 1988, having failed to install a sympathetic regime, the Soviet Union signed an accord with the United States, Pakistan and Afghanistan and agreed to withdraw its troops. The Soviet withdrawal was completed in February 1989. The civil war between rebellious factions continued until September 1996, when the Islamist Taliban militia captured Kabul and installed its regime.

**Sources:** 'Soviet Invasion of Afghanistan', Britannica, www.britannica.com/event/Soviet-invasion-of-Afghanistan; *National Geographic: Visual History of the World* (National Geographic, 2005) pp. 608–9.

Examples include the UN-mandated ISAF operation in Afghanistan, the AMISOM operation in Somalia and the anti-ISIS coalition in support of the Iraqi government from 2014 to 2020. The volume of such military support to governments engaged in civil conflict and consistent acceptance thereof by States, the United Nations and other international actors make it clear that, notwithstanding doctrinal support for either a principle of non-intervention in civil conflicts or conditional exceptions to that principle on the basis of so-called 'negative equality', there is in fact general acceptance that intervention in support of an incumbent government engaged in an internal armed conflict is lawful.[31] By contrast, any intervention devoid of lawful consent or other legal basis in a UNSC decision under Chapter VII or the right of self-defence is *ipso facto* illegal, as explained previously when discussing the prohibition on the use of force.[32]

### *12.2.5 Conclusion on Consent*

We have set out the legal basis for consent by a State to a military operation on its territory against a non-State entity as being an attribute of sovereignty and discussed the inherent conditions and restrictions flowing from the nature of sovereignty, as governed by peremptory norms and other international obligations applicable to the consenting State or the State receiving consent. The conditions for the granting of valid consent have also been discussed, including when a government is deemed capable of granting valid consent and which officials are typically authorized to grant consent, as well as whether there are any additional requirements regarding the form in which consent must be granted. In that context, we concluded that officials deemed capable of representing the State at the international level can issue valid consent and that the main tests for determining a government's competence to consent are whether it exercises reasonably effective control over a substantial portion of its territory and has the power to conduct international relations. Finally, we have discussed whether there is a legal barrier against inviting support for to a party to an internal conflict or providing such support and have concluded that while intervention on the side of an armed

[31] Examples of support for a principle of non-intervention in civil conflicts in legal doctrine (also referred to as 'negative equality') include Institut de Droit international, Session of Wiesbaden – 1975, 8th Commission, The Principle of Non-Intervention in Civil Wars, Resolution of 14 August 1975, www.idi-iil.org/app/uploads/2017/06/1975_wies_03_en.pdf; L. Doswald Beck, 'The Legal Validity of Military Intervention by Invitation of the Government' (1985) 56 *British Yearbook of International Law* 189–252. More recent support for the doctrine of 'negative equality' includes Buchan and Tsagourias, *Regulating the Use of Force* (n. 16), pp. 109–12. We do not share the view that intervention is precluded under the law for the reasons given above. Other authors who support the position that lawful consent is not precluded under international law in the context of an internal armed conflict include Dinstein, *War, Aggression and Self-Defence* (n. 6), pp. 125–6; Fox, 'Intervention by Invitation' (n. 8), pp. 828–9; Henderson, *Use of Force* (n. 6), pp. 364–5; A. Peters, 'Intervention by Invitation: Impulses from the Max Planck Trialogues on the Law of Peace and War' (2019) 79 *Zeitschrift für ausländisches öffentliches Recht und Völkerrecht* 635–41, at 637–9.

[32] See Chapter 4, Section 4.6, above.

group or other movement that is in conflict with the incumbent government contravenes the prohibition on the use of force and the principle of non-intervention, there is no legal prohibition as such against assisting a government that is engaged in an internal conflict.

## 12.3 The Policing of Territory in Reaction to Unlawful Incursions below the Threshold of Armed Attack

### *12.3.1 Introductory Remarks*

In Chapter 4 we concluded that there was no minimum threshold for forcible actions to constitute a 'use of force'. We also explained that in certain circumstances the unauthorized incursion of State aircraft or warships into State territory and the non-consensual presence of foreign military forces can constitute a use of force.[33]

In Chapter 6 we examined the possible relevance of self-defence in response to unauthorized violations of territory when discussing the different modalities of application of the right of self-defence.[34] There, we took the position that where there was a hostile incursion by foreign military aircraft into national airspace or by foreign military vessels into internal waters and it was evident that such unauthorized presence was deliberate, not due to error, *force majeure* or distress and posed a reasonably significant threat to the State's security and the intruding aircraft or vessels refused to leave after due notification and warning, then the use of force in self-defence would be justified. The same would apply to the non-consensual presence of foreign military forces on land territory in situations where it was clear that the presence was deliberate and the troops in question showed hostile intent or refused to be escorted out of the State's territory. We also pointed to the possibility that non-innocent passage of warships in the territorial waters of a State could trigger the right of self-defence in the event the violation posed a relatively serious threat to national security and the vessels concerned refused to desist from the prejudicial conduct and leave territorial waters without undue delay. An example would be the submerged passage of a foreign military submarine and its refusal to surface and identify itself when challenged to do so, where it was evident that the submerged

[33] See Chapter 4, Section 4.5.

[34] See Chapter 6, Section 6.5.2.

passage was not due to adverse weather and was hostile in nature.[35] In all of those scenarios a proverbial line has been crossed between mere violation of territory and a use of force constituting a severe enough threat to security to amount to an armed attack. What about situations below that threshold? These would include situations in which, on the basis of the facts and presumed intent of the intruding vessels, aircraft or military personnel, it is not clear that the intrusion poses a significant enough threat to warrant the use of force in self-defence. That is the topic we discuss in this second part of the chapter.

### *12.3.2 Legal Basis to Respond to Unlawful Territorial Incursion and Non-Innocent Passage in the Territorial Sea below the Threshold of Force and Armed Attack*

Violation of territorial sovereignty can be effectuated in different ways and involve a variety of actors. Here, we are concerned only with deliberate violations. Intrusions due to error, distress, *force majeure* or equipment or systems malfunction are not per se unlawful and will not be discussed.[36] Nor do we address violations of territory by commercial aircraft; non-innocent passage in the territorial sea by commercial or private vessels, or other acts involving unauthorized entry into a State's territory by non-State actors of all sorts for whatever purpose. In such cases, the State whose territory has been violated can have recourse to

[35] See T. Ruys, *'Armed Attack' and Article 51 of the UN Charter: Evolution in Customary Law and Practice* (Cambridge University Press, 2010), pp. 195–7; Dinstein, *War, Aggression and Self-Defence* (n. 6), pp. 214–15. For a contrary opinion, see R. Sadurska, 'Foreign Submarines in Swedish Waters: The Erosion of an International Norm' (1984) 10 *Yale Journal of International Law* 34–58. We are in agreement with the former point of view and do not think that the principle of sovereign immunity of warships stands in the way of the exercise of measures of self-defence in response to the hostile military incursion of a submerged submarine into a State's territorial waters.

[36] Distress and *force majeure* are recognized circumstances precluding wrongfulness in the law of international responsibility (see Chapter 15, below). An error or mistake of fact is not included as a circumstance precluding wrongfulness in the law of international responsibility (in contrast to criminal liability under international criminal law), but a navigational error and equipment failure have played a role in assessing wrongfulness in situations of *force majeure* or distress involving the unauthorized incursion of military aircraft or foreign warships. See, for example, ARSIWA Commentaries (n. 8), p. 77 (Commentary to Article 23), para. (5), referring to navigational error in relation to aerial intrusion incidents.

measures of law enforcement, alongside other means of settlement laid down in air service agreements or multilateral instruments such as the 1982 Law of the Sea Convention (UNCLOS).[37]

Deliberate violations of territory by State aircraft (especially military aircraft), foreign military or paramilitary personnel or foreign warships are not subject to law enforcement by the territorial State due to the immunity of such aircraft, personnel and vessels from criminal jurisdiction, as recognized in both conventional and customary international law and reflected in the maxim *par in parem non habet imperium*. Likewise, the law on the use of force does not apply in situations below the threshold for the use of force, and while that threshold is arguably low, it does not mean that any violation of territory or instance of unauthorized passage automatically constitutes a use of force. The question that then arises is what legal regime applies to measures aimed at halting such non-forcible instances of unauthorized incursion or passage inside another State's territory and what, if any, remedial measures the territorial State can take. By territorial State, we refer to the State whose territory is violated or in which the unauthorized activity takes place.

The relevant conventions suggest that territorial sovereignty has a bearing on the answer to this question, but provide few or no clues as to the legal basis for the taking of remedial measures by the territorial State or what these measures could practically entail. The 1944 Chicago Convention on Civil Aviation refers to the complete sovereignty of the State over its national airspace and defines where national airspace is located. It also sets out a strict division between commercial and State aircraft and makes clear that entry of State aircraft into another State's national airspace is always subject to specific authorization, which is an

[37] See, for example, Article 27 of the UN Convention on the Law of the Sea (Montego Bay, 10 December 1982) (UNCLOS), setting out the conditions for the exercise of jurisdiction over non-State vessels by the coastal State in the context of innocent passage. By contrast, State vessels enjoy sovereign immunity from the exercise of jurisdiction according to Article 32 UNCLOS and customary law. It should be stressed, however, that sovereign immunity does not remove the duty of foreign warships to respect coastal State law relating to the exercise of innocent passage and regulations pertaining to navigational safety in so far as these are compatible with the rights of States set out in UNCLOS and in customary law. Likewise, sovereign immunity does not preclude the taking of measures by the coastal State to prevent passage which is non-innocent on the basis of Article 30 UNCLOS (referring to the right of the coastal State to require a warship to leave its territorial sea in such cases) and does not preclude the responsibility of the flag State of a warship that has caused damage or loss in the context of its passage through the territorial sea.

attribute of sovereignty.[38] Likewise, UNCLOS makes clear which maritime areas adjacent to a State's coast form part of its territory and are subject to its sovereignty and what the rights of other States are in relation to navigation in the territorial sea.[39]

While some States take the position that the entry of foreign State vessels into the territorial sea is subject to prior authorization, or in any case notification, the better opinion is that innocent passage is in principle open to all ships, including warships, and that there is no duty to request authorization or give prior notification before engaging in innocent passage. This is reflected not only in the negotiating history of UNCLOS[40] but also in its text as finally adopted. In particular, Part Two, Section Three, of UNCLOS, which relates to the right of innocent passage by all vessels in the territorial sea, establishes in Article 25 the right of the territorial (coastal) State to take measures to prevent non-innocent passage and prevent non-authorized entry into internal waters. Article 31 affirms the right of the coastal State to require a warship to leave its territorial sea if the warship disregards laws and regulations pertaining to passage and refuses orders to comply with them. These provisions would be redundant if innocent passage by warships were subject to authorization.

The exercise of innocent passage is, however, subject to the conditions laid out in Articles 19–22 of UNCLOS, which are also generally reflective of customary law. Article 19's enumeration of actions which constitute non-innocent passage is a clear indication that innocent passage pertains to all vessels including warships, and there is no mention of a duty to seek authorization or provide prior notification when exercising that prerogative.

Although UNCLOS does not set out the status and rights of the coastal State in relation to its internal waters, it is clear, from Article 8, that all waters to the landward side of the baseline are internal waters and, from general practice, that internal waters are subject to the full sovereignty of the coastal State. Accordingly, what does the right of protection of the

[38] See Articles 2 and 3 of the Convention on International Civil Aviation (Chicago, 7 December 1944).

[39] Ibid., Articles 2, 17–19.

[40] For an overview of the main issues during UNCLOS negotiations, see UN Division for Ocean Affairs and the Law of the Sea, 'The United Nations Convention on the Law of the Sea: A Historical Perspective', https://tinyurl.com/3dbv772j. On the question of innocent passage of warships, see, for example, N. Klein, *Maritime Security and the Law of the Sea* (Oxford University Press, 2011), pp. 30–3.

coastal State consist of and what is its legal basis? By the same token, what can a State do if its airspace or land territory is deliberately violated by foreign military aircraft or personnel?

### 12.3.3 *The Right of States to Safeguard Their Territory from Unlawful Incursion and the Conditions Relating to the Exercise of That Right*

As stated at the beginning of this chapter, sovereignty bestows plenary authority over the territory of a State upon its government and the concomitant power to take measures to safeguard that sovereignty.[41] The exercise of this right is subject to the conditions set out in general international law, including, in particular, the prohibition on the use of force. It is also conditional on other relevant considerations, such as ensuring that the measures taken do not unnecessarily endanger human life, are aimed solely at ending the unlawful or prejudicial conduct by the intruding State and are proportionate to the nature of the violation of territorial sovereignty and the threat this poses in the prevailing circumstances.

At the same time, the power to safeguard sovereignty allows for the taking of coercive measures short of actual use of force. These include interception; escorting an intruding military aircraft or foreign warship out of the territory; and verbal and physical warnings, including warning shots to reinforce instructions given to a State aircraft that has intruded into national airspace or to terminate the unauthorized or non-innocent passage of foreign warships in the territorial sea or internal waters. Since these measures fall short of the actual use of force, they do not belong to the *jus ad bellum*, unless the situation escalates and/or the unauthorized foreign military presence is tantamount to an armed attack. Whether one views such measures as actions of territorial law enforcement constituting an exception to sovereign immunity or as applications of a *sui generis* right to safeguard territorial inviolability is secondary to the fact that States possess the right to halt unauthorized territorial incursion in situations which fall below the threshold for the use of force.[42]

[41] See nn. 2, 4, 5 above. Opinions concerning the legal basis for reacting to unauthorized intrusion vary from seeing any unauthorized intrusion by military personnel, aircraft or vessels as an (incipient) armed attack to viewing actions directed against such unauthorized intrusion as a form of law enforcement. For the former view, see, for example, Dinstein, *War, Aggression and Self-Defence* (n. 6), pp. 214–15. For the latter view, see Sadurska, 'Foreign Submarines' (n. 35), pp. 45–6, referring to sovereign immunity relevant to law enforcement.

[42] B. Simma et al. (eds.), *The Charter of the United Nations: A Commentary* (Oxford University Press, 2012), vol. 1, p. 215, states that Article 2(4) 'does not apply to military

In cases of unauthorized aerial intrusion by foreign State (in particular military) aircraft, the territorial State should – whenever possible – issue a notification that the aircraft is approaching or has reached national airspace and must adjust its course so as to avoid or leave the national airspace without delay. This can be accompanied by interception of the intruding aircraft by the territorial State's military aircraft to ensure the notification and instructions to leave national airspace are complied with. This is indeed a widespread practice among States, carried out on a regular basis. If the instructions are not complied with and the intruding aircraft refuses to end its unauthorized presence in the other State's airspace, a warning should be issued before resorting to any forcible measures, unless it is evident that the unauthorized presence is (part of) an armed attack, in which case no prior warning needs to be given. If such warning is also not complied with, and the unauthorized presence poses a significant threat to the State's security, the intrusion may amount to an armed attack and the territorial State may take action in self-defence (see Chapter 6, above). In such a case, the legal basis for taking action shifts from a general right of safeguarding territorial sovereignty short of the use of force to the exercise of self-defence aimed at ending the threat posed by the intruding military aircraft (*see* Fact Box 12.5).[43]

As concerns unauthorized incursions into internal waters or land territory, the two situations are similar, although the modalities of remedial action may be slightly different. Foreign warships deliberately entering internal waters without authorization can be intercepted by warships or Coast Guard vessels or the aircraft of the coastal State and escorted to the limits of the territorial sea. Unauthorized deliberate entry into internal waters will qualify not only as a violation of internal waters but also as non-innocent passage due to the use by the intruding warship

acts of protection against intruding persons ships or aircraft on the State's own territory'. Presumably, this is a reference to either a form of law enforcement or to a *sui generis* right of territorial protection where the incursion remains below the threshold of force. One of the authors of the present book has set out arguments for recognition of the right of States to take measures of armed retorsion in situations where sovereignty has been violated or a substantive right has been denied or is being contested as a measure of enforcement or affirmation of a right in situations which fall and remain below the threshold of a use of force amounting to an armed attack. See T. D. Gill, 'The Forcible Protection, Affirmation and Exercise of Rights under Contemporary International Law' (1992) 23 *Netherlands Yearbook of International Law* 105–73.

43 The classic article on aerial intrusion is O. Lissitzyn, 'The Treatment of Aerial Intruders in Recent Practice and in International Law' (1953) 47 *American Journal of International Law* 559–89. See also Ruys, '*Armed Attack*' (n. 35), pp. 191–4; Gill, 'Forcible Protection' (n. 42), p. 129.

### FACT BOX 12.5 THE U2 INCIDENT

On 1 May 1960 a U2 reconnaissance plane operated by the US Central Intelligence Agency was shot down over Soviet territory while on an aerial intelligence mission. The plane was stationed at a US base in Turkey and had taken off from Pakistan and flown some 2,000 km over Soviet territory before it was shot down. There had been a series of such missions starting in 1956, but Soviet air defences were unable to shoot down the high-flying aircraft until they developed surface-to-air missiles which could reach the high altitude at which the U2 flew. The pilot, Francis Gary Powers, and much of the surveillance equipment on board the aircraft were captured and over the following days the downing of the aircraft and the identity of the pilot and description of his mission were gradually made public by the Soviet authorities. The United States initially claimed the aircraft was a weather plane used by NASA, but once evidence of the identity of the pilot and the nature of his mission had been made public, it admitted, through a statement of a member of Congress who was aware of the aerial espionage programme, that the aircraft was on a surveillance mission. President Eisenhower subsequently confirmed this in a public statement on 11 May, defending the mission as 'distasteful but necessary'. The incident resulted in the failure of a four-power summit conference at Paris. On the first day of the conference, Soviet premier Khrushchev demanded an apology and the termination of aerial espionage over Soviet territory. US president Eisenhower refused to apologize, although he did say the U2 flights had been suspended and would not resume during his presidency. This was deemed unacceptable by Khrushchev, who left the conference after the first day.

In the Security Council, a draft resolution submitted by the Soviet Union characterizing the espionage flights as an 'act of aggression' received only two votes in favour (Poland and the Soviet Union), although various States agreed that the incident violated Soviet territory. An alternative draft resolution submitted by Ecuador reaffirming Charter principles of non-use of force and respect for sovereignty and territorial integrity was adopted unanimously, with the USSR and Poland abstaining. No State, the United States included, has ever argued, whether at the time of the incident or since then, that the Soviet Union did not have the right to shoot down the intruding aircraft. The incident led to an increase in Cold War tensions over several years until after the Cuban missile crisis of 1962. In any event, such flights soon became unnecessary with the advent of space-based reconnaissance satellites.

**Sources**: 'U2 Incident', *Britannica*, www.britannica.com/event/U–2-Incident; Q. Wright, 'Legal Aspects of the U2 Incident' (1960) 54(4) *American Journal of International Law* 836–54.

of the territorial sea to enter the coastal State's internal waters. Refusal to leave or other hostile or evasive acts on the part of the intruding warship(s) may render the intrusion a use of force. If the intrusion poses a significant threat to the State's security, it may amount to an armed attack and open the way for self-defence. This would also apply to unauthorized and deliberate incursion by foreign military personnel and remotely operated vehicles into the land territory of another State in the absence of a legal basis for such action. Interception and escort to the border with appropriate measures short of the use of force would be permissible. Refusal to comply would trigger the right of self-defence if the intrusion posed a significant threat to the State's security.

As regards the territorial sea, as said above, there is a right of innocent passage by all vessels, including warships. There is thus a presumption that the mere passage of a foreign warship in the territorial sea is lawful and does not constitute a violation of the coastal State's sovereignty. This presumption may be set aside if there is a clear indication that the passage of the foreign warship poses a significant threat to the coastal State's security. The following acts may pose such a threat: using or threatening to use weapons for any reason; deliberate interference with the coastal State's communications; deliberate interference with navigation by impeding access to the coastal State's ports or to the open sea from the coastal State's territorial waters; and reconnaissance or espionage activities aimed at the coastal State.[44]

Such violations would amount to non-innocent passage clearly prejudicial to the coastal State's security and would justify the expulsion of the warship(s) engaging in such conduct. This could be effectuated by interception and instructions to leave the territorial sea, including the use of warning shots to reinforce the message, if necessary. If the intruding warship(s) refused to comply or otherwise engaged in hostile or evasive actions, the coastal State would be justified in exercising self-defence, if this became necessary as a means of countering the threat to its security.[45] In cases of non-innocent passage by foreign warships falling short of constituting a significant threat to the State's security, the coastal State should exercise restraint and simply call upon the warships to cease the activity in question or leave the territorial sea. Examples of conduct short of a threat to national security could include non-compliance with

[44] Some States (such as China) take the position that any unauthorized passage by a foreign warship in a State's (claimed) territorial sea is in itself non-innocent. This view would render Article 19 UNCLOS redundant and should be rejected. In any case, whatever the position a State chooses to take regarding passage by foreign warships in the territorial sea, there is no justification for the use of force in the absence of specific acts posing a credible threat to the coastal State's security.

[45] In addition to the sources referred to above in nn. 35, 41, 42 and 43 see C. Moore, *Freedom of Navigation and the Law of the Sea* (Routledge, 2021), pp. 68–70.

navigational instructions or use of allocated sea lanes (unless this results in acute danger to navigational safety), passage by the warships in defensive formation and the use of surveillance radar, as well as other actions not necessarily related to passage which are not serious enough to constitute a threat to the State's security. In such cases, diplomatic protest and other non-forcible measures would normally suffice.

### *12.3.4 Conclusion on Measures to Safeguard Territorial Sovereignty*

It is sometimes posited that territorial incursions which fall short of constituting an unequivocal use of force amounting to an armed attack take place in a legal 'grey zone' or even leave the State whose territory has been violated defenceless or without any remedy. We reject that proposition and argue that in cases where a violation of territory is deliberate and constitutes a significant threat to a State's security, self-defence is justified when other measures short of force are insufficient to end the threat posed by the incursion. In other cases, the right of the State to safeguard its sovereignty and any relevant provisions from multilateral conventions relating to measures of self-protection are the legal basis for taking measures aimed at halting unlawful territorial incursions and allow for remedial 'police' measures short of the use of force.

# 13

# The Use of Force in the International Commons

## 13.1 Introduction

The term 'international commons' (or 'global commons') refers to those areas that do not form part of any State's territory and in relation to which all States share the same rights and obligations. They include the high seas, deep seabed, international airspace and outer space.[1] The term is merely descriptive in nature and does not in itself confer any legal status; this is regulated in specific conventions, such as the 1982 UN Convention on the Law of the Sea (UNCLOS), the 1944 Chicago Convention on Civil Aviation and the 1967 Outer Space Treaty, as well as, to some extent, in customary international law.

In addition to the previously mentioned maritime areas pertaining to the international commons, there are also several maritime zones (e.g. the exclusive economic zone (EEZ), continental shelf and contiguous zone) in which coastal States have certain jurisdictional rights, but which do not form part of the coastal State's territory, and where, aside from the exercise of those rights, the traditional high seas freedoms (of navigation, overflight, use for the laying of cables and pipelines and other activities, including military activities) are generally recognized.[2]

1 On the concept of international or global commons, see S. Buck, *The Global Commons: An Introduction* (Routledge, 1998); M. S. Soroos, 'The International Commons: A Historical Perspective' (1988) 12 *Environmental Review* 1–22. For a wider approach, including such concepts as 'shared natural resources' and 'biodiversity', see S. Ranganathan, 'Global Commons' (2016) 27 *European Journal of International Law* 693–717. In the context of this chapter, by 'international commons' we mean all spaces outside the exclusive or functional jurisdiction of any State. Since we include outer space, the term 'global' seems rather out of place.

2 For more information concerning each of these zones and the extent of coastal State functional jurisdiction over them and coastal States' rights to the natural resources located within them, see R. Churchill, V. Lowe and A. Sander, *The Law of the Sea* (Manchester University Press, 2022); M. Gavouneli, *Functional Jurisdiction in the Law of the Sea* (Nijhoff, 2007). In this chapter and elsewhere in this book, the term 'international waters' refers to all sea areas beyond the territorial sea of any State and includes both high sea and exclusive economic zone (EEZ) areas.

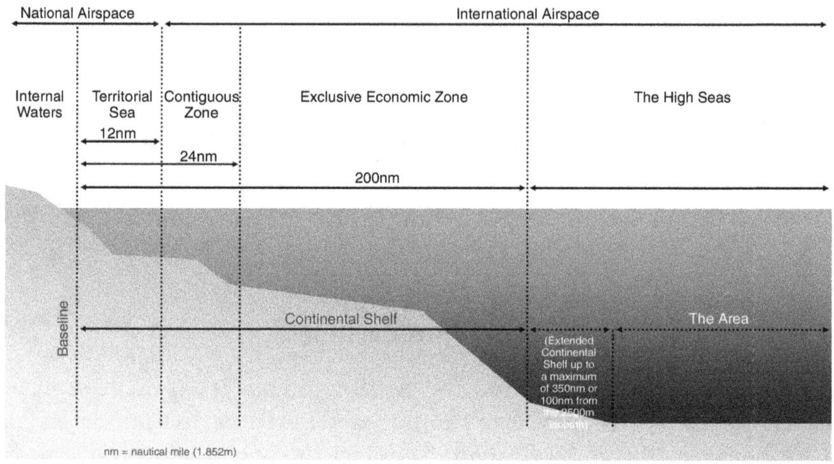


Maritime zones
Courtesy of Dr Valentin Schatz

The term 'international waters' is not a legal term either, but rather a descriptive one, denoting maritime areas not falling within any State's territory. The term 'territorial waters' is likewise descriptive and refers to maritime areas falling within the territory of a State. Territorial waters include the territorial sea, internal waters and, where relevant, the archipelagic waters of a State (see Figure).

Both the high seas and the EEZ are international waters, since they do not fall within any State's territory. But since the EEZ allows for sovereign rights and the exercise of functional jurisdiction by the coastal State over matters pertaining to natural resources and artificial platforms, as well as to marine pollution and marine scientific research, it does not form part of the international commons. The contiguous zone is the part of the EEZ adjacent to the territorial sea. As such, it allows for the exercise of functional jurisdiction over matters relating to customs, immigration and sanitary measures over (non-State) vessels destined for or leaving the territorial sea, in addition to the previously mentioned EEZ rights. The continental shelf is the seabed under the superjacent EEZ, extending in some cases beyond the outer limit of the EEZ; the coastal State has functional jurisdiction and sovereign rights pertaining to the natural resources located on and under the continental shelf. International straits falling within the territorial waters of the State(s) bordering them are governed by a set of rules allowing for unimpeded passage of all vessels. Under certain conditions, overflight by aircraft and the submerged passage of submarines are also allowed and, to the extent necessary, will be given attention in this chapter.

Finally, the continent of Antarctica is subject to a special legal regime, which provides for its complete demilitarization.

In this chapter, the rules relating to the use of force are considered in relation to the specific legal rules and regimes pertaining to the previously mentioned areas. They include the law of the sea, international air law and the international law relating to outer space, alongside certain other instruments such as the 1959 Antarctic Treaty. The purpose is not to explain the rules contained in these legal regimes in detail or to focus on specific disputes, but to give a general indication of how the law on the use of force applies in those areas and how the rules from those legal regimes impact on the law governing the use of force. The law of naval warfare (which forms part of the law of armed conflict) and its relationship to the law on the use of force will be given attention in Chapter 14.

## 13.2 Maritime Law Enforcement, the Use of Force and the Law of the Sea

### *13.2.1 The Law Enforcement Paradigm and Its Distinctness from the Use of Force*

The distinction between the concept of law enforcement and the use of force is a recurrent question, and one which is especially pertinent in the maritime context.[3] Law enforcement is normally associated with the maintenance of public order and combatting of crime on national territory under domestic law. Nevertheless, in the maritime domain it is also linked to the exercise of functional jurisdiction by coastal States in maritime areas adjacent to the coast on the basis of their jurisdictional competence to enact and enforce laws pertaining to specific activities within those maritime zones. This is regulated by UNCLOS, much of which is also part of customary law. In addition, the exercise of law enforcement jurisdiction in relation to international offences such as piracy, slave trade and maritime terrorism (provided for in UNCLOS and certain other international

[3] The terms 'law enforcement' and 'use of force' are used here to designate, respectively, the legal regime and factual context applicable to the exercise of jurisdiction and police powers, and the legal regime and factual context applicable to the use of armed force by States across an international frontier or demarcation line. These designations are derived from the use of comparable terms in the law of armed conflict and military operational law first introduced by Nils Melzer. See N. Melzer and G. Gaggioli, 'Conceptual Distinction and Overlaps between Law Enforcement and the Conduct of Hostilities', in T. D. Gill and D. Fleck (eds.), *The Handbook of the International Law of Military Operations* (Oxford University Press, 2015), pp. 63–92.

instruments) is also relevant. Finally, the enforcement of embargoes enacted by the UN Security Council (UNSC, Security Council) in the exercise of its powers to maintain international peace and security – while conceptually distinct from law enforcement – shares certain characteristics with it in terms of the permissible use of force in carrying out those tasks.

Most of the situations involving an application of force at sea take place in connection with one of these categories of law enforcement and as such require some attention. By contrast, the use of force between States at sea is comparatively rare, but when it does occur it is governed by the same rules as in any other domain, albeit subject to certain additional considerations arising from the division of the seas and oceans into different maritime zones.

Law enforcement on the territory of a State is based on the exercise of jurisdiction, which is primarily territorial in nature and linked to the notion of sovereignty. By contrast, extraterritorial law enforcement depends on the allocation, under international law, of authority to enact and enforce laws pertaining to specific activities or offences outside of the State's territory on the basis of (multilateral) treaties and/or customary international law. Virtually all extraterritorial law enforcement takes place in the maritime domain and is largely based on the aforementioned notion of functional jurisdiction.

States can exercise maritime law enforcement powers only in relation to non-State (commercial) vessels, given the immunity enjoyed by State vessels, in particular foreign warships and coast guard vessels.[4]

Law enforcement does not automatically involve the use of force. Nevertheless, force may be employed by a coastal State on the basis of its functional jurisdiction and within strict limits for purposes of non-consensual boarding and detention of an offending vessel and the arrest of persons involved in offences. For example, a coast guard, police or naval vessel can stop, search and detain a fishing vessel engaged in illicit fishing activity and take necessary action to prevent pollution of the marine environment or the exercise of unauthorized marine scientific research within the EEZ.

Aside from the exercise of functional jurisdiction by coastal States over matters UNCLOS defines as falling within such jurisdiction, flag States are allocated exclusive jurisdiction over vessels navigating outside the territorial sea of another State that sail under their registry and fly their flag. Naval

[4] See UN Convention on the Law of the Sea (Montego Bay, 10 December 1982) (UNCLOS), Articles 32, 95.

and coast guard vessels of any State also routinely approach merchant vessels on the high seas to query their identity and they have the right to board and search vessels whose identity is unclear or which are suspected of being engaged in piracy or certain other offences (see below).[5]

The use of lethal force in the context of law enforcement is strictly limited to situations where there is a direct and acute danger to life and/or the safety of the arresting vessel.[6] It will be for the competent courts of the (coastal) State exercising functional jurisdiction to determine, in the first instance, the legality of the arrest and impose any penalties for transgression of the (coastal) State's laws by the offending vessel(s), with UNCLOS dispute settlement procedures potentially coming into play later if the matter is taken up at inter-State level.

With regard to the exercise of law enforcement outside the context of coastal State functional jurisdiction, the main exceptions – other than law enforcement by flag States on board vessels flying their flag outside the territorial waters of another State on the basis of the principle of exclusive flag State jurisdiction – are the combatting of piracy, the slave trade and maritime terrorism in international waters (high seas or EEZ areas).[7] As far as piracy is concerned, the definition and competences contained in UNCLOS and earlier conventions are generally recognized as an expression of customary law. The slave trade is subsumed under the notion of piracy in the context of customary law. On this basis, public vessels of all States are authorized to take the measures necessary to suppress piracy in any maritime areas outside the territorial sea of another State, including the use of strictly necessary force to effect the arrest of suspected pirates and the seizure of any vessel engaged in piracy.

[5] On routine maritime security operations outside the exercise of functional jurisdiction by coastal States, see J. Kraska, 'Broken Taillight at Sea: The Peacetime International Law of Visit, Board, Search and Seizure' (2010) 16 *Ocean and Coastal Law Journal* 1–46. On maritime law enforcement in general, see A. H. A. Soons, 'Law Enforcement in the Ocean' (2004) 3 *WMU Journal of Maritime Affairs* 3–16. The right of peacetime approach and visit is regulated by Article 110 UNCLOS.

[6] On the use of force in the context of maritime law enforcement and enforcement of UN embargoes, see C. Moore, 'The Use of Force', in R. Warner and S. Kaye (eds.), *Routledge Handbook of Maritime Regulation and Enforcement* (Routledge, 2015), pp. 27–40.

[7] D. Guilfoyle, *Shipping Interdiction and the Law of the Sea* (Cambridge University Press, 2009), pp. 26–78. It should be pointed out that some States have entered into treaty regimes ('shiprider agreements') which allow for law enforcement to be exercised by public vessels of the other treaty party (or parties) – for example, in connection with the suppression of narcotics smuggling. Besides such treaty arrangements, a flag State can always consent ad hoc to the boarding and search of a vessel under its registry by a public vessel of another State.

In principle, the courts of all States are competent to prosecute pirates, but relatively few States have enacted domestic criminal laws for this purpose, which means that pirates are often put on trial in a jurisdiction in which such laws have been enacted and which is willing to take on the task.[8]

Law enforcement in relation to maritime terrorism can relate to the unlawful seizure of a commercial vessel by members of the crew or passengers on board the vessel. Law enforcement in this context is regulated by the 1988 Convention for the Suppression of Unlawful Acts against the Safety of Maritime Navigation (SUA Convention). The SUA Convention makes the exercise of enforcement jurisdiction on board a foreign flag vessel located in international waters subject to the consent of the flag State. Law enforcement in relation to maritime terrorism is otherwise governed by standards similar to those concerning the use of force in other law enforcement activities.[9]

### 13.2.2 *The Use of Force at Sea: Collective Security and Self-Defence in the Maritime Domain*

In contrast to maritime law enforcement, which involves the exercise of jurisdiction by a State in relation to non-State vessels and activities, the use of force in the maritime domain is primarily a State-versus-State activity (with some exceptions) and is wholly governed by international law. We are concerned here with the law governing the use of force in international relations; the law of armed conflict and its relationship to the *jus ad bellum* will be discussed in Chapter 14. With regard to the use of force, the same rules apply in the maritime domain as elsewhere. Consequently, force is prohibited unless it is lawfully based on one of the two exceptions to the prohibition on the use of force in international relations.[10]

[8] On prosecution of piracy, see M. Gardiner, 'Piracy Prosecutions in National Courts' (2012) 10 *Journal of International Criminal Justice* 797–821.

[9] Convention for the Suppression of Unlawful Acts against the Safety of Maritime Navigation, Protocol for the Suppression of Unlawful Acts against the Safety of Fixed Platforms Located on the Continental Shelf (Rome, 10 March 1988) (SUA Convention); 2005 Protocol to the Convention for the Suppression of Unlawful Acts against the Safety of Maritime Navigation (London, 14 October 2005) (2005 SUA Protocol). Under the 2005 SUA Protocol, the flag State is in certain circumstances presumed to have consented to the conduct of law enforcement on one of its vessels. However, adhesion to the Protocol remains limited in contrast to the SUA Convention, which numbered 166 parties as of late 2022.

[10] See Chapters 5 and 6, above.

Where the use of force is undertaken pursuant to a decision by the Security Council, it will have its basis in Chapter VII of the UN Charter. A prime example in the maritime domain would be an authorization by the Security Council to enforce maritime embargoes. Such authorization would empower the naval vessels of enforcing States to stop and board vessels heading to or coming from the embargoed State's ports and to conduct a search for embargoed goods or persons, whether at sea, to the extent this was feasible, or in a port of a co-operating or consenting third State. If the vessel refused to co-operate, the boarding could proceed without its co-operation or the consent of the flag State if the Council had so authorized. This would allow for the taking of measures necessary to bring the vessel under control, including the use of coercive measures closely resembling those allowed under the law enforcement paradigm, despite the clear conceptual difference between collective security measures and law enforcement measures.[11]

Although the Council has hitherto not specifically authorized a blockade as a belligerent measure, it is possible that an authorization to use 'all necessary means' to restore international peace and security could also include the imposition of a blockade, as in fact occurred in the Korean conflict.[12] Other measures covered by the use of force paradigm which could be authorized by the Security Council include amphibious landings and the provision of sea-based air and naval gunfire support to ground forces executing a Security Council mandate. In such cases, alongside the legal basis formed by the Security Council mandate authorizing enforcement action, the law of armed conflict and other relevant international law would also be applicable and would include the relevant provisions of UNCLOS.

The same general considerations would apply to the exercise of (collective) self-defence in a maritime context. The conditions for the exercise of self-defence are no different in the maritime domain than elsewhere, although the modalities of their application can differ somewhat.[13] An armed attack could consist of an attack launched from land, sea or air

[11] On the use of force in the enforcement of maritime embargoes authorized by the UNSC, see Moore, 'Use of Force' (n. 6). See also M. D. Fink, *Maritime Interception and the Law of Naval Operations* (Springer, 2018), pp. 191–226.

[12] E.J. Marolda, 'The Siege of Wonsan', *Naval History Magazine*, August 2023 https://www.usni.org/magazines/naval-history-magazine/2023/august/siege-wonsan.

[13] Self-defence applies to individual warships and naval aircraft (or formations of warships and/or aircraft) at the level of 'unit self-defence' (or 'on-the-spot reaction') in the event of an incidental attack on one or more military platforms. If the attack were part of a more general assault on the State operating the warships/aircraft, the right of self-defence at the level of a defensive war would be(come) applicable. See above Chapter 6, Section 6.5 on the modalities of self-defence. On the applicability of self-defence to an attack on a single

### FACT BOX 13.1 EMBARGOES AND BLOCKADES

**Embargo:** An embargo is an enforcement measure within the context of the UN collective security system which is taken pursuant to a decision by the Security Council under Article 41 of the Charter following a determination by the Council under Article 39 that there exists a threat to peace or that a breach of peace or act of aggression has occurred. An embargo is a restriction upon the transfer of specified goods, usually arms or petroleum products, to the embargoed State. It could also include a bar upon specific individuals or categories of persons (e.g. mercenaries) entering the embargoed State. If the Council authorizes enforcement of the embargo by one or more named States or by a regional organization, the States enforcing the embargo can stop, board, inspect and divert any vessel suspected of transporting embargoed goods or persons to the embargoed State, including without the consent of the master of the vessel or the flag State, if co-operation is not forthcoming. To this end, force strictly limited to what is required to bring the vessel under control and conduct an inspection may be used in the face of active resistance to a boarding party. Such force would fall within the law enforcement paradigm and be subject to the restrictions laid down by international human rights law. An aerial embargo has the same legal basis and purpose, but due to the different environment (air as opposed to sea) and the lethal consequences of applying armed force to civil aircraft in flight, no armed force can be used to enforce an aerial embargo against civil aircraft in the event that the interception of the aircraft meets with resistance.

**Blockade:** A blockade is a belligerent measure under the law of naval warfare during an international armed conflict and is subject to the rules and principles of the humanitarian law of armed conflict (IHL/LOAC). To the extent a blockade still constitutes a lawful measure of control, it is governed by a number of rules deemed by various naval warfare manuals, including the authoritative, but non-binding, San Remo Manual on International Law Applicable to Armed Conflict at Sea of 1994, to be customary international law. These rules include a duty to declare a blockade and notify mariners and airmen of its location through the appropriate international channels; the duty to enforce it impartially; and the requirement that it be effective in closing off the blockaded State's coast to all ingresses and egresses. According to these rules, it may be enforced by measures of control, including belligerent visit and search, capture of the enemy and, in some cases, neutral merchant vessels, seizure of the goods covered by the blockade, etc.

**Sources**: A. H. A. Soons, 'Enforcing the Economic Embargo at Sea', in V. Gowlland-Debbas (ed.), *United Nations Sanctions and International Law* (Kluwer, 2001), pp. 307–24; San Remo Manual on International Law Applicable to Armed Conflict at Sea (1994), Articles 93–104.

against one or more warships or military aircraft operating in international waters or international airspace above international waters or warships engaged in innocent passage through the territorial sea or lawful passage through an international strait. Any such attack would permit the exercise of self-defence, whether in the form of a localized defensive action at unit level in reaction to a discrete armed attack or at a higher end of the intensity scale if the attack were part of a larger and more intense armed attack on the State or its allies.

If a State bordering an international strait tried to interfere with or block lawful passage through that strait by military vessels (or aircraft where the regime of transit passage applied), the vessels and aircraft could take measures short of use of force to effectuate their passage. If this resulted in armed interference endangering the safety of the vessel or aircraft or otherwise amounting to an armed attack, it would justify the use of necessary and proportionate measures in self-defence.[14]

An issue which has led to disagreement and in some cases armed confrontation at sea, particularly in the South China Sea region, is whether the conducting of military activities within another State's EEZ is subject to prior notification or approval by the coastal State. While there exists a group of approximately eighteen States that subject military activities in their EEZs to restrictions or approval, this has no basis in UNCLOS or customary law. The text and the negotiating history of UNCLOS support the position of most States that, aside from the jurisdictional competence allocated to coastal States in respect of natural resources and the prevention of marine pollution or unauthorized marine scientific research, the

warship, see International Court of Justice (ICJ), *Oil Platforms (Islamic Republic of Iran* v. *United States of America)*, Judgment, 6 November 2003, ICJ Reports 2003, para. 72.

[14] In the *Corfu Channel* incident, the United Kingdom was exercising the right of passage through an international strait to affirm that right following an incident in which two warships had earlier come under fire from a shore battery. The Court held that passage in a state of readiness to respond to forcible interference, exercised as a demonstration of the right of passage through a strait, was compatible with international law. See ICJ, *Corfu Channel (United Kingdom of Great Britain and Northern Ireland* v. *Albania)* (Merits), Judgment, 9 April 1949, ICJ Reports 1949, p. 31. See also C. H. M. Waldock, 'The Regulation of the Use of Force by Individual States in International Law' (1952) 81 *Collected Courses of the Hague Academy of International Law* 455–517; C. H. M. Waldock, 'General Course in Public International Law' (1962) 106 Collected Courses of the Hague Academy of International Law 1–251, at 237–40; T. D. Gill, 'The Forcible Protection, Affirmation and Exercise of Rights under Contemporary International Law' (1992) 23 *Netherlands Yearbook of International Law* 105–173, at 161–2; C. Moore, *Freedom of Navigation and the Law of the Sea* (Routledge (2021), pp. 84–6.

traditional high seas freedoms of other States remain unaffected, as long as they have due regard to the coastal State's rights concerning navigation, overflight and other lawful activities, including military activities.

Hence, there is no legal basis for (armed) interference with routine naval exercises and other military activities that do not infringe upon the coastal State's rights and jurisdictional competence in its EEZ or amount to a threat or use of force against the coastal State.[15] To the extent necessary, the State conducting military activities in another State's EEZ can establish temporary safety zones and take other measures to affirm its right to engage in peacetime military activities in international waters and airspace, especially when confronted by armed interference by the coastal State. These measures can include the operational exercise of navigational rights by warships in the territorial sea and in international straits, as well as the exercise of the high seas freedoms provided for in the EEZ, including the conduct of routine naval exercises. Certain States perform these exercises as a matter of policy to demonstrate their opposition to coastal States' conditioning these activities on prior notification or permission. This is not, however, a licence to engage in provocative behaviour, such as live-fire exercises in proximity to the coastal State's public or commercial vessels or offshore platforms, interference in the exercise of rights pertaining to the coastal (or third) States or blockage of access to the coastal State's ports. If the coastal State disputing the right to engage in military activity escalates the situation by threatening the use of force or displaying aggressive conduct (such as ramming or attempting to board naval vessels), this would justify defensive measures short of the use of force. Where necessary, such defensive

[15] On the preservation of high seas freedoms outside the context of coastal States' rights over natural resources and the prevention of marine pollution and marine scientific research within the EEZ, the starting point is Article 58 UNCLOS, which sets out the rights to unimpeded and unrestricted navigation and overflight in the EEZ. On the outcome of UNCLOS negotiations concerning the balancing of interests between coastal and maritime States in the EEZ, see the statement of Ambassador Koh, who chaired the negotiations leading to UNCLOS and in 1984 stated that '[t]he solution in the Convention text is very complicated. Nowhere is it clearly stated whether a third state may or may not conduct military activities in the exclusive economic zone of a coastal state. But, it was the general understanding that the text we negotiated and agreed upon would permit such activities to be conducted'. Cited in J. van Dyke, 'Military Ships and Planes Operating in the Exclusive Economic Zone of Another Country' (2004) 28 *Marine Policy* 29–39, at 31. See also G. Galdorisi and A. Kaufman, 'Military Activities in the Exclusive Economic Zone: Preventing Uncertainty and Defusing Conflict' (2002) 32 *California Western International Law Journal* 253–302. For an overview of States that prohibit or subject to authorization military activities in their EEZ, see R. Pedrozo, 'Military Activities in the Exclusive Economic Zone: East Asia Focus' (2014) 90 *International Law Studies* 514–43, at 521–2.

measures could also include the use of gradual force to neutralize the immediate threat to the safety or integrity of the vessels, aircraft and their personnel.[16]

While it may be doubtful whether self-defence would apply in relation to an incidental attack on a merchant vessel, there is no reason to exclude the possibility that attacks directed against such vessels because of their link to the flag State or which caused significant damage to the vessel or injury to its crew or passengers could constitute an armed attack. Attacks directed against merchant vessels because of their link to the flag State are based on a similar rationale to those directed against a State's nationals because of the link of nationality. They are both potential means of exerting coercion on the (flag/nationality) State and can amount to armed attacks triggering the right of self-defence (see Chapter 8, above).[17] Another area where self-defence may become applicable is the protection of undersea critical infrastructure (such as pipelines and fibre-optic cables for telecommunications) from deliberate attack. Cables and pipelines provide critical services, but it is not likely that a State could cut off digital and telephone communications by severing cables, for in most cases communications would be simply re-routed. That also applies in most cases to pipelines which transport oil or natural gas, since there are usually multiple alternative energy sources. Cutting off or severely limiting a State's energy imports by sabotage of pipelines is not a realistic option for blocking energy supplies in most cases, despite the impact it might temporarily have on energy prices. Moreover, a cable or pipeline falls under the jurisdiction of the company or State organ which owns it, so it is not always easy to determine which State would be the victim of the attack. But in the event a concerted effort were made to sever a State's communications or energy supply by a deliberate attack on undersea infrastructure on which it was dependent, it would not

[16] See sources cited above in n. 14. If a State may assert its right of passage in an international strait which falls within another State's territorial sea, subject to a regime of passage as argued above, then it follows that it may also assert its rights in the EEZ, which is subject to a substantially more liberal regime relating to navigation than either transit or non-suspendable innocent passage in an international strait when it is subjected to forcible interference. See Moore, *Freedom of Navigation* (n. 14), pp. 97–9. For an example of such operational assertion of rights, see Office of the Staff Judge Advocate, Indo-Pacific Command, 'US Freedom of Navigation Program' (2021) 97 *International Law Studies* 70–5.

[17] On attacks against merchant vessels as armed attacks, see *Oil Platforms* (n. 13), para. 64, where the Court, although setting a fairly high threshold for an attack on one or more merchant vessels to qualify as an armed attack on the State, did not rule out this possibility. See also Y. Dinstein, *War, Aggression and Self-Defence* (Cambridge University Press, 2017), p. 219; T. Ruys, *'Armed Attack' and Article 51 of the UN Charter: Evolution in Customary Law and Practice* (Cambridge University Press, 2010), pp. 204–13.

be unreasonable to assume that this could trigger the right of self-defence to prevent and halt such an attack if the consequences were likely to be severe and protracted and if it were possible to establish which State was responsible for the attack.[18]

On the other hand, self-defence does not apply, as a matter of principle, to the (un)lawful exercise of law enforcement by a coastal State vis-à-vis a merchant or fishing vessel of another State within maritime zones forming part of its territory or subject to its functional jurisdiction. Disputes relating to the exercise of jurisdiction or the delimitation of maritime zones, such as the EEZ, do not, as a rule, give rise to the exercise of self-defence.[19] Where a dispute over the exercise of jurisdiction or the delimitation of a maritime zone leads to the intervention of one State's public vessels in waters where the same rights are also claimed by another State, this could lead to the taking of proportionate non-forcible measures to prevent usurpation of the (disputed) rights. Such measures could include escorting its fishing vessels or preventing the construction of platforms or other artificial structures within its EEZ. Should this result in the other claimant resorting to armed force to enforce its claim, that could amount to an armed attack, in response to which the right of self-defence would apply if no other means of dispute settlement were available.[20]

Where self-defence is applicable on account of an armed attack directed against State or merchant vessels, it will permit action aimed at halting the attack and neutralizing the threat of further attacks where such a risk exists. The law on the use of force and other relevant international law, including the law of the sea, would be relevant in subjecting the conduct of operations to certain geographical and other limitations. These restrictions are inherent in the principles of necessity and proportionality *ad bellum*, which are an integral part of the right of self-defence. In most cases, they will result in the use of force in self-defence being limited temporally and spatially to the duration and location of the attack.

The practical effect of the law of the sea on operations conducted under the use of force paradigm, whether in connection with maintaining international

[18] See D. Azaria and G. Ulfstein, 'Are Sabotage of Submarine Pipelines an 'Armed Attack' Triggering a Right to Self-Defence?, *EJIL:Talk!* (18 October 2022), https://tinyurl.com/ym843n7f.

[19] On the distinction between the use of force and maritime law enforcement, see P. Jimenez Kwast, 'Maritime Law Enforcement and the Use of Force: Reflections on Categorisation of Forcible Action at Sea in the Light of the *Guyana/Suriname* Award' (2008) 13 *Journal of Conflict and Security Law* 49–91.

[20] See above nn. 14, 16; Moore, *Freedom of Navigation* (n. 14), pp. 99–100.

peace and security pursuant to a UNSC decision or as a lawful exercise of self-defence, is that they must not infringe on the territory, including the territorial sea, of any State not actively engaged in the operation or which had not consented to the conduct of such operations on its territory. Moreover, operations should not interfere with the passage of vessels of all States through international straits and archipelagic sea lanes. Not only would such interference potentially infringe on the sovereignty of the State(s) bordering an international strait; it would also unduly impact on the rights of all States to passage through international waterways and to peaceful use of the sea for commerce and other lawful activities. Finally, the law of the sea provides for a balancing of State interests in the different maritime zones and any encroachment on the various rights of States in these zones must be limited both temporally and spatially to what is strictly necessary for a lawful use of force in the exercise of self-defence or under a UN mandate.[21]

## 13.3 The Use of Force in International Airspace and the Law of Civil Aviation

International airspace includes all airspace not located above the land territory or territorial waters of any State. All aircraft have the right to fly in international airspace, subject to agreed air traffic control regulations for civil aircraft. A civil aircraft is any aircraft which is not in government service for non-commercial purposes. State aircraft include military, police, customs and other aircraft engaged in government service. As discussed above in Chapter 12, State aircraft have no right to enter foreign national airspace in the absence of express authorization. State aircraft must operate with due regard for the safety of other aircraft but are not subject to international air traffic regimes. The primary legal instrument governing use of the air for civil aviation is the 1944 Chicago Convention on Civil Aviation, as amended on a number of occasions since its adoption.[22]

[21] This follows from the duty to respect the sovereignty of third States (i.e. not involved in the dispute), the rights of all States to unimpeded passage in international straits and the balancing of interests in UNCLOS, as well as being part of legal methodology in general. See B. Lindell, *Multi-Criteria Analysis in Legal Reasoning* (Edward Elgar, 2017), pp. 1–44; 'Fragmentation of International Law: Difficulties Arising from the Diversification and Expansion of International Law', Report of International Law Commission Study Group, finalized by M. Koskenniemi (2006), UN Doc. A/CN.4/L.682 and Add.1, paras. 27–43.

[22] The extent of national and international airspace is set out in Article 2 of the Convention on International Civil Aviation (Chicago, 7 December 1944) (Chicago Convention on Civil Aviation). Article 1 establishes sovereignty over national airspace. Article 3 sets out the distinction between civil and State aircraft.

## FACT BOX 13.2 CONVENTION ON THE LAW OF THE SEA (1982) – EXCERPTS

### Part II Territorial Sea and Contiguous Zone

*Section 1 General Provisions*

**Article 2 Legal status of the territorial sea, of the air space over the territorial sea and of its bed and subsoil**

1 The sovereignty of a coastal State extends, beyond its land territory and internal waters and, in the case of an archipelagic State, its archipelagic waters, to an adjacent belt of sea, described as the territorial sea.
2 This sovereignty extends to the air space over the territorial sea as well as to its bed and subsoil.
3 The sovereignty over the territorial sea is exercised subject to this Convention and to other rules of international law.

*Section 3 Innocent Passage in the Territorial Sea*

Subsection A Rules Applicable to All Ships

**Article 17 Right of innocent passage**

Subject to this Convention, ships of all States, whether coastal or land-locked, enjoy the right of innocent passage through the territorial sea.

**Article 19 Meaning of innocent passage**

1 Passage is innocent so long as it is not prejudicial to the peace, good order or security of the coastal State. Such passage shall take place in conformity with this Convention and with other rules of international law.
2 Passage of a foreign ship shall be considered to be prejudicial to the peace, good order or security of the coastal State if in the territorial sea it engages in any of the following activities:
   (a) any threat or use of force against the sovereignty, territorial integrity or political independence of the coastal State, or in any other manner in violation of the principles of international law embodied in the Charter of the United Nations;
   (b) any exercise or practice with weapons of any kind;
   (c) any act aimed at collecting information to the prejudice of the defence or security of the coastal State;
   (d) any act of propaganda aimed at affecting the defence or security of the coastal State;
   (e) the launching, landing or taking on board of any aircraft;
   (f) the launching, landing or taking on board of any military device;
   (g) the loading or unloading of any commodity, currency or person contrary to the customs, fiscal, immigration or sanitary laws and regulations of the coastal State;

FACT BOX 13.2 *(cont.)*

(h) any act of wilful and serious pollution contrary to this Convention;
(i) any fishing activities;
(j) the carrying out of research or survey activities;
(k) any act aimed at interfering with any systems of communication or any other facilities or installations of the coastal State;
(l) any other activity not having a direct bearing on passage.

**Article 20 Submarines and other underwater vehicles**

In the territorial sea, submarines and other underwater vehicles are required to navigate on the surface and to show their flag.

**Article 24 Duties of the coastal State**

1 The coastal State shall not hamper the innocent passage of foreign ships through the territorial sea except in accordance with this Convention. In particular, in the application of this Convention or of any laws or regulations adopted in conformity with this Convention, the coastal State shall not:
 (a) impose requirements on foreign ships which have the practical effect of denying or impairing the right of innocent passage; or
 (b) discriminate in form or in fact against the ships of any State or against ships carrying cargoes to, from or on behalf of any State.
2 The coastal State shall give appropriate publicity to any danger to navigation, of which it has knowledge, within its territorial sea.

**Article 25 Rights of protection of the coastal State**

1 The coastal State may take the necessary steps in its territorial sea to prevent passage which is not innocent.
2 In the case of ships proceeding to internal waters or a call at a port facility outside internal waters, the coastal State also has the right to take the necessary steps to prevent any breach of the conditions to which admission of those ships to internal waters or such a call is subject.
3 The coastal State may, without discrimination in form or in fact among foreign ships, suspend temporarily in specified areas of its territorial sea the innocent passage of foreign ships if such suspension is essential for the protection of its security, including weapons exercises. Such suspension shall take effect only after having been duly published.

Subsection C Rules Applicable to Warships and Other Government Ships Operated for Non-Commercial Purposes

**Article 29 Definition of warships**

For the purposes of this Convention, 'warship' means a ship belonging to the armed forces of a State bearing the external marks distinguishing such ships of its nationality, under the command of an officer duly commissioned by the government of the

FACT BOX 13.2 *(cont.)*

State and whose name appears in the appropriate service list or its equivalent, and manned by a crew which is under regular armed forces discipline.

**Article 30 Non-compliance by warships with the laws and regulations of the coastal State**
If any warship does not comply with the laws and regulations of the coastal State concerning passage through the territorial sea and disregards any request for compliance therewith which is made to it, the coastal State may require it to leave the territorial sea immediately.

**Article 32 Immunities of warships and other government ships operated for non-commercial purposes**
With such exceptions as are contained in subsection A and in articles 30 and 31, nothing in this Convention affects the immunities of warships and other government ships operated for non-commercial purposes.

### Part III Straits Used for International Passage

*Section 2 Transit Passage*

**Article 37 Scope of this section**
This section applies to straits which are used for international navigation between one part of the high seas or an exclusive economic zone and another part of the high seas or an exclusive economic zone.

**Article 38 Right of transit passage**
1 In straits referred to in article 37, all ships and aircraft enjoy the right of transit passage, which shall not be impeded; except that, if the strait is formed by an island of a State bordering the strait and its mainland, transit passage shall not apply if there exists seaward of the island a route through the high seas or through an exclusive economic zone of similar convenience with respect to navigational and hydrographical characteristics.
2 Transit passage means the exercise in accordance with this Part of the freedom of navigation and overflight solely for the purpose of continuous and expeditious transit of the strait between one part of the high seas or an exclusive economic zone and another part of the high seas or an exclusive economic zone. However, the requirement of continuous and expeditious transit does not preclude passage through the strait for the purpose of entering, leaving or returning from a State bordering the strait, subject to the conditions of entry to that State.
3 Any activity which is not an exercise of the right of transit passage through a strait remains subject to the other applicable provisions of this Convention.

FACT BOX 13.2 (*cont.*)

**Article 44 Duties of States bordering straits**
States bordering straits shall not hamper transit passage and shall give appropriate publicity to any danger to navigation or overflight within or over the strait of which they have knowledge. There shall be no suspension of transit passage.

*Section 3 Innocent Passage [in Straits]*

**Article 45 Innocent passage**
1 The regime of innocent passage, in accordance with Part II, section 3, shall apply in straits used for international navigation:
 (a) excluded from the application of the regime of transit passage under article 38, paragraph 1; or
 (b) between a part of the high seas or an exclusive economic zone and the territorial sea of a foreign State.
2 There shall be no suspension of innocent passage through such straits.

**Part V Exclusive Economic Zone**

**Article 55 Specific legal regime of the exclusive economic zone**
The exclusive economic zone is an area beyond and adjacent to the territorial sea, subject to the specific legal regime established in this Part, under which the rights and jurisdiction of the coastal State and the rights and freedoms of other States are governed by the relevant provisions of this Convention.

**Article 56 Rights, jurisdiction and duties of the coastal State in the exclusive economic zone**
1 In the exclusive economic zone, the coastal State has:
 (a) sovereign rights for the purpose of exploring and exploiting, conserving and managing the natural resources, whether living or non-living, of the waters superjacent to the seabed and of the seabed and its subsoil, and with regard to other activities for the economic exploitation and exploration of the zone, such as the production of energy from the water, currents and winds;
 (b) jurisdiction as provided for in the relevant provisions of this Convention with regard to:
  (i) the establishment and use of artificial islands, installations and structures;
  (ii) marine scientific research;
  (iii) the protection and preservation of the marine environment;
 (c) other rights and duties provided for in this Convention.
2 In exercising its rights and performing its duties under this Convention in the exclusive economic zone, the coastal State shall have due regard to the rights and duties of other States and shall act in a manner compatible with the provisions of this Convention.

FACT BOX 13.2 *(cont.)*

3 The rights set out in this article with respect to the seabed and subsoil shall be exercised in accordance with Part VI.

**Article 57 Breadth of the exclusive economic zone**

The exclusive economic zone shall not extend beyond 200 nautical miles from the baselines from which the breadth of the territorial sea is measured.

**Article 58 Rights and duties of other States in the exclusive economic zone**

1 In the exclusive economic zone, all States, whether coastal or land-locked, enjoy, subject to the relevant provisions of this Convention, the freedoms referred to in article 87 of navigation and overflight and of the laying of submarine cables and pipelines, and other internationally lawful uses of the sea related to these freedoms, such as those associated with the operation of ships, aircraft and submarine cables and pipelines, and compatible with the other provisions of this Convention.

2 Articles 88 to 115 and other pertinent rules of international law apply to the exclusive economic zone in so far as they are not incompatible with this Part.

3 In exercising their rights and performing their duties under this Convention in the exclusive economic zone, States shall have due regard to the rights and duties of the coastal State and shall comply with the laws and regulations adopted by the coastal State in accordance with the provisions of this Convention and other rules of international law in so far as they are not incompatible with this Part.

## Part VII High Seas

### *Section 1 General Provisions*

**Article 87 Freedom of the high seas**

1 The high seas are open to all States, whether coastal or land-locked.

Freedom of the high seas is exercised under the conditions laid down by this Convention and by other rules of international law. It comprises, *inter alia*, both for coastal and land-locked States:

(a) freedom of navigation;
(b) freedom of overflight;
(c) freedom to lay submarine cables and pipelines, subject to Part VI;
(d) freedom to construct artificial islands and other installations permitted under international law, subject to Part VI;
(e) freedom of fishing, subject to the conditions laid down in section 2;
(f) freedom of scientific research, subject to Parts VI and XIII.

FACT BOX 13.2 *(cont.)*

2 These freedoms shall be exercised by all States with due regard for the interests of other States in their exercise of the freedom of the high seas, and also with due regard for the rights under this Convention with respect to activities in the Area.

**Article 101 Definition of piracy**
Piracy consists of any of the following acts:

(a) any illegal acts of violence or detention, or any act of depredation, committed for private ends by the crew or the passengers of a private ship or a private aircraft, and directed:
   (i) on the high seas, against another ship or aircraft, or against persons or property on board such ship or aircraft;
   (ii) against a ship, aircraft, persons or property in a place outside the jurisdiction of any State;
(b) any act of voluntary participation in the operation of a ship or of an aircraft with knowledge of facts making it a pirate ship or aircraft;
(c) any act of inciting or of intentionally facilitating an act.

**Article 105 Seizure of a pirate ship or aircraft**
On the high seas, or in any other place outside the jurisdiction of any State, every State may seize a pirate ship or aircraft, or a ship or aircraft taken by piracy and under the control of pirates, and arrest the persons and seize the property on board. The courts of the State which carried out the seizure may decide upon the penalties to be imposed, and may also determine the action to be taken with regard to the ships, aircraft or property, subject to the rights of third parties acting in good faith described in subparagraph (a) or (b).

**Article 110 Right of visit**

1 Except where acts of interference derive from powers conferred by treaty, a warship which encounters on the high seas a foreign ship, other than a ship entitled to complete immunity in accordance with articles 95 and 96, is not justified in boarding it unless there is reasonable ground for suspecting that:
   (a) the ship is engaged in piracy;
   (b) the ship is engaged in the slave trade;
   (c) the ship is engaged in unauthorized broadcasting and the flag State of the warship has jurisdiction under article 109;
   (d) the ship is without nationality; or
   (e) though flying a foreign flag or refusing to show its flag, the ship is, in reality, of the same nationality as the warship.

2 In the cases provided for in paragraph 1, the warship may proceed to verify the ship's right to fly its flag. To this end, it may send a boat under the command of an officer to the suspected ship. If suspicion remains after the documents have been checked, it may proceed to a further examination on board the ship, which must be carried out with all possible consideration.

FACT BOX 13.2 (*cont.*)

3 If the suspicions prove to be unfounded, and provided that the ship boarded has not committed any act justifying them, it shall be compensated for any loss or damage that may have been sustained.
4 These provisions apply mutatis mutandis to military aircraft.
5 These provisions also apply to any other duly authorized ships or aircraft clearly marked and identifiable as being on government service.

**Part XVI General Provisions**

**Article 300 Good faith and abuse of rights**
States Parties shall fulfil in good faith the obligations assumed under this Convention and shall exercise the rights, jurisdiction and freedoms recognized in this Convention in a manner which would not constitute an abuse of right.

**Article 301 Peaceful uses of the seas**
In exercising their rights and performing their duties under this Convention, States Parties shall refrain from any threat or use of force against the territorial integrity or political independence of any State, or in any other manner inconsistent with the principles of international law embodied in the Charter of the United Nations.

Specific questions which receive attention in this chapter include so-called air-defence identification zones (ADIZ) located in international airspace, the enforcement of aerial embargoes, no-fly zones and other measures of aerial interdiction.

### *13.3.1 Air-Defence Identification Zones*

A number of States have instituted ADIZs in airspace adjacent to their national airspace, in some cases extending a considerable distance from their territory. An ADIZ is not inconsistent with international law if it is located in international airspace. ADIZ identification procedures are restricted to non-State aircraft wishing to enter national airspace. An ADIZ should not extend over any other State's territory and does not confer any jurisdictional rights other than denial of entry into national airspace to any aircraft not complying with ADIZ identification procedures. Some States send military aircraft to intercept aircraft that have entered their particular ADIZ without identifying themselves, but this does not imply any right of enforcement in international airspace. Any measures of enforcement are restricted to preventing unauthorized entry once the aircraft reaches national airspace and, in any event, may not result in the use of force against civil passenger aircraft except in the very restricted circumstances examined below. Accordingly, there is no duty to comply with ADIZ identification procedures unless one wishes to enter the national airspace of the State implementing the ADIZ. In contrast to maritime zones adjacent to territorial waters, an ADIZ does not confer any jurisdiction over foreign aircraft so long as they remain outside national airspace. Consequently, there is no such thing as a 'violation' of an ADIZ by any aircraft, since it does not confer any rights other than to establish the identity of an aircraft which wishes to enter national airspace.[23]

The unauthorized entry of military and other State aircraft into national airspace has been dealt with in Chapter 12. It is conceptually distinct from unauthorized entry of civil aircraft into national airspace in that it constitutes a violation of sovereignty at the very least, unless it can be considered a result of distress, *force majeure* or navigational error, and in some cases it can be deemed a use of force amounting to an armed attack.[24] By contrast, the unauthorized entry of a civil aircraft into national airspace does not violate the sovereignty of any State; nor, in itself, does it constitute a threat of or actual use of force. The violation pertains to air traffic regulations and aviation law rather than to State sovereignty or the law on the use of force. Consequently, the appropriate response is restricted to enforcing such laws and regulations and has no connection with the *jus ad bellum*. For civil aircraft that have failed to follow identification procedures, the State can either deny entry or order the aircraft to land at a designated airport to undergo immigration and customs controls. In any case, there are no grounds for using force against a civil aircraft that has simply entered national airspace without identifying itself.

[23] On air-defence identification zones (ADIZ) and their compatibility with international law, see Office of the Staff Judge Advocate, Indo-Pacific Command, 'Air Defense Identification Zones' (2021) 97 *International Law Studies* 7–11. See also M. N. Schmitt, 'Air Law and Military Operations', in T. D. Gill and D. Fleck (eds.), *The Handbook of the International Law of Military Operations* (Oxford University Press, 2015), pp. 354–74, at 358. For an examination of how conflicting ADIZ claims and procedures play out in the East Asia region, see M. Trent, *Over the Line: the Implications of China's ADIZ Intrusions in Northeast Asia* (American Federation of Scientists, 2020).

[24] See Chapter 12, Section 12.2.

### 13.3.2 Aerial Embargoes and No-Fly Zones

Aerial embargoes and so-called no-fly zones are measures implemented by the Security Council in the context of the maintenance of international peace and security and are binding on all States.[25] They should be distinguished from aerial blockades and exclusion zones. The latter are belligerent measures under the law of armed conflict in an international armed conflict and do not receive attention here.

An aerial embargo is a measure aimed at preventing specific goods or persons from entering a State's airspace. A no-fly zone is a measure ordered by the Security Council to prohibit and prevent use of a specified area of airspace by the aircraft of the designated State(s). If the Security Council has authorized one or more States, sometimes operating under the auspices of a regional organization or arrangement, to enforce an aerial embargo or no-fly zone, the question arises as to what this means in practical terms and, in particular, whether this would justify the use of force against aircraft violating the embargo or no-fly zone.

The use of force against aircraft is always potentially lethal, hence there is little scope for graduated measures other than the issuing of warnings by visual or other means. Consequently, any use of force in the context of enforcing an aerial embargo or no-fly zone is, by its nature, a measure that can be justified only where there is an overriding necessity to use force and no other options are available. This would be extremely rare in relation to a civil aircraft, especially one carrying passengers, save in the exceptional circumstances discussed in the following sub-section. Consequently, the usual means of enforcing an aerial embargo or no-fly zone vis-à-vis a civil aircraft that

[25] On aerial embargoes and no-fly zones in the context of UNSC measures, see T. P. McIlmail, 'No-Fly Zones: The Imposition and Enforcement of Air Exclusion Regimes over Bosnia and Iraq' (1994) 17 *Loyola of Los Angeles International and Comparative Law Review* 35–83. See also Schmitt, 'Air Law' (n. 23), pp. 358–9. An aerial embargo aimed at military aircraft would be of little or no practical value, since they do not normally carry cargo or passengers. If they did, the UNSC's mandate could provide for diversion and inspection of military aircraft that might be involved in transporting persons or goods covered by such an embargo and allow for the use of force to enforce such an embargo. But it is hard to see why such a measure would be chosen if the aim was to interdict military aircraft from flight to or over a particular area. A no-fly zone, by contrast, can include both civil and military aircraft, as was the case with the no-fly zone over Libya in 2011 based on UNSC Resolution 1973 (2011).

refuses to comply with orders to alter its course or land are limited to identification, monitoring and reporting the violation to the appropriate authorities.[26] Enforcement of a no-fly zone against military aircraft of the State targeted by the enforcement measures is another matter. If the Security Council has authorized use of force to prevent operations by the targeted State's military aircraft, this would justify the use of necessary force against military aircraft that attempted to violate the measure, if prior warnings had not been complied with. But even in such cases force should be used only if the violation were serious enough to justify lethal force and no other measures to de-escalate the situation were available.

### *13.3.3 The Use of Force against Civil Aircraft*

A number of incidents in which force was used against civil passenger aircraft (with predictable devastating results) resulted in an amendment of the 1944 Chicago Convention on Civil Aviation to prohibit the use of force against civil aircraft in flight. Such incidents include the downing of a Korean airliner over Soviet territory in flight from Anchorage to Seoul in September 1983 (see Fact Box 13.3). Article 3 *bis* of the Convention, adopted in 1984, introduced a prohibition on the use weapons against civil aircraft in flight and a duty not to endanger the safety and the lives of persons on board an intercepted civil aircraft, for example when it has strayed off course into national airspace, as was apparently the case with the Korean airliner.

[26] This follows from the fact the UNSC is bound by fundamental legal norms of a peremptory nature in the exercise of its enforcement powers. Shooting down a civilian aircraft without an overriding need to do so (discussed in the following section) would be in contravention of the right to life under international human rights law and the prohibition of attacks on civilian objects, to the extent the law of armed conflict was applicable, both of which are almost certainly peremptory norms. In that context, the rule of proportionality *in bello* would preclude the shooting down of a civil aircraft, even if it somehow became a military objective, unless the military necessity clearly outweighed the death of civilians on board and potentially under the aircraft. While some authors have opined that the Council may authorize the use of force against a civilian aircraft in violation of both IHRL and IHL/LOAC, we disagree for the reasons given here. See, for example, T. D. Gill, 'Legal and Some Political Limitations on the Power of the UN Security Council to Exercise its Enforcement Powers under Chapter VII of the Charter' (1995) 26 *Netherlands Yearbook of International Law* 33–138. For a contrary opinion, see M. N. Schmitt, 'Clipped Wings: Effective and Legal No-Fly Zone Rules of Engagement' (1998) 72 *International Law Studies* 239–95, at 267–8.

## FACT BOX 13.3 THE SHOOTING DOWN OF KAL FLIGHT 007

On 1 September 1983 a Korean Airlines (KAL) flight from New York to Seoul by way of Anchorage, Alaska, strayed well off course into Soviet airspace over the Kamchatka Peninsula and Soviet fighter planes were sent to intercept it. However, by the time they arrived, it had left Soviet airspace over Kamchatka and was over international waters, but it soon re-entered Soviet airspace over Sakhalin Island on its way to its final destination. A US Air Force Boeing 707 reconnaissance aircraft operating over nearby international waters was monitoring a Soviet missile launch at the time and it is probable that the Soviet air defences mistook the airliner for the surveillance aircraft. In any event, just before the airliner was to leave Soviet airspace, a Soviet fighter jet released two air-to-air missiles, which struck the Korean airliner, causing it to crash into the Sea of Japan some thirty miles off the coast of Sakhalin, killing all 269 persons aboard.

The US government reacted furiously, condemning the shooting down of a civilian airliner as 'an act of barbarism'. This representation of the event was maintained even after US intelligence agencies concluded that the airliner may well have been mistaken for the US military surveillance aircraft. The Soviets, for their part, initially denied responsibility but, faced with intercepted Soviet radio transmissions that the United States made public, later claimed the airliner was on an espionage mission for the United States. However, the Soviet pilot could see the aircraft when he decided to release the air-to-air missiles and noted that its navigational and strobe lights were blinking, which would suggest it was not engaged in aerial espionage. Whatever the case, the incident led to a renewed heightening of tensions between the Soviet Union and the United States.

The International Civil Aviation Organization (ICAO) started an investigation, which was initially inconclusive for lack of evidence. An amendment to the Chicago Convention on Civil Aviation was proposed, prohibiting the use of force against civil aircraft in flight, without prejudice to the rights and obligations of States under the UN Charter. This amendment entered into force in 1998 after receiving the requisite number of ratifications. Once the Cold War was over, the Russian government released the black box and flight data recorder, which they had recovered after the incident but had kept secret until then. On the basis of that information, the ICAO completed its investigation and concluded that the KAL airliner had probably gone off course owing to a human error when setting the autopilot. They also found no evidence of intelligence gathering by the aircraft.

**Source**: 'Korean Airlines Flight 007', *Britannica*, www.britannica.com/event/Korean-Air-Lines-flight-007.

Article 3 *bis* contains a proviso that it does not affect the rights and obligations of States under the UN Charter. This means that in cases of self-defence States retain the right to use force against a civil aircraft if it can be deemed to be engaged in an armed attack. It probably also does not preclude the shooting down of a civil aircraft in other cases where there is a significant threat to the lives of other persons or aircraft on the ground due to international terrorism or other criminal conduct.[27] This could arise if the aircraft had been hijacked and was being used as a flying, fuel-laden bomb capable of causing extensive casualties and destruction. This occurred in September 2001, when two airliners were deliberately flown into the World Trade Center in New York and a third struck the Pentagon in Washington, with a fourth airliner crashing before it could strike its target. In such cases, the use of force against a civil aircraft to prevent large-scale loss of life could be justified as either self-defence or an extraordinary law enforcement measure, depending on the nature of the threat.[28] It is otherwise unlawful to use force against a civil aircraft or engage in conduct which would endanger its and its occupants' safety, even where the aircraft has made an unauthorized entry into a State's airspace. In other words, Article 3 *bis* simply reinforces an existing prohibition on the use of force against a civilian aircraft – especially one containing passengers – save for an overriding necessity to do so foreseen in international human rights law, the law of armed conflict or the law on the use of force.

### *13.3.4 The Impact of Air Law on the Use of Force*

Just as the law of the sea impacts on the application of force in the maritime domain, so international air law influences the application of the law regulating the use of force in relation to both to a State's national airspace and the right of all States avail themselves of international airspace. In situations where force is applied – be it under a Chapter VII mandate of the Security Council to use 'all necessary

[27] On the amendment of the Chicago Convention on Civil Aviation to include Article 3 *bis*, see B. Cheng, 'The Destruction of KAL Flight KE007, and Article 3 *Bis* of the Chicago Convention', in C. Jui Cheng (ed.), *Studies in International Air Law: Collected Works of Bin Cheng* (Brill-Nijhoff, 2018), pp. 343–70.

[28] R. Geiß, 'Civil Aircraft as Weapons of Large-Scale Destruction: Countermeasures, Article 3BIS of the Chicago Convention, and the Newly Adopted German "Luftsicherheitsgesetz"' (2005) 27(1) *Michigan Journal of International Law* 227–56.

means' to address a particular threat to, or breach of, the peace or in exercising the right of self-defence – international air law, as well as general international law relating to respect for territorial integrity and non-intervention, would preclude the entry of military aircraft into the national airspace of a State not involved in the unlawful use of force. Where an armed conflict was under way, the rules pertaining to non-belligerent/neutral States would also be relevant to excluding use of the airspace of a non-belligerent State by a party to the armed conflict. International air law entitling all States to use international airspace, plus the principles of necessity and proportionality *ad bellum*, would also be relevant considerations in limiting any measures, such as the implementation of air-exclusion or no-fly zones, to what was strictly necessary to the conduct of operations without unduly interfering with normal civil aviation. Finally, as stated above, the prohibition on the deliberate use of force against civil aircraft, save where there are extraordinary circumstances, would apply during an armed conflict, just as it does in peacetime. Any operational zones that were implemented would have to be announced through the usual international channels to avoid the risk of civil aircraft entering them. If a civil aircraft were inadvertently to enter such a zone, it might be impossible for it not to be mistaken for a military aircraft, since visual identification may not always be possible. Nevertheless, the requirement to take feasible precautions in the circumstances would apply. Hence, air-exclusion or no-fly zones can never be equivalent to free-fire zones, although any aircraft that enters such a zone heedless of the danger it represents would not be protected from being shot down as a result of mistaken identification. Provided such an incident were not a deliberate use of force against a civil aircraft or the result of reckless disregard for its safety, it would not amount to a violation of air law, the law on the use of force or the law of armed conflict.[29]

## 13.4 The Antarctic Treaty System and the Demilitarization of Antarctica

The 1959 Antarctic Treaty and several subsequent agreements together form one of the most successful treaty regimes under international law, generally referred to as the Antarctic Treaty System (ATS). The ATS currently has fifty-three parties, twenty-nine of which have the status

[29] On the relationship between international air law and the law of military operations in general, see Schmitt, 'Air Law' (n. 23), p. 354.

FACT BOX 13.4 CHICAGO CONVENTION ON CIVIL AVIATION (1944) – EXCERPT

**Article 1 Sovereignty**

The contracting States recognize that every State has complete and exclusive sovereignty over the airspace above its territory.

**Article 2 Territory**

For the purposes of this Convention the territory of a State shall be deemed to be the land areas and territorial waters adjacent thereto under the sovereignty, suzerainty, protection or mandate of such State.

**Article 3 Civil and state aircraft**

(a) This Convention shall be applicable only to civil aircraft, and shall not be applicable to state aircraft.
(b) Aircraft used in military, customs and police services shall be deemed to be state aircraft.
(c) No state aircraft of a contracting State shall fly over the territory of another State or land thereon without authorization by special agreement or otherwise, and in accordance with the terms thereof.
(d) The contracting States undertake, when issuing regulations for their State aircraft, that they will have due regard for the safety of navigation of civil aircraft.

of 'Consultative Party' enabling them to participate in decision-making at consultative meetings held at regular intervals.[30] Article 1 of the Treaty reserves the Antarctic region (south of latitude 60 degrees South) for peaceful purposes and prohibits any military activity, including the establishment of military bases and performance of military manoeuvres or weapons testing. It does not prohibit the use of military equipment and personnel in support of scientific research. The ATS also prohibits nuclear explosions or the deposit of nuclear waste within the Antarctic region. Furthermore, it provides for an inspection regime allowing observers from contracting States to

[30] Antarctic Treaty (Washington, 1 December 1959). On the Antarctic Treaty Systems (ATS) and the status of the parties to the Antarctic Treaty, see Secretariat of the Antarctic Treaty, www.ats.aq/index_e.html. On the relationship between the ATS and other treaties, see P. Vigni, 'The Interaction between the Antarctic Treaty System and Other Relevant Conventions to the Antarctic Area' (2000) 4 *Max Planck Yearbook of United Nations Law* 481–542.

inspect any installation, vessel or aircraft at any time, including by means of aerial surveillance, to ensure compliance.

The reservation of Antarctica for peaceful purposes has existed for over sixty years. Even during the most tense periods of the Cold War and during armed conflicts between parties to the ATS, there were no significant breaches of this provision, whether by a State party to the treaty or any other State.[31] Likewise, while there is no consensus that the ATS has created an 'objective legal regime' binding *erga omnes,* there has to date been no opposition by any State to the demilitarized status of Antarctica.[32] Although there is a degree of ambiguity in the wording of the treaty provision relating to the demilitarized status of Antarctica, which on the one hand prohibits 'any measures of a military nature', while on the other hand allowing an exception for the use of military personnel and equipment 'for scientific research or any other peaceful purpose', this has not resulted in an objection or challenge to the demilitarized status of Antarctica. The fact that military vessels and aircraft can fly over and traverse waters in the Antarctic region does not amount to 'military activity' in breach of the provision. Likewise, the fact that some of the equipment used in Antarctic scientific research may also have a military use or function alongside its more strictly 'scientific' function, does not gainsay the clear object and purpose of the provision, which is to ban the use of weapons and other military action in the Antarctic region.[33]

The similarities and differences between the 'peaceful use' provision of the Antarctic Treaty and that contained in the Outer Space Treaty, and the way they have been interpreted and applied, receives attention in the following sub-section. For now, we can conclude that any use of force against a vessel or aircraft engaged in scientific research or a research station and its personnel would result in a serious breach of the

[31] H. H. Almond Jr, 'Demilitarization and Arms Control: Antarctica' (1985) 17 *Case Western Journal of International Law* 229–84. It should be noted that even during armed conflict, such as that between Argentina and the United Kingdom over the Falklands/Malvinas in 1982, no hostilities or military activities by the parties spilled over into the Antarctic Treaty region.

[32] B. Simma, 'The Antarctic Treaty as a Treaty Providing for an Objective Regime' (1986) 19 *Cornell International Law Journal* 189–207.

[33] A. D. Hemmings, 'Challenges to Substantive Demilitarisation in the Antarctic Treaty Area' (2020) 12 *Yearbook of Polar Law* 172–94, points out some of the ambiguities in the demilitarization provision of the ATS. However, while his point is well taken, we think the shortcomings are somewhat overstated since, despite these ambiguities, the demilitarization of the Antarctic Treaty region is, as we say, longstanding, uncontroversial and intact.

**FACT BOX 13.5 ARTICLE 1 OF THE ANTARCTIC TREATY (1959) – EXCERPT**

**Article I**

1 Antarctica shall be used for peaceful purposes only. There shall be prohibited, inter alia, any measures of a military nature, such as the establishment of military bases and fortifications, the carrying out of military maneuvers, as well as the testing of any type of weapons.
2 The present Treaty shall not prevent the use of military personnel or equipment for scientific research or for any other peaceful purpose.

demilitarized status under the ATS and would clearly contravene the prohibition to use force. No State has so far had any reason to engage in such action and it is unlikely that such action would ever occur. Whether that is due to the effectiveness of the 'peaceful purposes' provision in the Antarctic Treaty or other factors like the lack of military or strategic advantage in engaging in military action in the region – or to a combination of both – is secondary to the fact that the demilitarized status of Antarctica is uncontroversial and has been effective in preventing military rivalry from spilling over into the Antarctic region.

## 13.5 The Law on the Use of Force and Its Application in Outer Space

### *13.5.1 The Law of Outer Space and the Use of Force: Some Pertinent Questions*

The legal regime of outer space is contained in a number of multilateral treaties, the most important of which is the 1967 Outer Space Treaty.[34]

[34] Treaty on Principles Governing the Activities of States in the Exploration and Use of Outer Space, including the Moon and Other Celestial Bodies), (London, Moscow and Washington, DC, 27 January 1967) (Outer Space Treaty). The legal regime of outer space includes, in addition to the Outer Space Treaty, four other conventions and a number of UN General Assembly resolutions setting out several basic principles applicable to activities in outer space. At least some of these basic principles have acquired customary status, including the non-appropriation of outer space, the duty of international cooperation and open access to outer space for all States and the demilitarized status of the Moon and other celestial bodies, to name the most important. See UN Office for Outer Space Affairs, www.unoosa.org/oosa/en/ourwork/spacelaw/treaties.html.

**SUMMARY BOX 13.1 DESCRIPTION OF ORBITAL SPACE**

The portion of outer space adjacent to Earth, where satellites are in orbit and which ballistic missiles traverse between their launch and re-entry into the atmosphere prior to reaching their intended target or destination.

Article IV of the Treaty reserves the use of the Moon and other celestial bodies for exclusively peaceful purposes and prohibits the placement of military installations, the conducting of military activities and the testing of weapons on celestial bodies, as well as the stationing of nuclear weapons or other weapons of mass destruction in outer space.

This leaves considerable latitude for military uses of outer space that are not specifically referred to or prohibited, in particular in what we refer to as 'orbital space'.

Article III of the Treaty provides for the applicability of international law, including the UN Charter, in outer space and requires any use and exploration of outer space to be in the interest of international peace and security and the promotion of international cooperation. Accordingly, the prohibition on the use of force and its exceptions also apply in outer space.

These provisions give rise to several questions. First, how should the 'peaceful purposes' requirement be interpreted in light of the treaty text, its object and purpose and considering the extensive use of outer space, and in particular orbital space, for military purposes? How does the demilitarization of the Moon and other celestial bodies relate to the 'peaceful purposes' clause and to the growing importance and emphasis on 'permissible' military activities in outer space in the positions and practices adopted by a number of States? Finally, how could the law on the use of force be applied in conformity with the Outer Space Treaty, as well as with the UN Charter and other relevant international law? We address the first two questions in Section 13.5.2 and the third question in Section 13.5.3.

### *13.5.2 Interpreting the 'Peaceful Purposes' Reference in the Outer Space Treaty*

The Outer Space Treaty is not the only multilateral instrument regulating a portion of the international commons to contain a reference to peaceful use. Both UNCLOS (Article 301 among other provisions) and the Antarctic Treaty (Article I) contain provisions on the peaceful use of the portions of the commons to which they relate.[35] The reference to peaceful use in UNCLOS is generally seen as a repetition of the obligation to refrain from the threat or use of force contained in the UN Charter and does not add anything substantive to that obligation. It is in any case not related to a duty to refrain from any military use of the sea. The Antarctic Treaty, by contrast, specifies that no military activity may be undertaken in the region covered by the Treaty but does not prohibit mere traversal of Antarctic waters and airspace by military aircraft or vessels or the use of military personnel and equipment for scientific and other 'peaceful' purposes. This goes significantly further than UNCLOS in the direction of demilitarization.[36]

The provision contained in Article IV of the Outer Space Treaty with respect to the Moon and other celestial bodies resembles that of the Antarctic Treaty. It bans military exercises, weapons testing and the erection of fortifications and military bases on the Moon or other celestial bodies, as well as prohibiting the stationing of nuclear weapons or other weapons of mass destruction in outer space. In this respect, it lays down obligations (to refrain from the specified military activities) that are not significantly different from the obligation of peaceful use contained in the Antarctic Treaty. The other provisions of the Outer Space Treaty that refer to application of the Charter and the rest of international law to activities undertaken in outer space and the requirement to act in conformity with international peace and security have much more in common with the way this is set out in UNCLOS. In other words, the Outer Space Treaty does not ban military activities in outer space as such, but only with regard to celestial bodies like the Moon, leaving the way open to use of outer space for military purposes in conformity with the Charter or other relevant international law. Nothing in the rest

[35] On the notion of 'peaceful purposes' and how it relates to various treaties, see A. Proelss, 'Peaceful Purposes', in *Max Planck Encyclopedia of Public International Law* (Oxford Public International Law, 2021), https://tinyurl.com/yck4cae4. On the meaning of 'peaceful purposes' in UNCLOS, see R. Wolfrum, 'Restricting the Use of the Sea to Peaceful Purposes: Demilitarization in Being?' (1981) 24 *German Yearbook of International Law* 200–41.

[36] Proelss, 'Peaceful Purposes' (n. 35).

of the Treaty points in the direction of complete demilitarization of outer space.[37]

That being said, it may be argued that, with the exception of the areas of space reasonably adjacent to the Earth which we refer to here as 'orbital space' (between 100 and 35,790 km above the Earth's surface), where numerous military and dual-use satellites are not only present but have become indispensable for military purposes, the rest of outer space is irrelevant to any conceivable military purpose. Consequently, if military activities are banned on celestial bodies such as the Moon, the planets in the solar system and other celestial bodies, it makes no sense to allow military activities beyond orbital space. This is particularly true of interplanetary space, in which, from a military, scientific or normative perspective, there is no cogent reason to perform or allow military activities. Hence, we take the position that an interplanetary spaceship or other spacecraft engaged in scientific research, whether manned or unmanned, should not have any military function or carry any type of armament and should be seen as 'an envoy of mankind'. This would fit into the logic underlying the demilitarization of space activities on celestial bodies and the promotion of peaceful scientific research, without encroaching on the now well-established military use of orbital space.[38] This is, however, at present only an aspiration or argument in favour of a progressive interpretation of Article IV of the Outer Space Treaty and is not a statement reflecting established law.

[37] B. Cheng, 'Properly Speaking, Only Celestial Bodies Have Been Reserved for Use Exclusively for Peaceful (Non-Military) Purposes, but Not Outer Void Space' (2000) 75 *International Law Studies* 81–117, at 92.

[38] Ibid. Cheng makes a plea in the direction of demilitarization, while acknowledging the lack of consensus on the question (p. 110), as do some other authors. At present, this does not seem to be the prevailing interpretation, but as far as outer space beyond orbital space is concerned, there is no military activity as of yet and no cogent reason we can think of for interplanetary space having any military utility or purpose – hence our plea for a 'progressive interpretation' of Article IV of the Outer Space Treaty. The notion of 'envoy of mankind' is found, inter alia, in Article V of the Outer Space Treaty. The origins of this notion date back to the eighteenth century when Benjamin Franklin issued an order during the American Revolutionary War to all commanders of American vessels to regard Capt. James Cook and his vessel and crew as an envoy of mankind engaged in scientific research and exploration for the benefit of humanity. See US National Archives, Founders Online, https://tinyurl.com/56jx865z.

### 13.5.3 *The Military Use of Orbital Space and the Applicability of the* jus ad bellum

The area of outer space in which satellites are present (orbital space) has become steadily more militarized in recent years. Space-based assets in the form of satellites with military and dual-use functions have become increasingly important, and even indispensable for some armed forces.[39] In September 2021 there were approximately 4,550 operational satellites orbiting the Earth. Most of these (just under 3,800) were in 'low Earth orbit' between 100 km (the generally accepted point where outer space is considered to commence) and 2,000 km (roughly one third of the Earth's radius and considered the outer limit for low orbit) above sea level. Approximately 570 other satellites were in geostationary or geosynchronous orbit (altitude 35,786 km), used especially for telecommunications, with some 140 others in 'medium Earth orbit' (mostly on a semi-synchronous orbit revolving around the Earth in twelve hours at an altitude of 20,350 km). These are used primarily for global positioning systems (GPS) for navigation and certain military purposes such as target location. Finally, there were fifty-six satellites in a 'highly elliptical orbit' (meaning they traverse a course which at its lowest point is around 1,000 km above the Earth's surface and at its highest point 35,786 km out). These satellites are used for satellite communication, remote sensing and other applications and are particularly useful for coverage of higher latitudes, which are difficult for satellites in geostationary or geosynchronous orbit to reach, since they are positioned above the Equator.[40] Of the total number of

[39] On the (steadily increasing) military use of [orbital] space, see A. B. Carter, 'Current and Future Military Uses of Space' (1986) 489 *Annals of the New York Academy of Sciences* 5–17. M. N. Schmitt, 'International Law and Military Operations in Space' (2006) 10 *Max Planck Yearbook United Nations Law* 89–125; B. Skinner, 'Military Uses of Outer Space', *Space Security Index* (November 2020), https://tinyurl.com/4xknef8t; C. Mills, 'The Militarisation of Space', Research Briefing, UK Parliament House of Commons Library (14 June 2021), https://tinyurl.com/3ar82rmz. The military use of outer space and international law is the topic of two expert manual projects which were nearing completion in mid 2022. These are the Manual on International Law Applicable to Military Uses of Outer Space (MILAMOS), sponsored by McGill University in Montreal (Canada), and the Woomera Manual on the International Law of Military Space Activities and Operations, sponsored by the University of Adelaide (Australia). See, respectively, McGill University, www.mcgill.ca/milamos/about; University of Adelaide, https://law.adelaide.edu.au/woomera/.

[40] For a diagrammatic overview of operational satellites orbiting the Earth, see DEWESoft, 'Every Satellite Orbiting Earth and Who Owns Them' (18 January 2022), https://tinyurl.com/4ftkc2sk. For numbers of military satellites, see 'Modern Spy Satellites in an Age of Space Wars', *Deutsche Welle* (25 August 2020), https://tinyurl.com/m9jmd452.

satellites, probably somewhere between 15 and 20 per cent are used for military applications (intelligence, communications, navigation and other functions, such as weapons guidance).[41] The principal 'space powers' (i.e. States using outer space for military purposes) include the United States, China, Russia, the United Kingdom, France, India, Israel, Japan and Germany. The use of outer space for military and security purposes increases each year, so the importance of orbital space and satellite technology in the military and national security context cannot be overstated.

In view of this importance, it is reasonable to assume that an attack on the satellites of a State would be viewed as an armed attack if it had serious consequences. A military or governmental satellite is analogous to any other military platform, such as a warship, military aircraft or vehicle. While it has no crew, it has been placed in orbit to perform a military or governmental function, which in some cases may be deemed essential to the functioning of that State. While commercial satellites are more akin to commercial vessels or aircraft, many of them also play essential functions for a State and its economy, and to the extent an attack on such a satellite results in long-term and severe crippling of essential State functions, it could be viewed as an armed attack. At least one State has openly taken the position that an attack on its satellites with serious consequences could be deemed as an armed attack, and it is more than likely that other States would take a similar position.[42] Lower intensity (cyber) interference below the threshold of armed force, however, takes place on a regular basis without leading to force as a response.[43] While there have so far been no known instances of an attack resulting in the destruction or permanent disabling of a foreign satellite, it is increasingly probable that targeting of space assets would occur in the event of a major armed confrontation between States with appreciable military assets in orbital space. Several States have, or are likely to have, the capacity to target an adversary State's satellites in such a scenario now or in the near future.

[41] See C. Mills, 'Militarisation of Space' (n. 39), p. 6, stating that 15.5 per cent of satellites have a military or dual-use function.

[42] C. Petras, 'The Use of Force in Response to Cyber-Attack on Commercial Space Systems: Reexamining Self-Defense in Outer Space in Light of the Convergence of US Military and Commercial Space Activities' (2002) 67 *Journal of Air Law and Commerce* 1213–68. For official US policy on serious interference in or attacks on US space assets, see US Office of Space Commerce, 'National Space Policy of the United States of America' (December 2020), pp. 3, 4, www.space.commerce.gov/policy/national-space-policy/.

[43] J. Trevithick, 'U.S. Satellites Are Being Attacked Every Day According to Space Force General', *The Drive* (30 November 2011), https://tinyurl.com/ye4psx33. See also the discussion on low-level cyber-attacks in Chapter 11, above.

## FACT BOX 13.6 OUTER SPACE TREATY (1967) – EXCERPT

### Article I

The exploration and use of outer space, including the Moon and other celestial bodies, shall be carried out for the benefit and in the interests of all countries, irrespective of their degree of economic or scientific development, and shall be the province of all mankind.

Outer space, including the Moon and other celestial bodies, shall be free for exploration and use by all States without discrimination of any kind, on a basis of equality and in accordance with international law, and there shall be free access to all areas of celestial bodies.

There shall be freedom of scientific investigation in outer space, including the Moon and other celestial bodies, and States shall facilitate and encourage international co-operation in such investigation.

### Article II

Outer space, including the Moon and other celestial bodies, is not subject to national appropriation by claim of sovereignty, by means of use or occupation, or by any other means.

### Article III

States Parties to the Treaty shall carry on activities in the exploration and use of outer space, including the Moon and other celestial bodies, in accordance with international law, including the Charter of the United Nations, in the interest of maintaining international peace and security and promoting international co-operation and understanding.

### Article IV

States Parties to the Treaty undertake not to place in orbit around the Earth any objects carrying nuclear weapons or any other kinds of weapons of mass destruction, install such weapons on celestial bodies, or station such weapons in outer space in any other manner.

The Moon and other celestial bodies shall be used by all States Parties to the Treaty exclusively for peaceful purposes. The establishment of military bases, installations and fortifications, the testing of any type of weapons and the conduct of military manoeuvres on celestial bodies shall be forbidden.

The use of military personnel for scientific research or for any other peaceful purposes shall not be prohibited.

The use of any equipment or facility necessary for peaceful exploration of the Moon and other celestial bodies shall also not be prohibited.

Because of the unavoidability of collateral effects and resulting space debris, attacks on satellites using kinetic means (a missile with an explosive warhead aimed at the satellite) would not only be almost certainly unlawful under the law of armed conflict but also contravene the law on the use of force and other relevant international law (environmental law, telecommunications law, etc.), because these collateral effects would almost inevitably violate the rights of third States, especially if conducted on more than an incidental basis.[44] Other means of engaging satellites (such as through the use of high energy or laser weapons or the disruption or blockage of communication between the satellite and its ground station by cyber or electronic means) would avoid space debris, but if it were to have serious and irreversible consequences resulting in the permanent or long-term neutralization of the ability of the satellite to function, it would likely be unlawful. As self-defence, such use of force could be lawful only in the event of a large-scale attack on a State necessitating the neutralization of the attacking State's space-based military and militarily relevant systems. It is difficult to see how, outside the context of self-defence against such a large-scale attack, the use of force against satellites resulting in their permanent destruction or neutralization would be necessary or proportionate in *ad bellum* terms.[45] Likewise, it is even more unlikely, save in the event of a full-scale war, that the Security Council would authorize measures against the space-based assets of a State in connection with the maintenance or restoration of international peace and security (and that, too, belongs more in the realm of hypothetical rather than realistic scenarios). Consequently, while the *jus ad bellum* is undoubtedly applicable in outer space, it is not likely to provide a basis for the lawful use of force except in the event of a major armed conflict.

## 13.6 Conclusion

In this chapter, we examined the use of force parameters in areas beyond the sovereignty of any State and subject to specific regimes. These included areas designated as international commons, in which all States have the same

[44] B. Boothby, 'Space Weapons and the Law' (2017) 93 *International Law Studies* 180–214, at 206.

[45] We base this statement on our classification of the modalities of exercising self-defence. If an attack were low-level or restricted to a specific region, it would make no military sense (aside from it almost certainly being unnecessary and disproportionate in *ad bellum* terms) to expand the conflict into outer space. See Chapter 6, above.

rights and obligations, and covered certain maritime areas outside their territory, the high seas, international airspace, the Antarctic and outer space.

In relation to the exercise of maritime law enforcement, both in the context of the exercise of functional jurisdiction by coastal States in maritime areas and in the international commons, the use of force will be governed by the law enforcement paradigm and any law enforcement may be performed only in relation to non-State vessels. With reference to measures of control relating to civil aviation, we stated that while States may establish so-called air-defence identification zones in international airspace, these do not allocate jurisdiction over approaching aircraft other than for purposes of identification as a possible condition for entry into national airspace. We also maintained that, in contrast to the unauthorized entry of military aircraft into national airspace (which constitutes a violation of sovereignty and can amount to an armed attack allowing for forcible measures to end the unauthorized presence), the unauthorized entry of a civil aircraft does not violate a State's sovereignty nor give ground for using force against the aircraft, except in the most exceptional of circumstances.

We also discussed the fact that outside the context of law enforcement, the same rules apply to the use of force at sea as elsewhere, albeit with some significant differences to take account of the competing rights and interests of both coastal States and other States in the maritime domain. We noted that the specific treaty regimes and customary law pertaining to the law of the sea and commercial aviation can influence the extent to which force can be utilized and require States engaging in military activities in international sea and airspace to take account of other States' rights to freedom of (aerial) navigation and use of those spaces for other legitimate purposes. UNCLOS and the Chicago Convention on Civil Aviation do not prohibit the use of international waters and airspace for military purposes, but due regard must be given to the rights of all States to (aerial) navigation and other legitimate uses under the same treaty regimes and customary law. This has clear implications for the use of force in international waters and airspace, which apply alongside conventions and customary rules governing such use, as well as in relation to the application of force under the law of armed conflict (see Chapter 14, below).

Finally, we examined the legal regimes pertaining to Antarctica and outer space and determined that while the former is to all intents and purposes essentially demilitarized, that is only partly true of outer space. We argued that while military use of orbital space is established and generally accepted, the rest of outer space beyond the outer orbit of any satellite (including the Moon, planets and other celestial bodies) should be subject to the same degree of demilitarization as Antarctica. We consequently argued that any use of force in outer space should be restricted to orbital space, and then only in self-defence against large-scale armed attacks where such force is absolutely necessary.

# 14

# The Relationship of the Law on the Use of Force with the Law of Armed Conflict and Human Rights Law

## 14.1 Introduction

This chapter will examine the relationship between the law regulating the use of force (*jus ad bellum)* and the legal regimes that govern the actual application of force, both within and outside the context of an armed conflict. The former body of law is usually seen as being relevant only to the questions of whether and why the resort to armed force is lawful; whereas the legal regimes of international humanitarian law (which, together with the law of neutrality and the law of naval warfare, comprise the law of armed conflict (IHL/LOAC)) and human rights law are concerned with the conditions governing the actual application of force (how, where, for how long and to whom/what force may be applied), alongside their other functions of safeguarding human dignity and fundamental guarantees in the treatment of persons under the control of a State or other party to an armed conflict .[1] This division is based on the principle of belligerent equality in the application of the law of armed conflict and the related rule of combatant privilege for persons who qualify as combatants in armed conflicts between States (international armed conflicts). The principle of belligerent equality provides for equal application of the 'rights' and obligations in the law of armed conflict, irrespective of the causes of armed conflict or the legality of the resort to force by the State parties to an international armed conflict. Belligerent or combatant privilege provides for immunity from prosecution for members of the armed forces and certain other categories of persons for taking

[1] For an overview of the functions of both branches of the law, see M. N. Shaw, *International Law* (Cambridge University Press, 2021), chaps. 19 (pp. 982–1029) and 20 (pp. 1030–69). See also International Committee of the Red Cross (ICRC), 'The Same IHL Applies to All Warring Parties: Differentiating between *jus contra bellum* (Law Prohibiting the Use of Force) and *us in bello* (Law Limiting Effects of Warfare)', *How Does Law Protect in War?*, https://tinyurl.com/mryhw258.

part in hostilities in an international armed conflict, so long as the law of armed conflict is not violated (see Summary Box 14.1).[2]

Without in any way denying the validity of either the notion of belligerent equality or the rule providing for combatant privilege in the application of international humanitarian law to international armed conflicts, we will examine the nature of the relationship between the *jus ad bellum* and the legal regimes that govern the actual application of force. We will set out some observations on how the former remains relevant once force is applied and throughout its application, and how this relates to the law of armed conflict when the threshold of armed conflict is reached. In that context, we will discuss how the law regulating the use of force influences targeting. We will additionally discuss how human rights law as a body of law relates to both the law regulating the use of force and the law of armed conflict, and vice versa. We will also examine to what extent the law of neutrality is relevant to the use of force, in particular whether violation of neutrality or actions resulting in a State becoming a party to an armed conflict can provide a legal justification for the use of force as a counter-measure or as a consequence of a serious violation of neutrality by an erstwhile neutral State. We will try to show how the law regulating the use of force and the law of armed conflict interact with each other and influence the resort to and application of armed force, without conflating the two branches or gainsaying their respective functions and spheres of application.

[2] Belligerent equality is reaffirmed in the preamble to the Protocol Additional to the Geneva Conventions of 12 August 1949, and Relating to the Protection of Victims of International Armed Conflicts (Additional Protocol I) (Geneva, 8 June 1977): 'Reaffirming further that the provisions of the Geneva Conventions of 12 August 1949 and of this Protocol must be fully applied in all circumstances to all persons who are protected by those instruments, without any adverse distinction based on the nature or origin of the armed conflict or on the causes espoused by or attributed to the Parties to the conflict'. The rule of combatant immunity is laid down in Article 43 of Additional Protocol I. It is worth pointing out that most, if not all, of the supposed 'rights' that belligerents are said to have under the law of armed conflict (LOAC) are not 'rights' as this term is usually understood in international law. The 'right' to target enemy soldiers who are not *hors de combat* and other military objectives in accordance with IHL/LOAC, to detain enemy combatants as prisoners of war (POWs) or to capture enemy merchant vessels under the law of naval warfare are simply actions permitted, or more accurately not prohibited, under IHL/LOAC. No violation of the subject's rights occurs if the performance of these 'rights' is interfered with or prevented by the opposite party in the conflict actively resisting or avoiding being targeted or captured. No international responsibility is incurred for such interference or prevention of the performance of such rights.

This chapter is subdivided into three sub-chapters. The first consists of these introductory remarks. The second will discuss the general relationship of the law regulating the use of force with the law of armed conflict and the interrelationship between the law relating to the use of force, the law of armed conflict and international human rights law and examine their respective functions in relation to the targeting of persons and objects and discuss their essential complementarity. It will then go on to discuss the threshold of armed conflict under the law of armed conflict, as this is crucial in determining which legal regime is applicable to the employment of force in a given context. The third and final sub-chapter will examine the relevance and role of the law of neutrality, particularly in relation to the question of whether and in what circumstances a violation of neutrality provides a legal basis for use of force on the territory of a neutral State against the forces of another belligerent present on the neutral State's territory or can lead to a neutral State becoming party to an armed conflict. It will also discuss the impact of the law regulating the use of force on certain modes of warfare in the law of (maritime) neutrality and the law of naval warfare.

## 14.2 The Relationship between, and Respective Functions of, the *jus ad bellum*, the Law of Armed Conflict and Human Rights Law

### *14.2.1 The Role of Belligerent Equality in Determining the Relationship of the Law on the Use of Force with the Law of Armed Conflict*

The origins of the principle of belligerent equality can be traced back to the gradual replacement of just war doctrine by the principle of sovereignty and positive international law as the standards governing regulation of the resort to war in the course of the late seventeenth and first half of the eighteenth centuries. Once State sovereignty became the governing paradigm in the relations between European nations and the resort to war was seen as a prerogative of the State, the idea that all parties to a war were subject to the same rules (then known as the laws and customs of war) irrespective of the reasons for resorting to war became established law and reflected the principle of sovereign equality of States.[3] While this

[3] The separation between the law of war and justified recourse to war or *jus ad bellum* was a product of the Enlightenment; it resulted in the 'voluntary' positive law of nations gradually supplanting natural law just war theory as well as other developments such as the professionalization of armed forces in the service of the State and the desire to limit warfare to avoid the almost total lack of restraint which had characterized much of the warfare of the Reformation. Early theorists like Emmerich de Vattel and Christian Wolff reflected this in their writings. See E. de Vattel, *The Law of Nations or the Principles of*

is still true, the primary motivation nowadays for continuing the equal application of IHL/LOAC is to ensure the maximum scope of protection provided by that body of law, irrespective of the causes for resorting to armed conflict. There is general agreement as to the continued validity of the principle of equal application of IHL/LOAC, or belligerent equality, to the parties to an armed conflict, despite a minority view to the contrary on the part of some ethicists.[4]

Likewise, there is general agreement as to the respective functions of the two bodies of law. The *jus ad bellum* is primarily concerned with the question of the scope of the prohibition on the use of armed force and under what circumstances resorting to armed force is lawful. The prerequisites for lawful resort to force inform the legal basis of any use of force and do not restrict the applicability of the law of armed conflict. IHL/LOAC is first concerned with the regulation of the conduct of hostilities through rules determining which persons and objects may be lawfully targeted, what means and methods of warfare are permissible and how to limit the effects of hostilities on civilians and other protected persons and objects. Its second main function is to provide for the humanitarian treatment of persons who are not or no longer participating in hostilities, such as the wounded, prisoners of war and civilians who find themselves in the hands of the adversary. These rules do not affect the legality of the resort to armed force and are not dependent upon it.[5]

However, contrary to what is often presumed to be a total exclusion of the law relating to the use of force once the initial question of the legality of the resort to force has been determined, there is no rule in either body

*Natural Law: Applied to the Conduct and to the Affairs of Nations and of Sovereigns* (Oceana, 1964), bk III ('Of War'); C. Wolff, *Law of Nations Treated According to the Scientific Method* (Liberty Fund, 2017), chaps. 6 ('Of the Law of War of Nations') and 7 ('Of the Law of Nations in War'). See also S. Neff, *War and the Law of Nations: A General History* (Cambridge University Press, 2005), pp. 111–15.

[4] The view that the principle of belligerent equality should be modified or abandoned has been put forward by some writers on just war ethics, in particular those associated with the Oxford University Institute on Ethics, Law and Armed Conflict. See, for example, D. Rodin and H. Shue, *Just and Unjust Warriors: The Moral and Legal Status of Soldiers* (Oxford University Press, 2010).

[5] See sources cited above in nn. 1, 2. See also E. Crawford and A. Pert, *International Humanitarian Law* (Cambridge University Press, 2020), pp. 29–33. Traditionally, IHL/LOAC rules relating to the conduct of hostilities were referred to as The Hague Law, while the rules relating to humane treatment of persons affected by the armed conflict (wounded, POWs, civilians in occupied territory, etc.) were referred to as Geneva Law.

of law which says that they do not apply simultaneously once hostilities have commenced, or that the *jus ad bellum* ceases to have any relevance once force is applied and a situation of armed conflict is in progress. The principle of belligerent equality simply ensures that both 'sides' in an armed conflict are equally bound and protected by the rules contained in the law of armed conflict; it does not affect the applicability of any other body of law. Belligerent equality is about affording maximum possible protection against the effects of hostilities and to the persons affected by armed conflict, but it has no limiting effect on the continued applicability of the law regulating resort to force – or, for that matter, any other relevant body of law such as human rights law. The same is true of the related notion of combatant/belligerent privilege. This rule is related to the principle of belligerent equality and simply states that so long as the IHL/LOAC rules relating to the conduct of hostilities are respected, a member of the armed forces of a State party to an international armed conflict cannot be held criminally responsible for engaging in hostilities regardless of whether or not the resort to force by the State they adhere to was lawful under the *jus ad bellum*. It does not, however, in any way limit the applicability of the *jus ad bellum* once hostilities have commenced. In short, the separation of the *jus ad bellum* from the law of armed conflict does not affect their parallel applicability within their respective spheres of application.[6]

The answer to the question of whether the law relating to the use of force remains relevant once hostilities have commenced is not to be found in the principle of belligerent equality or any other rule of the law of armed conflict, but in the law regulating the use of force itself. The principles of necessity and proportionality *ad bellum*, which govern the right of self-defence and other lawful resort to force (e.g. on the basis of a mandate by the UN Security Council to use 'all *necessary* means' to achieve a particular objective), will not only shape the initial resort to force but remain relevant as long as force is being resorted to. For them to have any meaning, their regulatory effect must remain applicable as long as force is being used.

[6] One of the few writers who has acknowledged the parallel applicability of the *jus ad bellum* and the law of armed conflict or *jus in bello* without conflating them is Christopher Greenwood, former judge at the International Court of Justice (ICJ). He did so as long ago as the 1980s in the direct aftermath of the Falklands/Malvinas conflict. See C. Greenwood, 'The Relationship between the *ius ad bellum* and the *ius in bello*' (1983) 9 *Review of International Studies* 221–34.

SUMMARY BOX 14.1 BELLIGERENT EQUALITY AND COMBATANT PRIVILEGE

**The principle of belligerent equality** requires equal application of the 'rights' and obligations in the law of armed conflict, irrespective of the causes of armed conflict or the legality of the resort to force by the State parties to an international armed conflict.

**Belligerent or combatant privilege** grants immunity from prosecution to members of the armed forces and certain other categories of persons for taking part in hostilities in an international armed conflict, so long as the law of armed conflict is not violated.

Both bodies of law are relevant and applicable to any use of force within an armed conflict and have their distinct functions. In that sense, the two bodies of law are mutually compatible and complementary.[7]

### *14.2.2 The Impact of* ad bellum *Considerations on Targeting*

This general relationship and the continued applicability of *ad bellum* considerations of necessity and proportionality influence not only the lawfulness of the (initial and continued) resort to force but also the targeting of persons and objects, as well as the geographical and temporal scope of targeting.[8] Hence, while an action may be in conformity with IHL/LOAC (e.g. engaging warships, military aircraft or soldiers of the opposing party in conformity with the rules governing the conduct of hostilities), it may or may not be lawful from the perspective of the law on the use of force, as it may be disproportionate in *ad bellum* terms in relation to the scale of the attack or the execution of a mandate from the Security Council.

[7] Ibid., p. 233. For a more recent affirmation of their parallel applicability, see G. Cohen, 'Mixing Oil and Water? The Interaction between *jus ad bellum* and *jus in bello* during Armed Conflicts' (2022) 9 *Journal on the Use of Force and International Law* 352–90, https://doi.org/10.1080/20531702.2022.2059154. In favour of parallel applicability, see also E. Lieblich, 'On the Continuous and Concurrent Applicability of *Ad Bellum* and *In Bello* Proportionality', in C. Kreß and R. Lawless (eds.), *Necessity and Proportionality in International Peace and Security Law* (Oxford University Press, 2020), pp. 41–76.

[8] T. D. Gill, 'Some Considerations Concerning the Role of the *Ius ad Bellum* in Targeting', in P. A. L. Ducheine, M. N. Schmitt and B. Osinga (eds.), *Targeting: The Challenges of Modern Warfare* (Springer, 2016), pp. 101–19.

Under IHL/LOAC, persons who are subject to attack (combatants and civilians directly participating in hostilities) and objects which, due to their nature, use, purpose or location, make an effective contribution to military action, and whose destruction, capture or neutralization would confer a concrete and direct military advantage in the circumstances prevailing at the time the attack is planned and executed, are lawful military targets. This can be anyone in the armed forces or with a civil or military leadership function related to the direction of the conflict or conduct of hostilities, any military platform and any 'dual use' object which makes or likely will make a contribution to military action, such as bridges, roads, airfields and other facilities used for both civilian and military purposes. Attacks on military objectives by nature (military platforms, fortifications, etc.) are almost automatically considered to render a military advantage, even if located at a considerable distance from the area of operations. LOAC/IHL is considered applicable anywhere on the territory of belligerent States and in international waters and airspace wherever military objectives may be located. So, any attack on a lawful military objective in accordance with the IHL/LOAC rules governing the conduct of hostilities and targeting is lawful under that body of law. However, because *ad bellum* necessity and proportionality require that the use of force be both necessary, in the sense of countering an ongoing or imminent armed attack, and proportionate, in the sense of allowing the degree of force required to ward off the attack, it may well be unlawful under *ad bellum* law to target persons or objects that are lawful targets under IHL/LOAC. On the other hand, *ad bellum* considerations can never render a person or object subject to attack if it/they do(es) not qualify as a lawful target under the law of armed conflict. Hence, *ad bellum* considerations act as additional constraints on the targeting of persons and objects alongside the rules of IHL/LOAC relating to targeting, but they can never enable an expansion of targeting beyond what is permitted under IHL/LOAC.[9]

For example, although attacking an enemy headquarters or destroying the entire air defence system of a State that has engaged in a limited and localized attack on a single military unit or platform (such as a warship or flight of military aircraft) would not violate IHL/LOAC (if all conditions regarding targeting, precautions and minimization of collateral effects were met), such an action would be unlawful under the principles of necessity and proportionality within self-defence, since attacking such

[9] Ibid.

targets would be clearly unnecessary and disproportionate in the context of responding to such a localized attack.

Likewise, although the geographical and temporal scope of applicability of IHL/LOAC would allow for attacks directed against military objectives anywhere within the territory of the adversary State, or even in international waters and airspace if an international armed conflict were in progress, this might very well be neither necessary nor proportionate in relation to resisting an unlawful use of force by the opposing party, if the attack were not on a scale justifying the taking of such defensive measures (see Fact Box 14.1).[10] For example, in the conflict between Argentina and the United Kingdom over the Falkland/Malvinas islands in 1982, the British, relying on self-defence as the legal basis for re-taking the islands after the Argentine invasion, largely confined their operations within a geographical radius of 200 nautical miles from the islands and refrained from attacking military targets on the Argentine mainland, even though these would have constituted lawful military objectives under IHL/LOAC, assuming they were making an effective contribution to the military action. The exercise of self-defence to restore the *status quo ante* did not necessitate operations beyond the vicinity of the islands given the prevailing situation.[11] If Argentina had disposed of longer-range anti-ship missiles located on the mainland within range of the British task force, the situation would have been different. This would have permitted the neutralization of those hypothetical missile installations on the basis of necessity and proportionality *ad bellum*, in addition to their status as lawful military objectives under IHL/LOAC. In short, the question of whether a particular use of force is lawful under international law as a whole can be answered only by referring to all relevant sub-disciplines of international law and by taking the factual situation into consideration as well.

The rules relating to the conduct of hostilities under IHL/LOAC regulate the application of force at the tactical and operational levels. A combat engagement (referred to under IHL/LOAC as an 'attack') denotes an act of violence directed at the adversary, whether offensive or defensive in nature, and is to be differentiated from the notion of 'armed attack' in *jus ad bellum* (see Summary Box 14.2). A combat engagement is lawful under IHL/LOAC if it (i) is directed against a specific military objective or person(s) subject to attack; (ii) is carried out

10 Ibid., pp. 110–16.

11 Greenwood, 'Relationship' (n. 6), pp. 223–4.

**FACT BOX 14.1 THE SINKING OF THE GENERAL BELGRANO AND THE RELEVANCE OF THE JUS AD BELLUM TO TARGETING**

During the Falklands War of 1982, the United Kingdom declared an exclusion zone of 200 nautical miles around the Falklands and warned that ships and aircraft situated within it would be subject to attack. The clear implication behind this was, inter alia, to limit operations to the declared zone, at least in so far as no threat to the UK operation originated from elsewhere. This was connected to the United Kingdom's reliance on self-defence, whereby the principles of necessity and proportionality *ad bellum* would limit the scope of operations to what was required to expel the Argentinian forces occupying the islands and remove the threat of further operations by them against the islands or UK forces located there or in their vicinity.

On 2 May 1982, the Argentinian cruiser *General Belgrano* was torpedoed by a British submarine although it was situated outside the exclusion zone. British intelligence had intercepted an internal message from the Argentinian chief of naval operations ordering naval units to seek out the British task force and engage it. This was seen as a potential threat to the safety of the task force and permission was given by the then prime minister, Margaret Thatcher, to alter the rules of engagement to allow an attack on the *General Belgrano* by the British nuclear-powered attack submarine that was tracking it. Two torpedoes struck the Argentinian cruiser resulting in the sinking of the ship and the loss of 323 members of a crew of approximately 1,000.

In the controversy that followed the sinking of the ship most attention was paid to whether the action was necessary. The salient point in the discussion concerning the legality of the sinking of an enemy warship during an armed conflict was not whether it was a lawful target under the law of armed conflict but whether it was unnecessary and disproportionate under the right of self-defence. There was no doubt, including on the part of the commander of the *General Belgrano*, that it constituted a legitimate target under IHL/LOAC, but views differ as to whether it was a proportionate action in relation to the purpose of the British mission to retake the Falklands. Regardless of how one views the *ad bellum* necessity/proportionality of sinking the vessel, it illustrates the relevance of *ad bellum* considerations of necessity and proportionality in targeting.

**Sources**: 'Falkland Islands War', *Britannica,* www.britannica.com/event/Falkland-Islands-War; G. Alison, 'Britain Was Right to Sink the Belgrano', *UK Defence Journal* (27 January 2017), https://tinyurl.com/3tzxvs4t; C Greenwood, 'The Relationship between the *ius ad bellum* and the *ius in bello*' (1983) 9 *Review of International Studies* 221–34, at 223–4.

with all feasible precautions to avoid or minimize collateral effects on civilians and civilian objects; and (iii) does not cause excessive injury, death, damage or destruction of civilians and civilian objects in relation to the concrete and direct military advantage anticipated from that specific engagement on the basis of available information at the time the engagement is being planned and is conducted.[12] The overall military advantage of 'winning the war' is not included in this equation. Neither the scale or cause of the conflict nor the 'justice' of the causes of the adversaries has any bearing on whether an attack is lawfully conducted under IHL/LOAC.

On the other hand, the principles of necessity and proportionality *ad bellum* relate to the overall scale of the defensive measures in relation to the armed attack. This is true regardless of the modality of self-defence, which, as we have discussed in Chapter 6, can range from a localized response to a limited one-off armed attack to a full-scale war in response to a large-scale attack or invasion.[13] For example, an armed attack directed against a single tactical level military unit or platform (such as a warship) will allow the degree of force necessary to ward off the attack. In such situations, the application of targeting rules from IHL/LOAC (assuming it applies to such an armed incident) and the principles of necessity and proportionality within the right of self-defence will coincide, since the 'tactical' and 'strategic' levels of operations would be (virtually) identical. By contrast, in the event of a large-scale attack directed against the armed forces, population and territory of a State, necessity and proportionality *ad bellum* would allow defensive measures aimed at repelling the attack and expelling the invading forces from the defending State's territory, as well as military operations directed against the ability of the attacking State to regroup and renew the attack, until such time as a clear end to the necessity of self-defence came about through either a cessation of hostile activity or the taking of adequate measures by the Security Council. In such a case, the rules relating to the conduct of hostilities would govern the application of force at the operational and tactical levels, while the principles of necessity and proportionality *ad bellum* would govern the scale of the overall response at the strategic level.[14]

[12] Articles 49, 51, 52 and 57 of Additional Protocol I. For authoritative treatment of IHL/LOAC rules on targeting, see M. N. Schmitt, 'Targeting in Operational Law', in T. D. Gill and D. Fleck (eds.), *The Handbook of the International Law of Military Operations* (Oxford University Press, 2015), pp. 269–306. See also W. H. Boothby, *The Law of Targeting* (Oxford University Press, 2012).

[13] See Chapter 6, Section 6.5.2.

[14] For a quick guide to the levels of operations in military doctrine, see, for example, US Joint Chiefs of Staff, Joint Publication 1 (JP 1), *Doctrine for the Armed Forces of the United States* (25 March 2013, incorporating Change 1, 12 July 2017), pp. I-7–I-8, https://irp.fas.org/doddir/dod/jp1.pdf.

SUMMARY BOX 14.2 DISTINGUISHING THE DIFFERENT NOTIONS OF 'ATTACK'

**Armed attack: Article 51, UN Charter.** An 'armed attack' denotes a transboundary use of force that exceeds a *de minimis* level of gravity and is a precondition for the exercise of the right of self-defence. See Chapter 6 above for further discussion.

**Attack: Article 49, Additional Protocol I to the Geneva Conventions.** An 'attack' within the context of the law of armed conflict (IHL/LOAC) denotes an act of violence directed against the adversary, whether in offence or defence. It is synonymous with a 'combat engagement'. The IHL/LOAC rules on the targeting of persons and objects (distinction, proportionality and precautions in attack) are applicable to attacks in this context.

In either situation, the question of when the necessity of self-defence has terminated and what measures would be proportionate will be answerable only if necessity and proportionality *ad bellum* remain relevant throughout the entire application of force and not just in relation to the initial recourse to force. The same applies to the use of force on the basis of a mandate of the Security Council. The degree of force that would be necessary and proportionate to carry out the mandate would regulate the overall scale of the use of force, while the IHL/LOAC rules on the conduct of hostilities, if applicable, would primarily govern the actual application of force against specific military objectives.[15]

### 14.2.3 *The Function of Human Rights Law in the Regulation of the Use of Force between States and Its Relationship with the* jus ad bellum *and the Law of Armed Conflict*

International human rights law (IHRL) is of a more recent origin than the law on the use of force or the law of armed conflict, but has come to be recognized as playing an essential role in the application of armed force at the international level, both within and outside the context of an armed conflict. The key provision in IHRL relating to the use of force at the international level is, of course, the right to life set out in the UN Covenant on Civil and Political Rights and in regional human rights treaties.[16] The

[15] See T. D. Gill et al. (eds.), *Leuven Manual on the International Law Applicable to Peace Operations* (Cambridge University Press, 2017), pp. 91–104, 145–56.

[16] International Covenant on Civil and Political Rights (New York, 16 December 1966) (ICCPR).

right to life is a peremptory rule of both treaty and customary international law and prohibits the arbitrary deprivation of life. This translates into, first, the requirement of a legal basis for action that could result in the deprivation of life and, second, standards relating to the application of force ensuring that any action that could result in the deprivation of life is regulated to prevent unnecessary or disproportionate force and safeguard the lives of all affected individuals to the maximum extent possible in the prevailing circumstances.[17]

IHRL does not prescribe the situations in which it is lawful for a State to resort to force, nor does it purport to govern the conduct of hostilities once an armed conflict exists. It does, however, lay down a requirement for a legal basis for any use of force and sets a standard for the application of force in any situation, including in the context of armed conflict. It recognizes that acts undertaken within the context of the conduct of hostilities that conform to IHL/LOAC do not constitute arbitrary deprivation of life and are therefore, in principle, lawful. It is the general default standard for the application of force outside the context of the conduct of hostilities both during and outside armed conflict. For example, if a State is conducting a maritime interdiction operation in the enforcement of a UN embargo, the application of force for the purpose of enforcing the mandate will be governed by the standards of IHRL. The same applies to the maintenance of order in a UN peace operation or an anti-piracy operation conducted in accordance with the law of the sea. The IHRL standard also applies to the application of force not falling within the hostilities paradigm in the context of an armed conflict. For example, maintenance of public order in occupied territory would normally be governed by human rights law standards, unless it involved armed clashes between occupying armed forces and organized armed resistance movements.[18]

17 See UN Human Rights Committee, ICCPR, General Comment 36, Article 6: Right to Life (adopted 124th session, 2018), UN Doc. CCPR/C/GC/36, paras. 10–12.

18 Ibid., para. 13, which refers explicitly to law enforcement by military personnel. This includes all acts conducted outside the hostilities paradigm. On the legal and factual content of the hostilities and law enforcement paradigms, see N. Melzer and G. Gaggioli, 'Conceptual Distinction and Overlap between Law Enforcement and the Conduct of Hostilities', in Gill and Fleck (eds.), *Handbook* (n. 12), pp. 63–92. See also E. Pouw, 'Some Thoughts on the Notion of "Control" in "Choosing" the Paradigm of Hostilities or Law Enforcement as the Governing Legal Framework in the Use of Force in Military Operations: Is There Any', in R. Bartels et al. (eds.), *Military Operations and the Notion of Control under International Law: Lieber Amicorum Terry D. Gill* (Springer, 2021), pp. 195–217.

By and large, the question of whether a particular situation falls within the paradigm of the conduct of hostilities or the so-called law enforcement paradigm is one of fact. 'Hostilities' is a term of art in IHL/LOAC and refers to the application of the means and methods of warfare against the adversary party. Hostilities can exist only in the context of an armed conflict. The conduct of hostilities is relevant to situations where a party attempts to gain or maintain control over territory or neutralize or destroy the military assets of the adversary or its ability to conduct and coordinate military operations. It is, in simple terms, the conducting of 'attacks' (according to the IHL/LOAC usage of the term) against the military forces or other military objectives of the adversary and is governed by the rules of IHL/LOAC relating to the conduct of hostilities.[19] If the rules relating to the conduct of hostilities are observed, they do not clash with IHRL since, as stated, the conduct of hostilities in conformity with IHL/LOAC is not considered an arbitrary deprivation of life under human rights law.[20]

All situations involving the application of (potentially) lethal armed force but not constituting conduct of hostilities within the context of an armed conflict fall under the 'law enforcement' paradigm, which is primarily governed by human rights law. Generally speaking, this standard is (much) more restrictive, in terms of the allowable force, than IHL/LOAC rules are. That does not mean, however, that human rights law does not take account of the specific situations arising in the conduct of military operations. Accordingly, in volatile circumstances and where control is lacking, it does not necessarily require the same degree of restraint that would apply in domestic law enforcement. It remains, however, significantly more restrictive than the standard applicable under IHL/LOAC in the conduct of hostilities, involving notable differences in the way it is applied compared to IHL/LOAC. One such difference is that, under IHL/LOAC, so-called 'status-based targeting' is lawful

[19] T. D. Gill, 'Some Thoughts on the Relationship between International Humanitarian Law and International Human Rights Law: A Plea for Mutual Respect and a Common-Sense Approach' (2013) 16 *Yearbook of International Humanitarian Law* 251–66.

[20] See UN Human Rights Committee, General Comment 36 (n. 17), para. 64. What the Human Rights Committee means by its seeming qualification that force used in compliance with IHL/LOAC 'is, *in general*, not arbitrary' (emphasis added) is unclear. It is difficult to see how force used in compliance with IHL/LOAC could constitute arbitrary deprivation of life so long as we are dealing with application of force within the hostilities paradigm. Outside that context, the more restrictive standards of human rights law would apply in situations where the law enforcement paradigm applies due to the degree of control exercised by the party resorting to potentially lethal force.

and allows for the deliberate targeting of persons because they belong to the armed forces of the adversary.[21] Another major difference is the way the notions of proportionality apply under IHL/LOAC and human rights law, respectively (see Summary Box 14.3).

Under IHL/LOAC, proportionality refers to the prohibition of attacks on military objectives which would result in excessive incidental death or injury to civilians and/or collateral damage and destruction of civilian objects compared to the anticipated military advantage resulting from that attack.[22] Under human rights law, it (together with the human rights principle of necessity) refers to the duty to take all possible measures to limit the degree of force to be applied as far as possible; it restricts the use of deadly force to situations where there is a clear threat to life or public safety and no other course of action is feasible; and it requires a balance between the benefit of the use of force and the harm caused by its use.[23] This standard does not apply to the conduct of hostilities, because IHL/LOAC contains detailed provisions regulating hostilities under both international treaty and customary law. But there is no general precedence of one body of law over the other. IHL/LOAC and human rights law are largely complementary and both are relevant in the application of force. So, to the extent that there is a specific rule in IHL/LOAC governing the conduct of hostilities or other related matters (such as permissible weapons or status and treatment of prisoners of war), that rule will prevail over rules of general application.[24] For example, while tear gas and expanding bullets are permissible in some law enforcement situations (such as riot control or hostage rescue), their use in the conduct of hostilities is banned, and this takes precedence in that context.[25] Likewise, persons subject to attack under IHL/LOAC may be targeted in an armed conflict where the situation requires application of the

[21] 'Status-based targeting' is a term from military doctrine relating to the targeting procedure. It applies only in the context of armed conflict. It is a corollary to the principle of distinction codified in Article 48 of Additional Protocol I, which provides that attacks may be directed only against military objectives and persons subject to attack. Combatant members of enemy armed forces who are not *hors de combat* due to wounds, intent to surrender, etc. are, in principle, subject to attack at all times under IHL/LOAC.

[22] The principle and rule of proportionality under IHL/LOAC is codified in Article 51(5)(b) of Additional Protocol I.

[23] Proportionality under human rights law is part of the prohibition of arbitrary deprivation of life and is dealt with in UN Human Rights Committee, General Comment 36 (n. 17), para. 12.

[24] See references cited above in nn. 18, 19, 20.

[25] Melzer and Gaggioli, 'Conceptual Distinction and Overlap' (n. 18), pp. 87–9.

'hostilities paradigm', regardless of whether they pose a direct threat to the person targeting them at the relevant time, and persons captured on the battlefield become prisoners of war for the duration of the conflict.

At the same time, as said above, the law on the use of force remains relevant to the continued legality of the use of force for the duration of its use. Force used in lawful self-defence or pursuant to a Security Council mandate will have a legal basis. Therefore, it would not, in principle, constitute an arbitrary deprivation of life under human rights law.[26] Nevertheless, the *ad bellum* legality of the use of force does not directly affect the question of whether a specific act of force within the context of the military operations sanctioned by *jus ad bellum* has been undertaken in conformity with IHL/LOAC rules governing hostilities or IHRL outside hostilities. Hence, while a resort to force may be lawful, it is quite conceivable that the conduct of operations violates either IHL/LOAC or IHRL in the way it is applied.[27] This also works the other way round: a State may be using force in violation of the prohibition on the use of force but conducting its operations in conformity with IHL/LOAC or IHRL standards of necessity and proportionality. In any event, unless force is lawful under both the *jus ad bellum* and IHL/LOAC or IHRL, it is not lawful under international law as a whole. The different bodies of law are in that sense complementary and mutually reinforcing; they each play their respective roles in governing any resort to force and the way it is applied.

### 14.2.4 Threshold of Armed Conflict and the Application of Force

In the preceding sub-sections we discussed the respective roles of IHL/LOAC and IHRL as well as the notion of 'conduct of hostilities' in the context of an armed conflict. This begs the question of when an armed conflict can be said to exist. There is no definition of armed conflict that specifically sets out when an armed conflict commences. The closest

[26] UN Human Rights Committee, General Comment 36 (n. 17), para. 70, pointing to acts of aggression as *ipso facto* violations of the right to life. Consequently, armed action conducted in conformity with the law on the use of force would not constitute violations of the right to life if the force used also complied with the relevant legal regime of human rights law or IHL/LOAC, where either of these applied in an armed conflict. By contrast, a use of force which clearly lacked any basis in the law on the use of force would be prima facie arbitrary and therefore a violation of the right to life.

[27] Examples include the use of torture in the context of the resort to self-defence in response to the attack by Al Qaida on the World Trade Center and other targets on 11 September 2001.

SUMMARY BOX 14.3 NECESSITY AND PROPORTIONALITY IN DIFFERENT BRANCHES OF INTERNATIONAL LAW

### Necessity and proportionality *ad bellum*

**Necessity in the context of the exercise of self-defence** relates to the existence of an ongoing or imminent armed attack and the lack of feasible alternatives to ward it off.

**Proportionality in relation to the exercise of self-defence** refers to the duty to use no more force than required to ward off or forestall an imminent or ongoing attack from the same source within the proximate future.

**Necessity in the use of force under a Security Council mandate** relates to the existence of a threat to or breach of the peace or an act of aggression as determined by the Security Council. Necessity in this context is delimited by the decision of the Council under Chapter VII of the Charter authorizing use of necessary force to remove or suppress such threat to or breach of the peace; such decision may also mention specific purposes set out by the Council, such as the protection of civilians from unlawful violence.

**Proportionality in the use of force under a Security Council mandate** refers to the duty to use force proportionate to what is required to achieve the purpose set out in the decision of the Security Council authorizing the use of force.

### Necessity, humanity and proportionality *in bello*

**Military necessity** in the law of armed conflict is a foundational principle and allows application of force for the purpose of achieving the submission of the adversary within the limits set out in the rules of IHL/LOAC. It is built into the rules themselves, alongside the balancing principle of humanity. The latter principle sets limits on the means and methods of warfare and sets out basic guarantees of humane treatment of persons who are not, or no longer, participating in hostilities, such as prisoners of war, the wounded and sick who are *hors de combat* and civilians. Most of the rules of IHL/LOAC reflect a balance between these two foundational principles.

**The principle and rule of proportionality** in the law of armed conflict relates to the targeting of persons and objects constituting lawful military objectives and the expected incidental effects a specific attack would likely have on civilians and civilian objects. An attack that would cause excessive incidental harm to civilians and/or civilian objects compared to the concrete and direct military advantage anticipated from conducting the attack would violate this rule and is prohibited. The expected incidental effects and anticipated military advantage are calculated on the basis of the information available at the time the attack is conducted. This rule is set out in Articles 51(5)(b) and 57(2)(iii) of Additional Protocol I of 1977 and is a rule of customary IHL.

SUMMARY BOX 14.3 (*cont.*)

**Necessity and proportionality in the use of force under international human rights law**

**Necessity in relation to the use of (potentially) lethal force under IHRL** is a standard of strict necessity requiring that force (i) have a legal basis and lawful purpose (e.g. defence of others, arrest of armed suspects); (ii) be of last resort; (iii) be of the minimum degree required in the circumstances to achieve the lawful purpose; and (iv) stop once the purpose has been achieved or is no longer achievable.

**Proportionality in relation to the use of (potentially) lethal force under IHRL** is distinct from, albeit closely related to, the above standard of necessity. It serves to determine whether there is a balance between the benefits of the use of force and the possible consequences and harm caused by its use. For example, the use of naval gunfire or an anti-ship missile by a warship to sink a vessel (suspected of being) engaged in piracy, instead of disabling it and arresting the suspected pirates, would be disproportionate under human rights law. It would be excessive because the legitimate result (neutralization of the threat posed by piracy) could be achieved by a less intrusive measure and the benefit of the measure is outweighed by the impact on the infringement of rights – in this case, the near-inevitable death of the suspects.

**Sources**: M. N. Schmitt, 'Military Necessity and Humanity in International Humanitarian Law: Preserving the Delicate Balance' (2011) 50(4) Virginia Journal of International Law 795–839; J. C. van den Boogaard, 'Proportionality in International Humanitarian Law' (PhD thesis, University of Amsterdam, 2019), https://tinyurl.com/5n7ab63b; S. Casey-Maslen, Use of Force in Law Enforcement and the Right to Life: The Role of the Human Rights Council, Academy In-Brief No. 6 (Geneva Academy of International Humanitarian Law and Human Rights, 2016); D. Hart KC, 'Supreme Court on EU and ECHR Proportionality: Back to Basics', UK Human Rights Blog (27 June 2015), https://tinyurl.com/vcn96swj; Office of the High Commissioner for Human Rights, 'Basic Principles on the Use of Force and Firearms by Law Enforcement Officials' (7 September 1990), https://tinyurl.com/4wpnsec3; Amnesty International, 'Use of Force: Guidelines for Implementation of the UN Basic Principles on the Use of Force and Firearms by Law Enforcement Officials – Short Version' (August 2016), https://tinyurl.com/ynhtdybp.

thing to a definition is contained in the dictum of the International Criminal Tribunal for the Former Yugoslavia (ICTY) in the famous *Tadić* decision of 1995, where the Tribunal ruled that 'an armed conflict exists whenever there is a resort to armed force between States or protracted armed violence between governmental authorities and organized armed groups or between such groups within a State'.[28] This largely

[28] ICTY, *Prosecutor* v. *Dusko Tadić*, Case No. IT-94-1-AR-72, Appeals Chamber, Decision on Defence Motion for Interlocutory Appeal on Jurisdiction (2 October 1995), para. 70.

reflects the commentary of the International Committee of the Red Cross (ICRC), which takes the position that an international armed conflict is triggered by any clash between the armed forces of a State or, in its most recent commentary of 2016, even by the non-consensual presence of the armed forces of a State on the territory of another.[29] This approach would render any armed incident between States or unauthorized incursion by one State on the territory of another an armed conflict even in the absence of any use of force. Another approach was put forward by the Use of Force Committee of the International Law Association (ILA) in its 2010 final report on the notion of armed conflict and is reflected by and large in the practice of States. According to this position, minor armed incidents and small-scale violations of territory do not trigger an armed conflict unless this results in more sustained and intensive exchange of fire between the protagonists or occupation of the territory of one State by the armed forces of another.[30] The distinction is important to the extent that the first approach would extend the applicability of IHL/LOAC to any clash between States, while the second would exclude minor incidents from the notion of armed conflict and thus from the applicability of IHL/LOAC as a matter of law.

Both approaches have advantages and drawbacks. The ICRC approach ensures that the protective provisions of IHL/LOAC will apply to every situation involving an armed clash between States but makes IHL/LOAC provisions relating to the conduct of hostilities applicable to relatively minor incidents. This potentially expands the scope of the conflict on the basis of the exercise of 'belligerent rights'. The ILA approach avoids the application of the conduct of hostilities rules to minor incidents, making it harder to use IHL/LOAC as a shield to expand hostilities beyond what the situation requires, but does not provide a clear substitute for these, thereby leaving a potential regulatory gap, alongside perhaps less comprehensive protection of persons affected by an armed incident or who are detained in that context.[31] However, none of these approaches is clearly recognized as constituting the 'gold standard' enjoying general

[29] ICRC, Commentary on the First Geneva Convention of 1949 (1952), p. 32; ICRC, Commentary on the First Geneva Convention (2016), para. 237.

[30] International Law Association Use of Force Committee, 'Final Report on the Meaning of Armed Conflict in International Law' (2010), https://tinyurl.com/bdh835h6.

[31] For a discussion of the advantages and disadvantages of both approaches and the proposal of an alternative, see T. D. Gill, 'Some Reflections on the Threshold for International Armed Conflict and on the Application of the Law of Armed Conflict in Any Armed Conflict' (2022) 99 *International Law Studies* 698–730 (the alternative approach is proposed at pp. 706–18).

acceptance, although the ICRC approach probably comes closest to meeting that test. For our purposes, suffice it to conclude that any use of force beyond the most incidental will trigger an armed conflict and thereby the applicability of at least some of the LOAC/IHL conduct of hostilities rules. In determining which ones, the scale of the incident and the intensity of the use of force should play a role, alongside *ad bellum* considerations of necessity and proportionality, in determining how to apply the LOAC/IHL rules to the incident and to the personal, geographical and temporal scope of targeting.

## 14.3 Neutrality Law and the Law of Naval Warfare: Their Relevance and Relationship to the *jus ad bellum*

### *14.3.1 The Traditional Laws of Neutrality and Naval Warfare and Their Contemporary Relevance*

Under the law on the use of force and the law of war effective prior to the gradual prohibition of war during the interbellum period (see Chapter 3, above), there was a strict division between the law applicable to peacetime relations among States and the law applicable during war. The law of war was applicable to the relations between States which were belligerent parties to a declared war or situation that amounted to a 'state of war'. States not party to the war were considered neutral and were required to refrain from action that could be deemed assistance to a party. Neutral States had to maintain a policy of impartiality in their relations with the States that were actively engaged as belligerents.[32] As war was gradually banned during the first decade after the First World War, this concept of neutrality came under increasing pressure. During the initial stages of the Second World War, the United States, followed a policy of 'qualified' (or 'benevolent') neutrality prior to entering into the war, whereby it differentiated between States it deemed to be engaged in aggressive war in violation of the Kellogg-Briand Pact and States that it considered to be

[32] Indeed, up to and including the eighth edition of the most influential English-language treatise on international law of the first half of the twentieth century by Lassa Oppenheim, updated and edited by Sir Hersch Lauterpacht, there was a sharp divide between the law of peace and the law of war and neutrality, reflected in the treatment of the two bodies of law in two separate volumes, each dealing exclusively with one body of law to the virtual exclusion of the other. On the demise of the sharp divide between the law of peace and the law of war after the adoption of the UN Charter, see J. Kleffner, 'Scope of Application of International Humanitarian Law', in D. Fleck (ed.) *The Handbook of International Humanitarian Law* (Oxford University Press, 2013), p. 44.

acting lawfully in self-defence. On that basis, the United States supplied war materials to States engaged in war against the Axis powers and imposed an oil embargo on Japan during its war against China.[33]

With the adoption of the UN Charter and its provisions relating to the powers of the Security Council in the maintenance or restoration of international peace and security, the prohibition of the threat or use of force and the practice of States relating to collective self-defence alliances against the backdrop of the Cold War, the place of neutrality law within the overall legal system underwent further change. From being the default legal status of a State not actively engaged as a belligerent in a war, as had been the case throughout the period preceding the adoption of the UN Charter, it now became synonymous with a policy of non-alignment for those States that belonged neither to the Western alliance nor to the Soviet bloc in the context of the Cold War.[34] Since the end of the Cold War, only a handful of States have openly proclaimed themselves as being 'neutral', although at least some of the rules relating to neutrality are generally considered still to be relevant – to some extent – to determining the rights and obligations of States not party to an armed conflict in their relations with parties to an armed conflict. Some States have on occasion followed a policy of 'non-belligerence', which amounted to non-participation in a conflict while at the same time performing one or more acts which could not be reconciled with traditional neutrality, such as allowing passage through territory by belligerent forces, participation in application of embargoes imposed by the UN Security Council and so forth.[35] The status of qualified neutrality/non-belligerence has largely supplanted traditional neutrality, except for those States that choose to retain neutral status as a matter of policy or domestic law, such as Switzerland and Austria.[36]

[33] US Holocaust Memorial Museum, 'The United States: Isolation-Intervention', *Holocaust Encyclopedia*, https://tinyurl.com/2p8mdd47; H. Lauterpacht (ed.), L. Oppenheim, *International Law*, vol. 2 (Longmans Green, 1952), pp. 661–3.

[34] T. Fischer, J. Aunesluoma and A. Makko, 'Neutrality and Nonalignment in World Politics during the Cold War' (2016) 18(4) *Journal of Cold War Studies* 4–11.

[35] M. Bothe, 'The Law of Neutrality', in Fleck, *Handbook* (n. 32), p. 550.

[36] Since the end of the Cold War relatively few States have taken a position of traditional neutrality in relation to international armed conflicts. In some cases, third States have more or less ignored the existence of an armed conflict if it did not affect their interests. In others, varying degrees of support for one belligerent or the other have often been provided by non-belligerent States, as in the Iraq/Kuwait conflict of 1990–1, the intervention of NATO in Kosovo in 1999, the US invasion of Iraq in 2003, the 2008 war between Russia and Georgia, the Russian annexation of Crimea in 2014 and, most recently, in the latest stage of the Russia/Ukraine conflict that commenced in

## FACT BOX 14.2 ORIGINS OF THE TERMS (QUALIFIED) NEUTRALITY AND NON-BELLIGERENCE

**Neutrality:** Under the traditional law of neutrality, a State not wishing to become party to an armed conflict was a neutral State. Neutrality carried with it various rights and obligations. The most important obligation was the duty to maintain a policy of impartiality towards the belligerents in an international armed conflict and refrain from any action or omission that would aid or hamper one of the belligerents in their war effort. The most important right was the right to territorial inviolability, corollary to the duty of the belligerent parties to respect the neutral State's territory. The neutral State also had the right to conduct normal relations with all other States not party to the conflict, subject to some controls in relation to maritime commerce. The most important sources of the law of neutrality are the Hague Convention V of 1907 with respect to neutrality in the context of land warfare and the Hague Convention XIII of 1907 with respect to the law of naval warfare. These conventions, along with various State practices dating from the eighteenth and nineteenth centuries, are considered by some writers to (still) represent customary international law. The International Court of Justice (ICJ) and the International Law Commission (ILC) have both acknowledged the continued existence of the law of neutrality, without going into any degree of analysis or detail regarding the content of the principle under contemporary international law.

**Qualified or benevolent neutrality:** According to this term, which came into use under the influence of the nascent *jus ad bellum* in the early twentieth century, a State could make a distinction between a State it deemed an aggressor and a State it deemed a victim of aggression. From this viewpoint, the duty of impartiality meant that a State could consider itself 'benevolently neutral' and provide assistance to the defending State(s), short of directly becoming a party to the conflict. In such a case, it exposed itself to potential counter-measures by the other belligerent(s) disadvantaged by the action of the qualified neutral State. The United States followed a policy of qualified neutrality towards the participants in the Second World War prior to its entry into the conflict in December 1941.

**Non-belligerence:**
This term, which simply denotes a factual situation of non-participation in an international armed conflict, can be used to denote a situation that is identical to, or which closely resembles, that described above under qualified or benevolent neutrality. It is sometimes used to denote a situation where a State is obliged to modify the 'duty' of impartiality under traditional neutrality to the extent necessary to comply with a binding decision of the Security Council regarding the conflict under Chapter VII, such as observing an arms embargo imposed on one of the belligerents or allowing troops or war material to pass through its territory.

**Sources:** Hague Convention (V) Respecting the Rights and Duties of Neutral Powers and Persons in Case of War on Land (The Hague, 18 October 1907); Hague Convention (XIII) Concerning the Rights and Duties of Neutral Powers in Naval War (The Hague, 18 October 1907).

The traditional law of neutrality established a rather extensive set of rights and obligations for both neutral and belligerent States in their mutual relations where two or more States were engaged as belligerent parties to a war. A neutral State was under an obligation not only to refrain from acting in support of any of the parties to a war but also to proactively enforce its neutrality by preventing its territory from being used as a base of operations or a safe haven by one of the parties to a war. This included taking military action to safeguard its territorial inviolability from incursions by one of the belligerents and refusing use of its territory or territorial waters for the military operations of either side in a war and interning any troops who sought safe haven on its territory. A neutral State was allowed to carry on commerce with belligerents in a war, but was to refrain from supplying military weapons, munitions and other 'warlike materials' to the belligerents. On the other side of the ledger, the belligerent parties to a war were under an obligation to respect the neutrality of a State conducting itself in conformity with the law of neutrality. This included, first and foremost, a duty to respect its territory and refrain from any incursion, unless the neutral State failed to take adequate measures to safeguard its territory from being used as a base of operations or a safe haven by one of the belligerent parties.[37]

At sea, a fairly comprehensive set of rules of the law of naval warfare relating to belligerent visit and search, the capture of merchant vessels and blockade by belligerent parties to a war was applied prior to and during the two World Wars. It included a right of capture of enemy merchant vessels and internment of their crews as prisoners of war; a right of seizure of neutral goods on board enemy merchant vessels deemed contraband and of neutral vessels transporting goods deemed contraband destined for one of the belligerent parties; a duty of respect for neutral goods on board enemy merchant ships that did not fall within

February 2022. The last-named conflict, in particular, demonstrates how traditional neutrality has been supplanted by qualified neutrality or non-belligerence in the practice of a substantial number of States.

37 The traditional law of neutrality is set out in the Hague Conventions V and XIII of 1907 and in various military manuals, especially relating to naval warfare, which are considered by some experts to reflect customary international law. See Convention (V) Respecting the Rights and Duties of Neutral Powers and Persons in Case of War on Land (The Hague, 18 October 1907); Convention (XIII) Concerning the Rights and Duties of Neutral Powers in Naval War (The Hague, 18 October 1907). For a succinct overview of the rights and duties pertaining to traditional neutrality, see Bothe, 'Law of Neutrality' (n. 35), pp. 559–79. For a more comprehensive treatment, see J. Upcher, *Neutrality in Contemporary International Law* (Oxford University Press, 2020).

the category of contraband; a system of prize law; and courts aimed at adjudicating whether the capture of a merchant vessel had been carried out in accordance with this set of rules. The law of blockade allows (or at least allowed) a belligerent to completely cut off access to and exit from an enemy State's ports and coastline and the enforcement of this by forcibly preventing any vessel from breaching the blockade, including by capturing, and in some situations destroying, vessels that resisted measures of control. This blend of maritime neutrality rules and the law of naval warfare is still represented as customary law in the naval manuals of various States and in the opinion of some experts.[38]

Hence, neutrality law traditionally manifested much of its relevance in relation to the status of neutral vessels during an armed conflict with a significant naval dimension. Whether that is still true is open to question in view of the antiquated nature of many of the rules and practices of the traditional law of naval warfare. These rules, in so far as they concern the 'rights' of belligerents to conduct economic warfare through measures of control aimed at denying an enemy State use of the sea (through the capture of its merchant ships, blockade and the imposition of other restrictions on enemy and third-party commerce), are arguably no longer compatible with the other rules of IHL/LOAC requiring attacks to be directed solely against military objects and not against the economy of the enemy State as a sort of blanket category of military objective. These rules are also arguably incompatible with several other regimes under contemporary international law, such as human rights law and the rights of non-belligerent/neutral States to conduct lawful trade and commerce without undue interference from States engaged in an armed conflict. Many of the provisions of the law of naval warfare dating from the nineteenth and early twentieth centuries are clearly outdated and many of the practices described in naval warfare manuals have not, or only sporadically, been engaged in since the Second World War. To the extent that they have been engaged in, this has usually not been in

[38] The traditional law of naval warfare is restated in the naval warfare manuals of various States. See, for example, US Department of the Navy, Marine Corps and Coast Guard, *The Commander's Handbook of the Law of Naval Operations* (NWP1-14M, March 2022); UK Ministry of Defence, *Joint Services Manual on the Law of Armed Conflict*, Joint Service Publication 383 (2004), chap. 13 ('Maritime Warfare'). For a comparative law perspective on and analysis of the normative value of service manuals, see, for example, N. Hayashi (ed.), *National Military Manuals on the Law of Armed Conflict* (Forum for International Criminal and Humanitarian Law, 2010). The most authoritative expert manual is the San Remo Manual on International Law Applicable to Armed Conflicts at Sea (12 June 1994), https://ihl-databases.icrc.org/ihl/INTRO/560.

conformity with the rules of naval warfare set out in the same manuals.[39] The taking of merchant vessels as 'prize', the confinement of the crews of enemy merchant ships as prisoners of war for the duration of a conflict and the far-reaching effects of the traditional law of blockade on both the population of the blockaded State and the populations and economies of third States are all compelling reasons to give this area of the law a thorough rethink and to adjust and update the rules and discontinue practices that are no longer militarily necessary or compatible with contemporary law. Nevertheless, so long as these rules continue to be seen by some experts and States as reflecting customary law (albeit of a bygone era), they cannot be ignored. Therefore, (maritime) neutrality will remain relevant to some extent.[40]

The law of neutrality was and is agnostic in the sense that it aims to treat all parties to an armed conflict equally and impartially irrespective of the legality of the recourse to war by either side. That is difficult (if not wholly impossible) to reconcile with the UN Charter and contemporary law regulating the threat or use of force. If the Security Council has adopted measures under Chapter VII relating to an armed conflict,

[39] For example, the actions in the Iran-Iraq War of 1980–8 saw attacks on neutral vessels bound to and leaving the Persian Gulf region by both sides with scant regard for the rules of naval warfare. The Israeli blockade of Gaza is of doubtful legality for various reasons, not least of which is the enormous impact it has had on the civilian population. In the conflict in Yemen, the blockade imposed by Saudi Arabia and the other members of the 'Coalition' has had a devastating impact on the civilian population and the rules allowing for relief shipments have largely been ignored. On the 'tanker war' between Iraq and Iran, see, for example, 'Tanker War', Strauss Center for International Security and Law Strait of Hormuz Project, www.strausscenter.org/strait-of-hormuz-tanker-war/. On the Gaza blockade, see Office of the High Commissioner for Human Rights, 'How Can Israel's Blockade of Gaza Be Legal? UN Independent Experts on the "Palmer Report"' (13 September 2011), https://tinyurl.com/3sf2xsrb. On the blockade of Yemen, see Reliefweb, 'Torture in Slow Motion: The Economic Blockade of Yemen and Its Grave Humanitarian Consequences' (22 September 2022), https://tinyurl.com/3yhnrpmx.

[40] Criticism of various aspects of the law of naval warfare and maritime neutrality as anachronistic or incompatible with contemporary international law has been voiced by various writers, including one of the authors of this book. See, for example, S. Haines, 'War at Sea: Nineteenth-Century Laws for Twenty-First-Century Wars' (2016) 98(902) *International Review of the Red Cross* 419–47; A. Clapham, 'Booty, Bounty, Blockade and Prize: Time to Reevaluate the Law' (2021) 97 *International Law Studies* 1200–68; P. J. Drew, 'Can We Starve the Civilians? Exploring the Dichotomy between the Traditional Law of Maritime Blockade and Humanitarian Initiative' (2019) 95 *International Law Studies* 302–21; T. D. Gill, 'Rethinking the Scope of Application of International Humanitarian Law and Its Place in the International Legal System' (2022) 60 *Revue de droit militaire et de droit de la guerre/The Military Law and Law of War Review* 58–70.

they will clearly take precedence over any provisions of neutrality law. Yet, contrary to what is often assumed, the precedence of the Charter and the contemporary *jus ad bellum* does not stop there. For example, the duty of belligerent States to respect neutral territory does not have the independent legal significance it had prior to the prohibition on the use of force and the principle of non-intervention contained in the Charter and customary law. That duty is now anchored in these Charter provisions and customary law; the law of neutrality adds little or nothing in that respect.[41]

Under traditional neutrality law, a belligerent could forcibly intervene on a neutral State's territory to counter a violation of neutrality, such as the neutral State's supplying war material, intelligence or training to the opposing party or failing to intern members of an opposing belligerent party's armed forces present on its territory. This 'belligerent right' no longer has any basis in international law. Under traditional neutrality law, the consequence of a violation of neutrality was the exercise of 'belligerent rights', which included military intervention on the territory of the neutral State as a counter-measure in response to the failure of a neutral State to take action to uphold its neutrality. No such right of armed intervention survived the prohibition on the use of force. No State acting in violation of the prohibition on the use of force has a 'right' to enforce its unlawful act by implementing counter-measures, be they forcible or not, in response to a breach of neutrality law, since it has no rights that have been violated. This is a consequence of the legal maxim *ex injuria jus non oritur*. For States acting in conformity with the law on the use of force, a violation of neutrality by a State not party to the armed conflict would potentially provide a basis for the taking of acts of non-forcible retorsion or counter-measures in the form of sanctions or trade restrictions. If a violation of neutrality amounted to support for an act of aggression, it would constitute an unlawful act in itself.[42]

[41] Many commentaries on the impact of the UN Charter regime on the law of neutrality focus (almost) exclusively on the UN collective security system and its relationship to traditional neutrality. See Bothe, 'Law of Neutrality' (n. 35), pp. 551–4.

[42] For a contrary opinion, see ibid., pp. 558–9. The ICRC takes the position that if a neutral State fails to take action against belligerent forces on its territory by expelling or interning them, the opposing belligerent has the right of hot pursuit. See *Handbook on International Rules Governing Military Operations* (ICRC, 2013), § 13.6.2.6, p. 413. See also J. K. Davis, 'You Mean They Can Bomb Us? Addressing the Impact of Neutrality Law on Defense Cooperation', *Lawfare* (2 November 2020), https://tinyurl.com/ycxynrux. These arguments state that such a right of belligerent armed counter-measures, hot

There are only two recognized exceptions to the prohibition on the threat or use of force, neither of which permits forcible intervention on another State's territory as a result of a violation of neutrality. In fact, there is no duty incumbent on a non-belligerent State to refrain from supporting a State that is the object of an unlawful armed attack or aggression. If a State has the right to exercise collective self-defence in conjunction with, or at the request of, another State which is under attack, there is no plausible reason why it could not choose to engage in lesser forms of support such as the provision of weapons, training, intelligence and implementation of measures of economic and diplomatic coercion aimed at inducing the attacking State to desist from its attack or act of aggression. Although a resolution by the UN Security Council (or the UN General Assembly when the Security Council is unable to act) to the effect that State A is engaged in an unlawful use of force against State B would help in providing clarity and remove any doubt over which side is acting lawfully, it is not a precondition for providing assistance where, prima facie, a State is being subjected to an unlawful use of force by another.

On the other hand, support for a State that is acting unlawfully, particularly in violation of a peremptory rule such as the prohibition on the use of force, is itself a violation of international law, regardless of whether a resolution condemning the use of force has been adopted. A Security Council resolution adopted under Chapter VII would have binding effect, but it is not a condition for the applicability of the duty to refrain from supporting an unlawful use of force. Equally, a resolution adopted by the General Assembly or a regional organization or a declaration by a sizeable number of States proclaiming that a particular use of force was in violation of the Charter would be authoritative, if not in itself binding, but would likewise not create a duty to refrain from assisting a State engaged in the unlawful use of force. Such a duty has an independent basis in the law of international responsibility (see Chapter 15, below)[43] and has legal force without any need for a decision by the Security Council.

pursuit or any other name one may wish to give it exists – without explaining how it overrides a peremptory rule such as the prohibition of the use of force – even assuming such a right still does exist under the Charter.

[43] This follows from Article 16 of the Articles on the Responsibility of States for Internationally Wrongful Acts. See also International Law Commission, 'Draft Articles on Responsibility of States for Internationally Wrongful Acts, with Commentaries' (2001), in Report of the International Law Commission on the Work of Its Fifty-Third Session, UN Doc. A/56/10, pp. 65–7 (Art. 16).

In short, traditional neutrality law has lost much of its relevance in the contemporary legal order as a result of the UN collective security system and the contemporary law on the use of force. It has become redundant in relation to the duty to respect the territorial inviolability of a non-belligerent or neutral State. It gives no right of armed enforcement on the territory of a neutral/non-belligerent State acting in violation of neutrality law, and it does not stand in the way of assisting a State that is the victim of an unlawful use of force or add much to the duty of all States to refrain from assisting a State acting in violation of the law regulating the use of force. While it may still ensure some regulation and limitation of hostilities at sea, its legal relevance in a more general sense is limited. In fact, at present it is quite plausible that neutrality or any variant of it is as much a matter of policy as it is a question of international law. The present conflict between the Russian Federation and Ukraine is a clear illustration of this. A sizeable number of States have openly taken the position that the Russian invasion of Ukraine is unlawful and have imposed sanctions – or, at least, have not openly opposed the measures taken, especially by Western States, to sanction Russia. The Western group of States, besides sanctioning Russia, has additionally openly provided substantial support to Ukraine, including the provision of military equipment and training of Ukraine forces in the use thereof. On the other hand, a small number of States have openly supported Russia and some have even provided it with military equipment or other forms of support. Finally, a significant group of mainly non-aligned States, including Brazil, China, India, Indonesia, Nigeria, Saudi Arabia and South Africa, have continued business as usual with Russia – and Ukraine – and show varying degrees of support for one party to the conflict or the other. Turkey, with some success, has played the role of a mediator in the conflict. In short, States have done more or less anything short of openly entering the conflict, based on what they view as reflecting their international position and protecting their interests, with little to no reference to the law of neutrality.[44]

44 On the implications of the Russia/Ukraine conflict on the law of neutrality, see, for example, A. Cheatham, 'A Look at Neutrality Now – and After the Ukraine War', United States Institute of Peace (28 April 2022), https://tinyurl.com/mry6vxd9. On the way States have positioned themselves within the United Nations, see UN Regional Information Centre for Western Europe, 'The UN and the War in Ukraine: Key Information' (9 March 2022, updated 8 June 2023), https://tinyurl.com/2hdnww7c. On the positions of some key non-aligned States, see J. Guyer, 'Why Some Countries Don't Want to Pick a Side in Russia's War in Ukraine', *Vox* (9 June 2022), https://tinyurl.com/76cvk7tj.

The core questions that remain relevant to our discussion are, first, when does support provided by a State to a party in an armed conflict render that State a party to the same conflict and make it subject to attack under the law of armed conflict? Second, in relation to the law of naval warfare, when would imposition of a blockade or other measures of control (such as maritime exclusion zones) be permissible in relation to the law on the use of force? We now turn to answering these questions.

### *14.3.2* Jus ad bellum *and Support of Belligerent Parties by Neutral States*

If a non-belligerent/neutral State engages in acts of support towards a party to an armed conflict, the question arises as to what level of support would render that State a party to the conflict and what the legal consequences would be under both the law of armed conflict and the law on the use of force. The answer to the first part of the question relating to the threshold of actual participation is primarily factual. Certainly, direct participation in the conflict by launching attacks in support of one party against the other would have that effect. This would also usually – but not always – apply when a State allows its territory to be used as a base of operations for a party to the conflict to conduct attacks against the other. Other forms of support come in degrees and their aims and effects differ. Clearly, low-level material support would not render a non-belligerent a party to a conflict by any reasonable standard. Nevertheless, as the level of support increases to become crucial to the war-making capacity of a party, or takes the form of actually assisting that party in targeting decisions and other forms of conduct of hostilities, it could potentially render the assisting State a party to the conflict. Such a conclusion would also depend on the aims of the parties to the conflict and of the State(s) offering support. It would also depend on the effect that support has on the parties and their ability to conduct operations. At the end of the day, however, what is crucial is how the State 'disadvantaged' by the provision of support perceives the level of that support and whether it is willing to expand the conflict by 'adding' the supporting State to the 'list' of opposing parties and launching attacks against that State's territory to deter it from further support. In short, if one of the parties to an ongoing conflict sees a relatively substantial level of support as a *casus belli* and, after warning, commences to conduct hostilities against the supporting State, the latter becomes a party to the conflict. As long as the 'disadvantaged' party refrains from expanding the conflict to include the supporting State, the support will fall short of making the latter a party. This is because under the law of armed conflict, the existence of an armed conflict is a factually driven question. An armed conflict between two or more States exists if one or both engage in attacks (in the IHL/LOAC sense) against the other.[45]

From the perspective of the law on the use of force, the support given by one State to assist another State that is the object of a prima facie unlawful use of force by a third State does not violate any rule of international law. At the same time, no State is under any obligation to assist a victim of an armed attack, absent a treaty commitment to do so or a binding order from the Security Council to assist. Hence, a policy of (relative) neutrality to remain outside the conflict is permissible, and to that extent neutrality retains some significance. Obviously, the greater the level of support, the higher the risk that the opposing party will view the assisting State as a party to the conflict and expand the hostilities to include the assisting State(s). At the same time, if the initial use of force was an unlawful armed attack (that triggered the right of individual or collective self-defence), then the expansion of the conflict by the State that launched the armed attack would also be unlawful. A State engaged in an ongoing armed attack against another has no right of self-defence or other legal remedy against either the defending State or any State which comes to the latter's assistance, be that support direct or indirect. Hence, any action taken in furtherance of the unlawful use of force will only compound the illegality of that State's actions by expanding the conflict. Likewise, if the aggressor State is assisted by a third State, such assistance would be unlawful no matter what form it takes. If a third State were to intervene directly on the side of a State conducting an armed attack, it would become co-responsible for the unlawful use of force and its political leadership could become co-perpetrators in a criminal act of aggression.[46]

[45] See Section 14.2.4 above on the threshold of armed conflict. By either standard discussed, if two or more States engage in armed action of any intensity, this would trigger an armed conflict. In the absence of the threshold of armed conflict being reached, there is no armed conflict. For a discussion of whether support to Ukraine constitutes a violation of neutrality and whether this renders States supporting Ukraine a party to the conflict, see, for example, K. Ambos, 'Will a State Supplying Weapons to Ukraine Become a Party to the Conflict and Thus Be Exposed to Countermeasures?', *EJIL:Talk!* (2 March 2022), https://tinyurl.com/4kne39kt.

[46] See above nn. 41, 42. See also Chapter 15 on international criminal responsibility for the crime of aggression.

To sum up, from the perspective of the law of armed conflict, the provision of assistance by a State to a party to an armed conflict would result in the supporting State also becoming a party, if the opposing party considered the level of assistance to be a *casus belli* and proceeded to conduct hostilities against the supporting State, since the question of whether an armed conflict exists under IHL/LOAC is a factual one. From the more normative perspective of the *jus ad bellum*, the question of the legality of the support by a State to a party to an armed conflict would depend on which State could be reasonably seen as the perpetrator and which the victim of an armed attack or act of aggression. Should the evidence be unclear or inconclusive, it would behove third States to abstain from rushing in with assistance to one party or the other until the situation had been clarified.

### *14.3.3* Jus ad bellum *and Belligerent 'Rights' in the Law of Naval Warfare*

Finally, we turn to the question of when a resort to the law of naval warfare provisions relating to blockade and other measures of control (to deny use of the sea to an enemy State and cripple its economy) could be a permissible exercise of force under the *jus ad bellum* in so far as such measures retain any legality as methods of warfare under IHL/LOAC. It is clear that, due to their impact on both the target State and third States, such methods of warfare would be potentially lawful exercises of self-defence or enforcement powers under authorization of the Security Council only in cases of large-scale armed attacks or breaches of the peace where necessity and proportionality *ad bellum* would require and permit such far-reaching measures in the context of prolonged hostilities aimed at overcoming the attacking State and forestalling further attack. This would not apply, in principle, to less far-reaching measures of maritime interdiction (to prevent specific goods or persons reaching a State engaged in an armed attack) or other situations requiring enforcement measures by the Security Council to maintain international peace and security. Consequently, such less extreme measures should be resorted to instead of traditional blockades, because the former can be tailored to fit the situation and would not normally have the same impact on the welfare of the civilian population of the target State or the rights of third States to engage in maritime commerce as would traditional blockade law. Since the lawful objective of preventing military material and strategic goods from reaching the adversary can be fulfilled by less far-reaching measures of maritime interdiction, such as those employed in UN embargoes, there is no cogent reason to use more coercion than the situation requires. This would be an example of how *ad bellum* law can impose additional restrictions on the conduct of war over and above the rules contained in the law of armed conflict.

## 14.4 Conclusion

The relationship between the *jus ad bellum*, IHL/LOAC and IHRL can be summed up as follows. As regards the relationship between *jus ad bellum* and IHL/LOAC, the principle of belligerent equality signifies that the parties to an international armed conflict are subject to the same 'rights' and obligations under the law of armed conflict, but it does not imply that, once force is resorted to, the *jus* ad *bellum* ceases to be applicable throughout the duration of the use of force. The *jus ad bellum* will also be relevant, alongside IHL/LOAC, to targeting in the context of an armed conflict. As regards the relationship between IHRL and IHL/LOAC, a reasonably significant and/or protracted use of force between two or more States, or between a State and an organized armed group, would trigger the applicability of IHL/LOAC, and IHL/LOAC would be the legal regime primarily applicable to the conduct of hostilities between the parties to an armed conflict. Outside the context of the conduct of hostilities, the legal regime of IHRL is the default standard for the use of force both in an armed conflict where there is effective control over a particular area, individual or group of persons and in the context of law enforcement. With respect to *jus ad bellum* and IHRL, a lawful resort to force under the former would prevent the use of force being deemed arbitrary and therefore unlawful per se under the latter, provided it were applied in accordance with the human rights law standards of necessity and proportionality.

Concerning the impact of the *jus ad bellum* on the law of neutrality, we argued that while in the past neutrality required that a State not party to an armed conflict refrain from any action that would support or prejudice the war effort of the parties to an international armed conflict, this position is hardly tenable under the contemporary legal regime relating to the use of force. Not only do States have the right to directly assist the victim of an armed attack by engaging in collective self-defence at the victim's request, but there is equally no rule of international law that prohibits States from providing the same victim State with support not amounting to direct intervention. That being said, the law of neutrality retains some relevance, particularly in relation to the exercise of hostilities at sea, to the extent the partially antiquated law of naval warfare remains legally relevant.

As regards the rendering of support by a third State to a party to an armed conflict, to the extent that support to a victim of an unlawful attack or aggression constitutes (or is perceived as) a direct intervention in the conflict, it will clearly open the possibility that the disadvantaged belligerent party will view this as a reason to conduct hostilities against the intervening State. Unless and until hostilities are engaged in by either the 'disadvantaged' belligerent or a third State assisting one of the parties against the other party, no amount of assistance short of direct participation in the conflict will automatically render a State providing such assistance a party to the conflict.

Finally, the law of naval warfare provisions permitting measures directed against the commerce and economy of the adversary, such as blockades, should be limited to situations where the principles of necessity and proportionality *ad bellum* do not stand in the way of their application, due to the scale of the ongoing or imminent attack or serious nature of the threat to or breach of the peace, in so far as that body of law is still relevant and no other alternative is be feasible or adequate in the circumstances.

# 15

## International Responsibility for the Unlawful Use of Force: States, Organizations, Armed Groups and Individuals

### 15.1 Introduction

This chapter deals with international responsibility for breach of *jus ad bellum* obligations. The notion of responsibility is examined from the perspective of public international law for States and international organizations and from the perspective of international criminal law for individuals. When necessary, reference is made to the international law of armed conflict as well. This chapter does not delve into responsibility under domestic law or under private international law.

Traditionally, international responsibility concerned States alone as the only subjects of international law. The current *jus ad bellum* obligations are conceptualized, interpreted and applied in relation to State action. Gradually, however, international organizations have also acquired varying degrees of personality under international law. By virtue of their members being States, *jus ad bellum* obligations are also relevant in respect of such organizations. Moreover, since the end of the First World War the question of individuals possessing limited international legal personality for the purpose of their prosecution for initiating wars has also become relevant. As a result of a number of Nuremberg and Tokyo judgments in the aftermath of the Second World War and by virtue of the ICC Statute, individuals can under certain conditions incur criminal responsibility for their role in a State's act of aggression.

The responsibility of States, international organizations and individuals for breaches of *jus ad bellum* obligations are discussed below. The lack of legal personality of armed groups for *jus ad bellum* purposes is also touched upon briefly.

## 15.2 International Responsibility of States

### *15.2.1 The Basic Rules of State Responsibility*

All States enjoy sovereign equality. Their obligations as subjects of international law stem from the bilateral or multilateral treaties they adhere to and from international custom. When a State breaches such an obligation, it commits an internationally wrongful act, which triggers State responsibility if certain conditions apply.

The rules governing State responsibility were the object of several decades of codifying work by the International Law Commission (ILC), culminating in the adoption in 2001 of the Articles on Responsibility of States for Internationally Wrongful Acts (Articles, ARSIWA).[1] After their adoption by the ILC, the UN General Assembly took note of the ARSIWA and commended them to the attention of States 'without prejudice to the question of their future adoption or other appropriate action'.[2] While the ARSIWA have not been incorporated into a binding treaty, they are widely acknowledged as codifying customary international law and are frequently referenced by States, the International Court of Justice (ICJ), other international courts and international organizations.[3] For this reason, the present chapter will rely on the Articles to set out the basic rules of State responsibility.

According to Article 2 of the ARSIWA, an internationally wrongful act of a State is conduct consisting of an action or omission which '(a) is attributable to the State under international law; and (b) constitutes a breach of an international obligation of the State'.[4]

[1] Responsibility of States for Internationally Wrongful Acts, Annex to UN General Assembly (UNGA) Resolution 56/83 (12 December 2001), UN Doc. A/RES/56/83.

[2] Ibid., p. 2.

[3] See, for example, even before the ARSIWA were adopted in 2001, International Court of Justice (ICJ), *Case Concerning the Gabčikovo-Nagymaros Project (Hungary/Slovakia)*, Judgment, 25 September 1997, ICJ Reports 1997, paras. 46, 49, 79, 83. After the adoption of the ARSIWA, see for example, ICJ, *Case Concerning Application of the Convention on the Prevention and Punishment of the Crime of Genocide (Bosnia and Herzegovina* v. *Serbia and Montenegro)*, Judgment, 26 February 2007, ICJ Reports 2007, paras. 398, 401, 407, 414; European Court of Human Rights, *Kotov* v. *Russia*, Application No. 54522/00, Grand Chamber Judgment, 3 April 2012, paras. 30–2; Inter-American Court of Human Rights, *Case of Ruano Torres et al.* v. *El Salvador* (Merits, reparations and costs), Judgment, 5 October 2015, p. 46; UN General Assembly, 74th session, Responsibility of States for Internationally Wrongful Acts, Compilation of Decisions of International Courts, Tribunals and Other Bodies, Report of the Secretary-General, UN Doc. A/74/83 (23 April 2019).

[4] These elements were identified as early as 1938 by the Permanent Court of International Justice in the *Phosphates in Morocco* case, where the Court linked the creation of

In order to impute a breach of an international obligation to a State, the conduct in question must be attributable to it. Article 4 of the ARSIWA sets out the general rule for the attribution of conduct, according to which the conduct of any State organ shall be considered an act of that State under international law. Subsequent articles then set out additional rules attributing to a State the conduct of persons or entities exercising elements of governmental authority (Articles 5 and 7), the conduct of organs placed at the disposal of a State by another State (Articles 6 and 7), the conduct of a person or a group directed or controlled by a State (Article 8), the conduct of a person or a group exercising elements of governmental authority in the absence or default of the official authorities (Article 9), the conduct of an insurrectional or other movement (Article 10) and conduct acknowledged and adopted by a State as its own (Article 11).

The ARSIWA also set out the responsibility of States that knowingly assist (Article 16), control and direct (Article 17) or coerce (Article 18) another State in committing an internationally wrongful act.

Whether conduct attributed to the State is a breach of a particular obligation depends on the interpretation and application of the primary rules defining that obligation, and not on the rules of State responsibility. The rules of State responsibility do not require the presence of a mental (fault) or material (damage) element for a breach to be established and international responsibility to be incurred.[5] Whether such elements are required depends on the content of the primary obligation.

As codified in the ARSIWA, the wrongfulness of a State's breach of an international obligation may be precluded in certain circumstances – namely, in the event of consent (Article 20), self-defence (Article 21), counter-measures (Article 22), *force majeure* (Article 23), distress (Article 24) and necessity (Article 25).

international responsibility to the existence of an 'act being attributable to the State and described as contrary to the treaty right of another State'. Permanent Court of International Justice (PCIJ), *Phosphates in Morocco*, Judgment, 14 June 1938, PCIJ Series A/B No. 74, p. 28. The ICJ also identified these two elements in several cases; See ICJ, *United States Diplomatic and Consular Staff in Tehran (United States of America* v. *Iran)*, Judgment, 24 May 1980, ICJ Reports 1980, para. 56; ICJ, *Military and Paramilitary Activities in and against Nicaragua (Nicaragua* v. *United States of America)* (Merits), Judgment, 27 June 1986, ICJ Reports 1986, para. 226.

[5] International Law Commission, 'Draft Articles on Responsibility of States for Internationally Wrongful Acts, with Commentaries' (2001), in Report of the International Law Commission on the Work of Its Fifty-Third Session, UN Doc. A/56/10 (ARSIWA Commentary), p. 36 paras. (9)–(10) (Art. 2).

### FACT BOX 15.1 ARSIWA EXCERPTS

## Part One The Internationally Wrongful Act of a State

### *Chapter I General Principles*

#### Article 1 Responsibility of a State for its internationally wrongful acts

Every internationally wrongful act of a State entails the international responsibility of that State.

#### Article 2 Elements of an internationally wrongful act of a State

There is an internationally wrongful act of a State when conduct consisting of an action or omission:

(a) is attributable to the State under international law; and

(b) constitutes a breach of an international obligation of the State.

### *Chapter V Circumstances Precluding Wrongfulness*

#### Article 20 Consent

Valid consent by a State to the commission of a given act by another State precludes the wrongfulness of that act in relation to the former State to the extent that the act remains within the limits of that consent.

#### Article 21 Self-defence

The wrongfulness of an act of a State is precluded if the act constitutes a lawful measure of self-defence taken in conformity with the Charter of the United Nations.

#### Article 22 Countermeasures in respect of an internationally wrongful act

The wrongfulness of an act of a State not in conformity with an international obligation towards another State is precluded if and to the extent that the act constitutes a countermeasure taken against the latter State in accordance with chapter II of part three.

## Part Two Content of the International Responsibility of a State

### *Chapter I General Principles*

#### Article 28 Legal consequences of an internationally wrongful act

The international responsibility of a State which is entailed by an internationally wrongful act in accordance with the provisions of part one involves legal consequences as set out in this part.

FACT BOX 15.1 *(cont.)*

### Article 29 Continued duty of performance

The legal consequences of an internationally wrongful act under this part do not affect the continued duty of the responsible State to perform the obligation breached.

### Article 30 Cessation and non-repetition

The State responsible for the internationally wrongful act is under an obligation:
(a) to cease that act, if it is continuing;
(b) to offer appropriate assurances and guarantees of non-repetition, if circumstances so require.

### Article 31 Reparation

1 The responsible State is under an obligation to make full reparation for the injury caused by the internationally wrongful act.
2 Injury includes any damage, whether material or moral, caused by the internationally wrongful act of a State.

## *Chapter II Reparation for Injury*

### Article 34 Forms of reparation

Full reparation for the injury caused by the internationally wrongful act shall take the form of restitution, compensation and satisfaction, either singly or in combination, in accordance with the provisions of this chapter.

### Article 35 Restitution

A State responsible for an internationally wrongful act is under an obligation to make restitution, that is, to re-establish the situation which existed before the wrongful act was committed, provided and to the extent that restitution:
(a) is not materially impossible;
(b) does not involve a burden out of all proportion to the benefit deriving from restitution instead of compensation.

### Article 36 Compensation

1 The State responsible for an internationally wrongful act is under an obligation to compensate for the damage caused thereby, insofar as such damage is not made good by restitution.
2 The compensation shall cover any financially assessable damage including loss of profits insofar as it is established.

FACT BOX 15.1 *(cont.)*

### Article 37 Satisfaction

1 The State responsible for an internationally wrongful act is under an obligation to give satisfaction for the injury caused by that act insofar as it cannot be made good by restitution or compensation.
2 Satisfaction may consist in an acknowledgement of the breach, an expression of regret, a formal apology or another appropriate modality.
3 Satisfaction shall not be out of proportion to the injury and may not take a form humiliating to the responsible State.

### Article 38 Interest

1 Interest on any principal sum due under this chapter shall be payable when necessary in order to ensure full reparation. The interest rate and mode of calculation shall be set so as to achieve that result.
2 Interest runs from the date when the principal sum should have been paid until the date the obligation to pay is fulfilled.

### Article 39 Contribution to the injury

In the determination of reparation, account shall be taken of the contribution to the injury by wilful or negligent action or omission of the injured State or any person or entity in relation to whom reparation is sought.

## *Chapter III Serious Breaches of Obligations under Peremptory Norms of General International Law*

### Article 40 Application of this chapter

1 This chapter applies to the international responsibility which is entailed by a serious breach by a State of an obligation arising under a peremptory norm of general international law.
2 A breach of such an obligation is serious if it involves a gross or systematic failure by the responsible State to fulfil the obligation.

### Article 41 Particular consequences of a serious breach of an obligation under this chapter

1 States shall cooperate to bring to an end through lawful means any serious breach within the meaning of article 40.
2 No State shall recognize as lawful a situation created by a serious breach within the meaning of article 40, nor render aid or assistance in maintaining that situation.

FACT BOX 15.1 *(cont.)*

3 This article is without prejudice to the other consequences referred to in this part and to such further consequences that a breach to which this chapter applies may entail under international law.

## Part Three The Implementation of the International Responsibility of a State

### *Chapter II Countermeasures*

#### Article 49 Object and limits of countermeasures

1 An injured State may only take countermeasures against a State which is responsible for an internationally wrongful act in order to induce that State to comply with its obligations under part two.
2 Countermeasures are limited to the non-performance for the time being of international obligations of the State taking the measures towards the responsible State.
3 Countermeasures shall, as far as possible, be taken in such a way as to permit the resumption of performance of the obligations in question.

#### Article 50 Obligations not affected by countermeasures

1 Countermeasures shall not affect:
(a) the obligation to refrain from the threat or use of force as embodied in the Charter of the United Nations;
(b) obligations for the protection of fundamental human rights;
(c) obligations of a humanitarian character prohibiting reprisals;
(d) other obligations under peremptory norms of general international law.

2 A State taking countermeasures is not relieved from fulfilling its obligations:
(a) under any dispute settlement procedure applicable between it and the responsible State;
(b) to respect the inviolability of diplomatic or consular agents, premises, archives and documents.

#### Article 51 Proportionality

Countermeasures must be commensurate with the injury suffered, taking into account the gravity of the internationally wrongful act and the rights in question.

#### Article 52 Conditions relating to resort to countermeasures

1 Before taking countermeasures, an injured State shall:
(a) call upon the responsible State, in accordance with article 43, to fulfil its obligations under part two;
(b) notify the responsible State of any decision to take countermeasures and offer to negotiate with that State.

FACT BOX 15.1 (*cont.*)

2 Notwithstanding paragraph 1 (b), the injured State may take such urgent countermeasures as are necessary to preserve its rights.
3 Countermeasures may not be taken, and if already taken must be suspended without undue delay if:
(a) the internationally wrongful act has ceased; and
(b) the dispute is pending before a court or tribunal which has the authority to make decisions binding on the parties.

4 Paragraph 3 does not apply if the responsible State fails to implement the dispute settlement procedures in good faith.

Article 53 Termination of countermeasures

Countermeasures shall be terminated as soon as the responsible State has complied with its obligations under part two in relation to the internationally wrongful act.

Article 54 Measures taken by States other than an injured State

This chapter does not prejudice the right of any State, entitled under article 48, paragraph 1, to invoke the responsibility of another State, to take lawful measures against that State to ensure cessation of the breach and reparation in the interest of the injured State or of the beneficiaries of the obligation breached.

As reflected in the ARSIWA, when a State commits an internationally wrongful act whose wrongfulness is not precluded by any of the above circumstances, it becomes responsible for that act and is obliged to cease the wrongful conduct, offer guarantees of non-repetition (Article 30) and make full reparation for the injury (Article 31)[6] in the form of restitution, compensation and/or satisfaction (Articles 34–37).[7] In the event of a serious breach of a peremptory norm, further consequences may become relevant. In such cases, all States have an obligation to co-operate in bringing the breach to an end, not to recognize as lawful the situation

[6] See also PCIJ, *Factory at Chorzów* (Jurisdiction), Judgment, 26 July 1927, Series A No. 9, p. 21.

[7] See also PCIJ, *Factory at Chorzów* (Merits), Judgment, 13 September 1928, Series A No. 17, p. 47 (on restitution); *Gabčikovo-Nagymaros* (n. 3), p. 81 para. 152 (on compensation); *Case Concerning the Difference between New Zealand and France Concerning the Interpretation or Application of Two Agreements, Concluded on 9 July 1986 between the Two States and Which Related to the Problems Arising from the Rainbow Warrior Affair*, Decision, 30 April 1990, Report of International Arbitral Awards (RIAA), vol. XX, pp. 272–3 para. 122 (on satisfaction).

created by the breach and not to render aid or assistance allowing the responsible State to maintain the situation so created (Articles 40–1).[8]

In order to implement such forms of State responsibility, the defending State may resort to various measures, such as bilateral or multilateral agreements, judicial decisions, counter-measures or other individual or collective measures of self-help.

The application of these rules in the *jus ad bellum* context will be discussed below.

### 15.2.2 *Breach of* jus ad bellum *Obligations*

In the *jus ad bellum* context, States have several international obligations that they owe to the international community as a whole. First, as enshrined in Article 2(4) of the UN Charter and discussed in virtually all chapters of this book, States are to refrain from the use or threat of force. Second, when using force unilaterally, a State (or States acting collectively) may do so only in self-defence and within the treaty-based and customary limits of this right. Third, by virtue of Article 25 of the Charter, States must not interfere with military enforcement action and must comply with other collective measures imposed by the UN Security Council (UNSC, Security Council) under Chapter VII of the Charter (see Chapter 5, above).

The prohibition on the use of force is widely recognized as a peremptory (*jus cogens*) norm of international law (see Chapter 4, above).[9] The ARSIWA confirm this understanding.[10] Gross or systematic failure by a State to abide by the prohibition may amount to a 'serious breach' within the meaning of Article 40 of the ARSIWA.

Conduct that may amount to a breach of *jus ad bellum* obligations can vary from case to case. The list of acts prohibited by the Friendly Relations Declaration and the Definition of Aggression includes multiple examples of breach encompassing both acts and omissions.[11] In particular, a State can breach its *jus ad bellum* obligations by, inter alia, invading

[8] ARSIWA Commentary (n. 5), p. 87 para. (2) (Art. 28), pp. 114–16 (Art. 41).

[9] ILC, Report of the International Law Commission on the Work of Its Eighteenth Session, 4 May–19 July 1966, *Yearbook of the International Law Commission 1966*, vol. II (1966), pp. 247–8; *Nicaragua* (n. 4), para. 190; J. Crawford, *State Responsibility* (Cambridge University Press, 2013), p. 690; A. Cassese, *International Law* (Oxford University Press, 2005), pp. 202–3. For a definition of peremptory norms, see Article 53 of the Vienna Convention on the Law of Treaties (Vienna, 23 May 1969), https://tinyurl.com/34a9drf5.

[10] ARSIWA Commentary (n. 5), p. 85 para. (5) (Art. 26), pp. 131–2 paras. (1)–(5) (Art. 50).

[11] Declaration on Principles of International Law Concerning Friendly Relations and Co-operation among States in Accordance with the Charter of the United Nations,

or attacking another State; allowing its own territory to be used by a State to attack another; sending or organizing irregular forces for incursion into the territory of another State; organizing or participating in acts of civil strife or terrorist acts against another State or acquiescing to organized activities within its territory aimed at the commission of such acts; using force within the territory of another State based upon the consent or invitation of the receiving State but in contravention of the conditions provided by that State or beyond the withdrawal of the consent or the invitation; exercising self-defence in excess of its limits; and acting in contravention of collective measures imposed by the Security Council under Chapter VII.

As said above, whether such conduct is a breach of the particular obligation depends on the interpretation and application of the relevant *jus ad bellum* rules and not on the rules of State responsibility. For example, the assessment of whether a State breached its obligation to exercise self-defence within its limits when it used force against a non-State actor on the territory of another State will depend on the interpretation of Article 51 of the Charter and the customary right of self-defence, as well as on how that State applied these rules in that instance. The rules of State responsibility do not concern the content of *jus ad bellum* (or any other international) obligations;[12] they are instead secondary rules setting out the general conditions for holding a State responsible for committing an internationally wrongful act (Article 2) and for assisting, controlling, directing or coercing another State in committing such an act (Articles 16–18). These general conditions remain the same regardless of the content of the primary rules, which in our case are the *jus ad bellum* rules.

Both material and mental elements may play a role in assessing the existence of a breach in the *jus ad bellum* context. For instance, in order to determine whether the use of armed force exceeds a *de minimis* level and qualifies as an armed attack, the scale and effects of the damage caused are necessary considerations.[13] Likewise, proponents of humanitarian intervention argue that use of force with a genuine intent to halt human rights violations should be lawful; such an approach requires an assessment of the intent or mental element of the State engaging in humanitarian intervention. Moreover, the present authors' proposals to

UNGA Res. 2625 (24 October 1970); Definition of Aggression, UNGA Res. 3314 (14 December 1974).

12 ARSIWA Commentary (n. 5), p. 31 para. (1) (Gen. Cmt.).

13 See Chapter 6, Section 6.4.1, above.

take into consideration moral and policy considerations in mitigating or excusing certain instances of humanitarian interventions or reprisals also imply the taking into account of a mental element when deciding whether to attach legal consequences to a *jus ad bellum* breach.[14]

Whether a breach of a *jus ad bellum* obligation is 'serious' within the meaning of Article 40 of the ARSIWA depends on the particular instance. For example, a full-scale invasion of a State by another that involves flagrant violations of international law may amount to a serious breach, but this would have to be assessed taking into consideration the facts on the ground.

### *15.2.3 Attribution of Conduct in the* jus ad bellum *Context*

The ARSIWA rules of attribution set out above also apply in the *jus ad bellum* context and need not be further elaborated on. Attribution of conduct to a State is unproblematic in most cases where force is openly used by that State's armed forces against another State. That being said, in some cases States try to avoid attribution by the use of 'hybrid' tactics, such as when Russia seized Crimea in 2014 with troops not wearing nationality markings (see Chapter 11, above). More controversies arise in relation to the attribution of the conduct of armed groups to States in the *jus ad bellum* context. Most of the time this question becomes relevant in relation to the exercise of self-defence (i.e. whether an armed attack carried out by an armed group can be attributed to a State, justifying the exercise of self-defence against that State). These issues are discussed above in Chapter 6. In this chapter, we look at attribution in relation to the more general purpose of establishing State responsibility for the use of force by armed groups.

The nature and extent of the relationship that must exist between a State and an armed group in order for the conduct of the latter to be attributed to the former has been addressed by the ICJ and the ICTY. The ICJ differentiated between a 'complete control' and an 'effective control' test. According to the 'complete control' test, the conduct of an armed group is attributable to a State when the armed group is in a relationship of such complete dependence on the State that it cannot be considered otherwise than as one of its organs.[15] A separate means of attribution is based on the 'effective control' test, whereby the conduct of an armed

[14] See Chapters 7 and 9, above.

[15] *Nicaragua* (n. 4), para. 115; *Bosnian Genocide* (n. 3), para. 397.

group can also be attributed to a State when the group acts in accordance with a State's instructions or under its effective control in respect of each operation in which the alleged violations occurred.[16] This test reflects Article 8 of the ARSIWA, according to which the conduct of a person or group may be attributable to a State only if that person or group is acting on the instruction of the State or under its direction or control. The tests set out by the ICJ were criticized by some authors and two dissenting judges in the *Nicaragua* case for not fully corresponding to the reality in the international arena, where relationships between States and armed groups are increasingly complex, with support to armed groups being provided by States in various forms other than through instructions, control or direction.[17] In the context of determining whether an armed conflict was international or non-international, the ICTY found that the 'effective control' test was appropriate only in attributing the conduct of private persons performing specific acts on behalf of a State on the territory of another State. It held that the test was too restrictive when having to attribute the conduct of armed groups to a State. In such a case, the ICTY found that a test of 'overall control', where a State had a role in organizing, co-ordinating or planning the military action, in addition to financing, training, equipping or providing operational support for the armed group, was better placed than the 'effective control' test.[18] In judgments post-dating the ICTY findings, the ICJ reaffirmed the 'effective control' test,[19] which today remains the authoritative test for attributing acts of armed groups to States for purposes of international responsibility.

Neither the ARSIWA nor the above tests condone the attribution of an armed group's attacks to a State that merely supports, harbours or

16 *Nicaragua* (n. 4), para. 195; *Bosnian Genocide* (n. 3), para. 400.

17 K. Tibori-Szabó, 'Control and the Right to Self-Defence against Non-State Actors', in R. Bartels et al. (eds.), *Military Operations and the Notion of Control under International Law: Lieber Amicorum Terry D. Gill* (Springer, 2021), p. 90. Some of this criticism came from dissenting ICJ judges who opined that substantial State support falling short of effective control should be sufficient for attributing the armed group's conduct to the supporting State. See *Nicaragua* (n. 4), Dissenting Opinion of Judge Jennings at p. 543, Dissenting Opinion of Judge Schwebel at para. 171.

18 ICTY, *Prosecutor* v. *Dusko Tadić*, Case No. IT-94-1-A, Appeals Chamber, Appeals Judgment, 15 July 1999, paras. 118–20, 137, 145. See also Tibori-Szabó, 'Control and the Right to Self-Defence' (n. 17), pp. 90–1.

19 ICJ, *Legal Consequences of the Construction of a Wall in the Occupied Palestinian Territory*, Advisory Opinion, 9 July 2004, ICJ Reports 2004, para. 139; ICJ, *Armed Activities on the Territory of Congo (DRC* v. *Uganda)* (Merits), Judgment, 19 December 2005, ICJ Reports 2005, para. 160; *Bosnian Genocide* (n. 3), para. 406.

tolerates the activities or presence of that group on its territory. This does not mean, however, that such a State cannot incur international responsibility. As set out in Chapter 6, a core duty of the sovereign is to exercise vigilance over its territory and safeguard the interests of other States.[20] Furthermore, as said above, a State's *jus ad bellum* obligations can be breached by, inter alia, acquiescing to organized activities within its territory aimed at the commission of armed acts on another State's territory.[21] Failure by the State to abide by these obligations may give rise to international responsibility under the basic rule of attribution (i.e. imputing to that State the acts or omissions of its own organs that allowed these duties to be breached).

### *15.2.4 Circumstances Precluding Wrongfulness in the* jus ad bellum *Context*

In the *jus ad bellum* context, only consent and self-defence can preclude the wrongfulness of an otherwise unlawful use of force.

#### 15.2.4.1 Consent

According to Article 20 of the ARSIWA, valid consent by a State to the commission of an act by another State precludes the wrongfulness of that act in relation to the former State to the extent that the act remains within the limits of that consent. Article 20 reflects a basic principle of international law that a sovereign State has the power to consent to a particular conduct on its territory by another State.[22] As explained above in Chapter 12, in the case of a consensual or invited use of force by one State on the territory of another, no rule of international law is violated in principle. It lies within the sovereignty of the State to issue consent or a request to a foreign State or international organization to deploy military forces on its territory and conduct actions within the bounds of the consent and in conformity with general international law.[23] Such a use of force cannot be against the territorial integrity or

[20] See also *Island of Palmas Case (Netherlands, USA)*, Award, 4 April 1928, RIAA, vol. II, pp. 829–71; ICJ, *The Corfu Channel Case* (Merits), Judgment, 9 April 1949, ICJ Reports 1949, pp. 22–3.

[21] UNGA Res. 2625 (n. 11). See also *Nicaragua* (n. 4), para. 191.

[22] ARSIWA Commentary (n. 5), p. 72 para. (1).

[23] See Chapter 12, above. See also G. H. Fox, 'Intervention by Invitation', in M. Weller (ed.), *The Oxford Handbook of the Use of Force in International Law* (Oxford University Press, 2017), pp. 816–40.

political independence of the consenting State, nor is it inconsistent with the purpose of the United Nations. Therefore, it does not fall under the prohibition on the use of force enshrined in Article 2(4) of the Charter.

The conditions for a valid consent to the use of force and the limitations applicable to the ensuing consensual use of force are elaborated in Chapter 12 and need not be repeated here.

#### 15.2.4.2 Self-Defence

According to Article 21 of the ARSIWA, the wrongfulness of an act of a State is precluded if the act constitutes a lawful measure of self-defence taken in conformity with the UN Charter. As with consent, Article 21 reflects a pre-existing rule of international law, according to which self-defence is an exception to the prohibition on the use of force. The legal basis of self-defence is accordingly not in Article 21 of the ARSIWA but in Article 51 of the Charter and customary international law. Article 21 simply acknowledges that a State exercising its inherent right to self-defence does not breach the prohibition enshrined in Article 2(4) of the Charter and does not thereby commit an international wrongful act.

The conditions and limits of the exercise of self-defence are set out above in Chapter 6 and need not be repeated here.

#### 15.2.4.3 Other Circumstances Precluding Wrongfulness

None of the other circumstances precluding wrongfulness (counter-measures, *force majeure*, distress or necessity) are relevant to excusing or justifying use of armed force in contravention of the prohibition on the threat or use of force.

The prohibition on the use of force is recognized as a peremptory norm of international law. While, as said above, consensual or invited use of force does not fall under the prohibition, any non-consensual use of force does and can be lawful only if it qualifies as an exception recognized in the Charter (self-defence or collective security measures). Accordingly, any other justification, factor or circumstance cannot preclude the wrongfulness of a non-consensual use of force that does not fall under any of the two Charter exceptions. This is also reflected in Article 26 of the ARSIWA, according to which no circumstance can preclude the wrongfulness of an act that is not in conformity with an obligation arising under a peremptory norm of international law. Moreover, in relation to counter-measures as a specific category of circumstances precluding wrongfulness, Article 50 of the ARSIWA likewise states that they cannot affect the obligation to refrain from the threat or use of force embodied in the Charter.

The state of necessity, as a circumstance precluding wrongfulness, has sometimes been used to justify or excuse instances of humanitarian intervention. The present authors discussed and rejected this argument in Chapter 7 above, with the possible narrow exception of force used by a State to halt violations committed by one or more armed groups on the portion of the territory of another State over which the latter no longer retained any control. But such situations would most likely be either consented to by the government if it were still functioning or capable of being addressed by a Security Council authorization.[24] The present authors also opined that a state of necessity could be invoked to excuse an emergency evacuation of nationals from another State's territory when obtaining prior consent was not possible or feasible in the prevailing circumstances. This excuse was premised on the presumption that no armed force is used against the State where the evacuation is conducted and consequently such an emergency evacuation does not breach the prohibition on the threat or use of force, despite being a temporary trespass on that State's territory (see Chapter 8, above).

#### 15.2.4.4 The Limited Effect of Circumstances Precluding Wrongfulness

The fact that self-defence and consent can preclude the wrongfulness of an unlawful use of force does not mean that the State invoking these circumstances is exempted from its *jus ad bellum* obligations once the circumstance no longer exists. This general principle is reflected in Article 22(1) of the ARSIWA, but it is also a specific consideration in the *jus ad bellum* context. Self-defence is not a *carte blanche* for the use of force; once the necessity of self-defence ceases, the use of force becomes unlawful (see Chapter 6, above). Similarly, the use of force with the consent or upon the invitation of the territorial State must remain within the limits of such an agreement and must cease as soon as the consent or invitation is withdrawn (see Chapter 12, above).

Moreover, as reflected in Article 22(2) of the ARSIWA, self-defence and consent do not necessarily set aside the question of compensation of the territorial State for material loss caused by the intervening State.

24 See Chapter 7, above.

### 15.2.5 *Consequences of State Responsibility in the* jus ad bellum *Context*

The above-mentioned ARSIWA rules on the legal consequences of State responsibility also apply in the *jus ad bellum* context. Any State responsible for a *jus ad bellum* breach must cease its wrongful conduct and make reparations.

Cessation of wrongful conduct in the *jus ad bellum* context may entail, inter alia, withdrawing armed forces from the defending State's territory; ceasing aerial or naval attacks against the defending State's targets; ending the assistance of another State in using force unlawfully; discontinuing the direction or control of, or assistance provided to, an armed group to carry out attacks against a defending State; taking measures to oust an armed group from a State's territory; or ceasing to disregard obligations imposed by the Security Council under Chapter VII. In all of the above examples, if the circumstances so dictate, the responsible State may also be required to offer appropriate assurances and guarantees of non-repetition, which may include so-called territorial guarantees (i.e. recognizing the integrity and inviolability of a given territory as belonging to the defending State and pledging not to invade or annex it again).[25]

Reparations in the *jus ad bellum* context are also known as 'war reparations'. The practice of claiming and paying reparations in the aftermath of war dates back to ancient times and has developed as a sub-category of reparations obligations, also acknowledged under the law of armed conflict.[26] Accordingly, the principle that States must pay compensation when a belligerent party violates the laws of armed conflict is enshrined in the Hague Convention Concerning the Laws and Customs of War on Land and the Additional Protocol I of the Geneva Conventions.[27] War

[25] See, for example, Treaty of Mutual Guarantee between Germany, Belgium, France, Great Britain and Italy (Locarno, 16 October 1925) (Locarno Pact); 'Letter dated 24 October 1989 from the Permanent Representatives of Argentina and the United Kingdom of Great Britain and Northern Ireland to the United Nations addressed to the Secretary-General', UN Doc. A/44/678 (24 October 1989), with annexed 'Joint Statement issued at Madrid on 19 October 1989 by the delegations of the Republic of Argentina and the United Kingdom of Great Britain and Northern Ireland'.

[26] P. Sullo and J. Wyatt, 'War Reparations', in *Max Planck Encyclopedia of Public International Law* (Oxford Public International Law, 2015), paras. 1, 5–9, https://tinyurl.com/36s4wyva.

[27] See Article 3 of the Hague Convention (IV) Concerning the Laws and Customs of War on Land (The Hague, 18 October 1907); Article 91 of the Protocol Additional to the Geneva Conventions of 12 August 1949, and Relating to the Protection of Victims of International Armed Conflicts (Geneva, 8 June 1977) (Additional Protocol I).

reparations may entail restitution, monetary compensation and symbolic reparations, referred to in the ARSIWA as satisfaction.

In particular, restitution in the aftermath of an unlawful use of force may take the form of restoration or return of territory, property or persons. For instance, the 1919 Treaty of Versailles required Germany to arrange for the return of prisoners of war and interned civilians to their homes.[28] Likewise, the restitution of looted artworks following the Second World War has taken decades and is still ongoing.[29]

If restitution is impracticable, the responsible State may be required to pay compensation for any financially assessable damage.[30] Such compensation can be paid, inter alia, for aircraft shot down or destroyed or sunken ships; damage or destruction caused to infrastructure and civilian buildings; and the cost of medical treatment, pensions and other forms of assistance for victims or their dependents. For instance, the 1919 Treaty of Versailles required Germany to pay damages for certain categories of civilian damage, including damage caused by acts of cruelty, violence or maltreatment.[31] Likewise, in the *Corfu Channel* judgment, the ICJ awarded compensation to the United Kingdom for the damage caused to two destroyers and for the costs of pensions and other grants resulting from the deaths and injuries of naval personnel.[32] Likewise, in the *Armed Activities* judgment, the ICJ awarded compensation to the Democratic Republic of the Congo for damage caused by Uganda to persons, property and natural resources.[33] A compensation obligation may also carry

[28] Article 216 of the Treaty of Peace with Germany (Versailles, 28 June 1919) (Treaty of Versailles), Library of Congress, www.census.gov/history/pdf/treaty_of_versailles-112018.pdf.

[29] See, for example, E. Campfens (ed.), *Fair and Just Solutions? Alternatives to Litigation in Nazi-Looted Art Disputes: Status Quo and New Developments* (Eleven International, 2015); US National Archives and Records Administration, 'World War II Looted Art: Turning History into Justice', Google Arts & Culture, https://g.co/arts/AH5FQKTUrCQBqhSV9; T. O'Donnell, 'The Restitution of Holocaust Looted Art and Transitional Justice: The Perfect Storm or the Raft of the Medusa?' (2011) 22(1) *European Journal of International Law* 49–80; B. L. Hay, *Nazi-Looted Art and the Law: The American Cases* (Springer, 2017).

[30] ARSIWA Commentary (n. 5), pp. 98–9 paras. (1)–(5) (Art. 36).

[31] Treaty of Versailles (n. 28), Article 232. See also Sullo and Wyatt, 'War Reparations' (n. 26), paras. 11–13.

[32] ICJ, *The Corfu Channel Case* (Assessment of the Amount of Compensation Due from the People's Republic of Albania to the United Kingdom of Great Britain and Northern Ireland), Judgment, 15 December 1949, ICJ Reports 1949, p. 249.

[33] ICJ, *Armed Activities on the Territory of Congo* (Reparations), Judgment, 9 February 2022, paras. 132–366, 405–8.

a requirement to pay interest.[34] In the *Armed Activities* judgment, the ICJ decided that, should payment by Uganda be delayed, interest of 6 per cent would accrue on any overdue amount as from the day after the day on which the instalment was due.[35]

States responsible for breach of *jus ad bellum* obligations may also be required to make symbolic reparations or satisfaction. This can take various forms, such as acknowledging the breach, expressing regret or issuing a formal apology.[36] One of the most common modalities of satisfaction is a declaration of the wrongfulness of the act by a competent court or tribunal,[37] and this modality also applies in the *jus ad bellum* context. For instance, in the *Corfu Channel* judgment, the ICJ declared the British minesweeping operation a violation of Albanian sovereignty and stated that this was 'in itself appropriate satisfaction'.[38]

In relation to any serious breach of a *jus ad bellum* obligation, the consequences listed in Article 41 of the ARSIWA apply *mutatis mutandis* and in fact reflect several duties enshrined in the Charter and other international legal instruments. In particular, the duty incumbent on States to co-operate in bringing to an end through lawful means any serious breach (Article 41(1) of the ARSIWA) reflects the seminal duties to fulfil in good faith the obligations assumed in the UN Charter (Article 2(2) of the Charter), to settle international disputes by peaceful means (Article 2(3) of the Charter, Friendly Relations Declaration) and to co-operate with one another in accordance with the Charter (Friendly Relations Declaration). Furthermore, the duty not to recognize as lawful a situation created by a serious breach (Article 41(2) of the ARSIWA) translates into the *jus ad bellum* duty not to recognize as legal any acquisition of territory brought about by the use of force (Friendly Relations Declaration). This duty was also invoked by the UNSC in Resolution 662 (1991), where it called upon States and international organizations not to recognize the annexation of Kuwait by Iraq and to refrain from any action that might be interpreted as indirect recognition thereof.[39]

[34] ARSIWA Commentary (n. 5), pp. 107–9 paras. (1)–(12) (Art. 38).
[35] *Armed Activities* (n. 33), paras. 397–402, 409.
[36] ARSIWA Commentary (n. 5), Article 37(2), pp. 106–7 paras. (5)-(7).
[37] ARSIWA Commentary (n. 5), Article 37, p. 106 para. (6).
[38] *Corfu Channel* (n. 20), pp. 35–6.
[39] UNSC Resolution 662 (1991), para. 2.

### 15.2.6 *Means of Addressing Breaches of Obligation in the* jus ad bellum *Context*

Following the above discussion of the forms of State responsibility in the *jus ad bellum* context, the question now arises as to how a defending State (or the international community) can address and remove the consequences of a breach of an obligation? In other words, what may States faced with a *jus ad bellum* breach by (an)other State(s) do to ensure that the responsible State(s) cease their wrongful conduct and make reparations?

#### 15.2.6.1 Self-Defence

As the only unilateral exception to the prohibition on the use force, self-defence is not – strictly speaking – meant to be an implementation of State responsibility for breach of *jus ad bellum* obligations. A State's right of self-defence is triggered to defend that State's territorial integrity, political sovereignty and citizens from an armed attack (see Chapter 6, above). Nonetheless, these aims necessarily entail, and may lead to, the cessation of wrongful conduct by the State(s) responsible for the armed attack. For instance, the United Kingdom's exercise of self-defence against the Argentinian invasion of the Falklands Islands was aimed at restoring British sovereignty over the islands, which evidently entailed the ending of the Argentinian presence on those territories.[40]

For this reason, exercising self-defence may lead to the implementation of at least one form of responsibility: ceasing the unlawful use of force. But the relevance of this right as a means of implementing State responsibility is limited to the *jus ad bellum* context.

#### 15.2.6.2 Chapter VII Measures

The breach of *jus ad bellum* obligations may endanger international peace and security, in which case the Security Council is empowered to take non-forcible or forcible measures under Chapter VII of the UN Charter, if it determines that the existence of a threat to peace, breach of the peace or act of aggression so requires (Articles 39, 41–2 of the Charter) (see Chapter 5, above).

Like self-defence, Chapter VII measures are not – strictly speaking – meant to be an implementation of State responsibility for breach of *jus ad*

[40] K. Tibori-Szabó, *Anticipatory Action in Self-Defence: Essence and Limits under International Law* (Springer, 2011), pp. 153–5; E. Henry, 'The Falklands/Malvinas War – 1982', in T. Ruys and O. Corten (eds.), *The Use of Force in International Law: A Case-Based Approach* (Oxford University Press, 2018), pp. 361–72.

*bellum* obligations. They are – as stated in Article 39 of the Charter – aimed at maintaining or restoring international peace and security.[41] This aim, however, may also involve the cessation of wrongful conduct or reparations by the State(s) responsible for the unlawful use of force. In particular, under Article 41 of the Charter the Security Council may take non-forcible measures, including calling upon States to interrupt economic relations and various means of communication or to sever diplomatic relations with the responsible States. Under Article 42 of the Charter, the Security Council may take such forcible measures by air, sea or land forces as may be necessary to maintain or restore international peace and security.

It is under Article 41 of the Charter that the Security Council has over the years taken numerous measures that involved both cessation of wrongful conduct and reparations.

For example, in the late 1990s and the 2000s, the Security Council took several measures under Article 41 of the Charter against the Taliban regime in Afghanistan for, inter alia, providing a safe haven for Osama bin Laden and Al-Qaida, which was deemed to be a threat to peace. Such measures included a flight embargo, asset freezes and other financial restrictions.[42] One of the Security Council demands was that the Taliban 'cease the provision of sanctuary and training for international terrorists and their organizations'.[43] These measures were then implemented, not only by individual States but also by regional organizations such as the European Union (EU).[44] Similarly, the Security Council imposed sanctions against Iraq as a result of its invasion of Kuwait in August 1990. These sanctions included sweeping bans on the import and export of Iraqi products, including an arms embargo.[45]

41 See also Chapter 5, above.

42 See, for example, UNSC Resolutions 1214 (1998); 1267 (1999); 1333 (2000). After the Taliban regime was deposed, the UNSC continued to impose sanctions against the Taliban group as well as al-Qaida; see UNSC Resolutions 1388 (2002); 1390 (2002); 1456 (2003); 1735 (2006); 1988 (2011); 2082 (2012); 2160 (2014); 2255(2015); 2615 (2021).

43 UNSC Resolution 1267 (1999), para. 1.

44 See, for example, Council Regulation (EC) No. 881/2002 of 27 May 2002 imposing certain specific restrictive measures directed against certain persons and entities associated with Usama bin Laden, the Al-Qaida network and the Taliban, and repealing Council Regulation (EC) No. 467/2001 prohibiting the export of certain goods and services to Afghanistan, strengthening the flight ban and extending the freeze of funds and other financial resources in respect of the Taliban of Afghanistan, as amended several times, including in 2022, https://tinyurl.com/bddd3p67.

45 See, for example, UNSC Resolutions 661 (1990); 687 (1991); 1483 (2003); 1546 (2004). See also UNSC, 'Security Council Committee Established Pursuant to Resolution 1518

Furthermore, the Security Council has repeatedly called for reparations in response to unlawful uses of force.[46] For instance, the Council considered Lebanon entitled to redress for the destruction by Israel of the Beirut airport in 1968.[47] Similarly, the Security Council deemed as just Angola's claims to full compensation for the damage and destruction inflicted by the 1975 invasion of its territory by South African forces.[48] In relation to the Iran-Iraq War (1980–8), the Security Council recognized the magnitude of the damage caused by the conflict and requested the Secretary-General to assign a team of experts to study the question of reconstruction.[49] Despite the unequivocal language, none of these demands materialized, due in part to the non-imposition of a particular reparations regime. Perhaps as a consequence, when it came to the Iraq-Kuwait War (1990–1) the Security Council, alongside the aforementioned sanctions regime, also established a comprehensive reparations regime, which included an institutional structure for the management of claims (see Fact Box 15.2).[50]

#### 15.2.6.3 Negotiations and Agreements

One of the oldest forms of implementing State responsibility is through bilateral or multilateral negotiations between States and the adoption of treaties or other types of agreements setting out the details of the responsibility incurred.

Reparations in the aftermath of the two World Wars were recorded in treaties, such as the 1919 Treaty of Versailles, the 1945 Potsdam Agreement,[51] the 1947 Paris Peace Treaties[52] and the 1951 Peace Treaty

(2003)', detailing current sanctions regime against certain Iraqi entities and individuals, www.un.org/securitycouncil/sanctions/1518.

46 Sullo and Wyatt, 'War Reparations' (n. 26), para. 26.

47 UNSC Resolution 262 (1968), para. 4.

48 UNSC Resolution 387 (1976), para. 4.

49 UNSC Resolution 598 (1987), para. 7.

50 See UNSC Resolutions 674 (1990); 686 (1991); 687 (1991); 692 (1991). See also Sullo and Wyatt, 'War Reparations' (n. 26), paras. 28–30.

51 Conclusions of the Protocol of the Proceedings of the Berlin Conference of the Three Heads of Government of the USSR, US and UK (Potsdam, 1 August 1945).

52 Treaty of Peace between the Allied and Associated Powers and Italy (Paris, 10 February 1947); Treaty of Peace between the Allied and Associated Powers and Bulgaria (Paris, 10 February 1947); Treaty of Peace between the Allied and Associated Powers and Romania (Paris, 10 February 1947); Treaty of Peace between the Allied and Associated Powers and Finland (Paris, 10 February 1947); Treaty of Peace between the Allied and Associated Powers and Hungary (Paris, 10 February 1947).

**FACT BOX 15.2 REPARATIONS FOR IRAQS INVASION OF KUWAIT**

As a consequence of Iraq's invasion of Kuwait in August 1990, the Security Council created a comprehensive reparations regime, starting with the establishment of a compensation commission.

In Resolution 687 (1990), the Security Council reaffirmed that Iraq was liable for any direct loss, damage or injury as a result of the unlawful invasion and occupation of Kuwait. It therefore decided to create a fund for compensation for such damage and to establish a commission that would administer the fund (paras. 16, 18).

As a result, the United Nations Compensation Commission (UNCC) was created in 1991 as a subsidiary organ of the Security Council with a mandate to process claims and pay compensation for losses and damage suffered as a direct result of what the Security Council determined to be the unlawful invasion and occupation of Kuwait. The UNCC's task was to establish for each claim whether or not the damage was directly linked to the invasion and occupation. Governments, international organizations, companies and individuals could claim various types of damage before the Commission.

In total, the Commission received approximately 2.7 million claims seeking approximately USD 352.5 billion in compensation for death, injury, loss of or damage to property, commercial claims and claims for environmental damage resulting from Iraq's invasion and occupation of Kuwait. The Commission concluded its processing of claims in 2005, and the compensation totalled USD 52.4 billion, awarded to approximately 1.5 million successful claimants.

In January 2022, upon settling thc last rcmaining claim with an outstanding balance, the Government of Iraq fulfilled its international obligations to compensate all claimants awarded compensation by the Commission. The Security Council subsequently adopted Resolution 2621 (2022), which terminated the mandate of the Commission.

**Source:** website of the United Nations Compensation Commission, https://uncc.ch/home.

with Japan.[53] While the Treaty of Versailles was criticized as excessively onerous on Germany in respect of the amount of compensation demanded, the reparation agreements after the Second World War took into account the responsible party's capacity to pay such reparations.[54]

[53] Treaty of Peace with Japan (with two declarations) (San Francisco, 8 September 1951).

[54] See, for example, Articles 74A(3), 74B(3) of the Treaty of Peace between the Allied and Associated Powers and Italy (Paris, 10 February 1947); Article 14 of the Treaty of Peace with Japan (with two declarations) (San Francisco, 8 September 1951).

Treaties or agreements may also lead to a mutual renunciation of reparations, as in the case of the Falkland Islands War, where Argentina and the United Kingdom issued a joint statement in 1989 declaring, inter alia, that both governments 'undertook not to pursue any claim against the other, including nationals of the other, in respect of loss or damage arising from the hostilities and all other actions' in and around the relevant islands before 1989.[55]

#### 15.2.6.4 Judicial Process

International State responsibility claims can also be pursued before competent courts and tribunals. Article 36(2)(d) of the Statutes of both the Permanent Court of International Justice (PCIJ) and the ICJ lists 'the nature or extent of the reparation to be made for the breach of an international obligation' as one of the questions over which a State may give the Court jurisdiction through an optional declaration, but apart from this the Statutes give no guidance on the determination of remedies.[56] In the *Factory at Chorzów* judgment, however, the PCIJ held that jurisdiction to determine a breach had to imply jurisdiction to determine reparations.[57] Since then, the ICJ's competence to determine reparations, even without the explicit consent of the Parties, is well established.[58] Accordingly, the ICJ has ruled on requests for reparations in numerous cases, some directly or indirectly involving breaches of *jus ad bellum* obligations, such as the *Corfu Channel*, *Nicaragua*, *Oil Platforms* and *Armed Activities* judgments.[59]

Other courts, tribunals or commissions may also be set up or awarded competence by the relevant parties to adjudicate reparations claims arising from the breach of *jus ad bellum* obligations. For example, the Eritrea-Ethiopia Claims Commission was set up in 1998 by the two governments to 'decide through binding arbitration all claims for loss,

[55] 'Letter dated 24 October 1989 from the Permanent Representatives of Argentina and the United Kingdom of Great Britain and Northern Ireland to the United Nations addressed to the Secretary-General', UN Doc. A/44/678 (24 October 1989), with annexed 'Joint statement issued at Madrid on 19 October 1989 by the delegations of the Republic of Argentina and the United Kingdom of Great Britain and Northern Ireland'.

[56] Crawford, *State Responsibility* (n. 9), p. 615.

[57] *Factory at Chorzów* (n. 6), pp. 21, 25.

[58] Crawford, *State Responsibility* (n. 9), p. 616.

[59] See, in general, the following judgments: *Corfu Channel* (n. 32); *Armed Activities* (n. 33). See also *Nicaragua* (n. 4), paras. 283–9, p. 149 paras. (12)–(15); ICJ, *Oil Platforms (Islamic Republic of Iran* v. *United States of America)*, Judgment, 6 November 2003, ICJ Reports 2003, paras. 99, 124, p. 218 paras. (1)–(2).

damage or injury by one Government against the other' related to the armed conflict and resulting from 'violations of international humanitarian law, including the 1949 Geneva Conventions, or other violations of international law'.[60] The Commission was seated in The Hague, with the Permanent Court of Arbitration serving as registry. Between 2001 and 2009 the Commission delivered fifteen partial and final awards on liability. It concluded its work on 17 August 2009, when it delivered its final awards on damages.[61]

#### 15.2.6.5 Individual Measures of Self-Help

Besides negotiations and judicial process, States can also resort to certain individual measures of self-help to induce cessation of, or reparations for, the breach of a *jus ad bellum* obligation. Self-help as a concept of international relations dates back to the eighteenth and nineteenth centuries, when States that considered themselves wronged by another State's breach of obligations could take both non-forcible and forcible measures to remedy or punish that breach. Forcible measures could take the form of armed reprisals, other measures short of war or war itself.[62] With the advent of the prohibition on the use of force, these measures have been outlawed (see Chapter 9, above). Non-forcible measures of self-help have survived in various forms. Within the context of State responsibility, they remain one of the least developed areas of international law.[63] Such measures may today take the form of exception of non-performance, counter-measures or retorsions, although in practice it is often difficult to distinguish clearly between them.[64] What complicates matters further is that counter-measures and retorsions are often referred to as 'sanctions'. This term is quite confusing as it is used to describe UNSC measures adopted under Chapter VII of the Charter as well as – formally or colloquially – retorsions or counter-measures taken unilaterally or collectively by States or international organizations.

It is important to note that these measures are, in principle, meant to induce compliance by the responsible State with its international

[60] Eritrea-Ethiopia Claims Commission, https://pca-cpa.org/en/cases/71/

[61] Ibid.

[62] N. D. White and A. Abass, 'Countermeasures and Sanctions', in M. D. Evans (ed.), *International Law* (Oxford University Press, 2018), pp. 521–2.

[63] T. Ruys, 'Sanctions, Retortions and Countermeasures: Concepts and International Legal Framework', in L. van den Herik (ed.), *Research Handbook on UN Sanctions and International Law* (Edward Elgar, 2016), p. 23; White and Abass, 'Countermeasures' (n. 62), p. 521.

[64] Crawford, *State Responsibility* (n. 9), pp. 675–6.

obligations – namely, the cessation of the wrongful conduct and reparations for the breach. Accordingly, they are supposed to be temporary measures, to be rescinded once the responsibility of the target State has been implemented. More often than not, however, these 'temporary' measures last for years, because the responsible State continues its wrongful conduct. In such cases, these self-help measures become in practice substitute forms of international State responsibility. This is especially true of measures imposed in response to unlawful uses of force.

**Exception of Non-Performance** In the *jus ad bellum* context, the exception of non-performance does not apply, as this rule flows from the principle of reciprocity and is therefore limited to the suspension of performance of the same or a closely related obligation.[65] If a State breaches a *jus ad bellum* obligation, the prohibition on the use of force does not allow the victim State to suspend its own obligations under *jus ad bellum*. As described above, the only exceptions to the prohibition on the use of force are self-defence and Chapter VII measures, which are governed by specific rules and do not fall under the exception of non-performance.

**Counter-measures** Counter-measures involve non-compliance by one State with an international obligation owed towards another State, adopted in response to a prior breach of international law by that other State and aimed at inducing it to comply with its obligations of cessation and reparation.[66] They therefore also operate as a circumstance precluding wrongfulness, but, as discussed above, such measures cannot preclude the wrongfulness of an unlawful use of force.

Resort to counter-measures under international law is limited by a number of substantive and procedural safeguards, codified in Articles 49–53 of the ARSIWA. Accordingly, such measures must be commensurate with the injury suffered and must be directed against the responsible State. They must be taken in such a way as to permit the resumption of performance of the relevant obligation and must be terminated as soon as the responsible State has complied with its obligations.[67] Counter-measures are broader than the exception of non-performance, because the injured State's non-compliance is not limited

[65] Crawford, *State Responsibility* (n. 9), p. 678.
[66] Ibid., p. 685; Ruys, 'Sanctions' (n. 63), p. 33.
[67] Crawford, *State Responsibility* (n. 9), p. 686.

to a similar obligation. They are narrower than retorsions, because they involve an international obligation that the injured State chooses temporarily not to perform. But no State resorting to counter-measures can opt out of peremptory or fundamental obligations of international law, such as the prohibition on the use of force and the protection of fundamental human rights.[68]

The ARSIWA acknowledge that third States can invoke the responsibility of another State if the obligation breached is owed to a group of States or is owed to the international community as a whole.[69] The ARSIWA do not, however, recognize an entitlement of States other than the injured State to resort to counter-measures.[70] In practice, however, counter-measures have been used not only by a State that considers itself injured but also by third States in solidarity with the injured State.[71] Moreover, violations of peremptory norms like the prohibition on the use of force trigger the duty of States to co-operate in bringing the breach to an end by lawful means.[72] In the opinion of the present authors, such a duty could also accommodate the taking of counter-measures by a collectivity of States to end the unlawful use of force. Such counter-measures should (a) target solely the responsible State(s); (b) aim at inducing the responsible State(s) to cease the unlawful use of force; (c) be proportionate to the aim of inducing compliance and not take the form of excessive, arbitrary, abusive or irreversible measures; and (d) respect at all times the peremptory norms of international law.

Counter-measures, including against the breach of *jus ad bellum* obligations, can take various forms, such as the denial by the injured State of free passage in its territorial sea to all ships flagged in the responsible State or the denial by the injured State of landing rights provided for in a multilateral or bilateral agreement to any aircraft registered in the responsible State. The injured State could also conduct cyber operations against private entities in the responsible State that would otherwise violate the responsible State's sovereignty.[73]

68 ARSIWA Commentary (n. 5), pp. 131–4 paras. (1)–(15) (Art. 50).
69 Ibid., pp. 126–7 paras. (1)–(10) (Art. 48).
70 Ibid., pp. 137–9 paras. (1)–(7) (Art. 54).
71 Ruys, 'Sanctions' (n. 63), pp. 44–6.
72 ARSIWA Commentary (n. 5), pp. 113–14 paras. (1)–(3) (Art. 41(1)).
73 M. N. Schmitt, 'Lieber Institute White Paper: Responding to Malicious or Hostile Actions under International Law', Lieber Institute Articles of War (26 April 2022), https://tinyurl.com/mt9jy9yy. See Chapter 11, above.

**Retorsion** Retorsion can be defined as any retaliatory act by which a State responds, by an unfriendly act not amounting to a violation of international law, to either a breach of international law or an unfriendly act by another State.[74] Retorsions may entail breaking off diplomatic relations; expelling nationals, including diplomats, of the responsible State; restricting travel of nationals to and from the responsible State; discontinuing or reducing trade or investment relations; withholding or reducing economic assistance; or imposing heavy customs duties on goods imported from the responsible State. Such measures are also known as unilateral (economic) sanctions imposed by a State on another and are also applied as a response to the breach of *jus ad bellum* obligations. They can be applied by the injured State against the responsible State, but also by other States, in solidarity with the injured State, in order to induce the responsible State to cease the unlawful use of force or other *jus ad bellum* breach and make reparations.

For instance, the United States has imposed sanctions against Syria for, inter alia, sponsoring terrorism. These sanctions include blocking the US-based property, including funds, of the Syrian government and some of its nationals; prohibiting new investments in Syria by US persons; prohibiting the export or sale of services to Syria by US persons; and prohibiting the import of petroleum or petroleum products of Syrian origin.[75] Likewise, the United States has applied sanctions against Russia for the annexation of Crimea in 2014 and the invasion of Ukraine in 2022. These sanctions include travel restrictions for certain Russian nationals; prohibiting or limiting the financing of certain Russian banks, energy companies and other companies, including those involved in military or defence activities; and imposing export controls and blocking any US-based property, including funds, of certain Russian nationals.[76]

The difficulty with retorsions lies in determining whether they are indeed retorsions – and not counter-measures involving a breach of an international obligation. For instance, breaking off diplomatic relations would generally not entail such a breach. Conversely, the prohibition of commerce or investments, or the imposition of embargoes, may prove to be breaches of a bilateral or multilateral treaty between two or

[74] Cassese, *International Law* (n. 9). p. 310. See also ARSIWA Commentary (n. 5), p. 128, para. (3) (Countermeasures).

[75] US Department of State, 'Syria Sanctions', www.state.gov/syria-sanctions/.

[76] US Department of State, 'Ukraine and Russia Sanctions', www.state.gov/ukraine-and-russia-sanctions/.

more States.[77] In the latter case such measures amount to counter-measures and must accordingly remain within the applicable limits detailed above.

##### 15.2.6.6 Sanctions by International or Regional Organizations

International and regional organizations may also impose sanctions against a State in breach of a *jus ad bellum* obligation. The legal basis of these sanctions may derive from Chapter VII measures of the Security Council or from the legal instruments and policies of the organization itself.[78] For instance, past and present EU 'restrictive measures' (the formal description of sanctions) against the Taliban regime have been based on and/or supplemented Chapter VII measures adopted by the Security Council.[79] But the EU has also adopted sanctions against *jus ad bellum* breaches on its own initiative.[80] In particular, the EU has imposed comprehensive 'restrictive measures' against Russia for what it sees as the 'illegal annexation of Crimea in 2014, the decision to recognize the non-government-controlled areas of the Donetsk and Luhansk oblasts as independent entities in 2022 and the unprovoked and unjustified military aggression against Ukraine in 2022'.[81] As of late 2022, these measures include asset freezes and travel bans against 1,236 individuals and 115 entities; targeted economic measures against Russian financial, trade, energy, transport, technology and defence sectors, including the closure of EU airspace to all Russian-owned and Russian-registered aircraft; restrictions on media; diplomatic restrictions, including the cancellation of EU-Russia meetings; and visa restrictions.[82]

The EU has also imposed sanctions against Belarus and Iran in response to their assistance of Russia in the invasion of Ukraine.[83] Restrictive measures against Belarus entail individual and economic sanctions

[77] Ruys, 'Sanctions' (n. 63), pp. 24–5.

[78] N. Ronzitti, 'Sanctions as Instruments of Coercive Diplomacy: An International Law Perspective', in N. Ronzitti (ed.), *Coercive Diplomacy, Sanctions and International Law* (Brill-Nijhoff, 2016), p. 16.

[79] See Section 15.2.6.2.

[80] On EU sanctions regimes, see generally M. Gestri, 'Sanctions Imposed by the European Union: Legal and Institutional Aspects', in Ronzitti (ed.), *Coercive Diplomacy* (n. 78), pp. 70–102.

[81] European Council/Council of the EU, 'EU Restrictive Measures against Russia over Ukraine (since 2014)', https://tinyurl.com/58dnubdm.

[82] Ibid.

[83] European Council/Council of the EU, 'EU Restrictive Measures against Belarus', https://tinyurl.com/mshns6uw; European Council/Council of the EU, 'Iran: EU Restrictive Measures', www.consilium.europa.eu/en/policies/sanctions/iran/.

targeting a number of its nationals, restrictions on trade, a SWIFT ban applied to a number Belarusian banks, the prohibition of transactions with the Central Bank of Belarus, limits on financial inflows from Belarus to the EU and a prohibition on the provision of euro-denominated banknotes to Belarus.[84] Restrictive measures applied to Iran for the use of its drones by Russia build on previous sanctions against Iran for human rights violations and include the freezing of assets and travel bans.[85]

Sanctions (other than those stemming from Chapter VII measures) by international or regional organizations remain largely unregulated under the rules of international State responsibility. It is generally accepted that such sanctions may not violate peremptory norms of international law, but there is not much clarity on the legal basis, conditions and limits of such measures. Lawyers and legal commentators generally apply the same rules as those discussed under individual measures of self-help and scrutinize sanctions imposed by such organizations as either retorsion or counter-measures. As with the individual measures, it is often difficult to delineate the boundary between these categories. For instance, during the past decade the EU has imposed a wide range of autonomous economic and financial sanctions on Iran targeting nuclear proliferation activities.[86] While measures restricting or impeding trade relations are a typical example of retorsion, it has been argued in relation to some previous EU sanctions that they also involved the suspension of the performance of international legal obligations otherwise owed to Iran, such as commitments under bilateral investment treaties between Iran and European countries.[87]

Consequently, violations of *jus ad bellum* can trigger comprehensive and far-reaching sanctions regimes, which remain largely unregulated under international law, leaving their legitimacy and legality in the eye of the beholder.

## 15.3 Responsibility of International Organizations

The diversification of the subjects of international law brought about the recognition of a limited measure of international legal responsibility for

[84] European Council/Council of the EU, 'EU Restrictive Measures against Belarus' (n. 83).
[85] European Council/Council of the EU, 'Iran: EU Restrictive Measures' (n. 83).
[86] Ibid.
[87] N. J. Calamita, 'Sanctions, Countermeasures, and the Iranian Nuclear Issue' (2009) 42 *Vanderbilt Journal of Transnational Law* 1393–442; P.-E. Dupont, 'Countermeasures vs. Collective Security? The EU Sanctions against Iran', *EJIL:Talk!* (22 June 2012), https://tinyurl.com/2p9wpr87. See also Ronzitti, 'Sanctions' (n. 78), pp. 21–2.

entities other than States.[88] International organizations, created by States through treaties or other instruments for the purpose of exercising certain functions, possess international legal personality and may be held responsible for their acts.[89] The responsibility of international organizations is largely governed by the same general principles which apply to the responsibility of States; the Draft Articles on the Responsibility of International Organizations (DARIO), adopted by the ILC in 2009, are inspired to a very large extent by the ARSIWA.[90]

The question then arises as to whether international organizations such as the United Nations, the North Atlantic Treaty Alliance (NATO), the Organization of American States (OAS) and the EU are bound by the same *jus ad bellum* obligations as States.

It must be noted at the outset that the core *jus ad bellum* obligations binding States are equally applicable to any international or regional organization by virtue of its members being States. This does not mean, however, that the particular organization cannot create new obligations relating to the use of force, so long as they remain consistent with the core of the *jus ad bellum*. In fact, on the basis of the Chapter VII collective measures enshrined in the UN Charter, States have bestowed on the Security Council, an organ of an international organization, the power to take binding measures which may entail the use of force.

Regional organizations can also enact rules relating to the use of force so long as these do not contradict the UN Charter. For instance, Article 18 of the OAS Charter reaffirms the prohibition on the use of force and the exception of self-defence. Articles 24 and 25 of the OAS Charter then set out an obligation to act 'in furtherance of the principles of continental solidarity or collective self-defense' and in conformity with applicable treaties in the event of an act of aggression, armed attack, an extra-continental conflict, a conflict between two or more American States or any other fact or situation that might endanger the peace of America.[91] Similarly, Article 1 of the North Atlantic Treaty reaffirms the obligation to refrain from the use or threat of force and Article 5 of the same treaty sets

[88] A. Pellet, 'The Definition of Responsibility under International Law', in J. Crawford, A. Pellet and S. Olleson (eds.), *The Law of International Responsibility* (Oxford University Press, 2010), p. 6.

[89] ICJ, *Reparation for Injuries Suffered in the Service of the United Nations*, Advisory Opinion, 11 April 1949, ICJ Reports 1949, p. 179.

[90] Pellet, 'Definition of Responsibility' (n. 88), pp. 6–7.

[91] Articles 5(f) and 18 of the Charter of the Organization of American States (Bogota, 30 April 1948).

out the well-known collective defence clause of the alliance: 'an armed attack against one or more of [the Parties] in Europe or North America shall be considered an attack against them all and ... if such an armed attack occurs, each of them, in exercise of the right of individual or collective self-defence recognized by Article 51 of the Charter of the United Nations, will assist the Party or Parties so attacked by taking forthwith, individually and in concert with the other Parties, such action as it deems necessary, including the use of armed force, to restore and maintain the security of the North Atlantic area'.[92] The EU also has a mutual defence clause, enshrined in Article 42(7) of the Treaty of Lisbon, which states that 'if an EU country is the victim of armed aggression on its territory, the other EU countries have an obligation to aid and assist it by all means in their power'.[93] Article 6 of the Charter of the Arab League provides that in the event of aggression, or a threat of aggression, by one State against a member State, the latter may demand the immediate convocation of the League's Council, which shall then, by a unanimous decision, determine the measures necessary to repulse the aggression. If the aggressor is a member State, its vote shall not be counted in determining unanimity.[94]

The use of force by States in furtherance of the mandate or decision of an international organization raises complex questions of international responsibility. Would the member States be held responsible as individual States? Would the organization be held responsible concomitantly with the States, or would the responsibility of the organization preclude or mitigate the responsibility of its members? According to Article 7 of the DARIO, the conduct of a State organ that is placed at the disposal of an international organization shall be considered an act of the latter 'if the organization exercises effective control over that conduct'.[95] Furthermore, Article 8 of the DARIO provides that '[t]he conduct of an organ or agent of an international organization shall be considered an act of that organization under international law if the organ or agent acts in an official capacity and within the overall functions of that organization, *even if the conduct exceeds the authority of that organ or agent or contravenes instructions*' (emphasis added). These provisions do not preclude, however, the concomitant responsibility of the State itself for the conduct

92 Article 5 of the North Atlantic Treaty (Washington, DC, 4 April 1949).

93 Article 42(7) of the Treaty of Lisbon (Lisbon, 13 December 2007).

94 Pact of the League of Arab States (Cairo, 22 March 1945).

95 See also A. Tzanakopoulos, *Disobeying the Security Council: Countermeasures against Wrongful Sanctions* (Oxford University Press, 2011), pp. 34–45.

of the organ that it placed at the disposal of an international organization. For example, if a number of States act ultra vires in conducting a peacekeeping operation mandated by the Security Council, the States will be the ones incurring responsibility. Only if it is shown that those States acted in an official capacity and within the overall functions of the UN peacekeeping mission will the Security Council (and the United Nations) also incur responsibility, even though the States in question exceeded the limits of the peacekeeping mandate. In such a case, the Security Council could take remedial action, such as terminating the authorization of the States to implement the peacekeeping mandate or adopting additional measures to prevent further excesses. This has not materialized to date, but it is a possible scenario – save for a veto by a permanent member to protect its own organs or those of an ally State. In addition, the victim State could also demand a third-party arbitration and settlement, but this would have a slim chance of success given that the mandate stems from the Security Council.

If the international organization were to be held responsible (alone or in conjunction with its members), how could its responsibility be implemented? For instance, it has long been held that, while the Security Council enjoys wide discretion, its decisions are limited by the purpose and principles of the Charter as well as by peremptory norms.[96] Hence, could a State challenge the determination of the Security Council under Article 39 of the Charter that a threat or breach of peace or an act of aggression existed? Or could the content or proportionality of the measures adopted by the Security Council under Article 42 of the Charter be challenged? And if so, would there be a forum to hear such a challenge? In line with Article 34(1) of the ICJ Statute, only States may be parties in cases before the Court, so a State cannot bring a case against the Security Council as such. The Security Council could, however, submit its decision to judicial review by making a request for an advisory opinion of the Court.[97] While ICJ advisory opinions are not binding and have so far been underused as

[96] T. D. Gill, 'Legal and Some Political Limitations on the Power of the UN Security Council to Exercise Its Enforcement Powers under Chapter VII of the Charter' (1995) 26 *Netherlands Yearbook of International Law* 33–138, at 61–4, 68–72; E. de Wet, *The Chapter VII Powers of the United Nations Security Council* (Hart, 2004), pp. 133–310; B. Simma et al. (eds.), *The Charter of the United Nations: A Commentary* (Oxford University Press, 2012), vol. 2, pp. 1256–71. See also Chapter 5, above.

[97] According to Article 96(1) of the UN Charter, the General Assembly or the Security Council may request the ICJ to give an advisory opinion on any legal question.

a means of judicial review, they carry significant authority and it would be difficult for the Security Council to ignore a potential determination of illegality concerning one of its resolutions.[98] In any event, these issues have never arisen in practice, but they have received attention in academic literature.[99] Similar questions of judicial review of decisions could arise in relation to NATO, the OAS or the EU, if they used armed force. For instance, the Federal Republic of Yugoslavia brought cases before the ICJ against NATO members for alleged violations of their obligation not to use force against another State. Since none of those cases were tried on their merits, the ICJ has so far not ruled on the question whether and to what extent member States using force in furtherance of a NATO decision could be held responsible.[100]

## 15.4 International Responsibility of Armed Groups

The current international landscape clearly shows that armed groups, whether autonomous or semi-dependent on States, can play a substantial role in the use of armed force. As discussed above in Chapter 6, self-defence against autonomous armed groups is increasingly viewed as legitimate as a result of the rising number of armed attacks perpetrated by such groups.

The question then arises as to whether any of the discussed *jus ad bellum* obligations apply to such groups and, consequently, whether they can be held responsible for their acts. The simple answer is no; only States have *jus ad bellum* obligations, as subjects of international law or, as set out above, as members of international organizations (see Chapter 4, above). Armed groups do not have legal personality in *jus ad bellum*; they

98 de Wet, *Chapter VII Powers* (n. 96), pp. 55–68.

99 See generally de Wet, *Chapter VII Powers* (n. 96); Tzanakopoulos, *Disobeying the Security Council* (n. 95). In this respect Judge Jennings opined that 'Security Council decisions and actions should in no wise be regarded as enjoying some sort of "immunity" from the jurisdiction of the principal judicial organ of the United Nations'. ICJ, *Questions of Interpretation and Application of the 1971 Montreal Convention Arising from the Aerial Incident at Lockerbie (Libyan Arab Jamahiriya* v. *United Kingdom)* (Preliminary Objections), Judgment, 27 February 1998, Dissenting Opinion of Judge Jennings, ICJ Reports 1998, p. 110.

100 See generally the following cases: ICJ, *Legality of Use of Force (Serbia and Montenegro* v. *Belgium, Serbia and Montenegro* v. *Canada, Serbia and Montenegro* v. *France, Serbia and Montenegro* v. *Germany, Serbia and Montenegro* v. *Italy, Serbia and Montenegro* v. *Netherlands, Serbia and Montenegro* v. *Portugal, Serbia and Montenegro* v. *Spain, Serbia and Montenegro* v. *United Kingdom, Serbia and Montenegro* v. *United States of America).*

have limited rights and obligations only under international humanitarian law.[101]

Despite the fact that such groups are playing an increasingly significant role in the use of armed force, there has been no initiative in State practice to endow armed groups with any form of legal personality for *jus ad bellum* purposes. Any such discussion remains strictly academic for now and the foreseeable future.[102]

## 15.5 Individual Criminal Responsibility

### *15.5.1 The Crime of Aggression: Brief History and Definition*

*Jus ad bellum* obligations, including the prohibition of acts of aggression, concern States and not individuals. But States are run by individuals who issue orders, deploy troops, assign funds and make other decisions bringing about acts of aggression and other unlawful uses of force. For this reason, holding heads of State or government or other high-ranking military or civilian leaders responsible for starting wars and committing related crimes is not unknown in modern history. A plan to prosecute German emperor Wilhelm II for the 'supreme crime against international morality and the sanctity of treaties' was enshrined in Article 227 of the 1919 Treaty of Versailles.[103] While the emperor was never tried, the idea of prosecution for starting wars re-surfaced after the Second World War and bore fruit in the shape of 'crimes against peace'. The 1945 London Charter defined crimes against peace as 'the planning, preparation, initiation or waging of a war of aggression or a war in violation of international treaties, agreements or assurances, or participation in a common plan or conspiracy for the accomplishment of any of the foregoing'.[104] The Tokyo Charter contained a very similar definition

[101] J. K. Kleffner, 'The Applicability of International Humanitarian Law to Organized Armed Groups' (2011) 93(882) *International Review of the Red Cross* 443–61.

[102] J. d'Aspremont et al., 'Sharing Responsibility Between Non-State Actors and States in International Law' (2015) 62(1) *Netherlands International Law Review* 49–67; A. Nollkaemper and I. Plakokefalos (eds.), *Principles of Shared Responsibility in International Law: An Appraisal of the State of the Art* (Cambridge University Press, 2014).

[103] W. Schabas, *The Trial of the Kaiser* (Oxford University Press, 2018); K. Sellars, 'The First World War, Wilhelm II and Article 227: The Origin of the Idea of "Aggression" in International Criminal Law', in C. Kreß and S. Barriga (eds.), *The Crime of Aggression: A Commentary*, vol. 1 (Cambridge University Press, 2017), pp. 21–48.

[104] Agreement for the Prosecution and Punishment of the Major War Criminals of the European Axis, and Charter of the International Military Tribunal (London, 8 August 1945).

of crimes against peace.[105] Charges of crimes against peace were included in the indictments of the international military tribunals at Nuremberg and Tokyo and in one French and four US military trials held under Control Council Law No. 10.[106]

In the second half of the twentieth century the discussion concentrated on the concept of aggression in inter-State relations, with the UN General Assembly adopting Resolution 3314 defining aggression and providing examples of acts that qualified as such (see Chapter 4, Fact Box 4.2).[107] In line with Articles 2 and 3 of the resolution, these acts were deemed to qualify as acts of aggression regardless of a declaration of war, unless the Security Council, in conformity with the Charter, concluded that, in the light of other relevant circumstances, including the fact that the acts concerned or their consequences were not of sufficient gravity, it would not be justified to determine that an act of aggression had been committed.

The concept of prosecuting individuals for a crime of aggression took a prominent place in the negotiations leading up to the drafting and adoption of the Statute of the International Criminal Court (ICC).[108] At that time, however, no agreement was reached on a definition, so the crime of aggression was included in the list of crimes falling within the jurisdiction of the ICC, but the definition and conditions for the exercise thereof were left for later consideration at the first review conference. At the 2010 Kampala Conference, the ICC Statute was amended to include,

105 Charter of the International Military Tribunal for the Far East (Tokyo, 19 January 1946, as amended 26 April 1946).

106 *Government Commissioner of the General Tribunal of the Military Government for the French Zone of Occupation in Germany* v. *Hermann Roechling et al.*, in *Trials of War Criminals before the Nuernberg Military Tribunals under Control Council Law No. 10*, vol. 14 (US Government Printing Office, 1951–2), Appendix B, pp. 1061–143; *United States of America* v. *Carl Krauch et al.* (*Farben Case*), in *Trials of War Criminals before the Nuernberg Military Tribunals under Control Council Law No. 10*, vols. 7, 8 (US Government Printing Office, 1952); *United States of America* v. *Alfred Felix Alwyn Krupp von Bohlen und Halbach et al.*, in *Trials of War Criminals before the Nuernberg Military Tribunals under Control Council Law No. 10*, vol. 9 (US Government Printing Office, 1950); *United States of America* v. *Ernst von Weizsäcker et al.* (*Ministries Case*), in *Trials of War Criminals before the Nuernberg Military Tribunals under Control Council Law No. 10*, vols. 12–14 (US Government Printing Office, 1951); *United States of America* v. *Wilhem von Leeb et al.* (*High Command Case*), in *Trials of War Criminals before the Nuremberg Military Tribunals under Control Council Law No. 10*, vols. 10, 11 (US Government Printing Office, 1951).

107 UNGA Res 3314 (1974).

108 R. S. Clark, 'Negotiations on the Rome Statute, 1995–98', in Kreß and Barriga (eds.), *Crime of Aggression* (n. 103), pp. 244–70.

## FACT BOX 15.3 ARTICLES 8 BIS AND 25 OF THE ROME STATUTE OF THE INTERNATIONAL CRIMINAL COURT

### Article 8 *bis* Crime of Aggression

1 For the purpose of this Statute, 'crime of aggression' means the planning, preparation, initiation or execution, by a person in a position effectively to exercise control over or to direct the political or military action of a State, of an act of aggression which, by its character, gravity and scale, constitutes a manifest violation of the Charter of the United Nations.

2 For the purpose of paragraph 1, 'act of aggression' means the use of armed force by a State against the sovereignty, territorial integrity or political independence of another State, or in any other manner inconsistent with the Charter of the United Nations. Any of the following acts, regardless of a declaration of war, shall, in accordance with United Nations General Assembly resolution 3314 (XXIX) of 14 December 1974, qualify as an act of aggression: [there follows the list set out in the Definition of Aggression, Article 3(a)–(g); see Chapter 4, Fact Box 4.2, above].

### Article 25 Individual criminal responsibility

1 The Court shall have jurisdiction over natural persons pursuant to this Statute.

2 A person who commits a crime within the jurisdiction of the Court shall be individually responsible and liable for punishment in accordance with this Statute.

3 In accordance with this Statute, a person shall be criminally responsible and liable for punishment for a crime within the jurisdiction of the Court if that person:

(a) Commits such a crime, whether as an individual, jointly with another or through another person, regardless of whether that other person is criminally responsible;

(b) Orders, solicits or induces the commission of such a crime which in fact occurs or is attempted;

(c) For the purpose of facilitating the commission of such a crime, aids, abets or otherwise assists in its commission or its attempted commission, including providing the means for its commission;

(d) In any other way contributes to the commission or attempted commission of such a crime by a group of persons acting with a common purpose. Such contribution shall be intentional and shall either:

(i) Be made with the aim of furthering the criminal activity or criminal purpose of the group, where such activity or purpose involves the commission of a crime within the jurisdiction of the Court; or

(ii) Be made in the knowledge of the intention of the group to commit the crime;

(e) In respect of the crime of genocide, directly and publicly incites others to commit genocide;

FACT BOX 15.3 *(cont.)*

(f) Attempts to commit such a crime by taking action that commences its execution by means of a substantial step, but the crime does not occur because of circumstances independent of the person's intentions. However, a person who abandons the effort to commit the crime or otherwise prevents the completion of the crime shall not be liable for punishment under this Statute for the attempt to commit that crime if that person completely and voluntarily gave up the criminal purpose.

3 *bis* In respect of the crime of aggression, the provisions of this article shall apply only to persons in a position effectively to exercise control over or to direct the political or military action of a State.

4 No provision in this Statute relating to individual criminal responsibility shall affect the responsibility of States under international law.

inter alia, the new Article 8 *bis* containing a definition of the crime of aggression, Articles 15 *bis* and 15 *ter* containing provisions on the conditions for the exercise of jurisdiction and Article 25(3) *bis* setting out modes of liability for the crime of aggression (see Fact Box 15.3). The ICC's jurisdiction over the crime of aggression was activated in December 2017.[109]

### 15.5.2 The State Conduct Element in the Crime of Aggression

Many authors and commentators have already analysed and dissected the text, application and future potential use of Article 8 *bis* (1). It is not the purpose of this chapter to delve into all these discussions, most of which are better placed in works focusing on questions of international criminal law and procedure. For the purpose of this chapter, we look only at the role, if any, that certain *jus ad bellum* questions would play in the interpretation and application of Article 8 *bis*.

The crime of aggression, as defined in the ICC Statute, is intrinsically connected to the *jus ad bellum* prohibition on the use of force. Since this prohibition concerns inter-State relations, the crime of aggression necessarily requires the commission of an internationally wrongful act by a State. The crime thus has an intrinsic State conduct

[109] W. A. Schabas, *An Introduction to the International Criminal Court* (Cambridge University Press, 2020), pp. 140–8.

element,[110] which is reflected in the reference in Article 8 *bis* to an act of aggression, as defined and elaborated in the Definition of Aggression.

#### 15.5.2.1 Use of Force

The State conduct element in Article 8 *bis* can be understood as a pyramid construct. At the bottom lies the requirement of the use of armed force by a State. A threat of force does not accordingly form part of the definition.

#### 15.5.2.2 Act of Aggression

In order for this use of armed force to reach the next level and qualify as an act of aggression, it must be directed against the sovereignty, territorial integrity or political independence of another State, or it must be in any other manner inconsistent with the UN Charter. It follows that not every use of armed force necessarily qualifies as an act of aggression. Military incursions of a limited nature, such as cross-border rescue missions or the limited use of force against a trespassing foreign military force,[111] that cause neither loss of life nor significant damage or disruption in the target State fall below a *de minimis* level and are generally not regarded as being inconsistent with the prohibition on the use of force or other provisions of the Charter.[112] Likewise, as discussed above in Chapter 12, use of armed force by a State exercised on the territory of another State upon, and within the limits of, the latter's consent or invitation also falls outside the scope of the prohibition and is not in itself inconsistent with the Charter. Furthermore, use of armed force within the limits of the right of self-defence or for the implementation of Chapter VII measures cannot qualify as an act of aggression, as it is conducted on the basis of the two exceptions to the prohibition on the use of force enshrined in the Charter, as discussed above in Chapters 5 and 6.

Other unilateral uses of force, however, cannot be regarded as falling outside the scope of the prohibition. In particular, even if the armed force is not directed against the sovereignty, territorial integrity or political independence of another State and is instead aimed at ending egregious human rights violations on the territory of that State, the force used is still inconsistent with the Charter's Article 2(4) prohibition.[113] Similarly, if

[110] C. Kreß, 'The State Conduct Element', in Kreß and Barriga (eds.), *Crime of Aggression* (n. 103), p. 412.

[111] Ibid., p. 425.

[112] See also Chapters 6 and 8, above.

[113] See Chapter 7, above.

the armed force used exceeds the limits of self-defence or the parameters of the requesting State's consent or invitation, it amounts to an unlawful use of force and may therefore fall within the definition of an act of aggression.

#### 15.5.2.3 Manifest Violation of the Charter: Character, Gravity and Scale

Does this mean that such uses of armed force qualify as crimes of aggression? Not necessarily. The last level of the pyramid construct in the State conduct element of Article 8 *bis* requires that the act of aggression, by its character, gravity and scale, constitute a manifest violation of the UN Charter. The qualitative component of 'character' was added to confine the State conduct element to the core of the prohibition on the use of force. Accordingly, if the legality of a use of force is the object of genuine disagreement between reasonable international lawyers, it cannot, by its character, be a manifest or evident violation of the Charter.[114] Furthermore, the quantitative components of gravity and scale were added to signal the drafters' understanding that aggression was the most serious and dangerous form of the illegal use of force.[115] The scale component refers to the spatial and temporal dimensions of the use of force and to its intensity, while the gravity component concerns the number of human casualties, the scope of the disturbance to common life and the level of destruction.[116] All three components must be met in order for the act of aggression to be judged a manifest violation of the Charter.[117]

Once a finding is made that an act of aggression has taken place, the question arises as to the order in which the three components are to be assessed. This will depend on the magnitude of the force that qualified as an act of aggression. Most of the time, and as suggested by the language of Article 8 *bis* (1), when analysing whether the qualitative and quantitative components are met, character would come first. If this component is not met, it is unnecessary to analyse the remaining two elements. This is especially true in respect of armed force used for so-called benign purposes.[118] As proposed by the present authors in

[114] Kreß, 'State Conduct Element' (n. 110), pp. 523–4.

[115] ICC, Review Conference of the Rome Statute, Kampala, 31 May–11 June 2010, 'Annex III: Understandings Regarding the Amendments to the Rome Statute of the International Criminal Court on the Crime of Aggression', RC/10/Add.1, Understanding No. 6.

[116] Kreß, 'State Conduct Element' (n. 110), p. 520.

[117] ICC, 'Annex III' (n. 115), Understanding No. 7.

[118] Kreß, 'State Conduct Element' (n. 110), pp. 431–2.

Chapter 7 above, genuine humanitarian interventions, while unlawful under *jus ad bellum*, could nevertheless be accepted or tolerated, leading to a mitigation of responsibility as far as they are concerned. The same argument was made above in Chapter 9 in relation to surgical reprisals driven by imperative humanitarian considerations. These proposals arise from the very character of these uses of force as large-scale or surgical interventions to halt serious human rights violations. Because of their benign purpose, reasonable legal opinions are divided as to their legality; the present authors consider them unlawful but argue for their mitigation. Some authors advocate for their legalization, while others view them as unequivocally unlawful and illegitimate.[119] The division of opinions already shows that such uses of force cannot be manifest violations of the Charter, because the character component is not met. Consequently, it is difficult to see how humanitarian interventions or surgical reprisals driven by imperative humanitarian considerations would ever qualify as crimes of aggression under Article 8 *bis* of the ICC Statute.

Similarly, certain controversial uses of self-defence would not qualify as manifest violations of the Charter, as by their character they are not unequivocally seen as illegal. In particular, as discussed by the present authors in Chapter 6 above, States can exercise self-defence against autonomous non-State armed groups, including on the territory of States that are unwilling or unable to stop the conduct of the armed group, if the necessity and proportionality requirements are met. Although increasingly recognized, this is not a universally held position. Many States or commentators view such exercise of self-defence as an unlawful use of force and an act of aggression. It would be difficult, however, to show that self-defence thus exercised was a manifest violation of the Charter; reasonable legal opinions are divided on the topic and it is thus not evident to everyone that a State would be acting unlawfully if it defended itself against an autonomous armed group on the territory of a State that was unwilling or unable to tackle the problem. Consequently, it is difficult to see how such – albeit controversial – exercises of self-defence would ever qualify as crimes of aggression under Article 8 *bis* of the ICC Statute.

If the character component is met, the analysis still needs to show that the gravity and scale components are also met. For example, if the competent Chamber of the ICC found that the use of armed force by a State in

[119] See Chapters 7 and 9, above.

excess of the consent provided by the territorial State was manifestly illegal by its character, it could still find that the human casualties and scope of destruction was so minimal that the gravity component could not be met. Likewise, if the competent Chamber found that the use of armed force by a State in excess of the necessity requirement of self-defence was manifestly illegal by its character, it could still find that the spatial and temporal dimensions of the excessive use of force were inconsequential and the scale component could not be met.

Only once the State conduct element of the crime is established can the competent Chamber determine the individual responsibility of the accused for the crime of aggression.

### *15.5.3 Individual Criminal Responsibility for the Crime of Aggression: Highlights*

In order to qualify as a perpetrator of the crime of aggression under Article 8 *bis* of the ICC Statute, a person (a) must have been in a position effectively to exercise control over or to direct the political or military action of a State and (b) must have planned, prepared, initiated or executed the act of aggression.

Without delving into a rigorous criminal law analysis of the above conditions, a few *jus ad bellum*-related observations are called for. First, the crime of aggression is a 'leadership crime'. A regular member of the State's armed forces or central administration cannot be held criminally responsible under Article 8 *bis*. The person planning, preparing, initiating or executing the acts of aggression must have the ability to control or direct the action of a State.[120] This means that only high-ranking individuals who 'effectively' control or direct the political or military actions of a State can qualify as perpetrators. This does not mean that only heads of State or government can be held responsible. Article 8 *bis* does not require the highest level of ability to control or direct; heads of the military and defence apparatus and other high-ranking individuals with decision-making powers may be regarded as having sufficient control or direction over the aggressor State.[121]

[120] V. Nerlich, 'The Crime of Aggression and Modes of Liability: Is There Room Only for Principals?' (2017) 58 *Harvard International Law Journal*, https://tinyurl.com/h8hkf6eb.

[121] The ICC's Elements of Crimes for the crime of aggression provide in a footnote that '[w] ith respect to an act of aggression, more than one person may be in a position that meets these criteria'. Amendments to the Rome Statute of the International Criminal Court (11 June 2010) A-38544 U.N.T.S., Annex II, p. 21 n. 1.

Second, by virtue of Article 25(3) *bis* of the ICC Statute, forms of accessory liability for the crime of aggression are also limited to persons who are in a position to effectively exercise control over or to direct the political or military action of a State. This has been interpreted as effectively annulling the application of the standard forms of accessory liability, as provided in Article 25(3) of the Statute, to the crime of aggression.[122] While the qualification indeed narrows the pool of persons who could be accessories or accomplices for perpetration of an act of aggression, it does not mean that such liability is rendered impossible. The requirement of direction or control concerns the 'political or military action of a State' and not the perpetration of the crime of aggression. For example, a foreign affairs minister may have control over the international relations of a State, including in respect of measures taken in the context of an armed conflict, and may therefore be regarded as having control over the political action of that State. The same minister may, however, not be directly involved in the planning, preparation, initiation or execution of the act of aggression, and may thus be found to have been an accomplice rather than a principal perpetrator of the crime of aggression.[123]

Third, the conditions for individual criminal responsibility set out in Articles 8 *bis* and 25(3) *bis* of the Statute do not seem to envisage the prosecution of private persons as perpetrators or accomplices in crimes of aggression, except in the very exceptional circumstance of such persons effectively controlling or directing the political or military action of the aggressor State. This limitation flows from the very construct of the prohibition on the use of force, which is an international obligation incumbent on States. As the crime of aggression was created to protect this prohibition, it is logical that it entails a necessary State conduct element and requires that the persons held responsible be part of that State apparatus. Nonetheless, one cannot deny that nowadays private persons may play a substantial role in conducting, or at least aiding, wars. For example, multiple reports point to the substantial involvement of the powerful Wagner Group in supplying Russia with manpower in its war against Ukraine.[124] In the hypothetical situation of this war

[122] K. Ambos, *Treatise on International Criminal Law*, vol. 2: *The Crimes And Sentencing* (Oxford University Press, 2014), pp. 206–8.

[123] Nerlich, 'Crime of Aggression' (n. 120).

[124] BBC News, 'What is Russia's Wagner Group of Mercenaries in Ukraine?' (3 October 2022), www.bbc.com/news/world-60947877; Hajdin, N., 'Complicity in a War of Aggression: Private Individuals' Criminal Responsibility', *Just Security* (1 April 2022), https://tinyurl.com/bdfj5bhw.

ever becoming the subject of ICC trials, the executives of the Wagner Group would probably fall outside the scope of Articles 8 *bis* and 25(3) *bis*. Even if the Article 25(3) *bis* condition were interpreted more permissively as having to reflect the parameters of an accused's functions within the State apparatus (i.e. effectively controlling or directing some, but not all, aspects of the State's political or military action), it would be extremely difficult, if not impossible, to maintain and show that the executives of the Wagner Group controlled or directed any such aspects of Russian military or political action. Mere involvement in policy decisions would not be sufficient to satisfy the condition of Article 25(3) *bis*, even under the aforementioned more permissive interpretation.

## 15.6 Conclusion

State responsibility for *jus ad bellum* breaches follows the general principles of the law on responsibility. Questions remain as to the effectiveness of the various forms of implementing such responsibility, especially in relation to individual counter-measures and retorsions as well as collective sanctions. The responsibility of international organizations for *jus ad bellum* breaches is much more problematic, as there are no functioning mechanisms for implementing such responsibility. Armed groups, despite their increasing relevance in the *jus ad bellum* context, do not possess the legal personality and legal capacity to be held responsible for their acts of armed force. Finally, the ICC Statute creates the possibility of prosecuting individuals under international criminal law for perpetrating or assisting the crime of aggression, but such prosecutions are not foreseeable in the near future.

# PART V

# Concluding Remarks

# 16

# Conclusions

## 16.1 What We Set Out to Do

As set out in Chapter 1, we wrote this book out of a conviction that international law is a coherent and interlocking system (a proverbial 'metro map' with different coloured lines intersecting and serving different destinations), in which the law on the use of force (*jus ad bellum*) plays a central role. To this end, throughout this book we examined the *jus ad bellum* not only under a microscope but also through a telescope, to see how it is connected to the wider international legal system.

We started with a brief review of the historical evolution of the rules relating to the use of force (Part I), after which we delved into the contemporary scope (Part II) and controversies (Part III) of the *jus ad bellum*, before finishing with a wide-ranging analysis of the place of *jus ad bellum* in the international legal system (Part IV). The findings of these parts are detailed below.

We embarked on our microscopic and telescopic review with the hope that it would be a worthwhile contribution to the ongoing debate on issues relating to the use of force and thus benefit the relevant academic community. While we did not write this book in the form of a manual on how to apply the law in a practical setting, we aimed to provide clear takeaways on each topic we analysed, hoping that this would assist the practitioner community in providing usable answers to hard questions. Finally, we wrote this book in the hope that it would become an important research tool for any (post-)graduate-level student or PhD candidate who is interested in the topic.

In Section 16.2, we briefly summarize the main takeaway points for each chapter. On that basis, in Section 16.3 we then set out our conclusions regarding the function and place of the law regulating the use of force in the international legal system. Finally, in Section 16.4 we provide a brief analysis of the relevance of *jus ad bellum* in the light of the war between Russia and Ukraine.

## 16.2 Takeaway Points from the Chapters

In Part I, we provided an introduction to the book and a historical background to the contemporary legal framework governing the use of force.

In Chapter 1, we described the purpose, structure, intended audience and methodology of this book.

In Chapter 2, we followed through the history of the Western just war tradition, from its ancient roots to its Christian, and later secular, natural law precepts. We did this in recognition of the fact that this tradition forms the basis of the contemporary international law on the use of force. We concluded in this chapter that although the just war tradition was gradually replaced by positive law and a 'balance-of-power' system starting in the seventeenth century, many of its elements endured and remained at the base of the contemporary discourse on the morality and/or legality of war. For instance, the limitation of just causes to defensive wars has informed centuries of moral and legal doctrine on the legitimacy and legality of self-defence, culminating in today's Charter- and custom-based exception to the prohibition to use force. Equally, contemporary arguments favouring armed interventions for humanitarian purposes have, at their core, an implicit natural law and just cause rationale – a responsibility to protect people from large-scale human rights violations. Alongside these just war elements, other concepts presented in this chapter have also survived into contemporary law on the use of force. For example, the balance-of-power system embodied in the Concert of Europe foreshadowed the collective security systems of both the League of Nations and the United Nations in the twentieth century. Likewise, the nineteenth-century movement towards peaceful dispute settlement and the prevention of war laid the early foundations for twentieth-century efforts to regulate and prohibit war.

In Chapter 3, we traced the evolution of the law governing the use of force from the end of the First World War to the adoption of the UN Charter. We briefly evoked the creation of the League of Nations, as well as its successes, failures and final demise, along with the adoption and impact of the Kellogg-Briand Pact. The chapter shed light on the differences between the prohibitions at the core of the League Covenant and the Kellogg-Briand Pact, on the one hand, and the Charter, on the other. It also delved into the debate around and understanding given to the Charter drafters' prohibition on the use of force, which help in identifying the elements and considerations that lay at the basis of that ground-breaking rule introduced in the first half of the twentieth century. These conclusions served for the subsequent chapters' analysis of how that prohibition has since been interpreted and adapted.

In Part II, we examined the contemporary *jus ad bellum*, consisting of the prohibition on the threat and use of force and the two recognized exceptions to that prohibition.

In Chapter 4, we discussed the content and function of the prohibition on the use or threat of force. The text of Article 2(4) of the Charter has given rise to some controversy, but there is general agreement as to its meaning and the need to interpret the prohibition broadly.

The most important takeaway point regarding the prohibition is that it is almost universally acknowledged as having a peremptory character. That is more than just a label; it means that attempts to alter or do away with all or part of the prohibition are void unless the entire international community accedes to any changes. It also means that no use of force by a State against another State or across an international boundary or demarcation line has any claim to legality unless it can be plausibly based on one of the two generally acknowledged 'exceptions' to the prohibition or is an exercise of extraterritorial law enforcement with an established legal basis against a non-State actor. So, claims to use force for the settlement of territorial disputes, for the promotion of human rights and democracy, to 'de-nazify' a particular country or on any other pretext are illegal and fall under the prohibition. The importance of the prohibition on the threat or use of force should not be under-estimated; it is one of the defining features of the contemporary international legal order. It is what sets the current legal order apart from preceding eras when recourse to force was seen as a legitimate instrument of State policy or a measure of retribution for 'a wrong received'. Despite its obituary being repeatedly pronounced by international lawyers reacting to instances of its violation, the prohibition is nevertheless still alive and functioning nearly three quarters of a century after it was adopted – albeit not always as effectively as one would wish. It is undeniable that the rule has been repeatedly violated since it was adopted, but this is true of virtually any rule of law. Moreover, the fact that no State has ever repudiated the prohibition and that virtually all uses of force are based – justifiably or not – on one of the accepted legal grounds for use of force, so as not to appear in violation of this cardinal rule, merely reinforces the continued legal validity and importance of the prohibition.

In Chapters 5 and 6, the two recognized legal bases for the use of force were examined in depth. The UN collective security system and the right of self-defence are complementary to each other and in fact serve to underline the basic object and purpose of the Charter (i.e. to preserve peace and limit the use of armed force to collective measures and self-defence). In connection with the maintenance of international peace and security, we underlined that both the far-reaching powers of the UN Security Council (UNSC, Security Council) and the inherent and implicit limitations on those powers are built into the Charter and reflect the state of international relations. We also discussed how that system has evolved since the Charter was adopted and the role it plays in maintaining international peace and security through a variety of measures ranging from enforcement action to consensual peacekeeping. With regard to self-defence, we discussed its dual legal basis and the contending positions on several controversial issues, including authorship of an armed attack and the relationship of an armed attack to the use of force. We also examined how the principles of necessity, proportionality and immediacy apply in the *ad bellum* context, the modalities of exercising self-defence and the geographical and temporal scope of its application. There can be no doubt that contrary to what is sometimes argued, the right of self-defence performs an essential function and has a central place in the *jus ad bellum*. It provides States with sufficient scope to defend themselves, including against novel threats (such as digital or cyber warfare). Most importantly, notwithstanding the controversies alluded to above, the right of self-defence is well-settled law, on which there is general agreement. Nevertheless, it is important also to re-emphasize its fundamental purpose and scope. It is not, and should not be(come), a licence for a State to wage preventive war, a pretext for it to establish, maintain or reassert a modern-day version of imperial hegemony or an instrument of retribution for real or imagined past wrongs that may have been committed against it.

In Part III, we examined some of the most contentious issues relating to the use of force.

In Chapter 7, the question of whether there is a legally sanctioned right of humanitarian intervention to halt large-scale human rights violations was examined. We determined that, in the absence of a mandate by the Security Council, no recognized right allowing for such intervention exists, whether on the basis of an existing or emerging customary rule or on any other purported basis. Nonetheless, we opined that the unlawfulness of such interventions could be 'mitigated' in cases of large-scale human rights violations, where there was no likelihood of UNSC-mandated or -authorized enforcement measures and where the intervention was proportionate, in terms of both how it was conducted and its likely effects on internal and international security and stability. In such a case, the intervention – while remaining unlawful – could have a greater or lesser measure of legitimacy depending on the circumstances and the way it was conducted.

In Chapter 8, we discussed the legality of intervention for the purpose of rescuing and evacuating nationals of the intervening State in response to acute danger to their lives or safety. While we rejected a right of 'protection of nationals' as incompatible with the prohibition on the use of force, we concluded that in situations where there was an acute danger to the safety of nationals due to internal unrest or conflict, and the consent of the State where the nationals were at risk was unlikely, an emergency evacuation that was not directed against the State where the evacuation was taking place was excusable under the rubric of a 'state of necessity'. We also concluded that when nationals are directly attacked or taken hostage as a means of coercing their parent State, this can constitute an attack on their parent State justifying a proportionate and necessary forcible intervention in self-defence to neutralize the direct threat and move them to safety. A further condition for any such evacuation or rescue operation is that there is a genuine link of nationality.

In Chapter 9, we discussed armed reprisals outside a situation of armed conflict. After a brief overview of the history of reprisals by individuals or communities against foreigners or their communities, the chapter traced the evolution and legality of inter-State armed reprisals both before and after the adoption of the UN Charter. We concluded that since the adoption of the UN Charter armed reprisals in time of peace have remained prohibited under international law, despite various instances of State practice and doctrinal opinion proposing their limited legality in certain circumstances. Such instances of State practice included the 2017 and 2018 US air strikes against Syrian targets in response to the use of chemical weapons by the Syrian government. Despite such instances, we remained of the opinion that the evolution of post-Charter State practice did not signal the emergence of a new customary rule legalizing reprisals in certain situations. We nonetheless concluded that where there were overriding humanitarian considerations and no other feasible alternatives, reprisals resorted to in a proportionate manner to coerce a State to respect its obligations and stop egregious human rights violations could, to a certain extent, be excused and not condemned in any significant way.

In Chapter 10, we discussed the implications that weapons of mass destruction (WMDs) were purported to have for the international law governing the use of force. We looked at the definition of the term WMD and briefly mentioned past uses of such weapons. We then analysed a number of instances of State practice involving the use or threatened use of nuclear and chemical weapons, including in the war against Iraq, the 2007 Israeli air strike in Syria and the 2017 and 2018 US air strikes against Syrian targets. We also provided a brief overview of the role of nuclear deterrence in the *jus ad bellum*. On these bases, we drew conclusions on the implications of these instances had for the law governing the use of force. We concluded that any use of force against the possession or use of WMDs should also accord with Article 2(4) of the Charter and, in particular, with the exceptions thereto (i.e. collective enforcement measures and self-defence). We also emphasized that the reviewed instances of State practice had all pushed against, and in some cases clearly exceeded, the limits set out in the prohibition of force and the recognized 'exceptions' to it. They were precedents only in the sense that they happened. We concluded that the indisputably abhorrent effects of WMDs were not in themselves a justification for ignoring the law on the use of force and that the relatively narrow scope of the exceptions to the prohibition against the use force served the very important purpose of preserving international peace and security. We admitted, however, that the *jus ad bellum* was shaped by the will of States, which, if sufficiently consistent and coherent, could lead to new treaty obligations or new customary rules. In the case of WMDs, it remains to be seen whether their feared nature and effects will result in an alteration of the existing limits to the *jus ad bellum*.

In Chapter 11, the impact (or lack of impact) of new technologies and methods of warfare and (armed) coercion on the *jus ad bellum* was the focus of attention. There can be no doubt, we concluded, that the law applies just as much to them as it does to more conventional uses of armed force – albeit with certain modifications to take account of the different effects such technologies and methods of coercion pose. We concluded that cyber warfare is now generally recognized as being subject to the law relating to the use of force and that the modalities of its application are fairly well established. We also determined that 'autonomous weapons' incorporating artificial intelligence pose few challenges to the *jus ad bellum*, regardless of the controversy they may cause when it comes to the application of the law of armed conflict. This is because determinations relating to the use of force are matters of State policy, reserved in most cases to a State's leadership and not to any weapons system. Remotely controlled vehicles, especially aerial drones, have on the other hand increased the likelihood of the application of inter-State force because of their specific characteristics, including in situations where their use is of questionable legality. Hypersonic weapons, we determined, are also potentially destabilizing due to the difficulties they present when they are to be countered and the pressure they can exert on the temporal scope of self-defence. But they may also be somewhat over-hyped – as well as being hypersonic – since it remains unclear how well they are likely to be able to perform in reality. The present conflict between Russia and Ukraine has reportedly seen their use, but hitherto with little added effect as far as can be determined. Regarding hybrid warfare, we concluded that it is most effective in situations below the threshold of force, where the grey areas of the law allow ill-intentioned States to engage in forms of coercion that can disrupt their opponents and advance their interests, especially if there is a clear power gap between the State applying the pressure and its target(s). By contrast, once the threshold of open force is crossed, hybrid warfare becomes essentially another name for irregular warfare, which is nothing new or particularly challenging from a legal perspective.

In Part IV, we examined how the law relating to the use of force applies in relation to the legal regimes that govern State sovereignty, the use of the international commons and other areas subject to special legal regimes, the legal regimes that govern the application of force inside and outside the context of conducting hostilities in an armed conflict, the rights and duties of non-participating States in an armed conflict and the law of international responsibility. In connection with the latter, some attention was also given to the relationship between the *jus ad bellum* and the crime of aggression under international criminal law.

In Chapter 12, we first examined how the principle and rule of State sovereignty (defined, as in the *Island of Palmas* arbitral award, as independence, signifying plenary authority over the State's territory) provided the basis for a State's consent or invitation to another State or an international organization to conduct a military operation directed against a non-State entity on the former State's territory. The conditions for lawful consent or invitation were divided between those that are integral to the legal system, irrespective of any other considerations, and those that are dependent on the factual context or are of a more procedural character. There is, we argued, ample State practice demonstrating that States have the competence to lawfully consent to outside intervention or to request assistance in using force against a non-State entity on their territory, including in situations of internal armed conflict.

The exercise of this competence was conditional only on the intervening/consenting State not violating a peremptory norm of general application or any other rule binding on them.

Second, we examined how the principle of sovereignty and State authority over territory empowers a State to take action to, inter alia, halt any unauthorized incursion into its territory (including its national airspace and internal waters) by foreign military personnel, vehicles, aircraft or vessels; end any exercise of non-innocent passage by foreign warships in its territorial sea; and enforce the departure of any military unit, aircraft or vessel on its territory without its consent and any warship which refuses to comply with the regime of innocent passage after being summoned to do so. We determined that this power is inherent in the sovereign authority of the State over its territory and allows for measures of enforcement short of actual use of force. We also concluded that in the event an intruding military unit, aircraft or warship refuses to comply with instructions to identify itself and end its unlawful presence or passage and/or constitutes a reasonably significant threat to State security, this triggers the right of self-defence and allows the use of force to halt the incursion.

Chapter 13 explored the application of the law relating to the use of force in the international commons (consisting of the high seas, international airspace and outer space) and in certain areas subject to specific legal regimes (exclusive economic zone, international straits, Antarctica) and its interaction with the legal regimes that govern those spaces.

In relation to the maritime domain, we discussed how the paradigm of law enforcement has a primary role in regulating the use of force outside the comparatively rare instances of States engaging in hostilities at sea in the context of an armed conflict. In that context we discussed how the functional jurisdiction allocated to coastal States under the UN Law of the Sea Convention (UNCLOS) authorizes them to exercise law enforcement over non-State vessels in the maritime zones adjacent to their coast in relation to the specific rights they enjoy under UNCLOS. We also discussed how the rights of coastal States relate to the rights of other States to engage in lawful passage through their territorial waters and engage in the exercise of high seas freedom of navigation, overflight and other activities in the EEZ, provided they exercise due regard and avoid forcible interference.

With respect to the law relating to the use of force between States, we concluded that the same rights and duties regulating the use of armed force apply at sea as elsewhere, but that the specific legal regime of

UNCLOS and other relevant conventions calling for a balancing of the interests of all States, together with the specific characteristics of the maritime domain, require that States take all feasible precautionary measures – over and above those set out in the law of armed conflict in relation to targeting – to take account of and respect the rights enjoyed by all States when lawfully exercising force at sea.

As regards international airspace, we pointed out that all States have the right to engage in civil aviation and in military and related activities in international airspace. State aircraft must show due regard for air traffic control regulations, despite not being bound by them. They may not enter another State's national airspace without authorization. By contrast, civil aircraft do not violate a State's sovereignty by entering another State's airspace in violation of aerial regulations or entry requirements, and although they may be intercepted over national airspace and instructed to land, the use of armed force to enforce any such regulations or instructions against a civil aircraft in flight is – barring exceptional circumstances – strictly prohibited under the Chicago Convention on Civil Aviation, the law on the use of force and human rights law. Any use of force impacting on the rights of all States to use international airspace must be limited to what is strictly required to achieve the lawful goal of warding off an armed attack or carrying out a mandate authorized by the Security Council.

Outer space extending from approximately 100 km above the Earth's surface is open to use by all States, subject to the rules set out in the 1967 Outer Space Treaty (OST), which has come to reflect customary law binding all States. In contrast to the 1959 Antarctic Treaty, which reserves Antarctica for use to peaceful ends and effectively demilitarizes it, we pointed out that the OST does not preclude the use of outer space for military purposes. In the zone of 'orbital space' adjacent to the Earth's atmosphere there are several thousand operational satellites in orbit, a substantial number of which perform a military or dual-use function, so military use of orbital space is pervasive and well established. But we also concluded that the prohibition of military bases, exercises and weapons testing on the Moon or celestial bodies – viewed against the background of the infinite size of outer space and the object and purpose of the OST – are compelling reasons to view outer space beyond the narrow band of orbital space as an area reserved for peaceful purposes and that any interplanetary or other spacecraft engaged in scientific exploration is or should be immune from attack.

We also concluded that any use of force against a satellite in orbit would likely constitute an armed attack if it had significant long-term effects, and that a use of force against a satellite in orbit – that results in its physical destruction – would be disproportionate under the law on the use of force in all but the most overriding situations of necessity. Such use of force would inevitably violate the rights of third States under the law of outer space and the law of armed conflict on account of the long-term effects it would have on all other users and uses of space due to space debris potentially causing irreparable harm to other satellites, space vehicles and space platforms.

In Chapter 14, we examined how the law on the use of force (*jus ad bellum*) interacts with the law of armed conflict (IHL/LOAC/*jus in bello*) and international human rights law (IHRL). We also looked at how these three branches of law act in parallel not only to determine whether force may be resorted to but also to regulate how, when and where it may be applied. In that context, we discussed how the separation of the *jus ad bellum* from the *jus in bello* is based on the principle of belligerent equality. We explained that this principle signifies merely that the parties to an international armed conflict are subject to the same 'rights' and obligations under IHL/LOAC. It does not mean that once force is resorted, the *jus ad bellum* ceases to be applicable throughout the duration of the use of force. We also explained how this is relevant to targeting and to the geographical and temporal scope of the application of force. In this respect, *jus ad bellum* serves as a parallel and additional restraint to the targeting rules and principles under IHL/LOAC.

We also determined that, outside the context of the conduct of hostilities in an armed conflict, the legal regime of IHRL is the default applicable standard for the application of force both (i) within the context of an armed conflict where there is effective control over a particular area, individual or group of persons and (ii) in relation to the use of force in the context of law enforcement, such as enforcing an embargo at sea or conducting a peace operation that had not become party to an armed conflict. We pointed out that a lawful resort to force under *jus ad bellum* would prevent the use of force from being deemed arbitrary and therefore unlawful per se under IHRL, provided it complied with human rights law standards of necessity and proportionality – adjusted, where necessary, to take account of the specific circumstances, which might not necessarily be comparable to those obtaining in a domestic law enforcement situation. Nevertheless, those standards would always be substantially more restrictive than those under IHL/LOAC. In determining where the threshold of applicability of IHL/LOAC lies, we examined the contending positions and concluded that a reasonably significant and/or protracted use of force between two or more States, or between a State and an organized armed group, would in any event trigger the applicability of IHL/LOAC alongside the *jus ad bellum* and IHRL, and that it would be the primary applicable legal regime with respect to the conduct of hostilities between the parties to an armed conflict.

Finally, we examined how the *jus ad bellum* has substantially modified the obligations of States under the traditional law of neutrality. Where neutrality formerly required that a State not party to an armed conflict refrain from any action supporting or prejudicing the war effort of the parties to an international armed conflict, this position was hardly tenable under the contemporary legal regime relating to the use of force. Not only do States have the right to directly assist the victim of an armed attack by engaging in collective self-defence at the victim's request, but there is equally no rule of international law prohibiting them from providing support to the victim of an armed attack that does not amount to a direct intervention in the conflict. The law of neutrality does retain some relevance, however, particularly in relation to the exercise of hostilities at sea, in so far as the arguably partially antiquated law of naval warfare remains legally relevant.

As to the question of at what point the rendering of support by a third State would make it a party to the conflict, we argued that if the support given by a third State to a victim of unlawful attack or aggression constitutes (or is perceived as) a direct intervention in the conflict, it will clearly open the possibility that the disadvantaged belligerent party will view this as a reason to conduct hostilities against the intervening State under the principle of belligerent equality underlying IHL/LOAC. That, however, is a factually driven situation rather than a normative one, in that once hostilities are engaged in between two States, IHL/LOAC becomes applicable. We also determined that the law of naval warfare provisions permitting measures directed against the commerce and economy of the adversary, such as a blockade, would be limited to situations in which the scale of the ongoing or imminent attack or the seriousness of the threat to or breach of the peace were such that the principles of necessity and proportionality a*d bellum* did not stand in the way of their application – assuming that body of law was still relevant and there was no feasible or adequate alternative in the circumstances.

In Chapter 15, we discussed international responsibility for breach of *jus ad bellum* obligations. We examined the notion of responsibility from the perspective of public international law for States and international organizations and from the perspective of international criminal law for individuals. We also touched upon the lack of legal personality of armed groups for *jus ad bellum* purposes. We concluded that State responsibility for *jus ad bellum* breaches followed the general principles of the law on responsibility. Questions remained concerning the effectiveness of the various forms of implementing such responsibility, especially in relation to individual counter-measures and retorsions, as well as collective sanctions. We further found that the responsibility of international organizations for *jus ad bellum* breaches was much more problematic, as there were no functioning mechanisms of implementing such responsibility. Finally, we noted that the ICC Statute made it possible to prosecute individuals under international criminal law for perpetrating or assisting the crime of aggression, but that such prosecutions were not foreseeable in the near future.

## 16.3 The Function and Place of the Law Relating to the Use of Force in the International Legal System

International law is a complex system of interrelated legal sub-systems that share a common set of attributes and characteristics. This is what makes it a legal – as opposed to some other type of – construct. These attributes and characteristics include – to name but some of the most fundamental – the binding force of the rules contained in the system; the manner in which the rules come into being; the way they are recognized as such, interpreted and applied (including to whom, to what and, in some cases, when and where they are applicable); and the consequences of the rules being breached. The question of how to address some of the problems raised by the fragmentation of international law as a consequence of its continued expansion and specialization has received expert attention and guidance, notably from the International Law Commission and in the work of various scholars.[1] We have tried to apply their findings when examining the functioning of the law on the use of force. We did this on the premise that international treaties and rules of customary international law retain their validity when armed

[1] On the problems raised by fragmentation and the views of the International Law Commission, see 'Fragmentation of International Law: Problems Arising from Diversification and Expansion of International Law; Report of the Study Group of the International Law Commission, Finalized by Martti Koskenniemi', UN Doc. A/CN.4/L.682 and Add. 1 (2006).

force is resorted to and that therefore the rules belonging to other subsystems of international law are relevant to the interpretation and application of that body of law and vice versa. Moreover, since the law does not exist in a vacuum or a self-contained bubble, it is obviously influenced by and interacts with other factors. The law on the use of force is a case in point: the power relationships and conflicting and coinciding interests among States, the shared and conflicting values of States and their inhabitants, and the impact of historical experience and technological developments all have an influence on how the law is perceived, interpreted and applied.

The starting point for our examination of the function of the law on the use of force within the contemporary international legal system was the prohibition on the threat or use of force in the relations between States. The scope of the prohibition and its direct connection to the other fundamental purposes and principles set out in the UN Charter all point to the need to interpret the prohibition broadly and comprehensively. Furthermore, the prohibition must be viewed alongside the two recognized bases for using force in international relations: collective security measures under Chapter VII of the Charter and the right of States to defend themselves against armed attack. The prohibition and its recognized 'exceptions' are complementary and serve the same fundamental purpose – as well as providing the only legal bases for the use of force by one State against another. They serve as linchpins in the contemporary legal order, along with the principle of the sovereign equality of States and the fundamental principle of humanity underlying both human rights law and the law of armed conflict. Moreover, any resort to force is further regulated by the principles of necessity and proportionality *ad bellum*, according to which force must be limited to what is required to ward off (a threat of) an armed attack or address a threat or breach of the peace as determined by the Security Council. The same principles also have an impact on the scope of application of force, both within and outside the context of an armed conflict, including on the geographical and temporal dimensions of uses of armed force. That brings it into a direct relationship with both IHL/LOAC and IHRL, notwithstanding their separate spheres of application and distinct functions.

This means that any resort to force must comply with both the law on the use of force and the applicable legal regime(s) that govern its application. Although separate, the latter together determine the circumstances in which force may be resorted to and its personal, geographical and temporal scope of application. As we demonstrated, the law on the use of force is relevant not only to the question of whether and for what purpose armed force may be lawfully resorted to but also, alongside IHL/LOAC, to targeting and to how long and where force may be resorted to in any situation that involves the conduct of hostilities in an armed conflict. We also demonstrated that in any other situation where armed force is resorted to outside the paradigm of hostilities in an armed conflict, the default legal regime for the application of force is IHRL. In that context, the law on the use of force serves a dual function, as it provides a legal basis for resort to force and thus prevents it from being deemed arbitrary and *ipso facto* unlawful under IHRL. The law on the use of force also influences the determination of whether an actual application of force was necessary and proportionate in the sense that if it does not meet the requirements of necessity and proportionality *ad bellum* it will automatically be disproportionate under IHRL. Hence, whenever force is resorted to, there is interplay, not only between IHL/LOAC and IHRL but also between those two regimes and the law on the use of force, requiring that they be applied coherently and concurrently, albeit separately.[2]

Moreover, as we explained earlier, uses of force which partially or wholly occur in international waters, airspace or outer space will also interact with the legal regimes that govern those areas. Since these areas are shared and used by all States, the rights of all other States enter the equation and must be given due regard. This goes beyond the rather obvious obligation not to use force against the territory of a third State or against the vessels, aircraft and space vehicles and platforms under the flag of a third State. The rights and interests of these States must be given due regard by the State (or international organization) resorting to force. Hence, the States' rights as users of such common spaces, their commerce and other rights and interests must not be subjected to more interference or restriction than is strictly required to effectively ward off an armed attack or address a specific threat to, or breach of, the peace and security. The rights of non-participants in an armed conflict do not (temporarily) cease to apply simply because two or more States find themselves in a situation where force is being resorted to between them. We pointed out that neutrality law, as set out in the Hague Conventions V and XIII of 1907[3] and customary law dating back to the eighteenth and nineteenth

[2] See Chapter 14.

[3] Hague Convention (V) Respecting the Rights and Duties of Neutral Powers and Persons in Case of War on Land (The Hague, 18 October 1907); Hague Convention (XIII) Concerning the Rights and Duties of Neutral Powers in Naval War (The Hague, 18 October 1907).

centuries, used to be the governing standards between parties to an armed conflict and States outside that conflict. As a result of the contemporary *jus ad bellum*, the nowadays much increased interdependence between States and the exponential expansion of the scope of international law, neutrality law is no longer the primary answer to how the rights and interests of third States must be respected and given due consideration by States resorting to armed force. This means that in addition to, and where necessary in lieu of, traditional neutrality law, the rights and obligations of both participating and non-participating States in an armed conflict must also be found in the legal regimes that govern the use of force, the law of the sea, the law of civil aviation and the law relating to outer space, to the extent those regimes are relevant and applicable in a given situation.[4]

This interplay and interrelationship between different legal sub-systems poses significant challenges in determining how the rules of these sub-systems must be applied concurrently, how the obligations they impose and any rights they may generate relate to each other and how any conflicts that may arise between specific provisions or obligations can best be resolved. The tools of legal methodology will provide a basis for resolving such conflicts and indicating how the rules and principles from different legal regimes and sub-systems can best be interpreted and applied to ensure that they are each given all due consideration and that due regard is given to the rights and obligations of all parties. They will also assist in ensuring that no more force is used than the situation requires, with the least possible impact on any rights and obligations that are applicable to any affected party or individual under international law.

These tools include the rules governing the interpretation of treaty and customary law, legal principles such as the principle of complementarity, the obligation to give the fullest possible legal effect to any applicable rule and the principle of 'systemic harmonization or integration', which is one of the most useful and widely accepted ways of addressing the problems posed by legal fragmentation.[5] Essentially, this amounts to interpreting and applying any rule or principle that

[4] See Chapters 13 and 14.

[5] 'Fragmentation of International Law' (n. 1), paras. 33–43. On systemic harmonization/integration, see P. Merkouris, 'Principle of Systemic Integration', in *Max Planck Encyclopedia of Public International Law* (Oxford Public International Law, last updated August 2020), https://tinyurl.com/4f9d8uym. See also Article 32(2)(c) of the Vienna Convention on the Law of Treaties (Vienna, 23 May 1969), https://tinyurl.com/3rfzfupn.

arises in one instrument or sub-system in the light of any other applicable rules of international law that interact with it. Finally, where there is a direct conflict between two specific rules from different legal regimes, the principles of *lex posterior* and *lex specialis* can assist in resolving the conflict. Nevertheless, contrary to what is sometimes argued, the principle of *lex specialis* is not a trump card dictating that the rules of 'peacetime' international law are always overridden by those relating to the use of force and/or the law of armed conflict – even when there may be a direct conflict between the two. This will be the case only where there is a genuine conflict that cannot be resolved by harmonizing the rules and the only reasonable solution lies in setting a rule from one regime aside and giving precedence to a more specific rule in a given situation.[6]

To illustrate, in Chapter 13 we opined that the limitation of the military use of outer space to the orbital space in the OST means that the reservation of the Moon and celestial bodies for peaceful purposes applies also to lunar and interplanetary space. Consequently, we argued that in no circumstances can there be any cogent reason to allow outer space beyond orbital space to be used for military purposes, including armed force, and that astronauts engaged in space exploration should be treated in accordance with Article V of the OST, which recognizes them as 'envoys of mankind', requires that they be given every possible assistance and that they and their spacecraft must be returned without delay to the State of registry of the space vehicle in the event they land on another State's territory. On the basis of the principle of systemic harmonization and the rules of treaty interpretation, and given the function and scope of application of the *lex specialis* principle, the protected status of a space vehicle engaged in a mission of scientific exploration and the corresponding status of the astronauts as 'envoys of mankind' would take precedence over any rule allowing for the use of force against a space vehicle if it had a formal military status, or against the crew thereof as members of the armed forces, or their being made prisoners of war upon capture if there happened to be an armed conflict in progress and they fell into the hands of the adversary party upon re-entering the Earth's atmosphere and landed on enemy territory. The basic purpose underlying the law on the use of force would not allow for the use of force in such a situation, since using force against an unarmed space vehicle engaged in a scientific mission in no way contributes to warding off an armed attack. Likewise, no valid military purpose under IHL/LOAC

[6] 'Fragmentation of International Law' (n. 1), paras. 98–122.

would be served by setting aside the special protected status of astronauts under the Outer Space Treaty – unless the space vehicle and its crew were clearly engaged in a military mission that seriously and directly prejudiced the security of the State faced with this choice of either using force and/or capturing them or treating them as 'envoys of mankind' entitled to special protection.[7]

## 16.4 Relevance of the Law on the Use of Force in the Light of the War between Russia and Ukraine

Without going into an in-depth examination of the ongoing war between the Russian Federation and Ukraine, a brief examination of how the topics discussed in this book relate to that conflict may serve as a reminder of the central importance the law on the use of force plays, even when it is being manifestly violated, as in this case.

The armed conflict between Russia and Ukraine started in February 2014 when Russian troops employing techniques of hybrid warfare seized Crimea and an armed insurrection by ethnic Russian citizens of Ukraine, with the substantial backing and some direct participation of Russian forces, broke out in some parts of the Donbas region in east Ukraine. This insurrection settled down into a protracted and relatively low-intensity proxy war between Russia and Ukraine.[8] The seizure of Crimea constituted a direct armed attack (see Chapter 6); it was a serious violation of Article 2(4) and there is a good case for qualifying it as an act of aggression (see Chapters 4 and 15). The substantial Russian involvement in the Donbas insurrection and the level of its support and control over the separatists constituted an indirect armed attack (see Chapter 6), on top of the direct armed attack already mentioned. The use of hybrid tactics, including clandestine support for the separatists, cyber warfare and encroachment on Ukrainian use of the Black Sea relate directly to the examination of such means of coercion in Chapter 11.

In February 2022, Russia initiated a full-scale invasion of Ukraine on the pretext of responding to an alleged genocidal situation against ethnic

[7] This question was put forward by Prof. Marten Zwanenburg during his inaugural lecture at the University of Amsterdam on 14 December 2022. See M. Zwanenburg, 'Et inter astra vigent leges: Het juridisch kader voor militaire operaties in de ruimte' (2021) 190(4) *Militaire Spectator* 181–91, at 190, https://tinyurl.com/2u3t4dfs.

[8] N. Walker, 'Conflict in Ukraine: A Timeline (2014–present)' UK House of Commons Library Research Briefing (24 February 2023), https://tinyurl.com/zhw7frcy.

Russians in the Donbas and elsewhere in Ukraine (see Chapter 7) and under the guise of protecting ethnic Russian nationals viewed by Russia as its citizens (see Chapter 8). Russia based its 'special military operation' on self-defence in response to an alleged threat of attack posed by the expansion of the North Atlantic Treaty Organization (NATO) and Ukraine's wish to enter that alliance.[9] The criteria for a lawful invocation of the right of self-defence and the modalities of its application received comprehensive attention in Chapter 6. On the basis of those criteria, it is clear that Russia had no credible basis to rely on self-defence as a justification for its invasion; it is indeed Ukraine that has the right to rely on self-defence to repel the renewed and ongoing armed attack which commenced on 24 February 2022. Russia's invasion triggered widespread international condemnation in the UN General Assembly following a vetoed resolution in the Security Council.[10] The role of both these UN organs and the powers and limits of the Security Council in the maintenance of international peace and security were discussed in Chapter 5. Russia also alleged the existence of a US-supported biological weapons facility used to develop that category of banned weapons of mass destruction (WMDs), but without providing any evidence to support these allegations. There have also been repeated veiled threats by Russia that nuclear weapons could be resorted to if its existential interests were threatened. The topic of WMDs and their relationship to the law on the use of force was examined in Chapters 9 and 10.

The shooting down of a Malaysian airliner by a Russian surface-to-air missile battery over the Donbas in July 2014, the subsequent denials of Russian involvement, the international outcry and combined investigations by national authorities and international investigators are related to the discussion in Chapter 13 of the relationship between the law on the use of force and the law of civil aviation banning the use of force against civil aircraft.[11] Likewise, the blockage of the Black Sea and the export of grain is related to the discussions on the use of force at sea and its relationship to other legal regimes in Chapters 13 and 14.[12] The use of

[9] 'Transcript: Vladimir Putin's Televised Address on Ukraine', Bloomberg News, (24 February 2022), https://tinyurl.com/mw9rmz7n.

[10] UN News, 'General Assembly Resolution Demands End to Russian Offensive in Ukraine' (2 March 2022), https://news.un.org/en/story/2022/03/1113152.

[11] R. Lewis, 'Malaysia Airlines Flight 17', *Britannica* (6 January 2023), www.britannica.com/event/Malaysia-Airlines-flight-17.

[12] K. Ahmed et al., 'The Black Sea Blockade: Mapping the Impact of War in Ukraine on the World's Food Supply – Interactive', *The Guardian* (9 June 2022), https://tinyurl.com/mr44my8n.

force in relation to the use of outer space for military purposes is illustrated by Russia's cyber hack of Ukraine's communications modem immediately prior to its invasion in February 2022 and the resulting neutralization of the Viasat link used by Ukraine for reconnaissance purposes. Such cyber acts received attention in Chapters 11 and 13.[13] The use of drones and hypersonic weapons in the context of the armed conflict also received attention in Chapter 11.[14]

The continued relevance of the law on the use of force, IHL/LOAC and IHRL and the relative irrelevance of the law of neutrality were covered in Chapter 14. Their connection to the conflict in Ukraine is self-evident in view of Ukraine's insistence on expelling Russian forces from its entire territory in the context of repelling the armed attack and the numerous allegations of serious violations of humanitarian and human rights law by Russian forces, especially in relation to the indiscriminate attacks on civilian infrastructure and in territory occupied by Russian forces. The extensive support Western States are providing to Ukraine under the banner of 'non-belligerence', 'qualified neutrality' or 'all support short of direct intervention' in the conflict is impossible to rhyme with the traditional law of neutrality, as we also discussed in Chapter 14.[15] Finally, the law of international responsibility discussed in Chapter 15 is directly related to the extensive sanctions imposed on Russia by numerous States. The potential use of frozen Russian assets to compensate Ukraine for the massive damage that has been inflicted during the conflict would face significant legal plus more practical obstacles.[16] While the chances of prosecution of the Russian leadership for the crime of aggression, which was also discussed in Chapter 15, are presently remote, that possibility might play an indirect role in relation to the conflict that is not necessarily evident now.

This overview of the ways in which the topics covered in this book relate to an ongoing international conflict illustrates how the body of law we have examined retains its importance and relevance, even in

[13] S. Cohen, 'Acid Rain Malware and Viasat Network Downtime in Ukraine: Assessing the Cyber War Threat', *Just Security* (12 September 2022), https://tinyurl.com/y4tezv5z.

[14] D. Palavenis, 'The Use of Emerging Disruptive Technologies by the Russian Armed Forces in the Ukrainian War', Air Land Sea Space Application (ALSSA) Center (1 October 2022), https://tinyurl.com/6hb5tmf5.

[15] A. Cheatham, 'A Look at Neutrality Now – and After the Ukraine War', United States Institute for Peace (28 April 2022), https://tinyurl.com/mry6vxd9.

[16] C. Mortera Martinez and Z. Meyer, 'Using Sanctioned Russian Assets to Rebuild Ukraine Will Not Be Easy', Centre for European Reform (3 August 2022), https://tinyurl.com/mwz5u7sp.

a situation such as this where there is a large degree of consensus that the resort to force by Russia constitutes a major and egregious violation of the basic principle of non-use of force in international relations.

We hope that the analysis we have provided in the preceding pages has contributed to an increased understanding of the place of the law on the use of force within the system of international law and the vital role it plays in international relations.

# BIBLIOGRAPHY

## Books and Book Chapters

Alexandrov, S., *Self-Defense against the Use of Force in International Law* (Kluwer Law International, 1996)

Allison, G. T., *Essence of Decision: Explaining the Cuban Missile Crisis* (Little, Brown, 1971)

Ambos, K., *Treatise on International Criminal Law, Volume II: The Crimes and Sentencing* (Oxford University Press, 2014)

Augustine, *Political Writings*, trans. M. W. Tkacz and D. Kries, ed. E. L. Fortin and D. Kries (Hackett, 1994)

Bartlett, C. J., *Peace, War and the European Powers 1814–1914* (Palgrave Macmillan, 1996)

Baylis, J. and Smith, S., *The Globalization of World Politics* (Oxford University Press, 2001)

Beaulac, S., *The Power of Language in the Making of International Law: The Word* Sovereignty *in Bodin and Vattel and the Myth of* Westphalia (Brill, 2004)

Bellamy, A. J., *Just Wars: From Cicero to Iraq* (Polity Press, 2006)

Bigongiari, D. (ed.), *The Political Ideas of St. Thomas Aquinas: Representative Selections* (Hafner, 1969)

Boddens Hosang, J. F. R., 'Force Protection, Unit Self-Defence and Personal Self-Defence: their Relationship to Rules of Engagement', in T. D. Gill and D. Fleck (eds.), *The Handbook of the International Law of Military Operations*, 2nd ed. (Oxford University Press, 2015), pp. 476–501

Boddens Hosang J. F. R., 'Personal Self-Defence and Rules of Engagement', in T. D. Gill and D. Fleck (eds.), *The Handbook of the International Law of Military Operations*, 2nd ed. (Oxford University Press, 2015), pp. 478–81

Boddens Hosang, J. F. R., *Rules of Engagement and the International Law of Military Operations* (Oxford University Press, 2020)

Boothby, W. H., *The Law of Targeting* (Oxford University Press, 2012)

Bothe, M., 'The Law of Neutrality', in D. Fleck (ed.), *The Handbook of International Humanitarian Law* (Oxford University Press, 2013), pp. 550–80

Bowett, D. W., *Self-Defence in International Law* (Manchester University Press, 1958)

Bowett, D. W., *United Nations Forces* (Praeger, 1964)

Bowett, D. W., 'The Use of Force for the Protection of Nationals Abroad', in A. Cassese (ed.), *The Current Legal Regulation of the Use of Force* (Nijhoff, 1986), pp. 39–56

Boyd, A., *Fifteen Men on a Powder Keg: A History of the United Nations Security Council* (Methuen, 1971)

Brownlie, I., 'Humanitarian Intervention', in J. N. Moore (ed.), *Law and Civil War in the Modern World* (John Hopkins University Press, 1974), pp. 217–28

Brownlie, I., *International Law and the Use of Force by States* (Clarendon Press, 1963)

Brownlie, I., *Principles of Public International Law* (Oxford University Press, 1990)

Brownlie, I., 'Thoughts on the Kind-Hearted Gunman', in R. Lillich (ed.), *Humanitarian Intervention and the United Nations* (University of Virginia Press, 1973), pp. 139–48

Buchan, R. and Tsagourias, N., *Regulating the Use of Force in International Law: Stability and Change* (Edward Elgar, 2021)

Bull, S., *Trench: A History of Trench Warfare on the Western Front* (Osprey, 2014)

Carus, W. S., *A Short History of Biological Warfare: From Pre-History to the 21st Century*, Center for the Study of Weapons of Mass Destruction Occasional Paper No. 12 (National Defense University Press, 2017)

Cassese, A., *International Law* (Oxford University Press, 2005)

Cathcart, B., 'Command and Control in Military Operations', in T. D. Gill and D. Fleck (eds.), *The Handbook of the International Law of Military Operations*, 2nd ed. (Oxford University Press, 2015), pp. 259–68

Chan, K., 'The Ugandan-Tanzanian War – 1978–79', in T. Ruys et al. (eds.), *The Use of Force in International Law: A Case-Based Approach* (Oxford University Press, 2018), pp. 255–68

Chang, L. and Kornbluh, P. (eds.), *The Cuban Missile Crisis, 1962: A National Security Archive Documents Reader* (New Press, 1992)

Chayes, A., *The Cuban Missile Crisis* (Oxford University Press, 1974)

Cheng, B., 'The Destruction of KAL Flight KE007, and Article 3 *Bis* of the Chicago Convention', in C. J. Cheng (ed.), *Studies in International Air Law: Collected Works of Bin Cheng* (Brill-Nijhoff, 2018), pp. 343–70

Churchill, R., Lowe, V. and Sander, A., *The Law of the Sea* (Manchester University Press, 2022)

Clark, C., *Iron Kingdom: The Rise and Downfall of Prussia, 1600–1947* (Penguin Books, 2006)

Clark, C., *The Sleepwalkers: How Europe Went to War in 1914* (Penguin Books, 2012)

Clark, R. S., 'Negotiations on the Rome Statute, 1995–98', in C. Kreß and S. Barriga (eds.), *The Crime of Aggression: A Commentary*, vol. 1 (Cambridge University Press, 2016), pp. 244–70

Clausewitz, C. von, *On War*, trans. J. J. Graham, rev. A. J. Maude (Wordsworth, 1997)

Colbert, E., *Retaliation in International Law* (King's Crown Press, 1948)

Constantinou, A., *The Right of Self-Defence under Customary International Law and Article 51 of the United Nations Charter* (Sakkoulas, 2000)

Corten, O., *Le droit contre la guerre: L'interdiction du recours à la force en droit international contemporain* (Pedone, 2008)

Corten, O., *The Law against War: The Prohibition on the Use of Force in Contemporary International Law* (Hart, 2010)

Crawford, E. and Pert, A., *International Humanitarian Law* (Cambridge University Press, 2020)

Crawford, J., *Brownlie's Principles of Public International Law* (Oxford University Press, 2019)

Crawford, J., *State Responsibility* (Cambridge University Press, 2013)

D'Amato, A., *International Law: Process and Prospect* (Transnational, 1987)

Darcy, S., 'Revival of Classical Concepts? Retaliation and Reprisal', in M. Weller (ed.), *The Oxford Handbook of the Use of Force in International Law* (Oxford University Press, 2017), pp. 890–1

Dinstein, Y., *Non-International Armed Conflicts in International Law* (Cambridge University Press, 2014)

Dinstein, Y., *War, Aggression and Self-Defence*, 6th ed. (Cambridge University Press, 2017)

Doswald-Beck, L. (ed.), *San Remo Manual on International Law Applicable to Armed Conflicts at Sea* (Cambridge University Press, 1995)

Dougherty, R., 'St. Augustine on Natural Law', in J. Crowe and C. Y. Lee (eds.), *Research Handbook on Natural Law Theory* (Edward Elgar, 2019), pp. 57–75

Dubuisson, F. and Koutroulis, V., 'The Yom Kippur War – 1973', in T. Ruys et al. (eds.), *The Use of Force in International Law: A Case-Based Approach* (Oxford University Press, 2018), pp. 189–200

Ducheine, P., 'Military Cyber Operations', in T. D. Gill and D. Fleck (eds.), *The Handbook of the International Law of Military Operations*, 2nd ed. (Oxford University Press, 2015), pp. 456–75

Dunstan, S., *Entebbe: The Most Daring Raid of Israel's Special Forces* (Rosen, 2011)

Ferrell, R. H., *Peace in Their Time: The Origins of the Kellogg-Briand Pact* (Yale University Press, 1952)

Fink, M. D., 'The Application of Force in Maritime Interception Operations', in *Maritime Interception and the Law of Naval Operations: A Study of Legal Bases and Legal Regimes in Maritime Interception Operations* (Springer, 2018), pp. 191–226

Fiore, P., *Nouveau droit international public suivant les besoins de la civilisation moderne*, 2nd ed., trans. C. Antoine, vol. 1 (A. Durant et Pedone-Lauriel, 1885)

Fox, G. H., 'Intervention by Invitation', in M. Weller (ed.), *The Oxford Handbook of the Use of Force in International Law* (Oxford University Press, 2017), pp. 816–40

Fox, G. H., 'The Vietnamese Intervention in Cambodia – 1978', in T. Ruys et al. (eds.), *The Use of Force in International Law: A Case-Based Approach* (Oxford University Press, 2018), pp. 242–54

Franchini, D. and Tzanakopoulos, A., 'The Kosovo Crisis – 1999', in T. Ruys et al. (eds.), *The Use of Force in International Law: A Case-Based Approach* (Oxford University Press, 2018), pp. 594–622

Franck, T. M., *Recourse to Force: State Action against Threats and Armed Attacks* (Cambridge University Press, 2002)

Freedman, L., 'The First Two Generations of Nuclear Strategists', in P. Paret (ed.), *Makers of Modern Strategy: From Machiavelli to the Nuclear Age* (Princeton University Press, 1986), pp. 735–78

Funck-Brentano, T. and Sorel, A., *Précis du droit des gens* (Plon, 1887)

Gardam, J., *Necessity, Proportionality and the Use of Force by States* (Cambridge University Press, 2004)

Gavouneli, M., *Functional Jurisdiction in the Law of the Sea* (Nijhoff, 2007)

Gazzini, T., *The Changing Rules on the Use of Force in International Law* (Manchester University Press, 2005)

Gentili, A., *De jure belli libri tres* (Clarendon Press, 1933)

Gestri, M., 'Sanctions Imposed by the European Union: Legal and Institutional Aspects', in N. Ronzitti (ed.), *Coercive Diplomacy, Sanctions and International Law* (Brill-Nijhoff, 2016), pp. 70–102

Gill, T. D., 'The *Jus Ad Bellum Anno* 2040: An Essay on Possible Trends and Challenges', in M. Waxman and T. Oakley (eds.), *The Future Law of Armed Conflict* (Oxford University Press, 2022), pp. 25–40

Gill, T. D., 'Non-Intervention in the Cyber Context', in K. Ziolkowski (ed.) *Peacetime Regime for State Activities in Cyberspace* (NATO CCD COE Publications, 2013), pp. 217–38

Gill, T. D., 'Peace Operations', in T. D. Gill and D. Fleck (eds.), *The Handbook of the International Law of Military Operations*, 2nd ed. (Oxford University Press, 2015), pp. 153–60

Gill, T. D., 'The Security Council', in G. Zyberi (ed.) *An Institutional Approach to the Responsibility to Protect* (Cambridge University Press, 2013), pp. 83–108

Gill, T. D., 'Some Considerations Concerning the Role of the *Ius ad Bellum* in Targeting', in P. A. L. Ducheine, M. N. Schmitt and F. P. B. Osinga (eds.), *Targeting: The Challenges of Modern Warfare* (Springer, 2016), pp. 101–19

Gill, T. D., 'The Temporal Dimension of Self-Defence: Anticipation, Pre-emption, Prevention and Immediacy', in M. N. Schmitt and J. Pejić (eds.), *International Law and Armed Conflict: Exploring the Faultlines* (Nijhoff, 2007), pp. 113–55

Gill, T. D., 'When Does Self-Defence End?', in M. Weller (ed.), *The Oxford Handbook of the Use of Force in International Law* (Oxford University Press, 2017), pp. 737–51

Gill, T. D., Haaster, J. V. and Roorda, M., 'Some Legal and Operational Considerations Regarding Remote Warfare: Drones and Cyber Warfare Revisited', in J. D. Ohlin (ed.), *Research Handbook on Remote Warfare* (Edward Elgar, 2019), pp. 298–334

Gill, T. D. and Fleck, D. (eds.), *The Handbook of the International Law of Military Operations*, 2nd ed. (Oxford University Press, 2015)

Gill, T. D. et al. (eds.), *Leuven Manual on the International Law Applicable to Peace Operations* (Cambridge University Press, 2017)

Goodrich, L. M., *The United Nations and the Maintenance of International Peace and Security* (Brookings Institution, 1955)

Goodrich L., Hambro, E. and Simons, A. P., *Charter of the United Nations: Commentary and Documents* (Columbia University Press, 1969)

Graebner, N. A. and Bennett, E. E., *The Versailles Treaty and Its Legacy: The Failure of the Wilsonian Vision* (Cambridge University Press, 2014)

Gray, C., 'The Conflict in Georgia – 2008', in T. Ruys and O. Corten (eds.), *The Use of Force in International Law: A Case-Based Approach* (Oxford University Press, 2018), pp. 712–28

Gray, C., *International Law and the Use of Force* (Oxford University Press, 2018)

Greenwood, C., 'Legality of the Use of Force: Iraq in 2003', in M. Bothe, M. E. O'Connell and N. Ronzitti (eds.), *Redefining Sovereignty: The Use of Force after the Cold War* (Transnational, 2005), pp. 399–404

Greenwood, C., 'Self-Defence and the Conduct of International Armed Conflict', in Y. Dinstein (ed.), *International Law in a Time of Perplexity: Essays in Honour of Shabtai Rosenne* (Nijhoff, 1989), pp. 273–88

Grewe, W. G., *The Epochs of International Law* (De Gruyter, 2000)

Grimm, D., *Sovereignty: The Origin and Future of a Political and Legal Concept* (Columbia University Press, 2015)

Grotius, H., *De jure belli ac pacis libri tres* (Oceana, 1964)

Grunden, W. E., 'No Retaliation in Kind: Japanese Chemical Warfare Policy in World War II', in B. Friedrich et al. (eds.), *One Hundred Years of Chemical Warfare: Research, Deployment, Consequences* (Springer, 2017), pp. 259–71

Guilfoyle, D., *Shipping Interdiction and the Law of the Sea* (Cambridge University Press, 2009)

Guttry, A. de, 'The Iran-Iraq War – 1980–88', in T. Ruys and O. Corten (eds.), *The Use of Force in International Law: A Case-Based Approach* (Oxford University Press, 2018), pp. 315–28

Hajjami, N., 'The Intervention of the United States and Other Eastern Caribbean States in Grenada – 1983', in T. Ruys and O. Corten (eds.), *The Use of Force in*

*International Law: A Case-Based Approach* (Oxford University Press, 2018), pp. 385–94

Hall, W. E., *International Law* (Clarendon Press, 1880)

Halleck, H. W., *International Law or Rules Regulating the Intercourse of States in Peace and War* (H. H. Bancroft, 1861)

Hathaway, O. A. and Shapiro, S. J., *The Internationalists and Their Plan to Outlaw War* (Penguin Books, 2018)

Hay, B. L., *Nazi-Looted Art and the Law: The American Cases* (Springer, 2017)

Hayashi, N. (ed.), *National Military Manuals on the Law of Armed Conflict* (Forum for International Criminal and Humanitarian Law, 2010)

Heffter, A. W., *Le droit international de l'Europe* (H. W. Muller / A. Cotillon et Cie, 1883)

Henderson, C., *The Use of Force and International Law* (Cambridge University Press, 2018)

Henig, R., *The Peace That Never Was: A History of the League of Nations* (Haus, 2019)

Henkin, L., *International Law: Politics and Values* (Nijhoff, 1995)

Henkin, L., 'The Use of Force: Law and US Policy', in L. Henkin et al., *Right v. Might. International Law and the Use of Force*, 2nd ed. (Council on Foreign Relations Press, 1991), pp. 37–69

Henry, E., 'The Falklands/Malvinas War – 1982', in T. Ruys and O. Corten (eds.), *The Use of Force in International Law: A Case-Based Approach* (Oxford University Press, 2018), pp. 361–72

Heraclides, A. and Dialla, A., *Humanitarian Intervention in the Long Nineteenth Century: Setting the Precedent* (Manchester University Press, 2015)

Hessbruegge, J. A., *Human Rights and Personal Self-Defense in International Law* (Oxford University Press, 2017)

Higgins, R., *The Development of International Law through the Political Organs of the United Nations* (Oxford University Press, 1963)

Higgins, R., *Problems and Process: International Law and How We Use It* (Oxford University Press, 1994)

Hiscocks, R., *The Security Council: A Study in Adolescence* (Longman, 1973)

Hofer, A., 'The Suez Crisis – 1956', in T. Ruys and O. Corten (eds.), *The Use of Force in International Law: A Case-Based Approach* (Oxford University Press, 2018), pp. 36–47

Howard, M., *The First World War. A Very Short Introduction* (Oxford University Press, 2002)

Ilgen, T. L. (ed.), *Reconfigured Sovereignty: Multi-Layered Governance in the Global Age* (Ashgate, 2003)

Jennings, R. and Watts, A., *Oppenheim's International Law* (Oxford University Press, 2008)

Jessup, P. C., *A Modern Law of Nations: An Introduction* (Macmillan, 1948)

Jones, M. A., *The Limits of Liberty: American History 1607–1980* (Oxford University Press, 1983)

Joyner D. H., 'The Implications of the Proliferation of Weapons of Mass Destruction for the Prohibition of the Use of Force', in M. Weller (ed.), *The Oxford Handbook of the Use of Force in International Law* (Oxford University Press, 2017), pp. 1034–56

Keegan, J., *The First World War* (Bodley Head, 2014)

Keegan, J., *The Second World War* (Pimlico, 1997)

Kleffner, J., 'Scope of Application of International Humanitarian Law', in D. Fleck (ed.) *The Handbook of International Humanitarian Law*, 3rd ed. (Oxford University Press, 2013), pp.50–80

Klein, N., *Maritime Security and the Law of the Sea* (Oxford University Press, 2011)

Kolesnik, D. N., 'The Development of the Right of Self-Defence', in W. E. Butler (ed.), *The Non-Use of Force in International Law* (Nijhoff, 1989), pp. 153–9

Kreß, C., 'The State Conduct Element', in C. Kreß and S. Barriga (eds.), *The Crime of Aggression: A Commentary*, vol. 1 (Cambridge University Press, 2017), pp. 412–564

Kreß, C. and Nußberger, B., 'The Entebbe Raid – 1976', in T. Ruys and O. Corten (eds.), *The Use of Force in International Law: A Case-Based Approach* (Oxford University Press, 2018), pp. 220–33

Kritsiotis, D., 'The Intervention of India into (East) Pakistan', in T. Ruys and O. Corten (eds.), *The Use of Force in International Law: A Case-Based Approach* (Oxford University Press, 2018), pp. 169–88

Laffan, R. G. D., *Select Documents of European History: 800–1492* (Henry Holt, 1929)

Lagerwall, A., 'Threats and Actual Military Strikes against Syria – 2013 and 2017', in T. Ruys and O. Corten (eds.), *The Use of Force in International Law: A Case-Based Approach* (Oxford University Press, 2018), pp. 828–54

Laity, P., *The British Peace Movement* (Oxford University Press, 2002)

Lauterpacht, H., *The Function of Law in the International Community* (Oxford University Press, orig. pub. 1933, repr. 2011)

Lauterpacht, H. (ed.), L. Oppenheim, *International Law*, vol 2 (Longmans Green., 1952)

Lieblich, E., 'On the Continuous and Concurrent Applicability of *Ad Bellum* and *In Bello* Proportionality', in C. Kreß and R. Lawless (eds.), *Necessity and Proportionality in International Peace and Security Law* (Oxford University Press, 2020), pp. 41–76

Lillich, R., 'Humanitarian Intervention: A Reply to Ian Brownlie and a Plea for Constructive Alternatives', in J. N. Moore (ed.) *Law and Civil War in the Modern World* (John Hopkins Press, 1974), pp. 229–51

Lindell, B., *Multi-Criteria Analysis in Legal Reasoning* (Edward Elgar, 2017)

Longobardo, M., 'Robust Peacekeeping Mandates: An Assessment in Light of *Jus Post Bellum*', in C. Stahn and J. Iverson (eds.), *Just Peace after Conflict:* Jus Post Bellum *and the Justice of Peace* (Oxford University Press, 2020)

Lubell, N., *Extraterritorial Use of Force against Non-State Actors* (Oxford University Press, 2010)

Machiavelli, N., *The Prince* (Collector's Library, 2004)

MacMillan, M., *Paris 1919: Six Months That Changed the World* (Random House, 2003)

Mamiani, Count, *Rights of Nations or, The New Law of European States Applied to the Affairs of Italy* (W. Jeffs, 1860)

Mattox, J. M., *Saint Augustine and the Theory of Just War* (Continuum, 2006)

McDougal, M. S. and Feliciano, F. P., *Law and Minimum World Public Order: The Legal Regulation of International Coercion* (Yale University Press, 1961)

McGoldrick, D., *From '9-11' to the 'Iraq War 2003': International Law in an Age of Complexity* (Hart, 2004)

Melzer, N. and Gaggioli, G., 'Conceptual Distinction and Overlaps between Law Enforcement and the Conduct of Hostilities', in T. D. Gill and D. Fleck (eds.), *The Handbook of the International Law of Military Operations*, 2nd ed. (Oxford University Press, 2015), pp. 63–92

Meselson, M., 'From Charles and Francis Darwin to Richard Nixon: The Origin and Termination of Anti-Plant Chemical Warfare in Vietnam', in B. Friedrich et al. (eds.), *One Hundred Years of Chemical Warfare: Research, Deployment, Consequences* (Springer, 2017), pp. 335–48

Miller, D. H., *The Peace Pact of Paris: A Study of the Briand-Kellogg Treaty* (G. P. Putnam's Sons, 1928)

Mlodoch, K., 'The Indelible Smell of Apples: Poison Gas Survivors in Halabja, Kurdistan-Iraq, and Their Struggle for Recognition', in B. Friedrich et al. (eds.), *One Hundred Years of Chemical Warfare: Research, Deployment, Consequences* (Springer, 2017), pp. 349–62

Moir, L., 'Action against Host States of Terrorist Groups', in M. Weller (ed.), *The Oxford Handbook of the Use of Force in International Law* (Oxford University Press, 2017), pp. 720–30

Moir, L., 'Israeli Airstrikes in Syria – 2003 and 2007', in T. Ruys and O. Corten (eds.), *The Use of Force in International Law: A Case-Based Approach* (Oxford University Press, 2018), pp. 662–72

Moir, L., *The Law of Internal Armed Conflict* (Cambridge University Press, 2002)

Moore, C., *Freedom of Navigation and the Law of the Sea* (Routledge, 2021)

Moore, C., 'The Use of Force', in R. Warner and S. Kaye (eds.), *Routledge Handbook of Maritime Regulation and Enforcement* (Routledge, 2015), pp. 27–40

Moore, J. N. (ed.), *Law and Civil War in the Modern World* (John Hopkins University Press, 1974)

Morris, S. J., *Why Vietnam Invaded Cambodia: Political Culture and the Causes of War* (Stanford University Press, 1999)

Mougel, N., *World War I Casualties* (REPERES – Centre européen Robert Schuman, 2011)

Mueller, K. P. et al., *Striking First: Preemptive and Preventive Attack in U.S. National Security Policy* (RAND Project Air Force, 2006)

Myjer, E. P. J. and White, N. D., 'Peace Operations Conducted by Regional Organizations and Arrangements', in T. D. Gill and D. Fleck (eds.), *The Handbook of the International Law of Military Operations*, 2nd ed. (Oxford University Press, 2015), pp. 185–209

Neff, S. C., 'A Short History of International Law', in M. D. Evans (ed.) *International Law* (Oxford University Press, 2003), pp. 48–9

Neff, S. C., *War and the Law of Nations: General History* (Cambridge University Press, 2005)

Nollkaemper, A. and Plakokefalos, I. (eds.), *Principles of Shared Responsibility in International Law: An Appraisal of the State of the Art* (Cambridge University Press, 2014)

Nussbaum, A., *A Concise History of the Law of Nations* (Macmillan, 1947)

O'Connell, M. E., 'The Crisis in Ukraine – 2014', in T. Ruys and O. Corten (eds.), *The Use of Force in International Law: A Case-Based Approach* (Oxford University Press, 2018), pp. 855–72

O'Connell, M. E., 'The Prohibition on the Use of Force', in N. D. White and C. Henderson (eds.), *Research Handbook on International Conflict and Security Law* (Edward Elgar, 2013), pp. 89–119

Ohlin, J. D. (ed.), *Research Handbook on Remote Warfare* (Edward Elgar, 2019)

Oppenheim, L. F. L., *International Law: A Treatise*, vol. 1 (Longmans Green, 1905)

Orakhelashvili, A., 'The Cuban Missile Crisis – 1962', in T. Ruys and O. Corten (eds.), *The Use of Force in International Law: A Case-Based Approach* (Oxford University Press, 2018), pp. 99–106.

Pagden, A. andLawrance, J. (eds.), Vitoria, *Political Writings* (Cambridge University Press, 1991)

Pellet, A., 'The Definition of Responsibility under International Law', in J. Crawford, A. Pellet and S. Olleson (eds.), *The Law of International Responsibility* (Oxford University Press, 2010), pp. 3–16

Phillimore, R., *Commentaries upon International Law*, vol. 1 (W. Benning, 1854)

Phillimore, R., *Commentaries upon International Law*, vol. 1 (Butterworth, 1879)

Phillimore, R., *Commentaries upon International Law*, vol. 3 (W. Benning, 1857)

Phillips, C., 'Syria', in L. Arimatsu and M. Choudhury (eds.), *The Legal Classification of the Armed Conflicts in Syria, Yemen and* Libya (Chatham House, 2014), pp. 7–19

Phillipson, C., *The International Law and Custom of Ancient Greece and Rome*, vol. 2 (Macmillan, 1911)

Pijpers, B. M. J., 'Influence Operations in Cyberspace' (PhD thesis, University of Amsterdam, 19 January 2022) https://tinyurl.com/yckx2xas

Pouw, E., 'Some Thoughts on the Notion of "Control" in "Choosing" the Paradigm of Hostilities or Law Enforcement as the Governing Legal Framework in the Use of Force in Military Operations: Is There Any', in R. Bartels et al. (eds.), *Military Operations and the Notion of Control under International Law: Lieber Amicorum Terry D. Gill* (Springer, 2021), pp. 195–217

Pradier-Fodéré, P. L., *Traité de droit international public européen et américain, suivant le progrès de la science et de la pratique contemporaines*, vol. 1 (A. Durand et Pedone-Lauriel, 1885)

*Public Papers of the Presidents of the United States: John F. Kennedy, 1962* (US Government Printing Office, 1963)

Pufendorf, S. von, *De Jjre naturae et gentium libri octo*, vol. 2 (Clarendon Press, 1934)

Pufendorf, S. von, *On the Duty of Man and Citizen According to Natural Law* (Cambridge University Press, 1991)

Quigley, J., 'The Six Day War – 1967', in T. Ruys and O. Corten (eds.), *The Use of Force in International Law: A Case-Based Approach* (Oxford University Press, 2018), pp. 131–42

Quigley, J., *The Six Day War and Israeli Self-Defense* (Cambridge University Press, 2013)

Randelzhofer, A. and Dörr, O., 'Article 2 (4)', in B. Simma et al. (eds.), *The Charter of the United Nations. A Commentary*, vol. 1 (Oxford University Press, 2012)

Reichberg, G. M., Syse, H. and Begby, E., *The Ethics of War: Classic and Contemporary Readings* (Blackwell, 2006)

Roberts, A. and Sivakumaran, S., 'The Theory and Reality of the Sources of International Law', in M. D. Evans (ed.), *International Law* (Oxford University Press, 2018), pp. 92–6

Rodin, D. and Shue, H., *Just and Unjust Warriors: The Moral and Legal Status of Soldiers* (Oxford University Press, 2010)

Ronzitti, N., 'Sanctions as Instruments of Coercive Diplomacy: An International Law Perspective', in N. Ronzitti (ed.), *Coercive Diplomacy, Sanctions and International Law* (Brill-Nijhoff, 2016), pp. 1–32

Roth, B., 'The Illegality of Pro-Democratic Invasion Pacts', in G. Fox and B. Roth (eds.), *Democratic Governance and International Law* (Cambridge University Press, 2010), pp. 328–42

Ruys, T., *'Armed Attack' and Article 51 of the UN Charter: Evolution in Customary Law and Practice* (Cambridge University Press, 2010)

Ruys, T., 'Israel's Airstrike against Iraq's Osiraq Nuclear Reactor – 1981', in T. Ruys and O. Corten (eds.), *The Use of Force in International Law: A Case-Based Approach* (Oxford University Press, 2018), pp. 329–41

Ruys, T., 'Sanctions, Retortions and Countermeasures: Concepts and International Legal Framework', in L. van den Herik (ed.), *Research Handbook on UN Sanctions and International Law* (Edward Elgar, 2016), pp. 19–51

Schabas, W. A., *An Introduction to the International Criminal Court* (Cambridge University Press, 2020)

Schabas, W., *The Trial of the Kaiser* (Oxford University Press, 2018)

Schachter, O., *International Law in Theory and Practice* (Nijhoff, 1991)

Schmaltz, F., 'Chemical Weapons Research on Soldiers and Concentration Camp Inmates in Nazi Germany', in B. Friedrich et al. (eds.), *One Hundred Years of Chemical Warfare: Research, Deployment, Consequences* (Springer, 2017), pp. 229–58

Schmitt, M. N., 'Air Law and Military Operations', in T. D. Gill and D. Fleck (eds.), *The Handbook of the International Law of Military Operations*, 2nd ed. (Oxford University Press, 2015), pp. 354–74

Schmitt, M. N., 'Targeting in Operational Law', in T. D. Gill and D. Fleck (eds.), *The Handbook of the International Law of Military Operations*, 2nd ed. (Oxford University Press, 2015), pp. 269–306

Schmitt, M. N. (ed.) *Tallinn Manual 2.0 on the International Law Applicable to Cyber Operations* (Cambridge University Press, 2017)

Schrijver, N., 'The Ban on the Use of Force in the UN Charter', in M. Weller (ed.), *The Oxford Handbook of the Use of Force in International Law* (Oxford University Press, 2017), pp. 466–87.

Scobbie, I., 'War', in J. d'Aspremont and S. Singh (eds.), *Concepts for International Law: Contributions to Disciplinary Thought* (Edward Elgar, 2019), pp. 900–12

Scott, J. S. (ed.), *Selections from Three Works of Francisco Suarez* (Clarendon Press, 1944)

Sellars, K., 'The First World War, Wilhelm II and Article 227: The Origin of the Idea of "Aggression" in International Criminal Law', in C. Kreß and S. Barriga (eds.), *The Crime of Aggression: A Commentary*, vol. 1 (Cambridge University Press, 2017), pp. 21–48

Shaw, M. N., *International Law* (Cambridge University Press, 2021)

Simma, B. et al. (eds.), *The Charter of the United Nations: A Commentary*, 2 vols. (Oxford University Press, 2012)

Siracusa, J. M., *Nuclear Weapons: A Very Short Introduction* (Oxford University Press, 2020)

Sivakumaran, S., *The Law of Non-International Armed Conflict* (Oxford University Press, 2012)

Smuts, J. C., *The League of Nations: A Practical Suggestion* (Hodder & Stoughton, 1918)

Stone, J., *Aggression and World Order* (University of California Press, 1958)

Stowel, l E. C., *Intervention in International Law* (John Byrne, 1921)

Taylor, A. J. P., *The Struggle for Mastery in Europe 1848–1918* (Oxford University Press, 1954)

Teson, F., *Humanitarian Intervention: An Inquiry into Law and Morality* (Transnational, 1997)

Thomas, H., *The Spanish Civil War* (Penguin Books, 1965)

Tibori-Szabó, K., *Anticipatory Action in Self-Defence: Essence and Limits under International Law* (Springer, 2011)

Tibori-Szabó, K., 'Control and the Right to Self-Defence against Non-State Actors', in R. Bartels et al. (eds.), *Military Operations and the Notion of Control under International Law: Lieber Amicorum Terry D. Gill* (Springer, 2021), pp. 83–105

Tibori-Szabó, K., 'The "Unwilling and Unable" Test and the Law of Self-Defence', in C. Paulussen et al. (eds.), *Fundamental Rights in International and European Law* (Springer, 2016), pp. 73–97

Trapp, R., 'The Use of Chemical Weapons in Syria: Implications and Consequences', in B. Friedrich et al. (eds.), *One Hundred Years of Chemical Warfare: Research, Deployment, Consequences* (Springer, 2017), pp. 363–75

Trent, M., *Over the Line: The Implications of China's ADIZ Intrusions in Northeast Asia* (American Federation of Scientists, 2020)

Tsagourias, N., 'The US Intervention in Panama – 1989', in T. Ruys and O. Corten (eds.), *The Use of Force in International Law: A Case-Based Approach* (Oxford University Press, 2018), pp. 426–38

Tsagourias, N. and Buchan, R. (eds.), *Research Handbook on International Law and Cyberspace* (Edward Elgar, 2021)

Twiss, T., *Law of Nations Considered as Independent Political Communities: On the Rights and Duties of Nations in Time of Peace* (Oxford University Press, 1860)

Twiss, T., *Law of Nations Considered as Independent Political Communities: On the Rights and Duties of Nations in Time of War* (Oxford University Press, 1863)

Tzanakopoulos, A., *Disobeying the Security Council: Countermeasures against Wrongful Sanctions* (Oxford University Press, 2011)

Upcher, J., *Neutrality in Contemporary International Law* (Oxford University Press, 2020)

Vandenberg, A. H. Jr, *The Private Papers of Senator Vandenberg* (Houghton Mifflin, 1952)

Vasquez, J. A., *Contagion and War: Lessons from the First World War* (Cambridge University Press, 2018)

Vattel, E. de, *The Law of Nations or the Principles of Natural Law: Applied to the Conduct and to the Affairs of Nations and of Sovereigns* (Oceana, 1964)

Visscher, C. de, *Theory and Reality in Public International Law* (Princeton University Press, 1968)

Walker, N. (ed.), *Sovereignty in Transition* (Hart, 2003)

Walters, F. P., *A History of the League of Nations* (Oxford University Press, 1965)

Wampach, C., *Armed Reprisals from Medieval Times to 1945* (Nomos, 2020)

Watkins, A. C., *The Paris Pact: A Textbook for Schools and Colleges* (Harcourt Brace, 1932)

Weaver, R., *The Hundred Thousand Sons of St Louis: The French Campaign in Spain, April–October 1823* (Helion 2018)

Weinberg, G. L., *World War II: A Very Short Introduction* (Oxford University Press, 2014)

Weller, M., *The Crisis in Kosovo, 1989–1999: From the Dissolution of Yugoslavia to Rambouillet and the Outbreak of Hostilities* (International Documents & Analysis, 1999)

Weller, M. (ed.), *The Oxford Handbook of the Use of Force in International Law* (Oxford University Press, 2017)

Wet, E. de, *The Chapter VII Powers of the United Nations Security Council* (Hart, 2004)

Wheaton, H., *Elements of International Law: With a Sketch of the History of the Science* (Carey, Lea & Blanchard, 1836)

Wheeler, J., *Saving Strangers: Humanitarian Intervention in International Society* (Oxford University Press, 2002)

White, N. D., *Keeping the Peace* (Manchester University Press, 1997)

White, N. D. and Abass, A., 'Countermeasures and Sanctions', in M. D. Evans (ed.), *International Law* (Oxford University Press, 2018), pp. 537–62

Williams, P., 'The R2P Protection of Civilians and UN Peacekeeping Operations', in A. J. Bellamy and T. Dunne (eds.), *The Oxford Handbook of the Responsibility to Protect* (Oxford University Press, 2016), pp. 524–44.

Wolff, C., *Law of Nations Treated According to the Scientific Method* (Liberty Fund, 2017)

Woolsey, T. D., *Introduction to the Study of International Law* (Sampson Low, Marston, Searle & Rivington, 1879)

Zyberi, G. (ed.) *An Institutional Approach to the Responsibility to Protect* (Cambridge University Press, 2013)

## Journal and Yearbook Articles

'U.S. Drone Strike in Iraq Kills Iranian Military Leader Qasem Soleimani' (2020) 114 *American Journal of International Law* 313–23

Abi-Saab, G., 'Cours général de droit international public' (1987) 207 *Collected Courses of the Hague Academy of International Law* 9–463

Almond, H. H. Jr, 'Demilitarization and Arms Control: Antarctica' (1985) 17 *Case Western Journal of International Law* 229–84

Anderson, K., Reisner, D. and Waxman, M., 'Adapting the Law of Armed Conflict to Autonomous Weapons Systems' (2014) 90 *International Law Studies* 386–411

Aspremont, J. d' et al., 'Sharing Responsibility Between Non-State Actors and States in International Law' (2015) 62(1) *Netherlands International Law Review* 49–67

Badr, G. M., 'The Exculpatory Effect of Self-Defence in State Responsibility' (1980) 10 *Georgia Journal of International and Comparative Law* 1–28

Baker, S. G., 'Terrorism and the Inherent Right of Self-Defence' (1987) 10 *Houston Journal of International Law* 25–49

Barras, V. and Greub, G., 'History of Biological Warfare and Bioterrorism' (2014) 20 *Clinical Microbiology and Infection* 497–502

Beer, A. C. de and Tladi, D., 'The Use of Force against Syria in Response to Alleged Use of Chemical Weapons by Syria: A Return to Humanitarian Intervention?' (2019) 79 *Heidelberg Journal of International Law* 205–39

Beres, L. R., 'After the Gulf War: Israel, Preemption and Anticipatory Self-Defence' (1991) 13 *Houston Journal of International Law* 259–80

Bethlehem, D., 'Self-Defence against an Imminent or Actual Armed Attack by Nonstate Actors' (2012) 106 *American Journal of International Law* 770–7

Beyerlin, U., 'Die israelische Befreiungsaktion von Entebbe in völkerrechtlicher Sicht' (1977) 37 *Zeitschrift für ausländisches öffentliches Recht und Völkerrecht* 213–43

Blokker, N., 'Is the Authorization Authorized? Powers and Practice of the UN Security Council to Authorize the Use of Force by "Coalitions of the Able and Willing"' (2000) 11 *European Journal of International Law* 541–68

Blum, Y. Z., 'State Response to Acts of Terrorism' (1976) 19 *German Yearbook of International Law* 223–37

Boothby, W.H., 'Space Weapons and the Law' (2017) 93 *International Law Studies* 180–214

Bowett, D., 'Reprisals Involving Recourse to Armed Force' (1972) 66 *American Journal of International Law* 1–36

Brockmeier, S., Stuenkel, O. and Tourinho, M., 'The Impact of the Libya Intervention Debates on Norms of Protection' (2016) 30(1) *Journal of Global Society* 113–33

Brooks, R., 'Duck-Rabbits and Drones: Legal Indeterminacy in the War on Terror' (2014) 25 *Stanford Law and Policy Review* 301–16

Brunnée, J. and Toope, S. J., 'Self-Defence against Non-State Actors: Are Powerful States Willing but Unable to Change International Law?' (2018) 67 *International & Comparative Law Quarterly* 263–86

Butchard, P. M., 'Back to San Francisco: Explaining the Inherent Contradictions of Art. 2 (4) of the Charter' (2018) 23 *Journal of Conflict and Security Law* 229–67

Calamita, N. J., 'Sanctions, Countermeasures, and the Iranian Nuclear Issue' (2009) 42 *Vanderbilt Journal of Transnational Law* 1393–442

Campbell, J. S., 'The Cuban Missile Crisis and the U.N. Charter: An Analysis of the United States Position' (1963) 16 *Stanford Law Review* 160–76

Carnazza Amari, G., 'Nouvel exposé du principe de non-intervention (première partie)' (1873) 5 *Revue de droit international et de législation comparée* 352–89

Carter, A. B., 'Current and Future Military Uses of Space' (1986) 489 *Annals of the New York Academy of Sciences* 5–17

Cheng, B., 'Properly Speaking, Only Celestial Bodies Have Been Reserved for Use Exclusively for Peaceful (Non-Military) Purposes, but Not Outer Void Space' (2000) 75 *International Law Studies* 81–117

Christakis, T., 'Challenging the "Unwilling and Unable" Test' (2017) 77 *Zeitschrift für ausländisches öffentliches Recht und Völkerrecht* 19–22

Clapham, A., 'Booty, Bounty, Blockade and Prize: Time to Reevaluate the Law' (2021) 97 *International Law Studies* 1200–68

Clarke, M., 'China's Application of the "Three Warfares" in the South China Sea and Xinjiang' (2019) 63 *Orbis* 187–208

Cohen, G., 'Mixing Oil and Water? The Interaction between *j*us ad *b*ellum and *j*us in *b*ello during Armed Conflicts' (2022) *Journal on the Use of Force and International Law* 352–90, https://doi.org/10.1080/20531702.2022.2059154

Corten, O., 'The "Unwilling or Unable" Test: Has It Been, and Could It Be, Accepted?' (2016) 29 *Leiden Journal of International Law* 777–99

Corten, O. and Dubuisson, F., 'Opération "liberté immuable": Une extension abusive du concept de légitime défense' (2002) 106 *Revue générale de droit international public* 51–77

D'Amato, A., 'Israel's Air Strike against the Osiraq Reactor: A Retrospective' (1996) 10 *Temple International and Comparative Law Journal* 259–60

Deeks, A., 'Unwilling or Unable: Toward a Normative Framework for Extraterritorial Self-Defense' (2012) 52 *Virginia Journal of International Law* 483–550

Doswald Beck, L., 'The Legal Validity of Military Intervention by Invitation of the Government' (1985) 56 *British Yearbook of International Law* 189–252

Drew, P. J., 'Can We Starve the Civilians? Exploring the Dichotomy between the Traditional Law of Maritime Blockade and Humanitarian Initiative' (2019) 95 *International Law Studies* 302–21

Egerton, G., 'Collective Security as Political Myth: Liberal Internationalism and the League of Nations in Politics and History' (1983) 5 *International History Review* 496–524

Falk, R. A., 'The Beirut Raid and the International Law of Retaliation' (1969) 63 *American Journal of International Law* 415–43

Fischer, G., 'Le bombardement par Israël d'un réacteur nucléaire irakien' (1981) 27 *Annuaire français de droit international* 147–67

Fischer, T., Aunesluoma, J. and Makko, A., 'Neutrality and Nonalignment in World Politics during the Cold War' (2016) 18(4) *Journal of Cold War Studies* 4–11

Fleck, D., 'Rules of Engagement for Maritime Forces and the Limitation of the Use of Force under the UN Charter' (1988) 31 *German Yearbook of International Law* 165–86

Galdorisi, G. and Kaufman, A., 'Military Activities in the Exclusive Economic Zone: Preventing Uncertainty and Defusing Conflict' (2002) 32 *California Western International Law Journal* 253–302

Gardiner, M., 'Piracy Prosecutions in National Courts' (2012) 10 *Journal of International Criminal Justice* 797–821

Gardner, R. N., 'Neither Bush Nor the "Jurisprudes"' (2003) 97 *American Journal of International Law* 585–90

Geiß, R., 'Civil Aircraft as Weapons of Large-Scale Destruction: Countermeasures, Article 3BIS of the Chicago Convention, and the Newly Adopted German "Luftsicherheitsgesetz"' (2005) 27(1) *Michigan Journal of International Law* 227–56

Gill, T. D., 'The Forcible Protection, Affirmation and Exercise of Rights under Contemporary International Law' (1992) 23 *Netherlands Yearbook of International Law* 105–73

Gill, T. D., 'Humanitaire Interventie: Rechtmatigheid, Rechtvaardigheid en Legitimiteit' (2001) 94 *Militair Rechtelijk Tijdschrift* 221–41

Gill, T. D., 'Humanitarian Intervention: Legality, Justice and Legitimacy' (2005) 1 *Global Yearbook of International Law* 51–76

Gill, T. D., 'Legal and Some Political Limitations on the Power of the UN Security Council to Exercise its Enforcement Powers under Chapter VII of the Charter' (1995) 26 *Netherlands Yearbook of International Law* 33–138

Gill, T. D., 'Rethinking the Scope of International Humanitarian Law and Its Place in the International Legal System' (2022) 60 *Revue de droit militaire et de droit de la guerre / The Military Law and Law of War Review* 58–70

Gill, T. D., 'Some Reflections on the Threshold for International Armed Conflict and on the Application of the Law of Armed Conflict in Any Armed Conflict' (2022) 99 *International Law Studies* 698–730

Gill, T. D., 'Some Thoughts on the Relationship between International Humanitarian Law and International Human Rights Law: A Plea for Mutual Respect and a Common-Sense Approach' (2013) 16 *Yearbook of International Humanitarian Law* 251–66

Gill, T. D. and Tibori-Szabó, K., 'Twelve Key Questions on Self-Defense against Non-State Actors' (2019) 95 *International Law Studies* 467–505

Gordon, E., 'Article 2(4) in Historical Context' (1985) 10 *Yale Journal of International Law* 271–8

Green, J. A., 'The Article 51 Reporting Requirement for Self-Defense Actions' (2015) 55 *Virginia Journal of International Law* 563–624

Green, J. A., 'Fluctuating Evidentiary Standards for Self-Defence in the International Court of Justice' (2009) 58 *International & Comparative Law Quarterly* 163–79

Green, J. A., 'Questioning the Peremptory Status of the Prohibition of the Use of Force' (2011) 32 *Michigan Journal of International Law* 215–57

Green, J. A., Henderson, C. and Ruys, T., 'Russia's Attack on Ukraine and the *jus ad bellum*' (2022) 9 *Journal on the Use of Force and International Law* 4–30

Greenwood, C., 'International Law and the Pre-emptive Use of Force: Afghanistan, Al-Qaida, and Iraq' (2003) 4 *San Diego International Law Journal* 7–38

Greenwood, C., 'The Relationship between the *ius ad bellum* and the *ius in bello*' (1983) 9 *Review of International Studies* 221–34

Gross, L. M., 'The Legal Implications of Israel's 1982 Invasion into Lebanon' (1983) 13 *California Western International Law Journal* 458–92

Hafner, G., 'Report on Intervention by Invitation' (2009) 73 *Institute of International Law Yearbook* 302–39

Haines, S., 'War at Sea: Nineteenth-Century Laws for Twenty-First-Century Wars' (2016) 98(902) *International Review of the Red Cross* 419–47

Hakimi, M., 'Defensive Force against Non-State Actors: The State of Play' (2015) 91 *International Law Studies* 1–31

Hathaway, O. et al., 'Consent-Based Humanitarian Intervention: Giving Sovereignty Back to the Sovereign' (2013) 46 *Cornell International Law Journal* 499–568

Heinze, E. A. and Neilsen, R., 'Limited Force and the Return of Reprisals in the Law of Armed Conflict' (2020) 34 *Ethics and International Affairs* 175–88

Helal, M. S., 'The Myth of U.N. Collective Security' (2018) 32 *Emory International Law Review Recent Developments* 1063–97

Hemmings, A. D., 'Challenges to Substantive Demilitarisation in the Antarctic Treaty Area' (2020) 12 *Yearbook of Polar Law* 172–94

Henderson, C., 'The Bush Doctrine: From Theory to Practice' (2004) 9 *Journal of Conflict and Security Law* 3–24

Henkin, L., 'Kosovo and the Law of "Humanitarian Intervention"' (1999) 93 *American Journal of International Law* 824–8

Henriksen, A., 'Trump's Missile Strike on Syria and the Legality of Using Force to Deter Chemical Warfare' (2018) 23 *Journal of Conflict & Security Law* 33–48

Herik, L. van den andSchrijver, N., 'Leiden Policy Recommendations on Counter-Terrorism and International Law' (2010) 57 *Netherlands International Law Review* 531–50

Heyns, C. et al., 'The International Law Framework Regulating the Use of Armed Drones' (2016) 65 *International & Comparative Law Quarterly* 791–827

Hill, C., 'Remarks by Charles Hill' (under 'The Bush Administration Preemption Doctrine and the Future of World Order') (2004) 98 *American Society of International Law Proceedings* 329–31

Hillmann, H. and Gathmann, C., 'Overseas Trade and the Decline of Privateering' (2011) 71 *Journal of Economic History* 730–61

Hossain, K., 'The Concept of *jus cogens* and the Obligation under the UN Charter' (2005) 3 *Santa Clara Journal of International Law* 72–98

Huszti-Orbán, K. and Kalandarishvili-Mueller, N., 'Is it a Bird? Is it a Plane? Is it an Armed Conflict? The Classification of the Situation in Syria' (2012) 1 *Journal of International Law*, https://papers.ssrn.com/sol3/papers.cfm?abstract_id=2045696

Jacobson, M. R., 'War in the Information Age: International Law, Self-Defense, and the Problem of "Non-Armed" Attacks' (1998) 21(3) *Journal of Strategic Studies* 1–33

Jennings, R. Y., 'The Caroline and MacLeod Cases' (1938) 32 *American Journal of International Law* 82–99

Jimenez Kwast, P., 'Maritime Law Enforcement and the Use of Force: Reflections on the Categorisation of Forcible Action at Sea in the Light of the *Guyana/Suriname* Award' (2008) 13 *Journal of Conflict & Security Law* 49–91

Joyner, D. H., 'The Kosovo Intervention: Legal Analysis and a More Persuasive Paradigm' (2002) 13 *European Journal of International Law* 597–619

Joyner, D. H., 'The Proliferation Security Initiative: Nonproliferation, Counterproliferation, and International Law' (2005) 30 *Yale Journal of International Law* 507–48

Kamiński, M. A., 'Operation "Olympic Games": Cyber-Sabotage as a Tool of American Intelligence Aimed at Counteracting the Development of Iran's Nuclear Programme' (2020) 29 *Security & Defence Quarterly* 63–71

Kaplan, N. J., 'The Attack on Osirak: Delimitation of Self-Defence under International Law' (1982) 4 *New York Law School Journal of International and Comparative Law* 131–56

Kleffner, J. K., 'The Applicability of International Humanitarian Law to Organized Armed Groups' (2011) 93(882) *International Review of the Red Cross* 443–61

Kraska, J., 'Broken Taillight at Sea: the Peacetime International Law of Visit, Board, Search and Seizure' (2010) 16 *Ocean and Coastal Law Journal* 1–46

Krishnan, S., 'The Alleged Use of Chemical Weapons against the Syrian People' (2017) 21(2) *World Affairs: The Journal of International Issues* 22–33

Kunz, J., 'Individual and Collective Self-Defence in Article 51 of the Charter of the UN' (1947) 41 *American Journal of International Law* 872–9

Lanovoy, V., 'The Use of Force by Non-State Actors and the Limits of Attribution' (2017) 28(2) *European Journal of International Law* 563–585

Laursen, A., 'The Use of Force and (the State of) Necessity' (2004) 37 *Vanderbilt Journal of Transnational Law* 485–526

Lehto, M., 'The Fight against ISIL in Syria: Comments on the Recent Discussion of the Right of Self-Defence against Non-State Actors' (2018) 87 *Nordic Journal of International Law* 1–25

Letendre, L. A., 'Lethal Autonomous Weapons Systems: Translating Geek Speech for Lawyers' (2020) 96 *International Law Studies* 274–94

Lieblich, E., 'Intervention and Consent: Consensual Forcible Interventions in Armed Conflicts as International Agreements' (2011) 29 *Boston University International Law Journal* 337–82

Linderfalk, U., 'The Effect of *Jus Cogens* Norms: Whoever Opened Pandora's Box, Did You Think about the Consequences?' (2007) 18 *European Journal of International Law* 853–71

Lissitzyn, O., 'The Treatment of Aerial Intruders in Recent Practice and in International Law' (1953) 47 *American Journal of International Law* 559–89

Lowe, V., 'The Iraqi Crisis: What Now?' (2003) 52 *International & Comparative Law Quarterly* 859–71

Martens, F., 'Étude historique sur la politique russe dans la question d'Orient' (1877) 9 *Revue de droit international et de législation comparée* 49–77

Martin, C., 'Challenging and Refining the "Unwilling and Unable" Doctrine' (2019) 52 *Vanderbilt Journal of Transnational Law* 387–461

Marwah, O., 'India's Intervention in East Pakistan 1971–1972' (1979) 13*Journal of Modern Asian Studies* 549–80

McDougal, M. S., 'The Soviet-Cuban Quarantine and Self-Defense' (1963) 57 *American Journal of International Law* 597–604

McIlmail, T. P., 'No-Fly Zones: The Imposition and Enforcement of Air Exclusion Regimes over Bosnia and Iraq' (1994) 17 *Loyola of Los Angeles International and Comparative Law Review* 35–83

McKinnon, F., 'Reprisals as a Method of Enforcing International Law' (1991) 4 *Leiden Journal of International Law* 221–48

Meeker, L. C., 'Defensive Quarantine and the Law' (1963) 57 *American Journal of International Law* 515–24

Mendelson, M. H., 'The Formation of Customary International Law' (1998) 272 *Collected Courses of the Hague Academy of International Law* 155–410

Mobley, R., 'Pueblo: A Retrospective' (2001) 54 *Naval War College Review* 1–20

Myjer, P. J. and White, N. D., 'The Twin Towers Attack: An Unlimited Right to Self-Defence?' (2002) 7 *Journal of Conflict and Security Law* 5–17

Nydell, M. S., 'Tensions between International Law and Strategic Security: Implications of Israel's Preemptive Raid on Iraq's Nuclear Reactor' (1983–4) 24 *Virginia Journal of International Law* 459–92

O'Connell, M. E., 'Dangerous Departures' (2013) 107 *American Journal of International Law* 380–6

O'Connell, M. E., 'The Popular but Unlawful Reprisal' (2018) 44 *Ohio Northern University Law Review* 325–50

O'Donnell, T., 'The Restitution of Holocaust Looted Art and Transitional Justice: The Perfect Storm or the Raft of the Medusa?' (2011) 22 *European Journal of International Law* 49-80

Paret, P., 'Machiavelli, Fichte, and Clausewitz in the Labyrinth of German Idealism' (2015) XVII(3) *Ethics & Politics* 78–95

Pedrozo, R., 'Military Activities in the Exclusive Economic Zone: East Asia Focus' (2014) 90 *International Law Studies* 514–43

Peters, A., 'Intervention by Invitation: Impulses from the Max Planck Trialogues on the Law of Peace and War' (2019) 79 *Zeitschrift für ausländisches öffentliches Recht und Völkerrecht* 635–41

Petras, C., 'The Use of Force in Response to Cyber-Attack on Commercial Space Systems: Reexamining Self-Defense in Outer Space in Light of the Convergence of U.S. Military and Commercial Space Activities' (2002) 67 *Journal of Air Law and Commerce* 1213–68

Pierson, C., 'Preemptive Self-Defence in an Age of Weapons of Mass Destruction: Operation Iraqi Freedom' (2004) 33 *Denver Journal of International Law and Policy* 150–78

Ranganathan, S., 'Global Commons' (2016) 27 *European Journal of International Law* 693–717

Reisman, W. M., 'Humanitarian Intervention and Fledgling Democracies' (1994–5) 18 *Fordham International Law Journal* 794–805

Roberts, A., 'The Equal Application of the Laws of War: A Principle under Pressure' (2008) 90(872) *International Review of the Red Cross* 931–62

Roberts, G., 'The Uganda-Tanzania War, the Fall of Idi Amin, and the Failure of African Diplomacy, 1978–1979' (2014) 8 *Journal of East African Studies* 692–709

Rodley, N., 'After Bangladesh: The Law of Humanitarian Intervention by Military Force' (1973) 67 *American Journal of International Law* 275–305

Roscini, M., 'Cyber Operations as Nuclear Counterproliferation Measures' (2014) 19 *Journal of Conflict & Security Law* 133–57

Russell, R. L., 'Iraq's Chemical Weapons Legacy: What Others Might Learn from Saddam' (2005) 59 *Middle East Journal* 187–208

Ruys, T., 'The Meaning of "Force" and the Boundaries of the *jus ad bellum*: Are "Minimal" Uses of Force Excluded from UN Charter Article 2(4)?' (2014) 108 *American Journal of International Law* 159–210

Sadurska, R., 'Foreign Submarines in Swedish Waters: The Erosion of an International Norm' (1984) 10 *Yale Journal of International Law* 34–58

Sadurska, R., 'Threats of Force' (1988) 82 *American Journal of International Law* 239–68

Sapiro, M., 'Iraq: The Shifting Sands of Preemptive Self-Defense' (2003) 97 *American Journal of International Law* 599–607

Sapiro, M., 'Preempting Prevention: Lessons Learned' (2005) 37 *NYU Journal of International Law and Politics* 357–71

Sassoli, M., 'Autonomous Weapons and International Humanitarian Law: Advantages, Open Technical Questions and Legal Issues to Be Clarified' (2014) 90 *International Law Studies* 308–40

Schachter, O., 'The Lawful Resort to Unilateral Use of Force' (1985) 10 *Yale Journal of International Law* 291–4

Schmitt, M. N., 'Clipped Wings: Effective and Legal No-Fly Zone Rules of Engagement' (1998) 72 *International Law Studies* 239–95

Schmitt, M.N., 'Computer Network Attacks and the Use of Force in International Law: Thoughts on a Normative Framework' (1998–9) 37 *Columbia Journal of Transnational Law* 885–937

Schmitt, M. N., 'Drone Attacks under the *jus ad bellum* and *jus in bello*: Clearing the "Fog of Law"' (2011) 13 *Yearbook of International Humanitarian Law* 311–26

Schmitt, M. N., 'International Law and Military Operations in Space' (2006) 10 *Max Planck Yearbook of United Nations Law* 89–125

Schmitt, M. N. and Ford, C. M., 'Assessing U.S. Justifications for Using Force in Response to Syria's Chemical Attacks: An International Law Perspective' (2017) 9 *Journal of National Security Law & Policy* 283–303

Schwebel, S. M., 'Aggression, Intervention and Self-Defence in Modern International Law' (1972) 136 *Collected Courses of the Hague Academy of International Law* 413–97

Shapira, A., 'The Six-Day War and the Right of Self-Defence' (1971) 6 *Israel Law Review* 65–80

Simma, B., 'The Antarctic Treaty as a Treaty Providing for an Objective Regime' (1986) 19 *Cornell International Law Journal* 189–209

Simma, B., 'NATO, the UN and the Use of Force: Legal Aspects' (1999) 10 *European Journal of International Law* 1–22

Slaughter, A.-M., 'The Use of Force in Iraq: Illegal and Illegitimate' (2004) 98 *American Society of International Law Proceedings* 262–3

Soons, A. H. A., 'Law Enforcement in the Ocean' (2004) 3 *WMU Journal of Maritime Affairs* 3–16

Soroos, M. S., 'The International Commons: A Historical Perspective' (1988) 12 *Environmental Review* 1–22

Spiegel, H. W., 'Origin and Development of Denial of Justice' (1938) 32 *American Journal of International Law* 63–8

Steenhoven, N. van der, 'Conduct and Subsequent Practice by States in the Application of the Requirement to Report under UN Charter Article 51' (2019) 6 *Journal on the Use of Force and International Law* 242–72

Stoker, D. and Whiteside, C., 'Blurred Lines: Gray-Zone Conflict and Hybrid War – Two Failures of American Strategic Thinking' (2020) 73(1) *Naval War College Review* 13–48

Taft, W. H., IV and Buchwald, T. F., 'Preemption, Iraq, and International Law' (2003) 97 *American Journal of International Law* 557–63

Thakur, R., 'R2P after Libya and Syria: Engaging Emerging Powers' (2013) 36(2) *Washington Quarterly* 61–76

Thompson, A. W., 'Doctrine of the Protection of Nationals Abroad: Rise of the Non-Combatant Evacuation Operation' (2012) 11(3) *Washington University Global Studies Law Review* 627–68

Tladi, D., 'An Assessment of Bethlehem's Principles on the Use of Force against Non-State Actors' (2013) 107 *American Journal of International Law* 572–5.

Tladi, D., 'The Nonconsenting Innocent State: The Problem with Bethlehem's Principle 12' (2013) 107 *American Journal of International Law* 570–6

Tsagourias, N., 'Necessity and the Use of Force: A Special Regime' (2010) *Netherlands Yearbook of International Law* 11–44

Urs, P., 'Effective Territorial Control by Non-State Armed Groups and the Right of Self-Defence' (2017) 77 *Zeitschrift für ausländisches öffentliches Recht und Völkerrecht* 31–4

Vidmar, J., 'The Use of Force as a Plea of Necessity' (2017) 111 *American Journal of International Law Unbound* 302–6

Vigni, P., 'The Interaction between the Antarctic Treaty System and Other Relevant Conventions to the Antarctic Area' (2000) 4 *Max Planck Yearbook of United Nations Law* 481–542

Waldock, C. H. M., 'General Course in Public International Law' (1962) 106 *Collected Courses of the Hague Academy of International Law* 1–252

Waldock, C. H. M., 'The Regulation of the Use of Force by Individual States in International Law' (1952) 81 *Collected Courses of the Hague Academy of International Law* 455–517

Wedgwood, R., 'The Fall of Saddam Hussein: Security Council Mandates and Preemptive Self-Defence' (2003) 97 *American Journal of International Law* 576–85

Wilmshurst, E., 'The Chatham House Principles of International Law on the Use of Force by States in Self-Defence' (2006) 55 *International & Comparative Law Quarterly* 963–72

Wolfrum, R., 'Restricting the Use of the Sea to Peaceful Purposes: Demilitarization in Being?' (1981) 24 *German Yearbook of International Law* 200–41

Yoo, J., 'International Law and the War in Iraq' (2003) 97 *American Journal of International Law* 563–76

## Reports and Other Documents of the United Nations

'A More Secure World: Our Shared Responsibility; Report of the High-level Panel on Threats, Challenges and Change', UN Doc. A/59/565 (2004)

Human Rights Council, 'Report of the independent international commission of inquiry on the Syrian Arab Republic', UN Doc. A/HRC/21/50 (16 August 2012)

International Law Commission, Responsibility of States for Internationally Wrongful Acts, Annex to UN General Assembly (UNGA) Resolution 56/83 (12 December 2001), UN Doc. A/RES/56/83

Koskenniemi, M. (Chair ILC Study Group), 'Fragmentation of International Law: Difficulties Arising from the Diversification and Expansion of International Law', UN Doc. A/CN.4/L.682 and Add.1 (2006)

Office of the High Commissioner for Human Rights, 'How Can Israel's Blockade of Gaza Be Legal? UN Independent Experts on the "Palmer Report"' (13 September 2011), https://tinyurl.com/3sf2xsrb

## Reports and Resolutions of Other Organizations

Benes, E. and Politis, N., 'Report on the Protocol, Submitted to the Fifth Assembly' (1924) 23 *League of Nations Official Journal*, Spec. Supp. 479–502

Campfens, E. (ed.), *Fair and Just Solutions? Alternatives to Litigation in Nazi-Looted Art Disputes: Status Quo and New Developments* (Eleven International, 2015)

Davids Commission, 'Rapport Commissie van Onderzoek Besluitvorming Irak' (January 2010), https://tinyurl.com/2p89dh2u

Human Rights Watch, 'Death by Chemicals: The Syrian Government's Widespread and Systematic Use of Chemical Weapons' (1 May 2017), https://tinyurl.com/5ce6p7xs

Independent International Fact-Finding Mission on the Conflict in Georgia, *Report*, vol. II (September 2009)

Institut de Droit international/Institute of International Law, Session of Santiago – 2007, 10th Commission, Present Problems of the Use of Armed Force in International Law, Sub-group on self-defence, Resolution of 27 October 2007, www.idi-iil.org/app/uploads/2017/06/2007_san_02_en.pdf

Institut de Droit international/Institute of International Law, Session of Wiesbaden – 1975), 'Conditions of Application of Rules, other than Humanitarian Rules, of Armed Conflict to Hostilities in which United Nations Forces may be Engaged', www.idi-iil.org/app/uploads/2017/06/1975_wies_02_en.pdf

Institut de Droit International/Institute of International Law, Session of Wiesbaden – 1975), 8th Commission, The Principle of Non-Intervention in Civil Wars, Resolution of 14 August 1975, www.idi-iil.org/app/uploads/2017/06/1975_wies_03_en.pdf

International Commission on Intervention and State Sovereignty (ICISS), Report (2001)

Mills, C., 'The Militarisation of Space', Research Briefing, UK Parliament House of Commons Library (14 June 2021), https://tinyurl.com/3ar82rmz

UK Ministry of Defence, *Joint Services Manual on the Law of Armed Conflict*, Joint Service Publication 383 (2004)

US Department of the Navy, Marine Corps and Coast Guard, The *Commander's Handbook of the Law of Naval Operations* (NWP1-14 M, March 2022)

Walker, N., 'Conflict in Ukraine: A Timeline (2014–present)', UK House of Commons Library Research Briefing (24 February 2023), https://tinyurl.com/zhw7frcy

## News Items

Ahmed, K. et al., 'The Black Sea Blockade: Mapping the Impact of War in Ukraine on the World's Food Supply – Interactive', *The Guardian* (9 June 2022), https://tinyurl.com/mr44my8n

Aisch, G., Joseph, Y. and Singhvi, A., 'Which Countries Support and Which Oppose the U.S. Missile Strikes in Syria', *New York Times* (9 April 2017), https://tinyurl.com/yhf9kw5c

Al Jazeera, 'Russia Says It Used Hypersonic Missiles in Ukraine Again' (20 March 2022), https://tinyurl.com/n7puk5hw

Australian Broadcasting Corporation, 'What's the Big Deal about Hypersonic Weapons and Why Are Major Powers Vying for This Capability?' (28 October 2021), https://tinyurl.com/3xs6ubfe

Barnard, A. and Gordon, M. R., 'Worst Chemical Attack in Years in Syria; US Blames Assad', *New York Times* (4 April 2017), https://tinyurl.com/5erwtaak

BBC News, '"Little Green Men" or "Russian Invaders"?' (11 March 2014), www.bbc.com/news/world-europe-26532154

BBC News, 'Nuclear Weapons: Which Countries Have Them and How Many Are There?' (14 January 2020), www.bbc.com/news/newsbeat-51091897

BBC News, 'Syria Air Strikes: US and Allies Attack "Chemical Weapons Sites"' (14 April 2018), www.bbc.com/news/world-middle-east-43762251

BBC News, 'Syria War: At Least 70 Killed in Suspected Chemical Attack in Douma' (8 April 2018), www.bbc.com/news/world-middle-east-43686157

BBC News, 'What is Russia's Wagner Group of mercenaries in Ukraine' (3 October 2022), www.bbc.com/news/world-60947877

Bloomberg News, 'Transcript: Vladimir Putin's Televised Address on Ukraine' (24 February 2022), https://tinyurl.com/mw9rmz7n

Borger, J., 'Israeli Airstrike Was Aimed at Syrian Reactor, Report Says', *The Guardian*(15 October 2007), www.theguardian.com/world/2007/oct/15/syria.israel

CBS News, 'President Biden Warns Vladimir Putin Not to Use Nuclear Weapons: "Don't. Don't. Don't"' (16 September 2022), https://tinyurl.com/yevbjft6

CNN News, 'Syria Complains to U.N. about Israeli Airstrike' (11 September 2007), https://edition.cnn.com/2007/WORLD/meast/09/11/israel.syria/

CNN News, 'US Combat Mission in Iraq Ends' (31 August 2010).

Deutsche Welle, 'Modern Spy Satellites in an Age of Space Wars', https://tinyurl.com/m9jmd452

*Economist*, 'A New Low for Global Democracy' (9 February 2022), https://tinyurl.com/ysppzc4e

Goldenberg, S., Paton Walsh, N. and MacAskill, E., 'Iraq Weapons Inspectors Find Empty Chemical Warheads', *The Guardian*(17 January 2003), www.guardian.co.uk/world/2003/jan/17/iraq.ewenmacaskill

*Guardian*, 'Special Report Iraq, Iraq Timeline: July 16, 1979 to January 31, 2004', www.guardian.co.uk/Iraq/page/0,12438,793802,00.html

*Guardian*, 'UN Weapons Inspectors Arrive in Iraq' (18 November 2002), www.theguardian.com/world/2002/nov/18/iraq

International Committee of the Red Cross (ICRC), 'Syria: ICRC and Syrian Arab Red Crescent Maintain Effort Amid Increased Fighting' (17 July 2012), https://tinyurl.com/y46p759a

Korean Central News Agency of the DPRK, 'Israel Condemned for Intrusion into Syria's Territorial Air' (11 September 2007), in Federation of American Scientists, *A Sourcebook on the Israeli Strike in Syria, 6 September 2007* (8 September 2018), https://fas.org/man/eprint/syria.pdf

MacAskill, E. and Burkeman, O., 'Defiant Saddam Accepts UN Team', *The Guardian* (14 November 2002), www.theguardian.com/world/2002/nov/14/iraq.ewenmacaskill

Mazzetti, M. and Cooper, H., 'Israeli Nuclear Suspicions Linked to Raid in Syria', *New York Times* (18 September 2007), www.nytimes.com/2007/09/18/world/asia/18korea.html

Reuters, 'Chemical Weapons a Red Line in Syria, France's Macron Says' (29 May 2017), https://tinyurl.com/2p93ttv9

Silverleib, A., 'U.S. Combat Mission in Iraq Ends', CNN Politics (1 September 2010), https://tinyurl.com/yr9f8wh4

Simpson, J., 'Russia's Crimea Plan: Detailed, Secret and Successful', BBC News (19 March 2014), www.bbc.com/news/world-europe-26644082

Stone, M., 'U.S. in Hypersonic Weapon "Arms Race" with China – Air Force Secretary', Reuters (1 December 2021), https://tinyurl.com/yt39tsr2

Tidy, J., 'Predatory Sparrow: Who Are the Hackers Who Say They Started a Fire in Iran?', BBC News (11 July 2022), www.bbc.com/news/technology-62072480

Tiron, R., 'Hypersonic Weapons: Who Has Them and Why It Matters', Bloomberg (27 October 2021, updated 6 April 2022), https://tinyurl.com/3exbk924

Younge, G. and MacAskill, E., 'UN Team Finds Iraq Has Illegal Missiles' (13 February 2003), www.guardian.co.uk/world/2003/feb/13/iraq.garyyounge

## Blog Posts, Podcasts and Other Online Articles

Akande, D., 'Does Use of Chemical Weapons Justify Intervention in Syria?', *EJIL: Talk!* (27 April 2013), https://tinyurl.com/ex4sj4ze

Ambos, K., 'Will a State Supplying Weapons to Ukraine Become a Party to the Conflict and Thus Be Exposed to Countermeasures?', *EJIL:Talk!* (2 March 2022), https://tinyurl.com/4kne39kt

Azaria, D. and Ulfstein, G., 'Are Sabotage of Submarine Pipelines an "Armed Attack" Triggering a Right to Self-Defence?', *EJIL:Talk!* (18 October 2022), https://tinyurl.com/ym843n7f

Bilal, A., 'Hybrid Warfare: New Threats, Complexity, and "Trust" as the Antidote', *NATO Review* (30 November 2021), https://tinyurl.com/3c9eua3e

Callamard, A., 'The Targeted Killing of General Soleimani: Its Lawfulness and Why It Matters', *Just Security* (8 January 2020), https://tinyurl.com/3rw4wuj4

Chan, M., 'What Is the Difference between a Hydrogen Bomb and an Atomic Bomb?', *Time* (22 September 2017), https://time.com/4954082/hydrogen-bomb-atomic-bomb/

Cheatham, A., 'A Look at Neutrality Now – and After the Ukraine War', United States Institute of Peace (28 April 2022), https://tinyurl.com/mry6vxd9

Cohen, S., 'Acid Rain Malware and Viasat Network Downtime in Ukraine: Assessing the Cyber War Threat', *Just Security* (12 September 2022), https://tinyurl.com/y4tezv5z

Corten, O., 'Contre une invocation abusive de la légitime défense pour faire face au défi du terrorisme', RTBF (30 June 2016), https://tinyurl.com/47n3p9xb

Davis, J. K., 'You Mean They Can Bomb Us? Addressing the Impact of Neutrality Law on Defense Cooperation', *Lawfare* (2 November 2020), https://tinyurl.com/ycxynrux

Deeks, A., 'Chemical Weapons in Syria: Enough to Justify the Use of Force?', *Lawfare* (26 April 2013), https://tinyurl.com/yc38nztb

Deeks, A., 'How Does the Syria Situation Stack Up to the "Factors" That Justified Intervention in Kosovo?', *Lawfare* (7 April 2017), https://tinyurl.com/5pb9jbet

Deeks, A., 'Syria, Chemical Weapons, and Possible U.S. Military Action', *Lawfare* (10 December 2012), https://tinyurl.com/2d4jyzxw

Dunkelberg, A. G. et al., 'Mapping States' Reactions to the Syria Strikes of April 2018: A Comprehensive Guide', *Just Security* (7 May 2018), https://tinyurl.com/bdupuujj

Dunlap, C., 'Yes, the Attack on Syria Was Justifiable, and International Law Will Benefit from It', *Lawfare* (7 April 2017), https://tinyurl.com/254cm7mbo

Dupont, P.-E., 'Countermeasures vs. Collective Security? The EU Sanctions against Iran', *EJIL:Talk!* (22 June 2012), https://tinyurl.com/2p9wpr87

Galeotti, M., 'How Migrants Got Weaponized', *Foreign Affairs* (2 December 2021), https://tinyurl.com/3krnns2d

Goodman, R., 'What Do Top Legal Experts Say about the Syria Strikes?', *Just Security*, (7 April 2017), www.justsecurity.org/39712/top-legal-experts-syria-strikes

Greenwood, C., 'Self-Defence', in *Max Planck Encyclopedia of Public International Law* (Oxford Public International Law, 2011), https://tinyurl.com/2txyfx9j

Grieger, G., European Parliamentary Research Service (EPRS), 'China Tightens Its Grip over the South China Sea' (24 February 2021), https://tinyurl.com/2p8p6664

Guyer, J., 'Why Some Countries Don't Want to Pick a Side in Russia's War in Ukraine', *Vox* (9 June 2022), https://tinyurl.com/76cvk7tj

Hajdin, N., 'Complicity in a War of Aggression: Private Individuals' Criminal Responsibility', *Just Security* (1 April 2022), https://tinyurl.com/bdfj5bhw

Hakimi, M., 'The Attack on Syria and the Contemporary *jus ad bellum*', *EJIL:Talk!* (15 April 2018), https://tinyurl.com/y5n3sk3t

Harries, M., 'Putin's Brutal War Shows the Dilemmas of Nuclear Deterrence: Powerful Threats Could Too Easily Become Real Disasters', *Foreign Policy* (22 March 2022), https://tinyurl.com/3tn2ferk

Hongju Koh, H., 'Not Illegal: But Now the Hard Part Begins', *Just Security* (7 April 2017), www.justsecurity.org/39695/illegal-hard-part-begins/

Jeannesson, S., 'The Concert of Europe', in *Digital Encyclopedia of European History*, https://tinyurl.com/4xwu2esm

Jebb, B. and Jones, L., 'Little Blue Men in the South China Sea: Unmasking China's Maritime Militia' (podcast), Modern War Institute (5 June 2022), https://tinyurl.com/53h2sba6

Kuzio, T. and D'Anieri, P., 'Annexation and Hybrid Warfare in Crimea and Eastern Ukraine', *E-International Relations* (25 June 2018), https://tinyurl.com/mvvdsn4a

Merkouris, P., 'Principle of Systemic Integration', in *Max Planck Encyclopedia of Public International Law* (Oxford Public International Law, last updated August 2020), https://tinyurl.com/4f9d8uym

Milanovic, M., 'The Clearly Illegal US Missile Strike in Syria', *EJIL:Talk!* (7 April 2017), www.ejiltalk.org/the-clearly-illegal-us-missile-strike-in-syria/

Milanovic, M., 'The Syria Strikes: Still Clearly Illegal', *EJIL:Talk!* (15 April 2018), www.ejiltalk.org/the-syria-strikes-still-clearly-illegal/

Miracola, S., 'Chinese Hybrid Warfare: Commentary', Italian Institute for International Political Studies (ISPI) (21 December 2018), https://tinyurl.com/bdcprffu

Mortera Martinez, C. and Meyer, Z., 'Using Sanctioned Russian Assets to Rebuild Ukraine Will Not Be Easy', Centre for European Reform (3 August 2022), https://tinyurl.com/mwz5u7sp

Nerlich, V., 'The Crime of Aggression and Modes of Liability: Is There Room Only for Principals?' (2017) 58 *Harvard International Law Journal*, https://tinyurl.com/h8hkf6eb

Palavenis, D., 'The Use of Emerging Disruptive Technologies by the Russian Armed Forces in the Ukrainian War', Air Land Sea Space Application (ALSSA) Center (1 October 2022), https://tinyurl.com/6hb5tmf5

Peters, A., 'Passportisation: Risks for International Law and Stability', *EJIL:Talk!* (9–10 May 2019), https://tinyurl.com/nm37cvh7 (Part I), https://tinyurl.com/2munkm84 (Part II)

Ponta, A., 'Responsible State Behavior in Cyberspace: Two New Reports from Parallel UN Processes' (2021) 25(14) *ASIL Insights*, www.asil.org/insights/volume/25/issue/14

Proelss, A., 'Peaceful Purposes', in *Max Planck Encyclopedia of Public International Law* (Oxford Public International Law, 2021), https://tinyurl.com/yck4cae4

Roguski, P., *Application of International Law to Cyber Operations: A Comparative Analysis of States' Views*, The Hague Program for Cyber Norms Policy Brief (March 2020), https://tinyurl.com/3zxfs2wk

Schlochauer, H. J., 'Bryan Treaties (1913–14)', in *Max Planck Encyclopedia of Public International Law* (Oxford Public International Law, 1984), https://tinyurl.com/565kz4u5

Schmitt, M. N., 'Lieber Institute White Paper: Responding to Malicious or Hostile Actions under International Law', Lieber Institute Articles of War (26 April 2022), https://tinyurl.com/mt9jy9yy

Schmitt, M. N. and Ford, C. M., 'The Use of Force in Response to Syrian Chemical Attacks: Emergence of a New Norm?', *Just Security* (8 April 2017), https://tinyurl.com/54tr67f4

Shida, J., 'China is Set to Wage Hybrid Warfare' *World Insight* (21 December 2021, updated 6 December 2022), https://tinyurl.com/347f2zh7

Skinner, B., 'Military Uses of Outer Space' *Space Security Index* (November 2020), https://tinyurl.com/4xknef8t

Strydom, H. A., 'Weapons of Mass Destruction', in *Max Planck Encyclopedia of Public International Law* (Oxford Public International Law, 2017), https://tinyurl.com/2dzp59xb

Sullo, P. and Wyatt, J., 'War Reparations', in *Max Planck Encyclopedia of Public International Law* (Oxford Public International Law, 2015), https://tinyurl.com/36s4wyva

Tams, C. J., 'League of Nations', in *Max Planck Encyclopedia of Public International Law* (Oxford Public International Law, 2006), https://tinyurl.com/m7cxd4s8

Tomuschat, C., 'Uniting for Peace (2008)', UN Audiovisual Library of International Law, https://legal.un.org/avl/ha/ufp/ufp.html

Trevithick, J., 'U.S. Satellites Are Being Attacked Every Day According to Space Force General', *The Drive* (30 November 2011), https://tinyurl.com/ye4psx33

Weitz, R., 'Israel Airstrike in Syria: International Reactions' (James Martin Center for Non-Proliferation Studies, 1 November 2007), https://tinyurl.com/k48buy63

Wright, D. and Tracy, C., 'The Physics and Hype of Hypersonic Weapons', *Scientific American* (1 August 2021), https://tinyurl.com/2yb85s67

## Webpages and Other Online Sources

Airforce Technology, 'Harop Loitering Munitions UCAV System' (2 July 2015), www.airforce-technology.com/projects/haroploiteringmuniti/

Army Technology, 'Iron Dome Air Defence Missile System' (14 May 2021), www.army-technology.com/projects/iron-dome/

Bureau of Investigative Journalism, 'Drone Warfare', www.thebureauinvestigates.com/projects/drone-war

DEWESoft, 'Every Satellite Orbiting Earth and Who Owns Them' (18 January 2022), https://tinyurl.com/4ftkc2sk

European Centre for Countering Hybrid Threats, www.hybridcoe.fi/hybrid-threats/

European Council/Council of the EU, 'EU Restrictive Measures against Belarus', https://tinyurl.com/mshns6uw

European Council/Council of the EU, 'EU Restrictive Measures against Russia over Ukraine (since 2014)', https://tinyurl.com/58dnubdm

European Council/Council of the EU, 'Iran: EU Restrictive Measures', www.consilium.europa.eu/en/policies/sanctions/iran/

International Committee of the Red Cross, 'ICRC Position on Autonomous Weapon Systems' (12 May 2021), https://tinyurl.com/y3y9n272

International Committee of the Red Cross, 'The Same IHL Applies to All Warring Parties: Differentiating between *jus contra bellum* (Law Prohibiting the Use of Force) and *jus in bello* (Law Limiting Effects of Warfare)', *How Does Law Protect in War?*, https://tinyurl.com/mryhw258

International Committee of the Red Cross, 'San Remo Manual on International Law Applicable to Armed Conflicts at Sea', https://tinyurl.com/yc2yncsr

Raytheon, 'Phalanx Weapon System', https://tinyurl.com/y2hj5y96

Reliefweb, 'Torture in Slow Motion: The Economic Blockade of Yemen and Its Grave Humanitarian Consequences' (22 September 2022), https://tinyurl.com/3yhnrpmx

Strauss Center for International Security and Law Strait of Hormuz Project, 'Tanker War', www.strausscenter.org/strait-of-hormuz-tanker-war/

The Hague Program for Cyber Norms, 'Annex to March 2020 Policy Brief on Application of International Law to Cyber Operations: Comparative Analysis of States' Views' (2020), https://tinyurl.com/yranh3st

UN Regional Information Centre for Western Europe, 'The UN and the War in Ukraine: Key Information' (9 March 2022, updated 8 June 2023), https://tinyurl.com/2hdnww7c

US National Archives and Records Administration, 'World War II Looted Art: Turning History into Justice', Google Arts & Culture, https://g.co/arts/AH5FQKTUrCQBqhSV9

# INDEX

www.ingramcontent.com/pod-product-compliance
Lightning Source LLC
LaVergne TN
LVHW011658200926
848484LV00004B/979
* 9 7 8 1 0 0 9 4 0 7 3 2 8 *